Debating Nigeria
A Collection of Essays

Jideofor Adibe

Adonis & Abbey Publishers Ltd
St James House
13 Kensington Square,
London, W8 5HD
United Kingdom

Website: http://www.adonis-abbey.com
E-mail Address: editor@adonis-abbey.com

Nigeria:
Suites C4 & C5 J-Plus Plaza
Asokoro, Abuja, Nigeria
Tel: +234 (0) 7058078841/08052035034

British Library Cataloguing-in-Publication Data
A catalogue record for this book is available from the British Library

ISBN: 978-1-909112-69-8

Debating Nigeria
A Collection of Essays

Jideofor Adibe

ADONIS & ABBEY
PUBLISHERS LTD

Table of Contents

PREFACE xii

DEDICATION..xiv

BOKO HARAM

CHAPTER 1
Chibok Protest or 'Busy-bodies' at work?..17

CHAPTER 2
Chibok Girls: It's Time for Prisoner swap with Boko Haram........................21

CHAPTER 3
Explaining the Emergence of Boko Haram..25

CHAPTER 4
Possible Trajectories of the Boko Haram Conflict................................31

CHAPTER 5
Boko Haram in Nigeria: The Way Forward..35

CHAPTER 6
Boko Haram: 'Mission Accomplished' or 'Technically Defeated'? 39

CHAPTER 7
A Nation at war with itself...43

CHAPTER 8
In Search of Dr Stephen Davis 47

CHAPTER 9
Re-evaluating the Boko Haram conflict 51

CHAPTER 10
Relocation of Boko Haram Prisoners to Anambra State 57

CHAPTER 11
Re-thinking Boko Haram...61

CHAPTER 12
Now that the Americans are here...(1)..67

CHAPTER 13
Now that the Americans are here...(2)..69

UNITS OF THE FEDERATION

CHAPTER 14
Mile 12 Clash: Between Indigenes, Settlers and Citizenship rights 75

CHAPTER 15
Reflections on Anambra Guber Race 79

CHAPTER 16
Abuja Indigenes: The Fire Next Time? 83

CHAPTER 17
The 'deportation' of Nigerians from Lagos 87

CHAPTER 18
States vs. Federal Government 91

CHAPTER 19
Indigene/Settler dichotomy and Constitution Review..95

CHAPTER 20
States' Bankruptcy: Time to embrace the 'R' word? 97

CHAPTER 21
That Peace May Reign in Kogi State..101

NATION-BUILDING

CHAPTER 22
2015: Issues that will drive the Election 107

CHAPTER 23
2015: Year of the Long Knives? 111

CHAPTER 24
Re-engineering our Politics...115

CHAPTER 25
Between Quota and Federal Character Principle 119

CHAPTER 26
Nigeria: A Country in Perpetual Transition? 123

CHAPTER 27
The Balance of Stories..127

CHAPTER 28
Constitution Amendment: Did the people really speak? 131

CHAPTER 29
On The Purported Merger of Christian and Islamic Studies in Schools 135

CHAPTER 30
Can we really Afford this Democracy? 139

CHAPTER 31
Dousing Political Tension in the Land 143

CHAPTER 32
'Exhibitionist patriotism' as a Threat to our Democracy 147

CHAPTER 33
Murder of Uniport Students and the Culture of Impunity 149

CHAPTER 34
Nigeria: Master of the Shuffle Dance at 53 153

CHAPTER 35
Nigeria@56? Is this House really Falling? 157

CHAPTER 36
Did America really Predict Nigeria will break-up in 2015? 161

CHAPTER 37
A Nation at War with itself 165

CHAPTER 38
The Return of the Parcel Bomb 169

CHAPTER 39
Between Polemics and 'on the other hand' Narratives 173

CHAPTER 40
Oyerinde's murder: Between the Police and the DSS 177

CHAPTER 41
Should Nigeria be re-colonized? 181

CHAPTER 42
Wars without Blood: Should Hate Speech be Criminalized? (1) 185

CHAPTER 43
Wars without Blood: Should Hate Speech be Criminalized? (II) 189

CHAPTER 44
Anomie, Rage and Redemptive Suffering 193

CHAPTER 45
No Matter how Long you've been Travelling in the Wrong Direction 197

CHAPTER 46
Does 'who gets what' really Matter?… 201

CHAPTER 47
Re-launched WAI and the Dangers of Atavism...205

CHAPTER 48
Rumour-Factualization...209

ECONOMY

CHAPTER 49
Debating the Nigerian Economy..215

CHAPTER 50
Currency Crisis, Gloomy Economy and Hidden Opportunities 219

CHAPTER 51
Recession: Is the Worst Really Over? 223

CHAPTER 52
Beyond the Corruption Stories 227

CHAPTER 53
Nigeria in MINT: Time for a New Swagger?...231

CHAPTER 54
N60bn Mobile Palaver for Farmers 235

CHAPTER 55
EFCC: How not to Fight Corruption 239

CHAPTER 56
'Yuanising' the Nigerian Economy..243

PARTY POLITICS: PDP AND THE APC

CHAPTER 57
As Baraje's faction of PDP joins APC 249

CHAPTER 58
APC: Determination or Desperation?...253

CHAPTER 59
APC: Dreams Die First? 257

CHAPTER 60
APC will be making a mistake with Muslim-Muslim ticket 261

CHAPTER 61
Tambuwal will be the Nightmare Scenario for PDP 265

CHAPTER 62
Reflections on the PDP Crisis...269

CHAPTER 63
Has PDP shot itself in the Foot?...273

CHAPTER 64
Ekiti: APC as a Sore Loser 275

CHAPTER 65
APC Crisis and the Myth of Party Supremacy...279

CHAPTER 66
Re-thinking the National Assembly..283

CHAPTER 67
Bringing back 'Do-or- Die Politics'? 287

PERSONALITIES

CHAPTER 68
Buhari: Torn Between Two Contradictory Impulses?.......................................293

CHAPTER 69
When the President Returns...297

CHAPTER 70
Buhari's Quest for Emergency Economic Powers 301

CHAPTER 71
Am I Really a "Buhari Hater"?..305

CHAPTER 72
Osibanjo and the role of Intellectuals in Politics..309

CHAPTER 73
Reflections on Fayose's 'stomach infrastructure' 313

CHAPTER 74
Emefiele: Clueless or Just a Fall Guy? 317

CHAPTER 75
Achebe and the 'innocence' of Mortuary Narratives 321

CHAPTER 76
Alamieyeseigha's Pardon: Would you have acted Differently? 325

CHAPTER 77
As Ali Mazrui joins 'Hereafter' 329

CHAPTER 78
Remembering Ali A Mazrui (1) 333

CHAPTER 79
Remembering Ali Mazrui (II) 337

CHAPTER 80
Are we trying to pull down Barrack Obama? 341

CHAPTER 81
The call for Asari-Dokubo to be Arrested 345

CHAPTER 82
Between Edwin Clark and Nigerian Governors..349

CHAPTER 83
Deconstructing Babangida...353

CHAPTER 84
'Fayemi effect' and Intellectuals in Politics 357

CHAPTER 85
Governor Aliyu's Challenge 361

CHAPTER 86
Ike Ibeabuchi: The Greatest who never was..365

CHAPTER 87
Jack Straw, Governor Amaechi and the Nigerian Condition 369

CHAPTER 88
Between President Jonathan and Governor Amaechi..373

CHAPTER 89
When President Jonathan met ASUU Leaders 377

CHAPTER 90
Jonathan's reply to Obasanjo: Too Little, Too Late? 381

CHAPTER 91
Will Jonathan Stepping Aside Solve Nigeria's Problems?..................385

CHAPTER 92
Between Keshi, NFF and Bleaching Complex 389

CHAPTER 93
The Social Costs of Being Mandela..................393

CHAPTER 94
Observations on Obama's Presidency and re-election..................397

CHAPTER 95
How Obasanjo Achieved his third term Ambition..................401

CHAPTER 96
Obasanjo's Agenda for 2015 405

CHAPTER 97
Obasanjo v Jonathan: Cockcrow at Dawn..................409

CHAPTER 98
When Pastor Oritsejeafore Acquired his own Jet 413

CHAPTER 99
The Resignation of Pope Benedict XVI 417

CHAPTER 100
Sanusi's 'democratic-conflict' Theory 421

CHAPTER 101
Sanusi and the Perils of a Two-Party System..................425

CHAPTER 102
Sanusi has raised a very Important Question but… 429

CHAPTER 103
Margaret Thatcher: We Remember Differently..................433

CHAPTER 104
The Achebe book: A Preface 437

CHAPTER 105
The Mandela Example 441

CHAPTER 106
Manipulators of Public Perception: Between Olisa Metuh and Lai Mohammed..................445

CHAPTER 107
The re-invention of Goodluck Jonathan (I)..449

CHAPTER 108
The re-invention of Goodluck Jonathan (II)...453

CHAPTER 109
The re-invention of Goodluck Jonathan (III) 457

CHAPTER 110
Between Strongmen and Strong Institutions 461

CHAPTER 111
Atiku: Beyond the Call for Restructuring Nigeria 465

CHAPTER 112
Funny Quotes from Robert Mugabe..469

CHAPTER 113
Chinakwe: When the law became an ass 473

CHAPTER 114
A new broom at the NPA?..477

CHAPTER 115
Tinubu and the 'rational calculus of war'...481

INTERNATIONAL AFFAIRS

CHAPTER 116
Africa: From Military Coups to Constitutional Coups 487

CHAPTER 117
Can Happiness Really be Measured?..491

CHAPTER 118
As Boutros Boutros-Ghali bows out 495

CHAPTER 119
The Identity Crisis: Who is an African? (I) 499

CHAPTER 120
The Identity Crisis: Who is an African? (II)..503

CHAPTER 121
The Identity Crisis: Who is an African? (III) 507

CHAPTER 122
The military's misadventure in Burkina Faso..511

CHAPTER 123
Issues in Nigeria's Foreign Policy..515

CHAPTER 124
Nation-building: The Mandela and Nyerere Examples..519

CHAPTER 125
Lessons from the Scottish Referendum..523

CHAPTER 126
South Africa: Beyond Xenophobia and 'Market Dominant Minorities'........................527

CHAPTER 127
US-Africa Summit: Another Gesture Politics? 531

CHAPTER 128
Brexit, Bregret and Scaremongering..535

CHAPTER 129
AU Passport: Road to United States of Africa? 539

CHAPTER 130
Lessons from the 2016 US Presidential Election..535

CHAPTER 131
Till debt do us apart..547

Index..551

PREFACE

Debating Nigeria is a collection of articles mostly from my weekly column on the back page of *Daily Trust* - one of Nigeria's leading national dailies. Since July 2010 when I began writing the column, it has only failed to appear twice.

The idea to maintain a weekly column in a Nigerian newspaper came sometime in 2008, when, after some twenty years of living outside the shores of the country, I began making serious arrangements to return home. Like most Nigerian professionals in the Diaspora, there really comes a time when the motivation to keep living 'abroad' simply dries up and home – meaning the country of one's birth - begins to hold a magnetic attraction despite the persistence of the challenges that helped to prolong one's self-imposed exile. I started weekly column writing The *Daily Independent* before switching over to *Daily Trust* in 2010. The column was, at that time, one way of taking 'active' part in the developments at home.

I am grateful to *Daily Trust* for the opportunity provided through this column. I am equally grateful to the readers who often keep me on my toes by writing, texting or calling to commend or critique each output. These comments have proved extremely useful in helping me strive to become better with each work.

With a collection of articles written over a number of years, there is often a challenge of how to arrange them to give the work both coherence and a narrative logic. I believe the best approach to collections of this nature is to regard each article as being independent. The date each article is published is stated at the end of the article for context.

It is often said that journalism is history written in a hurry. I am not sure if column writing fits into that genre. As an academic, I try my best, with each piece, to embed it in sober research. Despite this, any errors of facts and interpretations in any of the articles are mine, and are deeply regretted.

Jideofor Adibe
Abuja, November 2016

DEDICATION

For my wife, Nkem

BOKO HARAM

CHAPTER 1

Chibok Protest or 'Busy-bodies' at work?

I was among those who criticized our government – both the federal government and the Borno State government - for not doing enough in the first three weeks or so of the abduction of the Chibok girls. My thesis was that the prevailing conspiracy theories about Boko Haram played a big role in that lethargy. I argued that in the north, the dominant conspiracy theory was that Jonathan was sponsoring Boko Haram either to make Islam look bad or to depopulate the north ahead of 2015 while in the South and among the supporters of the President, the passionate belief was (is?) that Boko Haram was created by Northern elites to undermine the presidency of President Jonathan. I argued that with these divergent explanations of the Boko Haram challenge, it was difficult to mobilize collective anger and action against the sect. I opined that because of the above President Jonathan and his loyalists probably did not believe there was any abduction until global attention focused on the girls and convinced everyone that they were indeed kidnapped. I also underlined that there were so many gaps in the initial abduction story that many people were really confused, giving conspiracy theorists a field day.

The #BringOurGirlsBack campaigners played a critical role in galvanizing the attention of the world on the fate of the abducted girls, with several countries, including USA, France, China, Britain offering various forms of military and technical assistance, which the Nigerian government accepted. Many people are obviously frustrated that weeks after the hype surrounding the arrival of foreign military and technical advisers to locate the Chibok girls with their assumed sophisticated technology for gathering intelligence, the girls have still not been released.

Though whatever the government is doing to release the girls remains shrouded in secrecy (they can always rationalize this on security concerns for the girls), I think it will be uncharitable to believe that all the foreign technical advisers that reportedly arrived in the country to help in the search for the girls are merely here to drink coffee and tea. In other words, the government and these foreign 'partners' must be doing something. It is highly unlikely, in my opinion, that the government which received deserved piss for its initial inertia on the matter would have so quickly abandoned efforts to locate the girls

For the above reasons, while I can understand the need for the #BringOurGirlsBack social media campaigners not to relent in their efforts so that the Chibok girls will not be pushed off media headlines, I fail to understand the continued relevance of street protests on the matter, especially by the affluent in Abuja. Are the protests meant to force the government's hand into a commando-style rescue action – something most people have counselled against to ensure the girls do not come into harm's way?

While I respect the right of people in a democracy to a peaceful assembly - I believe that banning such protests would be abridging our democratic space - it would seem to me that a more practical way of showing GENUINE concerns now would be to contribute in re-building Chibok or reaching out to the parents of the abducted girls to offer moral and material support. There are many in Chibok and other parts of north-east who have lost their means of livelihood or have been rendered homeless. Such people need support. There are also communities and groups that are reportedly taking the fight to Boko Haram. Such communities too will appreciate any form of logistic, moral and material support.

Since most of the Abuja protesters seem rather well-heeled, they must convince us that they are not merely busy bodies or opportunists trying to cash in on the sad fate that befell the Chibok girls to seek for relevance or hug the limelight. Talk is cheap. As the American playwright Charles Fuller would tell us: "To spend one's life being angry, and in the process doing nothing to change it, is to me ridiculous. I could be mad all day long, but if I'm not doing a damn thing, what difference does it make?"

Wasila Umar is no Heroine

In April, 2014, Nigerians were hit by news of a 14-year old Kano girl, Wasila Umar, who poisoned her 35-year old husband, Umar Sani, and three of his friends to death by putting rodenticide (popularly known as 'ota pia pia') in their meal.

On why she poisoned her husband, Wasila claimed, according to reports, that she did not love Umar Sani, who owned a provision store in their village and was a also a successful farmer. She reportedly hated the idea of being forced to marry Umar Sani against her will so after their wedding she started thinking of what to do to get out of the marriage. She finally settled on getting a rat poison, which she reportedly bought in the local market for N80. When she got home, according to the story, she hid the poison, bidding her time for the right moment. So when the opportunity presented itself, she sprayed the man's food with the poison when no one was looking. And in a village where people would often share food, thirteen others reportedly partook in eating the food. Three died, including her husband.

Wasila reportedly claimed she did not mean to kill her husband but only wanted to show him she did not love him so he would be forced to divorce her. She was said to have confessed of the poisoning when the police were called in following the deaths and complaints of stomach ache by those who ate the food.

Wasila was detained in various centres before she was charged to a magistrate court in Kano. Understandably her case attracted the attention of human rights activists, including the Federation of Women Lawyers in Nigeria which reportedly practically took over her upkeep and defence.

I support the effort of human rights activists in ensuring that Wasila's case was transferred to a juvenile court. But I strongly disagree with any effort to cast her as a victim or worse still as a sort of heroine for killing her husband as a form of resistance to child and forced marriage. In my opinion, Wasila, is both a victim and a villain. It is wrong to glamourize murder under any headline.

The way I see it, there are two issues at stake here – child marriage and murder. Though from stories my mother told me when she was alive, she must have been married at any age between 13 and 15, I am passionately opposed to child marriage (it probably would not be otherwise for someone who lived for 23 years in Europe). But it is important to separate the issue of child or forced marriage from the very depraved act she was said to have committed.

If the reports of the events were correct, then Wasila's action appeared premeditated to me – she went to market, bought the rodenticide, hid it for days, bade her time and sprayed the poison on her husband's food when no one was looking.

While the human rights community performs very important functions in any democracy, efforts must also be made in some of their campaigns not send the wrong message to others – in this case that it is acceptable to commit murder as a form of resisting actions we do not condone.

For the above reason, I am against any move to turn Wasila into a heroine of any sorts because she is not. She might have felt terribly wronged for being married out as a child – and worse still against her will - as she claimed, but who taught a 14-year old girl that rodenticide could be used as poison? Are there no better ways for a 14 year old to show her displeasure at being forced into an early marriage? I do not buy her explanation that she did not intend to kill her husband but only wanted to show him that she did not love him so he divorce her. How exactly was putting rat poison into the man's food meant to achieve that? If she could go to the market unhindered to buy the 'ota pia pia', does it not mean she had relative freedom to run way from her husband? It is rather worrying to me that there has not been equal condemnation that a child Wasila's age could be capable of plotting the alleged evil.

I agree that in a way Wasila is a victim of a society which denied her education and failed to do something about the poverty of her parents - conditions that obviously predisposed her to the sort of unacceptable action she was alleged to have taken. But there are several other child-brides who have adopted other forms of resistance without shedding blood.

Wasila's alleged action may have rightly focused attention on child and forced marriages. But we will miss the point if we also fail to strongly communicate in the Wasila Umar story that spilling of blood is an unacceptable way of making any point. I find it repugnant that while most of the stories dwelt on how much Wasila missed her mum, not one report I read said anything about her showing any remorse for spilling blood.

Daily Trust June 5, 2014

CHAPTER 2

Chibok Girls: It's Time for Prisoner swap with Boko Haram

It is over 60 days since more than 200 Chibok girls were abducted from their school. It is also more than 40 days since the country received sundry offers of military assistance from various countries including USA, Britain, China, France and Australia. These offers from the 'international community' raised flickers of messianic hopes of a quick release of the girls. But more than 40 days after these foreign technical assistance were offered and accepted, many are coming to the realization that even the 'international community' has no magic wand to wave before the abductors of the girls. Messianic hopes are quickly giving way to despondency or rather to the bitter realization that the terrorists are as determined, even not more determined, than those pursuing them.

In all these, the Chibok girls have become cannon fodders for all - from those seeking for relevance to the opponents of the regime who are only too happy to remind us that this is another instance of the regime's incompetence and to the government's apologists who will blame anyone but the government for why the girls are not yet released.

Amid all these came a yet –to- be denied report that Boko Haram leaders were interested in swapping the abducted girls for some of their activists and family members held in captivity. In fact the President was quoted as saying emphatically that his regime would not engage in any swap of prisoners with terrorists. That is of course what many presidents are expected to say – talk tough in public even if they are using third parties to conduct negotiations with those they swear publicly never to negotiate with.

We may never know if the Jonathan regime is in fact negotiating with Boko Haram or not. It is in fact understandable that for security reasons not all that the government is doing to secure the release of the girls will be in the public domain. However, whatever the efforts are, many Nigerians are feeling that those efforts, if any, are taking far too long to bear fruits. Sixty days is far too long to leave young and impressionable girls in the hands of deviants who operate from the other side of the moral divide. We cannot continue to wait ad infinitum for 'something' to happen. To paraphrase the British economist, John Maynard Keynes, in the long run, most of the girls will have reconciled themselves to their circumstances; some will have become pregnant while some will have become dead.

I now believe it is time to do a prisoner swap with Boko Haram. Though the entire idea of releasing terrorists suspected of committing monstrous atrocities is truly horrifying, under the present circumstances, the consequences of not doing a deal are worse than the consequences of doing one. We just have to imagine we are the parents or siblings of the abducted girls!

Throughout history, countries that are far tougher than us, who have engaged in asymmetrical warfare, have had, when the push came to shove, to swap prisoners with their 'weaker' adversaries. For instance as tough and hawkish as Israel is in its relations with its avowed enemies, it has been estimated that in the three decades to 2011, it released almost 8,000 detainees in exchange for captured Israeli soldiers and detainees. Some of the more famous of those prisoner swaps include the release of 4,600 Arab detainees in June 1983 in exchange for six Israeli soldiers held in Lebanon. In June 1984 it swapped 291 Syrians captured in battle and the remains of 72 Syrians for six Israelis and five bodies (only two of which were positively identified as Israelis). In May 1985 Israel released 1,150 Arab prisoners in exchange for three IDF soldiers held by the Popular Front for the Liberation of Palestine. In January 2004 Israel released 436 Palestinian and other Arab prisoners in a deal with Hezbollah for the return of Elhanan Tannenbaum, an Israeli businessman, and three dead IDF soldiers abducted on a border patrol in 2000. In July 2008 in return for releasing five men, Israel recovered from Hezbollah the bodies of two of its soldiers, captured in The Second Lebanon War in 2006. In October 2011, Israel swapped 25 jailed Egyptians for Ilan Grapel who was detained in Egypt on accusations that he was out to recruit agents and monitor events during the revolt that toppled Hosni Mubarak, an ally of Israel and the United States. Israel denied the allegations.

France's decision in 2010 to release Ali Vakili Rad, who was convicted in 1994 of killing the former Iranian Prime Minister Shahpour Bakhtiar so that Interior Ministry officials could execute a court order expelling him to Tehran, was suspected to be a prisoner swap. This is because shortly after his release and deportation, Clotilde Reiss, a 24-year-old French teacher who had been detained in Tehran since July 2009 on charges of espionage in connection with Iran's contested 2009 presidential election, returned home.

The USA also does swapping of prisoners. At the beginning of this month the country secured the release of Sergeant Bowe Bergdahl who spent five years in captivity. Bergdahl, who was held by the Pakistani Taliban militants was exchanged for five of the group's most deadly snipers who were being who were being held at the detention centre at Guantanamo Bay.

But even before this, there was the infamous Iran-Contra affair which came to light in November 1986. Under the Iran-Contra deal (which became Irangate when it leaked), senior Reagan administration officials secretly facilitated the sale of arms to Iran, the subject of an arms embargo, on the hopes that the arms sales would secure the release of several American hostages in Iran and also allow U.S. intelligence agencies to fund the Nicaraguan Contras.

In almost all instances of prisoner swap, more detainees from the weaker adversaries are released by the state – an indication that such states value the life of its citizen more than several or even hundreds of their asymmetrical foes.

Of course there are legitimate fears that releasing some of the detained Boko Haram members could bolster the fighting forces of the terrorists, further endangering the lives of citizens. But we can also pose the question of whether the arrest and detention of those Boko Haram is allegedly asking to be released in exchange for the Chibok girls has led to an abatement in their terrorism. If the detention of the arrested suspected Boko Haram members has done little to abate Boko Haram's terrorism, then we can also argue that their release may not significantly affect the trajectory of the conflict. If anything, it could be a confidence-boosting measure, something to assure Boko Haram, that the government may be willing to do a 'better' deal if they choose to embrace peace and dialogue.

Certainly given the atrocities and mayhem the sect has committed serially, this will understandably be a very bitter pill for many Nigerians to swallow. However there comes a time in the life of a nation when it has to stoop painfully low, not to conquer, but to demonstrate that it is capable of compassion and empathy. Many Nigerians feel that if the children of some high profile politicians were among those kidnapped, something would have been done a long time ago to secure their release. In essence that the Chibok girls are still with their abductors more than sixty days after they were whisked away and more than 40 days since some foreign military advisers arrived to help secure their release, underlines the fact that despite the posturing and grandstanding about ethnicity, religion and region, it is in one's class location in the scheme of things that we should seek valid explanations about who gets what, when and how.

There are also those who oppose any form of deal with Boko Haram over the Chibok girls on the ground that the government would lose face by so doing. True, the government may lose face momentarily – and only in the estimation of some - but so what? Given a choice between losing a face and losing lives and futures, which one should we go for?

Though it is the policy of most governments not to pay ransom to have kidnap victims released, we know that in real life ransoms are paid to ensure that victims are released alive. By embracing the option of prisoner swap, the government will also deny its traducers the opportunity for grandstanding or puffing for relevance. It will be horrifying to the government to contemplate how the citizens will perceive it if (God forbid) anything untoward happens to the girls. Such, in many climes will be enough to bring down a ruling government. Though all the levels of government – federal, Borno State government and local governments in Borno state share culpability in the way the Boko Haram challenge grew out of hand and led to the abduction of the Chibok girls, only the federal government has the right to do a deal with Boko Haram. In my opinion this is the time for the federal government to exercise that prerogative. In fact the more the delay in securing the release of the girls, the more the regime loses its legitimacy and makes hero of opportunists and soldiers of fortune trying to regain relevance from the whole sad episode.

Daily Trust, June 19 2014

CHAPTER 3

Explaining the Emergence of Boko Haram

Nigeria has experienced a number of tragedies in recent weeks: The terrorist group Boko Haram has claimed responsibility for a series of recent bombings in Abuja and the kidnapping of over 200 schoolgirls in Borno State (including eight more just this morning). While these events have had devastating impacts, Boko Haram's activities in Nigeria, and those of its splinter group Ansaru, are hardly new. Under a radical Islamic agenda, these militants have perpetuated violence across northern Nigeria since roughly 2009, aiming to rid the country of any "Western influence." As leaders from across the region gather in Abuja this week for the World Economic Forum on Africa, Boko Haram and the direction of this conflict in Nigeria have received increased attention.

This month, the Brookings Africa Growth Initiative is wrapping up a yearlong study on the impact of conflict on the agricultural sectors in northern Nigeria and Mali. I collaborated with Brookings on this study and put together a long-form exposition on the possible trajectories of Nigeria's conflict. While the full report moves toward publication, Brookings asked me to publish excerpts for *Africa In Focus* on 1) explaining the emergence of Boko Haram, 2) discussing possible scenarios of how the conflict could evolve, and 3) offering policy recommendations for curbing the violence. Please find below the first part of my analysis: how Boko Haram came about.

A Brief History of Boko Haram

Boko Haram members prefer to be known by their Arabic name—*Jama'atu Ahlis Sunna Lidda'awati Wal-Jihad*—meaning "People Committed to the Propagation of the Prophet's Teachings and Jihad." The group is believed to have been formed in the town of Maiduguri in northeast Nigeria, where the locals nicknamed its members "Boko Haram," a combination of the Hausa word "boko," which literally means "Western education" and the Arabic word "haram" which figuratively means "sin" and literally means "forbidden." While the popular belief is that it was founded around 2001 or 2002 by Mohammed Yusuf, some have argued that the sect was actually started in 1995 as Sahaba. The group claims to be opposed not only to Western civilization (which includes Western education) but also to the secularization of the Nigerian state. There is a fair consensus that, until 2009, the group conducted its operations more or less peacefully and that its radicalization followed a government clampdown in 2009, in which some 800 of its members were killed. The group's leader, Mohammed Yusuf, was also killed after that attack while in police custody.

Ansaru, whose Arabic name is *Jamā'atu Anṣāril Muslimīna fī Bilādis Sūdān* ("Vanguards for the Protection of Muslims in Black Africa"), is a breakaway faction of

Boko Haram. It first announced its existence on January 26, 2012 by distributing fliers in Kano, shortly after Boko Haram attacks in the city killed approximately 150 civilians, most of them Muslims. It is from this attack that some media reports described Ansaru's emergence as a reaction to the loss of innocent Muslim lives. From inception, Ansaru was believed to coordinate its operations in Nigeria with the northern Mali-based al-Qaeda in the Islamic Maghreb (AQIM) and the Movement for Unity and Jihad in West Africa (MUJWA). Both Boko Haram and Ansaru were declared as foreign terrorist organizations by the United States on November 13, 2013.

There are many popular explanations for the emergence and radicalization of Boko Haram. They can be summarized under some key categories as follows:

Conspiracy Theories

Several conspiracy theories are commonly used to explain the Boko Haram and Ansaru phenomena. These include:

(a) Northern politicians sponsor Boko Haram to make the country "ungovernable" for President Goodluck Jonathan.

This theory is very popular among commentators and leading politicians from the southern part of the country. President Jonathan is a southerner from the minority Ijaw ethnic group. According to the theory, people from the north, essentially the "core north" (i.e., the Hausa/Fulani), believe it is their birthright to govern the country, and, because a Christian southerner is in charge, they decided to sponsor Boko Haram as an instrument for destabilizing the Jonathan presidency. A major weakness of this theory is that much of the mayhem carried out by the sect has been in the north and against northern Muslims. If northern politicians really want to make the country "ungovernable" for President Jonathan, why would they do so by sponsoring a group which is disproportionately killing northern Muslims and literally destroying several parts of the north?

(b) President Jonathan sponsors Boko Haram either to mobilize support from the south and Christians or to weaken and de-populate the north ahead of the 2015 presidential election.

Another conspiracy theory is that Boko Haram is actually sponsored by the Jonathan administration to make Islam look bad or give the impression that the north is out to pull down his administration or make him fail as president of the country. This would be a way for the president to mobilize the support of his "southern and Christian brethren" behind his administration. A variant of this theory is that Boko Haram is actually sponsored by the government to weaken, destroy or reduce the population of the north ahead of the 2015 elections. A number of respected leaders from the north, including the governor of Adamawa state, Murtala Nyako, and governor of Sokoto state, Alhaji Aliyu Wamakko, have legitimized this theory by coming out to subscribe to it openly.

The major weakness of this theory is that nothing in the confessions of arrested Boko Haram members supports it. Again, it is befuddling why the insurgents, who are all Muslims (going by the identity of those captured), and campaigning under the cloak of Islamic revivalism, would allow themselves to be used by a non-Muslim to kill fellow Muslims. Again, nothing supports this, either on YouTube or in press releases by Shekau, the leader of the mainstream Boko Haram who is now thought to be dead, although his death is questioned due to his continued appearance in YouTube videos.

The Failed State Argument

Some people have suggested that Boko Haram is simply a symptom that the overarching Nigerian state has failed, or at best, is failing. The problem here is that there is no consensus on the meaning of "failed state," including how to operationalize it. The difficulty of defining a "failed state" is compounded by the fact that it is sometimes used as a tool of political blackmail. Anyone can focus on where a state is perceived as not doing well—such as in the provision of security, welfare or improving citizens' standards of living—and then conclude that the state in question has "failed" or is "failing." The argument that Boko Haram's terrorism is conclusive evidence that Nigeria has failed as a state appears exaggerated because "successful" countries like South Africa, the United States and Brazil also have serious security challenges. Despite Boko Haram's activities, it is a stretch to describe the complexities of a vast country, whose economy has been growing by an average of 7 percent since 2000 such that it now has the largest economy in Africa (and 26th largest in the world) as a "failed state."

The Human Needs and Poor Governance Theories

Human needs theorists such as John Burton [1] and Abraham Maslow [2] would argue that one of the primary causes of the protracted conflicts in Nigeria is the people's drive to meet their unmet needs. Those who have sought to explain the Boko Haram phenomenon within this framework point out that, despite a per capita income of $2,700 (before the recent rebasing of the GDP) and an impressive annual GDP growth rate for over a decade, the north has one of the poorest populations in Nigeria. Within the north itself, the northeast—the base of Boko Haram's operations—has one of the largest concentrations of people Franz Fanon would call the "Wretched of the Earth." [3] Many of these people are either unemployed or underemployed, and therefore suffer from various forms of what Ted Gurr would call "relative deprivation." [4]

Some analysts have also attributed the relative poverty of the north to "bad governance" by the governors of the states in the region who are accused of embezzling or misappropriating the funds that should have been channelled to the development of their states.

There are some merits in the human needs and poor governance arguments, but they cannot fully explain the audacity of Boko Haram's actions or why a similar group has not emerged in other impoverished parts of the country. Moreover, poor governance is not exclusive to the states in the north, and there is actually no evidence that the states in other parts of the country are better governed.

The Frustration-Aggression Hypothesis

Otherwise known as frustration-aggression displacement theory, [5] this hypothesis argues that frustration causes aggression, and when the source of the frustration cannot be challenged, the aggression gets displaced onto an innocent target. Many recent events appear to fit into this theory. For instance, recently suspended Central Bank of Nigeria Governor Sanusi Lamido Sanusi blamed the rise of Boko Haram partly on the way the revenues from the country's Federation Account—an account in which all the revenues that accrue to the Federation are paid into—are shared. Sanusi argued that the sharing is done in a manner that disadvantages the north. According to him, a "revenue sharing formula that gave 13 percent derivation to the oil-producing states was introduced after the military relinquished power in 1999 among a series of measures aimed at redressing historic grievances among those living closest to the oil and quelling a conflict that was jeopardising output. [...] There is clearly a direct link between the very uneven nature of distribution of resources and the rising level of violence."

While Sanusi's argument may be partly true, it cannot comprehensively explain why the Boko Haram type of violence is not generalized in the north or why several states in the south that also do not benefit from the 13 percent derivation have not taken to militancy.

Another popular variant of the frustration-aggression response is, that after the reintroduction of Shariah in the 12 northern states, there was a widespread disillusionment at to the way it was implemented, and members of the sect simply tapped into that frustration. As Jean Herskovits, an expert on Nigerian politics, said, "You punish somebody for stealing a goat or less but a governor steals billions of naira, and gets off scot-free."

There is also a belief that, in Nigeria's mode of sharing privileges, the Igbo control the commercial economy, the Yoruba the corporate economy, and the north political power. The loss of this power to the south from 1999 to 2003, when Olusegun Obasanjo, a Yoruba from the southwest who was president, and again since May 2010 following the death of former northern and Muslim President Umaru Yaradua, is therefore seen as a loss of the north's lever in maintaining the power balance. This is believed to have created frustrations into which Boko Haram could tap, especially following the fallouts from the ruling party's bickering over zoning and power-sharing arrangements as well as President Jonathan's decision to contest the April 2011 elections and possible plans to contest again in 2015.

Broader Crisis in Nigeria's Nation Building

A better and more comprehensive view of the Boko Haram and Ansaru phenomena is to see them as symptoms of the crisis in Nigeria's nation-building processes. While the bombings, kidnappings, and other unsavory acts linked to the sects are condemnable, it is important to underscore that Boko Haram is only one of several groups in the country that purvey terror and death because there is an increasing tendency to discuss the spate of insecurity in the country as if it all began and ended with Boko Haram or as if without Boko Haram Nigeria would be a tranquil place in which to live.

The truth is that there is everywhere in the country a pervasive sense of what the German-American political theorist Hannah Arendt called the "banality of evil." [6] Her argument is that the great evils in history are not executed by fanatics or sociopaths but rather by ordinary people who accept the premises of their actions and therefore participate in them on the grounds that those heinous actions were normal. This is the so-called notion of "normalizing the unthinkable" or the routinization of evil. This argument captures an important element of what is happening throughout Nigeria: Violent armed robberies across the entire country, kidnapping (especially in the southeast), turf war by militarized cults and gangs (in Bayelsa State), and senseless intra- and inter-communal "warfare" are all increasingly common. [7] The crisis in Nigeria's nation building mixes with the crisis of underdevelopment to create an existentialist crisis for many Nigerians. For many young people, a way of resolving the consequent sense of alienation is to retreat from the "Nigeria project"—the idea of fashioning a nation out of the disparate nationalities that make up the country—and instead construct meanings in primordial identities, often with the Nigerian state as the enemy.

Based on the above, any strategy for effectively neutralizing Boko Haram and Ansaru must be hinged on resolving the crisis in Nigeria's nation-building processes. Admittedly, this will require a sense of long-term scenarios and solutions, as nation-building takes time. In the interim there are short- and medium- term strategies the Nigerian state can pursue to contain the challenges posed by the two terrorist groups. These scenarios and strategies will be the focus of the next installments in this blog series.

Brookings, Africa in Focus, http://www.brookings.edu/blogs/africa-in-focus/posts/2014/05/06-emergence-of-boko-haram-adibe

CHAPTER 4

Possible Trajectories of the Boko Haram Conflict

I think it may be germane to start with what we all probably know, that scenario planning - also called scenario thinking or scenario analysis - is merely a strategic planning method used by companies and countries to make flexible long-term plans or to plan for eventualities. It is not a prophecy of what will happen or what one wants to happen. Quite often scenario mapping – just like futures studies - is based on a very important caveat – all things being equal (*ceteris paribus*), which is another way of saying, "if current trends continue". In real life however we all know that things are rarely equal and current trends rarely continue as they are.

The other important point to bear in mind is that virtually everything about Boko Haram is contested – from the meaning of its name (i.e. whether the translation of 'Boko Haram' should mean "Western education is forbidden or a sin" [a mere transliteration in my opinion] or "Western civilization is forbidden or a sin" – which I believe should be the correct interpretation - to when the sect was founded, the reasons for its radicalization, whether its assumed leader Shekau is dead or alive and whether many of the attacks assumed to be carried out by the sect were actually carried out by them.

We will build a number of scenarios under which the Boko Haram conflict will abate or decelerate and permutations under which the conflict could accelerate or widen.

Scenario 1: Attacks by Boko Haram Decline

Aftermath of the kidnap of the Chibok girls
There were high expectations that the global outrage caused by the kidnap of over 200 Chibok girls and the involvement of foreign countries (USA, UK, France, China etc.), in the efforts to locate and release them could lead to a deceleration of the conflict.

- If the U.S-led foreign military and technical assistance had been quick in locating the whereabouts of the abducted girls and freed them without many of the kidnapped girls losing their lives in the process or a heavy civilian casualty during any rescue operation, it would have bolstered the standing of the US-led foreign countries in the eyes of the Nigerian public and probably demoralized the insurgents, leading to a deceleration of the conflict.

- However if the foreign military advisers are unable, within a short frame of time, to locate and release the girls, it could embolden Boko Haram, and further raise the sect's profile within the international terrorism franchise. In this sense, one of the unintended effects of the foreign 'intervention' in the wake of the kidnap of the Chibok girls could actually be an acceleration of the Boko Haram conflict. For instance there is a feeling that the declaration of the sect as an FTO by the US in November 2013 had the unintended effect of glamourizing the sect within the international terrorism franchise, leading to more support to them and increasing the audacity of their actions.

President Jonathan stepping aside as President

There are many people, especially from the north, who seem to believe, for various reasons, that Jonathan is the 'trouble with Nigeria' and that once he steps aside, renounces interest in 2015 or is removed from office, the problems of Boko Haram will be solved.

- Since Boko Haram taps into some local grievances in parts of the north, especially feelings of being cheated resulting from the acrimonious PDP's zoning and power rotation arrangements (or that the north needs the political lever to balance the south's alleged domination of the economy and bureaucracy), Jonathan stepping aside to be succeeded by a northern Muslim, could address some of these grievances and choke off any latent local sympathy for the sect in the north-east, leading to a deceleration in the conflict.

- The problem with this option however is that Jonathan may not agree to any deal in this direction unless such will enhance his political stature. This is another way of saying that such a deal will have to involve very complex negotiations involving strategic stakeholders from the north, south-south, the south, Muslim and Christian communities – and possibly also major world leaders. This is because Jonathan's candidacy has grown much larger than him and anyone who fails to appreciate this will be completely missing the point.

- There is always a danger that concessions to the north in this regard could militarize other insurgency groups in the country who may come to believe that Boko Haram-type of violence may be needed to win concessions for their parts of the country. For instance there are those who believe that NADECO's heroic (in my opinion) but militarized campaign for the revalidation of the June 12 1993 election won by Abiola but annulled by Babangida led to the presidency being conceded to the Yorubas in 1999 and that the militants in the Niger Delta were pacified not only with a generous amnesty programme that turned many of the militants into billionaires overnight but also paved the way for the emergence of someone from the Niger Delta (Jonathan) first as Vice President and subsequently as President. In other words, any negotiation for Jonathan to step aside and for power to 'return to north' must be mindful to address the possible 'me-tooist' imitations by other insurgent groups in the country.

- If President Jonathan is hounded out of office or prevented from running (such as the Supreme Court disqualifying him as ineligible to contest), it could lead to a renewed militancy in the restive Niger Delta and also deepen the north-south (or north- south south) divide.

- If Jonathan runs and loses, there will be the usual cries of being rigged out, which will most likely renew militancy in the Niger Delta – even if the electoral tribunals and the Supreme Court affirm the loss.

- If APC loses the election, there will also be the usual cries of being rigged out, leading to post-election violence in the north, perhaps on a scale larger than what we witnessed in 2011.

- If APC unravels and many of the influential northern politicians are persuaded to return to PDP, this is unlikely to have any major impact on the trajectory of the conflict.

If Northern state governors and political leadership are empowered to be the faces of the fight against Boko Haram and arrested Boko Haram suspects tried under Sharia law

- This could immediately address the conspiracy theory prevalent in the north that Jonathan is sponsoring the sect either to make Islam look bad or to depopulate the north ahead of 2015 or that he is not doing enough to fight the insurgents because it is not 'his people' that are being killed. In essence the Northern political leadership being made the face of the campaign against Boko Haram will give them full ownership and responsibility for the fight against terrorism in the region. Also trying arrested suspected Boko Haram insurgents under Sharia law could convince them that their trial is not a Western conspiracy against them and Islam since the insurgents have openly rejected Western civilization, including its jurisprudence.

- Though this option appears to hold a good promise of leading to the abatement of the conflict in the short term, there are flipsides to it: Will the rest of the country accept it if (a) the insurgents are tried under Sharia and not found guilty? (b) If the northern political leadership recommends a generous amnesty programme for the insurgents along the lines of what the Niger Delta militants received? © If the northern political leadership tries its best but is unable to capture leading members of the sect or stem the tide of the conflict?

Scenario 2: Boko Haram accelerates and widens the Conflict

It is possible for the Boko Haram conflict to grow far worse than it is now. This trend could happen under at least four possible scenarios.

(a) If Boko Haram unleashes attacks in any of the southern states and it leads to massive retaliatory responses

- This scenario could throw ethnicity and regional clashes into the boiling pot, widening the conflict and possibly turning Boko Haram and other insurgency groups in the country into *de facto* regional and ethnic armies.

- **(b) If Boko Haram chooses to outsource its terrorism to Fulani herdsmen or infiltrates them.** This could lead to their operations spreading to other parts of the country beyond the northeast up to the south. The good news here however is that even if this happens, Boko Haram will lack the critical local infrastructure to sustain its terrorism in the south – as it has done in the north-east.

- **(C)If the United States and Europe become the faces of the fight against the insurgents.** Anti-Western sentiments could galvanize, turning into support for the terrorists if Western countries are made the faces of the fight against terrorism in the country, especially if their involvement results in massive deaths of the insurgents and non-combatants.

- **(d)If President Jonathan wins the 2015 election, especially if there is a feeling that he rigged himself to power.** This option could harden the political discontents in the north, further feeding the Boko Haram terrorists the oxygen to continue and possibly widen their insurgency. It is important to underline that the notion of 'free and fair election in Nigeria is largely subjective. Election is deemed 'free and fair' only if one's preferred candidate is declared the winner.

Adapted from a presentation to the executives of the oil company, Chevron, Lekki, Lagos, 7 June 2014.

Daily Trust, June 12, 2014

CHAPTER 5

Boko Haram in Nigeria: The Way Forward

On Monday, in a video showing 130 of the over 200 kidnapped Nigerian schoolgirls, Boko Haram announced that it would be willing to let the girls go as part of a trade for Boko Haram militants currently held by Nigeria. Later that day, Nigerian Interior Minister Abba Moro announced that Nigeria declined the offer, stating that the sect is not in any moral position to swap prisoners for the innocent girls. As I stated in an earlier blog, this kidnapping is only the latest in a long list of attacks against the Nigerian state and its innocent civilians. Boko Haram militants have been active around the country and especially in the northeast for many years. In fact, this week President Goodluck Jonathan also asked Nigeria's parliament to extend the state of emergency declared in May of 2013 in the northeastern states of Adamawa, Borno and Yobe—the ones most vulnerable and consistently victimized by Boko Haram—by another six months.

However, the tragedies in Nigeria and the conflict with Boko Haram require more than just responses to terrorist activities. Though foreign governments are now providing Nigeria with security and surveillance support, the conflict will not end until longer-term and deeply held grievances are addressed. The strategies adopted by the government should be divided into long-term measures aimed at neutralizing the groups and short- to medium-term measures aimed at containing them and their terrorism.

Long-Term Solutions to Battling Boko Haram: Resolving the Crisis in Nigeria's Nation Building

Nigeria, the most populous country in sub-Saharan Africa as well as the biggest economy, is facing a severe crisis in its nation-building process. Virtually every part of Nigeria claims it is "marginalized." Concomitant groups have been calling for the convocation of a "Sovereign National Conference"—a euphemism for a meeting to discuss whether Nigerians want to continue to live together as one country. Something nasty has happened to the effort to create "true Nigerians"—that is, Nigerians who privilege their Nigerian identity over the other identities they bear in the country. Thus, some people still believe that Nigeria is a "mere geographical expression," a nation only in name and with only very few "true Nigerians."

The struggle in nation building mixes with poverty, inequality and a lack of development in the country, creating an existential crisis for many Nigerians. As I stated in my previous blog, for many young people, a way of resolving this sense of alienation is to retreat from the "Nigeria project"—the idea of fashioning a nation out of the disparate nationalities that make up the country—and construct meanings in chosen primordial identities, often with the Nigerian state as the enemy. I have elsewhere [i] called this phenomenon the "de-Nigerianization process." In Nigeria, there is a heavy burden of institutionalized memories of hurt, injustice, distrust and even a disguised longing for vengeance by various individuals, ethnic groups, regions and religious groups. In this sense, actions that ordinary Nigerians rightly see as heinous are seen by some as normal, even heroic.

There is a feeling that this "de-Nigerianization process" is accelerating by leaps and bounds. No individual or political authority enjoys universally perceived legitimacy across the main fault lines and therefore the country is in desperate need of creating more "true Nigerians." If this trend continues, there is a high risk of a growing number of individuals and groups impairing or even attacking the Nigerian state. Already, some of those entrusted with the nation's common patrimony steal it blind; some law enforcement officers turn the other way if offered a little inducement; organized labor (including university lecturers) sometimes goes on prolonged strikes on a whim; students may resort to cultism and exam malpractices; and workers often drag their feet, refuse to put in their best and engage in moonlighting. It seems that everyone has one form of grouse or another against the Nigerian state and its institutions.

A long-term solution for containing Boko Haram's and Ansaru's terrorism, and for neutralizing them along with other insurgency groups in Nigeria, is to resolve the crisis in the country's nation-building processes. Terrorism will end when Nigerians come to see themselves as one people and develop that sense of what Benedict Anderson calls "imagined communities." For Anderson, a nation is a community socially constructed and imagined by the people who perceive themselves as part of the group. For him, a nation "is imagined because the members of even the smallest nation will never know most of their fellow-members, meet them, or even hear of them, yet in the minds of each lives the image of their communion."[ii]

Re-starting the stalled nation-building process is not going to happen overnight. The following measures, however, hold a good promise:

(a) I remain skeptical that the on-going ad hoc National Conference convened by the federal government to recommend solutions to the country's many challenges will succeed, because of deeply ingrained distrust among Nigerians. However, the conference, if well managed, could be a credible platform for all stakeholders to vent their grievances and frustrations with the Nigeria project. The catharsis will be useful as the country strives for long-term solutions to its nation-building problems. In the same vein, some recommendations from the conference, if implemented, could help mollify some aggrieved groups.

(b) Perhaps one of the long-term solutions to the Boko Harm challenge could come by default. The increasing wave of "Naija optimism" could help blunt the pull of the centrifugal forces. This is a wave of new hope around the country's economic prospects, typified in the recent inclusion of Nigeria in the MINT (Mexico, Indonesia, Nigeria and Turkey) emerging economies and the rebasing of its GDP, making it the largest economy in Africa and the 26th largest in the world. Because people instinctively want to identify with success, economic growth, especially if it is accompanied with more equitable distribution and people-oriented development could pacify irredentist pressures, as separatist forces may have to contend with the fear of leaving at the time the country is being tapped as among the likely future economic superpowers of the world.

(c) As Nigeria's economy develops, the various parts of the country could develop organic economic linkages that will help further the cause of the nation-building process. For instance, if the groundnuts produced in the north are used in the manufacture of peanut butter in the southeast, and the cocoa produced in the west is used for manufacturing chocolate drinks in the north, such economic linkages will help blunt interregional animosities and thus further the cause of national unity.

What Can Nigeria Do in the Meantime? Short- to Medium-Term Solutions to the Violence

In the short- to medium-term, the government should adopt a combination of *koboko* (Hausa word for whip) and "pieces of the National cake" (a Nigerian phrase for "patronage" or "co-optation into the system"). In Western speak, carrot and stick strategies. Some of the measures the government could take include:

(i) *Empowering the state governments in the north to lead the charge and be the faces of the fight against Boko Haram.* This could, if anything, address the conspiracy theory in the north that President Goodluck Jonathan's administration is funding Boko Haram either to make Islam look bad or to depopulate the north ahead of the 2015 elections. It is important to underline that the conspiracy theories have made it more difficult to mobilize collective anger against Boko Haram.

(ii) *Creating a Ministry of Northern Affairs*—just like the Ministry of Niger Delta Affairs— to help address the numerous challenges in the north, including the problems of poverty, unemployment, illiteracy and radical Islam. This establishment would be one way of winning the hearts and minds of the locals and cooling local grievances on which Boko Haram feeds.

(iii) *Conducting speedy and fair trials, under Islamic laws, of those found to be Boko Haram activists or funders* and letting the law have its full course. Having suspects stand for trial for months or even years creates a backlash, and often has a way of mobilizing sympathy for the suspects. It may also be strategic to try the suspects under Islamic laws since the sect members have openly rejected Western civilization, including its jurisprudence. Whatever punishment is meted to them under Islamic jurisprudence will not be seen as part of Western conspiracy against Islam.

(iv) *Instituting a sort of Marshall Plan for the northeast* aimed at winning the hearts and minds of the local populace. The plan should aim at providing quality education, building local capacity and providing jobs.

(v) *Exploring the option of offering amnesty to the more moderate members* of the sects while side-lining the hardliners and finding means to effectively neutralize them.

Conclusion

There is no quick fix to fighting terrorism anywhere in the world as the experiences in Afghanistan, Somalia, Yemen and other countries have shown. However, with the above recommended short- to-medium term strategies pursued concurrently with the long-term strategy of resolving the crisis in Nigeria's nation-building processes, Boko Harm's and Ansaru's terrorism can be contained, and the groups eventually neutralized.

Brookings, Africa in Focus, http://www.brookings.edu/blogs/africa-in-focus/posts/2014/05/14-boko-haram-nigeria-adibe

CHAPTER 6

Boko Haram: 'Mission Accomplished' or 'Technically Defeated'?

The recent declaration by President Buhari that the country has "technically won the war" against Boko Haram reminds one of George W Bush's 'Mission Accomplished' speech on May 1 2003.

The United States had invaded Iraq on March 20 2013, with a coalition that included American, Australian, Polish and Danish military troops. With the Iraqi capital Baghdad falling on April 20 2003 – much earlier than envisaged by the coalition - an elated President Bush could hardly contain himself. In a televised speech on May 1 2003, President Bush pompously announced the defeat of Saddam Hussein and a victory for the coalition. On the background during that speech was a banner that read "Mission Accomplished" displayed on the US warship/ aircraft carrier USS Abraham Lincoln (also known as Navy One), which had just returned from combat operations in the Persian Gulf.

As it turned out however that declaration was premature because most of the casualties in the conflict – both civilian and the military - occurred after that speech. For his army of critics, that speech was one more instance of President Bush's shallowness on how the real world works. Bush himself was to severally regret that 'Mission Accomplished' speech. For instance in January 2009 he was quoted as saying: "Clearly putting 'Mission Accomplished' on an aircraft carrier was a mistake."

Re-wind to Nigeria, December 2015.

Nobody doubts that President Buhari was very determined from the day he assumed office as the elected President to confront Boko Haram headlong. However when in September he gave the military a December deadline to defeat the terrorists, many felt that such a deadline could be counterproductive. For instance in my column of October 7 2015 entitled 'Re-thinking Boko Haram', I argued that while giving the military a deadline to crush Boko Haram could have a role to play in motivating the soldiers and re-assuring the civilian populace, I was not sure whether a failure to meet the deadline could be interpreted as a defeat for the country or not. The deadline suggested a simplistic binary of 'win' or 'lose'.

The deadline also not only wrongly assumed that the Boko Haram militants were enemies massed on the other side of a conventional war but also ignored both the history of terrorism and Boko Haram's specific history. The truth is that the current religion-inspired wave of terrorism (which was estimated to have started in 1979) has not really been completely routed in any clime. In fact scholars estimate that this wave may last until 2025 to be replaced by another wave. In other words, if history is a guide, then we can talk of defeating terrorism only in the sense that we talk of eliminating corruption and crime. Complete elimination of terrorism is utopia but reducing it to the barest minimum is possible and should be the goal. Let us remember that following the attack in the USA on September 1, 2001, President George W. Bush declared a war on terrorism with a boast that the war "would not end until every terrorist group of global reach has been found, stopped and defeated". More than 14 years after, can we say America has won or is winning the war?

To argue as – as some APC spokes persons are currently doing – that the President never said or suggested that Boko Haram attacks would end by December but only that the group would no longer be able to hold any Nigerian territory - is to indulge in opulent sophistry. For one this line of logic not only wrongly assumes that Boko Haram was not lethal before it began seizing territories about two or three years ago but also falsely assumes that Sambisa forest (Boko Haram's current stronghold) is not part of Nigerian territory.

I feel it would have been far more ennobling for the government to come clean and admit that its initial assessment of the situation had been faulty. Essentially therefore, apart from putting the integrity of the government on the line, the government's 'Boko Haram has been technically defeated' speech could raise the expectation of the citizens such that any attack by the group will be seen as another evidence that the government has lied to them. In other words, the claim that Boko Haram has been 'technically defeated' could lead to frustrations and under-appreciation of the gallantry and sacrifices of the soldiers fighting the terrorists.

Some of Boko Haram's attacks since the 'Boko Haram has been technically defeated' speech include: on Christmas day, just two days after Buhari's pronouncement, Boko Haram raided a village, killing 14 people. On December 27, the Daily Post reported of an intense battle between Boko Haram insurgents and the military over attempts by the insurgents to take over Maiduguri, the capital city of Borno State. On the same December 27, the Premium Times reported that the army arrested seven Boko Haram bomb makers in Kaduna. On December 28 several media outlets reported that about 30 people were feared dead in a suicide attack in Adamawa state.

Since its radicalization in 2010, Boko Haram has shown remarkable resilience and adaptability. On at least three occasions, the country thought the group had become routed – only to be disappointed.

The 'smart' way to remove fuel subsidy

The recent announcement by the Federal Government that effective   from January 1, 2016, Premium Motor Spirit (PMS), otherwise known as petrol or fuel, would be sold at N86 per litre by the Nigerian National Petroleum Corporation's (NNPC's) retail stations while other oil marketers would sell at N86.50 per litre, was a smart move by the government. The current official cost of fuel is N97 per litre – though the price is considerably more outside the major cities of Abuja and Lagos. The general belief is that the government has finally decided to remove fuel subsidy from January 2016 – despite its conflicting signals on the matter.

By hiding the bad news in good news – a perfectly legitimate strategy used by governments across the world - the government is probably hoping to tie the hands of those opposed to removing subsidies. By showing that the price of fuel should actually be lower despite the de-subsidization, the government probably hopes to remove the quivers from the arrows of the pro-subsidy lobby.

Though the Nigerian Labour Congress (NLC) said it would resist any subsidy removal, it is not certain that they will get the backing of most Nigerians on this. The fact is that several people who were opposed to removing subsidies have since shifted positions. In fact the 'shut down Nigeria' protests that followed the attempt by the Jonathan administration to substantially reduce the subsidy on fuel on January 1 2012 had led to the House of Representatives setting up the Farouk Lawan Ad Hoc Committee on Fuel subsidy which showed how the subsidy regime was turned into a haven for rent seeking and outright theft by a cabal of oil marketers. The government's own Aig-Imoukhuede-led committee report and the Nuhu Ribadu's oil subsidy report were no less damning of the oil marketers - who fought back ferociously in a manner that convinced many Nigerians that given how powerful they are, the only viable option to the scam was for the subsidy to go.

With long queues returning at petrol stations across the country, people were rather surprised that it took the Buhari government so long to act on the fuel subsidy matter. In this sense I do not share the sentiment that it would amount to hypocrisy for those who opposed the removal of fuel subsidy under former President Jonathan to now turn round to support it.

I have two concerns on this though: one, if the subsidy should go (as I believe it should), what then is the need for the government to impose price controls with threats against anyone who will sell above the recommended price? If the supply side is as it should be, then the price should be determined by demand and supply.

My other concern is that while we are doing away with one subsidy (fuel subsidy), we are introducing a couple of new ones – school feeding and N5, 000 per month to 'vulnerable' unemployed people. Just like the fuel subsidy, the possibility that a cabal of contractors would capture these new regimes is very high.

Daily Trust, December 30 2015

CHAPTER 7

A Nation at War With Itself

The recent bomb attack in a bus terminus at Nyanya, a bustling outskirts of Abuja, by a suicide bomber suspected to be a Boko Haram terrorist or sympathizer, was one too many. Perhaps more than any of the previous attacks by the sect, the Nyanya incident, which targeted people hustling to get to work at Abuja, aroused a collective sense of sorrow and outrage. Estimates of the dead and injured vary – depending on whom you want to believe. What appears obvious is that anywhere between 75 and 130 people lost their lives in that mayhem with some 150-200 others sustaining various degrees of injuries. Properties and means of livelihood lost in the carnage are yet to be estimated. The psychological trauma induced by the incident will live with many of the residents of Nyanya and beyond for a long time.

Barely 24 hours after the Nyanya attack, came another report that some unidentified gunmen suspected to be members of the terrorist organization, abducted more than 100 female students from a Government Girls Secondary School at Chibok Local Government Area of Borno State – the epicenter of the Boko Haram challenge. Reports of deaths in Bornu state have become a daily staple such that for many, those deaths, reported daily in the media, no longer shock or awe them – a classical indication of the 'normalization' or routinization of evil.

Our challenge as a nation is to refuse to allow such impunities to be 'normalized' by the frequency of their occurrences or the longevity of their existence. Retaining a sense of outrage against such impunities is the strongest statement that they are unacceptable and cannot be 'normalized' like other acts of impunity in the country.

But why will otherwise 'normal' people derive sadistic joy in the mass murder of people who have done them no wrong?

The German - American political theorist Hannah Arendt tells us that the great evils in history are not executed by fanatics or sociopaths but rather by ordinary people who accepted the premises of their actions and therefore participated in them on the grounds that those heinous actions were normal. She used this to explain why evil deeds tend to be everywhere in a society. She called this the 'banality of evil'. For her, those engaged in barbarous acts such as the Boko Haram terrorists accepted the premises of their actions as just – even if the rest of the society thinks otherwise. Acts of impunity against innocent Nigerians unfortunately reflects the federal – violent armed robberies across the entire country, kidnapping especially in the South-east and south-south, turf war by militarized cults and gangs in Bayelsa State, ritual murders everywhere, senseless intra and inter communal 'warfare' across several parts of the country and of course terrorism couched in religious revivalist rhetoric in parts of the North.

Despite the 'banality of evil' or the 'normalization of the unthinkable', in several parts of the country, there are reasons why the impunity purveyed by Boko Haram and groups acting in its name or sympathetic to its cause pose a special threat to the country:

One, though impunity couched in religious revivalism has been an integral part of the conflicts in Nigeria, especially in Northern Nigeria, Boko Haram and Ansaru were the first drivers of conflicts in the country to be declared terrorist organizations by the United States and the United Kingdom. Two, both are also the first purveyors of violence in the country to be strongly linked to international terrorist networks, essentially Al Qaeda in the Islamic Maghreb (AQIM) and possibly the Movement for Oneness and Jihad in West Africa, (MOJWA), - also known as Movement for Unity and Jihad in West Africa (MUJWA). MUJA was formed in 2011 allegedly because of the marginalization of Black Africans in AQIM.

Three, Boko Haram was also the first group to introduce suicide bombing in Nigeria. Use of suicide bombers had been unknown in West Africa because suicide is regarded as cultural anathema - until two high-profile attacks in Abuja - the June 2011 police headquarters bombing and the August 2011 United Nations headquarters bombing. Since then, suicide bombing has become part of the tools in the arsenal of the two groups. Four, the two terrorist groups were also probably the first purveyors of impunity in Nigeria with both international and domestic territorial ambitions. For instance while in 2011, Boko Haram's terrorism was largely confined to Nigeria's northeast by the end of last year (2013), Boko Haram- driven attacks occurred in most of the 19 States in the North, including the Federal Capital Territory of Abuja. Boko Haram suspects have also been arrested in Lagos. The group was equally linked to the kidnapping of the French Catholic priest, Georges Vandenbeusch, in Cameroun in November 2013 and to another kidnapping of a French family in the same area of Cameroun in February 2013. Flowing from the territorial ambitions of the two groups, the conflicts they trigger have wider national implications and by virtue of their links to international terrorist networks, also wider international implications than the traditional conflicts that the country is used to.

Fighting the new terrorism has been problematic not only because of their methods but also because of disagreements on why such a group came about. The conspiracy theories that seek to explain the phenomenon tap into the fears that are edged in our traditional fault lines:

There are several conspiracy theories about Boko Haram. One, which is popular among commentators from the Southern part of the country, is that the sect is sponsored by key Northern politicians to make the country 'ungovernable' for President Goodluck Jonathan, a Christian from the minority Ijaw ethnic group. One of the weaknesses of this 'theory' is that much of the mayhem carried out by the sect has been in the North and against Northern Muslims. It is in fact difficult to see the nexus between destabilizing governance in some Northern states and making the country 'ungovernable' for the Jonathan administration. But there are several who believe in such, making it difficult to mobilize that sense of collective outrage needed to tackle the menace. Obviously there are certain local grievances that revivalist movements tap into but that must not be confused with deliberate sponsorship.

Another conspiracy theory is that Boko Haram is actually being sponsored by the Jonathan administration to make Islam look bad or give the impression that the North was out to pull it down as a way of mobilizing the support of his 'Southern brethren' and Christians behind his administration. A variant of this is that Boko Haram is actually sponsored by the government to weaken or destroy the North. Those who believe in any of the variants of this conspiracy 'theory', essentially people from the North, point out that during the Abacha days, the government deliberately bombed some places and then blamed it on NADECO, which was campaigning for the re-validation of the June 12 election won by Abiola but annulled by the military regime of Ibrahim Babangida. This variant of the conspiracy 'theoriy' therefore believes that the Jonathan administration is borrowing a leaf from the Abacha regime.

One of the weaknesses of this theory however is that nothing in the confessions of some of the arrested Boko Haram members supports any of these conspiracy theories. Also it defies logic why a President should set part of his domain on fire, especially where one cannot determine the direction of such conflagration - just to weaken a particular religion or part of the country

While there are a number of other efforts at scholarly explanations of the reasons for the emergence and subsequent radicalization of the sect, I have always believed that a more comprehensive explanation will be to see the sect as a reflection of the crisis in our nation-building processes. The crisis in our nation-building conflates with the crisis of underdevelopment to create an existentialist crisis for many Nigerians. Therefore for many young people, a way of resolving the consequent sense of alienation is to retreat from the Nigeria project and construct meanings in chosen primordial identities - often with the Nigerian state as the enemy. This must not be confused with supporting or condoning Boko Haram and its ways but the need for us to dig deeper, including finding the local grievances that they tap into. We will need to fight both the symptom of the problem and the root cause simultaneously.

Fighting terrorism is never easy or straight forward anywhere in the world. Victory can hardly come easily or quickly. Often the challenge is to contain the group such that the society can continue to function normally despite the episodic impunities they purvey – the way the society has learnt to live with other impunities carried out intermittently by other groups. The key challenge we have with Boko Haram is that the mayhem by the group is not only spreading across the country but also becoming 'routinized'. And while this is happening, politicians are playing silly blame games while their foot soldiers complicate matters with their absurd conspiracy theories.

Daily Trust, April 17 2014

CHAPTER 8

In Search of Dr Stephen Davis

Dr Stephen Davis, the Australian hostage negotiator, who reportedly assisted the governments of Obasanjo and the late Yaradua in their negotiations with the irate Niger Delta militants, has been making headlines recently. Dr Davies was widely reported as implicating former Chief of Army Staff Gen Azubuike Ihejirika (Rtd) and former Governor of Bornu State Modu Sheriff as sponsors of Boko Haram. But contrary to earlier reports, Dr Davis has denied that he was engaged by the Jonathan administration to help in securing the release of the kidnapped Chibok girls. In an interview with Osun Defender of 8 September 2014, Dr Davis was quoted as saying: "I was not engaged by the Federal Government of Nigeria, any state government or any other party. I went to Nigeria in late April in an effort to facilitate a handover of the Chibok captives after discussing such a possibility with former commanders of JAS (Jama'atu Ahlul Sunnah Lih Da'awa wal Jihad otherwise known as JAS) and others close to Boko Haram" (Osun Defender, 7 September 2014).

There are many questions that beggar answers: why did Dr Davis choose to go public with his allegations instead of passing the information to relevant security agencies? I am not sure that many people believe his explanation that he went public with the names of the alleged sponsors of Boko Haram because he hoped that by so doing, he would bringing attention to the many other girls and boys kidnapped by Boko Haram.

The other relevant question is how reliable the information Dr Davis claimed he was given by leaders of Boko Haram are? Could they possibly be deliberately feeding him false information perhaps to get back at people they perceive as their enemies? Could the information he claimed they fed him possibly be a decoy – given that in his role as negotiator with Boko Haram, Dr Davis was a sort of double agent? It is sometimes difficult to know when one side is using a double agent to feed deliberate falsehood. During World War II for example, the Allied powers crafted a web of deceptions to the Germans through their double agents in Britain who were most trusted and relied upon for strategic warning by the Germans. One of those agents, the Spaniard, Juan Pujol Garcia, code-named 'Garbo,' had impressed his German intelligence superiors with the accuracy of his reports on Britain. Knowing how much the Germans trusted information from Garbo, they used him to pass the misinformation directly to Adolf Hitler that the Allied's attack on Normandy was just a diversion. And that decoy proved to be Germany's undoing.

Dr Davis' allegation, whatever his motive, appears to have added salt to the boiling pot of our problems. For a long time, prevailing conspiracy theories made the mobilization of collective anger against the sect rather difficult. And just when people are coming to the realization that Boko Haram presents a common challenge to all Nigerians, came Dr Davis' 'revelations'.

True, the hasty manner the DSS spokesperson Marilyn Ogar exonerated Gen. Ihejirika from the allegation against him while indicating that they would investigate Modu Sheriff made her vulnerable to charges of ethno-religious profiling. Yet, I find it preposterous that a Christian could be the sponsor of a sect with an avowed agenda of establishing an Islamic caliphate and that the leadership of Boko Haram would willingly allow themselves to be tools in the slaughter of largely fellow Muslims. What will be General Ihejirika's motive in sponsoring Boko Haram?

I also find it difficult to believe that Modu Sheriff could be the sponsor of Boko Haram - as we know the sect today.

The truth is that Boko Haram has evolved and mutated since 2009 when the group got radicalized following the killing of their leader Mohamed Yusuf in police custody. The Boko Haram of today is therefore not the same in essence and character with the Boko Haram which was declared a Foreign Terrorist Organization by the USA in November 2013. The Boko Haram that kidnapped the Chibok girls in April this year has since evolved further to a sect sophisticated enough to take on and humiliate our national army in a symmetrical battle.

Since the radicalization of the sect in 2009, the allegation has always been in the public domain that Modu Sheriff was among those suspected to have groomed and used the sect members as thugs when it was under the leadership of Mohamed Yusuf. One of the stories was that when the group got 'too big' for him he called on the government to move against them in 2009 and that it was on his orders that the killing of Mohamed Yusuf, while in police custody, was effected. If the allegation is true or if Boko Haram shares that belief, it could justify Modu Sheriff's claim that he is one of their targets – even if he was a sponsor of an earlier version of Boko Haram.

There are several examples of people who founded groups that later became victims or enemies of that organization. Sometimes an organization mutates in a form that is incompatible with the visions of the original founders. Two examples here readily come to mind:

The Zikist Movement, formed in 1946, was inspired by the militant nationalism of Dr Nnamdi Azikiwe (Zik of Africa). It embraced Zik and his party, the National Council of Nigeria and the Cameroons as 'our edifice of freedom'. But the movement evolved and mutated from idolizing Zik to being disenchanted by his 'gradualist' ways. In 1948 leaders of the Zikist Movement plotted an illegal action (without letting Zik know of it) which they hoped would result in the imprisonment of Zik. The hope of the Zikists was that Zik's imprisonment would spur the nation to positive revolutionary action. The Zikists got so radical that Zik had to denounce them as cantankerous followers and dissociated both his party, the NCNC, and himself from their activities. The Zikist Movement in turn mutated from idolizing Zik to being his ardent critic, with their newspaper, *African Echo*, taking regular pot-shots at their former hero. Despite the name of the movement and its early collaboration with Zik and his party, could Zik have been held responsible for the movement's later 'undue radicalism'? In fact, as early as 1948, the President of the Zikist movement, Malam Habib Raji Abdallah, had declared himself to be a free citizen of Nigeria, holding no allegiance to any foreign government and bound by no law other than Nigerian native law and the law of nations. Zik and other nationalists had not even started contemplating of the idea of independence at that time.

Another good example is the Nigerian Pyrate Confraternity formed in 1952 by Professor Wole Soyinka and six of his friends at the then University College Ibadan. The "Magnificent Seven", as they called themselves, claimed that the university was populated with wealthy students associated with the colonial powers and a few poorer students striving in manner and dress to be accepted by the more advantaged students. Thus when their fellow students protested against a proposal to build a railroad across the road leading to the university on fears that easier transportation would make the university less exclusive, the Pyrates successfully ridiculed the argument as elitist. Soyinka's Pyrate, which was modelled after such fraternities and sororities (from the Latin words *frater* and *soror*, meaning "brother" and "sister" respectively) in American universities, proved popular among students, even after the original members moved on. For almost 20 years, the Pyrates were the only confraternity on Nigerian campuses and were not known to be violent. However, as new confraternities were formed in the universities in the 1970s and 1980s, they became increasingly violent as they competed for turf. By 1990s, many confraternities in the universities largely operated as criminal gangs, or "campus cults". The point is that even though Wole Soyinka and his friends formed the Pyrate Confraternity, it was materially different from the fraternities that had evolved into cults in our Universities.

In essence just as it will be wrong to accuse Wole Soyinka of forming the Pyrates (if one has in mind what the confraternity has mutated to become), or blame Zik for the latter activities of the Zikist Movement, it will in the same vein be wrong to accuse Modu Sheriff of funding the Boko Haram of 2014, which is materially different from the Boko Haram under Mohamed Yusuf.

The above is not meant to be a defence of Modu Sheriff – just to put Dr Davis' allegations in perspective.

Meanwhile as we dissipate energy on this 'new revelation' without making sufficient efforts to interrogate their likely veracity, what we lose sight of is that Boko Haram is fast evolving from an insurgency to a movement, capturing towns in Bornu, Adamawa and Yobe states and humiliating our army in conventional battles. Therefore what the country urgently needs now is not finger-pointing and buck-passing but a realization that there is truly fire on the mountain.

Daily Trust, September 11 2014

CHAPTER 9

Re-evaluating the Boko Haram Conflict

Introduction

Many political analysts had projected that if Muhammadu Buhari, a Fulani Muslim won the March 2015 Nigerian presidential election, it could lead to the deceleration of the Boko Haram conflict because the local grievances into which those terrorists tap would be removed. Unfortunately, despite President Buhari's victory at the polls, the Boko Haram conflict has failed to abate. In fact, it has been estimated that between the time Buhari was sworn in as president on May 29, 2015 and the end of October 2015, more than 2,000 Nigerians have lost their lives to Boko Haram. These tragedies have occurred despite the fact that fighting the terrorists has clearly been one of the Buhari regime's top priorities.

In September 2015 Buhari gave the army a three-month deadline to defeat Boko Haram. That deadline clearly has come and gone, but Boko Haram has not. Though the Buhari government continues to argue that "technically" it has defeated Boko Haram, ostensibly because the group can "no longer mount 'conventional attacks' against security forces or population centres," several Nigerians—including myself—have scoffed at the government's triumphalism as rather premature. Indeed, while the government claims that the terrorists no longer control any territory in Borno State—the epicenter of Boko Haram's activities—Senator Baba Kaka Garbai, who represents Borno Central in Nigeria's Senate, claims that the terrorist group still controls "about 50 percent" of his state.

Boko Haram is well-known as a plague on the security of the Nigerian state since the group became radicalized in 2010. Officially it is estimated that between 2010 and July 2015, over 15,000 people lost their lives to the Boko Haram conflict—though some estimate the actual death toll between 2010 and 2014 could be anywhere between 100,000 and one million. In addition, the 2014 report of the Internal Displacement Monitoring Centre and Norwegian Refugee Council have estimated that over 3.3 million people have been displaced in the northeast part of Nigeria—or 10 percent of the 33 million internally displaced persons worldwide.

Over this time Boko Haram has evolved from being a small-time terrorist organization, hidden in the civilian population and using guerrilla strategies to a sophisticated, well-motivated group that overpowers the police and military for weapons, seizes territory, and engages the Nigerian military in conventional battle. Indeed, by January 2015, the sect had succeeded in establishing a mini Islamic state the size of Belgium. The continued resilience of Boko Haram under the Buhari government calls for a second look and re-evaluation of some of the earlier rumors and notions about the sect.

Death of conspiracy theories

The continued resilience of Boko Haram under Buhari's administration is debunking some conspiracy theories about the sect.

Indeed, before Buhari came to power a conspiracy theory popular in the southern part of the country was that the group was being sponsored by eminent northern politicians to make the country "ungovernable" for former President Goodluck Jonathan because he is a Christian and from a minority ethnic group in the south. If this theory were true, Buhari's victory over Jonathan would have mellowed the group. But it hasn't.

Another conspiracy theory was that Boko Haram was being sponsored or ignored by former President Jonathan—either to depopulate the north ahead of the 2015 general elections or make Islam look bad in order to enable the former president to use religion as a tool of mobilization for his candidacy. Boko Haram's continued mayhem long after Jonathan's loss of power negates any suggestion that he was sponsoring the group—or the similar claim that he deliberately did not do enough to stop them because it was a "northern problem." In fact, recently the army accused some influential indigenes of the northern state known as Borno of deliberately undermining their efforts to defeat Boko Haram because they were profiting from the situation.

These theories undermined any attempt at collective action against the sect. For instance, when Jonathan first declared a "state of emergency" in the northeastern states of Adamawa, Yobe, and Borno in May 2013 in a determined bid to fight the terrorists, some eminent northern elders declared that the measure, which included the imposition of curfews, the mounting of several roadblocks, and the shutting down of the states' communication infrastructures, amounted to a declaration of war against the north. In the same vein, when the Chibok girls were kidnapped, some key Jonathan supporters openly doubted the story, and believed it was part of a grand design by the north to bring down the Jonathan government.

With the election of a Muslim ruler and the death of such conspiracy theories as the above, the expectation is that Buhari has the social capital for a united action against the sect—so why is Boko Haram still posing a threat?

Underestimation of the strength and resources of Boko Haram

The resilience of Boko Haram under the Buhari administration suggests that there has been a gross underestimation by the government of the numerical strength, organizational efficiency, and motivation of the sect members. For instance, in October 2015, government leaders were shocked when a failed suicide bomber claimed that the sect was planning to attack Maiduguri with as many as 8,000 fighters—far more than what many people estimated the entire numerical strength of the sect to be. At one point, Theophilus Danjuma, a retired lieutenant-general and former defense minister, claimed that Boko Haram's ability to gather intelligence was

100 percent better than that of the Nigerian military. In fact in 2014, when Governor of Borno State Kashim Shettima claimed that Boko Haram fighters were better armed and more motivated than the Nigerian army fighting them, he was criticized by many Nigerians, including President Jonathan. These portraitures of Boko Haram contrast heavily with the former image of the sect in the popular imagination as a group of rag tag snipers, and poor and uneducated youth that probably did not number more than a few hundred.

Indeed, the underestimation of Boko Haram helped fuel the narrative that the Nigerian army fighting the terrorists was under-equipped, ill-motivated, cowardly, or heavily compromised. This underestimation also probably explained why the army, which Buhari vowed to better motivate and equip with more sophisticated weapons than Jonathan did, was given only three months in September 2015 to defeat the terrorists. In retrospect, that deadline was counterproductive because it unduly raised public expectations and put enormous pressure on both the military and the government. As Boko Haram's attacks have continued long after the expiration of the deadline, the government continues to try and save its face with the rhetoric that the sect had been "technically defeated." The truth is that terrorism is rarely easily defeated in any country.

What is clear is that what Nigeria needs first is a realistic estimation of the numerical strength of Boko Haram, its organizational forms, and intelligence-gathering methods to enable the government to devise realistic strategies for confronting and containing the sect. The idea that Boko Haram could be defeated within any specified time frame should be abandoned.

The continued resilience of Boko Haram

Like a phoenix, Boko Haram has shown incredible capacity for regrouping after suffering setbacks. There have been at least three occasions when a successful anti-Boko Haram strategy led to a lull in the group's murderous activities that was erroneously interpreted as a sign of the group's imminent annihilation.

The first time a lull in the group's activities was misinterpreted was in 2013 during the war against some al Qaida-linked insurgents in northern Mali, which was also thought to be a training base for Boko Haram and other terrorist groups. It was believed that many Boko Haram fighters relocated to northern Mali to fight with the insurgents against the combined troops from Benin, Nigeria, Senegal, Togo, and Niger. When the French later intervened and routed the insurgents, the general belief was that Boko Haram had been dealt a deadly blow because of the suspected high number of causalities of its members and the destruction of their training bases. But Boko Haram lived on.

The second occasion a lull in Boko Haram's activities was mistaken for imminent victory against the sect was when a "state of emergency" was declared in 2013 in the three northern states of Adamawa, Borno, and Yobe—believed to be the three foci of Boko Haram's activities. With the emergency rule, there was an increase in the number of troops deployed to the affected states; more road blocks were set up to search people and vehicles; and telecom networks were shut down to prevent the terrorists from using mobile telephones to communicate with one another and their informants. The general consensus was that the emergency rule was initially very successful in that it led to a sharp drop in the sect's murderous activities. However, like the previous occasion, Boko Haram quickly regrouped and hopes that the solution lay in a "state of emergency" quickly faded.

The third occasion Nigerians thought that Boko Haram was a minute away from complete destruction was after the joint military operations with Chad and Cameroon in February 2015. The initial successes of the joint operation goaded a euphoric Jonathan, who had then already conceded defeat in the March 2015 presidential election to boast in April 2015 that "the ongoing military operations in the northeast had already recorded huge successes, with two states completely free from the control of terrorists while operations in the third state had reached a concluding stage." However, long after Jonathan made this statement, many people, such as Senator Baba Kaka Garbai of Borno State, insist that Boko Haram still controls half of his state.

Conclusion

One of the main lessons in the fight against Boko Haram in Nigeria is that the sect has shown an incredible capacity for regrouping after major setbacks. It is not clear if the Buhari government, which has shown a single-minded determination to militarily defeat the terrorists, appreciates this fact. The truth is that terrorists, because of their methods, are not easily defeated. They can be contained in the short to medium terms—not completely routed as Buhari seems to believe. It is important that the government does not mistake a lull in the group's murderous activities as a sign of imminent defeat.

In the same vein, in its single-minded desire to be seen as defeating Boko Haram on record time—something the preceding government was unable to do for years—this government seems unmindful of the many potential 'Boko Harams' that are breeding across the country. Elsewhere I argued that a major explanation for the emergence of Boko Haram is the crisis in the Nigeria's nation-building, which has led to several alienated groups de-linking from the state into primordial identities, often with the Nigerian state as the enemy. Rather than deliberately engaging other alienated groups such as the new agitation for a Republic of Biafra or the regrouping of ex-Niger Delta militants, Buhari appears to regard such groups as deliberate plans to undermine his government. It was essentially the same mistake former President Jonathan made with Boko Haram.

Overall, while the Buhari government must be lauded for its determined fight against Boko Haram, it needs to be encouraged to expand the tools of such fight beyond securing quick military victory to putting the servicing of Nigeria's nation-building process in the front burner. It is in fact by re-energizing the country's nation-building process that it can win over several "de-Nigerianized" Nigerians (i.e.,

Nigerians that have de-linked from the Nigerian state into other primordial identities). This will ensure that other "Boko Harams" do not emerge across the country if, and when the present Boko Haram is defeated.

Brookings, Africa in Focus, http://www.brookings.edu/blogs/ africa-in-focus/posts/2016/02/29-reevaluating-boko-haram-conflict-adibe

CHAPTER 10

Relocation of Boko Haram Prisoners to Anambra State

As with everything that touches on our primordial identities, the story that the government has relocated 47 Boko Haram prisoners to Ekwulobia prison, said to be located in the heart of a sprawling town of about 500,000 people, in Anambra State, has become steeped in emotionalism and controversies. The umbrella Igbo socio-political organization, Ohaneze, as well as the Southeast Governors Forum and the Anambra State chapter of the Christian Association of Nigeria (CAN) have all weighed in on the matter, and as expected, condemned the move. The government, characteristic of its style of governance so far, maintains a deafening silence.

I will start with what I believe should be two precedent questions in the whole brouhaha before discussing the possible implications of that relocation for the president and by extension the cause of nation-building

The first of the precedent questions is whether the Ekwulobia prison is a federal institution and whether there is a practice of moving prisoners across the prison facilities. Not much information is available about the Ekwulobia prison in the public domain. However I was told by one of my PhD students who works in the prison system and is also writing his PhD thesis on the prison service that Ekwulobia prison is a medium security, single cell prison built according to United Nations guidelines with all the modern correctional facilities. It is obvious that the federal government is at liberty to move prisoners within its facilities scattered across the country. What is not clear is whether the Boko Haram prisoners allegedly relocated to Ekwulobia have been convicted or are awaiting trial and whether, short of sentiments, Ekwulobia prison is built to handle such class of prisoners.

The second precedent question is the government's rationale for moving such calibre of prisoners around the country and whether Boko Haram prisoners have been relocated before to other facilities across the country. This piece of information will be crucial in shaping the raging controversy. Unfortunately such information is not available in the public domain and the government's silence does not help matters. In fact the government's silence has given room to all sorts of conspiracy theories, which was not helped by the contradictory stories on the matter by those who claimed to be in a position to know – first the Prison Service denied the story as did Osita Okechukwu, a chieftain of APC. What appeared to corroborate the relocation story is the news that soldiers, rather than prison guards had taken over guarding the Ekwulobia prison. That news was never denied – to the best of my knowledge.

While I can understand the hysteria and panic occasioned by the relocation of the Boko Haram prisoners to Anambra State, the danger posed by the relocated terrorists appears, in my opinion, to be exaggerated. I was told that Ekwulobia prison is a well-fortified single-cell prison built according to United Nations guidelines and that it will be almost impossible, given the facilities in it, for a jailbreak to happen - unless with a high-level insider connivance.

The other fear of the locals - that having Boko Haram prisoners in Anambra State would make it easier for Boko Haram to export its brand of terrorism to Igboland - also appears exaggerated. The truth is that terrorists (just like insurgents) need certain key infrastructures to flourish in any environment: they need expert knowledge of the local terrains, a certain support (or turning of the other eye) from the local population and the ability to live a double life undetected. In Anambra state, such infrastructures will not be there for would-be terrorists. In fact the danger posed by the relocated Boko Haram prisoners is no more than the danger posed by the possibility that a Boko Haram activist could embed himself or herself among Fulani herdsmen and cause mayhem as the herdsmen traverse the length and breadth of the country. It is also no more than the danger posed by the possibility that a man dressed as an Ohaneze chieftain in Onitstha could turn out to be a disguised female suicide bomber. The point is that in the dire times we live, danger could come from any unexpected quarter. But it is no excuse for people to be paranoid.

I believe that one of the ways to douse the tensions is a requirement that residents of each town – both indigenes and non-indigenes - should be required to register with their community associations, town unions, trades and other associations. Political correctness should not prevent state and federal governments from asking individuals they suspect their movements to be identified by their relevant communities, religious or trade associations. In the UK, if you move from one area to another, you will need to notify the local authorities, and without such notification, you will not be assigned a GP or be able to access local services. Insisting that new arrivals in any community should be registered with both the authorities in the community and with relevant community groups or associations will help to curb the danger of infiltration by undesirable elements. I have absolutely nothing against being asked to register where I live or to be asked that my workplace should identify me whenever the need arises. Already people who want to access certain services are asked to go to their state liaison offices to be identified. So what is the big deal
in it?

Implications

Though I believe that the danger posed by the relocated Boko Haram prisoners is exaggerated, the relocation itself will have several implications for President Buhari and by extension the nation-building process:

One, is that after his successful rebranding as a statesman during the presidential campaign, the conspiracy theories making the round in Anambra state as a result of this relocation is re-defining Buhari to his pre- 2015 perception in some parts of the country as a parochial person. It should be recalled that one of the fear factors exploited by politicians in Igboland during the presidential campaigns was that Buhari would forcefully Islamize the country. Some are now interpreting the relocation of

Boko Haram prisoners as part of that alleged plan to Islamize Igboland or to punish the Igbos for not voting for him.

Two, is that with a section of the southwest loyal to Tinubu feeling already alienated from the Buhari regime, and with murmurings in the social media of a 'northernisation' plot in appointments made so far, the government has to consider whether further alienating other groups is good politics, especially when it has not made any effort to explain itself on the matter. It should be borne in mind that in politics perception always trumps intentions. In essence while the government may mean well by the relocation, it should realize that the road to hell was also paved with good intentions. It needs to explain itself and carry people along. In the absence of this, the people will believe whatever fits into the markers through which they filter realities.

Three, is that such relocation, and the conspiracy theories that it has spurned, could end up militarizing the insurgency group, MASSOB, and other insurgent groups in different parts of the country – this time with support of the local population who may be looking upon such groups to defend them against an imagined plan to export terrorism to their area. And once one insurgency group militarizes, the others follow suit in a sort of arms race. The government's silence on this relocation feeds these conspiracy theories which I regard as dangerous.

Four, the relocation also mocks and diminishes the few leaders of the APC in the south-east, especially Rochas Okorocha, the lone Governor of APC in the region as well as Senator Chris Ngige and Dr Ogbonna Onu who are prominent members of two of the legacy parties that merged to become the APC. The local argument is that if these figures are unable to influence the relocation, it means that the party does not take them serious because of their ethnic background. In essence, though APC is still struggling to transform itself from being a multipurpose vehicle for defeating Goodluck Jonathan into a proper political party, it will need friends and members. The relocation, especially given the government's silence on the matter, is a big campaign against the APC in the area.

Five, is the danger of the relocation inciting anti-Northern sentiments in the Southeast- and a tit-for-tat in the North against the Igbos. In the end, at a time most Nigerians are looking for a reconciler in the mould of Mandela to help re-establish faith in the Nigeria project, the government should really consider how its moves, no matter how well intentioned, aids or undermines the nation-building process. In all these, it will be borne in mind that for ordinary people, perception rather than intentions is all that counts. It is a crucial role of the government to help to shape the citizens' perception. And you cannot do this if the citizens do not understand the reasons or the vision that informs your policy choices.

Daily Trust, July 9 2015

CHAPTER 11

Re-thinking Boko Haram

On 20 September 2015 coordinated bomb attacks in the satellite towns of Nyanya and Kuje, near Abuja, claimed about 20 lives while over 40 others sustained various degrees of injuries. At about the same time another set of coordinated blasts rocked the town of Maiduguri, claiming about 80 lives with several others seriously injured. Just today (Wednesday, October 7 2015), 18 people were reportedly killed in Damaturu, Yobe state. The attacks by suspected Boko Haram terrorists have continued with regularity, despite the consensus that one of the areas President Muhammadu Buhari has shown great resolve so far has been in his determination to end the Boko Haram terrorism. Buhari in fact gave the military three months to defeat Boko Haram and end their insurgency and terrorism.

The continued resilience of Boko Haram under the Buhari regime - at a time when the soldiers battling them are believed to be well motivated and well-equipped - call for a re-thinking of some of our earlier notions about the sect:

One, the continued resilience of the terrorist sect negates some of the conspiracy theories that for long helped to undermine any concerted action against the group. For instance, among the prevailing conspiracy theories was that the group was being sponsored by eminent Northern politicians to make the country "ungovernable" for former President Jonathan because he is a Christian and from a minority ethnic group in the south. Buhari had been accused under this theory of being one of the sponsors of Boko Haram and the only evidence often adduced by the accusers was that he was 'nominated' by the sect as a negotiator when the Jonathan administration was exploring the option of dialogue with the group. If this 'theory' is correct, Buhari's victory over Jonathan in the last election would have mellowed the group. But it hasn't.

Another version of this conspiracy theory was that Boko Haram was being sponsored by former President Jonathan–either to depopulate the north ahead of the 2015 general elections or to make Islam look bad in order to enable the former president to use religion as a tool of mobilization for his candidacy. That Boko Haram has continued to cause mayhem despite the fact that Jonathan is no longer in power again negates any suggestion that he was sponsoring the group –or that he deliberately did not do enough to stop them because it was a "northern problem". In fact, rather than Jonathan being the sponsor as the conspiracy theorists claimed, the army recently accused some elders in Bornu state of deliberately undermining their efforts to defeat Boko Haram because they were profiting from the situation.

The above two conspiracy theories were so strongly believed that it made many Nigerians indirectly complicit in the murderous activities of Boko Haram. For instance when a state of emergency was first declared against Boko Haram in May 2013, some eminent Northern elders declared that the measure amounted to a declaration of war against the north. In the same vein, when the Chibok girls were kidnapped, some key supporters of the Jonathan regime openly doubted the kidnap story and believed it was part of a grand design by the north to bring down the former president's government. The belief in this conspiracy theory prevented the Jonathan administration from moving quickly to locate the girls after they were kidnapped.

Two, the resilience of Boko Haram attacks in the face of increased onslaught by the Nigerian soldiers and increasing loss of their members would suggest that we have all along underestimated both the numerical strength of Boko Haram, the level of motivation and sophistication of its members as well as the members' fighting spirit. I believe such underestimations largely account for what will appear to be exaggerations on the narratives of inadequate equipment for our soldiers and poor morale as explanations for why our 'otherwise gallant soldiers' were unable to finish off the supposedly rag-tag and ill-equipped snipers in a matter of days.

Three, giving the military a deadline to crush Boko Haram has a role to play in motivating the soldiers and re-assuring the civilian populace. However there could also be a wrongly-inputted cost if the soldiers fail to meet the deadline – out of no fault of theirs. If the soldiers are unable to meet the deadline given to them, will that amount to a defeat? Put differently can we really talk of an end to terrorism?

It will be wrong to think of terrorists as some enemies massed on the other side of a conventional war. Terrorism is merely a tactic often employed by a weaker side in an asymmetric war. The terrorists use 'terror' methods to shock and awe and to compensate for their relative weakness in both numbers and armoury. True, terrorism is a favoured strategy of insurgency groups. But just as you can have insurgency groups which do not use terror tactics so can you also have terrorists who are not backed by any insurgency groups. A good example of the latter was the Oklahoma City bomber Timothy McVeigh who on 19 April 1995 detonated a bomb that killed 168 people – the worst terrorist incident on American soil before 9/11.

Four, the possible trajectory of global terrorism, including the one purveyed by Boko Haram, could be gleaned from the history and evolution of terrorism itself. Scholars these days talk of the four waves of terrorism – the Anarchist wave believed to have started in Russia in the 1880s, the Anti-Colonial wave which began in the 1920s and lasted for more than 40 years, the 'New Left wave', which became greatly diminished with the collapse of Communism in the Soviet union, and the current religion-inspired wave, which started in 1979, and which some scholars predicted may last until 2025 to be replaced by another wave. In other words, terrorism is rooted in modern culture. If history is a guide, then we can talk of defeating terrorism only in the sense that we talk of eliminating corruption and crime. Complete elimination of terrorism is utopia but reducing it to the barest minimum is feasible and should be the goal.

If the above sounds depressing, then let's remember that following the attack in the USA on September 1, 2001, President George W. Bush declared a war on terrorism with a boast that the war "would not end until every terrorist group of global reach has been found, stopped and defeated". About 100 years earlier, when an anarchist assassinated the American President William McKinley in September 1901, McKinley's successor Theodore Roosevelt called for a crusade to exterminate terrorism everywhere. More than 100 years after the Anarchists started the modern wave of terrorism, it remains undefeated, only mutating in its form and choice of areas to manifest its ugliest sides.

Diezani: time to speak up

Growing up in Onitsha, Anambra state, in the 1970s, whenever I came to the scene of a fight I would team up with the weaker party without even trying to find out the cause of the fight. Despite being occasionally terribly bruised by such irrational choices, I have not fully weaned myself of that bad habit. And this explains why I have some sympathies for Mrs. Diezani Alison-Madueke, the former Minister of Petroleum Resources in her current travails. Is she able to catch any sleep these days?

Apart from being detained and granted bail by the London Metropolitan police on suspicions of money laundering, she has also been linked to mindboggling sleaze and outright theft of hefty sums of money. We variously read that $700m was found in her house, that she bought a mansion in London worth £12.5m, was looking to buy a £13bn apartment in Hyde Park London and so on and so forth. While I am often mindful that stories can be planted and that anyone can level any allegation during media trial, I am also livid like many people at the level of corruption linked to her – none of which she has denied.

Diezani is facing trial both in the court of law in the United Kingdom and in the court of public opinion in Nigeria. She needs to defend herself in both courts. If these damaging allegations against her in the media are not true, she needs to come forward immediately with her own side of the story. Silence is not golden in this circumstance.

Buhari's ministerial nominees: The devil's alternative

I always believed there is no way Buhari would win with his choice of ministerial nominees. Of particular interest to many are figures like former Governors Fashola, Amaechi and Fayemi, who were believed to have worked very hard for the success of Buhari at the polls but who are also being accused of corruption by their successors. Buhari had said he would not deal with anyone tainted (not necessarily convicted) of corruption charges. No one is sure of the extent of intrusion of politics in the travails of these former Governors in their respective states.

If Buhari did not include the three former governors in his cabinet, he would become vulnerable to charges of ingratitude or 'use and dump'. If he nominates them for ministerial appointments – as he has now done- then there is the moral issue of why he will not extend the same benefits of the doubts to others like Saraki who have been accused of wrong doing but have not yet been convicted by any court of law.

Daily Trust, October 7 2015

CHAPTER 12

Now that the Americans are here… (1)

The kidnap of the Chibok girls and the global attention it has generated may actually be a tipping point in the country's fight against terrorism. For far too long, the Boko Haram challenge has thrived largely because of the deep distrust and thinly veiled antagonisms that are embedded in the country's fault lines. This has helped to nurture several conspiracy theories - along the traditional fault lines - making the mobilization of collective anger and action against the murderous sect difficult. It is within this context that President Jonathan's handling and mishandling of the Boko haram challenge should be located. It is equally within this framework that the inability or unwillingness of the northern political leadership, especially the governors of the most affected states, to provide the necessary leadership or lead the charge in the fight against a group that is killing their subjects and mutilating their economies, should be understood.

The blame on how we got to the sorry state we are in today in the fight against the sect must go round – from the President to the political leadership in the north down to the rabble-rousers and peddlers of useless conspiracy theories on either side of the political divide. Politicians who thrive on grandstanding and finger pointing with the hope of reaping political capital out of the whole situation also share part of the blame. No one should really try to occupy the moral high ground in this matter or play the ostrich. True, President Jonathan shares the greatest blame because as the President and chief security officer of the country the buck stops or ought to stop on his table. But have we all done what we ought to have done or have we all been driven by feel good theories that blame everyone else but ourselves for everything that has gone wrong in the country, including the handling of the Boko Haram challenge?

I believe that President Jonathan has not handled the Boko Haram challenge as he ought to have done, not necessarily because he is weak but because he was probably captive to the conspiracy theory fervently believed by his loyalists and people from his own part of the country. For most of such people, Boko Haram is simply sponsored by the Northern political establishment to undermine his presidency. With this pervasive belief, the idea that the girls were kidnapped had to be interrogated using this theory: How come over 200 girls were abducted and no one saw them? Why was the school open when all other schools in the state had been closed down by the government because of insecurity, especially given that an official of WAEC claimed it warned the state government against conducting the exam on security grounds? How come Boko Haram operates freely in states under emergency rule? Exactly how many people were abducted? How come some girls were able to escape from the dreaded Boko Haram while others were not? There were so many gaps in the abduction story that many on President Jonathan's side must be pardoned for doubting whether there was indeed any abduction at all. Even the alleged story that the army got an advance warning of the kidnap was interpreted differently by adherents of the two dominant conspiracy theories. For supporters of the President, it was yet evidence that the security forces – the hierarchy of which is controlled by officers from the north –is part of the conspiracy that is undermining the Jonathan presidency. For those in the north who believe that Boko Haram is sponsored by the Jonathan presidency to depopulate the north ahead of 2015 or to make Islam look bad, the same gaps in the abduction story were used to buttress their position. The fervent belief that the Jonathan presidency was behind Boko Haram in the north largely explains why some called the declaration of state of emergency in Adamawa, Yobe and Borno as a declaration of war against the north and why Governors Murtala Nyako of Adamawa State and Wamako of Sokoto accused President Jonathan of carrying out genocide against the north.

One of the unintended effects of the Chibok abduction is that it has helped to pooh-pooh these conspiracy theories. Thanks to CNN, Al Jazeera and other foreign media houses, we now know that the girls were actually kidnapped. We have also seen the mothers of some of the victims speak to foreign media houses. We saw Shekau, thought to be the leader of Boko Haram, boast that he organized the abduction and showed about 130 of the kidnapped girls who had converted to Islam. And with his radical Islamic rhetoric, does he really look like someone to do the biddings of a Christian President? We also saw images of the carnage the sect wrought in Chibok and other parts of the north. The *Daily Trust* of 13 May 2014 in fact reported that residents of Rann, the headquarters of Kala-Balge local government area in Borno, repelled attacks by the sect with local implements, killing 200 of the insurgents. Do these pictures fit into the narrative that the sect is sponsored by northern leaders to undermine the Jonathan presidency? Hello conspiracy theorists! Can you now see that your hands are also steeped in the blood of the innocent?

Now that the Chibok kidnap has helped debunk the two dominant conspiracy theories – and everyone now calls the abducted girls 'our girls' – another conspiracy theory has reared its head: Boko Haram is now said to be the creation of America's CIA to whittle down Nigeria's supposedly growing influence in the continent. As Nigerians, we love feel good theories. It is never our fault so someone must be responsible for Boko Haram. Honestly I find this new conspiracy theory, which is attributed to Wikileaks, even more absurd than the now discredited conspiracy theories that supporters and opponents of Jonathan had revelled in. The truth is that Nigeria's greatest attraction to countries like USA, Britain or China is in the potentially huge market it presents because of its population and resources – human and material. What purpose will Balkanizing the country serve them? The truth is that for many Western countries, Nigeria is too big to fail, not only because of the huge refugee problems that will be created if it unravels but also because such a balkanization could destabilize the West African sub-region. If any Western country is competing with Nigeria in the West African sub-region or likely to be threatened by its rising influence, it will probably be France because of its interests in the French-speaking West African countries, not the USA or Britain. This must not be construed as a defence of the USA - just that this conspiracy theory makes no sense to me at all. But it is now widely reported in the mainstream media. And there are many enthusiastic subscribers to it. We are Nigerians. And of course it is never our faults!

The greatest loser in the Chibok abduction affair is President Jonathan. The fact that his security officials were not even sure of the exact number of people abducted and had contradictory narratives of what really happened gave the impression that he is not effectively in charge of the country. More importantly the fact that heads did not roll to demonstrate the President's rage at the way the matter was mishandled by those who ought to be in charge created the impression of a weak President. The shoddy handling of the Chibok abduction fed into the disappointment many felt, when, a day after the Nyanya bombing in April this year, the president went to Kano to smile, dance and campaign. I have no problem with the President travelling to Kano to keep to a pre-planned schedule to demonstrate that the terrorists must not be seen as winning. But to get into smiling and dancing when the mood of the nation demanded a solemn ambience was disappointing.

Again the international media focus on the Chibok kidnap overshadowed what should have been the President's moment of glory – hosting of the World Economic Forum, a celebration of real improvements in the country's macroeconomic environment as demonstrated in consistent GDP growth, the inclusion of the country in the MINT emerging economies and a re-basing of the country's GDP, making her the largest economy in Africa and the 26th largest in the world. Rather than celebrate the President, several world media ran editorials and commentaries very uncomplimentary of him and his handling of the abduction of the girls.

Additionally, the Chibok affair coupled with the President's inappropriate response to the Nyanya bombing appears to have sown disillusionment among his 'protest supporters'. There are indeed thousands of Nigerians who 'support' the President – not necessarily because they believe in his ability but because they feel he is being unfairly hounded, especially after the rather opportunistic and temperamental open letter to him from former President Olusegun Obasanjo. As one of such people told me recently, "the more I try to find reasons to support the President, the more he seems to take delight in disappointing me".

But let me return to the Americans.

Though a number of countries – China, Britain, the Netherlands, France and others - have pledged various forms of military assistance in locating the abducted girls, Nigerians seem rather enamoured by the involvement of Americans in the rescue effort despite the fact that they sent only seven Marine soldiers. What should we expect from this international rescue effort? Can they deliver? How will their involvement impact on our local politics and the politics of 2015? And what will be the way out of the Boko Harm challenge?

To be concluded next week.

Daily Trust, May 15, 2014

CHAPTER 13

Now that the Americans are here... (2)

The international media focus on the Chibok kidnap overshadowed what would have been the President's moment of glory – hosting of the World Economic Forum, a celebration of real improvements in the country's macroeconomic environment as demonstrated in consistent GDP growth over the past decade, the inclusion of the country in the MINT (Mexico, Indonesia, Nigeria, Turkey) emerging economies and a re-basing of the country's GDP, making her the largest economy in Africa and the 26th largest in the world. Rather than celebrate the President, several world media ran editorials and commentaries very uncomplimentary of him and his handling of the abduction of the girls.

Additionally, the Chibok affair coupled with the President's inappropriate response to the Nyanya bombing appears to have sown disillusionment among his 'protest supporters'. There are indeed thousands of Nigerians who 'support' the President – not necessarily because they believe in his ability but because they either feel there are no better alternatives out there or are enraged by a feeling that he is being unfairly hounded, especially after the rather opportunistic and temperamental open letter to him from former President Olusegun Obasanjo.

But let me return to the Americans.

Though a number of countries – China, Britain, the Netherlands, France and others - pledged various forms of military assistance in locating the abducted girls, Nigerians seem rather enamoured by the involvement of the USA in the rescue effort despite the fact that the country sent only seven marine soldiers to join about 60 others already in the country as part of America's counter-terrorism effort. What should we expect from this international rescue effort? Can they deliver? How will their involvement impact on our local politics and the politics of 2015? And what will be the way out of the Boko Haram challenge?

On the US-led foreign assistance in locating the abducted Chibok girls, my personal opinion is that if the U.S. soldiers are able to quickly locate the whereabouts of the abducted girls and free them without many of them losing their life in the process or without a heavy civilian casualty during any commando-style rescue operation (a commando-style move will be ill-advised in my opinion), it will boost the U.S.'s standing in the eyes of the Nigerian public. If however the bombings continue despite the hype about foreign military assistance in fighting Boko Haram and if the girls are not quickly located or released, US's standing in the eyes of Nigerians will be diminished while Boko Haram could become even more emboldened. Similarly if the foreign soldiers are perceived to be the 'face' of the campaign against Boko Haram, especially if such open involvement leads to civilian casualties, it could remind Nigerians of the aftermath of US's involvement in several conflict countries –

Afghanistan, Iraq, Libya - galvanizing in the process anti-American and anti-Western sentiments and serving as a basis of recruitment for Boko Haram. Already it remains a matter of conjecture whether the declaration of both Boko Haram and Ansaru as foreign terrorist organisations by the US in November 2013 – a move that was supposed to choke off the sources of funding to the sects - helped in fact in glamourizing the sects within the international terrorism franchise and thus paradoxically helped in attracting more logistic support to the groups. In essence while foreign technical know-how could help the country in its fight against terrorism, there are potential flipsides to this that Nigerian security forces should be mindful of.

I have severally argued that Boko Haram is one of the symptoms of the crisis in the country's nation-building processes. The long term solution to the Boko Haram challenge in my opinion is therefore restarting the stalled nation-building processes to create more 'true Nigerians' - that is, Nigerians who privilege their Nigerian identity over the other identities they bear. The crisis in the country's nation-building processes interfaces with the crisis of underdevelopment to create an existential crisis for many Nigerians. For many young people, a way of resolving this crisis and its embedded sense of alienation is to retreat from the 'Nigeria project' and construct meanings in chosen primordial identities—often with the Nigerian state as the enemy. I have elsewhere called this phenomenon a "de-Nigerianisation" process. In Nigeria, there is a heavy burden of institutionalised memories of hurt, injustice, distrust and even a disguised longing for vengeance by various individuals, ethnic groups, regions and religious groups. In this sense, actions that ordinary Nigerians rightly see as heinous are seen by some as normal, even heroic. In Nigeria, no individual or political authority enjoys universal legitimacy across the main fault lines. Nigeria is therefore a country in desperate need of creating more 'true Nigerians'. Terrorism by Nigerians against their own country will end or be drastically reduced when Nigerians come to see themselves as one people and develop that sense of what the University of Cornell emeritus professor Benedict Anderson called "imagined communities"

Re-starting the stalled nation-building process in the country is not going to happen overnight. The following measures, however, hold a good promise:

(a) Though I remain sceptical that the on-going National Conference convened by the federal government to recommend solutions to the many challenges facing the country will succeed because of deeply ingrained distrust among Nigerians, the conference, if well managed, could be a credible platform for all stakeholders to vent their grievances and frustrations with the Nigeria project. The catharsis will be useful as the country strives for long-term solutions to its nation-building problems. In the same vein, some recommendations from the conference, if implemented, could help in mollifying some aggrieved groups.

(b) Perhaps one of the long-term solutions to the Boko Harm challenge could come by default. The increasing wave of "Naija optimism" – a wave of new optimisms about the economic prospects of the country typified in the recent inclusion of

Nigeria in the MINT emerging economies and the rebasing of her GDP which made her economy the largest in Africa and the 26th largest in the world, could help to blunt the pull of the centrifugal forces. Because people instinctively want to identify with success, economic growth and development could pacify irredentist pressures, as separatist forces may have to contend with the fear of leaving at a time the country is being tipped as among the likely future economic super powers of the world.

(c) As Nigeria's economy develops, the various parts of the country could develop organic economic linkages that will help further the cause of the nation-building process. For instance, if the groundnuts produced in the north are used in the manufacture of peanut butter in the southeast and the cocoa produced in the west are used for manufacturing chocolate drinks in the north, such economic linkages will help to blunt inter-regional animosities and thus further the cause of national unity.

What Can Nigeria Do in the Meantime?

In the short- to medium- term the government should adopt a combination of *koboko* (Hausa word for whip) and "pieces of the National cake" ("patronage" or "co-optation into the system"). In Western speak carrot and stick strategies. Some of the measures the government could take include:

(i) Empowering the state governments in the north to lead the charge and be the faces of the fight against Boko Haram. This could, if anything, address the conspiracy theory in the north that President Goodluck Jonathan's administration is funding Boko Haram either to make Islam look bad or to depopulate the north ahead of the 2015 elections. It is important to underline that the conspiracy theories have made it more difficult to mobilize collective anger against Boko Haram.

(ii) Very quick trials, under Islamic laws, of those found to be Boko Haram activists or funders. Having suspects stand for trial for months or even years creates a backlash, and often has a way of mobilizing sympathy for them. It may also be strategic to try the suspects under Islamic laws since the sect members have openly rejected Western civilization, including its jurisprudence. This means that whatever punishment is meted to them under Islamic jurisprudence will not be seen as part of Western conspiracy against Islam.

(iii) Creating a special ministry for Northern Affairs and instituting a sort of Marshall Plan for the north-east aimed at winning the hearts and minds of the local populace. The proposed Marshall plan will also help to rebuild the damages done to these areas and their economies by the Boko Haram insurgency and equally provide assistance to those who have lost their businesses and means of livelihood to the conflict.

(iv) Exploring the option of offering amnesty to the more moderate members of the sects while side-lining the hardliners and finding means to effectively neutralize them.

Obviously there is no quick-fix to fighting terrorism anywhere in the world – as experiences in Afghanistan, Yemen, Somalia and other countries have shown. However with the above recommended short- to- medium term strategies pursued concurrently with the longer term strategy of resolving the crisis in Nigeria's nation-building processes, Boko Harm's terrorism can be contained while resolving the crisis in the country's nation-building processes will ensure that the sect and other insurgency groups in the country will be effectively neutralised.

Daily Trust May 22, 2014

UNITS OF THE FEDERATION

CHAPTER 14

Mile 12 Clash: Between Indigenes, Settlers and Citizenship rights

The recent ethnic/regional clashes between some Yoruba youths and some people of northern Nigeria extraction at Mile 12, Lagos, is the latest in a series of clashes between host communities (indigenes) and 'settlers' across the country. Lagos, given its population, and ethnic melting pot character, is understandably one of the cities in the country where frictions between the Yorubas who are the indigenes of the city and others (the settlers) are quite frequent. In these frictions, it is pointless blaming any group. The sons and daughters of the soil (the indigenes) cannot be blamed for feeling under siege or that they are not 'respected' enough in their 'homeland'. The 'settlers' on the other hand cannot be blamed for exercising their constitutionally guaranteed citizenship rights, which empower them to settle and do business in any part of the country as a matter of right – not favour. This feeling of entitlement on either side of the divide is often the basis of anti-immigrant sentiments in the West. We simply haven't found a workable third way around this problem.

The online newspaper The Cable reported that the ethnic/regional clash at Mile 12 Lagos on Thursday March 4 2016 (which continued for a few days after despite curfews and the closure of the market) had been a fairly regular occurrence. The Mile 12 market is famous for its perishable food stuffs – tomatoes, yams, cucumbers etc from the northern part of the country. Traders from the northern parts of the country are well represented in the market – if not the dominant group there. Scores were reported dead in the clashes and properties worth millions of Naira were destroyed. To stem the violence, the Governor imposed curfew and ordered the market closed – a wise move that also has the unintended consequence of having adverse economic effects on the traders at the market especially as most of the goods sold there are perishable food stuffs.

According to the The Vanguard of March 5, 2016, the Mile 12 fracas started brewing on March 1 2016 when an "Hausa" commercial 'Okada' rider who was riding against the traffic knocked down a Yoruba woman. The woman reportedly sustained severe injuries and the Okada rider was asked to take her to a hospital but he refused on the grounds that the motorbike association, which collects tolls from them, should take care of the woman. It is not very clear from newspaper stories why the Okada man insisted on this rather strange course of action because Nigerians are usually compassionate, especially towards the sick and the dying.

A fight was said to have ensued between the woman's co-tenants and the Okada rider who reportedly had the sympathy of people from his own regional/ethnic group. The paper reported that the matter was amicably settled by some community leaders. Unfortunately, however, the woman died the following day from the injuries she sustained. It was alleged that this fired some Yoruba youths into a revenge mission in defence of their ethnic in-group. The "Hausa" Okada rider also mobilized people from his own regional and ethnic groups and what ought to have been a simple matter quickly morphed into an ethnic/regional clash.

Since there is a tendency in the southern part of the country for all people from the north to be pigeon-holed as 'Hausa', especially if they are Muslims, it is not clear from the newspaper headlines if the Okada rider was really an Hausa man or merely someone from the north. Be that as it may, it is likely that the Yoruba youths that mobilized to fight for the woman who was knocked down by the Okada did so more out of a feeling that they were defending ethnic pride against the 'disrespect' and 'ingratitude' of 'settlers' than out of any pursuit of justice. For the Okada rider and his ethnic and regional brethren, it was probably more a fight to enforce their citizenship right of freedom to be treated like anyone else in any part of the country. And usually such clashes are preceded by the use of intemperate languages and profiling between the host community and the settlers. We will never know the role played by such intemperate language and profiling in the conflagration at Mile 12. As we all know identities that are perceived to be under threat are often very aggressively defended.

Let me mention that contrary to the impression in some quarters, the indigene-settler problem is found across the length and breadth of the country, even in villages that appear to have a homogenous population. It is however usually more politicised in some parts of the country because of the intersection of this dichotomy with other markers of identity such as ethnicity and religion. What the Mile 12 clash and others vividly tells us is that we need to revisit the indigene/settler dichotomy against people's desire to robustly enforce their citizenship rights.

It is true that several efforts have been made in the past to resolve this tension. For instance in 2010 the House of Representatives sought to deal with the problem 'once and for all' when Hon. Sama'ila Mohammed (ANPP, Plateau State) sponsored a Bill, which would give Nigerians the right to be indigenes of any local government area in Nigeria if that person or the person's parents migrated to that Local Government area before October 1 1960. Again during the discussion on amending the 1999 constitution in 2013 and 2014, one of the 'bold' proposals was for any Nigerian, who has lived in an area for ten years, to claim to be an indigene of that place.

Proposals such as the above only underscore the fact that indigeneship rights is quite often mistaken for citizenship rights – and it ends up worsening the relations between host communities and the "settlers". For instance chapter Four of the 1999 Constitution outlines the Fundamental Rights of all Nigerians, including the right to be free from discrimination while Section 41(1) gives every citizen the right to "move freely throughout Nigeria and to reside in any part thereof." Section 43 guarantees every citizen "the right to acquire and own immovable property anywhere in Nigeria." These are citizenship rights. There are no constitutional provisions that make these rights dependent on indigene status. The constitution is right not to make these rights dependent on indigene status. What however it fails to take into consideration is that the parameters of nationhood remains contested across the country and that people everywhere are protective of their culture and ways of life and would often feel – rightly or wrongly - that 'settlers' are harbingers of destructive values. This is why people defend aggressively their citizenship rights when they are living outside their 'homeland' but will be uncomfortable when other people come to their own 'homeland' to exercise their citizenship rights. We need to recognize this fact and use it as a point of departure in finding amicable solutions to the intractable problem of indigene/settler problem. With increasing urbanisation and changes in the demographics of many cities, the need to find more lasting solutions to the indigene/settler issue will become more urgent.

I do not believe that the law alone will be sufficient to solve the indigene/settler problem. In fact one of the likely but unintended consequences of too much reliance on the law to solve the problem will be the exacerbation of a sense of siege among members of the host community. This will in turn unwittingly create bottled up feelings and mark out members of the 'favoured' ethnic group as targets of misplaced aggression.

Encouraging effective dialogue between relevant associations of the host and settler community, developing early warning systems and rapid intervention forces would have helped in dousing the tension generated by the unfortunate Okada incident at Mile 12.

Daily Trust, March 10, 2016

CHAPTER 15

Reflections on Anambra Guber Race

This Saturday, 16 November, the people of Anambra State - or Anambrarians as some indigenes of the state like to be referred to - will go to the polls to elect a successor to Governor Peter Obi, the first governor of the state to be elected to a second term in office. There are many parallels between the 'machine' politics that prevails in Anambra State and the rancorous politics of Kano, Oyo, Adamawa and Bayelsa States. It is generally believed that no one wins and retains power in any of these states without having some rough edges or losing his or her innocence in the process.

What should we expect from Anambra State on Saturday? Raw violence is rarely a major theme in the politics of Anambra state. Rather contestants have a way of using (or abusing) court processes to create a stalemate if things are not going their way. Contestants were known in the past to negotiate with fellow contestants on the basis of the number of court injunctions they had secured in advance or capable of securing. So we should be looking out for a major court ruling – disqualifying one candidate or granting an injunction to another a few days to the election.

We should also be looking out for hi-tech rigging. Though INEC under Attahiru Jega has improved the transparency of the electoral processes, including the conduct of elections, given the role of the state as the chief instrument for dispensing privileges and for wealth accumulation, the stakes are simply so high that for many of the candidates, it will be a 'do or die' affair. It should therefore be expected that efforts will be made to rig the election though it may not be the old-fashioned way of ballot snatching or ballot stuffing. Special attention should be paid to the potential sabotaging of the electoral processes such as late or non-arrival of electoral materials in the perceived strongholds of some of the leading candidates and the possible manipulation of vote tallies at the collation centres.

One of the questions that obviously agitate the minds of many is who will emerge the winner? For full disclosure, it may be germane to state upfront that in the last two weeks or so my sympathy has been tilting towards Patrick Ifeanyi Uba, founder of Capital Oil, and the candidate of the Labour Party. I will however underline that I have never met or discussed with Uba or anyone working for him. I will elaborate later on why I feel Uba is the 'man of the elections'.

On paper the candidate to beat is Willie Obiano, not only because he is the candidate of the ruling APGA, but also because he has been endorsed by Peter Obi, who, in my opinion, has a slightly above average performance as a Governor. I am not especially a fan of Peter Obi but I give it to him that he has carried himself very well as the Governor of the State. For instance, his public persona does not display any ostentation – despite being stupendously rich. He remains the only Governor who is content to be addressed as 'Mr Peter Obi' - others are either 'Chief, 'Dr', 'Alhaji' or

'Comrade'. Also despite his deceptively girlish voice, Obi is a master of intrigues and a real trader at heart who has perfected the art of manipulating church, town union and ethnic politics to achieve political ends. Will Mr Obiano benefit from Obi's express endorsement or will he be hurt by it?

There is no doubt that in many parts of Anambra State Obi is already facing voter fatigue, which could rob off negatively on Obiano's candidacy. I am particularly irate that Obi who fought the political godfathers to a standstill in Anambra State chose to play godfather himself by plucking out Obiano, who is thought to be his business associate from Fidelity bank in which he has a major interest to be his successor. This, in my opinion, is poor political judgment because if anything has been conclusively proved in this country, it is that investments in political godsons rarely bring the expected outcomes. Obiano has also not shown he is prepared for the job and in one occasion could not even remember the name of his running mate. I strongly doubt that Obiano has what it takes to contain the sharks and political godfathers that lurch on the sides in the state.

For Tony Nwoye, the PDP candidate thought to be bankrolled by the original godfather of Anambra state politics, Arthur Eze, he simply does not have any pedigree to be a Governor. He neither has any academic qualification (he did not complete his medical studies) nor is he known to have run any business. His only 'qualification' was that he was President of the National Association of Nigerian Students (NANS). If Tony Nwoye wins, then Anambra state will witness a reminiscence of the Mbadinuju era when godfathers held the state hostage. I cannot help wondering why of all the candidates in its fold, the PDP felt it is Nwoye it should present as its candidate for a state as complex as Anambra, where the voters expect candidates to combine academic accomplishments with distinction in other fields of human endeavour.

Ngige remains one of the most popular politicians in Anambra State. He was certainly the first Governor to show that the State has enough money to pay salaries of civil servants as and when due. He won election into the Senate on his own recognition in a fierce contest with Professor Dora Akunyili despite (or because of – as some say) active support from Governor Peter Obi.

I doubt however if Ngige will live up to expectations if he is elected. He distinguished himself as Governor between 2003 and 2006 largely because his predecessor Dr Mbadinuju had set an exceedingly low bar of public expectation. My personal opinion is that Dr Ngige has had his moment of glory as Governor because the sequel to any drama, film or book rarely lives up to the original work. Besides, I do not see any hunger for the job in him. He appears to be running on past glory and did not demonstrate special preparation for the elections. A typical example was a recent televised debate between him and Ifeanyi Uba. He appeared cocky, pedantic and unprepared. And when he was asked to mention any constituency project he had attracted to the state, he could only mention a VIP toilet in a certain primary school. And clearly lacking on what to say further, he waved off the question and went and sat down. I was disappointed in his performance in that debate.

Though he may not win, my sympathy in the last two weeks has moved to Patrick Ifeanyi Uba. I was initially unsympathetic to his candidacy – a young 'money miss road' without education trying to buy Anambra State, I thought. I have since changed my opinion of him.

I have been very impressed by his doggedness, energy and preparedness for the job. Of course this could be because I had a rather low bar of expectation from him. During the debates however he was often the most articulate of the candidates and many who expected him to make many grammatical mistakes or to fumble because he does not have university education, were disappointed. Quite often he spoke with the specificities of statisticians - and on a flipside also with the hyperboles of a typical Nigerian trader. I also wish he does not go about calling himself or causing people to call him 'Dr' Patrick Uba. It is very unnecessary. He has made his mark in the business world, not in academics, and that honorific suggests a sort of inferiority complex – something his performance in the debates disproved.

Unlike other people of immense wealth from Anambra who are often content to play godfathers, Ifeanyi Uba, by offering himself as a candidate, took the bull by the horn. I see Uba's candidacy as a bold statement to the political godfathers in Anambra State – throw your hats into the ring if you want to be in politics and let people scrutinize you instead of hiding behind fellows that appear malleable in the hope of ruling by proxy. I am equally impressed that despite all that happened when his company was mentioned among the oil marketing cabals that defrauded the country through oil subsidies regime and his well-publicised problems with Coscharis, he refused to allow these to affect his ambition to rule the state.

Uba's wealth is both his greatest asset and heaviest albatross. Was it not the French novelist Honoré de Balzac who told us that behind every fortune lies a hidden crime? So whether it is Atiku or Uba, there will always be that public suspicion of the 'real' motive of the wealthy when they dabble into politics. And when that wealthy person is relatively young and one of his companies is known to be in trouble, then the public suspicion will only be reinforced. Unfortunately for Uba, not many people buy the argument that the wealthy are so accomplished that they will not be tempted to fiddle with state's resources. Euripides, the Greek tragic dramatist, tells us that while the poor are envious, the rich are usually greedy for more.

Whatever may be the outcome of the election, I feel that Ifeanyi Uba has made a bold statement. He may not win but he may have announced his presence on the national political stage.

The News Chronicle, November 14, 2013

CHAPTER 16

Abuja Indigenes: The Fire Next Time?

There are two emerging features of the Nigerian condition, which appear to complicate efforts to redress the perceived grievances of any group in the country: every Nigerian group has an elephantine memory of a long list of perceived institutionalised hurt. Each group also feels that only its own grievances are genuine and that others are either merely crying wolf or that any efforts to redress any other complaint will undermine its own campaign for 'justice'. In essence, the Nigerian condition is such that rather than join hands so that several historical wrongs are redressed the tendency whenever any group seeks redress for its own perceived historical wrong is to undermine such agitations by either a resort to obscurantist re-reading of history or a quick dusting up by each group of its own catalogue of perceived injustice. Even those who have obtained redress for their own perceived wrongs are often unwilling to see others' grievances attended to.

The second tragedy of the Nigerian condition is that an impression is unwittingly being created that unless your agitations are militarized, they will either not attract the desired attention of those in authorities or be treated with levity. In essence conflict prevention and early warning systems do not attract the attention of authorities because of a certain genetic preference for a fire brigade approach to problems.

It is within the above two specificities of the Nigerian condition that the current agitation by the indigenous peoples of Abuja and the various responses to them should be located.

Recently several newspapers reported that over 100 indigenes of the Federal Capital Territory (FCT) under the auspices of the Original Inhabitants Development Association of Abuja (OIDA) stormed the secretariat of the FCT Administration (FCTA) at Area 11 in Garki, half nude, on 9 October 2012, in protest over alleged marginalisation on "their father's land" (People's Daily, October 10 2010). The protesters, who reportedly stormed the Secretariat in four trucks, had a long shopping list: they wanted a Federal Capital City (FCC) caved out of the FCT and 20 percent 'derivation' on all sales accruing from allocable lands within the FCC. They also demanded 40 per cent of all land allocation to individuals within the FCC in the "interest of equity and justice". They said they would be willing to concede the 1,600 square kilometers of the Federal Capital City as drawn in the Abuja Master plan to Nigeria as the capital city of the nation but would want the remaining 6,400 square kilometers of the larger Federal Capital Territory to be granted a state status for the original inhabitants of the territory.

In another protest march in May this year, the OIDA claimed that "more than 90 per cent of Abuja indigenes are yet to be resettled", and said the situation has made life extremely difficult for their people amid the increasing expropriation of their lands by estate developers (Vanguard 13 May 2012). OIDA further claims there are 1.5

million original inhabitants spread in 858 villages and towns within the territory. Abuja indigenous groups include the Gbabyi (also known as the Gwari), Koro, Gade, Egbura, Gwandara, Bassa and the Gana- Gana people.

In what would amount to government's admission of its own lethargy on the issue, the FCT Minister Bala Mohamed, in an interview published by an online medium African Examiner on 13 October 2012 explained that "the indigene issue is a long story" and that when the Abuja concept was developed, the indigenes were supposed to be resettled outside Abuja and "that is why you have Sabo Wuse and other towns in the outskirts of the city". The Minister said the scheme failed when the government "discovered" it would need N145bn to offset the cost of the indigenes' housing projects and other entitlements. Consequently, said the Minister, the government decided to resettle them within the 8,000 km square of the FCT and is now "building settlements for them along Airport Road so that at the end of the day we can resettle those that constitute social development challenge."

If the above attributions to the Minister were correct, then no one is left in any doubt that the indigenous peoples of FCT have had a most tepid response to their demands for redress and compensations for the expropriation of their lands and resources by the federal government. And by the way when lands are expropriated from indigenous peoples by the state, what the affected people lose is not just their land and resources but also the destruction of their community and its history as well as their ancestral and spiritual attachments to their environment.

In the Preamble to the 2007 United Nations Declaration on the Rights of Indigenous Peoples, it was recognised that indigenous peoples have suffered from historic injustice as a result of inter-alia the dispossession of their lands, territories and resources, which logically prevents them from exercising their right to development in accordance with their own needs. Article 4 of that Declaration states that indigenous peoples, in exercising their right to self determination, should have a right to autonomy or self government in matters relating to their internal and local affairs as well as ways and means of financing their autonomous functions." Article 8(1) is specific that "indigenous peoples and individuals have the right not to be subjected to forced assimilation or destruction of their culture" while Article 11 (2) urges states to provide redress "through effective mechanisms, which may include restitution developed in conjunction with indigenous peoples with respect to their cultural, religious and spiritual property taken without their free, prior, informed consent, or in violation of their laws, tradition and customs".

I have a feeling that the federal government has not kept faith with the United Nations Declaration on the Rights of Indigenous Peoples in the way it has treated Abuja indigenes.

Some have argued that the decision to create the FCT and expropriate lands from indigenous peoples for that purpose was based on the 1978 Land Use Decree which vests all land on the government. True. But an action is not necessarily right because it was based on an extant law which in any case was a military fiat rather than a law that flowed from peoples' wishes. And to think that more than 30 years after the issue of compensation ought to have been resolved, the government appears to be still playing politics with the issue!

On the calculated compensation (mainly for economic trees), it may be necessary to ask whether the original level of compensation is fair enough given the present economic realities in the country and the current land prices in Abuja. My personal opinion is that compensation should be indexed to the current economic realities, including land prices in Abuja.

Just as people say that 'Niger Deltans' get angry when they come to Abuja and discover that 'Rome has been built in a day' using the oil wealth from their area, indigenes of Abuja also reserve a right to feel cheated given the current costs of the lands taken from them. This is a natural human feeling that deserves sympathetic ears.

It may be true that some of the Abuja indigenes engage in sharp practices such as selling same land to multiple buyers or denying the receipt of compensation when they had already done so. These, even if true, are insufficient to undermine their claim for fair treatment along the lines of the UN Declaration on the rights of indigenous peoples.

I have sympathy for the demand of Abuja indigenes for a sort of 'derivation' on their lands. Let's face it, historically various groups in the country have campaigned for and obtained 'derivation' for their assets: at the 1950 Constitutional Conference in Ibadan, the North insisted that because of their population, unless they received 50 percent representation in a planned National Assembly they would secede from the country and their demand was granted. Since then till date there has been a 'derivation' on population. In the same way, the people of Niger Delta campaigned for and have been enjoying 'derivation' (currently 13%) on revenue from oil found in their area. At a point the South-East and the South-West enjoyed 'derivation' on primary school enrolment in which they had advantages. Groups that are vulnerable to natural disasters also have reprieve in a special 'derivation' fund known as 'ecological fund'. So what is wrong in the indigenes of Abuja asking to be similarly treated? Even if many of their demands appear to be mere bargaining chips, there is an urgent need to listen sympathetically to them and make more convincing efforts to redress some of their grievances. And for a start, will it be a big deal if a portion of the statutory allocation to the FCT is reserved for improving their welfare? And why is a Permanent Commission to attend to their development needs too much when we have a number of such infrastructures for the Niger Delta?

Daily Trust, October 18, 2012

CHAPTER 17

The 'deportation' of Nigerians from Lagos

The last two weeks have been marked by very hot verbal exchanges between Yoruba nationalists and defenders of the Igbo polity. Not long ago, the two groups had also squared against each other over perceived uncomplimentary remarks on Chief Awolowo made by the late Professor Chinua Achebe in his book, *There Was a Country*. At issue in this round of exchanges was the said deportation of some Igbo destitute who were allegedly dumped on the River Niger by the Lagos State government via its agent, Kick Against Indiscipline (KIA). Depending on which side of the fence you are shouting from, the number of the 'deportees' varies from 12 to over 70. The cadences of the narratives also vary – again depending on where you pitched your battle tent.

There are two contending accents in this 'deportation' story. According to one version, echoed mostly by defenders of Igbo interests, KIA arrested over 70 Igbos from Lagos and callously dumped them on the Niger Bridge. Those who argue from this perspective see this as another instance of Igbo prejudice, if not an attempt at ethnic cleansing, especially after the Igbos have 'helped to develop Lagos'. Acting within the ambits of this framework, a furious (real or contrived) Governor Peter Obi reportedly wrote to President Jonathan about the incident, threatening to retaliate.

Another version of the story, mostly from defenders of Fashola or Yoruba interest, is that 12 or 14 destitute were removed from Lagos State in a bid to 're-unite them with their families' in their home states. They argue that three States, not just Anambra, were affected in the exercise. According to this version, before the destitute were returned to their states of origin, the Lagos State Government notified the Government of each affected State at least 90 days ahead of time to enable them make adequate arrangements to receive and rehabilitate their indigenes but Anambra State never replied to any of the letters from the Lagos State government on the matter. People who fire from this side of the trench also remind us that over 3,000 of such people had previously been 're-united' with their families in the northern part of the country. They also told us that Governor Peter Obi was being hypocritical over the whole issue because he had also 'deported' members of the mendicant profession from Akwa Ibom in 2011.

There are   obvious holes and contradictions in the two contending versions of events, which we need not waste space on.   Suffice it to add that the expected ethnicization and politicization of the issue has led the combatants to dig into their institutionalized memories of perceived ethnic hurt or ingratitude to mislead and indulge in wide exaggerations.

I personally find it difficult to believe that Governor Fashola deliberately targeted the Igbo or any other ethnic group with his KIA and its associated dream of making Lagos a mega city. Compared with the small- minded Governor Theodore Orji of Abia State who sacked virtually all non-indigenes employed by the state, Governor

Fashola comes across as a truly cosmopolitan Nigerian, continuing and expanding on former Governor Ahmed Tinubu's policy of incorporating non-Lagosians in the governance of the state. For instance Fashola's Commissioner for Economic Planning and Budget, Ben Akabueze, is Igbo just like the chief executive of the state's Infrastructure Maintenance and Regulatory Agency, Joe Igbokwe. His Personal Assistant on Media Mac Duruigbo is also Igbo.

My personal opinion is that the 'deportation' once more demonstrates our penchant for embracing expediency over the rule of law. For instance, in societies governed by the rule of law, those who contravene any law of the state such as on vagrancy, will be charged to court, and upon conviction, the courts will prescribe the form of punishment to be meted. There is something untoward and distasteful about carting away citizens or even persuading them to leave your state –whatever their offence. The argument that such people were being re-united with their families is spurious for it wrongly assumes that those being repatriated have families who will welcome and care for them. The truth is that the extended family system which used to provide such care function has considerably weakened and bottomed out in some cases. Had Governor Fashola been more sensitive to the Nigerian temperament, he should have handled the matter differently. For instance finding a temporary camp for those removed from the streets (and awaiting trial) but insisting that such people should bring in their relatives to help foot the bill for their accommodation and feeding, would probably have achieved the same result without unnecessarily raising the ethnic dust or risking that this minor incident will overshadow his legacy.

Fashola is however not alone in our love of fire-brigade approach to issues. For instance in the midst of the raging controversy over the deportation of the Igbos, the Vanguard of August 3 2013 reported that Governor Peter Obi personally supervised the demolition of a hotel in Onitsha where human heads were allegedly found. It is difficult to fault Governor Obi on this given the gravity of the offence and the public mood for an instant justice to be meted on the suspected culprit. However in saner countries where the wheel of justice turns quickly and is blind-folded, only a competent court of law could authorize such demolitions – however strongly people felt about the hotelier's alleged evil deeds. Part of the tragedies of the country therefore is that no one dares question what seems to work and what satiates the mood of the moment. We pick and choose when to compare our country with the likes of USA and Britain and when to emphasize our uniqueness which will render such comparison irrelevant.

The 'deportation' issue also raises salient questions about our federalism. Given that in a federal system, each federating unit is within its sphere of competence, independent, what will be the relationship between the citizenship rights of Nigerians and the rights of states to regulate the behaviour of citizens within its domain? Does a state government have the right to expel non-indigenes from the state, and if so, under what conditions?

Also buried in the punches and counter-punches from the deportation brouhaha is a demystification of the stereotype that destitution is a social problem synonymous with the Almajiris phenomenon, and therefore a problem for only a section of the country. As the folklore goes, the Igbo, especially those from Anambra state, are supposed to be so enterprising and so aggressively competitive that everyone does what is necessary to succeed because, in the people's culture, there is no excuse for failure. The truth, as unearthed by the 'deportation' issue, is that across the country, so many people are being left behind in the Darwinist competition for survival that underlies the spirit of capitalism. This means it might be time for the government to start evolving social programmes that deliberately target such people. Removing them from the streets because they are 'eyesores' is not a policy. Assuming that those 'repatriated' will be taken care of by their families (nuclear or extended) is to miss the point that the family system across the country is under stress and transformation.

The deportation issue also re-echoes the lingering confusion between citizenship rights and 'indigeneship'. For instance the claim that Lagos welcomed the Igbo with open arms and that they should not take the Yoruba sense of generosity for weakness is hogwash. The truth is that your citizenship rights enable you to live and own property in any part of the country – irrespective of the feelings of the indigenes of the place. In fact you do not even need to be a Nigerian to enjoy such rights. If you are a legal resident in the country and operate within the limits of the law, what you own in your place of domicile is not necessarily at the benevolence of the indigenes. Generosity arises when you are accepted as one of the indigenes and treated as such either professionally or in their social circles. Obviously common decency dictates that wherever we are, we should not make ourselves odious by being insensitive to the feelings of others and the environmental variables in which we operate. But this is a matter of social etiquette and wisdom, not of citizenship rights.

Similarly, there is an exaggeration when the Igbos argue that they developed Lagos or other parts of the country. While it must be conceded that probably no ethnic group is as much willing to invest outside their ethnic enclave as the Igbo, it must equally be admitted such is never borne out of any altruistic sense of 'bringing development' to any part of the country. It is mostly actuated by commercial interest, evaluation of available opportunities and expediency. With one of the highest population densities in West Africa, the Igbo are naturally diasporic, not out of any missionary interest in exporting development but as part of their survival kits.

With the November 2013 Governorship elections in Anambra State around the corner, it cannot be ruled out that some politicians have vested interest ethnicizing and politicising the 'deportation' matter. The calculation here could be that such will hurt Dr Chris Ngige, who has declared his interest in running under the APC and who is still seen as one of the top contenders to beat.

Daily Trust, August 8 2013

CHAPTER 18

States vs. Federal Government

Between the federal government and the state government, which one will you consider the monster - or the bigger monster? Which do you feel needs its powers to be curtailed? Which of the two arms of government would you regard as more efficient in the discharge of its constitutional duties? Which is more an agent of development and which is more an impediment to progress? Which one facilitates more primitive accumulation and corruption? In fact which of the two deserves its powers to be whittled down and to which organ shall the appropriated power be turned to?

Answers to these questions will be pertinent in helping us take a side in the periodic ding-dong between the States and the Federal Government in our peculiar brand of federalism. The States, in their overwhelming numbers and congregating under the Governors' Forum, routinely complain about the power of the federal government, including its power of the purse. They want something to be done urgently about it. The Federal government too often feels the States are just too powerful, almost like Leviathans. It wants to see their power and influence whittled considerably down. In fact the much touted reform of the PDP under Dr Okwesili Nwodo was thought to be aimed at cutting down the Governors to size, especially on the matter of the number of delegates to party congresses and convention they controlled and which gave them a disproportionate voice in the outcome of party primaries.

In popular and spontaneous analyses of politics in street corners, beer parlours, gardens and pepper soup joints, Governors do not seem to be particularly beloved. Apart from the infamous Security Votes associated with them (too bad no one talks about that of the presidency), there is often a consensus that virtually all state legislatures are rubber stamps of the Governors, that the State judiciary is usually in their pockets and that it is almost inconceivable that a State government will lose a case at a state High Court. In this sort of political analyses by the 'masses' it is also not uncommon to hear complaints that most Governors have refused to organise Local Government elections and that even among the few that did, the Governor's party and favoured candidates usually 'sweep the polls', (often in the Nigerian fashion), without even allowing the opposition any 'consolation victory'.

It is within the context of the suspicions, accusations and counter accusations between the States and the Federal Government that the current move by the Governors to whittle down the powers of the federal Government must be located. Recently it was reported that the Nigerian Governors Forum was working on a document detailing the powers and functions of the Federal Government that should be devolved to the states. According to the report, the Governors wanted some items removed from the Exclusive legislative list and placed under the Concurrent and

Residual lists. The Exclusive list contains items under the sole jurisdiction of the Federal Government; the Residual list is for states while items on Concurrent list can be legislated upon by both the States and the Federal Government.

Some of the items the Governors want to move to the Residual or Concurrent list include designation of securities in which trust funds may be invested, issues pertaining to labour, including trade unions, industrial relations and industrial disputes; prescribing a national minimum wage for the federation or any part thereof; industrial arbitration; prisons and stamp duties. Others include the power to declare public holidays, the formation, annulment and dissolution of marriages other than marriages under Islamic and customary laws.

Several issues are raised by the latest reported move by the Governors:

One, the altercation shows the duality of the States and the Federal Government. Both are simultaneously too weak and too powerful. They are too powerful in the sense that they are efficient as agents of private enrichment for people in power. They are also too powerful in the deployment of authoritarian muscles to abridge the democratic space and hurt opponents. They are however equally too weak because of their inability to discharge their constitutional functions efficiently or to be agents of material progress for the generality of the citizens.

Two, the altercation brings to fore the fact that really no one is satisfied with the structure of the federation. This should temper our knee-jerk tendency to label people who espouse certain proposals on how to restructure the country – from those clamouring for Sovereign National Conference to those pushing for Constitutional Amendments and even those calling for the dismemberment of the country. All share a basic premise that things do not work as they ought to in the country and that the structure of the country is partly to blame for this. I find it nauseating when self-appointed 'super patriots' feign anger at any proposal that will suggest a fundamental restructuring of the country, often accusing the purveyors of such proposals as 'wanting to break up the country' – as if Nigeria was the person's mother's personal property rather than a collective asset and liability. In the marketplace of ideas notion used to justify freedom of expression, it is often held that the truth will emerge out of the competition of ideas in free and transparent public discourses. This is why in mature democracies, even political ideas that shock and awe are protected speeches. In this sense accusing purveyors of ideas we do not accept of 'wanting to break up the country' is either blackmail or an indication that the accuser is unable to generate counter ideas compelling enough to compete effectively in this marketplace of political ideas.

Three, with the States and the Federal Government accusing each other of being too powerful, there is a logical question of how to reduce the powers of both without making them less efficient than they are now. My personal opinion is that if the States get more functions from the Exclusive or Concurrent list under the current structure, they will become even more inefficient in discharging their basic functions, especially under current fiscal federalism. Should the Local Governments, currently an appendage of the States, be strengthened? My proposal will be for the creation of an 'intermediate force' which should stand between the Federal Government and the States in terms of the powers they wield. Here the current six geopolitical zones easily lend themselves to play this role.

Four, I will recommend that only the federal government and the six geopolitical zones should be the units for sharing revenues from the Federation Account. The government of each of the six geo-political zones will be constitutionally empowered to determine whether it wants to have a bicameral legislature or not, the number of States and local governments it wants to have and which units within its boundary (States, Local Governments and Town Unions) will be used in sharing its own revenues and on which formula. I also favour granting such geopolitical zones the power to have their own police which will be subordinated to the federal police.

Five, there are, in my opinion, several advantages of using the six geopolitical zones as units for allocating political privileges and sharing money from the Federation Account: First, it will automatically reduce the size of government at the centre. Second, since the zones are sufficiently large, it will moderate the pull of the centrifugal forces by moving substantially the site of the contest from the centre to the geopolitical zones, which are likely to have challenging internal contradictions. Third, making the geopolitical zones the only units that share resources and privileges with the federal government will be a very close approximation of what some people call 'true federalism'. Fourth, perpetual cries of marginalisation by virtually all the units of the federation, which have undermined the country's nation-building project, will become muffled. I do not think there should be any fear that any geopolitical zone may one day break away from the federation because the internal contradictions in each zone will be a sufficient bulwark against such.

Six, I believe the greatest challenge we have in the country today is not poverty and underdevelopment but politics. Our nation-building is in deep crisis, with trust, a key ingredient in that building project, long evaporated. Nigeria has become a country without Nigerians as there appears to be a stampede to withdraw from the Nigeria project into primordial identities.

Seven, I strongly feel that in the short to medium term, the country will continue to need a creative application of the principles of zoning and power rotation arrangements both at the centre and the units to give the constituent nationalities of the federation that psychological sense of belonging. Nigeria is facing a lot of very serious challenges but I honestly do not believe the country is a lost case.

Daily Trust, November 29, 2012

CHAPTER 19

Indigene/Settler dichotomy and Constitution Review

The issue of indigene/settler dichotomy has been with us for a long time, periodically generating conflicts and violence in different parts of the country. Often the trigger to the conflicts is a contest over access and exclusion to critical resources and the entitlement that being an indigene confers in this binary. Contrary to the impression in some quarters, the indigene-settler problem is found across the length and breadth of the country, even in my village in Anambra State. It is however more politicised in some parts of the country because of the confluence of this dichotomy with other markers of identity such as ethnicity and religion.

In 2010 the House of Representatives sought to deal with the problem 'once and for all' when Hon. Sama'ila Mohammed (ANPP, Plateau State) sponsored a Bill for an Act, which would give Nigerians the right to be indigenes of any local government area in Nigeria if that person or the person's parents migrated to that Local Government area before October 1 1960. The Bill also sought to restrict the authority for the issuance of 'indigeneship' certificates to the Ministry of Internal Affairs instead of the current practice where it can only be issued by States and Local Government Councils.

The above was a radical Bill as are some of the current proposals which are being submitted to the National Assembly ahead of the planned review of the 1999 Constitution. One of the 'bold' proposals currently making the waves, is for any Nigerian, who has lived in an area for ten years, to claim to be an indigene of that place.

In a country like ours, where the nation- building process has stalled, if not in crisis, and where distrust is embedded in people's bone marrows, what is bold or good may not always be what is appropriate. This seems to be the case with the indigene/settler issue. This means that if we copy and paste practices from other environments, especially from countries where there is already a consensus on the parameters of their nationhood, we will only exacerbate the problem.

It is important to highlight the distinction between 'citizenship' rights and 'indigeneship' rights – as these tend quite often to be mixed up. For the former, there are already certain constitutional guarantees for all citizens in the country. For instance chapter Four of the 1999 Constitution outlines the Fundamental Rights of all Nigerians, including the right to be free from discrimination while Section 41(1) gives every citizen the right to "move freely throughout Nigeria and to reside in any part thereof." Section 43 guarantees every citizen "the right to acquire and own immovable property anywhere in Nigeria." There are no constitutional provisions that make these rights dependent on indigene status.

Indigeneship rights on the other hand are largely cultural, ancestral and genealogical. In very traditional cultural settings, the indigenes are the ones who would know which gods to appease if the unexpected happens in the community. Contrary to what some people believe, a variant of the indigene-settler dichotomy also exists subtly in the West. For instance an African or even American who naturalised in the UK would have a British passport but would never call himself or herself English or Scottish or Irish. Many naturalised Africans would often tell you they are Nigerians or Ghanaians but have British or American passports. Racism and xenophobia are often rooted in the binary of settler versus indigene.

My personal opinion is that to impose indigeneship on any community on account of how long a group has lived there is simplistic. People everywhere are protective of their culture and their ways of life and would often feel – rightly or wrongly - that 'foreigners' are harbingers of destructive values. Often some settlers will assimilate very well into the culture of the host community – speaking their language, inter-marrying with them and worshipping alongside them. Usually the offspring of people who assimilated well into the cultures of their host communities do not experience very much the negative politics around the indigene/settler dichotomy. A crucial question here is whether a settler living apart from his host community and preserving the ways of his forefathers which he came to settle with in the community, should really claim to be an indigene of the host community – in the cultural sense in which that terminology is often used. This is another way of saying that both the settlers and the indigenes need to be broad- minded. Settlers who want to aspire to the rights of indigeneship should make efforts to integrate into the cultures of the host community while the host community should be willing to embrace those who are willing to be assimilated. It is contradictory in terms for a settler to want to embrace multiculturalism (i.e. a 'separate but equal' cultural policy) and at the same time clamour for the gains of assimilation (indigeneship).

Among settlers in many communities, you will always find some who have assimilated so well into the culture of their host community that the indigenes accept them as part of them. The problem often is where there is a large settler community that has not assimilated but have lived in the area for a very long time. In such a situation, what will be required is a political solution to any challenges that may arise in the interaction between the communities. Legislating indigeneship is unlikely to solve such problems.

One of the likely unintended consequences of any effort to use the law to impose indigeneship on any community is that it could create a sense of siege, namely that the more diasporic parts of the country are being favoured to 'colonize' others. This will unwittingly create bottled up feelings and mark out members of such 'favoured' ethnic groups as targets of misplaced aggression. If such happens, it will be a sad reminder of the late general Aguiyi Ironsi's Decree No.34, which was borne out of fervent patriotism but which in its author's naivety failed to take sufficient cognizance of the prevailing environment of the time.

Daily Times, January 17 2013

CHAPTER 20

States' Bankruptcy: Time to embrace the 'R' word?

The Chinese are said to use two brush strokes to write the word, 'crisis'. It is said that for them one brush stroke stands for danger while the other stands for opportunity. The critical question here is: what opportunity does the current economic crisis present to the country? I am using the virtual bankruptcy of our states to epitomize the current economic crisis.

Declining revenue from oil and consequently smaller receipts from the Federation Account is often blamed for the current economic crisis. For instance while the N305 billion shared by the three tiers of government in May 2016 was higher than the N281.5 billion of the preceding month, the marginal increase hardly improved the states' balance sheets. Also though the state governments may get more money with the flotation and consequent depreciation in the value of the Naira, their receipts are unlikely to be enough to solve their cash problems, especially as inflation continues to gallop to the high heaves. Unemployment, says the National Bureau of Statistics, grew from 10.4 per cent to 12.1 per cent in the first quarter of 2016, a figure that does not take into consideration underemployment and disguised unemployment

The bankruptcy of the states is further reflected in the fact that 27 of our 36 states are currently unable to pay the salary of their workers – arguably the most basic of their functions. In some states, workers are owed more than twelve months' salaries. For instance lecturers at the Tai Solarin College of Education, Omu Ijebu in Ogun state are said to be owed 13 months' salaries as at the end of June 2016. Across the country, teachers and lecturers in several state-owned institutions are owed months of salary. And students who paid tuition in such institutions naturally feel angry that they are not getting value for money – if they are lucky for their institutions to be open and running skeletal services. Other state employees are not faring better.

The unviability of our current states has other far-reaching implications: for instance can we really have the moral unction to preach anti-corruption gospel to workers who have not been paid for months and who have families to feed? This is why we argue that corruption is not just caused by moral lapse but is largely systemic. It is another way of arguing that states' inability to meet their basic obligations to their employees undermines loyalty and legitimizes corruption in the eyes of such workers. And add to the mix other problems created by the bankruptcy of the states – inability to pay contractors, high indebtedness of the states, lack of employment opportunities and inability to provide basic development infrastructure. The bankruptcy of the states also creates legitimacy crisis for the federal government – despite its penchant for blaming all the current challenges on the past government. For many people, the failure of the sub states is the same as failure of the Buhari government because the buck stops at his table.

The above are among the reasons why I feel it has become urgent for the government to find a lasting solution to the current problem of the bankruptcy of most of our states. Bailouts, even on generous terms, are at best palliative measures that are in themselves unsustainable and a sharp reminder of the unviability of those states queuing to meet the conditions for accessing them. And it is unrealistic to keep hoping that revenues from oil would bounce back to the levels they were two or three years ago. This is unlikely to happen soon – unless there are unexpected major crises in key oil producing countries.

The truth is that oil revenue on which the country depends for some 80 per cent of its revenue has for long masked the unviability of our 36- state system and the structure of the country on which it rests. So in many ways it is good, as the Igbo would say, for the wind to blow harshly so that the anus of the fowl would be exposed. We need to see in the crisis the opportunity to finally admit to ourselves that the current structure has failed.

I know that the 'R' word conjures different emotions among different people in our highly polarized and emotionally charged environment. I have in fact read about people who threaten that any talk about restructuring the country is an invitation for war or for the dismemberment of the country. Threats like these – age-old bargaining strategies by the different regional factions of the elite – now sound passé given the economic challenges facing the country. The irony with these threats though is that quite often those issuing them do not look strong enough to give anyone a good slap.

It has in my opinion become imperative to seriously consider a structure of the country in which fewer units will partake in sharing revenue from the Federation Account. I will align myself with the proposal that the current six geopolitical zones should replace the current 36-state system. Under this arrangement each zone will be at liberty to create as many states and local governments as it wants without these partaking in sharing the revenue from the federation account.

With the six geopolitical zones as the only units to share revenues with the federal government, there will be reduction in the number of bureaucracies in each zone and concomitantly reduction in the cost of governance. Perhaps with this sort of arrangement, the various geopolitical zones will be in a better position to provide infrastructure, invest in development projects and turn the country into a 'federation of economies' or what some people inappropriately call 'true federalism'. This system will also be in a better position to promote national integration. For instance, with larger markets in each zone, if the cocoa produced in the south-west is used in the manufacture of chocolate in the North-west, the people from the two zones will increasingly over time come to appreciate their economic interdependence. Economic linkages and interdependencies among the different geopolitical zones will in turn attenuate the anarchic nature of our politics.

The President should look into allegations of 'northernisation' policy

The social media is awash with reports of how the Buhari government has been favouring the North, especially Northern Muslims, in its appointments. Internet warriors and social media activists revel in such stories. Mistakes in this regard – whether of the head or of the heart – will only amount to giving ammunition to the government's critics with which they will happily take pot shots at the regime.

While every regime in the country has had to face similar allegations of favouritism in various degrees since 'ethnic/religious watching' became part of our political culture, the Buhari government should recognize that perception is everything in politics and should therefore take deliberate measures to ensure that instances of proven imbalance are addressed as quickly as possible.

The President should remember what happened during his First Coming. His coup was so popular that the late Dele Giwa recommended that all the politicians being tried for corruption should simply be given the 'Rawlings treatment'. Ironically, a few months after, the activities of the 'ethnic/regional and religious watchers' 'convinced' a significant portion of Nigerians from the southern part of the country that the regime was discriminating against them and favouring the Muslims from the North. With time, virtually every action of that government was analysed in the southern part of the country using the prism of ethnicity, regionalism and religion. The result was legitimacy crisis which paved the way for the Babangida coup. The politicians from the south who were jailed for corruption all came out as heroes and heroines.

Certainly the Buhari government does not need these distractions. It already has a plateful of these. Therefore it needs to do all it can to avoid getting entangled in further distractions.

Daily Trust, 7 July 2016

CHAPTER 21

That Peace May Reign in Kogi State

It is almost certain that the last has not been heard of the recent judgment of the Court of Appeal sitting in Abuja, which upheld the judgment of the Election Petition Tribunal that Alhaji Yahaya Bello was duly elected as the Governor of Kogi State. It will be recalled that Bello was nominated by his party, the All Progressive Congress (APC) to replace Abubakar Audu, who died before the conclusion of the November 21 2015 governorship polls. Audu was clearly in the lead in the elections when INEC declared it "inconclusive", arguing that the margin of his lead was less than the total number of cancelled votes. After Audu's sudden death, INEC asked APC to name his replacement for a supplementary election. The party after several horse trading in which the internal political configurations of Kogi state played out, selected Alhaji Yahaha Bello, who contested the governorship primaries with Audu. James Faleke, who was Audu's running mate, felt that he should have been the rightful choice and declined Bello's offer to be his running mate in the supplementary election slated for December of that year. Contesting without a running mate, Bello defeated the incumbent Governor Captain Idris Wada in the supplementary election.

Both Wada and Faleke challenged Bello's election in the Election Petitions Tribunal chaired by Justice Halima Mohamed. Not only did Wada allege "gross irregularities" in the elections, he also asked the tribunal to determine whether Bello was qualified to be declared Governor when he had not taken part in all the electoral processes that led to the supplementary poll. He also argued that Bello went into the December 5, 2015 supplementary poll without a running mate. Faleke on his own contended that the governorship election was concluded on November 21 2015 and that Bello could not inherit the votes which he and Audu got as a joint ticket. He contended that he (Faleke) should be declared the governor of the state following Audu's death.

The tribunal dismissed Faleke's contentions for lack of merit. For Wada, it argued that he lacked the *locus standi* to challenge the process that produced Bello as APC's governorship candidate in the state since he was not a member of the party.

The ruling of both the Election Petitions Tribunal and the Appeal Court in the Bello case raises a number of interesting issues: For instance the ruling that Faleke cannot lay claims to the votes polled before the death of Audu because the votes were meant for the party and not for the candidates contesting the elections, is likely to renew conversations on whether legislators who decamp to other parties under any reason should retain their seats. Following the ruling in the Bello case, it could be argued that the law recognises only parties, not individuals, in the legislature. This means that there may be need for conversations on the appropriate relationship between an individual contesting for office under the banner of a party and the party itself as well as the relationship between the party which sponsored a candidate for office and that candidate after winning office. Right now this relationship seems vague and the ruling in the Bello case has only amplified that vagueness. What is the real meaning of party supremacy as intended by framers of our constitution?

Another interesting issue from the Appeal Court ruling of August 4 2016 is on the wider implications of Section 141 of the 2010 Electoral Act (as amended). It should be recalled that Section 141 of the 2010 Electoral Act was more of a legislative intervention following the 'injustice' in the Amaechi vs. PDP case, where Rotimi Amaechi, who did not present himself to the Rivers State's electorate, was declared the Governor of Rivers State on the argument that he should have been the rightful governorship candidate of the party in Rivers, rather than Celestine Omehia. Section 141 of the 2010 Electoral Act was therefore a legislative intervention to ensure that only candidates who participated in all the processes in the election could benefit from the spoils of election. The interpretation of this section in the Bello case appears to suggest the need for another legislative intervention to clarify certain gray areas not envisaged by that section.

Initially the Faleke camp believed that section 141 of the Electoral Act would be used against Bello, since he merely participated in the primaries and not in the election proper and therefore could not be said to have participated in all the processes of the election. But Faleke was to learn that he too did not fully comply with that section because he did not take part in the party's primaries that produced Audu as the party's governorship candidate as he was chosen as Audu's running mate only after the conclusion of the primaries. I believe that section 141 of the Electoral Act as interpreted in the Bello case raises the question of whether a Governor elect who is suddenly appointed to a higher office (as Atiku was in 1999) should be succeeded by his Deputy or runner-up to such a Governor during the primaries – bearing in mind that most running mates are appointed only after the conclusion of the primaries?

As many Nigerians eagerly await the legal fireworks at the Supreme Court, the generality of the people of Kogi state will be praying for a rapid conclusion of this process so that the government will settle down to the many challenges confronting the state. Obviously with concurrent judgements from both the Election Petitions Tribunal and the Appeal Court, Bello appears to be a in a strong position since his opponents will now have to show that there had been miscarriage of justice at the two lower courts.

I am happy that after the Appeals Court ruling Governor Bello sued for peace and called on Faleke and Captain Wada and others challenging his declaration as the Governor of the State to join him in the onerous task of rebuilding the State. The Governor needs to demonstrate that his extension of the olive branch to his opponents was not mere rhetoric or even subtle triumphalism. Not only should he genuinely reach out to his opponents he should also reach out to members of his party in the state. It should be recalled that members of the state's party executive not long ago passed a vote of no confidence on him and asked him to resign for allegedly sidelining them in appointments and embracing the opposition PDP. Paradoxically a key plank of Bello's victories at both the Elections Petitions Tribunal in the state and in the Appeals Court ruling was the supremacy of the party. Now given the notion of party supremacy embraced by both the Elections Tribunal and the Appeal Court, it will be an interesting conversation, whether a Governor should be made to resign if members of the state executive of his party pass a vote of no confidence on him and ask him to resign.

Prosecuting election petitions is not only a big distraction, it also does not come cheap. Most states of the federation, including Kogi state, are currently in financial distress. The state is for instance one of 11 states dragged to the International Criminal Court for non-payment of salaries by the rights group Socioeconomic Rights and Accountancy project (SERAP). Since the discovery of crude oil deposits in the boundary areas of Kogi, Anambra and Enugu States, the affected communities have hardly known peace. Criminality is on the rise (as in most other states of the federation) – just as unemployment and growing poverty.

There can only be one state governor at a time. While it can be argued that the legal challenges in the state are beneficial to our jurisprudence and help in deepening our democracy, at the end of the day what most peace- loving people in the state yearn for most is the forging of elite consensus on how to resolve the numerous developmental and social challenges facing the state.

Daily Trust, August 11, 2016

NATION - BUILDING

CHAPTER 22

2015: Issues that will drive the Election

2015 is already here. The political partisans have rolled out their drums and mobilized their foot soldiers. As you read the news and listen to news commentaries these, it is becoming increasingly difficult to know which ones are genuine news stories and features and which ones are planted by these partisans.

All things being equal, the presidential election will be a two horse-race between the ruling PDP and the APC, which was formed from a merger of three regionally based parties – the Action Congress of Nigeria (A.C.N), the All Nigerian Peoples Party (ANPP), the Congress for Progressive Change (CPC) and a faction of the All progressives' Grand Alliance (APGA). I use the words 'all things being equal' deliberately because whether the election will be truly competitive or another walkover for the ruling PDP will depend on how APC handles any grievances from its primaries to select its presidential flag bearer. If the primaries end on a note of acrimony that leads either to the splintering of the APC or its emasculation, the ruling PDP will win with an even greater margin than it did in 2011. But APC has so far defied all doomsday predictions. Few gave it any chance of lasting this long as a cohesive entity so it may yet disappoint the undertakers who have been eagerly waiting to sing its *nunc dimittis*.

The strength of the APC is not that it is offering anything new – because it is not. There is no material difference between the two main parties – the difference between the two is in fact like the difference between 12 and one dozen. The uniqueness of the APC however is that it is the first time in our political history that major opposition parties merged to make a bold bid for power. We may differ on what constitutes the glue that has held the party together this far – an alliance to 'return' power to the north, the desire to save Nigerians from PDP's 'misrule' or a shared dislike for President Jonathan and/or the PDP?

To underline the similarity between the two parties and that no one ought to shed any sweat for either, I read recently that the APC approached a Federal High court in Abuja, asking for the seats of the six Ekiti lawmakers who recently defected to the PDP to be declared vacant. I thought to myself: Hang on; was it not the same APC who vehemently opposed the moves by the PDP to declare the seats of 37 members of the House of Representatives who defected to the APC vacant and also opposed calls by the PDP on Speaker Tambuwal to resign for defecting to the APC?

Given the similarity between the two parties, it may be germane to speculate on the issues which are likely to drive the campaigns of both parties (expressly or subtly)?

North-South, Christian-Muslim divide

The fault lines of region, ethnicity and religion run deep in Nigeria. Virtually every part of the country has institutionalized memory of hurt or feelings of injustice, which they often feel will be best addressed if one of their own wields power at the center, preferably as the president. Similarly, there is a pervasive fear that the president of the country will use the powers of his office to privilege his region, ethnicity or religion— if not to punish or deliberately disadvantage others.

To allay fears of domination, most of the political parties have written or unwritten zoning and power rotation arrangements. However as with virtually everything Nigerian, solutions thrown at problems quickly become bigger problems than the original problems they were meant to address. And so it has been with the PDP's zoning and power rotation arrangements. Feelings that Jonathan's candidacy in the April 2011 elections cheated the north of its turn of producing the president for eight years is a very powerful sentiment among some voters in the north which will play a crucial role in the elections.

There is a contrarian sentiment among Jonathan's supporters. For them, in the 39 years between the time the country gained independence in 1960 and the inauguration of the Fourth Republic in 1999, the north ruled the country for about 36 of those years and should therefore be patient for that "historical injustice" to be redressed first. This is another way of saying that they should be patient for President Jonathan, who is from the south-south – the area of the south that produces the oil on which the country depends for its revenue - to complete two terms of eight years.

Another powerful sentiment that will play crucial role in the elections is that in Nigeria's peculiar mode of allocating privileges, the south is believed to have economic advantages over the north. In fact Nigeria is sometimes described as a country that runs on two unequal wheels. In 2013 for instance, the Russian investment banking firm Renaissance Capital produced a report titled, 'Nigeria Unveiled', which painted the picture of Nigeria's economy as moving on two wheels - a thriving South with rising income, lower unemployment and better educated citizens and a poorer and less educated north (Business Day, 13 May 2013). Based on this economic imbalance, the north's dominance of power before 1999 was justified as a lever to balance the south's assumed economic advantage. For those who believe in such power balance, the fact that the south has held the presidency for 12 of the 15 years the country has been under civil rule since 1999 means that the north has lost its leverage in the north-south equation.

Jonathan's performance in office

Jonathan's performance in office will be a campaign issue. However, measuring a regime's performance in a highly polarized country like Nigeria is often a very subjective undertaking. For Jonathan's supporters, he is the best President the country has ever had who has not only managed to grow the country's economy by an average of six percent per year – despite the Boko Haram challenge - but has also led it into being the largest economy in Africa and the 26th largest in the world. Jonathan's supporters will also mention the regime's success in containing the ebola epidemic which seems to have become the template for confronting that challenge across the world.   For his critics however, his "incompetence" is reflected in the high unemployment rate, generalized insecurity in the country and the deepening suspicion among the different ethnic groups in the country.

Boko Haram/Insecurity

For his critics, Boko Haram is evidence of Jonathan's incompetence while for his supporters, it is evidence of the siege laid on his government by powerful politicians from the Muslim north for it to fail.   In the unlikely event that the Boko Haram challenge is contained before the election, it will remove one arrow in the amour of Jonathan's critics while for his supporters, it will add to his perception of competence.

Money and power of incumbency

Money plays a very important role in Nigerian politics – in campaigning, media reach and vote buying. Here the PDP has clear advantage: not only has it federal resources to use as patronage, it also controls key institutions like the police, the army and the anti-corruption agencies like the Economic and Financial Crimes Commission, which could be used to harass political enemies. Money alone however will not be sufficient to determine the outcome of the election. Where the voters are sufficiently animated by a certain cause, the role of money in influencing the outcome of an election will be muted. However where the elections are close, the role of money, especially in vote buying and other material inducements such as distribution of bags of rice, will become quite important in influencing the outcome

Who wins?

APC's strategists will be banking on harvesting rich votes from the populous northwest (18 million votes), north-east (11 million votes) and southwest (13.5 million votes) for victory. For PDP, it will be counting on the fact that it has more Governors (21 compared to APC's 14 states) and hold good majorities in both the Senate and the House of Representatives. It has also made remarkable progress in the battle ground south-west where it now controls two states to APC's five and has also shown strengths in Osun and Oyo. The PDP will equally be banking on a good showing in Lagos with sizeable Igbo population who are thought to be among President's Jonathan's key supporters.

To win APC will have to find a way of ensuring that voting takes place in all of the populous north-east, that the PDP does not get up to 20 percent of the votes in the

North-west and North-east or alternatively that the APC does far better than is currently being projected for it in the South-west, south-south and the south-east.

Three months is more than a life time in politics. APC's chances will largely depend on whether it emerges from its presidential primaries stronger or weaker and the narratives it will articulate to sentimentally draw voters to itself.

Given the centrality of the state and the role of state power in accumulation and the distribution of privileges, we will not need a soothsayer to know that that the outcome of the election will be contentious and that whoever loses will blame his faith on rigging or INEC's partiality or incompetence.

Daily Trust, November 27, 2014

CHAPTER 23

2015: Year of the Long Knives?

The Night of the Long Knives is an expression often used to refer to the purge that took place in Nazi Germany between 30 June and 2 July 1934 when the Nazi regime carried out a series of politically motivated assassinations against leading figures of both the left-wing Strasserist faction of the Nazi party and prominent conservative anti-Nazis, including former Chancellor Kurt von Schleicher and Gustav Ritter von Kahr who had suppressed Hitler's Beer Hall putsch in 1923.

In modern usage, the phrase 'the knives are out' refers to a situation when people are being unpleasant about someone – or in an extreme case, trying to harm that person. Saying that the 'the knives are out for Mr. A', suggests that Mr. A has come under a barrage of criticisms or has made himself odious. Using the metaphor of long knives to refer to 2015 suggests expectations of violence, upheavals and even Armageddon consequent upon the presidential election during the year.

There have been several apocalyptic portraitures of the presidential election that will take place during this year. There are at least five main reasons why 2015 is generally feared to be a year of the long knives:

One, elections are generally anarchic in the country because of the zero-sum nature of our politics, the centrality of the state and the role of state power as the critical ingredient of wealth accumulation, elite formation and the dispensation of privileges.

Two, the successful formation of APC against all odds and predictions meant the coming into being of a viable opposition party that could give the PDP a run for its money. APC defied all odds, including a generalized apprehension that selecting the party's presidential flag bearer would be its Achilles heels. While it is not yet Uhuru for the APC, there is no doubt that PDP is getting into the election in a weaker position than it was in 2011. For the first time in the country's political history, you have an opposition party that has structures across the country. The APC is especially strong in the populous North-west, North-east and south-west. Some of the relevant questions that may help crystallize the likely outcome of the presidential elections include: How will our fault lines of religion, ethnicity and regionalism interface in the contest between the APC and the PDP, which peeled of rhetoric, are basically two sides of the same coin? Will certain critical elites in the North support Buhari's candidacy, and if they don't, will their non-support be significant enough to sway victory to Jonathan? Given the current anti Jonathan sentiments in the north, will Jonathan count on PDP states in the north to deliver the votes to him? With the south-west regarded as an APC stronghold, and Governors Amaechi and Okorocha holding forte for the party in Rivers and Imo State respectively, can Jonathan still count on solid Christian and southern support? Will the new APC platform provided to General Buhari and the aggressive rebranding of his candidacy be enough to allay the old suspicions of him in the south and among Christians? And what role will the power of incumbency play in determining the outcome of the election?

Three, there are fears that the presidential elections may stoke the latent tensions between the north and south. The relations between the north and south, which were ever characterized by mutual suspicion, hit a new low in 2011 with the decision of President Jonathan to contest the 2011 elections. Some people in the north felt that the decision short-changed the region of its chance of completing its 'turn' of producing the president of the country for eight years after Obasanjo had taken the south's 'turn' of serving for eight years. For some in the north, another four years for President Jonathan would mean that in the current civilian dispensation (which started in May 1999), the south will have served for 17 years while the north will have served for only three. Southern irredentists however also counter that in the 39 years between 1960 (when the country got its independence) and 1999, the north ruled for about 35 years to the south's four years. Remarkably the two main candidates in the presidential elections reflect the main contending fault lines of region and religion.

Four, there are those who believe that America predicted that Nigeria would disintegrate in 2015 – even though no one has been able to come forward with any concrete evidence on where and when the so-called prediction was made. For such people, 2015 is the predicted year of the country's Armageddon.

Five, is the tendency for elections to aggravate the structures of conflicts in newly democratizing societies such as ours. Not only do newly democratizing societies retain authoritarian impulses from their dictatorial past, the various nationalities that make up the country often have institutionalized and bottled up memories of hurt and injustice. Elections, especially ones in which stakes are as high as they appear to be now, often unleash such bottled up feelings.

Though I believe the dangers of post- election violence in the Muslim north is real if Buhari loses the election and that the chances of renewed militancy in the restive Niger Delta is equally very high if Jonathan loses, there are several reasons why I believe the doomsday predictions are unlikely to happen:

First, Nigeria has been a master of hanging on the precipice for a very long time such that hanging on a cliff has become the country's comfort zone. I recall that the American journalist Karl Maier believed that the unravelling of the country was imminent and consequently titled his book: *This House Has fallen: Nigeria in Crisis.* More than 14 years after the book was first published, Nigeria is still standing, even if many of its political problems remain largely unresolved.

Second, there is a feeling that our democracy is actually maturing despite its noise. For instance compared to the impunities that characterized the Obasanjo era, including political assassinations, political imposition of favoured candidates and garrison commander/do-or-die politics, one can argue that our democracy is actually evolving very fast and that many are gradually developing democratic ethos and sentiments. For instance, compared to before, the electorate seem to now respect people who lose gallantly and display spirit of sportsmanship. The sour loser syndrome is gradually getting out of fashion. In this sense, though the likely outcome of the election will be contentious, the emerging new spirit among the electorate may not be favourable to very protracted contentions over the outcome of the elections.

The biggest winner in the 2015 election is Buhari – irrespective of the outcome of the election itself. Though Buhari had previously unsuccessfully contested for the presidency three times, there has, until now, been very little effort to market him beyond the Muslim north where he has cultic followers. This paradoxically helped to accentuate the label of him in the south as a northern irredentist or Muslim fanatic. Of course some of the retired General's gaffes did not help matters. Now the APC provides him a broader platform that makes it possible for him to travel to different parts of the country and be welcomed and lionized by leading regional elites. And with this Buhari is acquiring the image of a national leader accepted by various regional factions of the elites. This contrasts with earlier perceptions of him as a lone ranger, one incapable of working in concert with others to achieve a common goal. Coterminous with the advantage of a national platform provided to him, there is also a serious re-branding of the Buhari brand. I was very impressed with the photo of him on several websites wearing a suit – and looking like a respected school principal. I never knew I would ever see Buhari wear a suit. The retired general now also wears the traditional attire of different ethnic groups he visits – something his handlers in the past would probably have regarded as hypocrisy. The popular perception of the old Buhari among his admirers was that like the late Chief Obafemi Awolowo, he did not believe in "the little lies that people call diplomacy". This and his numerous gaffes were naively marketed by his admirers as political virtues.

Buhari's re-branding goes beyond new sartorial acquisitions. In the presidential debate in 2011, Buhari seriously underperformed. He was inarticulate and did not display much knowledge about both domestic and international affairs. The re-invented Buhari is however different. In Port Harcourt on 6 January 2015 to flag off his presidential campaign, the re-branded Buhari was in his new elements. Wearing the south-south traditional attire with their traditional fedora hat to match, Buhari was an orator. He spoke eloquently and without his trademark stern demeanour or reading from any prepared speech   Time will however tell how this re-branding of Buhari will impact on the elections.

Daily Trust, January 8, 2015

CHAPTER 24

Re-engineering our Politics

James Carville, the American political strategist coined the phrase "The economy, stupid" as one of the three messages to be used as sound bites in Bill Clinton's successful 1992 presidential campaign against George H.W. Bush. The other two were "Change vs. more of the same" and "Don't forget healthcare". It can be argued that in most of the industrialized countries, the driving force of their politics has remained "the, economy stupid." And here we are looking at 'economy' in its various manifestations – from unemployment and mortgage concerns to issues bothering on healthcare and immigration.

In contrast to most of the industrialized countries, it could be argued that the fundamental challenge in most of the underdeveloped economies of Africa is not poverty or issues of the economy but politics in all its manifestations – from the politics of leadership recruitment and its ancillary of 'who gets what, when, how, why and where' to the politics of nation-building and its embedded contrariness. In fact during Ghana's struggle for political independence from Britain, the late Kwame Nkrumah admonished his fellow Ghanaians to "seek ye first the political kingdom, and all things shall be added to you". Though Nkrumah was among the radical Africanists who embraced what they called 'African socialism', Nkrumah's dictum turned the doctrinaire Marxian dictum of 'economic determinism' on its head by privileging politics over economics. In essence, the trouble with Nigeria is the character of its politics.

In this era of 'change', it is important that the government pays adequate attention on how to change the character of our politics: Why is our politics too anarchic? Why do politicians want to sit tight beyond their tenures? Why do we need to rig elections if it is all about service? Why does identity politics almost always trump issues-based politics?

To blame the PDP for the character of our politics or to sanctimoniously present the APC as an embodiment of progressive politics is to be manipulative with language and logic. I do not see any fundamental difference between all the parties in the country.

The truth is that owing to the centrality of power in fragile and polarized states like Nigeria, the struggle for it is anarchic. Power is not only a veritable means of individual material accumulation and distribution of privileges, the constituent units of the country also believe that winning power is a prerequisite for redressing the perceived injustices they suffered. They also fear that if another ethnic or regional group is allowed to win power at their expense, that group will use the power to privilege its own primordial groups or to punish and disadvantage the others.

In a situation such as the above, suspicion is pervasive and no individual or institution enjoys universal legitimacy across the fault lines. There is hardly consensus on anything, including the parameters of nationhood, a regime's performance in office or the notion of merit.

No matter the integrity of the electoral umpire, the outcome of elections is bound to be contentious – simply because of the character of our politics. This is not to suggest that integrity and competence of the electoral umpire does not matter. It does. But in terms of contribution to the acceptance or otherwise of the outcome of an election, the competence and integrity of the electoral umpire will probably account for about 20 per cent while the invisible hands of the character of our politics will account for about 80 per cent.

What will be done to re-engineer the character of our politics?

The way we treat those who lose elections and concede defeat will go a long way in determining whether losers will accept defeat or make it a do-or-die affair. If losers perceive that the winners are going to use instruments of state power to come after them, it will encourage sit-tightism. This is why some of us have been consistent in arguing that former President Jonathan and indeed others who lost elections should be treated with respect and dignity. This is not incompatible with 'probing' any aspect of the tenure of such leaders, if the new regimes must. But care must be taken to ensure that their being called to account for their time in office is not seen as a witch-hunt. Governance is a continuous process. Each government is expected to make its mark and also make its mistakes. It is the job of a succeeding regime to correct such mistakes while building on the achievements of the previous regime. Any new government must inevitably also make its own mistakes – hopefully to be corrected by the regime that will come after it.

Related to the above is that while ethnicity, religion and region are mere masks used by the elites in the struggle for power and lucre, over time these categories have become 'ideologized' such that they have now acquired objective existence of their own. This is why you have ethnic, religious and regional entrepreneurs who will analyse our politics through these identity markers. This means the need for certain sensitivity among our national leaders on how some of their policies, no matter how well-intentioned, could be decoded, especially by those who do not share same primordial identities as them. It will always be a delicate balance because leadership is not a popularity contest. Good intentions are certainly not enough justifications for policies especially in a polarized and low-trust society as ours.

Since suspicion that the group that comes to power will use state power to privilege its in-groups and disadvantage others is pervasive, a way out of this is to strengthen the Federal Character Commission and make it independent along the lines of INEC. An invigorated FCC will be crucial in attenuating the anarchic character of our politics as it will help to remove the cloud of suspicion around wielders of political power. This will especially be so if it also becomes a requirement that the agency's imprimatur will be a prerequisite for the National Assembly approving most federal appointments by the President or approving the budget for capital expenditures.

Strategies should also be evolved for winning back 'de-Nigerianized' Nigerians. The truth is that there are several individuals and groups who feel alienated from the Nigerian state and have chosen to delink from it into certain primordial identities, often with the Nigerian state as the enemy. Contrary to what many people think, Boko Haram, Indigenous Peoples of Biafra (IPOB) and other insurgency and separatist groups are not the only groups that have de-linked or attempting to delink from the state. The politician who corners what should be a common patrimony, the policeman who looks the other way on a little inducement, the civil servant who moonlights and is hardly on seat are all displaying the same symptoms of 'de-Nigerianization' as Boko Haram. Preaching only patriotism to these individuals and groups when they are angry with the state will not be helpful. They need channels to ventilate their grouses. They need agencies to hear their own sides of the story. They need to be engaged.

One of the fears for newly democratising societies such as ours is that liberal democracy could aggravate the structures of conflict in the short to medium terms. The fear is that bottled up feelings that were not allowed expression under periods of authoritarianism may now be let loose, leading to aggressive challenges to the state and separatist movements. We are witnessing such a scenario in the country now. But experiences from other countries show that it is much better to draw the ideas espoused by the leaders of such movements into the marketplace of political ideas and outcompete them than banning them or using a high-handed approach on them. It is often more dangerous to drive the ideas purveyed by such groups underground where they will be romanticised and the purveyors of such ideas turned into heroes and heroines. This is why in advanced democracies hate groups such as the KKK in the USA and the British National Party in the United Kingdom are never banned. Rather efforts are made to draw their ideas into the marketplace of political ideas where they are outcompeted.

More importantly the government needs to put servicing the country's nation-building process in the front burner by establishing a special agency in the presidency to drive this. In fact unless a president focuses on creating a nation – in words and deeds - his policies, no matter how well-intentioned, will be distrusted and politicised because people have different markers and lenses for filtering reality. In this respect, several measures put in place in the past to further the cause of building unity in diversity in the country such as the country's federalism, the NYSC, unity schools, creation of states and local governments – need urgent review to ensure they are still optimally contributing to the objective of nation-building.

Daily Trust, April 7, 2016

CHAPTER 25

Between Quota and Federal Character principle

This reflection is a continuation of my last week's piece on how to re-engineer our politics to make it less anarchic and more oriented towards nation-building. As I argued, there is pervasive fear that the ethnic group/region that wins power at the centre will use it to privilege its in-group or to disadvantage the others. It is largely because of such fears, which are sometimes also expressed as 'the fear of domination' or 'fear of marginalization' that our Constitution guaranteed that federal appointments and the distribution of amenities should reflect the 'federal character' of the country.

Unfortunately the federal character principle, which was first enshrined in the 1979 Constitution and retained in the current 1999 Constitution, has been very misunderstood or deliberately abused. One of the most common mistakes is to confuse it with a quota system. This is wrong. There are basic differences between the goals of a quota system and the goals of a 'federal character' principle. A quota system indicates a result that is pre-determined and inflexible. For instance our Constitution ensures that in the appointment of Ministers each state of the federation must have at least one minister. This is a quota system. Federal character principle however is geared towards creating a rainbow nation. It is the taking of deliberate steps to ensure that appointments at federal levels and the distribution of amenities reflect the diversity of the country. The Federal Character Commission was established in 1996 to implement and enforce the Federal Character principles.

Another common mistake with the notion of 'federal character' is the wrong assumption that it is an instrument to ensure proportional representation. It was never the intention of the federal character principle that the staff strength in each federal parastatal must reflect the population strength of different areas of the country or that there must be state, regional or ethnic parity in the workforce of each federal government agency.

It is also wrong to equate the 'federal character principle' to the affirmative action philosophy as practised in the USA or positive discrimination as practised in the UK. For instance while affirmative action is used mainly to correct perceived historical wrongs such as the historical discrimination against Blacks and women, the philosophy behind the federal character principle is not to correct any historical injustice (every part of the country has its own stories of injustice anyway) but simply to give every part of the country the proverbial sense of belonging through unity in diversity. The 'Federal Character' principle therefore is a statement of goals not a call for quota, proportional representation or an instrument for redressing historical wrong. It is instructive to note that apart from Ministerial appointment where the Constitution explicitly made the states the unit of representation, the unit of representation under the federal character principle is not stated.

The Daily Trust of April 13 2016 reported that Dr Shettima Bukar Abba, the Acting Executive Chairman of the Federal Character Commission charged the Nigeria Police Force to ensure strict compliance with the principle of federal character in its on-going exercise to recruit 10,000 Nigerians into the force. Dr Abba reportedly charged the Police Service Commission to take special note of states like Bayelsa and Ebonyi states as well as the North-east zone which he said were not adequately represented in the current nominal roll of the police force. The chairman of the Police Service Commission Mr. Mike Okiro reportedly assured Dr Abba that "all the local government areas in Nigeria would be represented in the exercise." Here Mr Okiro gave the impression that local governments rather than states are the units of representation under the federal character principle which I am not sure is correct.

The truth is that in diverse countries like Nigeria, skills and resource endowments are rarely evenly distributed among the different cultural areas and regions. Rather they tend to be complementary. For instance people from riverine areas may naturally look for a career in the Navy such that they may come to dominate the force. I think it will be a misapplication of the federal character principle in such a hypothetical instance to deny people from such areas deserved promotion just to create room for others at the top. The goal in such a situation will be to deliberately ensure that future appointments will redress the imbalance. In fact for the federal character principle to be properly applied without turning it into a quota, it may be necessary to take a broad view of the gamut of available federal appointments and the distribution of amenities rather than focus narrowly on one or two sectors. The truth is that every part of the country has got areas where, for historical reasons, they are preponderant and areas where they are underrepresented. This is why media sensationalisation of geographic representation in one or two sectors of the economy is biased reporting.

Senator Ben Bruce, the 'Common Sense Senator' appears to be among those who confuse the federal character principle with a quota system. The Senator was quoted by the Daily Mirror of September 17 2015 as saying:

"Nigeria must make progress though tribe and tongue may differ. The only way to do that is by saying goodbye to ethnicity and hello to merit. Compare the progress that Nigeria made before the quota system (1960-66) and the retrogression we have made since 1966 till date. The difference is clear.

"Federal Character cannot make an electrical power station work. It can't make refineries work. Only merit can ensure this. As a result of Federal Character, Nigeria Airways went from 30 aircraft to bankruptcy and a debt of over $60m by the year 2000. Quota System and Federal Character lead to a sense of entitlement in beneficiaries and resentment in others. Merit is a better way of life…"

It is difficult for me to see how an asprirational instrument designed to service the nation-building process is creating all the problems listed above by the Senator. Also the federal character principle uses states as basis of representation not ethnicity as the Senator wrongly suggested. The Senator equally forgot that what he called 'merit' is relative and subjective in a fractious and low trust society like ours. Again contrary to the Senator's glorification of the 1960-1966 era, it was actually an era where the 'fear of domination' was the driving force of our politics.

Zoning and Power rotation

Just as the 'federal character principle, 'zoning' and 'power rotation', which were introduced by the defunct NPN in 1979 and explicitly embraced by the PDP (and implicitly by other parties) in this dispensation, are also criticised by 'merit advocates.' The two concepts are related but not the same. Zoning means asking a particular area of the country to produce a specified political office holder to the exclusion of others who are not from that zone while power rotation is an arrangement where designated areas are to take turns in producing designated political officeholders for an agreed number of years. The aim of zoning and power rotation is simply to avoid what Alexis Tocqueville, the French political thinker and historian called the 'tyranny of the majority' in his treatise on possible threats to representative democracy in America. In countries where the basis of nationhood remains contested or where the state is made up of an agglomeration of different ethnic nationalities, the notion of 'concurrent majority'- in which great decisions are not arrived at through numerical majorities but often require agreement or acceptance by the major interests in the society – is quite popular. In such states, contrivances like 'government of national unity', the need to reflect the 'federal character' of a country in appointments and 'zoning' and 'power rotations' are often popular political vocabularies. Essentially therefore, zoning and power rotation, if creatively applied, cannot also be threats to merit. Rather, they are meant to be supplements to other Constitutional instruments such as the federal character principle in the nation-building process. In fact, if properly applied both zoning and power rotation, which are contrivances by political parties, can also ameliorate the anarchic nature of our politics and remove the threat of majority tyranny. Just as zoning and power rotation could lead to rule by incompetent people, it could also improve the quality of governance if it leads to the various zones competing to produce candidates that will excel, and in the process do the geo-political zone proud.

Daily Trust, April 14, 2016

CHAPTER 26

Nigeria: A Country in Perpetual Transition?

This reflection was inspired by a report in the Daily Post of January 11 2016 where Pastor Tunde Bakare, founder of the Latter Rain Assembly was reported as urging President Muhammadu Buhari to implement the recommendations of the 2014 National Conference. According to the report, Pastor Bakare told the president: "Let it be known that in spite of the rejection of our pre-election call for a transition period, Nigeria is now a nation in transition.

> This transition period will predictably be followed by a revolution which will, in turn, be followed by a reformation that will eventually usher in the desired transformation of our nation.

Bakare re-echoed some popular sentiments about the Nigerian state: the first is an intuitive belief that despite current challenges, in the end things will be OK. In Pidgin-speak, Nigerians will generally say "E go better". This eternal optimism or the ability to see the light at the end of the tunnel, or "suffering and smiling", perhaps partly explains why Gallup Poll found in 2011 that Nigerians were the world's happiest people - or most optimistic nation or the happiest place to be in the world.

The second sentiment is a shared belief that there will be an 'intervening moment' before this light in the tunnel is manifested. For some this 'intervening moment' will be either a 'revolution', a 'transformation' (such as adopting the recommendations of a National Conference to transform the structure of the country) or the coming into power of a reform-minded leader. Essentially there appears to be a consensus that there will be a rupture with the present way of doing things before the New Nigeria will emerge. One of the flipsides to this is that virtually every leader the country has had justifies his policies, including retrogressive ones, as representing the needed rupture with the present way of doing things. It is probably the reason why every government in the country, including at the state and local government levels likes to give the impression that its predecessors did nothing good and that 'real governance' is only starting with it.

Aside from the above sentiments, the notion of Nigeria as a country in transition also masks a number of salient issues:

One, is a certain tendency to blank out any question of when Nigeria was ever in a state of equilibrium. The truth is that you cannot talk of transition without knowing your take-off point or where you are transiting to. Knowing your take-off point is a crucial metric for measuring any progress or retrogression.

Two, Nigerians seem to have a high consciousness of the journey but a vague notion of the nature of the destination. This has often led to finger-pointing by different parts of the country on which part (or parts) of the country is (are) slowing down the journey. Several parts of the country that have threatened secession have often implied that without the others 'slowing them down'; their journey to the unspecified destination would have been faster.

Three, in the discourse of Nigeria as a country in transition, there is often a confusion on whether the country, ever troubled, is just hanging on a cliff or whether the cliff is in fact the country's comfort zone. When the American journalist Karl Maier published the book *This House Has Fallen: Midnight in Nigeria* (2000), the clear impression was that the country was about to implode. More than 15 years after the book was published, the country is still standing, its problems largely unresolved. In fact the country's problems rarely get resolved. In the run-up to the 2015 general elections, there were predictions that the elections would lead to the unravelling of the country. The election came and went. Nigeria did not unravel neither did it emerge stronger from the election. It is still hanging on the precipice – as it has always done. The country remains as divided as ever and paradoxically the sense of optimism that "e go better" also remains as strong as ever.

Four, Nigeria has been caught between the mood swings of the 1980s and 1990s – often regarded as the lost decades for Africa and the Afro-optimism of 2000s. In the decade 2000 until recently, there was an overwhelming Afro optimism where suddenly Africa became the beautiful bride of the world, with six of the ten fastest growing economies in the world being in the continent. Nigeria benefited immensely from the Afro-optimism of the era. In 2005 for instance Jim O'Neil, then a former Goldman Sachs analyst included Nigeria in the Next 11 (N-11). These were eleven countries – Bangladesh, Egypt, Indonesia, Iran, Mexico, Nigeria, Pakistan, Philippines, Turkey, South Korea, and Vietnam which Jim O'Neill identified in a research paper as having a high potential of becoming, along with the BRICs, the world's largest economies in the 21st century. In January 2014 O'Neil again popularized the notion of MINT economies - a neologism referring to the economies of Mexico, Indonesia, Nigeria and Turkey, which he believed would be the next break-out economies. Nigeria's inclusion in MINT simply meant the country took over the spot of South Korea in the MIKT economies. To add to the wave of Naija-optimism, Filipino billionaire, Enrique Razon, was quoted as declaring during the closing activities at the World Economic Forum in Davos, Switzerland in 2014 that year that Nigeria was the best place to invest that year. During 2014 Nigeria also became the largest economy in Africa following the rebasing of its GDP. Outside the shores of the country, Nigerians walked with more swagger as the wave of 'Naija-optimism was clearly discernible. Suddenly there was a collapse in the price of crude oil. A new sheriff came to town and there have been subtle suggestions that nothing ever was got right by his predecessors. There have been revelations of mind boggling diversions of public funds suggesting that contrary to the image, those who governed the country before did nothing but steal the country blind. Nigeria, we are told is broke, and must begin a new transition.

Five, Nigeria is classified as a democratising rather than a democratic country. It is a country in transition from autocracy to democracy. We are told that some of the features of a democratizing society include the tension between democratic consolidation and democratic reversal and between the expansion and the contraction of the democratic space. In democratising societies, the structures of conflicts are aggravated because of the bottled up feelings that were denied expressions during the periods of dictatorship. But a cynic can also ask when the country ever was without tensions? In democratizing societies there are authoritarian impulses that make it difficult to decipher whether the country is consolidating its democracy or relapsing into its authoritarian past. What appears obvious is that it is in transition.

Six, Nigeria has also been in perpetual war against corruption. There is always a notion of a transition to a period when corruption will become very minimal. Every regime in the country has made fighting corruption a key feature of its policy options. Yet revelations by each succeeding regime 'probing the preceding' one often suggests that corruption has not become less despite all the grandstanding about fighting corruption. We remember Obasanjo's Jaji Declaration (during his First Coming), Shagari's Ethical Revolution, Babangida's MAMSER, Abacha's Failed Bank Tribunal and Obasanjo's EFCC and ICPC (in his Second Coming). Buhari is now waging his own war against the malaise. Each regime approaches the 'fight' with a sense of moral outrage. The true test of success however is not in how much money an agency has recovered from 'looters' or in revealing how officials stole the country dry – as important as these may be - but whether the fight succeeds in making the country less corrupt. So far there is nothing to suggest that the incidence of corruption has become less despite each regime's moral outrage and the existence of contraptions like EFCC and ICPC. In this sense Nigeria remains in transition with respect to the fight against corruption.

A crucial question following the above is when Nigeria will move from its permanent transition mode to permanently resolve at least one of its numerous existential problems.

Daily Trust, January 13 2016

CHAPTER 27

The Balance of Stories

One of the famous quotes often attributed to the late Chinua Achebe, master story teller extraordinaire, is this one about the lion and the hunter: 'Until lions learn (or Until lions learn) to produce their own historians, the history of the hunt will continue to glorify the hunter'. Deconstructed, we are told that - lions are very strong animals indeed. They get their priorities wrong – if not being plainly stupid – because they go about showing off their strength, believing that they are both feared and admired for their strength without knowing that they are indeed being ridiculed for what they would consider their asset. In this tale, only the hunter writes or tells stories of his encounters with the lion and naturally makes himself the hero of such encounters while lions have no history and are not smart enough to produce historians that will document their encounters with human beings – for a balance of stories.

There is a play of this lion and hunter aphorism in George Orwell's *Animal Farm* (1945). In this allegorical and dystopian novel, shortly after the animals successfully carried out a revolution which overthrew their human masters in the Manor Farm to establish a rule of the animals, there was a need for some reconstruction work in the farm. A horse, known as the Boxer, was the pillar of the work, and his maxim, anytime new challenges in the reconstruction were presented by the pigs, leaders of the new animal kingdom, was, 'I will work harder'. As the Boxer's strength deserted him owing to a combination of age and illness, the leadership of the new animal kingdom, duly sold him off to the butcher. In this tale, for the pigs, the Boxer was only good for his strength and nothing else. The Boxer, in the aforementioned novel, obviously did not make any attempt to tell his own side of the story on why he was willing to work extremely hard without complaining.

I have had a little more time to reflect on the lion and hunter tale and the whole issue of balance of stories. It would seem to me that we are rather too quick to judge and conclude that lions have produced no historians and that every available history of the hunt glorifies the hunter. What seems to have happened, in my opinion, is that we simply created a stereotype, based on our understanding and what we read, and concluded that the history of the hunt necessarily glorifies the hunter. Have we for instance made any effort to understand the ways of the animal kingdom and the language of the lions? Is it possible that in their kingdom and in their language, every lion and lioness is a professor of history who regales in telling their young ones (cubs) how a mere belch (roar) from them makes human beings freeze in fear and death?

Take again the relationship between chicken and man. Most people love chicken and eggs and take it as a matter of course that the whole essence of a fowl's life is to service the appetite of man. But is it possible that in the chicken kingdom they have their own history that they looked at men dying in their numbers out of malnourishment and then being selfless creatures, they collectively decided to offer themselves as sacrificial lambs to provide proteins to save human beings from their miserable existence – just as Jesus Christ died on the cross in Christian religion for the atonement of man's - sins? In other words, while as humans we are often too quick to assume that chickens have no brains and only live to provide meat and eggs for us, is it possible that in the chicken world, they see themselves as saints who willingly give up their lives just to save man from dying of malnourishment?

In fact while humans see themselves as the most advanced creature, is it possible that in the animal kingdom they laugh at us as being too lazy? Come to think of it: as a hunter, man can hardly run fast enough to catch any game and will need a dog to help him; he can hardly overpower any decent animal on his own and may need the aid of a gun or matchete; man is too lazy to carry a reasonable load and may require the assistance of a donkey or a lorry. How are we sure that in the animal kingdom we are not simply derided as lazy fools?

What am I driving at with all these stories? I am simply referring to the issue of stereotypes, which is often based on an incomplete or biased interpretation of others' reality by non-members of the group. Let me give a practical example. As an Igbo, I know for instance that if you return from say a town or foreign travel and tell your people that you came back empty- handed because your hosts were unfriendly or did not want to give you any opportunities for advancement, your people are likely to retort to your face, "are you not an Igbo man?" In essence, they are reminding you that in the Igbo culture there is no excuse for failure. In fact, I remember that in my secondary school, Oraifite Secondary school, in Anambra State, the school's motto was a Latin translation of, 'find the way or create one'. In the school, in my days, you would get into trouble if you ever answered any question with, 'I don't know'. But it was acceptable to answer, 'give me time or days to find out the answer'.

Now among non- Igbos, if you are called an 'Igbo man', it could mean you are aggressively competitive or love money too much. Here again we encounter an imbalance in stories – between the Igbos' notion of themselves and the others' perception of them. Again, there are some ethnic groups that cherish certain values which they want to be central in their historiography. A culture may for instance preach that being at peace with oneself and one's community and seeing life as transient are nobler than engaging in aggressive pursuit of materialism. Here while members of this culture may extol themselves for not being materialistic and accommodating, non-members of the culture may deride them as 'lazy people'.

Stereotypes exist in every society and could sometimes be a way of helping people organize or pigeon-hole reality. There is rarely a group in the world, including the remote village in our country, which does not have one stereotype or the other attached to it. The problem is often when this stereotype enters the political domain or conflates with hypocrisy to lead to hate speech. This seems to be what is currently happening in the country, with Nigerians seemingly enjoying profiling and pouring invectives on one another whenever they congregate in their in-group to discuss the Nigerian condition. And if you think this is only a past-time of the uneducated and those who believe the world revolves around their ethnic enclave, you may be disappointed. Just read the 'comments' that follow most articles online – whether in newspapers, blogs or on the numerous online news-and features aggregator sites on the country, and you will marvel at the capacity of educated Nigerians, including Diaspora-based ones, who are presumably living in 'civilized' countries, to write from their base animal instincts. When you read the comments in some articles published online, you often find the irony of people who complain of being insulted freely insulting others, you find groups who cry of marginalization shouting down on others who may complain of any marginalization, you find people who accuse others of having ruled longer than others boasting that their own group would rule for the next 100 years. Net effect: the widening of the social distance among the people from the different fault lines that make up the country and an exacerbation of the crisis in the country's nation-building.

Unfortunately stereotypes can neither be legislated against nor eliminated in any society. Even its politicised variant – hate speech - is difficult to deal with, especially in free speech jurisprudence. Often what is required is for people not to take themselves too seriously, to be able to just laugh off certain jokes that bother on stereotyping and of course for people to make better attempts at understanding why certain things matter more to others than it does to them. Perhaps, if we had been a little more sensitive or more humble, we would not have quickly concluded in the lion and hunter tale, that the lions have not produced historians. May be that aphorism would have read differently: 'Man's inability to decode the language of lions or access the universe of the animal kingdom, has given the impression that lions have not produced their own historians. Capitalising on this, the history of the hunt in the human kingdom, always glorifies the hunter'.

Daily Trust, June 27 2013

CHAPTER 28

Constitution Amendment: Did the People really speak?

There are a number of matters arising from the results of the peoples' public session on the Review of the 1999 Constitution, which was formally presented in Abuja on 18 April, 2013, by the Ad Hoc Committee of the House of Representatives on the Review of the 1999 Constitution. The public sessions, which were flagged off by Speaker Aminu Waziri Tambuwal on November 8, 2012, took place on November 18, 2012, across the 360 federal constituencies in the country. The public presentation of the collated results was initially billed to hold on January 31, 2013.

According to the aggregated results, 275 constituencies opposed rotational presidency while 80 were in favour, and five were undecided. The results also showed that about 210 constituencies rejected that a provision be inserted in the constitution to make the Office of President rotational among the six geo-political zones of the country while, 147 constituencies supported the idea and three constituencies claimed they were undecided. Other outcomes of the public sessions included a finding that a majority of the constituencies support the idea of independent candidacy, financial autonomy for state houses of assembly, abolition of joint state/local government account, abolition of state independent electoral commissions and reducing the immunity enjoyed by key political office holders like the President, Vice President, Governors and Deputy Governors. Majority of the constituencies, according to the findings, will like to see a separation of the office of the Attorney General of the Federation from the position of the Minister of Justice.

While the philosophy behind the public sessions – to ensure that the discordant voices of Nigerians are captured on the contentious issues of our time, to guarantee that any amendment to the constitution reflects the wishes of the generality of Nigerians – is unassailable, care must be taken not to take these results at their face value. In fact, reeling out figures to show that an aggregate number of constituencies support one idea or the other may be impressive on paper (after all figures don't lie, some would say), but, in reality figures are not always neutral arbiters in contentious situations. They can be employed to service ideological proclivities and hidden agendas. Remember Darren Huff?

In a very influential book, How to Lie with Statistics (1954), the American writer, Darrell Huff, discusses the funny business of lying with figures, telling us how intentional or unintentional errors could lead to inaccurate conclusions. The book, which was meant to be an introduction to statistics for the general reader, quickly became one of the most widely read statistics books in history- despite the fact that the author was not a statistician. I suspect that the popularity of the book had to do with the fact that using graphs and figures to prove one's point could make one look really clever.

I am not suggesting that the Ad Hoc Committee of the House of Representatives on the Review of the 1999 Constitution, which organised the public sessions, manipulated the figures. I don't think they did. The Deputy Speaker of the House of Representatives, Hon. Emeka Ihedioha, who superintended the exercise, is from all intents and purposes, an honourable man. I am however concerned that the way some of the questions were framed disposed the respondents to particular answers. Let me just take three examples from the questions presented to the respondents:

'Should Section 214(1) be amended to enable the establishment of a State Police?' The way this question is framed wrongly presupposes that the respondents know the arguments for or against state police. Because people are naturally apprehensive of change, an instinctive response to a question formulated in this manner by 'ordinary' Nigerians, will be 'no'. My personal opinion is that this question would have been more useful if it was predicated with a synopsis of the key arguments, for and against state police. For instance wouldn't it be more useful if the question was formulated thus: 'Some people have blamed the pervasive insecurity in the country to the fact that State Governors, though formally designated as the Chief Security Officers, are in reality not so because they do not control the police in the State. Will you therefore support an amendment to Section 214 (1) to enable the establishment of a State Police, which will be firmly under the Control of the Governors'?

Another question read: 'Should the Office of the President or Governor of a State be filled purely on merit, instead of zoning?.' According to the collated figures, 224 constituencies answered 'yes' while 135 answered 'no'. I have some issues with this question as I indeed do with several others. For one, the question implies wrongly that zoning is incompatible with merit. It also appears to confuse 'zoning' with 'power rotation'. More importantly, the question made no attempt to define for the respondents what it means by 'zoning' or provide a synopsis of the key arguments for or against the option. I believe that different respondents would have answered differently, if, for instance the question was cast this way: 'Some have argued that in a polarized society such as ours with different cleavages, the principle of zoning - the idea that key public offices should be shared in such a way as to reflect the character of the society – should be used in determining who becomes the President of the country or Governor of a State. Do you agree?'

I found some of the questions framed by the Ad Hoc Committee of the House of Representatives on the Review of the 1999 Constitution to be too convoluted, too legalistic or with double-barrel meanings – which could be quite confusing to the respondents. Take for instance the question: 'Should Section 308 be amended to make the immunity provision for the President, Vice President, Governor or Deputy Governor cover only civil proceedings while in office?' Now, how many non-lawyers really know what 'civil proceedings' mean?

I am not trying to undermine the efforts of the Ad Hoc Committee of the House of Representatives on the Review of the 1999 Constitution. My position is that we should thread with caution the apparent conclusions from the public sessions on the review of the constitution because they seem to undermine the efforts made so far in forging a nation from the mosaic of nationalities that make up the Nigerian state. Is it not for instance surprising that at a time that the clamour for 'true' federalism appears to be reaching a new crescendo with its concomitant sporadic agitations for 'resource control' and 'sovereign national conference' (all pointing to a quest for greater decentralization, if not a looser form of federation), the conclusions from the aggregated opinions of an overwhelming majority of the constituencies seem to point in the opposite direction. With the obvious endemic crisis in our nation-building project and a resultant massive de-Nigerianization process which it has triggered I find it rather surprising that a majority of the constituencies seem to favour options that will only lead to greater centralization of power. I am for instance taken aback that most constituencies are opposed to the use of zoning in the election of the President and Governors – when this principle has always been applied in our political history and is in fact given legal teeth by the constitutional provision that the 'federal character' of the country must be reflected in all public appointments. As mentioned earlier, 'zoning', should not be confused with 'power rotation' – the idea that the various units in the state or country should take turns in taking a shot at certain political offices.

I also feel that the question on 'indigeneship' confuses 'indigeneship' with citizenship rights, which are quite extensively provided for in the constitution. I believe 'indigeneship' can only be achieved through assimilation to the culture of the host community, such that, if they accept you as one of them, you will, so to say, be inducted into the ways of pacifying their local deities. In the United Kingdom for instance, you can acquire a British citizenship after meeting certain conditions. However, the fact that you are now 'British citizen' does not make you an English man or woman because this is a belonging of another type, bothering on shared culture and ancestry. My personal opinion is that if we get this issue of indigene-citizenship dichotomy wrong based on supposed preferences of a majority of the constituencies, we will create another problem – namely the fear of domination by groups which are more diasporic than others and the concomitant backlash against such groups.

In conclusion, while I applaud the initiative of the Ad Hoc Committee of the House of Representatives on the Review of the 1999 Constitution in taking these discussions to the grassroots, we must not be unmindful of the unintended methodological shortcomings of the exercise in interpreting the collated results from the public sittings.

Daily Trust, May 9, 2013

CHAPTER 29

On The Purported Merger of Christian and Islamic Studies in Schools

Nigeria can be anything but boring. The country often reminds one of the title of one of Dr Anezi Okoro's novellas – *One Week, One Trouble* (African University Press, 1972). In that novella, the lead character Wilson Tagbo, a brilliant and determined chap, had gained admission into a secondary school during the colonial days. In his quest to turn the period of his studentship into a journey for self discovery, the young man had several run-ins with the school authorities almost on a weekly basis.

As it was with Anezi Okoro's *One Week, One Trouble*, so it is with Nigeria. Every week brings its own simmering discord and contentious issue.

Over the past few weeks matters that dominated the headlines have included the purported $6bn loans and currency swap deal with China, the radicalization of 'Fulani' herdsmen as a new terrorist group, the trial of Senate President Saraki by the Code of Conduct Tribunal, agitations for Biafra by the Indigenous Peoples of Biafra, Boko Haram, Buhari's foreign trips and the debate on whether the Naira should be devalued or not. The current 'trouble with Nigeria' is the reported move by the Ministry of Education to merge the teaching of Christian Religious Studies (CRS) with Islamic Studies (IS) under a new subject to be known as Religion and National Values (RNV).

I use the word 'purported' deliberately because, to the best of my knowledge, there is no official confirmation or denial of this story – not even on the website of the Federal Ministry of Education. However given the tendency for this government to either allow the media to go to town with stories and then deny such stories after they have gained currency (as happened with the issue of $6bn loan and currency swap with China) or to stake a position and then do a U-turn (as happened with the issue of Nigeria joining a Saudi-led Islamic coalition against terrorism), anything is possible with this story. It is on this premise that I feel that certain observations on the matter are germane:

One, the idea to 'merge' the teaching of CRS with IS actually predates the Buhari regime. It all started with the Universal Basic Education (UBE) Programme, which was introduced in Nigeria in September, 1988. In 2008 the Federal Government through the Nigerian Educational Research and Development Council (NERDC) introduced the 9-Year Basic Education Curriculum (BEC) in schools which sought to realign all extant Primary and Junior Secondary School Curricula to meet the key targets of the UBE programme. The structure of the 9-Year Basic Education Curriculum was such that the number of subject offered ranged from ten to sixteen. Between 2008 and now, the country witnessed two major curriculum reform initiatives at the Basic Education level, namely: the 9-Year Basic Education Curriculum (BEC) (September 2008- August 2014); and the Revised 9-Year Basic Education Curriculum (September 2014 –Present). The Revised BEC comprises ten subjects namely English

Studies, Mathematics, Basic Science and Technology, Religion and National Values, Cultural and Creative Arts, Business Studies, Nigerian Languages, Pre-vocational Studies, French and Arabic.

Two, it is not clear how the Revised 9-Year Basic Education Curriculum, which theoretically came into force in September 2014 and under which the RNV subject was introduced, has been enforced across the country. It is also not clear whether the current speculation is merely a kite being flown by the government about its desire to more strictly enforce the teaching of RNV or whether it has something else under its sleeve in this matter. At least one blogger has argued that the idea behind the new RNV subject was not to merge the teaching of the two dominant religions in the country but that the new subject has several themes, some of which are compulsory such as social studies, civic education and security education while the themes on CRS and IS will be taught separately. We await further clarification on this.

Three, since religion is a matter of faith and belief, its discussion in a multi-religious, multi-ethnic and low-trust society like ours often risks touching extremely sensitive nerves. It could in fact be hypothesized that any initiative that verges on religion and which is fiercely opposed by both leading Muslims and Christians is already dead on arrival. This appears to be the inevitable fate of RNV – whether it is merely a kite being flown by the government or not. For instance two prominent religious leaders, the Sultan of Sokoto, Alhaji Sa'ad Abubakar, and the Archbishop of the Catholic Archdiocese of Lagos, Alfred Adewale Martins, have condemned any move to merge CRS and IS under any guise. In the same vein, the Muslim Rights Concern, (MURIC) has warned the Federal Government against any merger of the teaching of the two faiths in school. MURIC drew the attention of the government to both the letter and spirit of Section 38 (ii) of the 1999 Constitution which states that "No person attending any place of education shall be required to receive religious instruction …if such instruction …relates to a religion other than his own, or a religion not approved by his parent or guardian." There are also concerns that RVN could actually contravene the Child's rights Act of 2003, which preserves the right of the child not to be exposed to any religion contrary to that of his parents or guardians.

Four, those who promote the RNV assume wrongly that allowing students to study about Christianity and Islam will automatically promote religious tolerance. The premise of this logic is erroneous. It is akin to arguing that the colonial anthropologists who pioneered the study of African cultures would be less racist than their counterparts who had never been to Africa. As experience showed, they were often more racist than their fellow citizens who never visited Africa. For instance Joseph Conrad, who wrote the infamous novel *The Heart of Darkness* (1902), which caricatured African customs, had travelled extensively in India, Singapore, Australia and Africa as a seafarer and had 'studied' African cultures. Collapsing the teaching of CRS and IS under RNV is therefore more likely to promote feelings of superiority and intolerance than religious amity. How will for instance ordinary Nigerians in a predominantly Muslim state in the north react to a Christian teaching them about CRS or IS under the RNV? And how will a student in a predominantly Christian state in the southeast or south-south react to a Muslim teaching them about CRS or IS under the RNV? It is difficult not to believe that students will under the RNV be forced to study comparative religions which could be problematic on its own especially in a society like ours, and given the age-group that is targeted. Based on this, I believe that those who fashioned the RNV were either genuinely ignorant of the depth of the religious fault line in the country or were being deliberately mischievous.

Five, the impression one gets is that those who designed the idea of RNV want religion to be taught as an academic subject (secular study of religious beliefs) – rather than as theology (designed to teach morals). If this assumption is correct, it immediately raises the question of how the adherents of one faith will feel when their faith is being critiqued from a secular perspective, especially if the teacher is not someone who shares the same faith as them. Even if the teaching of morals is stretched to be part of the objectives of collapsing the teaching of both CRS and IS under RNV, it raises the question of how this can be done given instances of different moralities preached by the two religions such as on polygamy? One may also want to know why Traditional African Religion is omitted from the RNV.

Six, there is also the question of where we will find teachers with the requisite skills and training to teach both CRS and IS and at the same time teach the other components of RNV such as social studies, Civic Education, Security Education, Consumer Education, Disaster Risk Reduction Education and Peace and Conflict Education? Even if we accept that 'separate classes should be run for CRS theme and IS theme' as one blogger argued, where do we get enough adjunct lecturers to teach the two religions across the country? RNV therefore is a poorly conceived programme that should never be allowed to see the light of the day, especially by a government which is already being accused of implementing religious and ethno-regional agenda.

Daily Trust, April 28 2016

CHAPTER 30

Can we really afford this Democracy?

I can understand if, from the title of this piece, you conclude that I am nursing some nostalgia for military regimes and their authoritarian impulses. This is certainly not my drift. On the contrary, I believe that the seed of many of the problems we confront in this country today - from mistrust to cries of marginalization and the crisis of nation-building they engender – were sown by the military when they used soldierly fiat and decrees to impose rules and structures that would never have seen the light of the day in a free contest of ideas. I am rather worried at the cost of our democracy – which is increasingly being corrupted to 'democrazy' and 'mob rule' as well as the tendency of this bastardized form of governance to aggravate the structures of conflict in our country.

Let me take this one step at a time. On April 10 2013, the Minister of Information, Labaran Maku disclosed that the Federal Executive Council had approved the sum of N2.1 billion for the printing of 33.5 million Permanent Voters Card for the Independent National Electoral Commission (INEC), which had earlier printed 40 million of the said cards at the cost of N2.6 billion. We were further told that the Permanent Voters' Card would be used only for the 2015 and 2019 elections after which they would be replaced by the National Identity Cards. Apart from the tantalizing technical term of 'biometric features' which the cards are said to possess and which its proponents argue will imbue transparency in the entire electoral process through a proper identification of voters, those who are not, or who refuse to be intimidated by the invincibility often ascribed to technology and its jargons, will not be afraid to ask some critical questions: is a proper identification of voters the only way elections can be rigged? Will plugging just one process in an election that comprises several processes, and which could be rigged at any stage, even at the stage of result collation or announcement, really worth the whopping sum being allocated to it? If banks and other institutions can accept drivers' licence and other forms of identification, why can't individuals whose names are on the voters' register in an area be asked to come forward with any acceptable form of identification as is the case in several countries? And if INEC really wants to play as safe as possible, why not use the temporary voters' card issued in 2011 and update it for those who did not get the card in 2011 or who were then not qualified to vote? And don't forget that by 2015 there may be new demands and new budgetary allocations to take into consideration those who may just have qualified to vote.

My personal opinion is that elections will remain a do-or-die affair in the country for as long as the state remains the major means of production and material accumulation and de-accumulation. The President or Governor can decide today to turn one pauper into a billionaire or a billionaire into a pauper. The stakes during elections are simply so high that it cannot be anything else but anarchical. The late

Kwame Nkrumah of Ghana put this more euphemistically when he counseled Ghanaians to seek first the political kingdom and every other thing would be added unto them.

Not surprisingly therefore the cost of our democracy and the seeking of political offices that can be said to constitute its superstructure tend to be far more expensive than you have in other countries. For instance while in the run-up to the April 2011 elections, INEC insisted and received N87.7 billion ($576.9 million) for registering about 70 million voters, Bangladesh, a fellow developing, corrupt and populous country spent only $65 million, (about N9.7billion) for a similar exercise of biometric voters registration of some 80 million voters conducted over a period of 11 months in 2008. In 2010 Canada, spent 19.2 million Canadian dollars (or roughly N2.8 billion) to register 23 million voters. If we multiply this by three to approximate the 70 million voters registered by INEC, the cost would still be about N8.6bn for 69 million voters compared to the N87.7 billion spent by INEC to register 70 million voters.

One Opeyemi Agbaje of the Resource and Trust Company Limited estimated that in 2011 the average cost of public holidays on the national economy for the four days' holiday declared during the April 2011 elections was N270.85 billion, while the average cost of public holidays on the economy for Bauchi and Kaduna where gubernatorial elections were postponed was estimated at N3.66 billion. He also estimated that the average cost of the public holidays declared for the re-run of elections in four Local Government Areas in Imo State during that period was N350 million.

Though the April 2011 elections were infinitely better than the charades that Professor Maurice Iwu presided over as INEC chairman, it remains unclear to me whether the improvements were the result of the huge investments into the conduct of the elections or whether it was because the bar of expectation was set very low for Professor Jega after he aborted the elections mid-way on April 2 2011. My strong feeling is that irrespective of the investment in the elections, the extent to which it will be free or fair will depend on the body language of the President and on Nigerians themselves. We are the problem of our elections, not the processes. The cost of conducting elections is just a tiny fraction of the cost of our democracy. You have to factor in the cost of maintaining the President, the Ministers, Governors and their and their commissioners and aides as well as the legislators and at the national and state levels and the cost could be mind-boggling.

The second limb of my concern with our democracy is its implications for nation-building.

One of the main attractions of democracy is its free speech component – the ability of people to speak their minds without censorship. Freedom of expression - a broader concept than freedom of speech - is sometimes used as a synonym not just for freedom of verbal speech but also for any act seeking, receiving and imparting information or ideas, irrespective of the medium used. Free speech is of course never absolute in any jurisdiction primarily because it competes with equally important values such as the right to privacy, the protection of people's reputation or the need to protect the society from potential harm from unrestrained hate or obscene speech. In general four key arguments are put forward to justify a free speech principle – the importance of discovering the truth, free speech as an aspect of self-fulfilment, free speech as being indispensable for citizens to participate in a democracy and the belief that there is a strong reason to be suspicious of the government. It is in general also believed that suppressing free speech could heighten the suspicion of authority, destroy the important civic education of tolerance and drive underground the suppressed speech where it could be romanticised in more dangerous forms. Besides, suppressing free speech is contrary to the marketplace of ideas theory popularized in the dissenting judgment of Holmes J in *Abrams v US* where he declared that the "ultimate good desired is better reached by free trade in ideas, that the best of the truth is the power of the thought to get itself accepted in the competition of the market and that truth is the only ground upon which their wishes safely can be carried out."

In societies where the basis of statehood are agreed upon, the British and American models of democracy and the periodic elections that underpin them will no doubt be deepened by an almost unfettered freedom of speech. I am not so sure this is the case in societies like ours where the basis of statehood remains sharply contested. With deep institutionalized memories of hurt and suspicions by the constituent nationalities, the British and American models of democracy often end up strengthening the pull of the centrifugal forces in the society. One of the consequences is often a concerted attack on the state and its institutions by various constituent units of the state, each claiming it is marginalized or not getting a fair deal from the Nigeria project. The crisis of nation-building tends to be more severe in the country under 'democracies' than under the military.

Having lived under military dictatorships in Nigeria, I can never nurse any nostalgia for what is a good riddance. I am however arguing that it may be time that we began to look at the cost of elections and the implications of our type of democracy for nation-building. This may lead to a new debate on whether there is possibly a third way where we can preserve the freedoms that democracy guarantees without the concomitant threats to the corporate existence of the state which it seems to engender in our type of societies. Some have argued that the current challenges in our democracy project is temporary and that in the long-run everything will be OK as our democracy matures. This may be true. But was it not the British economist John Maynard Keynes who told us that in the long run we are all dead?

Daily Trust, April 25, 2013

CHAPTER 31

Dousing Political tension in the land

The political war drums are already being rolled out – ahead of 2015. There is understandably palpable apprehension in the land. No one really knows what 2015 holds for the country. Only the future can tell.

Elections are always contentious in the country – and understandably so. As Kwame Nkrumah, Ghana's first President and doyen of his country's nationalist struggle would say, "seek ye first the political kingdom and every other thing shall be added unto you". Nigerian politicians appeared to take that dictum to heart. And can you blame them? Whoever is in control of state resources wields enormous power and influence. Not only has he (usually a 'he') the power to transform a pauper into a billionaire overnight and a billionaire into a grovelling charlatan in a matter of days, every senseless huff he utters is guaranteed to generate the loudest but feigned rib-cracking laughter and proclaimed the funniest or wisest thing ever uttered on earth by a coterie of favour seekers and hangers on. Simply put politics is anarchical in the land because state power is both a means of production and the shortest cut to wealth accumulation and elite formation.

2015 has a special salience. For the first time in our political history the outcome in the 2015 cannot be easily predicted. The result will be quite close; guaranteeing that whichever side is proclaimed to have lost will cry foul and perhaps take the laws into their hands. This is why I believe that there is an urgent need to begin the process of dousing the tension ahead of the elections. I shall return to this.

Two recent events have enormous implications for the build-up to 2015 – Governor Murtala Nyako's letter to the Northern Governor's forum and Buhari's reaction to the recent Nyanya terrorist attack.

Nyako's letter to Northern governors implying that Boko Haram was a creation of Jonathan and accusing him of genocide against the North has been rightly condemned by many people. I share strongly that condemnation, including the thinly veiled attempt to incite the North against a section of the country. Between Governor Nyako's outright incitement and the equally unacceptable attempt by the PDP to incite the people against APC and Buhari by blaming them for the Nyanya bombing, it is difficult to know which is worse. But these are ominous signs of what lie ahead as 2015 approaches.

But reading Olusegun Adeniyi's, 'Who is Nyako Speaking for?' (ThisDay, 24 April 2014), a broader perspective to the face-off emerged. Adeniyi argued that Nyako's memo could not have been borne out of any altruism. Recalling that both Nyako and Jonathan were buddies, Adeniyi traced the genesis of the quarrel to the appointment of Bamanga Tukur as PDP's national chairman against Nyako's wish – and despite the fact that the Adamawa Governor had swum against the tide in the North to deliver his state to Jonathan in 2011. Jonathan was said not only to abandon Nyako when he needed him most but also reportedly looked the other way when Bamanga Tukur dissolved the State Exco of the party in a bid to take away the party structure from the Governor. In essence Nyako's letter was actuated not by altruism but malice. Playing the regional card was therefore in my opinion a convenient mask to cover what was essentially a quarrel between two former friends. An important lesson here is for our politicians to be mindful that there are consequences for using and dumping others. And this includes politicians who, without scruples suck up to political godfathers only to turn round to play the saints after double-crossing their benefactors. While I strongly condemn Nyako's rather thoughtless letter, I also believe it will be counterproductive for security agencies to harass him or for him to be removed as Governor under the pretext of implementing a full state of emergency. It will only exacerbate the tension in the land.

Another major event was Buhari's letter on the Nyanya car bombing. In an article entitled 'Nyanya Bomb Blast and the Fight Against Terrorism in Nigeria' and circulated widely to the media, Buhari wrote: "We cannot allow these merchants of death to make us numb to the tragedy they manufacture. Those who were killed were not merely numbers on a page."

The highly commended letter from Buhari embodies at least three important lessons: one, that his handler (or a new handler) is coming around to appreciate that the General needs a re-invention and that previous image management strategies - if there were any - really did not work. Can we just not notice how one single letter rendered impotent the ill-advised move by the PDP to blame the General of being behind the Nyanya suicide bombing? Today people eulogise the statesmanlike letter while no one paid any heeds to his threat to sue the PDP if it did not withdraw the allegation. That should be an important lesson to the hawks around the General who like to talk tough and threaten everyone (the other side is equally guilty of this). Two, the   tone of the letter and the reactions to it, shows a certain latent admiration for Buhari across the fault lines. My personal opinion is that Buhari is a good product that has not been properly managed and packaged. Politics is a battle of the heart and mind. Politicians are often prone to gaffes and Buhari has had his own fair share of it.. Had Buhari been better managed, the presidency of this country would probably have been his for the asking – whether he is 80 years old or not. Hopefully the letter on Nyanya bombing should be a turning point for him. But he must go a step further. He needs to find ways to win critical segment of the elites, especially in the North, on side. He has to find a way to make them feel comfortable with him and his potential presidency because for as long as the critical elites distrust him for so long will they do all they can to undermine him. I have often heard some of the General's supporters talk of the elites fearing Buhari as if it is something to be celebrated in politics. The masses are important but in every democracy the critical elites have a big say on who gets to power. You need to be allowed to get power first before you can deploy it to the good of the society.

Three, Buhari's Nyanya letter is a sign that even as we fear 2015 there are still voices from the contending parties that will know when to do the needful to prevent the country from falling into the abyss.

This now brings me on what we should do to douse the enveloping tension. My suggestion is for the constitution of men of integrity – preferably outside the state structure – who will develop a taxonomy of what will constitute inflammatory speech or unacceptable conduct by politicians and eminent Nigerians. Such men and women should have the capacity to rise above the active controversies of the day and see issues from their multifaceted dimensions. They will fashion out modes of approaching the culprits – no matter how highly placed – with suggestions on how they can offer remedy for their unacceptable speeches or conduct. Despite the wide entrenchment of constructivist thinking and the triumph of one-dimensional writers, the country still abounds with individuals who can be objective and see issues from several perspectives – the Wole Soyinkas, Emeka Anyaokus, Christopher Kolades, Dangiwa Umars and even my fellow Daily Trust columnist Mahmud Jega. It is all too obvious from what has been going on that like the restored Bourbon dynasty in France after the abdication of Napoleon, our politicians have learned nothing and forgotten nothing.

An ode to our Soldiers

Two days ago, at about 7am, I was told someone was looking for me. When I opened the door, I saw a tall, lanky man, dressed in military uniform standing by the door. He was just a lance corporal – the lowest rank in the army. He started with apologies for coming to disturb – which was calming because you never really know if what you write earnestly will get you into trouble.

Put simply the man was asking around for a University lecturer around the area to discuss one or two issues regarding his master's thesis. I took a long look at the likeable young man and then his rank. He sensed my disbelief and in the next ten minutes or so we chatted: He enlisted in the army as a recruit more than fifteen years ago. He had, through his own efforts and sponsorship completed his first degree and about completing his master's. Despite knowing that his degrees would not earn him promotion, he had trudged on, bent on improving himself. He got the first promotion after 12 years in the army – and that was to the lowest rank, a lance corporal. From him I learnt there are several graduates, who entered the army or police as recruit and will remain on the same low rank for over ten years, doing their duties, obeying the last order, and sometimes laying down their lives so we can sleep in peace. So when next you see that army man or police corporal, can you spare a moment and say, 'well done for today'?. There are bad eggs in the police and the army. But given the conditions under which they work, they deserve even more respect and understanding.

Daily Trust, May 1, 2014

CHAPTER 32

'Exhibitionist patriotism' as a Threat to our Democracy

There are several ways in which some of our elected officials are becoming potent threats to our democracy. One way they do this is by unwittingly nursing and voicing nostalgia for our authoritarian past under what could be called 'exhibitionist patriotism'. Exhibitionist patriots like to hawk their love for the country – as if the rest of us love the country less than they do or that we are merely their appendages in the hierarchy 'Nigerianness'.

For instance the Vanguard (online) of 18 September 2013 quoted the Senate President David Mark as directing the 'security agencies to track down those beating the drums of war towards the 2015 general election, saying such actions were treasonable and should be treated seriously'. In a speech delivered at the resumption of the Senate from a two- month recess, the paper quoted the Senate President as saying: "It is disheartening that even though the general elections of 2015 are two years away, political jobbers, sycophants, and hustlers have prematurely seized the political space, and are being allowed to set the tone of national discourse."

Not long ago, the Governor of Niger State, Babangida Aliyu was also quoted as calling on security agencies to arrest former Niger Delta militant Asari Dokubo for allegedly threatening conflagration unless Jonathan is elected for a second term in office in 2015.Several top politicians and government officials frequently indulge in this 'exhibitionist patriotism', which on face value, is spurred by deep love of country but which on deeper reflection could be one of the most potent threats to our democracy. Such calls not only smack of nostalgia for our authoritarian past but also an invitation to a culture of 'prior restraint' and its associated muffling of free speech.

'Prior restraint' (also known as 'prior censorship' or 'pre-publication censorship') is censorship imposed, usually by a government, on expression before that expression actually takes place. It is like arguing that speech which is yet to be uttered or published, will stink if uttered or published. Prior restraint is said to have a 'chilling effect' on free speech because people will be restrained by fear of sanction from fully expressing themselves. And when it is realized that free speech and its associated marketplace of ideas is the foundational block of democracy, then the threat posed to our society by those nursing nostalgia for our authoritarian past will be better appreciated.

An alternative to 'prior restraint' is to allow the expression in question to take place and then to take appropriate action afterward if the expression is found to violate the law, regulations, or other rules. In several vibrant democracies in the world such as the United States, prior restraint by the government is forbidden by the constitution – subject to such exceptions as threat on national security. Usually for prior restraint to be permitted, such must have to pass the 'clear and imminent danger' test – that is the authority in question must prove that without such a prior restraint, there will be a CLEAR and Imminent danger to the society. This is clearly not the case with certain calls for people who express ideas that offend or shock. Tolerance of such offensive, awful or shocking ideas is often an indication of how far a democracy has matured.

In Anglo-American jurisprudence, prior restraint is considered a particularly oppressive form of censorship because it prevents the restricted material from being heard or distributed at all. Though other forms of restrictions on freedom of expression such as actions for libel, defamation or contempt of court can also have a 'chilling effect' on free speech, however because they are implemented after the offending material has been published or uttered, they do not impoverish the marketplace of ideas in the same way that prior restraint does.

In the marketplace of ideas theory of free speech, ideas compete in the political marketplace – just as goods also compete in open markets. There are at least four main reasons why freedom of speech is cherished in democracies: One, it is believed to be crucial in the quest to discover the truth. Two, it is regarded as an aspect of self-fulfillment. Three, it is seen as being indispensable for citizens to participate effectively in a democracy. Four, there is a strong suspicion of government - a suspicion that gets heightened any time free speech is muffled by officialdom.

While it is true that newly democratizing countries such as Nigeria often exhibit tendencies from their authoritarian past, we must recognize that democracy is a noisy enterprise and that in the competition of ideas in the political marketplace, even ideas that 'shock and awe' are seen as enriching the marketplace. This means therefore that the 'exhibitionist patriotism' of calling for the arrest of people who have expressed strong or offensive ideas, which however unacceptable they may be, do not pose any 'clear and imminent danger' to the society, is a disservice to our democracy. Such calls are also exhibitions of intolerance – the very negation of the whole basis of democracy. This is why in several mature democracies, fringe groups such as racist organizations like the KKK in the US or the British National Party in the UK, are never banned. Rather the ideas they espouse are drawn into, and outcompeted in the marketplace of political ideas. This ensures that the purveyors of such ideas do not go underground to romanticize ideas that are already outcompeted in the marketplace of ideas.

Daily Trust, September 19 2013

CHAPTER 33

Murder of Uniport Students and the Culture of Impunity

Impunity, in international law of human rights, usually denotes the persistent failure to bring perpetrators of human rights violations to justice. This failure on the part of authorities is in itself a denial of the victims' right to justice and redress. In essence, the victims of impunity endure two wrongs: the wrongs inflicted on them by those who choose to trample on their inalienable rights and the wrong done to them by a failure to give them justice by punishing those that trampled on their natural or human rights.

When impunity has become so embedded in any social system that it is regarded as a way of life or 'normal', people talk of the 'culture of impunity'. In this sense the culture of impunity can be regarded as a synonym for what the German-American political scientist Hannah Arendt called the 'banality of evil'. Her explanation of this thesis is that the great evils in history are not executed by fanatics or sociopaths but rather by ordinary people who accepted the premises of their actions and therefore participated in them on the grounds that those heinous actions were normal. This is the so-called notion of 'normalising the unthinkable' or the 'routinisation of evil'. It is within the context of this prevailing culture of impunity or 'culture of normalising the unthinkable' in the land that the murder of four students of the University of Port Harcourt by youths in Omuokiri-Aluu must be situated. It is remarkable that this culture of impunity is especially prevalent in countries that lack a tradition of the rule of law or where corruption is so endemic and pervasive that even the judiciary and its allied justice system are believed to be commoditized. A key manifestation of this culture of impunity is people's knee jerk resort to self-help either in self-defence or to ward off perceived threats.

The stories of what happened at Omuokiri-Aluu are fuzzy and conflicting. The version of the story on which apparently the youths or the vigilante group in the community acted upon was that the four students were either cultists or thieves who stole laptops. The other version is that two of the four boys went to the community to spend a night with a friend but on their way back they met the other two who agreed to accompany them to retrieve money a student and indigene of Aluu owed one of them. This is not abnormal among young people, especially students in a culture of impunity where self-help is the norm. If this version is correct, perhaps in the scuffle that ensued, the debtor felt overpowered and over-numbered and had to what most people under such a circumstance would do: scream 'armed robbers!' to mobilize support. Again this is not a defence of the dastardly act in the community which reportedly claimed that it had been under siege by armed robbers and cultists but to place the reaction of the villagers in its proper context.

It is in fact immaterial which of the competing narratives on what triggered the horrendous murder of the four students is correct. The key issue is the response to their alleged crime. Even if we take the version of the members of the Aluu that the four were thieves (not even armed robbers since they were not apparently armed), there are questions of people taking law into their hands, and even if they must, whether the punishment is proportional to the crime. However when impunity has become a way of life – as it seems to have become in the land- the issue of proportionality is often seen as a luxury by those who feel they must do whatever they must to 'send a message' and ward off threats in the absence of government or anyone else to protect them.

Growing up in Onitsha in the 1970s and 1980s, I remember that armed robbers periodically terrorised the town. After living perpetually in fear of the men of the underworld, residents suddenly came up with the idea of 'Boys Oyee' - a periodic clarion call for solidarity to go after the bad boys. Those who felt they were up to it would gather and chanting 'Boys Oyee', would go after those identified as criminals. Usually those identified would be killed in a most horrendous manner – often by beating them to pulp, stripping them naked, lacing them with tyres and setting them ablaze. The ring leaders of the 'Boys Oyee' - those who had the 'courage' to draw the machete, pour the petrol or set those laced with tyres on fire were often regarded as heroes in the town. I cannot remember complaints about the dastardly manner in which those identified as criminals were killed. The 'joy' was often that the town would be guaranteed 'peace' from miscreants – at least for a while. 'Boys Oyee' is nothing more than a signal that in a Hobbesian State of Nature, characterised by the absence of government which our country seems to have degenerated to, the only thing that seems to work is self-help because the government is not there to help you. Village vigilantes throughout Nigeria came into being because the State has proved incapable or unwilling to secure the life and property of citizens. And various communities across the country use various versions of the 'Boys Oyee' method to either defend themselves or ward off what they consider threats to cherished values.

And by the way this culture of impunity and the barbarity it spurns in its wake manifests in several other realms: when, as writers or word slingers, we prosecute, judge and condemn with venom someone accused of crime or even corruption but who has not been convicted by a competent court of law, we turn ourselves into vigilantes, fighting with the weapon at our disposal. That too is impunity. When a 'big shot' throws his or her weight around and secures some goodies for his or her ward disregarding that the rights of others are being trampled upon while beneficiaries cheer the big shot, that too encourages impunity.

It is understandable and even predictable that students of University of Port Harcourt should seek revenge on members of Omuokiri-Aluu community. The authorities of the University have wisely closed down the institution to allow emotions and tempers to cool. As difficult as it may be - given the sordid manner in which the four were killed - painting the entire Aluu community black will only increase the temptation for vengeance via self-help which paradoxically will encourage the same culture of impunity that led to such acts.

I believe there are several, more important questions we should be asking in order to prevent such from happening again:

One, the students were apparently beaten for a considerable length of time. Was the police aware of the beating, and if so, what effort did they make to remove the boys from the community for their safety?

Two, if it is true that the community has been under siege by armed robbers and cultist, what measures did the police in the village take to allay the fears of the community? How many crimes were committed in the village in the last one year and how many of the perpetrators of such crimes were fished out and brought to justice?

Three, there are some communities in the country that engage in witch-hunting – often based on those identified by a 'babalawo' or Pastor to be a witch. Quite often those identified as witches are buried alive, sometimes with their heads showing or stoned to death. What measures have been taken to bring perpetrators of such crimes to justice and to send a message that such is not acceptable?

Four, how come this culture of impunity is so entrenched in a country where people love to flaunt their religiosity? Is it possible that this entrenchment of the culture of impunity will generate a counter intuitive response to pompous outward display of piety by our people?

I believe that the perpetrators of the dastardly crimes in Aluu must be fished out and speedily brought to justice to serve as deterrence to others. I am a firm believer in capital punishment for those who carry out acts of premeditated murder. So those found guilty should face the music. However I believe that since versions of what happened with the four University students at Omuokiri-Aluu also happen regularly across the length and breadth of the country, we need to go beyond our horrors and moral grandstanding to find out why evil appears to have become truly banal in our land and why people's sensibilities are becoming numbed to acts of horror and barbarity. Simply put we need to find out why people do not trust in government and its institution and increasingly resort to self-help.

Daily Trust, October 11, 2012

CHAPTER 34

Nigeria: Master of the Shuffle Dance at 53

October 1, just two days ago, was the commemoration day of Nigeria's 53 years of existence, since independence in 1960. A number of commentaries gave the impression that Nigeria just turned 53 years old on that day. The assumption in this manner of thinking is Nigeria was zero (0) years on independence on October 1960 – a mathematical impossibility. Honestly I am not sure if the year Nigeria got her political independence could be the watershed for calculating the age of the country or the time the North and South was amalgamated into one country in 1914 or even when Flora Shaw, the girlfriend of the then colonial Governor-General Frederick Lugard suggested the name in 1898 to designate the British protectorate on the River Niger.

Reading through the various commentaries on whether there is anything to celebrate at 53 reminded me that we all wear tainted binoculars through which we filter the realities that confront us. In this sense, both those who see nothing to celebrate, and those who believe that everything is OK with the country tend to see the country from a very narrow prism. The cup is either full or empty. There are only two shades of colours: black and white.

Does the Country Really have anything to Celebrate About?

I am not too sure that I agree with analysts who postulate that the greatest achievement of the country is that it has remained together despite many challenges. I see no creative input from the entity called Nigeria or anything suggestive of an effort from such a position. Rather it conjures the sense of fatalism which we generally use to rationalize our inactions, complacency and plain incompetence.

In my opinion the greatest achievement of the country – and this is not down to any effort from the country – is the generalized belief among Nigerians that things ought to be better. This is what the American political scientist Ted Gurr would call 'relative deprivation'— "the tension that develops from a discrepancy between the 'ought' and 'is' of collective value dissatisfaction." Ted Gurr titled his book *Why Men Rebel*. In the Nigerian context the crisis of relative deprivation and its consequences is a major reason why the country cannot afford to continue on its path of complacency and inaction. And it is something positive in my book since any major change will necessarily have to start with a sharp dissatisfaction with the way things are as against the way people believe they ought to be.

To give an example: when I was growing up in Onitsha in the 1970s, each time NEPA – the precursor of PHCN- 'brought the light' after prolonged power outage that would last for days, everyone would scream 'up NEPA!'. There was no sense of anger at the power outage – at least not in the little world I knew. If NEPA 'took the light' again, there would be a few sighs of 'NEPA!' and everyone would reach out for their lanterns or candles. I studied in secondary school (1975-1980) with lantern and even when the school got a generator around 1979, it was still a luxury to be enjoyed for a few hours at nights. If the generator was not turned on for weeks, no one complained. Even in my university days (1980-1984), lanterns and candle lights were still common accessories. It was accepted that it was the prerogative of NEPA to 'bring' and 'take' 'light' whenever it chose.

Now Nigerians rightly get angry because there is no regular power supply. The same crisis of expectation that we see in the electricity generation and distribution sector we also see in the other sectors of the national life. In the political arena, people complain about the structure of the country and make various recommendations, including calls for a sovereign national conference. The intense hunger among Nigerians to bridge the gap between 'what is' and 'what ought to be' in the country, often expressed in different ways, is in my opinion the country's greatest achievement. It suggests that things cannot continue for too long to be the way they are. Something has to give in.

Nigeria embodies several paradoxes some of which feed into the crisis of Gurr's relative deprivation, helping on the one hand to engender hope and on the other hand to put pressure on the country to bridge the gap between 'what is' and 'what ought to be'. One of this is poverty amid huge potential. Apart from the country's huge population, which could potentially be translated into a huge market, on December 12 2005, Jim O'Neill, a Goldman Sachs investment bank economist in a research paper listed Nigeria among the Next Eleven (also known as N-11). These were a group of 11 countries - Bangladesh, Egypt, Indonesia, Iran, Mexico, Nigeria, Pakistan, Philippines, Turkey, South Korea, and Vietnam which O'Neill identified as having a high potential of becoming, along with the BRICs/BRICS, the world's largest economies in the 21st century. The criteria that Goldman Sachs used were macroeconomic stability, political maturity, openness of trade and investment policies, and the quality of education.

As politicians are wont to do, the Obasanjo regime tried to reap political capital out of this by suggesting that the country's elevation to the Next Eleven was due to its management of the state and economy. Nigerians love the hurrah effects that are suggested from such elevations. For them, it is an indication that the gap between what is and what ought to be is about being bridged. However as the material circumstances of the people continue to deteriorate despite the whiffs of optimism from such elevations, the crisis of relative aspiration is only deepened. And as this happens, systemic pressure is intensified. The systemic pressure itself is a warning sign that Nigeria, ever the master of hanging on the precipice without falling over, can no longer continue to count on its luck. Unbeknown to the Goodluck administration, each time it plays its politics of GDP growth - how the economy has been doing well under its management - it unwittingly increases the crisis of relative deprivation among the people, which in turn puts pressure on the regime to bridge the gap between 'what is' and 'what ought to be'.

Another evidence of the sort of 'revolution' that has taken place in the minds of Nigerians is with respect to their analysis of why things are the way they are today. Not too long ago, the weeping boy for almost all of the country's woes was colonialism or neo-colonialism. It was largely a feel-good theory that blamed everyone but Nigerians for the lapses and shortcomings in the country. Now people blame the country's leadership. Implicit in this is a transition from a feel-good analysis to a certain belief that even if someone helped to push us down, the ultimate responsibility to get up is our own. I foresee a situation where in the next couple of years people will move from blaming the government to sharing the blame with the government. This, in my book, is revolution of the mind, which can only increase the systemic pressure for change.

The prevailing condition of 'relative deprivation' in the country operates on a substructure of real challenges on the ground. The first in my opinion is a country where nothing – or just a few things work. On top of this is that it is a low trust economy – no one trusts anyone, not even that contracts duly signed by concerned parties will be observed. In a low trust society, the tendency to cut corners or resort to self -help tends to be very high. No one trusts the police or other state security apparatuses; you do not trust that if you deliver your goods to a customer he will transfer the money to your account as he promised just as the business man does not believe that if he transfers the money first, the goods will be delivered. Trust on government is even worse than the deep distrust among citizens and various ethnic and religious groups. When for instance the Academic Staff of Universities complain that the government reneges on agreement, people often laugh and wonder to which group the government has ever kept its promise. And the truth is that many of those who accuse the government of reneging on promises are themselves masters of doubletalk, of saying one thing and doing the other. The society is therefore one piece of chaos, with people openly professing their trust only in God.

There is security challenge and serious infrastructure deficits. But worse than these, is that there is a rapid de-Nigerianisation process, with people stampeding out of the Nigeria project into primordial identities where they seek to negotiate meaning for their lives, often regarding the Nigerian State as the enemy. If this trend continues, we risk having Nigeria without Nigerians.

What is the way out? President Jonathan has now bowed to the pressures from some quarters and inaugurated a committee for a National Conference. I am among those who believe that such a conference could become a platform for a vocal minority – the usual suspects – to grandstand and complicate the search for solution to the myriad of challenges that confront the country. I truly hope I am proved wrong.

Daily Trust, October 3, 2013

CHAPTER 35

Nigeria@56? Is this House Really Falling?

When Karl Maier published his book This House Has Fallen: Midnight in Nigeria (2000), I was probably among the first people he gave an advance copy of the book months before it was formally published. I was at that the Books Review Editor of the London-based monthly magazine, Africa Today. Maier, a former correspondent for the UK's Daily Independent called a few times to ask for my opinion of the book before I got to review it. I was unequivocal that some aspects of it appeared contrived and unbelievable. I subsequently did what could be called a very negative review of the book. To his credit, my dim review of the book did not stop him from inviting me to a party he held for his girlfriend which turned out to be just another opportunity for a healthy disagreement on several aspects of the book.

Maier's book appeared to me at that time to be more popular for its doomsday title than for any rigorous analysis of the Nigerian political condition. Accepted, he interviewed several movers and shakers of the society. I felt however that like most reportages and travel writings, Maier in several instances elevated the institutional manifestations of a phenomenon to its defining characteristics, thereby missing the point. I also accused him of peppering his reportage to enthral his publishers and the British reading public.

In October 2003, some eight years after Karl Meier's book was published, a survey of more than 65 countries published by the UK's New Scientist magazine suggested that the happiest people in the world lived in Nigeria. Nigeria had not imploded rather it inhabited the happiest people in the world, according to the survey. We flaunted the results of the survey directly wherever we could and by innuendo where social etiquette would frown at boastful behaviours. We were unconcerned about the 'scientificness' of the survey and very few of us took issues with the New Scientist that published it.

Nigerians appear to have a contradictory relationship with the Nigeria project. They seem to despise and loathe the country, which appears to have made hanging on a cliff its comfort zone. This is probably why they are simultaneously among the most patriotic people (especially for those living outside the country) and among the harshest critics of the Nigeria project. They have a way of uniting against outsiders who try to interfere. For instance when the late Muammar Gaddafi tapped into what he saw as a declining faith of many Nigerians in the Nigeria project to suggest that the country should be balkanized along its religious fault line, most Nigerians, even those that have represented centrifugal tendencies, jumped on him as they also did with the supposed prediction by America that the country would disintegrate in 2015. This suggests that despite our differences we seem to have become so used to one another that, like in most dysfunctional marriages, we bicker and threaten divorce all the time and at the same time paralyzed by fear of the unknown if our wishes for divorce were to come true.

Yet, we must also ask ourselves for how long we will continue to celebrate that we have survived yet another year on a cliff. Onlookers are getting tired of holding their breath, afraid that we might trip over the cliff.

I have always believed that the problem with Nigeria project is politics, not economics or underdevelopment or poverty. We are on the cliff because though every part of the country feels marginalized we have a zero-sum attitude to solving the country's problems. Once an effort is made to solve the problem of one area, others go into their institutional memories to retrieve cases of injustices and marginalization which must be concurrently addressed. In the end the country moves in circles, with problems mutating, rather than being effectively solved. All this calls for a forum where Nigerians can talk, air out their grievances, even if for catharsis. If the word 'restructuring' engenders distrust, we will need to construct new vocabularies that will enable us engage one another. Certainly if we continue to do what we have always done, then we will continue to get what we have always got, which is to hang on a cliff. Those think that the country's history in the 1960s is better, are just being nostalgic.

Dasuki and the ECOWAS Court Ruling

The recent ruling by the ECOWAS Court asking the federal government to release immediately the former National Security Adviser Sambo Dasuki, who has been in detention for nearly one year, has been making the headlines. The federal government said it was yet to comply with the ECOWAS Court order because it was still studying the   judgment.
Some have argued that the judgment given by the Court in favour of Dasuki does not have force of law in Nigeria since the National Assembly is yet to domesticate the Revised Treaty and Protocols relating to the Court. This may be true. In fact, states whether in municipal or international law pick and choose which court judgments to obey and which to ignore. This is why some have questioned whether enforcement or observance of court judgments is a sufficient defining characteristic of law. So if the Nigerian government chooses to ignore the judgment from the ECOWAS Court, it will only have joined a long list of countries that routinely disobey national and international court orders.

But there is a reason why I do not think it is right for the Buhari government to disobey the court judgement: many people still distrust his claim to being born again democrat. To disobey the judgment will therefore hand powerful ammunition to his critics. Besides I do not really see what purpose the continued detention of Dasuki, El Zakyzaky and Nnamdi Kanu serves except to blight the government's human rights record, which is actually not bad when compared with the records of fellow former military Head of State Olusegun Obasanjo. In this era of the globalization of the rule of law, it will be unwise to literally invite the international community to engage the government on its democratic credentials.

Be Careful with Kenyan Airways

I travelled to Kenya on July 14 2014 to attend a conference in Nairobi on the intellectual legacies of the late Kenyan political scientist Ali Mazrui. From the conference I was to travel to London for a one- week holiday. The organisers of the conference understandably booked me on Kenyan Airways for the Abuja to Nairobi limb of the trip. I had no problem with that. After boarding we were delayed for over an hour. Many of us were tensed with the prolonged delay in departing and wondered whether they had detected some technical problems with the aircraft. No one said anything to us which heightened the sense of anxiety.

It was only when we got to Nairobi that we learnt that the aircraft had exceeded its luggage limit and was therefore refused departure. It eventually had to randomly take off some luggage from the aircraft – without informing the owners of the luggage – before it was allowed to depart for Nairobi. I found out at Nairobi that my luggage was unfortunately among those randomly taken off the aircraft. . Apart from the suit I wore and my laptop, every other thing I was travelling with was in the luggage that I checked in.

I lodged a complaint and after formalities and filling of some papers, I was given $100. In Kenya, the $100 could barely buy you a decent shirt and slippers.

The following day I made concerted efforts to ensure that my luggage would be returned to me as soon as possible but to no avail. On July 17, precisely the day I was to leave for United Kingdom, I got a message from Kenyan Airways telling me that they could not even locate my luggage in Abuja. I was simply pissed off.

I never heard again from Kenyan Airways until July 25, the day I was to leave UK for Nigeria. They had called to tell me that my luggage had arrived in Nairobi. I was taken aback because I had told them of my itinerary. I asked them to return the luggage to my residence in Abuja, which they promised to do.

I never heard anything again from Kenyan Airways until about August 14, (one month after I boarded their aircraft) when I received a call from them asking me to come to the airport with my ID card to claim my luggage. I felt that was cheeky of them and insisted that they should deliver the luggage to my home. Though they eventually complied, they behaved as if they had done no wrong and saw no reason for profound apologies and compensation.

Daily Trust, October 6, 2016

CHAPTER 36

Did America really predict Nigeria will break-up in 2015?

I was in the bar section of Nicon Hilton Abuja about a week ago to meet a friend. He had called just after a few minutes after my arrival at the hotel to apologize he would be about one hour or so late. That meant I had a lot of time to while away while waiting for his arrival.

As I waited over a glass of red wine, I found myself seated quite close to two gentlemen and a lady. I was not deliberately eavesdropping on their conversations but they were not helping matters by not keeping their voices low. From their dictions and the way they chose their words, they were apparently well educated and well- travelled.

One of the gentlemen, in resplendent designer suit, was talking about the crises that crisscross the country and was making allusion to a supposed American prediction that Nigeria would break up in 2015. "You need to read that book. I was very saddened for days after reading the book. The facts were there and their conclusions were based on facts", the taller of the two men declared authoritatively. He also volunteered to lend the 'book' - I am not sure if he volunteered to lend it to the other gentleman with him or to the lady.

I nearly gate-crashed into the conversation but restrained myself, knowing it would be bad manners to do so.

The gentleman's authoritative position on the supposed prediction that Nigeria would break up in 2015 however reminds me that there is hardly a day you do not have commentaries in leading Nigerian newspapers and the broadcast media about this phantom American prognosis. Prominent political leaders have keyed into the falsehood, using it when it suits them to showcase their contrived patriotism.

With the conflation of the current crises rocking the PDP, (which has led to the party splintering into two factions) and the aggressive permutations for the politics of 2015, more people are talking about this supposed American prediction.

But did America really make this prediction? The definitive answer is 'no'.

I have decided to review the document on which this supposed American prognosis was extracted. The gentleman I mentioned earlier who talked about the 'book' where he read such and even promised to lend it to his companions simply lied through his tongue. There is no such book. What you have is a 17-page report, a summary of the outcome of a one-day conference of 'US experts on Africa' convened in January 2005 and sponsored by the country's National Intelligence Council to discuss likely trends in Sub-Saharan Africa over the next 15 years. This document is freely available on the Internet and can be accessed by 'Googling', 'Mapping Sub-Saharan Africa's Future'.

But what do I hope to gain by defending America, especially now that with its impending intervention in Syria, it seems to be returning to its bad behaviour of playing the opportunistic global cop? This is not a defence of America. However by putting the record straight it enables us also to reflect on the processes we use in arriving at our version of truths – compared to the processes used to do so in other climes governed more by rationality. Whereas 'rational' societies place premium on critical inquiries in the search for truth, for us we seem to arrive at our own version of truth through what I will call 'rumour factualization' – you repeat one rumour or lie consistently enough and it suddenly becomes treated as both fact and truth– be it on our population figure, rate of inflation, number of people living below the poverty line or anything for that matter.

Back to the document, 'Mapping Sub-Saharan Africa's Future'. As indicated earlier, participants at the one-day conference of 'US experts on Africa' were asked to discuss likely trends in Sub-Saharan Africa over the next 15 years. Quite a number of the predictions were banal, and wouldn't have required any knowledge of the emerging field of future studies by any average intelligent high school student to predict such. For instance on AIDS, it predicted: "Regarding AIDS, even with relatively optimistic assumptions about a vaccine and the roll-out of antiretrovirals (ARVs), it is clear that there will be very large increases in the number of people who will die in the next ten years given weak medical care distribution systems."

Though the participants in the conference were obviously downbeat about Africa's possibilities within the period under focus, they also discussed what they called 'upside surprises'. These included a surprise improvement in the management of petroleum resources by the oil-producing countries in the continent, scientific advances in agriculture along the lines of those that helped Asia in the 1960s and 1970s and technological breakthroughs that would help to contain the scourges of AIDS, malaria and other infectious diseases.

The famous or infamous prediction about Nigeria breaking up in 2015 is on page 16 of the document under 'downside risks'. Given the certainty with which many people believe a prediction was made, this is worth quoting in full:

"Other potential developments might accelerate decline in Africa and reduce even our limited optimism. The most important would be the outright collapse of Nigeria. While currently Nigeria's leaders are locked in a bad marriage that all dislike but dare not leave, there are possibilities that could disrupt the precarious equilibrium in Abuja.

"The most important would be a junior officer coup that could destabilize the country to the extent that open warfare breaks out in many places in a sustained manner. If Nigeria were to become a failed state, it could drag down a large part of the West African region.

"Even state failure in small countries such as Liberia has the effect of destabilizing entire neighbourhoods. If millions were to flee a collapsed Nigeria, the surrounding countries, up to and including Ghana, would be destabilized. Further, a Failed Nigeria probably could not be reconstituted for many years—if ever—and not without massive international assistance."

It is obvious from the above quote that what the participants did was scenario mappings – as opposed to arriving at a particular conclusion based on deductions from research. The outcome of any futures research (also known as futurology or futurism) and scenario mapping depends largely on the underlying assumption – change that premise and the conclusion changes immediately.

How quickly the tale of America's supposed prediction of the break-up of Nigeria graduated into the 'truth', Nigerian style, reminds me of 1975 when I was in the final year in primary school at Onitsha. Rangers International of Enugu, the darling team of most Igbo at the time, had just been walloped 3-1 by Mehalla of Egypt. It was an exceedingly sad day in Onitsha and beyond with most people wearing sad faces. By the following day however, a consoling explanation had been found on why Rangers, were defeated so resoundingly. This 'truth' quickly spread: Rangers lost only because each time the goalkeeper Emmanuel Okala wanted to catch the ball, it would turn into five balls or an elephant, ensuring a goal would be scored whatever his effort. Each purveyor of the 'new truth' had 'authoritative' sources, with some claiming they heard so directly from 'close friends' of some Rangers' players. Mehalla, in this narrative, had subdued Rangers with very powerful juju, and though there were no mobile phones then, this 'truth' quickly spread throughout Igboland.

Instances of 'rumour-factualization' in the country are legion: Not long ago there were stories that if you answered a call from a particular number you would die; that if you enter 'Okada' motorcycle and wore their helmet you would turn into a yam tuber, that if you shook someone's hands, the person could mystically steal your manhood. Usually the purveyors of the tales would cite 'authoritative' sources – if the person did not claim being an eye witness to the event.

Now compare our process of truth discovery through 'rumour factualization' with just one instance of what happened in the United Kingdom in the 1950s when one 'Dr Carl Kuon Suo' was peddling a manuscript called *Third Eye*. Just before the manuscript was published by Secker & Warburg in 1956, its author changed his name to Tuesday Lobsang Rampa. In the book, which turned out to be an instant best seller globally, the author claimed to have been a *lama* in Tibet and narrated a purported experience of growing up in a monastery there from the age of seven. Dr Rampa also claimed that during that period a small hole was drilled into his forehead, which aroused his 'third' (or 'inner') eye, giving him very strong powers of clairvoyance.

The spirit of critical inquiry forced Heinrich Harrer, an Austrian mountaineer and Tibetologist, to hire a private detective, Clifford Burgess, to investigate Dr Rampa and his claims. The detective was able to unmask Dr Rampa as Cyril Henry Hoskin, an Englishman who was born in Devon, and whose father was a plumber. It was also found that contrary to the claims in the book Mr Hoskin had never been to Tibet and spoke no Tibetan. Caught red-handed, Dr Rampa did not deny that he had been born as Cyril Hoskin, but claimed that his body was now occupied by the spirit of Lobsang Rampa. Curiously as an undergraduate in Nigeria in the 1980s, Lobsang Rampa's *Third Eye* was a sort of fashion accessory to a certain category of students who claimed to be seeking spiritual enlightenment.

Daily Trust September 5, 2013

CHAPTER 37

A Nation at War with Itself

The recent bomb attack in a bus terminus at Nyanya, a bustling outskirts of Abuja, by a suicide bomber suspected to be a Boko Haram terrorist or sympathizer, was one too many. Perhaps more than any of the previous attacks by the sect, the Nyanya incident, which targeted people hustling to get to work at Abuja, aroused a collective sense of sorrow and outrage. Estimates of the dead and injured vary – depending on whom you want to believe. What appears obvious is that anywhere between 75 and 130 people lost their lives in that mayhem with some 150-200 others sustaining various degrees of injuries. Properties and means of livelihood lost in the carnage are yet to be estimated. The psychological trauma induced by the incident will live with many of the residents of Nyanya and beyond for a long time.

Barely 24 hours after the Nyanya attack, came another report that some unidentified gunmen suspected to be members of the terrorist organization, abducted more than 100 female students from a Government Girls Secondary School at Chibok Local Government Area of Borno State – the epicenter of the Boko Haram challenge. Reports of deaths in Bornu state have become a daily staple such that for many, those deaths, reported daily in the media, no longer shock or awe them – a classical indication of the 'normalization' or routinization of evil.

Our challenge as a nation is to refuse to allow such impunities to be 'normalized' by the frequency of their occurrences or the longevity of their existence. Retaining a sense of outrage against such impunities is the strongest statement that they are unacceptable and cannot be 'normalized' like other acts of impunity in the country.

But why will otherwise 'normal' people derive sadistic joy in the mass murder of people who have done them no wrong?

The German - American political theorist Hannah Arendt tells us that the great evils in history are not executed by fanatics or sociopaths but rather by ordinary people who accepted the premises of their actions and therefore participated in them on the grounds that those heinous actions were normal. She used this to explain why evil deeds tend to be everywhere in a society. She called this the 'banality of evil'. For her, those engaged in barbarous acts such as the Boko Haram terrorists accepted the premises of their actions as just – even if the rest of the society thinks otherwise. Acts of impunity against innocent Nigerians unfortunately reflects the federal – violent armed robberies across the entire country, kidnapping especially in the South-east and south-south, turf war by militarized cults and gangs in Bayelsa State, ritual murders everywhere, senseless intra and inter communal 'warfare' across several parts of the country and of course terrorism couched in religious revivalist rhetoric in parts of the North.

Despite the 'banality of evil' or the 'normalization of the unthinkable', in several parts of the country, there are reasons why the impunity purveyed by Boko Haram and groups acting in its name or sympathetic to its cause pose a special threat to the country:

One, though impunity couched in religious revivalism has been an integral part of the conflicts in Nigeria, especially in Northern Nigeria, Boko Haram and Ansaru were the first drivers of conflicts in the country to be declared terrorist organizations by the United States and the United Kingdom.

Two, both are also the first purveyors of violence in the country to be strongly linked to international terrorist networks, essentially Al Qaeda in the Islamic Maghreb (AQIM) and possibly the Movement for Oneness and Jihad in West Africa, (MOJWA), - also known as Movement for Unity and Jihad in West Africa (MUJWA). MUJA was formed in 2011 allegedly because of the marginalization of Black Africans in AQIM.

Three, Boko Haram was also the first group to introduce suicide bombing in Nigeria. Use of suicide bombers had been unknown in West Africa because suicide is regarded as cultural anathema - until two high-profile attacks in Abuja - the June 2011 police headquarters bombing and the August 2011 United Nations headquarters bombing. Since then, suicide bombing has become part of the tools in the arsenal of the two groups. Four, the two terrorist groups were also probably the first purveyors of impunity in Nigeria with both international and domestic territorial ambitions. For instance while in 2011, Boko Haram's terrorism was largely confined to Nigeria's northeast by the end of last year (2013), Boko Haram- driven attacks occurred in most of the 19 States in the North, including the Federal Capital Territory of Abuja. Boko Haram suspects have also been arrested in Lagos. The group was equally linked to the kidnapping of the French Catholic priest, Georges Vandenbeusch, in Cameroun in November 2013 and to another kidnapping of a French family in the same area of Cameroun in February 2013. Flowing from the territorial ambitions of the two groups, the conflicts they trigger have wider national implications and by virtue of their links to international terrorist networks, also wider international implications than the traditional conflicts that the country is used to.

Fighting the new terrorism has been problematic not only because of their methods but also because of disagreements on why such a group came about. The conspiracy theories that seek to explain the phenomenon tap into the fears that are edged in our traditional fault lines:

There are several conspiracy theories about Boko Haram. One, which is popular among commentators from the Southern part of the country, is that the sect is sponsored by key Northern politicians to make the country 'ungovernable' for President Goodluck Jonathan, a Christian from the minority Ijaw ethnic group. One of the weaknesses of this 'theory' is that much of the mayhem carried out by the sect has been in the North and against Northern Muslims. It is in fact difficult to see the nexus between destabilizing governance in some Northern states and making the country 'ungovernable' for the Jonathan administration. But there are several who believe in such, making it difficult to mobilize that sense of collective outrage needed to tackle the menace. Obviously there are certain local grievances that revivalist movements tap into but that must not be confused with deliberate sponsorship.

Another conspiracy theory is that Boko Haram is actually being sponsored by the Jonathan administration to make Islam look bad or give the impression that the North was out to pull it down as a way of mobilizing the support of his 'Southern brethren' and Christians behind his administration. A variant of this is that Boko Haram is actually sponsored by the government to weaken or destroy the North. Those who believe in any of the variants of this conspiracy 'theory', essentially people from the North, point out that during the Abacha days, the government deliberately bombed some places and then blamed it on NADECO, which was campaigning for the re-validation of the June 12 election won by Abiola but annulled by the military regime of Ibrahim Babangida. This variant of the conspiracy 'theoriy' therefore believes that the Jonathan administration is borrowing a leaf from the Abacha regime.

One of the weaknesses of this theory however is that nothing in the confessions of some of the arrested Boko Haram members supports any of these conspiracy theories. Also it defies logic why a President should set part of his domain on fire, especially where one cannot determine the direction of such conflagration - just to weaken a particular religion or part of the country

While there are a number of other efforts at scholarly explanations of the reasons for the emergence and subsequent radicalization of the sect, I have always believed that a more comprehensive explanation will be to see the sect as a reflection of the crisis in our nation-building processes. The crisis in our nation-building conflates with the crisis of underdevelopment to create an existentialist crisis for many Nigerians. Therefore for many young people, a way of resolving the consequent sense of alienation is to retreat from the Nigeria project and construct meanings in chosen primordial identities - often with the Nigerian state as the enemy. This must not be confused with supporting or condoning Boko Haram and its ways but the need for us to dig deeper, including finding the local grievances that they tap into. We will need to fight both the symptom of the problem and the root cause simultaneously.

Fighting terrorism is never easy or straight forward anywhere in the world. Victory can hardly come easily or quickly. Often the challenge is to contain the group such that the society can continue to function normally despite the episodic impunities they purvey – the way the society has learnt to live with other impunities carried out intermittently by other groups.   The key challenge we have with Boko Haram is that the mayhem by the group is not only spreading across the country but also becoming 'routinized'. And while this is happening, politicians are playing silly blame games while their foot soldiers complicate matters with their absurd conspiracy theories.

Daily Trust April 17 2014

CHAPTER 38

The Return of the Parcel Bomb

The recent report that the police detonated a parcel bomb addressed to the Minister of Finance, Dr. Ngozi Okonjo-Iweala will obviously heighten the pervasive sense of insecurity in the land. Where can Nigerians now hide and feel secure? Travelling by road and returning safely to one's home is often regarded as God's divine favour - given the frequent carnages on the roads and the menace of armed robbers. Many say their last prayers before flying on our air spaces. In some parts of the North, the fear of bombs and killings by Boko Harm and groups acting in its name is the beginning of wisdom. In several states in the South, everyone now appears to have a certain kidnap value – some are kidnapped because of millions of Naira ransom to be extracted while others are reportedly seized and allowed to 'bail' themselves with re-charge cards. Across the country, in your home, office or public space, armed robbers and sadists can strike any time with fury, killing and maiming as if human lives were worth less than those of chickens. Or should we talk about inter-communal and indigene/setter feuds that erupt occasionally in different parts of the country and which often pits neighbours against one another?

With the widespread sense of insecurity comes, in typical Nigerian fashion, fear mongering and merchandising. For instance at the height of Boko Haram's bombings, several text and email messages were being circulated warning people not to buy oranges, garden eggs, yams and other food items from the North because Boko Haram had allegedly put poison in them. Never mind the near impossibility of poisoning millions of food items that come from different sources in the North and for which the group allegedly doing the poisoning could also be victims. But this is Nigeria.

Back to the parcel bomb. There are conflicting stories about the incident. While the Post-master General of the Federation Ibrahim Mori Baba for instance affirmed the incident of the parcel, he could not confirm if it was a bomb or not – according to several reports. However, an un-named Nigeria Postal Service official was quoted by the Guardian of 4 February 2012 as saying that they came to work in the morning on Monday (4 February 2013) and noticed a funny looking package with two N50 postage stamps on it in front of their premises and notified their boss who promptly invited the anti-bomb squad. This source was further quoted as saying that when the anti-bomb squad came they controlled human movement around the area and went into work with their instruments and after a while they heard an explosion, followed by another explosion. For this source therefore, the parcel was a letter bomb. The FCT Commissioner of Police, Mr. Aderenle Shinaba apparently had a different take on the incident. While he admitted that there was something that was packaged in carton that looked like bomb at the gate of NIPOST in Area 10, he claimed that their investigations showed that the parcel had nothing to do with improvised explosive device (IED).

Despite the conflicting stories on whether the parcel was a bomb or not, what is clear is that the intent of the sender of such a parcel was not a love message but to kill or scare. And the greater danger is that it could unwittingly inspire mischief makers and terrorists into realizing that the postal system, including courier services, could be another channel for conveying their evil designs.

To be sure, parcel or letter bomb has been part of the arsenal of terrorists and mischief makers for as old as there has been a Post office. For instance as early as the 18th century, the Danish historian Bolle Willum Luxdorph in his diary of 19 January 1764 noted that one "Colonel Poulsen residing at Børglum abbey was sent by mail a box. When he opens it, therein is to be found gunpowder and a firelock which sets fire unto it, so he became very injured." Again as early as 1915, Thomas R. Marshall, Vice President of the United States, was the target of an assassination attempt by letter bomb. In 1947 several letter bombs were sent to President Harry Truman in the White House by Zionist terrorists which fortunately were all intercepted. On August 17 1982, Ruth First, a South African communist and anti-apartheid activist was killed by a parcel bomb mailed by the South African government to her home in Mozambique. In April 2011 in the UK, Neil Lennon and two high profile fans of Celtic Football Club were sent parcel bombs. The two suspects in the case recently bagged a five year jail term each for the crime.

In Nigeria, parcel bombs were virtually unknown until October 19, 1986 when the flamboyant journalist Dele Giwa, one of the founders of the iconic *Newswatch* magazine was killed by such a bomb. Since then, there has been only one such recorded incident in the country. This was on December 22 2009 when a bomb exploded on a man at the Onipanu area of Lagos. The man was said to have walked into the building housing Superscreen Television in Onipanu part of Lagos State (Ikorodu road), with some parcels containing bombs, one of which accidentally went off, blowing off his fingers and his face. The man claimed that he was asked to deliver the parcel to the most senior person in the TV station.

One of the lessons of the letter bomb story should be not only to call our attention to the extensive insecurity in the country but also to alert us to the fact that some of our flanks remain dangerously porous amid the banality of evil in the country. It should be recalled that when Ngozi Iweala's mother Professor Kamene was kidnapped last year, the Co-ordinating Minister of the Economy fingered oil marketers - though there was nothing from the statements of the arrested suspected abductors that pointed to the complicity of the fuel subsidy cabal. It is instructive that the suspected parcel bomb was again addressed to the Finance Minister, which naturally raises questions and suspicions. If appointed public servants must be able to do their job with the necessary boldness, it behoves on the government to move decisively and unmask the person or persons behind the parcel. While this is not necessarily an endorsement of the manner in which the Finance Minister does her job, the fact is that unless public officials are assured of their security, including protection from intimidation, they cannot give their best.

I am by the way not impressed by the grand-standing of the Post-Master General of the Federation, Malam Ibrahim Mori Baba who reportedly said: "The issue is that on Friday [1 February 2013], somebody just came, we couldn't understand whether that person was a sane person or insane and wanted to get to the post office, but, unfortunately, for him, the gate was closed and he couldn't have access to our building and he left the parcel. This is because there are processes that have to be done and these processes are that we weigh it and, then, determine how much you will pay; we also have to examine it in your presence" (Blueprint, online 5 February 2013). Yes, the Post Office may have 'processes' but the truth is that the 'Nigerian factor' stands tall there - as in virtually every other public institution in the country. A determined mischief maker or terrorist can still get such a parcel bomb through the postal system despite the alleged 'processes'. After all every Ministry, Department and Agency in the country have 'processes' for ensuring transparency in both employment and utilization of allocated resources which are just simply largely observed in the breach. Therefore rather than a triumphant beating of the chest as the Post-Master General seemed to have done, the incident should be a wake-up call for extra security measures to ensure that the Post Office, including courier agencies, are not unwittingly utilized by merchants of death to perpetrate mayhem.

With people, especially those in authority positions and the high and mighty now likely to be afraid of opening their mails and parcels, it becomes necessary to wonder where one can go looking for succour in the country. The spaces appear to be further shrinking - from physical insecurity to material insecurity, including food insecurity. Nigeria is in dire need of being fixed. And the country cannot be fixed without the issue of extensive insecurity in the land being addressed.

It is true that many of the problems of insecurity in the country pre-date the Jonathan administration. What Nigerians want to see and believe is that the situation is getting better, not worsening, and that the government is on full throttle in addressing the problem. Right now Nigerians and the government appear to be on different pages on the matter.

Daily Trust February 7, 2013

CHAPTER 39

Between Polemics and 'on the other hand' Narratives

I did not set out to make this a philosophical inquiry, though by its nature, it is bound to be. The spur for this piece were reactions from some of my readers, who would sometimes challenge me to 'come out and take a bold stand' on issues instead of hiding behind words and academic semantics. One of the comments to my last week's piece, by one Musa Aliyu, on 'When Stella stepped on those banana peels', captured this line of accusation crisply: "Jideofor, as always, you tend to subtly cover your stand…." My good friend, Udenta O Udenta, a master polemicist, has long teased me about the 'on the other hand' predilections in most of my writings for newspapers. 'On the other hand' predilection in Nigerian-speak means that I tend to concede so much to every perspective in an argument that my own position is either blurred or is "cleverly hidden" between words. However when critics challenge me to 'come clean and take a stand' or to "put grammar and 'on the other hand' aside and shoot straight like a man" my reply has always been that I set out in most of my newspaper articles to be an analyst rather than a polemicist. Is there any difference between the two or is it just another obfuscation from me?

Let me preface my answer to the above question with a story about the elephant and some blind men. There are various versions of this story. A version in Jaina dharma – an Indian religion that prescribes a path of non-violence towards all living beings - has it that six blind men were asked to determine what an elephant looked like by feeling different parts of the elephant's body. The blind man who feels a leg says the elephant is like a pillar; the one who feels the tail says the elephant is like a rope; the one who feels the trunk says the elephant is like a tree branch; the one who feels the ear says the elephant is like a hand fan; the one who feels the belly says the elephant is like a wall; and the one who feels the tusk says the elephant is like a solid pipe.

In this elephant and blind men tale, the disputants eventually took their case to their King who calmly and unemotionally told them: "All of you are right. The reason every one of you is telling it differently is because each one of you touched the different part of the elephant. So, actually the elephant has all the features you mentioned".

Now back to my attempt to distinguish between the polemicist and the analyst: In the elephant story above, each of the six blind men is a polemicist to the extent that each argued forcefully that his notion of reality was the correct one while insisting that the others' conceptions were definitely wrong. A polemic is a contentious argument that is intended to establish the truth of only a specific understanding and the falsity of any contrarian position. Polemicists believe in zero-sum- game, one side winning for them equals to the other side losing, hence they have a singular and passionate devotion to proving the truth of their lineal understanding of the world and the falsity of whatever is contrary to it. Unlike the polemicist, the analyst (the king in the elephant story) aims at finding a common ground for disputants or arriving at a 'higher truth' by bringing together the versions of truth purveyed by the disputants in any controversial issue. In other words, 'on the other hand' is the analyst's way of ensuring that all contending perspectives are interrogated and something conceded to each in the quest for truth or common ground. While the polemicist aims to win an argument, the analyst strives for objectivity, if not scientism, by trying to see reality from as many facets as possible. This often requires empathy – trying to put yourself in the position of each disputant while unemotionally viewing reality from the lenses through which the disputant filters reality.

A key question here is whether striving for objectivity means that one must also be value neutral? My personal opinion is that maximizing objectivity in social research or write-up does not necessarily require total value neutrality but rather a commitment to certain social values. Here what motivates a particular write-up or social project becomes very important.

Let me illustrate with one of the criticisms of my last week's piece on Stella Odua. Obviously as a columnist, I am grateful that readers bother to comment on my writings, whether praise or acerbic criticism. In this sense this write-up should be seen not as a defence of the criticisms but an extension of the conversations triggered by my last week's piece and others.

One of the commentators on my piece on Stella Odua called to express his disappointment that I chose to defend Stella Odua because she is my fellow Igbo. However when I asked the gentleman whether ethnicity was also a factor when I became probably the first person to come to the 'defence' of Farouk Lawan when he was accused by Femi Otedola of demanding and receiving bribe from him, he fell silent. Actually my piece on Farouk, 'Why We Should Rally Behind Farouk Lawan' (Daily Trust, 21 June 2013), was not a defence of Farouk but an argument that I suspected the invisible hands of the oil cabals in Lawan's ordeal and that we should focus on fighting the cabals first and returning to ask Farouk questions later. Similarly my piece on Stella did not in any manner seek to defend the allegations of corruption and inflation of contract. Rather I suspected that the enemies she made from certain ethnic groups compounded her woes. This remains my position on her ordeal. I believe I would have taken the same position if Stella Odua were from any other ethnic group. Saying this does not amount to condoning any wrong doing. If she is found culpable of any offence, she should obviously be made to pay for it but we should not pretend that her ordeal has not been conflated by ethnicity.

Let me return to the argument about the polemicist and the analyst and declare that neither is superior to the other. It all depends on the context and what the society wants to achieve at a particular point in time. For instance, when propaganda is needed to engender ethnic or national pride or to mobilize the populace or a section of it towards a given cause of action, the polemicist will be preferred to the analyst who may not be able to arouse enough emotions in the citizens with his 'on the other hand' analyses. When however the search is for a common ground, reconciliation or a set of compromises that will satisfy all disputants, then the analyst will trump the polemicist. The thing I find nauseating about many of our political polemicists however that while is purveying their arguments with all the passion and grammar that they can muster, they often deny any merits in the grouses expressed by others. For instance a Nigerian polemicist complaining against the 'marginalization of 'his people' will quite often shout down anyone else who also complains that his or her own group is equally marginalized. This therefore tends to turn what should be national conversations into shouting matches and finger pointing.

We can also see polemical tendencies in action – not just at the level of rhetoric and write-ups but in practical politics. In the realm of practical politics, Obasanjo and Babangida may probably represent the two extremes of the polemical and analytical traditions. While Obasanjo is known to have a single- minded devotion to any objective he wants to achieve (polemics), Babangida would more likely listen to many perspectives on the issue before making up his mind (or even if he had already made up his mind on what to do). Thus while Obasanjo's 'garrison politics' involved militarizing politics to achieve a given end, Babangida's analytic approach would lead him into organizing a national debate about whether the country should embrace IMF/World Bank's facilities or not. It was also probably the same analytic approach that informed his strategy of aligning with any group to achieve a particular objective and quickly moving out of that alliance as soon as that objective was accomplished. This particular strategy made several groups believe, rightly or wrongly that he had sympathetic ears to their cause. Obasanjo would not have patience for such diplomatic niceties. In fact Babangida's two political parties – 'one a little to the left' and the 'other a little to the right' may not just be talking about ideological spectrum but of conceding something to each of the disputants in an argument.

Whether the analytical leader or the polemical leader is better will of course be a matter of taste. For Babangida, while his supporters will argue that but for the annulment of the June 12 elections won by Abiola, he would have been the greatest Nigerian leader in terms of political engineering; his critics will accuse him of cunning and of trying to please everyone. Similarly while Obasanjo's supporters would say there was no dull moment in his regime, his critics would accuse him of overheating the polity with his garrison (polemical) approach to politics and governance.

Daily Trust October 31, 2013

CHAPTER 40

Oyerinde's Murder: Between the Police and the DSS

The recent report that Governor Adams Oshiomhole of Edo State and the Minister of Justice Muhammad Bello Adoke nearly got into a physical fight on March 12 2013 - just before the National Executive Council meeting that day - over the alleged procedural flaws in the investigations of the murder of Comrade Olaitan Oyerinde should be a source of concern to Nigerians. Comrade Oyerinde was until his cruel assassination on May 4 2012 the Principal Private Secretary to the Edo State Governor.

One of the contentious issues in the investigation is that both the police and the Department of State Security (DSS) have different suspects for who allegedly confessed to the crime. And since it is almost impossible for two sets of suspects to have killed the deceased same day, there is clearly something wrong somewhere, which justifies the public cynicism towards the reports and to Governor Oshiomhole's anger about the 'shoddy' manner that the investigation was conducted. It also, in many ways, justifies the decision of the Civil Society Organization, Edo State, to bring a petition against the Nigerian Police on alleged complicity and improper investigation. The civil society organization could have also been miffed by the arrest of one of their own - Reverend David Ugolor, a bosom friend of the deceased and also the Executive Director of African Network for Environment and Economic Justice (ANEEJ).

Who do we believe between the Police and the DSS?

A critical issue here is the public perception of competence and integrity between the two organisations. In this respect, the Police are terribly disadvantaged, for even if they did a superb job, their public perception index is so low that even a ragtag vigilante group, concocting lies of bravery in contest with the NPF, is more likely to be believed than the Police. In this sense the Police do not have any chance of winning this case in the court of public opinion. In fact anytime the police find themselves competing with rival agencies, including village vigilante groups on investigations, narratives or anything else, you can close your eyes and declare the results without even bothering to read those accounts. And each time the police lose out in such competitions – as they are bound to do irrespective of the real merits of their case - the public confidence in them wanes the more, making it more difficult for the Force to carry out its statutory functions and demoralizing officers who genuinely want to make a difference.

The above should not be misconstrued as a wholesale approbation of the police investigation into the murder of Comrade Oyerinde. But I must say this: given the image of the Police, I was rather surprised at the systematic way in which they structured their written presentation – with virtually no grammatical error or typos, over several pages, structured almost like a mini dissertation and with some intellectual sophistication to it. They started by defining the allegation, then the highlights of the allegation, mode of presentation, their methodologies of investigations and how they arrived at their conclusions. They even have an additional six-page report entitled 'Additional comments arising from the brief submitted by Conference of Non-Governmental Organizations on 13 February 2013' in which they did a point-by-point rebuttal of the arguments of both the Civil Society Organization, which is accusing them of shoddy investigation and of the DSS, which believes that its set of suspects represent the true killers of Comrade Oyerinde. The DSS's written brief is structured differently, with emphasis on the profiling of the suspects rather than on the methods of its investigations.

Comrade Adams Oshiomhole, the highly vocal governor of Edo State, swore that he would see to it that the murderers of Comrade Oyerinde would be fished out. Such a posture by a high political authority has often led to a quick police action and quick arrests, often raising questions about the class character of our justice system. According to the Police, their detectives arrived Benin City on 4 May 2012 at about 11pm - the same day as the deceased was murdered. The flipside to this type of marching order however is that with a number of competing agencies involved, the desire to achieve quick results could lead to the sort of discrepancies in investigations as we saw between the Police and the DSS' investigations in the Comrade Oyerinde's case. Under our extant laws, the powers to investigate such crimes as murder lie with the Nigerian Police Force while the power to gather intelligence lies with the State Security. It will seem that in the competition for limelight and quick results, the statutory boundaries are often not respected.

The Police have argued that none of the items recovered from the DSS suspects had any bearing to what were stolen from the Oyerindes. It also accused the DSS of not handing over the case files of the suspects it handed over to the police. On its part the DSS used innuendos to accuse the Police of shoddy investigations and of using 'analogue' methods in its work.

On the controversial arrest and detention of Rev David Ugolor, the Police said it based its actions on a number of investigative procedures: he was the last to be seen with the deceased and they had a number of business relationships, including police allegation that Rev Ugolor was building a house for the deceased in Benin. Though I do not believe that the motive why Rev Ugolor should want his friend to be killed was very clearly established by the Police, I also found the defence that he couldn't have been involved in the murder because he was the deceased friend extremely weak. In many advanced societies, the wife or husband is often the first suspect when the other suddenly dies or is murdered. I also find it difficult to understand why the police should be accused of trying to cover up the real killers of Oyerinde or of trying to divert public attention by arresting Rev Ugolor. If the Police want to do that – and there is a general belief that such is not beneath them - they do not need to arrest Rev Ugolor to do so. In any case, there is nothing from the DSS investigation or set of suspects that suggested that characters other than hoodlums of various shades were involved in the conspiracy, robbery and murder of Oyerinde. So the case of cover-up appears difficult to sustain.

Clearly the unfortunate assassination of Comrade Oyerinde Olaitan, is proving to be one of the test cases of criminal investigations in this country, offering the country an opportunity to have a second look at the agencies entrusted to fight crime and the knee-jerk politicisation of several cases of murder. If the Police did all they claimed to have done in their report into their investigation of the murder of Oyerinde, then it would appear the police efforts are not sufficiently appreciated – despite the gaps here and there in both the Police and the DSS reports.

The police cannot completely exonerate themselves from the crisis of confidence that the force elicits in the public imagination. There are uncountable stories of police corruption, of suspects who went to seek succour in police stations being found dead, of trigger happy police people at check points and their 'accidental discharges'. One of the consequences of this is that even the remarkable works by the police are overshadowed by the Force's poor reputation. Curiously this poor image feeds into the generalised distrust of the Police, accentuating in the process their low rating in the competence perception index by the public. The current spat with Governor Adams Oshiomhole and the DSS is therefore another lose-lose situation for the police. No matter their effort or the merits of any report they present, no one will believe them because the public seems to have made up their minds about them. Yet in any efficient society the police are always at the forefront of crime detection and crime-bursting. We cannot expect an efficient police force where the crisis of confidence in them is reinforced every day. There is therefore an urgent need for the police to re-invent themselves and for the general public to begin to adjust their perception of the Police, giving them the benefit of the doubt when they deserve such.

The Oyerinde case also illustrates the lack of confidence in our judiciary. Ordinarily those who suspect a cover- up in police investigation would hire a tough attorney. The late Johnny Cochran, who represented OJ Simpson during the latter's jury trial (November 2 1994 – October 3 1995) over the alleged murder of his estranged wife Nicole Brown Simpson was able to show that the police were racist in their investigations and used that to secure acquittal for OJ Simpsom. In a country where the belief in the justice system is strong, the spat between Governor Oshiomhole, the DSS and the Civil Society Organization, Edo State on the one hand and the police on the other, would have been substantially settled in court without any one losing sight of what should be the real focus of any investigation or activism: to find the real killers of Comrade Oyerinde Olaitan.

Daily Trust March 14, 2013

CHAPTER 41

Should Nigeria be Re-Colonized?

Let me start this piece with boring you with some personal details and fragments of my autobiography. They will help to contextualize the drift of the article.

When I entered the University of Nigeria, Nsukka in 1980, as a young teenager fresh from secondary school, part of my expectations was to learn enough of jaw-breaking words – the type that Achebe called the 'English that filled the mouth. Professor Okwudiba Nnoli, who taught 'Introduction to Political Science' ('Pol Science 101) insisted that everyone in the class must buy, read, summarize these three books - Frantz Fanon's *The Wretched of the Earth*, Walter Rodney's *How Europe Underdeveloped Africa* and Okwudiba *Nnoli's Ethnic Politics in Nigeria.*

It was amazing how books could completely overhaul and mould the minds of impressionable young adults. We were repeatedly warned to be wary of 'bourgeois scholars' and their works because they were the intellectual representatives of the propertied class whose ideas, however disguised, were just meant to perpetuate the status quo. The 'good' Nigerian scholars with the 'right consciousness' and who employed the right 'analytical categories' were the likes of Claude Ake, Ikenna Nzimiro, Bade Onimode, Bala Usman, Okwudiba Nnoli and Comrade Ola Oni. Former INEC chairman Professor Humphrey Nwosu was among the lecturers in the department that we barely tolerated. By the time we completed the first two semesters, almost the entire class had become a bunch of unruly radicals and there were complaints from the 'bourgeois scholars' in the department that Nnoli had completely 'corrupted the minds of these youngsters'.

One day one of the lecturers that we barely tolerated came to teach about colonialism. After listing what he called the 'evils of colonialism', he wrote on the board, 'The benefits of Colonialism', hoping to discuss the other side of the coin, even if they were unintended. He had hardly completed writing the sentence when one of us screamed in disgust, 'What?' Suddenly hissings and sighing filled the class room and by the time you could say 'Jack Robins', we had packed our bags and left the classroom, abandoning the teacher to teach the 'benefits of colonialism' to himself. For weeks we refused to attend the man's class until the Head of Department intervened. How could, we argued among ourselves, any educated person talk about the 'benefits of colonialism'?

Fast forward to London, late 2002. I met the Ethiopian scholar, Mammo Muchie, who now holds concurrent professorial chair in Denmark, Oxford and South Africa. Both Mammo and I were regular contributors to the influential *New African*, monthly magazine. Its editor, the Ghanaian Baffour Ankomah, had brought us together when he learnt I was planning to set up a publishing company.

Mammo and I met at a time when Afro-pessimism was pervasive. Thabo Mbeki, had just popularized the notion of 'African Renaissance', first articulated by Cheikh

Anta Diop in his collection of essays, *Towards the African Renaissance: Essays in Culture and Development, 1946-1960.* The British press had derided the notion of 'African Renaissance', with some mockingly asking 'when did Africa ever have its naissance?' Mammo and I agreed that we should use the new publishing company, Adonis & Abbey Publishers (www.adonis-abbey.com), to soldier for Africa. We agreed that the fundamental problem in Africa was the failure of the nation-building in various African countries and the lack of unity among Africans. Mammo's book, the second I published, was aptly titled *'The Making of the Africa-Nation: Pan Africanism and the African Renaissance.* In June 2004 I set up a semi-academic, bi-monthly journal called *African Renaissance*, where we often brought leading African scholars – Ali Mazrui, Kwesi Prah, Helmi Sharawy, Gamal Nkrumah (Kwame Nkrumah's son), Mammo Muchie, Bankie Forster Bankie, Kimani Nehusi, Marcel Kitissou and others to robustly discuss the African condition and reply the Afro-pessimists. Goaded by the relative success of the journal, we decided to dabble into academic journal publishing to enable African academics set their own research agenda and combat the high mortality rate of journals published by Africans. *African Renaissance*, a quarterly which I still edit, is today one of the longest surviving social science journals published by any African. Adonis & Abbey Publishers on their own have published or incubated more peer-reviewed and indexed journals than probably any African publisher.

Fast forward again to 17 May 2013. I am billed to attend 'the scramble for Africa conference, hosted by the Africa Institute of South Africa, Pretoria (May 20-21 2013) and after that to give two other public lectures in Durban and Pietermaritzburg hosted by the University of Kwazulu. As I flew to catch a connecting flight from Lagos to Johannesburg, I was secretly praying that I would miss my flight. Is something happening to the fire of pan-Africanism that had for long been aflame in my soul?

In Pretoria, on a guided tour of the city's museums and historical sites, I whispered a question to some African conferees: 'We are all Africans and no one is listening. Among ourselves, do you really think that without Apartheid, South Africa would have been a country that works?' This was a 'family affair', so we told one another what we believed was the truth. Later in the evening, I whispered another question to three other Nigerian participants over dinner: 'If a plebiscite were to be organized in Nigeria over the question, "would you want Nigeria to be re-colonized", how do you think our people would vote?' There was unanimity that an overwhelming majority of 'ordinary Nigerians' would ask them to come back.

Meanwhile, Mammo Muchie, who was one of the organizers of the 'Scramble for Africa' conference, was still his old ebullient self, totally married to the cause of Africa. Why has Mammo's pan Africanism remained resilient while I seem to be getting tired? Has it anything to do with my relocating to Nigeria? If Mammo, who had been living out of Ethiopia for nearly 40 years had returned home, would the fire of pan Africanism still be burning bright in his soul?

Today (May 21 2013), the African American I had asked his opinion about a possible colonization of any part of Africa confronted me with my own question: 'Adibe, if there is a referendum for Nigeria to be re-colonized, how would you vote –

yes or no'? I was speechless for a minute or so. I thought of telling him I would abstain from voting, but realizing the implications, quickly told him I would vote 'No'. To vote 'Yes' I reasoned, would be to legitimate the racist ideology of the inherent inferiority of the Blackman to other races. It would also deny the possibility of the country ever getting its act together and doing the right thing. But there is enough frustration for one, in moments of emotional flourishes, to give up and call on the colonial masters to simply come back. What is your take on the question of whether Nigeria should be re-colonized?

My preferred framework for analyzing Africa's problems has always been the nation-building paradigm. But in my beloved Nigeria, I am now honestly beginning to wonder whether the fundamental problem of Nigeria is in fact not the Nigerian.

CHAPTER 42

Wars without blood: Should hate speech be criminalized?

Hate-filled profiling seems to have reached a new high in the current democratic dispensation with Nigerians apparently reveling in pouring invectives on one another whenever they discuss the Nigerian condition. The triggers for such warring with words are often predictable: if it has to do with the Civil War, Igbo nationalists will square with the rest of the country; if it is about Boko Haram and its alleged sponsors, self-appointed defenders of the North will be up in arms with equally self-appointed defenders of the South; if it has to do with resource control and oil politics, the North squares it with the South-south. The Igbos and the Yorubas frequently pick on each other as we saw recently with the alleged deportation of Igbo destitute from Lagos. In these exchanges, religion, region and even town union politics are all sucked into them.

Reading through the 'comments' that follow most articles published online, especially on contentious political issues one cannot help but marvel at the capacity of educated Nigerians, including Diaspora-based ones, to write from their base animal instincts. Hate speech is so pervasive in Nigeria that it is doubtful if there are many Nigerians that are completely free from the vice.

Hate speech employs discriminatory epithets to insult and stigmatize others on the basis of their ethnicity, religion, region, gender, sexual orientation or other forms of group membership. It is any speech, gesture, conduct, writing or display which could incite people to violence or prejudicial action. The wide prevalence of hate speech in the country has given rise to concerns that the profiling that is embedded in such speeches could aggravate the structures of conflicts in the country and complicate the nation-building process.

Ironically regulating hate speeches may be counter-productive as it could conflict with the free speech principle on which any country's democracy project is based. Hate speech therefore presents the country with the Devil's Alternative.

True, free speech - the ability of people to speak their minds without censorship - is never absolute in any country even in the most mature democracies such as the United Kingdom or the USA. But it is often seen as a necessary condition for the enjoyment of democratic ideals as it provides and guarantees the space for public discussion and debate. It is also argued that it is only through an unfettered competition of ideas in the political marketplace, including ideas that shock and awe, that the truth could be discovered. Free speech is equally regarded as an aspect of self-fulfilment – a value to be enjoyed for its sake. Additionally, free speech proponents argue that citizens harbour such a strong suspicion of the government that any attempt to regulate free speech will only heighten that suspicion.

Below are selected hate speech-laden comments from three recent stories in the media:

1) 'The bitter truth about the Igbos' by Femi Fani Kayode

This was an ethnic bile-loaded article published on Premium Times on August 8, 2013 and reproduced by several media in the country. The article, written by Femi Fani Kayode, a one-time Minister of Aviation during Obasanjo's civilian presidency, was apparently spurred by an alleged 'deportation' of Igbo destitute from Lagos and claim by former Governor of Abia State, Orji Uzo Kalu that the city of Lagos is a 'No Man's Land'. The article renewed the media war between the Igbos and the Yorubas following the publication of Chinua's Achebe's controversial book, *There was a country*. Selected comments on the article (unedited):

'Truth is Bitter'

> Once upon a time they claimed that they were "jews" and that they "migrated" from Jerusalem, then they claimed "there was a country" when in fact they were dreaming by river niger, now the new figment of their imagination is that they "own" Lagos. " Igbos do not have the capacity to disintegrate this country: as a politician, we are used to the antics of the Igbos. Preceding every election, they will make such claims, but once the election comes, they will fight to be vice president, Senate president and minister. So for me, the Igbos can make all the claims they want to make, but they are not going to disintegrate Nigeria. The first attempt to disintegrate Nigeria was precipitated by the Igbos, and till today, they are still suffering for it. So, I'm not sure they would allow the same mistake to be made the second time.

armrod Femi

> All the villages in igboland are better than towns in yorubaland. I dare you to go to igboland villages and compare it with Ibadan that have rusty zinc and Ibadan has been a capital since the time of regional government.
>
> Go to Nnewi no town in this country house the kind of industry that was solely built by Igbos. Go to Aba you will see the wonders of Igbos. Go to Abiriba reputed to be small London. When Igbos was denied airport they built their own with community effort through the able leadership of De Sam Mbakwe. You are a bush man you don't travel the only place you know is Lagos and am sure that you are a visitor in Lagos like some Igbos. Igbos have claimed their contribution in lagos which is obvious. Now I dare you to point to me any revenue generated economic base develop and built by Yorubas in Lagos or anywhere in Nigeria. Yes Igbos have menace of kidnapping so also yoruba. Let's check Efcc and compare lists of corrupt suspect yoruba top the list.
>
> To remind you that Igbos started afresh to build their economy after civil war with only 20 pounds. But Yorubas are still crawling in development. The only place they claim is Lagos which was developed with the help of Igbos. Today they are praying for Igbos to go back to their land so that they can claim their investment shame on you!!!!

2) 'Why Niger Delta oil theft can't stop by Boyloaf'

In this article published in the Vanguard of September 7 2013, one of the ex-militant leaders in the Niger Delta, Ebikabowei Victor Ben, alias 'General Boyloaf', was quoted as saying that oil theft in the Niger Delta would not stop until the Federal Government takes appropriate steps to compensate the natives of the region. Boyloaf said that oil theft soared in the region because the owners of the land where the oil facilities crisscross did not feel any sense of belonging after many decades of oil production. Boyloaf was further quoted as saying: "Let me seize this opportunity to appeal to our northern brothers not to mistake our resolve to maintain peace in the Niger Delta region as a form of weakness. Nobody should blame our people when they react forcefully on issues associated with these matters and many other unwarranted attacks on our sons and daughters by those who think they own Nigeria and our commonwealth and think that the Niger Delta people must continue to be subservient to them. A word is enough for the wise,"

Selected comments on the article (unedited):

muhammad zuezz

wow! hehehehehee! I just pity people from that part of Nigeria. the level of environmental pollution is unprecedented, yet they are breaking pipes anyhow and proud of it. The smart ones among them try to blame it solely on Shell. Just know that when the oil finishes, nobody is going to clean up your mess.

In all this the Niger delta governors are to blame! with the 13%, they can really make things work if they so wish! I really pity you Niger deltans. we may be poor in the North, but my grandfathers farm will always there for me in the future, with a clean environment. forget about the the current blood money you are making by oil theft, it won't last!

Udoabasi _Africa

You truly lack proper home bringing. Niger-Delta is built already. All the people need is control of their resources. Have the Niger-Delta people asked you to build the region for them before? Mention the place you built in Nigeria for years you have been ruling. I believe you have been hearing of national and international events happening in Rivers, Bayelsa, Cross River, Akwa Ibom, and Delta States every week. That means that it is built and it is fit for use by Nigerians more than many other states. Stop building Niger-Delta and build your region or your keep your insult and parochial sentiments to yourself. Have you seen the federal govt build Almajeri school or any Primary school for Niger-Deltans? It is built in the North. Have you seen the federal govt build VVF hospital to treat babies you marry and impregnate and they cannot deliver but have tear and bursts of female organs, making urine, facccs mix together, it is built in the North.

Have you seen the federal govt. bring in Drs. to treat lead poisoning, meningitis and poliomyelitis in the Niger-Delta? It is happening in the North.

Have you seen the federal govt. lower the cut-off point or literally removed cut-off point for Niger-Delta students? It is happening in the North. Have you seen the federal govt. build dams in the Niger-Delta? It is happening in the North.

Between 1999 and present day, about four states in the Niger-Delta have built Independent Power plant for electricity generation and no state in the North has done that? Examine yourself to see who rather cries.

Daily Trust January 16, 2014

CHAPTER 43

Wars without blood: Should hate speech be criminalized? (II)

In the first instalment of this piece, I discussed the dangers of hate speech, and with selected examples, showed that it is something that every part of the country is guilty of. I also showed the inherent problematic of trying to contain hate speech in an environment in which the protection, defence and sustenance of the country's democracy rests mainly on free speech being guaranteed and defended.

In this second and final segment, I look more closely at the tension between free speech and hate speech, including how some countries have tried to resolve this tension. I conclude by recommending some palliative measures:

There are two main perspectives in the debate on whether free speech should be restricted – the Libertarians, who favour protecting the rights of the individual to free speech and the Communitarians who believe that certain restrictions on free speech may be necessary to protect the community. For Libertarians, an almost unfettered free speech is needed to avoid the danger of condemning people simply because of the beliefs they hold and express. They equally argue that criminalizing views that are objectionable and offensive is the slippery rope to censorship. Restricting free speech, they equally argue, not only forecloses open debate but is also counter-productive especially as it risks making martyrs of people who have bigoted opinions.

Communitarians counter that a society that allows hate speech to go unpunished is one that tolerates discrimination and invites violence. They often cite examples with decades of hateful anti-abortion rhetoric in the US, which led to assassination of providers. They further contend that hate speech has no redeeming value, and that people should not pretend that it occupies a rightful spot in the marketplace of ideas or has anything to do with 'rational debate'.

The debate can be quite impassioned. What is not debatable is that in multi-ethnic and fragile societies like Nigeria, hate speech could very easily aggravate the structures of conflict, which will in turn complicate the nation-building process. Many countries who are confronted with the dangers of hate speech have sought to find ways of enacting laws and creative policies that will discourage bad behaviour and insensitive remarks without punishing bad beliefs. But it is not always an easy balancing act.

For instance though the International Covenant on Civil and Political Rights (ICCPR) - a multilateral treaty adopted by the United Nations General Assembly on December 16, 1966 and which came into force from March 23, 1976 - encourages countries to prohibit any advocacy of national, racial, ethnic or religious hatred, in practice hate speech is difficult to prohibit. In the US for instance, hate speech is protected as a civil right (aside from the usual exceptions to free speech such as defamation, incitement to riot, and fighting words). In fact laws prohibiting hate speech are unconstitutional in the United States as most often fail legal challenges based on the First Amendment of the Country's Constitution which prohibits the restriction of free speech. In the US law courts, even 'fighting words' - which are categorically excluded from the protection of the First Amendment - are not that easy to separate from hate speech.

An insight into how the American jurisprudence protects hate speech is in the way the law treats the Ku Klux Klan – one of the worst purveyors of racial hatred in that country. In a landmark case, Brandenburg v. Ohio (1969), the arrest of an Ohio Klansman named Clarence Brandenburg on criminal syndicalism charges, based on a KKK speech that recommended overthrowing the government, was overturned in a ruling that has protected rascals of all political persuasions ever since. In a unanimous judgment, Justice William Brennan argued that "the constitutional guarantees of free speech and free press do not permit a State to forbid or proscribe advocacy of the use of force or of law violation except where such advocacy is directed to inciting or producing imminent lawless action and is likely to incite or produce such action." In another important case, *Snyder v. Phelps* (2011), Westboro Baptist Church, which has achieved some notoriety for celebrating the 9/11 attacks and picketing military funerals, was sued by the family of Lance Corporal Matthew Snyder who was killed in Iraq in 2006 for intentional infliction of emotional distress after it picketed during the Corporal's funeral. In an 8-1 ruling, the U.S. Supreme Court upheld Westboro's right to picket.

In the United Kingdom, Section 18(1) of the Public Order Act of 1986 (POA) states that "a person who uses threatening, abusive, or insulting words or behaviour, or displays any written material which is threatening, abusive, or insulting, is guilty of an offence if: a) he intends to thereby stir up racial hatred, or; b) having regard to all the circumstances racial hatred is likely to be stirred up thereby." Among the panoply of other British hate speech laws is Section 5 of the POA, which makes it a crime to use or display threatening, abusive, or insulting words "within the hearing or sight of a person likely to be caused harassment, alarm, or distress thereby." Under this Section 5 of POA, Harry Taylor, an atheist who placed drawings satirizing Christianity and Islam in an airport prayer room, was convicted in April 2010 and given a six-month prison sentence.

In The Netherlands, which is long considered a bastion for the freedom of thought and expression, Articles 137(c) and 137(d) of the country's Criminal Code prohibits making public intentional insults, as well as engaging in verbal, written, or illustrated incitement to hatred, on account of one's race, religion, sexual orientation, or personal convictions. In The Netherlands, the most prominent hate speech case to date is that of politician Geert Wilders, who was indicted by the public prosecutor in 2009 for his public comments about Muslims and Islam, and his release of a short film documenting what he called 'inflammatory passages' in the Qur'an.

In France, Section 24 of the country's Press Law of 1881 criminalizes incitement to racial discrimination, hatred, or violence on the basis of one's origin or membership (or non-membership) in an ethic, national, racial, or religious group. In 2005, politician Jean Marie Le Pen, runner-up in the 2002 presidential election, was convicted of inciting racial hatred for comments made to *Le Monde* in 2003 about the consequences of Muslim immigration in France.

Is hate speech less in countries that try to use the law to fight the menace than say the US where free speech is regarded as protected speech? This is debatable. What is clear is that laws can sometimes exacerbate the problem. A good example of this is what happened in the Australian state of Victoria where a law banning incitement to religious hatred led to Christians and Muslims accusing each other of inciting hatred and bringing legal actions against each other which only served to further inflame community relations.

I agree that Nigeria should do something urgently about hate speech but my personal opinion is that outright criminalization could exacerbate the problem. Just imagine if Junaid Mohammed, Edwin Clarke, Chudi Uwazurike, Gani Adams, Ango Abdullahi, Dokubo-Asari, Oritsejeafor etc are convicted of hate-speech. Certainly, their religious affiliations and ethnic and regional homelands will come out smoking, and we will all be taken through a journey of Nigeria's political history and a documentation of non-members of the ethnic/regional/religious group, who made 'more hateful speeches' in the past without anything happening to them. The affected ethnic/regional/religious group will then count the conviction of its self-proclaimed champion and advocate as another instance of the 'injustice, hatred and victimization' it suffers in the country.

I will recommend the following measures: There is an urgent need to develop, in conjunction with critical organs of the society such as media owners and practitioners, a taxonomy of what constitutes hate speech. Media houses through their unions should incorporate these as part of good journalism practice and impose sanctions on erring members who publish or broadcast hate speech-laden materials. The National Orientation Agency, in concert with civil society groups and community leaders, should also embark on a campaign against the use of hate speech. In the same vein, Internet Service providers should be encouraged to bring down blogs and websites they host which publish, promote or give unfettered space for the expression of hate speech. Above all it should be impressed upon the political leadership at all levels that a deep distrust of the government is at the heart of the sort of free speech jurisprudence they have in the United States and that Nigerians have the same level of distrust of their governments.

Perhaps one of the most effective ways of combating hate speech is to ensure that purveyors of such speeches are marginalized. For instance in the UK, while the racist British National Party and the ideas it purveys are not banned, it will be political suicide for any politician to be seen to associate with the party's members. In Nigeria hate speech mongers are adopted as regional and ethnic heroes.

More importantly Nigerians should learn to laugh at themselves. This is already happening in some ways with our comedians who dish out jokes based on ethnic and regional profiling. In fact it could be argued that since every region and ethnic group in the country is both a victim and a victimizer when it comes to hate speech, they countervail and cancel out one another.

Daily Trust January 23, 2014

CHAPTER 44

Anomie, Rage and Redemptive Suffering

It was Emile Durkheim, the French sociologist and philosopher who coined the term 'anomie' to refer to a situation where the conditions for happiness are absent. Our own Wole Soyinka was to further popularize the word in his second (and last novel), *A Season of Anomie* (1973).

News streaming from various media outlets suggest that we may be indeed facing a season of anomie as things continue to get from bad to worse on the things we all value or are generally believed to be indicators of well-being: electricity generation dropped to 1400 megawatts from 5000 megawatts in December 2015 at a time the tariff was jacked up by 45%; figures from the National Bureau of Statistics show that the number of unemployed rose by 518,000 to over 1.45 million in the first quarter of the year, pushing the unemployment rate to 12.1 per cent from 9.9 per cent in September 2015. Meanwhile Nigeria has lost its 'crown' as Africa's largest producer of oil as its daily output fell to below 1.4 million barrels per day (bpd) from 2.2 million bpd. Angola which produces about 1.7 million bpd is now Africa's largest oil producer. In 2014 and 2015, Nigeria was named the third fastest growing economy in the world by CNNMoney (with China and Qatar respectively taking the lead at 7.3 per cent and 7.1 per cent of GDP growth). In 2014, the country was included in the MINT emerging economies. MINT is a neologism referring to the economies of Mexico, Indonesia, Nigeria and Turkey which were predicted by British economist Jim O'Neil, to be the next breakout economies in the world. O'Neil had in 2011 coined the acronym BRIC to refer to the economies of Brazil, Russia, India and China as emerging economic powers. According to the IMF's World Economic Outlook for 2016 (as revised in April 2016), Côte d'Ivoire is now the fastest growing economy in Africa while Nigeria is not even among the first 15. At 2.3 per cent, our GDP growth rate is the poorest since the inception of democracy in the country in 1999 and we are just one more quarter of negative GDP growth away from being officially declared as being in recession. In virtually every other social and economic indicators we are in the negative territory. Prices of virtually everything have gone to the mountain tops at a time governments routinely are unable to pay workers their salaries. The country is far more polarized today than it was last year.

How do we explain the above? We all wear binoculars through which we filter the maze of realities that daily hit us. Depending on the shade of your binoculars, in this season of anomie, it is either that the Buhari regime has squandered its goodwill and led us to a blind alley or that the present hardship is merely redemptive suffering, a necessary penance before we can start enjoying the dividends of change. In the latter explanation, if rage is becoming pervasive in the land, it is only because corruption is fighting back as the Buhari regime ratchets up its brand of fighting corruption.

Precisely because of my belief that truth is relative (meaning that what people earnestly believe is the truth for them), my ideological inclination has always been towards reaching out to people who differ from us or even carry out actions we regard as heinous. Johanna ('Hanna') Arendt, the German-American political theorist explained this nicely in his classic work, *Eichmann in Jerusalem: A Report on the Banality of Evil* (1963). Arendt tells us that the great evils in history were not executed by fanatics or sociopaths but rather by ordinary people who accepted the premises of their actions and therefore participated in them on the grounds that those heinous actions were normal. This is the so-called doctrine of 'normalising the unthinkable' or routinization of evil. This means that rather than dismissing people who act funnily or heinously as criminals, it may pay more to try to understand their rationalizations for their 'heinous' actions, and from there construct ways of engaging them. In this instance one may want to know whether members of Boko Haram accept that they are terrorists. Do members of the Niger Delta Avengers believe its members are common criminals or that no one has wronged them and therefore they have nothing to avenge? Do those agitating for Biafra truly believe that they are doing it for money or self-promotion? What justifications do herdsmen have to insist on their rights to enter into other people's farms to graze their cattle while others who forcefully enter into others' private property could be accused and even charged to court for trespassing?

Posing questions like the above in a bid to solve intractable conflicts is not pacifism. It is soft power at work – understanding why people behave the way they do and utilizing that knowledge to get them to see the world from your perspective. It is much more effective both as a conflict resolution strategy and also as a means of getting people to help you accomplish a desired outcome. Raw power alone as a strategy for pacifying 'troublesome' populations has since become passé. We only need to look at the Western powers' interventions in Iraq, Libya and Syria to understand the limits of raw power in achieving desired outcomes

In this season of anomie, macho grand-standings are erroneously called voices of 'change', while cautionary voices are denounced with such epithets as being 'Jonathanian' or resisting change. It is the old strategy of those who appropriate change to enthrone their perverse version of dictatorship. We found these in McCarthyism in the USA in the 1950s and in both Communist Russia and China where those who called for honest conversations were labelled counter-revolutionaries.

The truth is that in this season of anomie – more than at any time in our history – we need honest horizontal conversations on how to get the country out of the valleys and put it on a path of sustainable growth and development.

As the hardship bites harder – whether it is interpreted as redemptive suffering or evidence that we are being led to *cul de sac* – the polarizations are deepening, sometimes with frightening reverberations. Take the story that Jonathan has gone on exile to Côte d'Ivoire allegedly because he got reports that the EFCC was planning to arrest him on corruption charges. Though the former President was reported to have denied that he had sought for asylum anywhere, there are those who believe that arresting the former President would send a powerful message that no one is above the law and that incumbents of power positions must be prepared to answer for their deeds in office. Others would ask which of the former Presidents or Heads of States have been so humiliated in our history and how such an arrest would impact on the politics of identity and possible aggravation of militancy in the Niger Delta. Yet others (including my humble self) would worry on how such an arrest could resolve the tension between sending signals to political officeholders and deepening our democracy? Will those who lose elections in future be willing to accept defeat if he is arrested or humiliated or will our politics become more anarchic as incumbents fear the consequences of losing to the opposition? How will the international community react to the events such an arrest could trigger?

Certainly there are those baying for the blood of their supposed oppressors and class enemies and any policy that shames the mighty will always be hailed by such people. I do not mean that anyone is above the law. But what is right may not always be politically expedient in our type of clime. When some forces were pushing for Professor Jega to be removed as Chairman of INEC in the run-up to the 2015 on spurious allegations that he had become compromised or for the Jonathan government to use Buhari's certificate controversy to disqualify him from contesting the election, some cautionary voices (including my humble self) opposed such move for their possible unintended effects.

If the story of possible arrest of Jonathan is kite flying, then the government should carefully mull its possible unintended consequences.

Since great leaders emerge in periods of crisis, the challenge for the Buhari regime is to find creative ways of connecting with the various contending social forces and their grievances. We need to transform the rage and anomie in the land into opportunities for conversations.

Daily Trust, May 26, 2016

CHAPTER 45

No Matter how Long you've been Travelling in the Wrong Direction...

There is a saying that no matter how long you have been travelling in the wrong direction, the best solution remains to turn back. This was what came to my mind when I read the story that the government had eventually decided to 'remove' subsidies on premium motor spirits otherwise known as petrol or fuel.

By the time Buhari was sworn in as President on May 29 2015, there had been more or less a consensus that the subsidy regime was a cesspool of corruption and deserved to be done away with. The Farouk Lawan, Aig-Imoukhede and Nuhu Ribadu investigations into various aspects of the oil industry and subsidy regime had revealed mind-boggling corruption. There was therefore a huge expectation that doing away with the subsidy regime would be a priority for the new Buhari government especially as the government came to office with massive goodwill, bountiful legitimacy and the 'blessing' of long queues in filling stations, with fuel selling in many places for more than N200 per litre.

A number of reasons could explain Buhari's inability to act decisively on the issue: he was known to have assiduously opposed subsidy removal under Jonathan, and so could have assumed that to turn around to embrace what he had opposed all along, would undermine his integrity – his key marketing point among his supporters. The President also probably felt that the subsidy regime ran into problem under former President Jonathan because of corruption and that sanitizing the system of corruption could make subsidies on petrol sustainable. There is equally the fact that the majority of his supporters are ordinary Nigerians and he might have felt that any policy that seriously hurts his primary constituency would be an act of betrayal.

The point is that the Buhari regime eventually had to do the 'needful' but in a manner that left bitter taste in the mouth. The announcement of the price hike was more of an ambush – just as the Jonathan administration did in January 2012.

I don't think there is any reason for Buhari to appear apologetic for previously supporting removal of subsidies and then changing his mind later in the light of changing circumstances or new evidence. It is only change that does not change and a person who refuses to change as circumstances change will be called inflexible.

I believe however that the current crisis engendered by the fuel price hike should be another learning curve for the government and an opportunity for deep reflection on its approaches to governance:

One of the lessons the government should learn from the current crisis is not to allow its functionaries to speak in discordant tune – as it does so often on several issues. For instance when on January 18, 2016 the federal government reduced the price of fuel from N97 to N86.50k per litre, it claimed that the reduction was due to an implementation of the revised component of the Petroleum Products Pricing

Template for PMS and household kerosene. The Minister of State for Petroleum Dr Ibe kachukwu was later to announce that fuel subsidy had been removed through some form of ingenuity and that the country was saving $1bn in subsidy removal and $1bn in fuel importation. The government also thumped itself on the chest that "for the first time", our refineries were ready to work, that crude was being pumped from Brass to Port Harcourt, that pipeline was being used for the first time in 10 years and that crude was being pumped to Ilorin for the first time in ten years. Though the announcements did little to shorten the length of the queues in filling stations, they somehow gave the impression that the situation was under control. Dr Ibe also gave several unmet deadlines on when the queues in filling stations would disappear. Then 'gbaaam' came the announcement from the blues that the price of fuel had been increased to N145 per litre. People were understandably furious. The thinking in many people's mind was: Did they not say they had creatively removed fuel subsidy? As if to add to the confusion, the Vice President Professor Yemi Osibanjo claimed that contrary to reports, that the government had not removed any subsidies and that what it did was to withdraw the monopoly hitherto enjoyed by the NNPC to allow free market sales and that the decision was because of the non-availability of foreign exchange for the independent marketers to import fuel. Days after the Vice President's personally signed statement on the new fuel price Dr Ibe appeared to contradict him when he was quoted by Thisday of May 16 as saying that the federal government would have had to cough up N16.4 billion every month to offset the subsidy claims of oil marketers "had it not taken the decision to remove the subsidy on petrol." This pattern of contradictory talks and signals from top officials of the government has been common with this government.

Another important lesson for the government, which goes beyond the issue of removing subsidies but which I believe is creating problems for the regime is its approach for fighting corruption. It is well for the EFCC to thump its chest on the amount of money it claimed it recovered from suspected corrupt individuals. But what the EFCC is unable to tell us is the cost of its 'fight'. Not only do I believe that its system of media trial is de-marketing the country, there is a suspicion that wealthy individuals are unduly being cautious about spending money. Both effects are hurting the economy and Nigerians. I wish the President had honoured his earlier pledge that he would not be unduly concerned with what people did in the past but would look forward. This would not have been incompatible with his determination to recover looted funds. Obasanjo recovered looted funds in the early life of his regime without much ado. The President seemed to have succumbed to those baying for the blood of real and imaginary oppressors.

With labour threatening strike over the fuel price increase and crises suddenly becoming pervasive all over the land amid increasing hardship, the government should consciously make friends and engage with aggrieved groups – rather than revelling in a macho image and setting up numerous social forces against it or regarding voices of dissent as voices of those trying to undermine the regime. Most Nigerians believe the government means well. The government should therefore do more to cultivate even those who oppose it to be able to have the necessary space to leave a lasting legacy.

Military solution alone cannot assuage the issue of grievances, including with insurgency groups like Niger Delta Avengers and Biafra agitators. Related to this is that the government should go soft on the tendency to demonize the former President. History teaches us that the identity that is perceived to be under threat is the one most vociferously defended. In the wake of the 2015 presidential election for instance many analysts warned of possible renewed militancy in the Niger Delta if Jonathan lost and possible prolonged post-election violence in several parts of the North if Buhari lost. A common recommendation to overcome this from many analysts was for whoever won the election to treat the other as a co-winner. This has not happened under this regime. And it does not necessarily mean that the former President should not be made to account for his time in office. But it should be done with respect for the office he occupied. We cannot rule out the possibility that at least part of the causes of the renewed militancy in the region is because of that demonization. It should be recalled that the Yoruba came out to fight for revalidation of Abiola's mandate after an election he won was annulled not necessarily because he was loved by them (he constantly opposed Awolowo, the people's icon) but because that annulment was regarded as a slight on ethnic pride. We know what followed with NADECO and others. We can therefore assume that some of the neo-insurgents in the region are reacting out of a perception that their identity is being maligned. Today neo insurgency activities have reduced oil production from 2.2mbd to barely 1.4 mbd – at a time the country's economy is in dire straits.

While the government deserves credit for carrying the fight to Boko Haram, it will be unhelpful for it to defeat the group only to confront other Boko Harams in other parts of the country.

Daily Trust, May 19, 2016

CHAPTER 46

Does 'who gets what' Really Matter?

The inspiration for this reflection is a robust conversation I had with someone regarding my last week's column. A sub theme in the column was on 'Buhari should look into allegations of northernisation policy'. My friend, let's call him Ahmed, said he was disappointed that someone of "my intellectual calibre", a supposedly "cosmopolitan academic" should concern himself with the petty issue of 'who gets what' in Nigerian politics. He called the politics of 'who gets what, when, how and why' purely an "elite game", since a "poor farmer from Daura, practically gets nothing from coming from the same village as Muhammadu Buhari, the President of the country." He added that, if anything, coming from the same village as Buhari would add to the array of environmental and societal inconveniences the poor farmer suffers such as an added discomfort from traffic congestion and the inevitable ubiquity of security and secret service personnel whenever the President visits. For him therefore, he would not really mind if Buhari appointed all his operatives from Daura provided such people were qualified, are men of integrity and would deliver results. He said he would similarly not have been concerned if former President Jonathan appointed only people from Otuoke. His problem with Jonathan, he said, was that the former President was so grossly incompetent that most of his appointees were mediocre while he lived in awe of the few competent ones.

I agreed with my friend that the politics of 'who gets what', or 'ethnic/regional/religious watching' is an elite game which only benefits the various regional, ethnic , religious and social factions of the same elite. If people from say Anambra, Ekiti or Borno complain that they were left out or 'marginalized' in key federal appointments, they are essentially saying that the factions of the same Nigerian elite from these states had been excluded or marginalized in such appointments, not the ordinary people from those states who would never be appointed to the positions in question.

I elaborated that ethnicity and regionalism and the related 'ethnic/regional/religious watching' only exist in the context of the struggle for scarce socioeconomic resources by the same Nigerian elite. This means that Nigerians are fine when they engage in horizontal relationships – intermarrying, comingling, and conniving to loot the treasury- but not in vertical relationships that deal with citizens' relations with the state and the intra -elite competition for access to critical state resources. And this is why social scientists often point at the colonial urban centres as the cradle of ethnicity – or what some people inappropriately call 'tribalism' in Nigeria. It was in those colonial enclaves that the various ethnic groups for the first time came into intense contact with one another and struggled for the scarce resources from the colonial order such as scholarships or the location of infrastructure by mobilizing ethnic sentiments as veneers to mask the intra-elite character of such struggle. For instance, prior to the formal institution of colonialism, there was no consciousness of being Yoruba, Igbo Ibibio or Hausa/Fulani. It was in the colonial enclaves that such consciousness developed.

The above were the common grounds I shared with Ahmed in his contention that the politics of 'who gets what' and the concomitant 'ethnic/regional and religious watching' is just an elite game that sensible people should not fall for.

My point of divergence with Ahmed is that I went further to argue that even though ethnicity originally existed only in the context of the struggle for the scarce resources moderated through state power, over time, it has acquired an objective character, and exists independent of the original cause. I argued that it is within this context that one should understand ethnic/regional/religious watching in political appointments. It is also within that context that it is wrong to call it 'just an elite game'. In other words, ethnicity/regionalism over time becomes ideological. Ideology typically is like a pair of binoculars through which the people who share the ideology filter information from their political world. As an ideology, ethnic and regional concerns shape the actions of the adherents of the ideology and also provide a guide for their political behaviour.

In the above sense Ahmed was wrong that it does not really matter 'who gets what and when' in the authoritative allocation of values in the society. This is because ethnic/regional watching as an ideology means that perception of marginalization or exclusion by a group fuels a sense of otherness, and with that a proclivity to 'de-Nigerianize' (i.e. de-link from the state and regard the state as an enemy). This is why, in my opinion, it is dangerous to play the politics of 'it is our turn' as it not only undermines the nation-building process but also accentuates the anarchic character of our politics. Twenty years, they say, is not eternity. Those who feel excluded will bide their time to revenge when it gets to their turn.

Let me mention that I am usually suspicious of people who claim to be ethnically and regionally blind or 'de-tribalized' – such as my friend was trying to imply. The truth is that people are emotive about their primordial identities and any identity that is perceived to be under threat is the one most vociferously defended by the people that share such an identity. Therefore anyone telling you that his or her primordial identity does not matter is being less than honest. Being proud of one's primordial identity such as one's ethnic or religious group does not necessarily mean that one is an ethnic, regional or religious bigot. It becomes a problem when it is conflictual in form, that is, when you see the interaction between people of your ethnic, regional and religious identity and others as a zero-sum game – a competition in which 'your people' must either win or lose. When ethnic/regional watchers convince the rest of the in-group that their homeland is under threat by discrimination and marginalization, the hitherto harmless pride in one's ethnicity and regional identity morphs into dangerous bigotry.

One issue I agreed with Ahmed is on the need to find ways of breaking the vicious cycle of the 'politics of our turn' – where the group that captures state power believes it needs to use such power to privilege its in-group or redress the group's perceived historical wrongs. The oft repeated justification for the 'politics of our turn' is that the previous regime did the same –an argument readily bandied around by those defending Buhari against accusations of favouring the North, especially Northern Muslims, in his political appointments. The corollary to this argument is that the next group that captures state power has a right to use state power precisely in the same manner – to privilege its in-group and address the group's perceived historical wrongs against it. I believe that for this country to make any meaningful progress, the country needs to break this vicious cycle.

This is why very early in the Buhari regime some of us were goading him to be a reconciler, a statesman who will reconcile and unite a fractious country, rather than a sheriff brandishing koboko to whip sense into the heads of those suspected of being corrupt. Don't misunderstand me. I am not against fighting corruption. I have been a consistent critic of the style, which is the same 'gra-gra' used by previous governments. I do not believe any of the past efforts at fighting corruption (which assumed that the problem is a simple matter of moral lapses on the part of the corrupt) has worked – otherwise fighting corruption would not have continued to be a big policy plank of all the governments in the country from independence till date.

Though the Buhari government has lost tremendous goodwill since coming to power – and has not helped matters in some ways – I still believe that the President will eventually re-invent himself to play the role of a statesman and a reconciler. Leaders can be radicalized or de-radicalized by system dynamics at any time in their tenure. Intrigues and back-stabbing are the soul of politics. Some will bring out the animal in a leader, other forms of experience in power can humanize the President or change his perspective. I remain hopeful that surrounded by the right people, Buhari may still surprise his critics.

Daily Trust, July 14, 2016

CHAPTER 47

Re-launched WAI and the Dangers of Atavism

It was quite expected that it would happen if he won the Presidency. When he came to power in December 1983 via a military coup, fighting corruption and indiscipline were the regime's signature marks. Hundreds of high profile politicians, businessmen and civil servants were jailed for allegedly being corrupt. Queue culture was forcibly instilled during the early phase of the regime's War Against Indiscipline (WAI), with stern-looking soldiers flogging or taking the laws into their hands to discipline straying bloody civilians.

Buhari's supporters often hailed those moves as part of the efforts at 'sanitizing' the system. They would often reminisce on how Nigeria would have become vastly different today if Buhari was not toppled by the Babangida coup. Fighting corruption and indiscipline are at the core of the Buhari brand.

When the Minister of Information and Culture Lai Mohamed gave notice about plans to re-launch WAI, he said it would be rebranded to 'Change Begins with Me (CBWM)' and that it would aim at instilling public morality, social order and civic responsibilities in Nigerians.

On August 8 2016 the Director General of National Orientation Agency (NOA), Dr. Garba Abari, launched the WAI Brigade. Dr Abari was quoted as saying that the "the body would aid civil intelligence gathering in the area of insecurity, violence, kidnapping, and other forms of social vices". The NOA DG also claimed that the President decided to re-launch the WAI Brigade because it was particularly successful when it was first deployed in 1984 as a way of correcting disorderly conducts of citizens.

I have a few issues with the government's re-launching of WAI:

One, it is not quite clear to me if the new WAI Brigade will be sharing the job of the police and the Department of States Services in gathering intelligence and if so, how that function relates to war against indiscipline? It is also not quite clear to me the nexus between the functions of the WAI Brigade as spelt out by Dr Abari and Lai Mohamed's indication that a re-launched WAI would focus on Change Begins with Me (CBWM), that is to say, on the individual.

Two, proponents of a new WAI seem to forget that Nigeria of the mid 1980s is vastly different from today's Nigeria. For instance it could be argued that at the time Buhari launched WAI in 1984, the country was far less polarized than it is today. The crisis in the country's nation-building had not reached an alarming proportion as it has today, where several individuals and groups are de-linking from the Nigerian state and regarding the state as their enemy. Besides, while at the time of the first WAI Nigerians largely suffered from what the American political scientist Ted Gurr would call relative deprivation (such as when people's aspirations are either rising or constant but the capacity to meet those aspirations are stagnant or declining), today most Nigerians suffer from existential crisis (where people are questioning the very foundation of their lives as a result of lack of hope). Many are unable to see any light at the end of the tunnel. It is therefore questionable whether what people need now is preaching.

Three, the notion that WAI under Buhari's first coming was very successful can be interrogated. Besides the contradiction in a military government (which displayed the highest form of indiscipline by supplanting a democratically elected government) teaching civilians about discipline, Buhari did not stay long enough in power for WAI to be routinized. It is precisely at the stage of routinization of a policy and programme that its robustness is tested.

Four, it could be argued that the decision to bring back WAI – about 32 years after it was first launched- smacks of lack of creativity. The world has vastly changed from what it was in 1984 and 1985. It is like trying to bring back town- criers at a time the revolution in communication technology has rendered such mode of mass communication obsolete.

Five, launching another 'war' when we are yet done or even convincingly winning the many 'wars' the government is currently prosecuting – War Against Corruption', War Against Boko Haram, War Against Pipeline Vandals, War Against Hunger etc – brings to mind the government's rather militaristic approach to issues. There is an implicit but wrong suggestion that society can only be changed through 'war' and coercion. And by the way, not everyone agrees that the regime's identified problems on which it is warring against are actually the real problems. Similarly in this era where hard power is gradually giving way to soft power in the resolution of issues, why is the regime not also considering peace initiatives like launching 'peace ambassadors'? The truth is that 'koboko' approaches that depend on the personality of the President rather than the routinization of law observance, even if they work, will be temporary.

Six, I am among those who believe that Buhari is sincere in his desire to 'fix' Nigeria. But I have issues with some of his strategies. The retired general seems concerned more about outcomes rather than the processes, hence everything is 'war against'. Enduring change often requires a greater focus on processes than on outcomes.

Seven, a big part of the problem of indiscipline is systemic: I do not believe that there is anything in the genetic make-up of Nigerians that make them more undisciplined than people from other parts of the world. People would often behave in accordance with how functional or dysfunctional their system is. For instance if citizens of the so- called advanced countries were to live in a society where nothing works and nothing is guaranteed to work, they will be guaranteed to manifest as much indiscipline as the average Nigerian. This is not to justify indiscipline but to say that there are enabling conditions in the environment that facilitate indiscipline and which must be tackled too. How do you for instance preach to a civil servant who has not received six months' salary not to moonlight or to come regularly to work?

IBB At 75

I was very impressed with the tone of the congratulatory message sent to the former military President, Ibrahim Babangida, by President Buhari. In a message said to be signed personally by the President, he was quoted as saying: "There is hardly any major episode in Nigeria's short history where your name and contribution does not feature." In an interview to *The Interview* magazine recently Buhari reportedly said he was overthrown by the duo of Babangida and Gusau because he was about to probe them. That interview gave the impression that Buhari was still nursing grievances for his ouster from power. The tone of the President's congratulatory message has however doused suggestions of Cold War between them. That was a statesmanlike statement Sir.

I have always believed that despite their shortcomings, Babangida and Obasanjo are the two most cosmopolitan leaders the country has produced. They also arguably understand Nigerians better than most. Their achievements may be overshadowed by their shortcomings but I believe that history will be kind to both men. Happy birthday Sir and May the good Lord grant you many happy years ahead.

The PDP Crisis

Was the police wrong to try to prevent the PDP from holding their convention at the Sharks stadium, Port Harcourt – the initial venue of the convention? The party later reconvened at the Rivers State Secretariat of the PDP on Aba road and held the convention. The police action led to accusing fingers being pointed in different directions, including to the APC, in a typical Nigerian fashion.

Though it is not beneath the APC to mastermind such (as the PDP was also suspected of doing at different times during its 16-year reign), the issue of two courts of co-ordinate jurisdiction giving two contradictory ruling, should really be a matter of the Judicial Council to resolve, not the police. In my opinion, by being proactive to prevent any break down in law and order, the police was doing its duty.

But much has been made of the crisis in the PDP. Such crises are not abnormal in politics. Political parties are essentially aggregations of groupings and tendencies, which compete for influence, power and ascendancy within the party. The APC faces similar challenge – the challenge of managing success and distributing the sinecures of victory. Also politicians are not Mother Theresa. They are political investors who invest in the political processes with the hope of reaping a certain outcome – though these are often cloaked in nationalistic terms. Whatever happens, there is no cause for worry. We should be watching out for the possibility of aggrieved groupings in both the APC and the PDP coming together either to form a new political party or to breathe new lease of life into any of the smaller existing parties such as the Labour Party or APGA.

Daily Trust, August 18, 2016

CHAPTER 48

Rumour-Factualization

"If you tell a lie big enough and been repeating it, people will eventually come to believe it". This was one of the quotes attributed to Joseph Goebbels, Hitler's propaganda chief, though versions of this were also attributed to Lenin and Hitler.

In our country, there are so many lies that have acquired the toga of truth simply because they were repeated often enough. I have called this process 'rumour factualization',

One of these lies or myths (I believe 'myth' sounds more respectable) in the run-up to the 2015 elections in the country was that America predicted that Nigeria would disintegrate in 2015. In an article entitled 'Did America really predict Nigeria will break-up in 2015?', published in the Daily Trust on September 5 2013, I challenged this myth and argued that no such document existed anywhere – even though several people claimed to have read it. I argued that the closest to such prediction was a 17-page report, which was the summary of the outcome of a one-day conference of 'US experts on Africa' convened in January 2005 and sponsored by the country's National Intelligence Council to discuss likely trends in Sub-Saharan Africa over the next 15 years. Though participants in the one-day scenario mapping conference were obviously downbeat about Africa's possibilities within the period under focus, they also discussed what they called 'upside surprises'. I believe that the rumour that America predicted the disintegration of the country in 2015 probably originated from that conference, which was more like futures studies. But the lie that America predicted that the country would disintegrate in 2015 was repeated so often that it acquired the toga of truth – or became 'rumour- factualized'.

Today I will like to interrogate two popular myths that are repeated so often that they are acquiring the toga of facts.

- Previous governments made no efforts to diversify the economy
- Going back to farm is the solution to unemployment and youth restiveness

I am aware that choosing to interrogate the above myths may make me susceptible to accusations of defending the PDP since the above coincidentally are part of the mantras of the government of the day. My honest aim is not to defend or indict any party but to provide contrarian narratives to current discourses. That has been my pattern. In free speech jurisprudence, it is believed that it is only through unfettered and robust exchanges in the marketplace of ideas that the truth will be discovered. In any case, I have always set for myself three rules of responsible column writing: Have I done my research? Am I expressing an opinion earnestly held? Am I using respectful and sensitive language? Since I have ticked the three boxes, I feel I should interrogate these myths despite the risks of being labelled.

Previous governments made no efforts to diversify the economy

A very common mantra these days is that Nigeria is a monocultural economy and that past governments made no efforts to diversify the economy, which made the country susceptible to the vagaries of oil fortune in the global oil market. I believe this is only partially true.

A lot of information about the structure of the Nigerian economy came out in 2013 when the country re-based its GDP. After the rebasing, the revised GDP for 2013 became N80.2 trillion (or US$509.9 billion) –an increase of about 89 per cent based on the old GDP estimates for 2013 which was N42.4 trillion (or US$269.5 billion). True the new GDP numbers only mean that we were measuring our economic activities better, not that we became rich overnight. But the rebasing clearly showed that the country's economy is more diversified than previously reported and that the structure of the Nigerian economy has also changed significantly. For instance while previously agriculture accounted for 33% of GDP and services accounted for 26 per cent, with the rebasing, it was found that agriculture accounted for only 22 per cent of GDP while the services sector increased to 51 per cent of GDP. The services sector covers activities such as transportation, information and communications, arts and entertainment, financial and insurance services, real estate, public administration, education and health services. The rebased figures also showed that oil & gas accounted for 15.9 per cent, manufacturing 6.7 per cent, telecoms 8.7 per cent and Nollywood 1.2 per cent. Prior to the rebasing, the contribution of crude oil and natural gas to the nominal GDP was 40.86 per cent in 2011, 37.01 per cent in 2012 and 32.43 per cent in 2013. The entertainment industry, as typified by Nollywood, was not previously seen as a significant contributor to the GDP.

Based on the above, though oil remains the country's main source of revenue and chief foreign exchange earner, it is not actually correct to argue that the economy has not diversified or that no effort has been made in the past to diversify the economy. In Saudi Arabia, OPEC's largest producer, the oil and gas sector accounts for 48 per cent of the GDP. Qatar's oil and natural gas account for about 55 per cent of the GDP

Again, in the discussion of the diversification of the country's economy, there is often a tendency to narrow diversification to agriculture and solid minerals. It is often said that the country is blessed with 44 solid minerals in commercial quantities across the length and breadth of the country. I believe it is important to look at diversification beyond replacing one natural resource with another or even increasing the number of the resources in the basket. Just like oil is said to be the devil's excrement, so is the fortune of any commodity, including agricultural products, unpredictable. In fact unlike oil which has the OPEC cartel, several commodities do not even have a cartel to help them shore up prices in periods of low demands.

Based on the above, it is not exactly true to say previous governments have not made any efforts at diversification when the successes of the banking, telecoms and entertainment sectors are all too glaring.

Going back to farm is the solution to unemployment and youth restiveness

It is common these days to read repeated mantras urging the youth and unemployed people to go back to agriculture. Agriculture is also held up as a potential source of huge foreign exchange earnings – especially with the current weak earnings from oil.

I have issues with this. For instance the assumption that agriculture will boost our foreign exchange earnings seems exaggerated because before you can earn foreign currency, you must have exported something. Though we have exportable crops like cocoa, cashew nuts and palm fruits, many of these are not easily exportable because of the existence of non-tariff barriers in the potentially importing countries. Besides, these crops are at the mercy of the buyers who determine the prices at which they want to buy. Agricultural produce face the same, if not worse, boom and bust cycles as oil.

In the same vein, asking all young and unemployed people to go into farming (actually peasant farming) is to wrongly suggest that these young people do not have their own dreams. It could be argued that a big part of the crisis among young and unemployed people is what the American political scientist Ted Gurr would call 'Relative Deprivation'. This is the tension between your actual state and what you feel you should be able to achieve. It is, as Gurr would put it, the "perceived discrepancy between value expectations and value capabilities." Following from this, I am not sure it would work asking a young man who dreams of being a computer programmer to embrace farming that he absolutely has no interest in. In any case how many of the return-to-farm advocates are preaching the same to their own children?

My other issue with the current glorification of farming is that it seems to represent forward to the past. The truth is that as countries develop, the share of the population working in agriculture starts to decline. This explains why less than 5 per cent of the population in the rich countries are engaged in agriculture while more than 60 per cent of the population in poor countries are in agriculture. Remarkably through technological advances, the small percentage in agriculture in developed countries produces more than enough for their country's population. The target in agriculture should therefore be how to achieve huge productivity increase through mechanised farming, not for everyone to return to agriculture, regardless of whether they are interested in farming or not.

Daily Trust, September 15, 2016

ECONOMY

CHAPTER 49

Debating the Nigerian Economy

Nobel laureate Wole Soyinka, who has become a sort of deity to several functionaries of the APC-led federal government, raised the stakes when he called for an "emergency economic conference" to find ways of fixing the economy. During a visit to the Minister of Information and Culture Lai Mohammed in mid February this year, Professor Soyinka was quoted as saying: "Recovery is going to take quite a while...the President should call an emergency economic conference, with experts to be invited. Consumers, producers, labour unions, university experts, professors, etc.

"I think we really need an emergency economic conference, a rescue operation bringing as many heads as possible together to plot the way forward" (Sahara Reporters, February 18 2016). There are rumours that President Buhari has hearkened to the call by Soyinka for the economy to be debated and that a formal debate on the economy will be organized any time from now.

I have issues with this.

One, implicit in the call for the economy to be debated is an innuendo that managing the economy is beyond the capacity of the President and his team which therefore necessitates a need to broaden the pool of talents that will debate and hopefully agree on the magic elixir for the country's economic woes. As Professor Soyinka is uncharacteristically too soft on the Buhari government, the innuendo is being stretched even further by Buhari's critics who suggest that Soyinka's call for an economic conference is a polite vote of no-confidence on the APC-led federal government.

For others, especially members of the civil society, Soyinka's call has animated them into calling on President Buhari to quickly constitute his economic team. The question shifted to the 'capacity' of the President's economic team when Mr Laolu Akande , the Senior Special Assistant to the Vice President on Media and Publicity revealed that contrary to what some people think, the President does indeed have an economic team, which he said had been put in place since the inauguration of the Federal Executive Council (FEC) last November.

Two, the call for a debate on the economy implies wrongly that we have not been debating the economy. The truth is that we have been debating the government and its policy options right from its inception on May 29 2015. Opinion writers, newspaper editorials and columnists have been taking various positions on the government's policy options – from the Treasury Single Account (TSA), to whether the naira should be devalued or not through government's proposals for school feeding and to pay unemployed graduates a monthly stipend of N5,000. If these robust interrogations of the government's policy options are not debating the economy, what should we call them?

Three, instituting a formal debate on the economy could create additional problems for the Buhari government. True, there could be momentary respite for the government because its most ardent critics are likely to focus on hijacking and framing the debate. Here it is important to learn the lessons from Babangida's attempts to democratize the debate on whether the country should embrace the IMF/World Bank supported facilities in the mid 1980s. Largely because there was no official attempt to frame the debate (assuming such was possible), street populism triumphed and it was quickly wrongly framed as whether the Nigeria should "take IMF loan or not". The overwhelming populist response was that Nigeria "should not take the loan". People said they were ready to make sacrifices including making financial contributions in lieu of the government taking the loan. But the truth is that the issue at that time was not about the IMF loan per se but securing the imprimatur of the two Bretton Woods institutions on the country's economic programme. The imprimatur of the IMF and the World Bank on a country's economic programme had become a condition for even rescheduling a country's debt or opening new letters of credit. This was the so-called notion of 'cross-conditionalities'. When therefore Babangida, who really had no choice, eventually embraced the IMF/World Bank facility in 1986 despite the outcome of the formal debate on the issue, his critics counted the debate as another act of deception or one of the regime's 'Maradonic' moves against Nigerians. What is most likely to happen if a formal debate is organized is that the vocal minority and civil society activists will hijack the debate and frame it as they want. What if the recommendation from such a debate ends up asking the President to sack all his Ministers or even for him to resign?

Four, the call for the economy to be debated may in some ways be an expression of nostalgia for Obasanjo's Second Coming. Obasanjo had in 2003 established an economic reform group that became known as the 'Dream Team'. The team was made up of bold and confident technocrats who enjoyed Obasanjo's unfettered political cover. The team was led by Ngozi Okonjo-Iweala, the Minister for Finance who was recruited from the World Bank. He was complemented by a crop of erudite academics. While no one doubted that several members of the team were accomplished, it is not clear how they would have performed if they had not enjoyed as much political cover as they got from Obasanjo. Therefore any criticism of President Buhari's economic team must also include a qualifier on whether members of the team have sufficient elbow-room to take risks. Rather than a formal debate on the economy, the members of his economic team need more elbow room to take risks. The debate on the economy should be between them and relevant think-tanks and consultants. They can of course invite relevant groups for inputs and advice or bounce off ideas on the public. It should not be an all-comers' affair.

Five, while I believe Obasanjo is clearly the best leader the country has produced so far – despite what one columnist called "his lack of grace" - it should be borne in mind that his first few years in office were dogged by the sort of despair that some people now have about the Buhari government. For instance when Obasanjo increased the minimum wage to N7,500 on May 1 2000 without first examining the capacity of states to pay, the country erupted into agitations and strikes for almost a year. There were also sectional grumblings and agitations against the government, including from some northern state governors that decided to introduce Sharia law and also from Odi and Zaki Ibiam. It took Obasanjo a few years to take full control of his government.

Though I am one of the critics of the Buhari regime I do not believe the regime is beyond redemption. As I pointed out elsewhere, it takes a while after an aircraft has taken off before it can to get to a cruising height. Buhari is still full of unsustainably high energy levels and still has many political IOUS to settle. Eventually these will settle down and he will find his bearing provided he is willing to learn from his initial missteps and mistakes.

Buhari's foreign trips

Buhari's foreign trips have continued to generate intense debates. A crucial rhetorical question posed by the President supporters is whether a President needs to be at home to solve the country's problems. His supporters justify the trips on grounds that the President's foreign trips are necessary to attract foreign investments and broker agreements on repatriating looted funds. Buhari's critics also have their own rhetorical question: Does a President, in this era of revolutions in information technology, need to be undertaking so many foreign trips to accomplish the said objectives? The truth is that a President's foreign trips do not come cheap. For a president whose frugal ambience helped to propel him to Aso Rock, it is very important that he is not seen as enjoying himself while the generality of the masses are suffering and are being urged constantly to have patience or make more sacrifices. Perception is everything in politics.

Daily Trust, March 3, 2016

CHAPTER 50

Currency Crisis, Gloomy Economy and
Hidden Opportunities

The times are hard. There is a consensus that the economy has tanked – at least in the short term. The naira has lost much of its value in the real (or parallel) forex market. As usual we bicker on who is to blame. Overlooked in the finger pointing is the old cliché that necessity is the mother of invention and that every crisis creates its own opportunities. As Thomas Edison, the American inventor and business man would say, opportunity is missed by most people because it is generally dressed in overalls and looks like work. Peter Drucker, the Austrian-born American management consultant would say that the entrepreneur always searches for change, responds to it and exploits it as an opportunity. The Nigerian bus conductor would remind us that Nigeria is tough but that those who live in it are made of iron. The American author Napoleon Hill would say that our opportunity may be right where we are. The crucial question therefore is beyond the economic gloom, how do we partake in the available opportunities created by the current currency crisis and the gloomy economic outlook?

The first consolation is that we are not alone in what APC politicians like to call 'the mess we are in'. The truth is that it is simplistic to blame the PDP for all that has gone wrong in the country, including the current economic crisis. Ironically by framing the current economic crisis as a PDP legacy, there is an expectation that an APC government headed by a man that is generally believed not to be corrupt will fix things quickly. And because this has not happened and is not likely to happen overnight, there is an increasing frustration that is already morphing into legitimacy crisis in some quarters. Like those who blame all our problems, including the inability of some women to find husbands and some men to find wives on the past government, expectations that Buhari has a sort of magic wand to fix our problems overnight are also simplistic.

The truth is that several countries are seriously hurting. All exporting economies – whether they are exporting manufactured goods or simply commodities as we do are not finding things easy. For instance exporters of manufactured goods such as China are suffering because of the weakness in Europe and to a lesser degree the USA. Mineral and oil exporters have been particularly hard hit because of declining commodity prices.

In a very incisive article in the Geopolitical Futures of January 26 2016 entitled, 'The Export Crisis: The 10 Worst Hit Countries and the 5 Most at Risk', George Friedman ranked Nigeria the eighth worst affected behind China, Russia, Saudi Arabia, South Korea, Australia, Zambia and Angola in that order. Like Nigeria, Russia is heavily dependent on its oil revenues, with oil and gas accounting for about 70 per cent of total export revenues. It is often said that Russia loses about $2 billion in revenue for every dollar fall in the oil price. In Venezuela, which relies on crude sales for roughly 96 percent of its exports and more than half of the country's gross domestic product, it is estimated that for every dollar off the price of oil, the government loses as much as $700 million in estimated revenues a year. Though it is estimated that we need oil prices of about $119 a barrel to balance our budget, oil prices currently straddle between $39 and $40 per barrel. It is therefore obvious that much of the current economic challenge is caused by external shock. My argument is not that PDP did not get a few things wrong or that Buhari's and CBN's economic policies are beyond reproach. My argument rather is that insufficient weight is given to the international context of the current crisis and that not enough attention is paid to the opportunities created by the crisis.

While some companies are already grabbing these opportunities with both hands most of us remain the 'wailing wailers'. For instance the Deputy Managing Director of Tempo Pulp & Packaging Ltd, Nassos Sidirofagis, a Greek national who runs a manufacturing firm in Nigeria was quoted by the Vanguard of January 26 2016 as saying that due to the CBN's demand management policies that included the banning of the importation of 41 items, local patronage has increased, leading to a 70 per cent increase in capacity utilization. For Mr Sidirofagis, the CBN's policy was the "game changer because as a Nigerian company, we are also competing globally and locally".

It is within the above context that the current 'Made in Nigeria' campaign should be located. The Senate President Bukola Saraki recently promised that the National Assembly would support locally produced items including garments, wears and cars. He also promised that the Public Procurement Act would be amended by the 8th National Assembly to make it mandatory for the government to patronize 'Made in Nigeria' goods. In the same vein, Aisha Abubakar, the Minister of state for Trade, Industry and Investment has proposed a 'Patronize Naija Product Campaign', as a way of encouraging local manufacturers. Equally, Ben Bruce, 'the Common Sense' Senator has created a hashtag: #BuyNaijatoGrowtheNaira to trump support for locally made goods. Senator Bruce and some members of the National Assembly have gone a step further by purchasing Made in Nigeria cars. The wife of the President Muhamadu Buhari, Hajiya Aishat Buhari, equally keyed into the 'Made in Nigeria' train. Recently she commissioned the Erisco Foods Lagos Factory. The factory is said to be the largest tomato paste factory in Africa and the fourth largest in the world with installed capacity of 450,000 metric tonnes per annum.

Elite-led campaign for locally made goods is all well and good. But more needs to be done beyond the rhetoric, grandstanding, photo-op and our instinctive search for new mantras and catch-phrases as the magic elixirs to our problems. I will recommend the following:

One, the government should define what it means by 'Made in Nigeria'. Since many 'locally manufactured' products even in the industrialized economies still have substantial foreign inputs, we need to know what percentage of locally sourced materials must be in place for a product to be called 'Made in Nigeria' It is important not to mistake local re-packaging or assembling for local manufacture. The government will then design different incentive packages for companies with certain percentages of local content.

Two, for Nigerians to maximally take advantage of the opportunities in the current economic challenges or for the Made-in-Nigeria Campaign to work, credit must be available at affordable rate to local producers. In this connection the CBN needs to take a second look at the current nine per cent cost of borrowing policy from commercial banks to manufacturers. It also needs to fast track the commencement of operations by the recently established Development Bank of Nigeria, which is dedicated to industrial development.

Three, a big challenge for most policies in Nigeria is sustainability. Though some people mentioned as belonging to Buhari's Economic Management team are honestly uninspiring, once economic policies have been thoroughly debated by those competent to do so and a decision is taken, the government should avoid quick reversals. This is different from being inflexible which happens when one clings to a course of action even against superior argument or evidence that the chosen path is not working. Since every new policy is expected to disadvantage some of the current beneficiaries, a fight-back using different tools, channels and tactics should be expected. This is where the ability of the President to provide maximum political cover to those who are fronting the policy becomes an imperative. Certainly without Obasanjo's generous political cover, El-Rufai's restoration of the Abuja Masterplan or Soludo's bank consolidation would not have been possible.

Four, though the debate on whether the naira should be devalued or not is both complex and largely ideological (each option has its merits and downsides), what is not in doubt is that there is need for measures to bridge the gap between the official and parallel market rates. The Nation newspaper of 27 February 2016 reported that the CBN is targeting a N200 per dollar rate for the parallel market. It also claims that the CBN has the capacity to sustain the current downward pressure on the major foreign currencies and that the apex bank's aim is "to ensure that the divergence between the official and parallel rate does not exceed N3". Certainly if the CBN is able to do this, the debate on whether the Naira should be devalued or not will become a moot point because the black market is the 'real' foreign exchange market. It also means that the temptation for arbitrage and round tripping by those fortunate enough to get foreign currency at the official exchange rate will be reduced.

CHAPTER 51

Recession: Is the Worst Really Over?

With Nigerians waddling through what is generally regarded as the country's worst economic crisis in over two decades, the CBN Governor, Godwin Emefiele, has just dangled what some would regard as a ray of hope to suffering Nigerians. Speaking while playing host to members of the Newspaper Proprietors Association of Nigeria recently, the CBN Governor reportedly told them that Nigerians had seen the worst of the economic crisis and that the economy would be fully out of recession by December this year and would be on a part of growth. The apex bank governor was quoted as saying: "I repeat, the worst is over, Nigeria's economy is on the path of recovery and growth. If you are a bystander, you are losing... join the train now before it leaves you."

The first impulse is to yawn. We have heard this sort of apparently 'unfounded optimism' several times before from government officials, haven't we? Governments at every level in this country have a penchant for claiming that their policies are the magic elixir that would usher the elusive el Dorado that their predecessors in office failed to actualize. I believe that bogus promises are among the reasons for the deep distrust of governments across the world. In countries like the US, this distrust of government is one of the bases for their fierce defence of the freedom of speech. One of the arguments of free speech advocates is that it is only through unfettered competition of ideas in the political marketplace and the freedom to 'interrogate all interrogatables' that the truth can emerge. So can Emefiele's bold assertion that the worst is over hold up to scrutiny?

One of the bases for the CBN Governor's optimism is his claim that the liberalisation of the foreign exchange (Forex) market had begun to pay off. He claimed that the country had recorded $1 billion capital inflows from foreign investors since the market took off almost three months ago. In our highly import dependent economy, there is no doubt that the forex crisis (typified by the massive depreciation in the value of the naira against the major currencies) is both a cause and effect of the economic crisis. So a cynic can legitimately ask: if there has been inflow of over $1bn dollars since the liberalization of the forex why has the naira not begun appreciating or stabilizing in value? Another legitimate question is whether the disparity between the official exchange rate and the parallel market rate has not created a huge opportunity for arbitrage and round-tripping, which in turn are disincentives for investing in the productive sectors of the economy? Supporters of the CBN would counter that the policy is still working through the system and that the apex Bank is working on the unintended consequences of that liberalisation. The point to be noted here however is that every major policy often holds good opportunities of turning things around just as its unintended consequences could also derail such a policy – no matter how sound such a policy may be at the theoretical level.

Despite legitimate grounds for scepticisms over the government's claims, I have some grounds for sharing in the CBN's optimism:

One is the apparent increasing self confidence of the CBN Governor. This is typified by the decision to hold the interest rate unchanged at 14 per cent – despite criticisms, including from very influential quarters,(such as the Finance Minister who publicly called for a cut in the interest rate) that such is undermining the need for the private sector to secure loans at cheap rates to reflate the economy. In the past the CBN indulged in many policy somersaults – often abandoning policies once they came under barrage of criticisms – rather than having the nerve to see such policies work through the system. Though no one can be very sure in an environment like ours with many intervening variables if any policy introduced would work or not, I see the decision of the CBN Governor not to lower the interest rate as demonstrating a new found confidence and therefore commendable. It is also possible he had just secured more legroom to operate. In holding the MPR steady at 14 percent (the MPR is the rate at which the CBN lends to commercial banks and often determines the cost of funds in the economy), the CBN argued that to further lower the rate would worsen inflationary conditions. It also argued that in the past the MPC had cut rates to encourage lending to the private productive sectors but found that rather than the banks using the available liquidity to provide credit to agriculture and manufacturing sectors, the rate cuts only "provided opportunities for lending to traders who deployed the same liquidity in putting pressure on the foreign exchange market which had limited supply thus pushing up the exchange rate." On the argument that cutting interest rate would help the public sector to borrow at lower rates to boost consumption and investment spending, the CBN argued that "while it was expected to stimulate growth through aggressive spending, doing so without corresponding efforts to boost industrial output by taking actions to deepen foreign exchange supply for raw materials will not help reduce unemployment, nor would it boost industrial capacity."

I am not so much persuaded by the CBN's arguments as by the confidence displayed – given the calibre of the critics of the CBN's interest rate policy (I was one of the critics). The CBN also told the newspaper owners that it would take more than managing monetary policies to get the country out of recession and called on the fiscal authorities to improve fiscal activities "especially the active implementation of the 2016 Federal Budget and payment of salaries by states and local governments". The apex bank equally called for tax incentives to stimulate both the supply and demand sides of economic activities.

I feel that the Finance Minister and the CBN having divergent views in public on interest rates is healthy – though it would have been better if they had debated their positions behind closed doors and reconciled such. What this seems to suggest however is that the two authorities are beginning to find their voices. A few months ago, this would probably not have happened.

Two, another source of optimism for me is the apparent increasing realisation by the President that he has no magic wand that will solve the country's economic problems overnight and that there are limitations to what his charisma (or famed body language) could do. This is evident in some of the noticeable changes about him. For instance he is no longer vocally critical of devaluation of the Naira. More importantly, he was reportedly praised by Obama for the country's new forex policy. And Nigerian leaders love it when they are praised by leaders of the major world powers, especially by leaders of the USA and the UK! The cumulative impact of these may be that the President will become less meddlesome in affairs of the Bank as the media often accused him of doing. This will in turn give both the monetary and fiscal authorities more room to engage in robust idea exchanges.

Three, there is also evidence that the President is gradually softening his politics and rhetoric – even if slowly. I had in one of my articles argued that some of our current economic challenges are in part the economic manifestations of the president's hard politics. Some of his politics such as his approach to the Niger Delta issue and his government's constant demonization of former President Jonathan arguably helped to create the Avengers whose activities in turn helped to cut the country's oil production at a time of low prices. As the President softens his politics, it is likely to impact positively on some of the underlying political bases of the current economic crisis. I have argued variously that system dynamics would eventually humanize the President and turn him into a statesman.

Four, another major source of optimism for me is the resilience of Nigerians and their adaptability to circumstances. The country has since adapted to hanging perpetually on the cliff. While the country is often said to be tough, Nigerians pride themselves in being made of malleable irons. Nigerians survived the IMF/World Bank imposed structural adjustment programme of the mid 1980s and early 1990s. Already there are emerging coping strategies to the current economic crisis.

Five, while some of the CBN's positions such as its support for the partial sale of some state assets will remain controversial – given the experiences of such asset disposals under Obasanjo – the logic of life would seem to support its assertion that he who is down needs not fear further fall. As the CBN Governor put it: "We are already in the valley, the only direction is to go up to the hill and government is doing everything possible to move up the hill as quickly as possible."

Daily Trust, September 22, 2016

CHAPTER 52

Beyond the Corruption Stories

Corruption stories have been the dominant theme of governance since the Buhari government came into being more than eight months ago. In many ways this is not surprising. His candidacy was marketed on his well-known integrity and apparent incorruptibility. Buhari was also reported to have said that he would like to be remembered as a President who fought corruption to a standstill.

One of the most recent of the corruption stories is the one from the Minister of Information Lai Mohammed who was reported as saying that about 55 persons looted N1.3 trillion in seven years. To lend credibility to these figures the Minister sought to speak with the specificity of a statistician by breaking the figures down:

"15 former governors allegedly stole N146.84 billion; four former ministers allegedly stole N7 billion; 12 former public servants, both at federal and state levels, were said to have stolen N14 billion. Apart from public officials, 19 persons in banking and business were indicted in this looting. Eight of these were banking officials who allegedly stole N524 billion, and 11 businessmen who helped themselves to the tune of N653 billion."

Not to be out-done, the Economic and Financial Crimes Commission was also reported to have said that the country recovered more than $2 trillion that had been looted from the national treasury over the last twelve years. Dasukigate and the alleged $2.1 billion meant for arms procurement which was reportedly shared among friends and cronies is now an old tale.

Apart from the question of the veracity of the above huge figures, there are several unanswered questions around these apparently unending corruption stories: What is the real reason for these corruption stories? Is it to de-market the PDP? Or to mobilize a sense of outrage against impunity? Or to appropriate a moral high ground by playing the ostrich? Is it because the APC-led government is truly enraged by the cases of corruption it met on the ground? Or is it because corruption stories are the government's comfort zone?

Largely because the country is deeply polarized it is highly unlikely that Nigerians will ever agree on why corruption stories have completely drowned other conversations on how to resolve other compelling challenges that the country faces.

Anyone conversant with my writings will obviously know I have been a consistent critic of the system of fighting corruption in the country - from as far back as the days of Nuhu Ribadu's EFCC. There are a number of issues to ponder about in the current corruption stories:

One, is corruption really the fundamental problem of the country? I have never believed so. It is more a symptom of a more fundamental problem. I have consistently argued that what the country needs more than anything else is reconciliation and re-energizing the nation-building process because unless this is done, any solution thrown at the country's numerous problems will only quickly become part of the problems. Is it then any wonder that some are already sneering at the current corruption fight as being selective? Selectivity is of course embedded in any form of fight against corruption in our type of society because no government will realistically be expected to move against its core supporters and sponsors. This creates a big room for those currently being accused of corruption – including those who know that they are guilty as charged - to use 'selective justice' and 'persecution' to turn themselves into heroes and heroines as soon a new government replaces this one. That has been the standard practice in the country's history of fighting corruption.

Meanwhile, while we are regaling in the numerous corruption stories foreign news headlines create a profile of a country on the verge of implosion. For instance the highly influential bi-monthly Foreign Policy Magazine of 8 February 2016 titled its story on Nigeria: 'Nigeria Is Coming Apart at the Seams'. Similarly Wikistrat, the crowd-outsourcing consulting firm (founded in Australia in 2009 but headquartered in the United States) recently opened a forum on Nigeria, which it titled 'Nigeria: From Opportunity to Crisis'. A key question we must ask ourselves therefore is whether the numerous corruption stories are accentuating a certain negative profile of the country in the international imagination. Put differently, are we unwittingly de-marketing the country with these corruption stories and the fantastic figures of stolen money being bandied about?

Two, is also the question of what we have benefited from the corruption stories? How many people have been convicted as a result of the corruption stories? Have we really established the necessary frameworks for fighting corruption? What became of the idea of corruption courts that were mooted several months ago? Have we defined what we mean by corruption and separated it from impunity?

Three, the corruption stories raise the question of the place of 'name and shame' or media trial in a country like ours. Why are 'ordinary people' fascinated by such corruption stories that will at least show that the super-rich are only rich at their expense? Does name and shame really deter corruption in a country like ours? If so, why is it that 'budget rats' are being accused of padding the 2016 budget proposal despite the current corruption stories and the no-nonsense mien of the President on matters of corruption?

Four, there are legitimate fears that the promotion of competitive stories of corruption may be turning the regime into a single issue government. In the process, the country is missing an opportunity for earnest conversations on how to find solutions to her other and even more compelling challenges. For instance most of the current Ministers are made to look 'ordinary' because the hot stories are about corruption. They do not seem to have enough space to engage the public on what they do or want to do for their ministries. Compare this with the Obasanjo era and even under Jonathan when some Ministers were allowed to become 'celebrities' who could bounce off ideas on the populace. Who are the 'celebrity' ministers in this dispensation?

Five, while the corruption stories may, at least in part, be aimed at mobilizing the citizens' sense of outrage against impunity, the steady stream of such stories can also paradoxically numb that sense of outrage. For instance, with the humongous sums being mentioned in the corruption stories, if you come across a story where one is sentenced to a jail term for stealing say N2m, the instinctive feeling is that the punishment is disproportionate to the crime. Suddenly N2m seems like a peanut compared to the figures that are being bandied around in the steady stream of corruption stories.

Six, the country needs to do an impact analysis of the previous efforts at fighting corruption? How do you know if we are winning the war? It is wrong to assume that just because you have scared those prone to corruption to go underground, that you are winning. In the same way, the amount of money recovered by the contraptions used in fighting corruption may be important but hardly a reliable metric for measuring the success or otherwise of any fight against corruption. The metric should be: has it lessened the incidence of corruption? Unfortunately such a question cannot be answered by any regime waging such a war because our experience is that it is the succeeding regime that determines how corrupt the preceding regime was.

I am not against fighting corruption. I will however have preferred a conditional amnesty (you can call it plea bargaining) for those facing certain cases of corruption allegation. Those who have committed impunity will simply have to face trial quietly. Media trial and politicising the fight against corruption ends up polarizing the country the more. We can still achieve the same objective without the unnecessary 'gra gra' and a narrative that is couched on the simplistic binary of 'good guys versus the bad guys'.

Daily Trust, February 10, 2016

CHAPTER 53

Nigeria in MINT: Time for a New Swagger?

It has been a flourish of good news for the country, especially in sports and on the economy fronts: In football, the Super Eagles under Keshi have been doing so well (despite their drop in FIFA ranking) that many Nigerians believe that Nigeria winning the World Cup in Brazil this year is not just a pipe or malaria-induced dream. There was equally the 2013 class of the Golden Eaglets under Manu Garba, (regarded by many Nigerians as the best ever in that category from Nigeria), which won the Under-17 World Cup Competition in the United Arab Emirate last year. The come-back victory against Morocco by the home-based Eagles at the ongoing African Nations Championships, CHAN, in South Africa, has been attributed to that resilience of the Nigerian spirit. The Team B Super Eagles were down 3-0 in the first half of the game only to come from behind to win 4-3.

On the economy, though most Nigerians do not seem to feel it, if the plethora of foreign endorsements is anything to go by, the economy is growing well, if not doing well. The most celebrated of these external endorsements in recent times is the inclusion of the country in the MINT emerging economies.

MINT is a neologism referring to the economies of Mexico, Indonesia, Nigeria and Turkey. The term was originally coined by the Boston-based asset management firm Fidelity and popularized by the British economist Jim O'Neil, a former Goldman Sachs analyst, who had in 2011, coined the acronym BRIC to refer to the economies of Brazil, Russia, India and China. BRIC was later turned to BRICS when South Africa was bracketed into the group.

What is instructive about the four countries listed in the MINT club is that they are all members of the Next Eleven (also known as the N-11). The N-11 are eleven countries – Bangladesh, Egypt, Indonesia, Iran, Mexico, Nigeria, Pakistan, Philippines, Turkey, South Korea, and Vietnam – identified by Jim O'Neill in a research paper on December 12 2005 as having a high potential of becoming, along with the BRICs, the world's largest economies in the 21st century. At the end of 2011, the top four countries in the N-11 – Mexico, Indonesia, South Korea and Turkey (also known as MIKT) made up 73 percent of all Next Eleven GDP. The combined GDP of the BRIC economies is $13.5 trillion compared to MIKT's $3.9 trillion. MINT simply means that Nigeria has taken over South Korea's spot in MIKT.

To add to the current wave of Naija-optimism, Filipino billionaire, Enrique Razon, was recently quoted by Daily Newswatch as declaring during the closing activities at the recent World Economic Forum in Davos, Switzerland, that Nigeria is the best place to invest in 2014. Razon, who controls a $4.7 billion fortune, according to the Bloomberg Billionaires Index, has reportedly signed a deal to develop and operate a port in Lagos, Nigeria, by 2016, investing $225 million in the venture. He is walking the talk. In recent years, Nigeria has been the darling of frontier investors due to attractive yields and a steady currency.

What can we make of this unprecedented wave of Naija-optimism, especially the recent inclusion of the country in the MINT emerging economies? There are a number of observations:

One, the countries aggregated in the club share certain features in common. For instance all are populous countries, with a preponderance of young people. The average age of the population in Nigeria for instance is 18 and 27 in Mexico compared for instance to the United Kingdom where the average age is 40. Members of MINT are also strategically located: Indonesia is the heart of Southeast Asia, Mexico benefits from proximity to the USA, Turkey is located at the intersection between the Middle East and the West and has attributes from both divides while Nigeria is probably the most buoyant illustration of a rising African continent. Economically, three members of the MINT Club - Mexico, Indonesia and Nigeria - are commodity producers and only Turkey isn't. This contrasts with the BRIC countries where two - Brazil and Russia - are commodity producers and the other two - China and India - aren't.

Two, MINT countries are also very different in several respects: In terms of wealth, Mexico and Turkey are at about the same level, earning annually about $10,000 (£6,100) per head. This compares with $3,500 (£2,100) per head in Indonesia and $1,500 (£900) per head in Nigeria. They also differ widely in the quality of education in their countries, the level of development in infrastructure and social services, the life expectancy and the ease of doing business in the countries – among others.

Three, MINT countries face varying political and economic challenges. For instance as woeful as the country's economic condition may appear, Nigeria is the only MINT economy running a current account surplus -- US$5,016 million in the second quarter of 2013. There are leadership and economic challenges in Indonesia and political issues in Turkey. In essence, we shall not just focus on the numerous challenges the country faces to doubt her potential to 'make it' or even the wisdom of including the country in such a club. Challenges and opportunities often sit side by side. In other words, we shall look beyond the debate of whether we deserve being in MINT to assessing the opportunities and threats that come with such inclusion.

I see a number of opportunities and challenges from such inclusion:

On the positive side, the MINT acronym might induce the members to develop their own economic-political club – just as the BRIC countries did. There will be obvious benefits from such networking, including the self-fulfilling prophecy bit of it. If the MINT countries start working collaboratively and conspiratorially as the next big economic powerhouses as they are tipped to be, they will be seen by the rest of the world as such. Perception could be everything.

Also the inclusion of Nigeria among the MINT economies could spur the country to struggle to become a member of the G20 – as other MINT economies are already.

In fact Nigeria's inclusion in the MINT economies increases the chances that it will be accepted into the G20 because, as mentioned earlier, perception is everything.

The inclusion of the country in MINT may also affect the character of the country's domestic politics. Largely because people instinctively want to identify with success, the inclusion may temper the pull of the centrifugal forces and pacify irredentist pressures as separatist tendencies may have to contend with the fear of leaving at a time the country is being tipped as among the likely future economic power houses of the world.

The flipside to the above however is that the country's inclusion in MINT could also intensify the crisis of relative deprivation in the country. In other words, it could deepen the current frustration among many people in the country. The thinking for some could be: 'if Nigeria is doing this well, and the benefits are not trickling down to me, then it is either the government or a few individuals or ethnic group are cornering the benefits at my expense'. Simply put, Nigeria's inclusion in MINT also embeds a probability of an intensification of the 'scape-goating' of others.

The inclusion of the country in MINT could equally deepen the current anti-Nigerianism among many Africans. Already, our unilateral declaration of our country as the 'Giant of Africa' and reflecting same in the swagger in which we walk as well as the condescending manner in which we talk to other Africans, has not made us the darling of fellow Africans. The fear is that the inclusion of Nigeria in MINT could increase the swagger in our walks even more and make some of us even louder and more condescending towards others than previously, fuelling in the process anti-Nigerian sentiments. True, Nigerians' self-confidence, which often wrongly manifests in superiority complex towards other Africans, has been identified as one of the reasons why they are among the most successful minority groups in such countries as USA and the UK. However we cannot get very far if other Africans do not think much of us largely because of our arrogance and over-bearing attitude.

But just before we develop that extra swagger, it may be germane to give ourselves some doses of reality check: With MINT, O'Neill, was merely painting an economic picture that will take shape over decades and generations. His observations should therefore be seen in that very long-term light and with a recognition that such analytical prognoses are usually predicated on a crucial caveat - 'all things being equal' (i.e. if the current trends continue unchanged). As we all know from experience, things are rarely equal.

Daily Trust January 30, 2014

CHAPTER 54

N60bn Mobile Palaver for Farmers

This is not the best of times for the Minister of Agriculture Dr Akinwumi Adesina, a man – I must state my bias upfront - that I admire. A few days to the end of last year, Ibukun Idusote, Permanent Secretary, Federal Ministry of Agriculture, was reported as saying that the Federal Ministry of Agriculture would procure ten million mobile phones, worth about N60 billion, from China and the US for free distribution to rural farmers across the country. Idusote was also quoted as saying that the plan was part of the Ministry of Agriculture's "e-Wallet project under which the ministry officials would be able to educate, inform and communicate with the farmers in the rural areas across the country on the latest and best agricultural practices, as well as the current prices of commodities in the market". Understandably a flurry of negative reactions followed the announcement, which perhaps forced Dr Adesina to issue a press statement through his Special Assistant on Media and Strategy, Olukayode Oyeleye, saying that Mr Idusote had been misquoted. The Minister said there was no way he could have approved such a project, because "the government's focus has been to create jobs in Nigeria, not to export them."

I do not see anything wrong in using subsidies and freebies to incentivize workers, including farmers. That is often the practice in many Western countries that hypocritically frown at any government effort in Africa to make things a little easier for its populace through subsidies. In Europe for instance, the Common Agriculture Policy (CAP) – a system of European Union agricultural subsidies and programmes used a whopping 46.7% of the entire EU's budget in 2006 to subsidize agriculture in 2006. CAP's aim is to provide European farmers with a reasonable standard of living and to provide rural heritage. Under CAP, there is both a direct subsidy payment for crops and land which may be cultivated with price support mechanism including guaranteed minimum prices, import tariffs and quotas from certain goods outside the EU. The US has a similar subsidy regime for its farmers.

It is understandable that the highly urbanc Dr Adesina, who has extensive experience in working in international agricultural centres, including as Vice President (Policy and Partnerships) for the Alliance for a Green Revolution in Africa (AGRA), an organization established with support from the Rockefeller Foundation and the Bill and Melinda Gates Foundation, would be inspired by the freebies enjoyed by Western farmers. What the mobile phone plan probably did not factor in is the exceptionally high level of distrust of government – especially when it comes to money. There are certainly several legitimate questions to be asked about the project, especially as what was apparently an effort at damage control by the government, was not convincing. The 'damage control' did not deny plan for a free ten million mobile phone for farmers. In the new media, some Nigerians now daub the yet-to-be purchased phones, 'Jona-phones' (from President Jonathan's name).

Some of the relevant questions Nigerians are asking about the project include: How did the government establish that there are ten million peasant farmers in Nigeria? If, as widely reported in the media, the project would cost N60 billion (meaning N6, 000 per phone) is this value for money especially when some phones could be bought locally for as cheap as N2,000? Was the whole project spurred by a desire to award contracts and the kick-backs and kick-forwards that often arise from such? Are Nigerian peasants literate enough to read text messages on their phones? If I own a small garden in my house, do I qualify to get one of such phones? Are there alternative investments with such amount of money which could have been more beneficial such as using it to provide agricultural extension services to farmers in their local languages while simultaneously providing jobs to others in the process?

Apart from understandable anger from the populace, there are now also several conspiracy theories concerning the projects – trust us Nigerians. One of such 'theories' now making the waves in the cyberspace is that the project is part of President Jonathan's attempt to bribe Nigerian farmers ahead of his anticipated re-election bid in 2015. Another is that it is part of the white elephant projects' being created with the aim making money available to the PDP ahead of the 2015 presidential elections. I do not believe in any of these conspiracy theories. My feeling is that the phone plan for farmers it is a good project, but which was not properly thought-through before being unveiled.

Re: Sanusi has raised a very important question but…

Below are some of the readers' reactions to my last week's column on Lamido Sanusi Lamido.

'Dear Jideofor,
Your article on Sanusi was a very brilliant one. Every paragraph is loaded with sense. Your opinions have validated my feelings about CBN governor. I hope he will take some lessons from your article. That done, he might become the best CBN governor Nigeria ever had.'
(Email, no name: lijakan2000@yahoo.com).

'Please allow me to be more simplistic (naive) by suggesting that the remaining 50% will be more conscious of competition when they wake up to the realisation that they are, equally, dispensable if they do not perform. To the contrary, instead of holding out for higher pay-off (bribes), they should double or higher their efficiency. Remember, it was inefficiency that led to the underperformance ("not enough to do" - in your words). It is all in implementation. Also, for the remaining 50%, the professionalism should be in the form of awareness that the jobs must be earned and not entitlements and that unemployment is the deterrent for non-performance. Therefore, there should be no need to raise their pay scales to meet world standards – as you alluded. Nigeria is not or should not be competing with the rest of the world's labour market (with the level of well-educated unemployed workforce [we currently have]). You are simply demanding your compensation's worth of work.

Finally, although I said from the onset that Sanusi can defend himself, he should not wait until he becomes auditor-general or would I suggest the he uses one as his mouth-piece? Someone has to speak up, and personally I do not mind him doing so; you call it gaffes, I call them bombshells.'
(Email, Istiphanus, imagaji@mymts.net)

'Sir, I read your Thursday column on Daily Trust (3/01/2013) with relish. Thanking you very much sir for your educative and informative piece. You simply made my day in a special way'
Mansur Kotorkoshi (text message)

'Compliment of the season, Mr. Jideofor. On Sanusi and his questions, you really said all about him. I hope he will read this masterpiece about himself and take necessary corrections. Continue to educate Mr Jide. Your passionate weekly follower from Kaduna.'
Text message, no name: 08036290431.

'Your column omitted the key drainpipes on the nation's resources. Check Wiki's number of aides [for political office holders] who also front for contracts. See what is spent on [political] aides, Board Members etc. What is spent on one political appointee monthly can offset the wages of a whole department of an MDA'.
(Text message, Nator, Abuja).

'Hi Jideofor. Your Thursday column on Prince Sanusi is absolutely correct. Sanusi favours neo-classical thinking against a Keynesian approach. President Obama adopts a Keynesian thinking. I enjoyed your piece'.
(Text message, no name: 08107972195).

'Good piece as usual. But you should have summed up as follows:
Radical + Conservative = Confusionist'.
(Text message, no name: 080820773356).

'Sanusi has never got it right lately. As far as it is glaring, the recent issue of N5000 bill and his call for the sack of 50 per cent of [the country's] workforce lacks sincerity of purpose and were misplaced priorities. Or is it that the few capital projects affected by high current expenditure in budgets are even implemented in the first instance? So what is Sanusi's point?
(Text message, Bagudu, Minna).

'Always right, Sanusi: When in the year 2000, I met the man at Arewa House function, I was least deceived by his Queen's English. It was not what people around

were seeing that was on my vision. It was the real Sanusi of 1950s and 60s. The very one that forced many Kanawas out of his emirate because of his pseudo scholastic arrogance and intolerance. So what is wrong with dismissing the entire Nigerian civil servants as long as the decayed institution he represents will [not be affected]?
(Text message, Muhammed Mansour Hassan, Kaduna).

'I have read your column on Sanusi and have one question: why is the civil service bloated? I believe you know the answer. I agree with Sanusi on the assumption that as long as there is no conducive environment for people to turn to, government work will always stand out. The robotic response of those in power [to the challenge] of creating the desired environment coupled with the NLC's misplaced priorities should be revisited. No retreat, no surrender'.
(Text message. Muktar, Katsina).

Daily Trust, January 10 2013

CHAPTER 55

EFCC: How not to Fight Corruption

In an article for *Daily Independent* in 2009, I took the position that the shutting down of the Economic and Financial crimes Commission, (EFCC), the financial crime buster, famous or infamous (depending on where you stand on the arguments), for hustling the high and the mighty, was only a matter of time. My argument then was that the 'quango' was not doing anything its moribund predecessors did not do. Obasanjo's Jaji Declaration during his First Coming, Shagari's Ethical Revolution, Babangida's MAMSER, Abacha's Failed Bank Tribunals and Buhari's War Against Indiscipline all did the same 'garagara' in their days before they closed shop. No, it was not just a simple matter of non-sustainability of policies. Even before the curtain was drawn on those contrivances they were showing considerable fatigue from fighting the symptom of a more fundamental social malaise.

The truth is that the EFCC – just like its predecessors- fundamentally but erroneously treats corruption as a moral lapse rather than an inherently systemic problem that is exacerbated in climes where the nation-building process has manifestly failed – as in Somalia – or engulfed in deep crisis - as in Nigeria and several other African countries. EFCC's problem is worsened by a conflation of the supposed fight against corruption with political vendetta.

Given my long-held pessimistic view of EFCC's prospects, it is understandable that I should come back to this topic when I read the Punch of 16 October 2013, which had the instructive headline: 'EFCC broke, can't pay lawyers'. I had captioned my 2009 piece, which I mentioned earlier, as 'War on Corruption: Why the EFCC will Fail'.

The truth is that the EFCC failed a long time ago. Failure here is relative. In my opinion, the best way (methodologically speaking) to assess any organization set up to fight any societal malaise, is to use the 'before' and 'after' benchmark - that is to pose the question: what was the situation before such an organization was set up, and what happened after it was set up? Procedural issues like how much money it succeeded in confiscating from people or how it has forced public figures to find other avenues of concealing their loot are really mere details. In any football match, no matter how technical a team is or how entertaining its football is, what really counts is the score-line.

There is of course a sense in which the EFCC may be said not to have failed completely, especially under Nuhu Ribadu, its pioneer chairman. This was in the domain of 'naming and shaming' through media trial. Ribadu prosecuted, tried and convicted many suspects even before it had begun the process of evidence gathering. The logic appeared to be simple: since the Nigerian justice system is not blind – as it should be - but moves with the speed of a snail as it sniffs for lucre with a torchlight that assesses an accused's social standing and proximity to critical political power centres, such a system could be bypassed and judgment taken directly to the court of public opinion. Media trial suits Nigerians' morbid glorification of instant justice. True, some on the wrong side of the critical power wielders do get hassled by EFCC to help whip them into the line of the man calling the shots. For many Nigerians the art of publicly humiliating the high and mighty levels such people to the ground where they started while shaming the justice system for allowing itself to be both commoditized and politicized.

My feeling is that EFCC has been retained by subsequent regimes since it was set up by Obasanjo because it satisfies the demands of international donor agencies and investors for the government to be seen as fighting corruption – in a 'garagara', Nigerian style. So the EFCC's 'garagara', especially when it succeeds in arresting and making a scapegoat of a high ranking public official that has fallen out of favour before a presidential visit to the US or Europe, can be regarded as a qualified success if such makes the President earn some praises from his hosts. In this sense, it is just a monkey game.

But EFCC's symbolic successes must be distinguished from the substantial success expected of it. This substantial success can be framed in just one question: has corruption become less in the country since the EFCC was established? Anecdotal evidence, and the country's rankings on Transparency International's Corruption Perception Index, will suggest that it has not. On the contrary my feeling is that the malaise has grown worse and we should become emboldened to ask the EFCC tough questions. In fact the report that the EFCC is now broke and cannot pay its lawyers should raise two further questions: How much is really spent on running the EFCC annually? Is the country getting value for money from that?

A major reason why the EFCC has failed is that it is using exactly the same strategies employed by its predecessors – treating corruption as a moral lapse rather than more of a systemic problem. Fighting corruption cannot work when the issue of the crisis in the country's nation-building is unresolved. It cannot work when the justice system is rotten. And it cannot work when the agency has to keep an eye on how ethnic watchers will react to some of its prosecutions. Resolving the crisis in the country's nation-building and the ancillary issues that interface with it is clearly outside the mandate of the EFCC. This is why I believe any other contrivance in its image will also fail – unless the precedent questions are first answered.

The government is still regarded as 'no man's land – akin to the way working in the colonial enclave was regarded as 'white man's work' – something, just from its name alone, tells volume of how alienating people regarded it. Developing any emotive attachment to such work was regarded as stupidity, not smartness. What was regarded as being really clever was the ability to outsmart that system – whether through foot-dragging, moonlighting or corruption and nepotism. For many Nigerians, the government conjures the image of 'the white man's work'. We cannot address this problem without getting back to the crisis in our nation-building project.

The EFCC compounds its problems by spreading itself too thin. The agency wants "to curb the menace of the corruption that constitutes the cog in the wheel of progress; protect national and foreign investments in the country; imbue the spirit of hard work in the citizenry and discourage ill-gotten wealth; identify illegally acquired wealth and confiscate it; build an upright workforce in both public and private sectors of the economy and; contribute to the global war against financial crimes." Today the EFCC is also a debt collector. If the EFCC were to show the sort of prudence it preaches, I would have expected the agency to engage lawyers only on 'no win, no fee' basis.

I have long canvassed for a conditional amnesty for all that are standing trial for corruption. And why not? Several countries including Russia have tried that option. Besides if we can grant amnesty or plead for amnesty to be granted to brigands with blood in their hands, why not do the same to those who are standing trial for corruption? Their loot can help to reflate the economy rather than their hiding these away in foreign banks or using such to buy real estates in exotic places. Besides, with the conflation of corruption with vendetta, no one knows where the fight against corruption stops and where vendetta starts. Additionally, as Nigerians talk of a National Conference to discuss whether the 'federating units' still want to continue to live together, everyone deserves a new beginning.

Assuming that Nigerians decide that they want to continue living together, amnesty should be used as a therapy to heal wounds and to start afresh. All over the world amnesty programmes have been used to deal with problems that appear intractable. In 2004 for instance, George W Bush enacted a tax amnesty programme, which allowed US corporations to bring home, tax-free, the billions of dollars they stashed away in tax havens. The US also routinely offers amnesty to illegal immigrants who met certain conditions. Similarly, the Italian government in October 2009 launched a tax-amnesty plan, which allowed Italians to repatriate funds deposited in tax havens. In 2006, the government of Colombia granted amnesty to some 21,000 paramilitaries linked to drug cartels. In South Africa, the Truth and Reconciliation Commission offered amnesty to people who confessed and apologised for crimes committed under apartheid. Just before he became gravely ill and subsequently died, Yaradua also offered amnesty to militants of the Niger Delta in exchange for their laying down their guns. These instances suggest that there is a history of granting amnesty to people who have broken the law, including people who have committed murders, in exchange for everlasting peace or to ensure a new beginning.

Once the crisis in the country's nation-building is resolved - which I see as the fundamental problem facing the country - fighting other challenges, including corruption, will become much easier. And with some luck, a Nigerian version of Mandela or Nyerere will emerge to unite a fractious nation and lead the charge.

Daily Trust, October 17, 2013

CHAPTER 56

'Yuanising' the Nigerian Economy

The talk in town these days is about President Buhari's recent trip to China and the deals, loans and currency swap that resulted from that trip. Of particular concern to many people, is the reported naira and renminbi (also known as the Yuan) swap deal, which is expected to ease trade transactions between China and Nigeria. But beyond the rhetoric and the obfuscation around technicalities, what is this deal all about? And will it really 'crash' the value of the dollar against the naira as some people believe?

In this piece, we will look at the pros and cons of the deal and allow the reader to decide for himself or herself.

Basically a currency deal is an agreement between two central banks, at least one of which must be an international currency issuer, to trade in their own local currencies and pay for import and export trade at pre-determined rates of exchange without the use of a third currency such as the United States dollar or the British pounds. Usually the aim of a currency swap deal is to provide the parties with temporary liquidity in foreign currency. One peculiarity of Buhari's deal with China however is that it was not cemented between the Central Bank of Nigeria and its Chinese equivalent, the Peoples Bank of China (PBoC), but with the Industrial and Commercial Bank of (ICBC), the world's largest lender by total assets and market capitalisation. It is not clear why the deal is not between the CBN and PBoC just as information on the nature, size, duration, effective commencement date, the cost of the deal and the interest rate are not yet in the public domain.

It is important to underline that Nigeria is not the only country to have signed such a currency swap deal with China. In fact since 2008, China has signed such a deal with nearly 30 countries, with the biggest of such deals being the 400 billion Yuan currency swap with Hong Kong in November 2014. In April 2015, the South African Reserve Bank announced it had signed a three-year bilateral swap agreement with the People's Bank of China for the exchange of local currencies of up to R57 billion. In fact since 2014 when the Yuan was recognised as a likely global reserve currency, Ghana, South Africa and Zimbabwe have integrated the currency into their financial markets.

In many ways Buhari's recent currency swap deal is a continuation of the moves initiated by Sanusi Lamido Sanusi, the current Emir of Kano, when he was the Governor of the CBN. It should be recalled that in 2011 Sanusi had indicated that a small percentage of the country's foreign reserves would be held in the Chinese Yuan. At the time, the country's $32 billion in reserves were held 79 percent in dollars and the rest in Euros and Swiss francs. As late as 2014, then CBN's Deputy Governor Kingsley Moghalu was reported as saying that the CBN was looking to increase the percentage of Yuan foreign reserves in its possession from 2 percent to 7 percent. Moghalu was further quoted as saying: "It was clear to us that the future of international economics and trade will shift in large part to business with and by China. Ultimately the renminbi (Yuan) is likely to become a global convertible currency."

Potential benefits

For supporters of the currency swap, the deal will enable Nigerians who trade with China to pay for their goods in Chinese Yuan, bypassing the current transaction cost of having first to obtain the US dollars, which will subsequently be exchanged for the Yuan to pay for such goods. Supporters of the deal also believe that apart from easing the pressure on the demand for dollars, the deal could actually lead to increased investment flows from both China and the United States. The argument here is that if the deal shores up the value of the Naira against the dollar, it will actually encourage American investors to invest in our economy, because fewer dollars will yield more Naira for investments. Supporters of the deal also believe that with the Yuan not only being available in the commercial banks but also in the bureau de change (BDC) segment it will mean more business for the BDC operators as most other African countries will come to Nigeria to source for Yuan.

Concerns

Just as the currency swap deal is being enthusiastically welcomed in some quarters, some have also expressed strong concerns about it.

One lingering concern is why the deal was consummated with the ICBC, rather than with the PBoC as is the standard practice with currency swap arrangements. Critics have also expressed concerns that an overvalued Naira and unrestricted access to the Yuan might encourage unfettered importations and dumping from China (already infamous for dumping inferior goods in the country), which will further stifle our local industries. The "flooding" of Nigerian markets with cheap Chinese goods may particularly adversely affect the local textile industries, which are already struggling. The fear therefore is that the currency deal may reinforce Nigeria's position as a dumping ground for goods from China and undermine the import-substitution efforts of the Federal Government.

With the rivalry between the West and China in Africa, there are equally concerns that the deal may not be acceptable to the West as it may affect their own trade balance with Nigeria. How will the West respond? Will they offer more and improved terms of trade to Nigeria or will they choose to wield the big stick? Does Nigeria have the leverage to play the beautiful bride by playing China against the West for its benefit as several African countries did between the East and the West during the Cold War?

Critics are also sceptical about the touted expected greatest benefit from the deal – the strengthening of the naira against the dollar. For many critics, for the China deal to be able to have such an effect on the naira against the dollar, the country would need first to enhance its productive base. It is also argued that despite the deal a devaluation of the naira against the US dollar remains likely this year because the swap arrangement is not capable of addressing the disparity between the naira's official exchange rate of N197-N199 to the dollar and the parallel market's rate of $1 for about N320. Some critics equally believe that it is rather too hasty to accumulate a substantial portion of the country's foreign reserves in the Chinese currency in view of its volatility and suspected manipulation coupled with the fact that it is not yet an international reserve currency. There are also concerns about the speculated exclusion clauses in the deal such as that requiring that it precludes Nigeria from dealing with 'any other China' (such as Taiwan). In the same vein critics worry that with Chinese exports accounting for about 80 per cent of the total bilateral trade volumes between the two countries, Nigeria may not reap much benefit from the deal given the large trade imbalance in favour of China while China will be the main beneficiary.

Overall, the issue with every deal is not so much about who benefits more but whether the country has got the best deal within the limits of its available options. Unfortunately since the details of President Buhari's currency swap deal are not yet in the public domain and we are yet to see how this works in practice (not just on paper), it will be difficult to take a categorical position on it. The encouraging thing however is that since several of the countries that had entered into such a currency swap deal in the past renewed it at the expiration of the initial term (usually three years), we can surmise that there must be something beneficial in it to warrant these countries doing an 'Oliver Twist'.

Daily Trust, April 21, 2016

PARTY POLITICS: PDP AND THE APC

CHAPTER 57

As Baraje's Faction of PDP joins APC

There is a new wave of optimism in the camp of the All Progressives' Congress (APC) and its supporters following news of the merger of the Baraje faction of the PDP with the party. The merger with APC was announced in a communiqué read by the national chairman of the New PDP, Alhaji Abubakar Baraje following a four-hour long meeting at the Kano Governor's Lodge in Abuja. Among those at the meeting were the governors of Rivers, Kano, Kwara, Adamawa and Niger. The Niger State Governor, Babangida Aliyu was said to have left the meeting mid-way, apparently because he rejected the idea of merging with the APC.

The euphoria that greeted news of nPDP's merger with APC in some quarters reminds one of the run-up to the latter's registration when it attracted all manner of positive epithets, including as a mega unification of all the credible opposition parties in the country. Since its registration however, the party has not really lived up to its pre-registration media hype. Its candidates have not done exceptionally well in recent elections, including in the last local council elections in the Federal Capital Territory where, fresh from the euphoria of being registered, it missed the opportunity of creating a bandwagon effect that could have come with a very strong performance. Also rather than being pro-active to drive the debates, it has mostly been reactive.

Be that as it may, APC has good grounds for feeling elated by the news of the merger with the Baraje faction of the PDP. Certainly to gain about three (or is it two?) State Governors in one fell swoop brings with it inestimable war-chest, party structures - and let's face it- rigging machines and manuals. Apart from the President of the country, State governors are pearls of inestimable value in our brand of politics. No sustainable rigging can take place in a State without the knowledge or connivance of the State Governor.

The merger with Baraje's faction of PDP will also improve the media visibility of the APC. This is not just because of the news of the merger. The truth is that since its formation early in the year, the nPDP has been competing for media opposition space with the APC despite their apparent collaboration. Given the very audacious manner in which the nPDP came into being, and the roulette dance and hide-and-seek game it was playing with the main PDP, its moves created the sort of suspense that enthrals the media. This means that it managed to eclipse APC as the main opposition to the ruling PDP. The merger therefore creates an opportunity for APC to find creative ways of sustaining media interest in what it does – not simply by reacting to moves by the government or the ruling PDP. It was obvious though that the nPDP had to berth at a point because it could play its game of suspense only for so long. It was clear it was beginning to run out of options against a government that was hell bent on clamping down on it especially after the court judgment which ruled that the it was an illegal entity.

Just as there is often post-merger blues when two companies or organisations merge, the APC will face a whole range of problems following the merger with the nPDP. For instance while the new governors in the fold will inevitably increase the party's war-chest and rigging ability (I honestly believe that all parties rig or attempt to rig and that sitting governors control the main rigging machine in each state), they are also used to controlling the party structures in their states. It will in fact be anomalous to find a state where the governor (who is usually the main financier of the party in the state) is not the leader of his party (i.e. in charge of the party structures). The challenge here is that there are people who had been building or controlling such structures in the states of the 'new' Governors and may not take too kindly to being displaced.

There has been a suspected conflict of visions and agendas among the various parties that merged to form the APC. For instance while most of the Northern governors and other influential Northern politicians in the APC may have as their primary agenda the return of power to the North, for the South-west and the rump of APGA in the merger, the agendas may be different. How will this conflict of agendas play out especially with regards to the cohesion of the party? And how will the merger with the nPDP affect the politics over this conflict of agendas which some feel may be APC's Achilles' heels?

Apart from the conflict over agendas, there is also a big potential for a challenge of the national leadership of the APC. Right now the assumption is that Buhari is the anointed presidential candidate while Tinubu is the leader of the party. The speculation has been rife that all the Northern Governors doing their second term in office have presidential ambitions. If this is true, and if Buhari is APC's anointed candidate, then there could be a problem because while Buhari is very popular with the masses in several parts of the North, especially the North-west, it is not clear that he elicits such loyalty from the mainstream Northern elites. This means in essence that it cannot be taken for granted that the Northern Governors that recently joined the APC via the merger with the Baraje faction, will be willing to sacrifice their own ambitions for Buhari. In fact, it can be speculated that some may be joining the APC with the sole aim that it will offer them a platform to run for the presidency. If this speculation is right, then how the APC resolves the inevitable tension and needed adjustments resulting from this merger will determine how far it can go in its journey of being a credible alternative to the ruling PDP.

There is also a real possibility that the merger with the nPDP will end up diminishing the APC. Already some Governors, including those of Niger State, Jigawa states have dissociated themselves from the move to merge with the APC. This has dampened the sense of collective action that had existed for some time around the nPDP. Nothing has also been heard from the former Vice President Alh. Atiku Abubakar, who led the walk-out during the PDP convention that birthed the nPDP. If a number of influential members of nPDP dissociate themselves from the merger, it will create the impression that there is something which the dissenters strongly object in the APC. Such dissentions can conflate with the way the PDP handles the inevitable leadership tussles to create a wave of decampments from the APC either back to the PDP or to another party. If this happens, APC will feel emasculated because its strength lies principally in being seen as a cohesive and viable alternative to the PDP.

The APC also has to face the real possibilities that many of the disaffected PDP politicians who join its fold are there either to enhance their bargaining power with the PDP (which will inevitably go on the offensive to poach back some of its members 'stolen' by the APC) or as a vehicle to realize their own individual ambitions. This means essentially that their hearts may not really be in the party. Because the APC is still trying to build membership and trying transform from being an agglomeration of regional parties, decampments will hurt the APC far more than it will hurt the PDP, which despite its faults, remains the only true national political party, whose existence is not based on anyone's ambition or charisma. This means essentially that the PDP is better placed to recover more quickly from any setback than the APC – at least for now.

Again as the presidency has clearly demonstrated, it is not averse to wielding the big stick – including punching below the belt if it feels pushed to the wall. This means that it remains to be seen how many of the leading members of defecting nPDP will react when the government really comes after them with a combination of inducements, adverse security reports (real or contrived) or the EFCC. As experience from our recent political history has shown, most Nigerian politicians have a price tag and with 2015 around the corner, the government may be willing to meet the various politicians at their points of need.

More importantly the decampments of Northern Governors from the PDP could weaken the North's influence in the party. This means that if APC fails to play its cards well and atrophies in the process, the quest for power to return to the North may become a tougher proposition.

Daily Trust, December 5, 2013

CHAPTER 58

APC: Determination or Desperation?

The recent announcement by the leading opposing parties that they were dissolving their parties in favour of a mega party, the All Progressive Congress (APC) took Nigerians by surprise. True, Nigerians were not unaware of its coming but very few expected that it would emerge that fast. In the country's political history, talks of opposition parties uniting have been a perennial dream concocted often on the eve of elections but which usually turn out to be malaria-induced, coming to nothing in the end. During the last presidential election for instance some two years ago, the media were abuzz with stories of an impending merger between Buhari's CPC and the Tinubu-driven ACN. The talks however collapsed on the eve of the election largely due to irreconcilable differences amongst the leadership of the two parties.

The fact that both the CPC and the ACN remained locked in merger talks after the 2011 elections despite the failure of their first planned merger could mean that both parties strongly believe they need each other. That ANPP, on whose platform Buhari sought the presidency twice and allegedly was stabbed on the back on each occasion was part of the merger plan speaks volume of the level of determination – or desperation - depending on where you stand on the issue. Also the fact that most of the non-PDP Governors have endorsed the merger cannot simply be dismissed with a wave of the hand. In this country, Governors are like the sea monsters, Leviathans. They play very crucial roles in the outcome of any presidential election, including the rigging of such elections. In essence, even if for some other reasons APC atrophies or unravels before 2015, it has already recorded a milestone as it is probably the first time that major political parties are announcing a merger in the country's political history.

Several observations could be made about the new mega party:

One, for supporters of a two party dominant system such as in the USA– where only two parties are electorally viable while others are not precluded from contesting by law if they met certain conditions – the emergence of APC, if it endures till the 2015 election, will be a dream come true. It will, among other advantages, simplify the electoral process and reduce the cost of conducting elections. The flipside however is that the voices of certain cause groups – groups that are in the race not necessarily to win power but to highlight certain issues during the campaign such as environmental concerns or local peculiarities – will often get muffled.

Two, is the crucial question of whether APC can live up to its media hype? From all indications, the overriding concern of the people behind the new party is how to dislodge the PDP - or more correctly President Goodluck Jonathan - from power. There is nothing intrinsically wrong with that, especially for a regime that is generally believed to have performed far below expectation. The trouble is how to convince the populace that they will be a better alternative and how to manage the submerged contradictions that will flare up once this task is accomplished or fails to be accomplished. For instance shed of all rhetoric and grandstanding, is the APC any different from PDP – ideologically and otherwise? I honestly don't think so. I see no material difference between PDP-controlled states and those controlled by the opposition. However in the sea of mediocrity, you have a few Governors across the party lines striving to do their best.

Three, can the APC survive till 2015? This is a legitimate question, given the strong characters that are driving the new party. My take on this is that if the glue that holds the new party is desperation, then it will likely seriously atrophy or even unravel before 2015. Former President Shehu Shagari is not a philosopher king by any stretch of the imagination. But after the 1979 elections, when the opposition groups started talking about mergers and alliances to stop him from being sworn in, he did say that 'anything done out of desperation is bound to fail'. And he was right. The effort crumbled. If on the other hand the parties that merged were genuinely determined to change the lot of Nigerians from what they like to call PDP misrule, then they need to do far more to show us how the new party will be ideologically different from PDP. Grandiloquent phrases or appropriating the word 'progressive' cannot be a substitute for genuine ideological conviction. In this wise, Nigerians await, not just the manifesto of the new party but will be on the watch out for its likely key drivers.

Four, if APC enters the 2015 elections as a major force, can it unseat the PDP? While the next presidential election is still more than two years away – more than more than a life time in politics - if the current political arithmetic holds, APC will be in control of 11 States while PDP will be in control of 23. In reality however the fate of APC will be tied to a number of variables including the choice of its presidential candidate and whether President Jonathan decides to run or not. Since the party is most likely to present a Northerner as a presidential candidate – the Southwest will be constrained from doing so because of Obasanjo's eight-year presidency which only ended in 2007 - Buhari will appear to be the most popular choice. Buhari's cultic following in the region however will cut both ways: while it could help mobilize and energize the voters in the North, it may have the opposite effect in other parts of the country. This is because historically individuals with cultic following in one region such as the late Awolowo in the South West and the late Ojukwu in the Southeast tend to be deeply distrusted by others. The crucial question here is whether Tinubu's famed organisational skills will be sufficient to convince voters in the Southwest to vote for parties rather than individuals during the presidential election.

Five, the APC has to work hard to get beyond the current thinking that it is an alliance of the North and South-west. This could be one of the party's vulnerable spots, to be used by the PDP. Despite the PDP's failures and shortcomings, it is still perceived as a national party with strong presence in all parts of the country. It is not tied to the charisma of any individual. With the power of incumbency, it remains the party to beat. In fact the current joke in town is that since the major opposition parties are fusing into APC to unseat the PDP, the latter may be pushed into a merger or alliance with such critical organs of the state as the Nigeria Police Force, NPF, the Directorate of State Service, DSS, as well as the Independent National Electoral Commission, INEC, to scuttle their dream.

Six, states, religion and regions are false analytical categories. For instance does senate president David Mark, whose hometown is quite close to Enugu State really have more in common with a Sokoto farmer than with other non-Northerners simply because they belong to the same accident of geography called 'North?' Does a Professor from Anambra State have more in common with an Abakiliki mechanic he can hardly understand his language than with other Nigerians simply because they both belong to the same accident of geography called the 'East'? Despite being false analytical categories, ethnicity, religion and region have been turned into ideologies, meaning that they have now acquired independent existence and are therefore real. The crucial question here is how will ethnicity and our religious parochialism conflate with the political arithmetic that largely informed the formation of APC? Already APGA, which is factionalized claims that the Igbos were not invited as stakeholders in the new party. How will APC contain the ethnic/religious watchers? How will the PDP counterattack? What will be the mobilizational instruments for both the APC and PDP? Will the PDP resort to the use of agencies like EFCC to intimidate and emasculate the opposition pretty much the way Obasanjo did under Ribadu? In the last election, supporters of President Jonathan were able to mobilize regional and religious sentiments on the argument that the North has ruled the longest and 'should not see it as their birth right'. Can such a strategy work this time around especially in the face of the President's lacklustre performance and quarrel with critical political tacticians such as Obasanjo? If APC holds till 2015 and Jonathan decides to contest, what is certain is that it is going to be a slugfest.

Daily Trust, February 21, 2013

CHAPTER 59

APC: Dreams Die First?

Two developments the past two weeks have grave implications for the All Progressives Congress, (APC), which was conceived and born with unbridled euphoria and fanfare. The party made history as the first in our country to be conceived through the consolidation of major existing political parties. Hitherto, the idea of opposition groups coming together to form a mega party that will be strong enough to give the ruling party a run for its money had remained a pipe-dream. The pattern had been that such a dream would get hyped to the high heavens as each presidential election (or federal elections before 1999) neared only to fizzle out when it came to walking the talk. The main promoters of the idea usually bulked at the prospect of being politically diminished or having one of their rivals elevated at their expense. Better, they often reasoned, to be a big fish in a small pond than a small fish in an ocean. To APC's credit, it defied all odds, skilfully avoided all the carefully laid banana-peels, shouted itself hoarse that it was being sabotaged and through a combination of resilience, blackmail and intimidation, made it to the finishing line. "A new dawn has been heralded in our political firmament", appears to be the collective sigh of relief from civil society and pro-democracy groups. For proponents of a two-party dominant system, it was a new dawn in our democracy.

The sigh of relief and its associated triumphalism however appears to have come too early. It just reminds one of George W. Bush's 'mission accomplished' after the toppling of Saddam Hussein's regime in Iraq in 2003. As it turned out, George W Bush clearly mistook the changing of gear in Iraqi resistance to surrender.

When APC was being conceived, the permutation seemed to be that Buhari would bring to the table his cultic followership from some sections of the North; Tinubu would use his organizational skills to deliver the South West while disaffected members of the PDP, especially some of the Governors, would jump into the new ship. In this simplistic math, sentiments alone could be used to build enough elite consensus to topple the PDP, which it must be admitted, has been behaving badly, sometimes irresponsibly, because there is no one to give it a good fight at the national level. With the possible exception of the South-west (which necessarily has to play a catch-up to other parts of the country in this regard if our democracy must mature fully) and the South-south, (which is basking in the euphoria of having one of their own on the 'top'), sentiments alone will no longer be enough to build elite consensus in any zone. With the society becoming increasingly individualistic, and with an expanding elite base, better education and better exposure, you can only build a temporary coalition of elites (not elite consensus) by appealing to their selfish interests and fears.

This is the ace the party in power at the centre holds. Which of course does not mean it cannot be defeated. Ruling parties have been defeated in a number of African countries in recent time. But it will involve creating such a sense of outrage against the ruling party that other elites will subsume their personal interests and ally themselves to the agenda. Unfortunately, the parties that formed the APC were guilty of nearly all of the sins of PDP, including the lack of internal party democracy, so it will be difficult for APC to fight from the vantage of a high moral ground.

The difficulty of finding a common cause around which elite consensus could be built and the lack of clear moral or ideological dividing line between the APC and the PDP can perhaps explain why the 'brief case' political parties are not taking a cue from APC to consolidate. It may also explain the recent unveiling of two new political parties linked to critical elites from the North - People's Democratic Movement and the Voice of the People reportedly by some disaffected PDP Governors (they have since denied this - not that they would admit it even if it were true). Though INEC had declared that they receive an average of five requests from parties seeking to be registered per week, the PDM and the VOP were linked to politicians with sufficient clout and resources to factionalize the elites the APC so much need to put up a brave fight against the PDP.

With the apparent political anger in the North for being 'denied' the presidency in 2011, the new parties, all of which are linked to Northern politicians, clearly show that no political zone in the country is what it used to be or can ever be. Society is dynamic and virtually every part of the country has evolved into a society where individualism and self-interest are beginning to trump community, ethnic or regional agenda – despite the occasional postures by politicians. As the old order crumbles, it becomes more difficult to have personalities who can command the total allegiance of the critical elites in any part of the country (except to a lesser extent the south west). In this sense, those who moan the lack of unity (essentially lack of elite consensus) in their ethnic or regional homeland miss the point and live in a past which can never be reclaimed.

What we often call ethnic or regional unity is merely elite consensus. Various ethnic and regional groups appear 'united' when their 'super' elites - those who are proximal to the centres of power and critical resources have additionally three crucial Cs – being Conscious (of their political agenda), Cohesive and Conspiratorial. In the past, the likes of Zik, the Sarduana of Sokoto and Awo, and their senior allies met these conditions and therefore served as unifying symbols of their people. It will be difficult to replicate the 1960s when one or two super elites in an area s will serve as the rallying points.

How do all these relate to the APC?

As mentioned earlier, it would seem that part of the thinking of the APC at conception would be that Buhari would bring his cultic followership in some parts of the North to the table. The registration of PDM and the rumoured plans to register VOP allegedly by some Northern governors clearly underline the lack of elite consensus on how to 'return power to the North'. In the 1960s when the various regional factions of the elites were surrogates of one or two super elites, it was easier for such elites to exhibit the three critical Cs. This means in essence that were this to be the 1960s, the task of returning power to the North would have been a piece of cake. Similarly, despite MASSOB and threats of reincarnating Biafra in the east, it will be difficult to find any leader who can galvanize Igbo support on a sustainable basis for such. The society has moved on, with a relative parity in the power of various geographical and ethnic elites. These days it is easier to build a short term coalition of elites - where people who do not necessarily like one another come together to achieve a particular purpose and move away from that alliance as quickly as possible. But for this to happen you must be able to clearly appeal to their selfish interests or fears.

In essence, while Buhari's charisma and a certain anger in some parts of the North could be a rallying point in the quest for 'power to return to the North' in 2015, whether such could be achieved without finding a way to bring the critical elites in the North into the APC fold or another fold will remain to be seen.

For President Jonathan and the PDP, they will be happy, (if they are not the conspirators) in these moves that may end up removing the quiver from the APC's arrow. They can count on the support of most, if not all, the Governors in the East, because of the region's age-old philosophy that the 'goat should follow the man with the palm frond' (the Governors from the East supported Yaradua vocally even when he had become terminally ill and quickly wiped their mouths to sing the Alleluia of Jonathan whom they did not want to be made the Acting President) - after Yaradua died.

In essence, if the PDM overcomes its current controversies and manages to become a respectable political party, and if the VOP or any other party which is linked to key political actors comes on-board, the APC will become seriously emasculated and the idea of a two dominant party will become still born. The losers will be the leaders of the parties which essentially fused into the A.C.N. as such leaders will have to struggle to create new political platforms for themselves.

The above scenario means that APC should return to the drawing board – as the premise on which its membership recruitment and mobilization of popular support was based now seems suspect. Of course the PDP is not invincible and ruling parties elsewhere have in recent times been routed. But in all such instances the opposition had a popular outrage and managed to sustain a coalition of critical elites. The APC urgently needs to find out why heavyweight political elites who are disaffected with the PDP are not rushing into its fold and do whatever it can to regain the momentum.

Daily Trust, August 29, 2013

CHAPTER 60

APC will be making a Mistake with Muslim-Muslim Ticket

As the All Progressives Congress (APC) prepares for its ward, state and national congresses, the media have been awash with speculations that the party may have settled on retired General Muhammadu Buhari and former Governor of Lagos State, Bola Tinubu, as its presidential and vice presidential candidates respectively. A number of the country's leading newspapers, citing 'usually reliable sources' within APC, claimed that in zeroing in on Buhari and Tinubu, the party's strategists relied on the calculations that Buhari, who remains very popular at the grassroots level in most parts of the North-west and North-East, will be banking on an estimated 44,848,911 registered voters (accounting for 61 per cent of total registered voters of 73,528,040 in the 2011 election). In contrast, the North-central, South-south and the South-east zone combined (seen as Jonathan's strongholds) has only 27,735,678 registered voters. Throw onto this 2,941,214 votes cast for Jonathan in the South-west and Edo State in 2011- the bulk of which in this calculation, will now be re-directed to Tinubu and the APC will be coasting home to an easy victory!

Let me say immediately that I do not believe in this media speculation. Politicians are masters of decoy, filibuster and selling dummies. They rarely show their hands, and when they do, it will be necessary to closely inspect what they are offering. APC is peopled with so many politically smart operatives to make the mistake of fielding a Muslim-Muslim ticket. My instinct therefore tells me that the story was deliberately planted as a decoy so that when the party chooses its presidential candidate and running mate, they will come as a surprise to Nigerians. They may be calculating on giving Nigerians something to keep them busy – as Babangida did with the political class with his transition to nowhere – to give the party the peace of mind to prepare for its ward, state and national congresses.

But assuming that the party merely wants to fly a kite, I believe there are a number of fallacies in that permutation. For instance while Buhari remains very popular in the North West and North- east, it will be simplistic to assume that the preponderance of voters in the North West and North east will give him such a lead as to cancel out whatever deficits he may have from other zones. Experiences from the 2011 elections do not support such an argument. Similarly such a permutation may not have factored in the possibility of votes from the two zones and other zones in the country being divided by the emergence of a third relatively strong party, which also fields a Northern Muslim as a presidential candidate. The truth is that APC is an aggregation of political parties, groupings and tendencies. To its credit, the party has so far held together – much to the surprise of most people who did not give it a chance. However because of its nature, it is much easier for disaffected groupings within the party to move into any of the existing briefcase parties and overnight turn such a party into relatively formidable force.

People who use the Muslim-Muslim ticket of MKO Abiola and Alhaji Babagana Kingibe as an example that Nigerians may not mind about such a ticket miss the point. True, the Abiola-Kingibe ticket won but there were several reasons for this: One, Abiola, a Yoruba was the top of the ticket, meaning that at a time of a clamour for power shift to the south, he was seen more in the South as a Southerner, while his religious faith was also mollifying to some in the North. Two, that the Abiola-Kingibe ticket won does not necessarily mean that they would have ruled successfully if the election was not annulled. No one should under-rate the power of ethnic and religious watchers. For instance even though the Buhari coup was very popularly received, with some like the late Dele Giwa even calling for the overthrown politicians to be shot, ethnic watchers quickly went to work and very gradually succeeded in turning sentiments against the regime. Maverick Arthur Nzeribe for instance, in his book, *Nigeria Another Hope Betrayed* (1984), tried to 'show' that Buhari was favouring Muslims and the North and was against the South and Christians. Though from all indications it was an unfair allegation, the ethnic and religious watchers helped in no small ways in engulfing the regime with legitimacy crisis. One of the consequences of this was that all the politicians from the south who were herded into long prison terms for corruption by the Buhari Idiagbo regime came out of prison as heroes.

In essence the Buhari-Idiagbo regime was the first time in the country's political history we had someone from the same region (North) and the same religion (Muslim) rule the country. Whatever unfair religious labeling Buhari is tarred with today probably stemmed from the activities of ethnic/religious watchers during his regime. And this was despite the fact that the regime was one of the most determined regimes in the country to get things right and that Buhari himself uttered one of the most patriotic sentiments ever expressed by any Nigerian leader when he said: 'This generation of Nigerians, and indeed future generations, have no other country but Nigeria. We must remain here and salvage it together'.

Before Buhari made the mistake of having a fellow Muslim and Northerner as his second in command, the late Chief Awolowo, a Christian Yoruba, made a similar mistake in 1979 when he chose the late Philip Umeadi, a Christian Igbo as his running mate. It is sometimes tempting to speculate on what would have happened if Awolowo has emerged the President of the country in 1979.

It must not be forgotten that though religion – just like ethnicity- is only politicized in the context of the struggle for the scarce socioeconomic resources by the different ethnic and regional factions of the elites, over time, it has acquired an objective character such that it now becomes, so to speak, an objective reality. In other words, while it is true that being of the same faith or ethnicity as the President or Vice President of the country does not add an extra cup of garri to the shopping basket of the average Nigerian, however the hurrah effect of feeling that one of one's own is there could be salutary to development. This means that citizens that feel that 'their own' is there are more likely to accept the explanations of why a regime is performing sub-optimally or to believe that a regime is performing even when such is not backed by objective data. I believe this is what Nigerian politicians mean when they talk of giving 'Nigerians a sense of belonging'. Additionally, tolerance cannot happen in a multi-ethnic and multi-faith society without sensitivity to the feelings of others. Given the current crisis in the country's nation-building – and the increasing politicization of religion – a Muslim-Muslim, or Christian-Christian ticket will not be seen as being sensitive enough.

Urgent task for the new CBN Governor

Congratulations to Godwin Emefiele, whose appointment as CBN Governor was recently confirmed by the Senate. It seems that we currently have three CBN Governors – the suspended Governor Sanusi Lamido Sanusi (SLS) whose tenure expires in June this year, the Acting CBN Governor Mrs Sarah Alade and of course Mr Emefiele, whose tenure formally starts when that of SLS ends.

I believe that both Chukwuma Soludo and SLS met different challenges at the CBN during their times and rose to the task. They were both successful, in my opinion, as CBN governors, but also contributed to the problems of the CBN as an institution. While Soludo's bank consolidation helped to give our banks confidence by raising their profiles, his style also turned the position of CBN Governor to that of a celebrity. In the same vein while Sanusi was successful in cleaning up the post-merger blues from Soludo's consolidation exercise, he brought unnecessary political activism and 'roforofo' to the job. A key challenge therefore for Emefiele is to return the position of CBN Governor to what it should be - a non-celebrity position, where the incumbent of the position should be seen more than he is heard and where he completely eschews political activism.

Congratulations to Bishop Matthew Kukah

Congratulations to Bishop Matthew Kukah who was appointed Chairman of the Governing Council of the Nasarawa State University, Keffi. The Council will be inaugurated in Lafia on Monday April 7, 2014 after which the inaugural Council Meeting will hold in Keffi later the same day.

Daily Trust, April 3, 2014

CHAPTER 61

Tambuwal will be the Nightmare Scenario for PDP

I had a tough argument with a reader who had a very dim view of my last week's article in which I opined that APC would be making a mistake if it opts for a Muslim-Muslim ticket as was being speculated in the media. After fending off his charge that my supposed bias against APC beclouded my judgment in the said article, I also put him on the spot by charging that his obvious uncritical APC sympathy made it difficult for him to see the party's potential missteps, including those that could literally amount to the party digging its own grave. We eventually agreed to disagree on a number of issues. On his suggestion that I should recommend a 'winning' ticket for the APC, I demurred, arguing that it would be unethical for a columnist to try to force the hand of a party on its choice of candidates or influence voters' preferences. The way I see it, our duty as public intellectuals, is to provide enough analytical information and clarify the issues at stake sufficiently enough for policy makers or voters to make their own choices.

Based on the above, my zeroing in on a putative Tambuwal presidential candidacy does not amount to an endorsement or forcing the hands of APC. My interest is to show the likely implications of his candidacy in the 2015 race against President Jonathan, who is yet to formally throw his hat into the ring. This will of course be without prejudice to other potential presidential candidates in the party, several of whom are eminently qualified for the job.

There are reasons I believe that a Tambuwal presidential candidacy will bring unusual excitement to the campaigns and will valorise the base of both parties. In saying this, I am assuming that Tambuwaal, who was helped to the Speakership with opposition votes and has remained 'grateful' ever since, is either a closet APC chieftain or could be easily co-opted into the party. He is young and boyish - only 48 years old. He is also courageous, charismatic, speaks well and has been able to hold the House together for some three years. His greatest strength is that while he has a national name recognition by virtue of being the Speaker of the House of Representatives, he does not have the baggage that other potential presidential candidates who have held high public offices in the past have. The PDP will therefore struggle to find a major attack line against him that will stick.

If Tambuwaal, who is from the North-west is endorsed by Buhari and Atiku, chooses as his running mate an older Christian with the requisite governmental experience (to make up for his lack of real administrative experience and to allay the anxiety of those who may be worried about his relative youth), then the campaign for 2015 will get really exciting. He may not win but such a ticket will effectively forestall the emergence of a third relatively strong party in the North. My instinct tells me that any major misstep by APC, (which must be given credit for holding together for so long against all odds and predictions), will lead to mass defections, not of individuals as happened to the PDP but of the various groupings and tendencies that came together to form the party and give its current swagger. Defections of such groupings are unlikely to be back to the PDP – as it will amount to one swallowing one's vomit. If such disaffected groupings move to any party, especially if the defections include one or two governors who will bring with them a good war chest, the beneficiary political party will become bolstered overnight.

Tambuwal will be the PDP's nightmare not only because of the aforementioned factors going for him, but also because he can tap on sentiments to harvest bountifully from the rich votes in the North-west and Northeast without his candidacy generating negativities in other parts of the country.

But even a Tambuwaal candidacy will face an uphill, but not insurmountable, task in trying to defeat a likely Jonathan candidacy. The PDP has the advantage of incumbency and with it tremendous leverages, including the *koboko* (EFCC, ICPC etc.) to whip some politicians into line and also pieces of the 'national cake' to co-opt others. Besides, Jonathan can match Tambuwaal youth-for-youth and feature for feature. He may not be the most inspiring speaker in the world but at 56 he is quite young for a man of his political experience and the office he occupies. In the rare occasions he dresses in suits or T-shirts, his good and boyish looks come to the fore (one sometimes wonders why his handlers do not exploit such symbolisms frequently enough). In several countries these days, a candidate's age and looks are all part of the likeability factors that sway voters. This is another point those pushing for Buhari-Tinubu ticket should be sensitive to (Buhari is 71 while Tinubu is 62, which means that the ticket is also not generationally sensitive).

It must be pointed out that recent developments in the country's macroeconomic environment and other spheres of national life are already making some people revise their impressions of Jonathan as an underperforming President: whether by luck or design, under his watch Nigeria replaced South Korea in the MIKT economies to change the acronym to MINT (Mexico, Indonesia, Nigeria and Turkey). Under him the country won the African Cup of Nations and also won the World Cup in the under 17 category. In the same vein, the inflow of foreign direct investment under him in three years is more than all that Obasanjo achieved in eight years. These are in addition to the impacts of the recent re-basing of the country's GDP. True, you cannot eat GDP and the size of the economy does not equate to the economic wellbeing of a country. Yet, it is the G8 countries, (made up of the eight largest economies in the world) that rule the world – not the richest countries in the world (measured by GDP per capita where little known countries like Qatar, Luxembourg and Switzerland hold sway). If the Eagles do well in the World Cup in Brazil, Jonathan's corruption and unemployment perception flanks will remain vulnerable but the wind will certainly be on his back and the momentum on his side as the race for 2015 heats up.

Let me say that a voter's preference for one candidate over others often depends on the person's analysis of the major challenges facing the country. Across all democracies – emerging or mature - sentiments play a big role in voters' preferences but such sentiments often interface with other objective issues in determining the aggregate support a candidate gets. In essence, sentiments alone, especially in the face of active political marketing and rubbishing by the parties during campaigns, cannot be sufficient to win elections. A candidate supported on sentimental grounds alone can be so rubbished by good opposition strategists that the candidate's initial enthusiastic supporters will have a buyer's remorse just before the elections.

Several voters will embrace a presidential candidate based on their assessment of what they consider to be the most urgent task facing the country. Those who believe that corruption is the major problem of the country (I see corruption as only the symptom of a more fundamental societal malaise) and who admire a soldier-like battle against the ailment (a wrong strategy in my opinion), will continue to nurse a nostalgia for Buhari's War Against Indiscipline and Ribadu's EFCC. On the other hand, those who believe that the country's problem is having a visionary leader may not mind voting for a leader who may have been accused (rightly or wrongly) of corruption in the past if they believe the candidate has that vision thing. In the same vein, those who believe that the country's major challenge at this point is the crisis in its nation-building (I belong to this category) will be looking for a non-divisive, statesmanlike father- figure who can reconcile a fractious nation. Both Tambuwal and Jonathan can lay claim that they are unifying personalities – Jonathan has a humble, non-aggressive personality while Tambuwaal, by holding the House well in three years and being successful in networking across the fault lines, has also proved he is a unifying personality. This is why I see a contest between the two personalities as likely to be very exciting.

Killjoys and the Re-basing of the Nigerian economy

For too long, our country, which daubed itself the 'giant of Africa', has been the butt of jokes: we have been called 'Sleeping giant', 'Giant with feet of clay' and a country of '419ers'. Now that we have an opportunity of a counter narrative we should be allowed to enjoy it a bit before the fun is spoilt by naysayers and 'on the other hand' analysts. The truth is that with these developments, and despite continuing challenges in other sectors of life such as security, poverty and unemployment, no one can look the country in the face again and call it 'sleeping giant'. It would also help the country's quest for a permanent seat in the Security Council of the United Nations, blunt the pulls of the centrifugal forces in the country and further the attraction of the country to foreign investors. Just like any nation that won a major football tournament, we shall return to the weaknesses of the team despite the victory – but only after we have been given some time to savour the 'victory'.

Daily Trust, April 10, 2014

CHAPTER 62

Reflections on the PDP Crisis

The political space has been abuzz with excitement for many and gloom for some since the last convention of the Peoples' Democratic Party (PDP), in which the former Vice President Alhaji Atiku Abubakar led seven Governors and some political notables to stage what seemed to be a pre-planned walkout from the party's Convention at Eagles square. The group later congregated at the Yaradua Centre, Abuja where they announced that the PDP as we know it has become factionalized, and that their version of the party would be known as the 'New PDP' under the chairmanship of Alhaji Abubakar Baraje. They articulated their grouse perceive the lack of 'internal party democracy' in the party, especially under the chairmanship of Alhaji Bamangar Tukur.

With the factionalization of the PDP some commentators are prematurely (in my opinion) announcing either the death of the party or its total enfeeblement. Many have also expressed strong concerns about the implications of the PDP crisis for our democracy and even for the corporate existence of the country. My personal opinion is that concerns about the latter are overstretched because our country has long perfected the art of hanging on a precipice without actually falling over the cliff.

The way I see it, democracy is a noisy enterprise driven by the principle of the 'marketplace of ideas' – a metaphor that was first developed by John Stuart Mill in his book, *On Liberty,* first published in 1859. Like in any open market for goods and services, especially Nigerian open markets, haggling between traders and buyers could be aggressive – just as sharp disagreements and occasional exchange of blows among the traders or between the traders and buyers, are regarded as 'normal'. The PDP crisis is therefore absolutely normal in politics. Across the world, including in the US and the UK, major political parties tend to have their sharp internal squabbles and fissures, including factionalisations. During election periods in the US and elsewhere, the political atmosphere is usually so charged that the uninitiated might fear the worst.

But why are many people apparently joyed at the putative emasculation of the PDP, which appropriated to itself the toga of being the largest – not the smartest - political party in Africa? There is a conflation of factors: one, is the issue of our fault lines and the associated geo-politics, including the unfinished business of zoning and power rotation from the 2011 elections. President Jonathan's loyalists have been quick to point out that an overwhelming majority of those who walked out were from the North and that the seemingly carefully planned walkout was aimed at embarrassing or intimidating the President from contesting the 2015 elections. The other major factor is voter fatigue. The PDP has bestraddled Nigeria's political space like an octopus since the current political dispensation started in 1999. In every State of the country, it is either the party in power or the main opposition. Add to this the fact that it is the party in control of the centre and its association with the distribution of lucre and privileges at the highest level. Because the party has become entrenched for so long, people appear fatigued with it - just as the party itself has become lethargic and complacent. In this sense, the factionalization of the party may be the necessary shock it needs to wake up and reform or become atrophied.

A relevant question here is why the other parties are seemingly immune to the sort of popular anti-PDP sentiments that abound in our media. The simple answer, in my opinion, is that virtually all the opposition parties operate as 'cause groups', tapping into ethnic or regional grievances and solidarity (A.C.N and APGA,) or rests on the charisma of their founder or leading member (CPC). The PDP, despite its numerous shortcomings, remains the only national political party in the true sense of the word. It is not dependent on ethnic/regional solidarity or the charisma of anyone, not even the founding fathers of the party, for its membership recruitment and retention. The party's tragedy however is that it neither has any emotionally charged cause that drives nor is it animated by any set of well- articulated philosophy. This gives the impression that the only cause that unites the members is the search for lucre and privileges and a desperate bid not to lose out in the power game.

The truth however is that the difference between the PDP and any of the major opposition parties is just like the difference between twelve and one dozen. For instance, on the main grouse on which the PDP splintered – lack of internal party democracy – the worst culprit in this regard appears to be the defunct Action Congress of Nigeria (A.C.N.), now the senior partner in the newly formed APC, where an oligarchical group would unilaterally decide who would fly the party's flag at any election, often based on the candidate's Awoist or NADECO credentials. How many of the opposition parties have ever had the national chairman or BOT chairman of their parties changed through an election? And which of the parties can therefore morally call out the others on matters of internal party democracy?

Another important question is how the PDP crisis will impact on our political space. While it is still early days, what can be conjectured following what fellow Daily Trust columnist Adamu Adamu once called the 'Obasanjonisation' of Jonathan, is that the PDP and the presidency will mimic the Obasanjo style and fight venomously back a la Obasanjo. The Ota Farmer had a knack of combining brute force with extreme cunning. The PDP, perhaps in cahoots with the presidency, has already shown it would follow the Obasanjo line: most likely the security agencies sealed off the proposed secretariat of the nPDP, just as Obasanjo did in 2006 when a splinter faction from the PDP under Chief Solomon Lar and Alhaji Shuaibu Oyedokun opened a factional office in Mabushi, Abuja. Again if the Presidency and the Bamangar Tukur faction of the party were to follow the Obasanjo template, the real fight back would only commence after the two factions have 'reconciled'. Obasanjo developed a strategy of luring his opponents to lower their guards through phantom reconciliations and then delivering deadly political uppercuts when such opponents have been lured into a false sense of security. I foresee a short term strategy of the PDP using a combination of co-optation, exclusion and wielding the big stick to factionalize the Baraje group. Eventually if the PDP itself does not atrophy – and I don't see this seriously happening- it will move against anyone associated with the new faction. In essence the 'New PDP' should know it has crossed the proverbial Rubicon and must finish the fight it started or its leading members will be seriously bruised as the PDP and an Obasanjonised Jonathan fight back. However whether the nPDP has the capacity to 'fight to finish' in our type of society where everyone seems to have a price tag remains to be seen.

Again just as Obasanjo moved against many of his political benefactors, I won't be surprised if some aides of the presidency move against Obasanjo who has already been accused of igniting the fire – and dare heavens to break loose. If this happens, this is really where the PDP crisis will have serious implications. Obasanjo may not be the darling of his Yoruba kinsmen but as they say in my village, it is only when you molest a madman that you will realize he/she has brothers, sisters and relatives.

Another issue that remains to be seen is how the nPDP will interface or wriggle out of the current efforts to box it into the politics of the country's fault lines and the unfinished politics of zoning and power rotation from the 2011 elections. What appears obvious is that the circumstances that birthed the New PDP cannot be divorced from the aggressive permutations for 2015. I would worry if the New PDP came about on the eve of the 2015 elections because the passion will be hot going into elections, with high potentials for election violence. But with some clear two years before the elections, the passions will have been settled, the PDP will either have reformed or atrophied and the leaders of the walkout will either have been dealt with (Nigerian style) or firmly ensconced in a new party, where they will necessary get as much as they give in terms of verbal exchanges and contestation of ideas.

Daily Trust September 12, 2013

CHAPTER 63

Has PDP shot itself in the Foot?

The recent report that the PDP's National Executive Committee (NEC) has zoned the party's chairmanship position to the North-East geo-political zone after earlier zoning its presidential flag bearer to the north in 2019 - has raised the question of whether the party has shot itself on the foot. My simple answer to this is 'yes'. First, there are group dynamics in politics which cannot be wished away anywhere in the world. Zoning is not just a recognition of the salience of group dynamics and identity politics, it is also meant to be a supplement to other constitutional measures of nation-building such as the use of the Federal Character principle to ensure fair representation of all areas of the country in the distribution of federal jobs and amenities. In Nigeria's political parlance, it is a means of giving every part of the country 'a sense of belonging'. It is, contrary to the thinking in some quarters, not antithetical to merit - provided the principle is applied creatively. Even political parties that do not explicitly embrace zoning and power rotations, make efforts to practice the principles implicitly. I am a firm supporter of the creative use of the principles of zoning and power rotation to supplement other constitutional measures of building unity in diversity in the country. I am also a firm supporter of the use of quotas and other positive discrimination measures when necessary because in a federation like ours, it must be recognized that resources and talents are never evenly distributed spatially but are often available in a complementary manner among the geographic spaces.

For the above reasons, I understand why the PDP, just like its progenitor, the National Party of Nigeria (NPN) explicitly embraced zoning. But I fail to understand why the party should zone its chairmanship position to the North-east after zoning its presidential candidate to the north for 2019 and vice presidential candidacy to the southeast during the same period. My suspicion is that it was done to benefit the current interim chairman of the party and apparently its new financier, Modu Sheriff, who is also reportedly interested in being the party's presidential flag bearer in 2019. I have nothing for or against Modu Sheriff's ambition. But in terms of political strategy I believe the PDP goofed by this decision.

Strategically, it makes more sense for the PDP to give a sense of co- ownership (not just a sense of belonging) to critical areas that will be battle grounds in 2019. From all indications, the Southwest, with its huge voting population, will remain a key battle ground in 2019 as it was in 2015 and zoning the party's chairmanship position to the zone would have strengthened the PDP's hand there. In fact it is by strengthening the party in areas where Buhari currently has weak or fledgling support and incentivising such areas to remain within its fold that the party can be competitive in 2019. It cannot be competitive by the rather uphill task of trying to unseat Buhari in his strongholds of the Northwest and Northeast by dangling the chairmanship and presidential candidacy of another party before the electorates there. I am not arguing that the PDP should give up on the Northwest and Northeast without a fight but the truth is that Buhari's supporters in these two geopolitical zones are unlikely to abandon him irrespective of how he performs in office. They have demonstrated a remarkable loyalty to him as a person since he began contesting for the presidency in 2003 and any good political strategy must recognize that remarkable loyalty. I do not see Buhari's support base in the two zones being massively eroded in 2019 - irrespective of how he performs in office. In any case, performance, in a polarized country like ours, is like self-fulfilling prophecies. Both supporters and opponents will have enough 'evidence' to buttress their stand.

The current PDP leadership appears to be repeating the mistake made by the Jonathan administration in taking the Southwest for granted or not sufficiently incentivising the zone. In fact, Jonathan began to lose the Southwest when it allowed the 'Tambuwal coup' (which led to the Southwest losing the position of Speaker of the House of Representatives zoned to it) to stand and not doing enough to compensate them and give them a sense of co-ownership of the party when he failed to topple Tambuwal. As I argued in a report for Brookings' Foresight Africa before the election: "The APC gets much of its strength from tapping into anti-Jonathan sentiments in the Muslim north and grievances among the Yoruba who feel that the Jonathan administration has ignored them in key political appointments." The report, which was entitled 'The 2015 Presidential Elections in Nigeria: Issues and Challenges' was published in January 2015 (though it was submitted for publication in November 2014). A crucial question for the PDP strategists therefore is how has the party been able to address the perceived alienation of the South-west from the party? Certainly the decision of the PDP to zone both the chairmanship of the party and its presidential candidacy in 2019 to the north and the Vice Presidency to the southeast does nothing to even acknowledge that it advertently or inadvertently marginalized such a critical geopolitical zone under Jonathan.

The PDP's strategy is probably hinged on making the 'north' feel ownership of the party as a way of competing effectively against Buhari in 2019 - if he chooses to run. If this was the party's thinking, then it is unlikely to bear fruit. It is true that the PDP is in a pretty bad shape now: it is being effectively de-marketed by APC's propaganda machine amid allegations of financial heist and monumental corruption against the past regime. Additionally potential financiers seem to be living in fear of the EFCC. It is therefore understandable that the PDP will be happy to embrace anyone with enough cash and courage to come to its aid. But to be competitive, the party needs to look beyond its present condition.

I foresee the party going the way of the defunct ANPP - moving from the largest opposition party to becoming an effeminate opposition and eventually withering away. I also foresee the emergence of another opposition political party, most likely through mergers, which will try to bring new narratives to the current political discourse.

Daily Trust, May 5 2016

CHAPTER 64

Ekiti: APC as a Sore Loser

Last week I celebrated Fayemi for conceding victory to Fayose in a most gracious manner. In that article I also wondered why the idea of the gallant or gracious loser has not really become engrained in our political culture despite the fact that those who conceded defeat honourably, given the relative novelty of such gestures in the country, were always rewarded with public approbation and adoration. Ironically in almost all the instances where a loser, especially in governorship elections, conceded defeat graciously, something always happened to spoil the fun. We are already seeing signs of this in the widely celebrated détente between the victor Ayo Fayose and the vanquished Dr Kayode Fayemi.

In his concession speech, Fayemi said: "It is my belief that we must all start imbibing attitudes that will make us avoid activities that can threaten our peaceful co-existence. We must also avoid the bad loser syndrome. I believe we need to build this democracy to a mature end, rather than pull it down." A bad loser syndrome is an affliction which makes a loser whine and accuse everyone else but himself or herself of being responsible for his or her loss. Essentially at a time people are expressing optimism that the adulation given to Fayemi for being a gracious loser could be a cure for the bad loser syndrome, the All Progressive Congress (APC) quickly reminded us that old habits die hard. The party, which likes to appropriate the progressive sobriquet to itself, said it would challenge its defeat in court and that though Fayemi conceded victory, the party was not willing to toe the same path of honour.

It may be tempting to pose the question of why I am descending harshly on APC when the party has merely indicated it will exercise its constitutional right to challenge the outcome of the election in courts. The simple answer is that I believe that for our elections to be sanitized, we need to entrench the 'Fayemi effect' and for the 'Fayemi effect' to be entrenched we should all see it as our collective responsibility to come hard on both the sore loser and the triumphant winner. In that eulogy to Fayemi I opined: "It should be the duty of the Nigerian media and Nigerians to take on both the sore loser and the triumphalist victor if we are serious about sanitizing our politics. Both the sore loser and the triumphant victor must be seen and treated as problems to the democratic processes in the country. We must begin to find answers to the question of why the phenomenon of the gallant loser has not become entrenched in our political culture despite the fact that Obasanjo became a global statesman by merely handing over power to a democratically elected government in 1979."

APC claimed that the grounds for such a challenge would be the 'militarization' of the electoral process. In a communiqué after the party's inaugural National Working Committee meeting held at the party's National Secretariat in Abuja and read by the party's National Publicity Secretary, Alhaji Lai Mohammed about two days after Fayemi's famous concession, the party said that " in order to prevent a recurrence of what happened in Ekiti, especially the militarization of the process, the harassment and intimidation of citizens, especially those in opposition, my party has decided to challenge in court some of these constitutional breaches and will also encourage our leaders and supporters, who were arrested, harassed and intimidated to seek the enforcement of their constitutionally-guaranteed fundamental rights that were recklessly abridged by the security agencies." (Vanguard June 26 2014).

While I can understand the need for damage control by APC, especially with the coming governorship election in Osun on August 9 2014, it can also be argued that the party's non acceptance of the results helped to create the conditions that may lead to a quick breakdown in the spirit of camaraderie exhibited by Fayemi and Fayose after the election was won and lost. It is only natural that Fayose and his group would respond in kind to APC's lack of grace in defeat. Had APC been able to restrain itself and conceded defeat in as much gracious manner as Fayemi did, it would have earned it more respect from Nigerians. However by choosing to do otherwise, it not only put Fayemi in a difficult position but also allowed cynics to revel in the gossip that the party wants to resort to the courts because its leader Bola Tinubu has proven adept in "winning governorship elections through judicial processes".

My personal opinion is that the grounds of objection by APC may actually be the reasons why many people felt the Ekiti election was perhaps INEC's best outing so far. In my opinion, it was good judgment to keep governors (whether PDP or APC) away from states conducting elections (except the governor of the state conducting the election) because the truth is that in this country state governors are not ordinary citizens. Their presence and the accompanying gravitas not only serve as distractions, the incredible war chest they carry around could also corrupt the entire electoral process. Additionally governors hold the rigging manuals for elections in Nigeria. I therefore strongly feel that INEC should institutionalize the idea of the President; Governors (other than the Governor of the State where elections are taking place) should not be allowed to visit another state conducting elections on the polling day or even a day or two before that. Yes, this could be an abridgement of their constitutional right of free movement but that little derogation in their constitutional entitlement must be seen as a small price for the nuisance they are capable of causing if allowed into election venues on a polling day or even a day before.

Something should also be said about the putative swagger Fayose is already developing, which could further poison the relations between him and Fayemi, making future losers not to take the high moral ground. Given the public adulation that followed the manner Fayemi conceded, Fayose, goaded perhaps by jealousy or a feeling that a loser is being treated better than the winner, was alleged to have declared that Fayemi's concession was a mere publicity stunt. He was quoted by the Vanguard of June 27 2014 as saying: "The governor said I am conceding to defeat. Let me be realistic with you, there is a difference between propaganda and reality. I have been calling the governor since after our meeting but he hasn't picked the call" (Vanguard, June 27, 2014).

There is also a feeling that Fayose is seeing himself as a co-Governor of Ekiti State – even though he still has more than three months before he is sworn him. For instance he took umbrage at the reported attempt by Governor Fayemi to create new Local Government Areas and to offer some people jobs before his tenure expires. Fayose said that would be creating problems for the incoming administration, which may well be true. The point however is that Fayemi remained the executive Governor of Ekiti State until October when he (Fayose) will be sworn. He can of course reverse aspects of Fayemi's policies he does not like when he is sworn in. But to act as a co-Governor of the state when he is merely the Governor elect, will be testing the patience of Fayemi. One would obviously expect Fayemi to consult the governor-elect in certain critical decisions. But it is his prerogative on whether he should consult Fayose or not – just as it will be Fayose's prerogative on whether he will retain any of Fayemi's policies when he is sworn in.

Daily Trust, July 3 2014

CHAPTER 65

APC Crisis and the Myth of Party Supremacy

Much has been written about the current crisis rocking the All Progressives Congress (APC), with some people expressing concerns about a possible disintegration of the party. The crisis, as serious as it may appear, is normal and expected – even if the party had lost the presidential election.

The truth is that the APC was never a political party in a classical sense of the word. It was and remains a fragile coalition of disparate groups and groupings united by a common ambition to defeat President Jonathan and the former ruling party, the PDP. It was to that extent merely a multipurpose vehicle for capturing power. With that objective achieved, it is normal that the secondary contradictions that were papered over during the 'struggle' would come to the fore.

As the APC re-engineers to become a true political party rather than a coalition of disparate interests, it will not be abnormal for many of the founders to leave the party or be pushed out. This is what is meant by the dictum that every revolution, like Saturn, devours its children. History bears this out: the Cultural Revolution in China, the Night of Long Knives in Nazi Germany, Stalin's purge in Russia or the case of Imre Nagy, the highly respected former Hungarian head of state, who was the symbol of the country's uprising against Soviet rule in 1956 but who ended up being hanged for treachery by his country's communist leaders. Though the APC was more of a mass movement, parallels can be drawn between it and revolutionary movements that often aggregate different tendencies to win power first before dealing with the contradictions within the movement. The PDP itself is unlikely to remain the same. I expect the party to be captured by new forces who will re-engineer it according to their image.

Amid its crisis, I was surprised that the APC failed to realize that the 2015 presidential election was fought on the shadows of the PDP's zoning controversy of 2010/2011 which it benefitted immensely from. Consequently one had expected the party to take the issue of zoning very seriously by, for instance, zoning its offices shortly after the election rather than dithering on the issue and allowing powerful interests to coalesce and go after their own interests. No matter how romantic we want to be, 'federal character principle', 'zoning' and 'power rotation' arrangements have become key organizing principles of our political economy and important periscopes for assessing any regime. Romantics or opponents of these organizing principles often fail to realize that what they call 'merit' and 'competence', in a polarized society like ours, are socially constructed and do not exist outside the framework of the markers through which people filter realities. This is another way of saying that these are subjectively determined in a polarized society like ours and will always depend on where one stands in the fault lines and the active controversies of the day.

There is a very important lesson to be drawn from the APC's electoral victory at the national level and the crisis that followed the party's victory:

Largely because the party was the first opposition political party in the country to defeat a ruling party at the national level, its template for that success will for some time be a reference manual. The general perception is that APC was an alliance between the dominant elites in the South West and a charismatic leader capable of galvanizing huge support in the North West and North East (what some people call the 'core north'). It is expected therefore that in future, parties aiming for electoral success at the national level will now have to look for broad alliances among other geopolitical zones. This may seriously dilute the notion of any region having a permanent ally and even the tyranny of the majority ethnic groups such as through a successful coalition of different ethnic minority groups. If the APC's victory leads to the pattern of inter-ethnic and inter-regional alliances among the elites becoming more dynamic than hitherto, it will not only advance the cause of nation-building but will also infuse integrity into the political process because groups without history of treachery will be highly courted.

But how does the APC resolve its festering crisis?

The President reportedly called on the feuding politicians to "sheath their ambitions." With all due respect, I am not sure this will be an effective way of resolving the dispute because it assumes, not correctly in my opinion, that politicians are primarily driven by a sense of altruism and patriotism. In my opinion, any serious analysis of the political behaviour of Nigerian politicians must start from their enlightened self interest. Politicians do not "sheath their ambitions". They retreat if the structural constraints do not permit the realization of such ambitions or the cost of pursuing that ambition has become unbearable. This is what the 19th century Prussian General Von Clausewitz would call the 'rational calculus of war' (matching the means against the objectives of war). For politicians, politics, just like war, is an instrument for achieving an objective. Since politicians are not in politics for the heck of it, you cannot sermonize to them to forget their ambitions (especially when you have achieved yours and you are not offering any compensation to those who "sheath" their own ambitions) and expect them to obey you.

It is true that Buhari's charisma among the northern voters drove the process of the APC becoming a mass movement (despite making more money available to candidate Buhari and providing a more national platform, the new party added a mere three million votes to what Buhari had consistently achieved on his own since 2003). Despite this, other groupings and tendencies in the party – the Tinubu group, the 'New PDP' Governors that defected to the party and energized its base etc- could also claim that without their contributions, the party would perhaps not have succeeded and are therefore entitled to the 'sinecures of war'.

Party supremacy

A battle cry in the current crisis in the APC is the doctrine of 'party supremacy'. But what does this really mean? Does party supremacy for instance mean that the APC should select ministers and advisers and foist them on President Buhari?

There are two main perspectives when Nigerians brandish the phrase 'party supremacy': There are those who believe that before an election, the supremacy of the party over its candidates for offices should be unquestionable but that once the candidates win elections, they should be allowed to be guided by the national interest – meaning that such people should be allowed to follow their conscience. There are however others who believe that the decision of a political party must be abided by its members before and after elections because the party provided the platform on which its elected members ascended to power.

Both perspectives represent only partial views of reality. For instance, in parliamentary system where the notion of the supremacy of the party is strongest, there is what is called 'conscience' or 'free' vote where parliamentarians are allowed to follow their conscience in voting. In the run-up to the Iraq war in 2003 for instance, several Tory and Labour MPs in the UK defied their parties and voted against the war.

For those who believe that the party should be supreme at all times, this is often based on an erroneous assumption that in our type of societies parties are structured and institutionalized around core beliefs or that they are neutral arbiters in the intra-elite competitions for power, glory and lucre. Thus while many people know what the Labour and Conservative parties stand for in the UK or what the Republicans and the Democrats stand for in the USA, the same cannot be said of our parties. Like the general society where the absence of strong institutions means that organizations are often controlled by the 'strong man' or a cabal, Nigerian parties are also controlled by strong individuals and oligarchs. In essence what people call 'party supremacy' is merely the projection of the interests of the 'Big man' oligarchic group that controls the party structures at any point in time. Let me give an example:

Shortly after Jonathan became the President following the death of Umaru Yaradua, Vincent Ogbulafor, who was then Chairman of the ruling PDP was shoved aside after declaring that going by the party's zoning and power rotation arrangements, it would be the turn of the north to produce the president in 2011. Not long after Jonathan entrenched himself in power, the entire leadership of the PDP favoured his running for President in 2011- despite the reported earlier party arrangement which ceded to the north the right to produce the president in 2011. So which of these two contradictory stands of the PDP could be taken as the party's doctrine on which its supremacy should be enforced?

The point in the above is that it is wrong to have a romantic notion of any Nigerian political party as an impartial arbiter in the intra elite struggles and feuds over power and lucre. The truth is that 'party supremacy' is a projection of the wishes of the Big Man or oligarchic group that funds and controls the party. This is largely why powerful individuals and groups who have the confidence and resources often 'rebel' against the use of such veneer by their rivals to gain advantage.

Daily Trust, July 16, 2015

CHAPTER 66

Re-thinking the National Assembly

The inspiration for this piece came from a conversation with an elder statesman who felt it was time for President Buhari to 'sanitize' the National Assembly. Reminding me that former President Obasanjo had recently accused the National Assembly of corruption and that former CBN Governor Lamido Sanusi had also alleged that as much as 25 per cent of the federal budget is spent on the two chambers of the National Assembly, the elder statesman said it was time to do away with one of the chambers of the National Assembly in order to "reduce the level of corruption and impunity going on there."

For supporters of President Buhari, the politics that followed the submission of the 2016 budget in December 2015, the 'discovery' that the original budget submitted was 'missing', the accusations that the budget had been 'padded' and the finger pointing and grandstanding between the Executive and the National Assembly that ensued are additional reasons why the National Assembly should be cut to size. And one of the common proposals on how this could be done is to turn the national legislature into a unicameral one (that is with only one chamber instead of the Senate and House of Representatives as we have now). Some additionally want it to be a part time job.

There is also an economic angle to this. With declining revenues and workers across the country being owed salaries, some are murmuring about the N115bn allocated to the National Assembly in the 2016 Budget. The image of the National Assembly has not been helped by recent media reports that the Upper chamber went on a buying spree of exotic cars at the cost of over N4.7 billion – at a time Nigerians are suffering and struggling to buy fuel. With many Nigerians angry and baying for the blood of any suspected oppressor, it is not surprising that more Nigerians appear to be questioning the rationale for wasting scarce resources on a two-chambered National Assembly, when they believe that one chamber can conveniently do the job.

I feel that the anger against the National Assembly as an institution is misplaced. I also believe that a one-chamber National Assembly will create more problems than it will solve for several reasons:

One, the history of bicameral legislature (i.e. one with two chambers) is one of the most compelling arguments for its preference over a unicameral one.

The modern bicameral system has its roots at the beginning of constitutional government in 17th century England and later in the 18th century on the continent of Europe and in the United States. The English parliament became bicameral out of a realization that the interests of the nobility and clergy were distinct from those of the common people. Following from this, when the British colonies were established in America, the colonial assemblies were also bicameral in recognition that they were to serve two distinct interests: those of the mother country and those of the colonists. In fact after America's declaration of independence in 1776, it opted for a bicameral national legislature – the Senate and the House of Representatives – because one of the greatest fears of the framers of the U.S. Constitution was that of 'federal tyranny'. For this reason, not only did they ensure that that there would be executive, legislative and judicial branches to check one another, they also wanted a federal system of states to serve as a counterweight to the federal government. As a continuation of such checks and balances, a national legislature was not just for making laws and supervising the executive and the judiciary but its bicameral nature was also to ensure that the two chambers acted as a check on each other to forestall 'legislative tyranny'.

Two, in bicameral legislatures such as Nigeria and the USA, the House of Representatives is comprised of members who represent population districts within each state, while members of the Senate represent the states themselves. If we were to do away with one chamber, will Kano state feel it is fair if it has the same number of representatives as Ebonyi State? And will Ebonyi state not feel it is tyrannical if Kano is given more than twice the number of representatives than it has in such a one-chamber legislature? In a country like ours, a bicameral legislature could therefore also be seen as a great compromise between very populous and thinly populated states.

Three, there is an additional reason why I feel we ought to retain a bi-cameral legislature – it offers an opportunity for a second thought on a piece of legislation. Sometimes a chamber could pass a bill on the heat of the moment and since to become law in our country such legislation needs to be passed by both chambers, there is always an opportunity to re-think ill-considered or hurriedly conceived legislations rather than having to embark on the usually time-consuming process of Constitutional amendment when a bill is discovered to have been passed in error. It is of course true that a bicameral National Assembly could increase the risk of a gridlock in needed political reforms. But legislation being hastily passed into law.

Four, I also do not believe that having a bicameral legislature has much to do with the huge cost of maintaining the National Assembly or that making it a part-time job will result in any substantial saving. Most of the suspected costs in the National Assembly do not come from the wages of the legislators.

Five, I will argue that in an emerging nation like ours, there are several special interests and contending forces that play critical roles in the economy and nation-building project, which ought to be specially represented in one of the chambers of the national legislature. I will propose that the Senate shall continue to mirror the equality of states (the number for each state could be reduced to two) while the House of Representatives should continue to reflect the population of states. Provision should however be made for appointed members to represent special interests in one of the chambers such as those of manufacturers, organized labour, women, the physically challenged and even militant and insurgency groups. I believe that by drawing groups that espouse ideas that 'shock and awe' into the competition of the political marketplace, the 'glamour' that goes with their ideas when they operate underground will be removed while offering the nation an opportunity to better understand the viewpoints of their proponents. In Canada for instance, the country's

105 Senators are not elected but appointed by the Governor General on the advice of the Prime Minister.

Now that the budget has been passed...

The excitement that attended the signing of the Budget by the President gave the wrong impression that a Budget is a bank cheque that is going to be cashed and money would start flowing. The truth is that a budget is merely a statement of estimated expenditures and revenues. There is no certainty that the projected revenue – even from borrowing- will be met. For instance while the budget was based on estimated oil production of 2.2million barrels per day (mbd), following the two recent attacks at Chevron facilities, it is thought that production has already dropped to as low as 1.69 mbd. The projected revenue from oil in the face of the suspected drop in production could therefore only be met from an increase in the price of oil. The budget was based on oil price of $38 per barrel while it is currently selling for between $43 and $45.

Obviously, if money could be found to fund the N1.57trn capital expenditure in the budget, it will trickle down and ease a few things. But we should be a little more realistic about what the budget is capable of accomplishing. The current hardship won't go away overnight because some of the hardships have structural causes while others are compounded by the government's economic policies.

A major lesson from the 2016 budget however is that the executive needs to learn to cultivate the National Assembly. The grandstanding and finger-pointing between the two arms of government was unnecessary and reflects the poor relationship between them. In the past, it is not uncommon for errors to be discovered in the budget after submission to the National Assembly but resolving such had never been as acrimonious as we saw with the 2016 Budget. In the end the politics damaged both the Executive and the National Assembly in the eyes of many Nigerians. I believe the politics damaged the Executive more than it did the National Assembly.

Daily Trust, May 12, 2016

CHAPTER 67

Bringing back 'Do-or- Die Politics'?

I have not particularly been a fan of the Jonathan presidency. I have nothing against him as a person. If anything, I admire his very simple demeanour - no offensively expensive attire and everything about his person radiates simplicity and humility – well as much humility as the demands of the office permit and the need to have the necessary rough edges to ward off those seriously after his job or eager to pull him down.

My reservations stemmed mostly on a principled opposition to his stance on the zoning controversy in the run-up to the April 2011presidential election and my belief that he has underperformed in office. I however always give him one credit: the improvement in the credibility of elections since Professor Attahiru Jega became INEC chairman, I believe, owes more to President Jonathan than to any integrity that the electoral umpire might have brought with him to the office. In my opinion, in our type of society and the peculiar brand of democracy it spurns, elections are free and fair to the extent that the express instructions or body language of the president permit. In Local Government elections, it is transparent only to the extent that the Governor of the State wants it to be. Until now, there has been nothing to suggest that the President sees elections as a 'do-or-die' affair. I recall that when Professor Jega cancelled the National Assembly elections on April 2 2011, mid way into the exercise, President Jonathan was said to be in his home state of Bayelsa, in a queue, waiting to cast his vote, meaning he was not even consulted before the cancellation. If the President was miffed by that 'insult', he never expressed it publicly. Under a 'strong' President like Obasanjo, such an embarrassment would have been probably enough for his removal from office, if not making him a guest of the EFCC, on real or contrived allegations of corruption. President Jonathan earned a lot of my respect by the way he handled the situation – despite the fact that Jega's INEC had literally blackmailed the country into getting every Kobo he asked for.

In the past I had written about the re-invention of Jonathan since the April 2011 elections – from a public persona of simple, almost naïve president who does not mind changing his mind several times on an issue to one who is increasingly becoming 'Obasanjonized'. This is not altogether a bad thing because I still regard Obasanjo as a great leader, the best the country has had - despite his shortcomings and lack of grace. In our type of society, without developing some necessary rough edges and being able to firmly mete out sanctions to those who deserve it, all manner of obstacles, under various ideological, political, religious, ethnic and ideological persuasions, will be contrived to block your options. In Nigeria, turning the other cheek when slapped – as espoused by most religions – will be an invitation for more and deadlier slaps. Which was why the late Mokwugo Okoye, a member of the firebrand Zikist Movement during the nationalist agitations for independence, declared that he had chosen to meet Moses (who advocated an eye-for-eye when slapped) and Jesus Christ (who preached 'turning the other cheek') half-way, by plucking out the eyes of those who slapped him, not as revenge as Moses preached, but as a deterrence to others.

I have argued in an earlier piece that the ding-dong between Governor Amaechi and President Jonathan is just politics, in furtherance of their personal ambitions for power and glory and not anything actuated by any higher philosophy. I disagreed with the argument that it was heating up the polity but felt that it rather provided a needed entertainment, which our politics has largely been denuded of since the Fourth Republic. Unlike in the Second Republic where we had political entertainers like the late K.O. Mbadiwe (the self-styled man of timber and calibre), Dr Chuba Okadigbo (famed for his grandiloquence), the fast-talking Uba Ahmed and others with fanciful names like Mamman Ali Makele and Alhaji Alhaji Alhaji, our current crop of politicians are even incapable of giving us quotable quotes. Most are simply boring. Apart from few dog-fights such as provided in the epic battle between former President Obasanjo and his Vice Alhaji Atiku Abubakar, political news in the current dispensation have lacked any entertainment value. Until the current face-off between the presidency and Governor Amaechi, there have hardly been political sagas, with enough in-built suspense, that will force the electorate to monitor closely how the whole story will end. In essence, such political dog fights have a way of increasing political participation and the education of the electorate.

The fallout from the recent elections of a new Chairman of the Governors' Forum however appears to be introducing a macabre dance step to what I had all along seen as a mere political entertainment. Both Governor Amaechi and his opponent in the election - Governor Jonah Jang of Plateau State, who is widely believed to be sponsored by the Presidency, claimed victory. My concern with this development is that what I consider the greatest legacy of the Jonathan presidency – eschewing a do-or-die politics appears now to be under threat. This is an ominous sign for 2015.

The reaction of the presidency to the 'humiliation' that Governor Amaechi defeated its anointed candidate is truly frightening – not because Amaechi is completely blameless because he is not. At least he should share part of the blame for flouting his party's directives, going on a frontal fight with the Big Man in our type of society (rather than fighting him sideways as survivalists do) and for subtly fraternizing with the opposition party. The concern however is that whereas in the past President Jonathan had been among the first to congratulate any candidate who defeated his anointed one – as happened with Ikedi Ohakim in Imo State and elsewhere - in the just concluded NGF election, a splinter group was formed, apparently with the active connivance of the presidency, each claiming to have won the election. On top of this, he was immediately suspended from the PDP by the party's National Working Committee.

This immediately brings the memory of Côte d'Ivoire as we approach 2015. In that country, Laurent Gbagbo, who was the country's President from 2000 until his arrest in April 2011, lost the 2010 presidential election to Alassane Ouattara but refused to vacate. If the putative APC is able to overcome all the obstacles on its way and manages to defeat the President in the 2015 election (if he decides to run), are we going to face the Côte d'Ivoire scenario? The outcome of the recent NGF election, which pitted not just the presidency against Governor Amaechi but also the putative APC against the rump of the PDP loyal to President Jonathan, ought to highlight this question as demanding urgent answer in our political agenda.

There are several losers in this debacle between the presidency and Governor Amaechi. One sure loser will be the PDP, which by suspending Governor Amaechi shortly after the controversial election, lent credence to the perennial charges against it by the opposition parties that it lacked internal democracy. How can a party justify suspending a member, a Governor for that matter, without even the formality of inviting such a person to disciplinary hearing? This is giving the opposition a big ammunition to grandstand – even though internal party democracy in the various opposition parties is no better.

Another loser will be Governor Akpabio of Akwa Ibom State. Though I am suspicious of the media marketing of the achievements of various Governors (I call them Bill Board Governors), Governor Akpabio, with his peculiar theatrics and biography conflating with clever media marketing of his achievements in Akwa Ibom, comes across as a likeable character. However this epic ends, Akpabio will be seen rightly or wrongly as someone used to factionalize the Nigerian Governors Forum, and a Governor, who like a 'small boy', was being used to teleguide the biddings of the Presidency. How could such an apparently intelligent fellow allow himself to be so diminished?

I am also surprised that Governor Jang agreed to vie for the Presidency of the NGF at this time, knowing that he would be automatically seen as the candidate of the presidency. Already labelled - fairly or unfairly - as a 'divisive figure' in Plateau State by his critics, doesn't Governor Jang realize that being a factional chairman of the NGF would accentuate his label as a 'divisive figure'?

For President Jonathan, the controversial outcome of the NGF elections could cut both ways: while it would probably force more PDP supporters to sympathize with the APC – overtly or covertly - it could also send a signal that the weak President Jonathan, being trampled upon by all and sundry, is gone for good, and that the new President Jonathan will be willing to fight you toe-to-toe, if you fall out of line or dare him. In essence, as Jonathan transmutes from a President who wants to be loved (including for not wearing shoes to school), to one who engenders fear (especially among those lusting after his job), two critical questions are raised: which of these two personas will secure the presidency for him in 2015? Which one is better for our type of society and its peculiar brand of democracy?

Daily Trust, May 30 2013

PERSONALITIES

CHAPTER 68

Buhari: Torn Between Two Contradictory Impulses?

While hosting State House correspondents to a lunch recently at the Presidential Villa, Abuja, as part of the activities to mark his one year in office, President Buhari reportedly said he never expected that former President Goodluck Jonathan would concede defeat so easily after the March 2015 presidential election as he did. The President reportedly said:

"For him to have conceded defeat even before the result was announced by the Independent National Electoral Commission, I think it was quite generous and gracious of him…. Gen. Abdulsalami recognised the generosity of Jonathan to concede defeat and said we should go and thank him immediately and that was the first time I came here."

I was really touched when I read this. For me, it shows a conciliatory side of the President that did not exactly flourish during his first year in office. Buhari, it should be recalled, had gone to court to challenge the outcome of each of the three previous elections that he lost. He therefore knew what he was talking about, including the sort of pressure that Jonathan as a sitting President probably had to withstand to make that historic concession. It is precisely because of that noble gesture from Jonathan that several Nigerians, (including my humble self), felt that whatever his other shortcomings, Jonathan deserved to be treated as a statesman (even if he had to be asked to account for his time in office). True, conceding defeat is no big deal in climes where both the democratic and nation-building processes have matured. But in climes like ours where such a gesture is a rarity, it becomes an act of statesmanship. It is like telling the truth or having integrity in climes where such are scarce commodities. What could be normal in other climes could be revolutionary acts in others.

There was another glimpse of the conciliatory side of Buhari when he famously declared that he belonged to everybody and to nobody. He also promised that he would not look into the past but would draw a line on what people did from the time he was sworn into office. It appeared that this putative Mandela-like side of Buhari had to contend with the 'tough Buhari' personage of his first coming, which is apparently very much beloved by his fanatical supporters. The tough Buhari personage was expected to cart as many people as possible into jail, to be single-minded in fighting corruption using the sort of 'gragra' that characterised his first coming and to brook no nonsense and dialogue with no one (as such would be signs of weakness). From all indications those pushing for Buhari to live up to his tough man personage triumphed in his first year in office, for shortly after being sworn in office, he reversed himself and announced that he would probe the Jonathan regime. He also refused to grant bails to Sambo Dasuki and Nnamdi Kanu – despite their reportedly meeting their bail conditions. He equally reversed himself and declared that it would be unrealistic to expect that those who gave him five percent votes would get the same treatment as those who gave him 95 percent support. Alienated groups like agitators for Biafra and Niger Delta neo militants were given notice that they did not know who they were dealing with. With these, those pushing for Buhari to live up to his tough man image triumphed over those who felt that given his age and experience, the role of a Mandela would come natural to him. Mandela, it should be recalled forgave those who drove the Apartheid system in South Africa and jailed him for 27 years. He disappointed many Blacks who felt that his ascendancy would be used to right historic wrongs and seek vengeance. It is Mandela's singular effort in unifying a deeply fractured South Africa that made him a living saint even among White South Africans. He also became one of the greatest moral authorities in the world until his transition on December 5 2013.

For me Buhari's one year in office will be better assessed by the extent to which a particular brand of Buhari which dominated the period succeeded or failed.

When Buhari apologized to Nigerians over the illegal sacking of some vice chancellors by the Minister for Education, I argued in an article entitled 'Buhari's apology: Opportunity for another re-invention' (Daily Trust, March 31 2016), that it was an opportunity to re-invent the President so that his softer side would drive his policies. Buhari has since 'softened' up on several other key policy issues that people, who still have the notion of 'a tough and inflexible' Buhari of his first coming would never think is possible: He has approved huge increase in the pump price of fuel after opposing such a measure for years, he has given implicit consent to the devaluation of the naira and reneged on several campaign promises. Buhari is likely to be concerned whether his concessions to realities means watering down the Buhari personage his supporters deify. But I believe he needs not be a prisoner of supporters' conception of him.

Buhari needs to free himself from the control of the hawks and become a reconciler because I sincerely believe that the triumph of the 'tough man' side of Buhari in his first one year in office has been at a huge cost. For example when Nnamdi Kanu, leader of one of the Biafra agitation groups, was incarcerated and denied bail, very few people had ever heard of his name. Some of us warned that holding him in detention for a prolonged period would only turn him into a mythical figure among his followers which would aggravate the separatist agitation he champions. The fear of such unintended effect is precisely why in advanced democracies hate groups like the British National Party or the KKK in the USA are never banned or their leaders incarcerated but rather efforts are made to draw the ideas they espouse into the market of political ideas and outcompeted. But those pushing for the 'tough' Buhari personage apparently triumphed and today Biafra agitation, which has been there since the 1990s, as, at best, a largely non-violent irritation, has metamorphosed into something else. I still feel the government's response was mistaken because we have a template on how separatist agitations are dealt with and defeated in other places.

What can be said about Nnamdi Kanu can also be said about the continued detention of Dasuki – despite court orders to get him released. Despite the mind-boggling sum Dasuki is said to have embezzled, will the country really lose anything if he is granted bail as ordered by the courts, with perhaps his passports seized? For the Niger Delta Avengers and other insurgents, it was long predicted that there would be a resurgence of militancy in the Niger Delta if Buhari won and a prolonged post-election violence in parts of the Northeast and Northwest if Buhari lost because of the politics of identity. A common recommendation by analysts was that whoever won should reach out to the loser and treat him like a co-winner. There are indications that a part of Buhari wanted very much to do that (for example from his opinion of Jonathan cited earlier in this piece and from his statements that he belonged to everyone and to no one). Somehow the hawks and hardliners seemed to have held Buhari captive in his first year in office. .

For the hawks and hardliners pushing for a final solution against all the obstacles on the President's way, they should be reminded that it will take just one major international newspaper to label the President a dictator or accuse the army of human rights abuses for the remaining goodwill we have in the global community to be squandered.

I believe that most Nigerians want President Buhari to succeed – at least with the hope that such success will trickle down to their dining tables and pockets. For me, the tough Buhari personage who ruled in the first year of the regime's four -year tenure only recorded commendable success in fighting Boko Haram. In my opinion, the 'gra gra method' of fighting corruption has not only de-marketed the country but is also generally counter-productive – despite figures of recovered loots from EFCC. The tough and unyielding Buhari also failed in my opinion in the areas of rebuilding the economy and uniting Nigerians. Even the commendable success against Boko Haram is vitiated by the fact that as Boko Haram recedes in the Northeast, it is being reconstituted in other parts of the country – through groups like pro-Biafra activists, Black Avengers in the Niger Delta and murderous herdsmen across the country.

CHAPTER 69

When the President Returns

The recent news that President Buhari has taken ill and travelled to England to treat a discomforting left ear infection called Meniere Disease has brought to the fore the compassionate side of Nigerians. After the story, first reported by Premium Times on June 4 2016, was finally confirmed by the presidency, the social media began trending with compassionate 'get well soon' messages and prayers for the president's quick recovery.

The concerns and compassions, even from the President's most ardent critics, (and most of these concerns appear genuine to me) tell me that the 'banality of good deeds' must be a necessary complement to what the German-American political theorist called the 'banality of evil'. Arendt had argued that the great crimes in history were not committed by psychopaths but by ordinary men and women who accepted the premises and rationalizations of those deeds. I believe that the 'banality of good deeds' could be explained by the fact that there is a spark of divine or God's DNA in all of us which pushes us into morally uplifting deeds. The 'banality of evil' competes for space with this 'banality of good deeds' in pretty much the same way that the flesh and spirit part of us compete for space and dominance.

This tension between good and evil deeds is probably what the American politician Edward Wallis Hoch had in mind when he famously declared:

> "There is so much good in the worst of us,
> And so much bad in the best of us,
> That it hardly behooves any of us
> To talk about the rest of us"

Hock reminds us that the best of us are capable of mean and mischievous acts just as the worst of us, including terrorists and armed robbers, are capable of noble acts.

The outpouring of compassion for the President's illness reminds one of a similar outpouring of 'get soon' messages to Ibrahim Babangida, when in 1987 he was hospitalized in the American Hospital in Paris, France, for a condition known as radiculopathy, (which had something to do with an injury he sustained on his left foot during the Civil War). The irony here is that Babangida had become a bit unpopular at that time because he had a year before (i.e.1986) introduced the highly unpopular IMF/World Bank-supported structural adjustment programme (SAP), which many blamed for emasculating the middle class and further pauperizing the citizens. There is therefore a parallel between the economic hardship of the time and the current economic difficulties in the country. Babangida really had very little choice on the matter of SAP because the era was dominated by the doctrine of 'cross conditionalities' (i.e. if the two Bretton Woods institutions do not approve your economic policies you cannot reschedule your debts, open new letters of credit or even get aids and grants from major donors) Like Babangida, Buhari's medical trip is coming at a time of economic hardship and also when his popularity is on the wane.

I believe that another reason that Nigerians showed much compassion and empathy for both Babangida and Buhari's ill-health is that both leaders did not try to pretend that they are super humans who are incapable of getting ill. It is nothing to be ashamed of that one is ill – even if you are President or Governor.

While I join millions of Nigerians in wishing our President quick recovery, I also believe the period of his rest will give him an opportunity for sober reflection. One year in office may be still within that stretch of the learning curve, but it is also a period long enough for one to begin to decipher what has worked so far and what has not, including where one has made mistakes.

From the early years of this regime, I have been a consistent advocate that the President should be a reconciler and should re-think the rhetoric of 'probe', which essentially only assuages those baying for the blood of their assumed regional, ethnic and class enemies. We can still achieve the same goal using less polarizing means or means that unduly overheat the polity while entertaining a few that regale in media trial.

Related to the above is that the president should also reflect on how he deals with dissidents and groups it disagrees with. The presidency should for instance consider whether the continued detention of Nnamdi Kanu is serving any meaningful purpose or unduly turning him into a hero and radicalizing his followers. He should also consider whether the nation really gains anything by the continued detention of Sambo Dasuki and El Zakzaky. I am happy the government has announced it is suspending the militarization of the Niger Delta in favour of exploring peaceful resolution of whatever grievances the Niger Delta Avengers and other neo militants say they have. I believe we should also assess whether, given the damage the group has already done to the national economy, the negotiation option shouldn't have been our first line of engagement.

While I join Nigerians in commending the President for transferring power to the Vice President as required by the Constitution during his time of being away (unlike what the cabal around President Yaradua did before his death and what some Governors did in the last dispensation), the President's illness also draws eloquent attention to the gross information mismanagement in his government. For instance, when the information was first broken that Buhari was ill, the SSA Media to the President, Femi Adeshina, an otherwise affable man, claimed the news was a figment of the imagination of their purveyors and proclaimed that the President was as fit as a fiddle. A few days later, he swallowed his vomit and tweeted that the President would indeed be travelling abroad for medical treatment. Adeshina, who is increasingly turning himself into a gaffe machine, also reportedly claimed that the Biafra agitation arose because President Jonathan lost the election to Buhari. The implication of this is that Biafra agitation was aimed at destabilizing the Buhari regime. This is the sort of simplistic analysis that former President Jonathan fell for regarding Boko Haram. He was convinced that Boko Haram was formed by some northern politicians to destabilize his government even when some of us maintained that the sect was symptomatic of groups delinking from the Nigerian state and regarding the state as the enemy.

The truth is that Biafra agitation was there from the inception of this Republic. At a time the then Governor of Anambra state Peter Obi had to give a shoot-at-sight order on members of MASSOB, which was championing the agitation. Like most insurgency groups, MASSOB later factionalized into IPOB and other groups. The relevant question therefore is not when or why it was formed but the reasons for its radicalization and growing membership.

Some of us had expressed concerns that the detention of Nnamdi Kanu, the leader of IPOB, would only turn him into a mythical figure and radicalize his followers and that it is precisely for this reason that even hate groups like British National Party in the United Kingdom or the KKK in the USA are never banned or their leaders clamped into detention. Rather such groups are kept on the fringe of society by drawing their ideas into the marketplace of political ideas and outcompeting them.

When the President has fully recovered and returns home, we should also encourage honest conversation on the small matter of medical tourism. We should accept the argument that our hospitals cannot be brought to world standard overnight. But it will be difficult to convince many Nigerians that the Villa Clinic cannot be so equipped that it will become unnecessary for top government officials to seek medical treatment abroad.

In Memoriam: Enejere, Ali and Keshi

When I entered the University straight from secondary school in 1980, one of my memorable lecturers at the University of Nigeria, Nsukka, at that time was Dr Emeka Enejere. We nicknamed him Hobbes because he thought us 'Western Political Thoughts' and we found Hobbes' ideas quite mesmerizing. Unlike most lecturers, Dr Enejere was highly accessible to students and had no airs about him

We spoke about two weeks before his death. He had told me he was receiving chemotherapy at home every other week. I promised to visit him – which regrettably I did not manage to do. I was shocked when I got a text message from his family announcing his transition. Dr Enejere was an affable, deeply intelligent and lively scholar. May his gentle soul rest in peace.

Though I never met Muhammed Ali and Stephen Keshi, news of their transition was equally shocking. Their deaths were such that remind us of our own mortality. May their souls rest in peace.

Daily Trust, June 9, 2016

CHAPTER 70

Buhari's Quest for Emergency Economic Powers

Since Reuters broke the news on August 22 2016 that the government would be seeking for emergency powers to enable it fix the economy, Nigerians have been debating the pros and cons of that yet- to- be confirmed Bill. Though officially the government continues to claim it is unaware that such a Bill is on the pipeline, with the Nation, a paper owned by Asiwaju Bola Tinubu and regarded as pro-APC reporting the story same day as Reuters' and quoting unnamed government sources, many Nigerians feel it has gone beyond rumours and speculations.

According to The Nation newspaper of August 22 2016, an executive Bill entitled: 'Emergency Economic Stabilisation Bill 2016' would be presented to the National Assembly when the Senate and the House of Representatives resume from vacation on September 12. The paper claimed that in the Bill, the President would ask for sweeping powers to set aside some extant laws and use executive orders to roll out an economic recovery package within the next one year. According to the paper the President would specifically ask for 'emergency powers' to abridge the procurement process ostensibly because the extant law on procurement does not allow contract award earlier than six months after decision. The government is also said to be uncomfortable with the current provisions of the law which forbid it from mobilizing contractors with more than 15 per cent of the total contract sum. The Bill, the Nation claimed, would allow the government to mobilise contractors with 50 per cent of contract sum, making it easier for it to push for faster completion of projects.

The planned emergency powers, it was equally claimed, would also enable the government to amend certain laws such as the Universal Basic Education Commission (UBEC) Act so that states that cannot access their cash trapped in the accounts of the Commission because they cannot meet the counterpart funding requirements would be able to do so. It is estimated that about N58 billion is trapped in UBEC's coffers because many states cannot provide the required 50 per cent of counterpart funding. Through the planned Bill, the government would seek an amendment to the law so that states will pay only 10 per cent as counterpart funding. The proposed Bill would equally enable the President to allow virement of budgetary allocation to projects that are urgent without going back to the National Assembly as well as embark on radical reforms in visa issuance at Nigeria's consular offices.

With the economy in dire straits, there is no doubt that the government needs to do something urgently. In fact, recent provisional figures from the National Bureau of Statistics make a very grim reading. According to the NBS, during the second quarter of this year, the country's Gross Domestic Product declined by 2.06 per cent (year-on-year) in real terms compared to the growth rate of 0.36 per cent recorded in the preceding quarter and the 2.35 per cent recorded in the corresponding quarter of 2015. The NBS also reported that the total value of capital imported into the country in the second quarter of the year was a paltry $647.1m – which represents a decline of 8.98 per cent relative to the first quarter and a decline of 75.75 per cent relative to the second quarter of 2015. The statistics agency underlined that this provisional figure was the lowest level of capital imported into the economy on record and also represented the largest year on year decline. The NBS's figures clearly show that the country is on a rapid downward slide on virtually all economic and social indicators.

Supporters of the proposed Bill therefore argue that given the country's current economic condition, the President should be supported with whatever power he seeks to get things fixed.

I believe that many of the arguments on which the proposed (or rumoured) emergency economic powers are built make sense. For instance I am persuaded on the argument about changing the extant laws on UBEC to reduce the counterpart funding obligations of states from 50 per cent to 10 per cent. There is no doubt that there is a need for flexibility in the application of some of our extant laws – given the current economic climate. What remains debatable is whether wide-ranging emergency economic powers are what the government should be hankering after.

In fact the proposed or rumoured Bill on Emergency Economic Powers for the President raises a number of fundamental issues:

One, nay-saying to any government project or proposal – no matter how utilitarian or sophisticated the argument used in selling such – is quite normal and underlines the general distrust of governments everywhere especially by civil society activists. This is worse in Buhari's case because of his authoritarian antecedents as a military dictator and a lingering suspicion about his conversion as a democrat. His critics would remain suspicious of why he wants wide- ranging emergency powers when he could have asked for amendments of specific Acts or sections of the Constitution to achieve the same aim. I think the Bill will be a tough sell for the government, no matter how well its intention is. And I remain among those who believe the President means well for the country but is yet to find his mojo.

Two, while the current government might not have created what APC chieftains like to call the 'mess we are in'; it has not really been able to halt the country's economic, social and political decline. Rather the government appears to be on perennial trial- and- error runs, sometimes with policies that are contradictory and also with frequent policy somersaults – all of which end up worsening the country's condition. The fear therefore is whether the proposed Bill, if passed by the National Assembly, will not be another trial and error stuff that will be haphazardly implemented or even abandoned midstream – compounding the problems they were theoretically meant to solve.

Three, apart from questions of whether the President really needs sweeping emergency powers to resolve the country's economic problems, there is even a more fundamental question of whether the current economic challenges are not merely economic manifestations of the President's politics –or at least amplified by the President's politics. For instance, to what extent has the government's unintended de-marketing of the country through its probe rhetoric contributed to the drying up of foreign capital inflows in the country? To what extent has the regime's mode of fighting corruption – which is gra-gra driven rather than institution-driven, discouraged those with the money from coming out to invest? I do not support corruption but I have remained a consistent critic of the EFCC/ICPC gra-gra method of fighting corruption over the years. For one, I have remained unconvinced that their system either works in deterring corruption or has benefitted the economy – otherwise each new government at both state and federal levels would not be indulging in the sport of accusing its predecessor of monumental corruption. My belief is that while the current gra-gra method of fighting corruption may appeal to those baying for the blood of their class, regional and ethnic (real and imagined) enemies, it has discouraged those with the money to spend and reflate the economy. I have over the years called for conditional amnesty for those accused of corruption and a change in our way of fighting the malaise into something that is institution-driven and devoid of the razzmatazz of media trials. It is also difficult to separate the current system of fighting corruption with political vendetta. Essentially therefore, any attempt at seriously resuscitating our comatose economy must encompass retooling the President's brand of politics.

Four, I do not believe that the economy is the President's forté – and it must not necessarily be so. I also do not believe he has the best team he is capable of assembling to tackle the current economic challenges. But the President has a critical resource – an impressive force of personality and charisma to provide political cover to those working for him and willing to take risks. Therefore another key requirement in any serious attempt to turn around the economy is assembling people with impressive credentials from different ideological spectrum to be in his economic team. The President will also need to give such people real leg-room to engage in robust economic and political debates among themselves. The president should limit his role to providing political cover to members of the team once they have agreed on certain options – rather than being seen as dictating to them what to do in specific circumstances. I also believe that the government can benefit from a redefinition of loyalty, which does not have to mean fear of the leader. I think true and enduring loyalty should mean above anything else subordinates being encouraged to respectfully tell the leader the truth or to contribute their honest conviction to the vibrancy of the leader's think-tank.

Daily Trust, September 1, 2016

CHAPTER 71

Am I Really a "Buhari Hater"?

There were several reactions to my last week's column entitled 'Buhari's Quest for Economic Emergency Powers'. One of the points that attracted the most commentaries was the poser: "… apart from questions of whether the President really needs sweeping emergency powers to resolve the country's economic problems, there is even a more fundamental question of whether the current economic challenges are not merely economic manifestations of the President's politics – or at least amplified by the President's politics. For instance, to what extent has the government's unintended de-marketing of the country through its probe rhetoric contributed to the drying up of foreign capital inflows in the country? To what extent has the regime's mode of fighting corruption – which is gra-gra driven rather than institution- driven, discouraged those with the money from coming out to invest?"

Some of the reactions were critical of my criticisms of the regime's mode of fighting corruption. I was reminded that the President's anti-corruption fights have won kudos from world leaders and from a recent Buharimeter from the Centre for Democracy and Development. There were the usual accusations that I was driven by "sentiments" and of "hating the President, and consequently have chosen not to see anything good in his government".

I have always believed that every opinion expressed by any columnist or opinion writer is merely a modest contribution to the vibrancy of our marketplace of political ideas, which is the infrastructure on which our democracy project rests. Consequently I do not expect that ideas I express will not be aggressively interrogated. If I can take the liberty to interrogate the government and its policies who am I that people should not use various modes of expressions, including unorthodox modes such as name-calling and plain insult, to express their displeasure at my ideas? Anyone who throws his hat into the public square should not complain if people match or kick it.

I will however like to address today the persistent allegations by a certain group of 'Buharimaniacs' that my writings are animated by a supposed hatred for President Buhari. It is true that I have been a persistent critic of Buhari's fight against corruption. But so was I a critic of both Jonathan and Obasanjo's ways of fighting corruption as a simple search of some of my articles on corruption will show. In fact the titles of some of these articles are not pretentious about my cynicism for such 'wars'. Good examples of such articles include "War on Corruption: Why EFCC Will Fail" (2009). "Corruption: Time for General Amnesty?" (2010), "Is Corruption Really the Problem"? (2013). Under Jonathan, I consistently dismissed the war against corruption as a charade and called for conditional amnesty for all accused of corrupt practices so that the nation could reset the button on the fight against the malaise. The three articles cited above (and there are more) will vividly show that those who revel in accusing me of hating President Buhari because I criticise his system of fighting corruption are either being ahistorical or grossly unfair in their criticisms. That every regime has made the fight against corruption its key policy plank and yet the vice seems to continue unabated vindicates my position that we have been fighting the symptom of a more fundamental malaise using inappropriate tools (which I call gra-gra method).

Another area I have been critical of the Buhari government is on the general thrust of his government. This again derives from my own belief on what constitutes the fundamental problem of our country. I have always taken the position that the fundamental problem facing the country is the crisis in our nation-building process – not corruption or even poverty. In fact in 2012, at the height of the Boko Haram crisis, I gave a well- received public lecture at the Institute for Security Studies, Pretoria, South Africa entitled: "Boko Haram as Symptom of the Crisis in Nigeria's Nation-Building'. In that paper I wrote:

> "My position is that a more comprehensive explanation of the Boko Haram phenomenon is the crisis in our nation-building project. While the bombings and other unsavoury acts that are linked to the sect are very condemnable, it is germane to underline that Boko Haram is only one of several groups in the country that purvey terror and death. This is not an apology for their actions, but there is increasing tendency to discuss the spate of insecurity in the country as if it all began and ended with Boko Haram – or as if without Boko Haram Nigeria would be a tranquil place to live in.....
>
> "Virtually every part of Nigeria claims it is 'marginalised' and there are concomitant groups calling for the convocation of a Sovereign National Conference (a euphemism for a meeting to discuss whether Nigerians want to continue to live together as one country or not). This is a clear indication that something nasty has happened to the effort to create Nigerians to populate the geographical expression called Nigeria...
>
> "My personal opinion is that the number of Nigerians being alienated from the Nigeria project and therefore regarding the state as a legitimate target is increasing by leaps and bounds. If this trend continues, we risk having Nigeria without Nigerians as everyone seems to carry out an attack on the Nigerian state using whatever means at the person's disposal".

Essentially, I was as critical of nation-building under Jonathan as I am under Buhari. I was never called a Jonathan hater. Can it therefore be that those accusing me of hating President Buhari are either intolerant of criticisms or suffering from group-think?

Many of us who believe that the fundamental problem of the country is how to unite a fractious nation expected Buhari to be Nigeria's version of Mandela or Julius Nyerere. We were looking for a unifier, a father figure, not a new sheriff in town. We wanted to see conscious and sensitive efforts at re-uniting Nigerians after an acrimonious election. But rather than this happening, it seemed that President Buhari was quickly captured by hawks who wasted no time in demonizing the former President and saturating the public space with probe rhetoric. I am not against probing anyone but I do not believe that using the razzmatazz of media trial either helps the cause of reconciling Nigerians, fighting corruption or even promoting justice. The only thing it does, in my opinion, is to satisfy those haying for the blood of their supposed class, regional and ethnic enemies. I have been critical of the Buhari government on this as I was critical of Jonathan, including on the radicalization of Boko Haram as my quote from my article above shows.

Many of us who gave several public lectures or wrote commissioned papers on the 2015 elections warned that if Jonathan lost the election, it could trigger renewed militancy in the Niger Delta while post election violence would likely happen in many parts of the North if Buhari lost. Most of the recommendations on the way out was for whoever won the election to treat the other as a co-winner. I believe the Buhari government could have done things differently in this regard. In our highly polarized environment, identities that are perceived to be under threat are often the ones most vociferously defended. Perhaps if things were handled a little differently, there could probably be no Avengers and other neo militants in the Niger Delta today and our crude oil production could not have been crippled the way it is. The same could also be said about the President's statement about "97/5%" support and the unfortunate decision to virtually exclude some groups from his kitchen cabinet. That decision created certain sentiments which opportunistic groups gladly tapped into. In essence therefore, I believe there is a nexus between the president politics and the current economic crisis – or at least its perception. Nexus however does not necessarily mean causation.

Having said the above, I also believe that a leader can be radicalized or de-radicalized by system dynamics. The current economic crisis therefore presents an opportunity for introspection. Though there is evidence that the President's politics is gradually changing and the blame game and probe rhetoric are losing their initial allure, I am still optimistic that the President will eventually find his mojo, re-align with some political forces and surprise his critics. But he can only do so if we continue to hold him accountable and keep him on his toes – irrespective of the blackmail from those who want to create imaginary enemies for him. As I wrote in the same column last week, loyalty does not have to mean fear of the leader or subscription to groupthink. Enduring loyalty "should mean above anything else subordinates being encouraged to respectfully tell the leader the truth or to contribute their honest conviction to the vibrancy of the leader's think-tank."

Daily Trust, September 8, 2016

CHAPTER 72

Osibanjo and the Role of Intellectuals in Politics

How has Vice President Yemi Osibanjo, a Senior Advocate of Nigeria and former Professor of Law at the University of Lagos fared as an intellectual in politics? The role of intellectuals in politics is often a controversial one. Do intellectuals do well in politics or do they just see the public realm as an extension of their imaginary world as some argue?

In addition to being an intellectual, Osibanjo is also a Pastor, which means he is expected to be a moral authority and play morally and truth-driven politics. Essentially therefore Professor Osibanjo's actions and utterances as Vice President could be assessed simultaneously by several constituencies that may use contradictory metrics in their assessments: How loyal has he been to the President who plucked him out of relative obscurity and elevated him to be the nation's number Two? How far has he lived up to the expectations of the religiously inclined who expect him to bring a certain moral unction to politics? And in a polarized environment like ours, how does he balance the expectations of his particularistic group with what the rest of the country expects of him? Can he satisfy the expectations of the intellectual community who expect a certain analytical rigour in his framing of issues, if not anti-establishment posture and rhetoric from him?

Since this piece is essentially about Professor Osibanjo as an intellectual it may be germane to briefly define what I mean by the term. The late Kenyan political scientist Ali Mazrui defined an intellectual as someone who is fascinated by abstract ideas and who has acquired some skill, through formal education, for handling such abstract ideas. Usually when we talk of intellectuals we often think of academics or those involved in the business of publicly trading ideas. Intellectuals are believed to find the most fulfilment and happiness in the life of the mind. Mazrui believed that an intellectual can degenerate into being an 'ex-intellectual' such as when such a person ceases to be fascinated by abstract ideas or loses his capacity for dealing with such ideas.

While supporters of intellectuals in politics will argue that if politics is merely a space meant to provide solutions and guidance for a country, then intellectuals, because of their skills, ability to see the larger picture and their love of ideas, and principles ought to be more involved than they currently do. Their critics will however argue that intellectuals are often fascinated with public attention and recognition, including the tendency to take contrarian positions simply to prove that they are smarter than everyone else. Following from this, critics argue that because intellectuals often confuse the imaginary realm with the real world, their mind-set and training often encourage the treatment of problems from vantages that are neither practical nor realistic.

How has Osibanjo fared as an intellectual in politics?

We can say that from his rhetoric and public postures he has so far eschewed any temptation to play the smart intellectual, who is contrarian. He speaks in sound bites – like typical politicians and the Buharimaniacs in the social media – even though he knows intellectuals despise such as extremely simplistic analyses. In terms of publicly demonstrating loyalty to the President, I think the Vice President has done remarkably well. In my book that is a big virtue.

I am however not very sure that the Vice President has been sufficiently sensitive to the expectations of his other constituencies. And he does not necessarily need to meet those expectations by being disloyal to the positions and body language of the President and the mantras of the government. Let me give just three examples:

On June 28 2015, the Daily Trust reported that the Vice President criticised the setting up of the Federal Character Commission and declared that

> "henceforth employment and appointment into political offices in the country should be based on merit and not where anyone hails from". The Daily Trust further quoted him as saying: "Where you come from should not be criteria. Let us de-emphasise this issue of federal character and place more emphasis on merit. For instance, I take my health seriously, therefore, if I am ill I should not just look for a medical doctor from my state but for the best, irrespective of his state of origin".

The above statement was made at a time President Buhari was under heavy criticism for alleged lop-sidedness in political appointments. The Vice President's position was therefore probably meant to be a subtle defence of the President – something which any loyal deputy is obligated to do in public even if he disagrees with such a position in private.

Though the Vice President later said he was quoted out of context, the way his criticism of the Federal Character principle was crafted was bereft of the sort of analytical rigour expected of a distinguished intellectual of his standing. He could still have defended the President with a much more sophisticated argument – at least an argument that recognises that the Federal Character principle is one of the instruments of nation-building in a diverse country like Nigeria. It can even be argued that the Vice President himself is a beneficiary of the Federal Character principle he was said to have inveighed against.

Recently the Vice President also used the same sound bite approach to dismiss the clamour for the restructuring of the country. He was quoted as saying that even "if states are given half of the resources of the Federal Government, the situation will not change. The only change is to diversify the economy." On July 12, a day after he reportedly made the statement, the Vanguard reported that the Pan-Yoruba socio-political organisation, Afenifere, faulted the Vice-president. In a statement by its National Publicity Secretary, Yinka Odumakin, Afenifere reportedly said:

"While we understand that the learned Professor, who is from the zone that has been loudest on this call may have come under pressure to lend his voice to the upholders of the status quo that has brought Nigeria to this sorry pass, we would like to respectfully admonish him to be sure footed on the subject before he speaks next time."

On the Niger Delta Avengers, the Punch of July 6 2016 quoted the Vice President as saying that the

"Niger Delta Avengers are not freedom fighters, they are not fighting for any freedom, they only fight for their pockets. You can't be blowing up pipelines and compound the problem of the region and be saying you are fighting for freedom."

The Vice President may have some points here but given his positions as an intellectual and a Pastor, perhaps a different narrative is expected of him. And it does not have to differ from the position of the President, which I believe he is right to give unquestionable loyalty.

I think the handlers of the Vice President are yet to appreciate the fact that there are high expectations of the VP and that he plays to different constituencies. This means that they should eschew the sort of pedestrian sound bites he has been using to frame interpretation of serous national issues. For instance, on the call for 'restructuring the country', would it have hurt anyone if the Vice President for instance had said something like: "change is the only constant in life and every individual and organisation needs to constantly adjust and upgrade to meet current challenges. This too is restructuring. So on the call for restructuring, I believe the first hurdle is for all of us to agree on what we mean by restructuring so that everyone will be on the same page. Agreeing on what we mean by restructuring will help us know which elements of the proposed restructuring are needed at this point in our history and which ones will compound our problems"?

On the Niger Delta Avengers, would the Vice President have lost anything if he had said something like: "There are in several parts of the country seemingly good grounds for anger and we will respect people's rights to feel aggrieved. But the solution will always be to dialogue rather than compound the problem by blowing up the pipelines". Formulations like this will bring out the VP's compassion as a pastor and satisfy the expectations that intellectuals are expected to empathize with the weaker parties in any conflict – even if they disagree with their methods of expressing their grievances.

As a Pastor I also expect the Vice President to have more issues framed in moralistic terms because a Man of God is expected to bring special moral traction into politics. It will seem that right now the Vice President has focused on only one constituency – showing his loyalty to the President, which is virtue in my opinion but not good enough for his other constituents.

Daily Trust, August 4, 2016

CHAPTER 73

Reflections on Fayose's 'stomach infrastructure'

When Fayose defeated Fayemi in the Ekiti State Governorship election in 2014, I took it personal. Apart from a chance meeting with Kayode Fayemi in London around 1998/1999 when he was still the boss of the Centre for Democracy and Development, I never met him in person. Yet, like many 'public intellectuals', who deeply respected Dr Fayemi's poise and polished mannerism, that defeat appeared personal. The election was framed as a contest between a 'grassroots politician' and an intellectual.

In an article in this column on June 26 2014 entitled 'The "Fayemi effect" and intellectuals in politics', I wrote:

> "One of the lessons from Fayemi's loss therefore is for intellectuals planning to dabble into politics to start creating new narratives that will drive political discourses. Grassroots politicians in Nigerian parlance tend to be short-term oriented – they build new universities even when existing ones are not well equipped because it is what the people can relate with; they prioritize the building of roads over investing in qualitative education because the voters cannot immediately see the effect of the latter and the impact may not be felt before the next elections.
>
> "Grassroots politicians may know how to win the votes with 'amala', 'tuwo' or 'garri' politics but it is not certain they know what it takes to build a society that will be competitive in the 21st century. Therefore the danger of glamorizing 'grassroots' politicians is not only the unacceptable subtext that we need to lose our individual identities in order to thrive in politics but even the more dangerous innuendo that the gratification of the immediate physical and sensory needs of the masses is the only way to be a good politician.
>
> "What then happens to the age- old adage that leadership is not - and ought not to be - a popularity contest? In a largely illiterate and poor society like ours, both the visionary leaders and the grassroots politicians have complementary roles to play: we need the 'grassroots politicians' to remind the visionary leader (intellectual) that in the long-run the people will be dead if their immediate needs are not gratified; we also need the visionary leader to remind the grassroots politicians that a society that is not driven by a big vision will forever remain ordinary."

While I still stand by the crux of my argument on the need for both the grassroots politicians and intellectuals in politics to work together, my opinion of Fayose has since changed drastically – and for the better. I had seen him more as a rabble-rouser or show-man. Today, I see him more like el-Rufai in Kaduna state, who will stake a conviction and stand by it irrespective of whose ox is gored.

Rather than allow himself to be ridiculed or intimidated for being an apostle of 'stomach infrastructure' – the way the late Adedibu was ridiculed for being an apostle of 'amala politics' - Fayose, proud of his polytechnic education in a state that is known for its high attainments in education, has taken the concept mainstream. To drive home the fact that he was not ashamed of the accusation that he was an apostle of 'stomach infrastructure', he appointed a Special Assistant on Special Duties and Stomach Infrastructure in 2014. During last Christmas he was said to have distributed about 80,000 chickens, 100,000 bags of rice and cash gifts to the people of Ekiti state under its stomach infrastructure programme. His supporters even accused the national leader of the All Progressives Congress Asiwaju Tinubu, who distributed certain goodies to those in need during last Christmas, of copying 'the stomach infrastructure' programme of Ekiti State without attribution.

In politics, language can be used to frame a discourse. For instance to accuse a leader of possessing weapons of mass destruction (WMD), conjures the image of an impending Armageddon, in which the person accused of possessing the WMD is elevated to a potent threat to humanity such that anyone willing to take out such a leader will be seen as performing a humanitarian service.

Fayose's 'stomach infrastructure' is a new framing for a commonplace practice. Vote buying, crowd renting, distributing wrappers, bags of rice, salt and money are common practices during election periods but these banal practices needed to be couched in morally acceptable frames and defended. This is what Fayose has probably succeeded in doing with his 'theory of stomach infrastructure'. According to him, "while physical Infrastructure and urban renewal will continue to play its own role in the development of any nation, it "is only the living who are hale and hearty that can enjoy such Infrastructure." It can then be argued that 'stomach infrastructure' is a kind of welfare that targets the individual and his/her stories and not a programme that targets the collective.

In a sense Fayose's stomach infrastructure is akin to the notion of 'liberation theology' which was popular among Latin American Catholic priests in the 1970s and 1980s and which was based on the notion that the priests and the church needed to help liberate people's stomachs from the pangs of hunger before trying to liberate their souls from possible damnation.

With the notion of stomach infrastructure going main stream, it may be germane to speculate on how this can be refined so it can become part of the country's welfare packages:

One, 'stomach infrastructure' is different from traditional welfare packages such as El Rufai's school feeding programme or plans by the federal government to pay 'qualified' unemployed graduates a monthly stipend. While it can be argued that welfare packages target the collective, stomach infrastructure' targets the individual and his/her own unique stories and challenges. Also while there is officialdom and some form of paperwork for official welfare packages, stomach infrastructure is ostensibly driven by empathy and compassion and bypasses bureaucracy and red tape. This implies therefore that what was hitherto left for our 'dash' culture and extended family system to take care of is now recognized as part of government's obligations. People have individual stories that cry for immediate attention.

Two, it is wrong to assume that stomach infrastructure alone will be sufficient to determine electoral outcome. There are circumstances by which voters may be animated by other causes that 'stomach infrastructure' will become inconsequential in determining electoral outcomes. We saw that with Buhari's supporters from 2003 when he began contesting for the presidency of the country.

Three, we can a hypothesize that when 'stomach infrastructure' is driven by genuine compassion, its potency in winning over citizens will be qualitatively different from when it is driven by cold calculation or when it is being used as a sort of 'bribe' to voters.

Four, as the 'theory of stomach infrastructure' goes mainstream, a crucial question is whether it debases citizens or undermines our democracy?

The key message of Fayose's theory of 'stomach infrastructure' however is to remind us of the dictum by the British economist John Maynard Keynes, who famously reminded us that in the long-run we are all dead. In essence, governments should strive to ameliorate the immediate sufferings of the people while trying to implement a grand vision that will hopefully bring rewards in the long-run. Governments should also recognize that there are certain unique individual stories and challenges that do not always lend themselves to be solved through a bureaucracy.

The troubling happenings at NOUN

The Sahara Reporters of 22 February 2016 reported that some students of the National Open University of Nigeria have been expelled by the authorities ostensibly for trying to unionize to oppose certain ills in the university such violation of students fundamental rights.

The report by Sahara Reporters may be only a tip of the iceberg of the several ills at the NOUN where the institution apparently takes advantage of the university's peculiar structure to abuse students and deny them of their rights. Not only are there frequent complaints of sundry fees imposed by the University, it is not uncommon for students to turn up for examination at designated centres and be ordered to go to another centre several kilometres away for the exam. At other times, students can sit for examinations and their results for the subjects they sat for may not appear on their portal several months after while other students who sat for the same examination in other centres will have seen their own results. Quite often the students will have no one to complain to or there will be subtle threats by arrogant officials of consequences if they continued to pester them. For instance several students who sat for examination in October/November 2015 at the Study Centre, Central Area, Dutse, Abuja are yet to see to see the results of their ICT-based exam while their colleagues in other centres have seen theirs.

The government needs to intervene to ensure that a good idea such as NOUN is not destroyed by official arrogance and incompetence.

Daily Trust, February 24 2016

CHAPTER 74

Emefiele: Clueless or Just a Fall Guy?

This reflection was inspired by the 'crisis of confidence' that currently surrounds the Central Bank Governor, Godwin Emefiele, over his continued stewardship of the apex bank following what we now call 'Dasukigate' and the massive depreciation in the value of the Naira at the Black or parallel market. For instance the Serving Overseer of the Latter Rain Assembly, Pastor Tunde Bakare, who was also Buhari's running mate in the 2011 presidential election argued that it would be unfair to prosecute Sambo Dasuki, the immediate past National Security Adviser for allegedly misappropriating the money meant for arms purchase while the CBN governor, who released the money to Dasuki, was allowed to remain in office. In a similar note, Professor Chukwuma Soludo, former Governor of the Central Bank alleged that former President Jonathan ran the Central Bank of Nigeria (under Emefiele's watch) like the Ugandan maximum leader Idi Amin who, in a movie had to order the country's equivalent of our CBN Governor to print more money whenever he was told his country was going broke.

Questions have also been raised about Emefiele's competence, with suggestions that he is underperforming. Joseph Sanusi, who was appointed CBN Governor by Obasanjo shortly after being sworn in as President in 1999 for instance argued that it was wrong for the government to foist commercial bankers who were previously regulated by CBN Deputy governors on the latter as their bosses when such commercial bankers have not imbibed the institutional culture of central banking. Joseph Sanusi was already Deputy Governor of the CBN when he was elevated to head the apex bank. Emefiele who was appointed as CBN Governor on June 3 2014 was until his appointment the Chief Executive officer and Group Managing Director of Zenith Bank. He had been Deputy Managing Director of the bank since 2001 before he was appointed to take over from Jim Ovia as the Bank's MD in 2010.

I do not know Emefiele from Adam and my aim here is not to defend his tenure as CBN governor. Rather my objective is to interrogate some of the allegations against him – moral impropriety over the Dasukigate, not standing up to former President Jonathan who allegedly turned the CBN into an ATM and for allegedly not providing convincing leadership in the current economic crisis as epitomized by the huge depreciation in the value of the Naira at the parallel markets and the criticism that dogged the CBN's ban on the importation of 41 items, including tooth picks. It is hoped that by interrogating these events the proper lessons that should be learnt from them will not be lost in our simplistic desire to find a culprit.

Dasukigate

For me the key lesson from 'Dasukigate' goes beyond the alleged sharing of mouth-watering sums of money meant for arms purchase to the issue of how security votes for President and Governors are used. I learnt that the National Security Adviser manages the security vote of the President and that traditionally there is an 'elongated' definition of 'security' – for both the President and State Governors. In other words, while ordinary Nigerians may conceptualize security strictly in physical terms – the physical protection of the Governors and the President - it would seem that the designers of the idea of 'security vote' borrowed from the United Nations Development Programme's (1994) notion of 'human security', where anything that is capable of threatening the happiness of an individual - including the inability of a man to find a wife or vice versa could be securitized (i.e. become a security issue). In other words, what constitutes security appears to be left at the discretion of those who enjoy such a privilege – creating a huge room for abuse. In this sense 'Dasikugate', more than anything raises question about the meaning of 'security', the management of security votes and the sources of campaign finances for political parties – not just for the PDP.

Turning the CBN into an ATM of the President

That the CBN Governor allowed the carting away of huge sums of money from the apex bank's vaults on the say-so of former President Jonathan without apparently raising objections may be less Emefiele's fault but more because of the 'banana republic' character of the state. In banana republics the word of the maximum leader is law. And Nigeria till this day still exhibits the symptoms of a banana republic – including at the state levels where the Governors are the equivalent of sea monsters.

In banana Republics, which agency head, whether CBN Governor or not can really stand in the way of the instructions or even the body language of the maximum leader? Therefore an important takeaway from this is that our institutions, not any individual, are just too weak to resist any irrational demand of the maximum leader.

Import bans and the collapse in the value of the Naira

Banning the importation of certain items such as tooth picks and Indian incenses as a way of conserving foreign currencies may play well with national pride but they are also bound to attract criticisms from critical global media and financial analysts which are quickly reproduced at the national level or reinforce other existing disaffections. This is not to deny that some of the Bank's policies are not rather bizarre - such as preventing people who sourced foreign currencies from the 'black market' or elsewhere from paying such money into their local domiciliary accounts (the policy has now been reversed).

On the collapse in the value of the Naira at the parallel market, one does not need to be an economist to know that the slump in crude prices from the highs of over

$100 per barrel to less than $30 per barrel will have adverse effects on the supply of foreign currencies. The economy is not only highly dependent on oil for its foreign exchange earnings; the country is import dependent, if not addicted. For instance while the CBN's monthly foreign earnings have fallen from an average of $3.2 billion to an average of about $1 billion per month import bills have ballooned in the last ten years – from N148.3bn in 2005 to N917.6bn in 2015, an increase of 519 per cent. About 40% of official forex demand in the country is for the importation of refined petroleum products

It is possible that CBN's mode of handling the current economic crisis may not be optimal. But a key question is whether there is enough room for the policy makers to choose alternative policy options without being constrained by the President's famed body language and preferred policy options. As we know the president brand of economics appears to be cynical of 'market determinism' and favours command and control.

Who do we need as CBN Governor?

More than anything else, the moral and competence questions surrounding Emefiele's continued leadership of the apex bank raises an even more fundamental question of the sort of personality we need as CBN Governor. Joseph Sanusi, who became CBN Governor from the rank of Deputy Governor of the Bank argued that future CBN Governors should be appointed only from among the Deputy Governors of the Bank. However whether the head of an organisation or firm should be appointed from within or outside the organisation has always been controversial. Suffice it to add that two of the most distinguished (in my opinion) of the country's CBN Governors - Professor Chukwuma Soludo and Sanusi Lamido Sanusi - (now Emir of Kano) did not come from within the Central Bank. While Soludo had a background in the academia, Lamido Sanusi, like Emefiele, had a background in commercial banking. Remarkably while Soludo was a full time academic, both Lamido Sanusi and Emefiele had stints in academia before joining commercial banking. Lamido Sanusi briefly taught economics at Ahmadu Bello University Zaria (1983-1985), while Emefiele taught Finance and Insurance at the University of Nigeria Nsukka and the University of Port Harcourt before joining Zenith bank.

The three are different personality types. While Soludo was a flamboyant academic – he turned an otherwise innocuous position of CBN Governor into a celebrity position – he was very much an establishment person who wanted to be both seen and heard. Sanusi on the other hand was not only a flamboyant man who a wanted to be both seen and heard, he was basically an anti-establishment person who did not mind expressing his views on any political issue. I once described him as a "radical in a conservative job". Emefiele on the other hand appears to be a throw-back to CBN Governors in the pre-Soludo and Sanusi era. He is neither flamboyant nor does he give the impression that he is eager to be seen and heard – like his last two predecessors.

A crucial question here is whether the apparent dissatisfaction with the way Emefiele does his job is, at least partly, a misplaced merely nostalgia for Soludo and Lamido Sanusi?

Daily Trust, January 27 2016

CHAPTER 75

Achebe and the 'innocence' of Mortuary Narratives

The recent transition of literary giant Albert Chinualumogu Achebe has led to an uncommon outpouring of encomiums. Achebe's transition came less than a year after his last major work, *There was a country: A Personal History of Biafra* (2012) has stirred controversy in the country. His critics argued that the work diminished him from being Nigeria's gift to the literary world to an 'Igbo-phile'.

This piece is not so much a tribute to Achebe as an interrogation of the mortuary respect that followed his transition with a focus on the contrarian perspectives of Professor Ibrahim Bello-Kano whose intervention was couched in elegant academic aesthetics and published by several print and online media.

Why do the dead, even those we have reservations about when they lived always attract adulation? There are two key explanations – one based on myth and the other on rationality. The rational explanation is that the dead cannot defend themselves while the myth is that if you say evil against the dead their spirit will continue to haunt you until you join them in the hereafter.

Contrary to the belief in some quarters that respect to the dead is a specific African tradition, it is actually a universal practice, dating to antiquity. For instance the phrase 'mortuary respect' dates from the 4th century and is often attributed to Diogenes Laërtius' work 'Lives *and Opinions of Eminent Philosophers*' (ca. AD 300) where a Greek aphorism, 'Don't badmouth a dead man' was attributed to Chilon of Sparta, one of the Seven Sages of ancient Greece. There is also the Latin phrase 'De *mortuis nihil nisi bonum,*' which roughly translates to "Of the dead, nothing unless good". In English language there are several aphoristic phrases like: "Speak no ill of the dead", "Of the dead, speak no evil", and "Do not speak ill of the dead". The 18th century English writer and poet Samuel Johnson was famously quoted as saying: "He that has too much feeling to speak ill of the dead…will not hesitate…to destroy…the reputation…of the living."

Should a public intellectual necessarily be bound by the custom of mortuary respect? I do not think so. I believe a public intellectual owes it to his craft (excuse my apparent lack of gender sensitivity here but it is all to make things easier), to detach himself from mass hysteria, outrage or encomium and search for and expand on anything he feels has been missed out in the flourish of emotionally-driven mass euphoria. If a public intellectual's reasoning and choice of analytical categories lead him to a conclusion contrary to what is regarded as the popular position, then duty calls to take and defend that position. It takes courage to stand alone.

It is in the above respect that the contrarian intervention of Professor Ibrahim Bello-Kano receives my maximum respect. In that intervention, which is written in a compelling language that leaned here and there on the obscurantist literary form, he questioned the literary merits in Achebe's novels. I agree with most of his comments, including some of his comments on *Anthills of Savannah*, Achebe's last novel, generally thought to have been written when Achebe had either lost interest in writing novels or his skills in the craft had gone into terminal decline.

Despite agreeing with most of Professor Bello-Kano's critical comments on Achebe's works, I must quickly add that none of those comments is original. As a matter of fact in 2006, my publishing firm, Adonis & Abbey Publishers (www.adonis-abbey.com) - a publisher of academic books and journals since March 2003 - published an even more critical work on Achebe's writings entitled *Achebe: The Man and His Works* by Rose Mezu, a Professor of English, Women studies and Comparative Literature at Morgan State University, Baltimore, Maryland, USA. Between 2007 and 2010, the same company incubated and published the academic journal, *African Performance Review* for the African Theatre Association, where on every issue, I read with relish scholars 'tearing apart' the works of such great literary giants as Achebe, Soyinka, Osofisan and *Ngugi wa Thiong'o*.

Professor Bello-Kano's critique of Achebe's *Trouble With Nigeria (1983)* for neglecting the influence of system dynamics when Achebe claimed that the 'trouble with Nigeria is squarely that of leadership', is spot on. But it is also not original. In fact the structure-agency debate in the social sciences (the capacity of individuals to act independently and make free choices contra a patterned set of arrangements which influence or limit available choices and opportunities) has been ongoing since 1903 when the German non-positivist sociologist Georg Simmel published his seminal essay, 'The Metropolis and Mental Life'. The younger Achebe had in fact in *No Longer At Ease* (1960), through the character Obi Okonkwo, identified the trouble with Nigeria as being systemic. In that novel, Obi Okonkwo was such an independently minded character that when his community sent him to England to study law – at a time the voice of the elders approximated the voices of the gods – he disobeyed them, followed his heart and read English. Obi Okonkwo also had the courage to stand alone on several fronts, to the disappointment of his community: He married an 'osu'- which was an abomination among his people, he refused to use his position in the civil service to favour 'his people' in employment and he hated to his marrows the deeply entrenched corruption in public life. However, despite Obi Okonkwo's moral Puritanism, he was forced by certain societal pressures to take his own bribe and was caught. In this work therefore Achebe demonstrated that the problem with Nigeria, at least in terms of corruption, was systemic and not that of moral lapse or leadership.

The type of contradiction between what Achebe saw as the 'trouble with Nigeria' in *No Longer At Ease* (1960) and in his booklet of the same title is not uncommon among great thinkers and writers. Karl Marx, generally regarded as one of the greatest political, social and economic thinkers of all time, grappled with such contradictions in his works. For instance in his 'materialist conception of history', Marx gave the impression that socialism would succeed capitalism independent of men's will because capitalism, following the 'immutable law of history', would sow the seeds of its own destruction. By the time Marx and Engels published the Communist Manifesto in 1848, Marx had shifted his position and had come to believe that the socialist era would only come about through proletarian revolution. In the structure-agency debate (on which of the two is the key propellant of history), it could be argued that while the younger Marx, just like the younger Achebe favoured 'structure', the older Marx, just like the older Achebe, favoured 'agency'.

Several of Professor Bello-Kano's critical comments on Achebe's last work, *There was a Country: A Personal History of Biafra, are* legitimate. Certainly the book has flaws – on interpretation, generalizations and even proofreading. However one senses a desire by Professor Bello-Kano to hide behind academic aesthetics to soldier for the North. For instance I find his efforts to smell out any hint of the inferiorization of the North in *Anthills of Savannah*, quite stretched. The impression one gets is that the whole contrarian piece was inspired and animated by this desire to soldier for 'his people'. Given the brilliance that shone in the Professor's piece, this is most disappointing as it is an appropriation of the day-job of 'area boys', internet warriors, ethnic-watchers, one-dimensional journalists and such ethnic/regional contraptions as the Arewa Consultative Forum, the Ohaneze, the OPC and others. In advanced countries, Professors of Bello- Kano's standing try to find new frameworks and theoretical constructs that will raise the level of the conversation and discourse such that bigoted ideas are marginalized. This is why in several such countries, racist organizations like the KKK or British National Party are never banned but the ideas they purvey are equally never mainstreamed because the acceptable analytical categories and frameworks ensure that they will remain marginalized.

By electing to soldier for a piece of geography using the same ethnic and regional pedestals he inveighed against as his tools of counter narratives, Professor Bello-Kano becomes guilty of the same reductionism, of seeing issues mostly in terms of the static binary of 'we versus them' which he accused Achebe of. The irony is that most of those who soldier for pieces of geography in every part of the country dare not go to stay for a longer period in their village, and will, in private conversations, frankly tell you that 'my people are terrible'.

Since the 'withering away' of the Nigerian left, there has been a yawning dearth of efforts to develop an alternative vision of society and new analytical constructs away from this essentialist constructions of ethnicity and religion. And when public intellectuals, who ought to know, join the rat race of ethnic and regional finger-pointing, it becomes unfortunate.

Achebe's last book is flawed but it has already done a great service to the country. War propaganda on both sides of the conflict meant that each side has its own story, including of heroes and villains. Achebe's book by generating counter narratives, has forced many of us to revise what we thought we knew about the war, which was led mostly by young radicals and rascals in their 20s and early 30s.

Daily Trust, April 4, 2013

CHAPTER 76

Alamieyeseigha's Pardon: would you have Acted Differently?

The recent presidential pardon of Diepreye Solomon Peter Alamieyeseigha, Governor of Bayelsa State, from 29 May 1999 to 9 December 2005, has generated an understandable sense of outrage across the country. Alamieyeseigha is credited with plucking President Jonathan from total political obscurity and making him his Deputy throughout the duration of his Governorship. From that happenstance, fate took over and the rest, as they say, is now history.

In my opinion what could be considered as 'sustainable' outrage against Jonathan's action was the obvious filial connection between the two - Alamieyeseigha was his political benefactor and his fellow Ijaw. The argument that the pardon is a setback against the fight against corruption is however neither here nor there because the presidential prerogative of mercy is bestowed on people who are accused of committing crimes or have been convicted of committing crimes – not on innocent people. It is not a prize award or national honour for distinguished service to the nation but a show of mercy on the beneficiaries. It is like arguing that because US Presidents routinely pardon drug barons such a show of mercy constitutes a setback in the global fight against illicit drugs.

Largely because of the lack of any scientific method of determining who will benefit from presidential pardons, most of such acts of mercy are inherently controversial. In the US Article II Section 2 of the country's Constitution, empowers the President to "grant reprieves and pardons for offences against the United States, except in cases of impeachment." While a reprieve reduces the severity of a punishment but retains the guilty pronouncement of a court, a pardon removes both punishment and guilt. This heightens a pardon's controversial nature.

Historically US Presidents have used the power of pardon to heal rifts in their national psyche as George Washington did when he pardoned leaders of the Whiskey Rebellion. James Madison similarly pardoned Lafitte's pirates after the War of 1812; Andrew Johnson pardoned Confederate soldiers after the Civil War; Harry Truman pardoned those who violated World War II's Selective Service laws; and Jimmy Carter pardoned Vietnam War draft dodgers. In Nigeria those who fought on the Biafran side during the Civil War (1967-1970) were granted pardon just as Niger Delta Militants received amnesty from the late President Yaradua. You do not necessarily need to have been 'convicted' of a crime by a court of law to be granted pardon as these instances clearly illustrate.

Apart from the above type of pardon, virtually every other form of pardon evokes controversy. For instance there was a sense of outrage across the world in 1992 when President George Bush (Snr) pardoned six Reagan administration officials involved in the Iran-Contra Affair. George Bush (Snr) was considered a close associate of one of the beneficiaries, Caspar Weinberger, who served as Secretary of Defence while Bush served as Vice President under Reagan. Weinberger and others had all been convicted for illegally conducting arms sales with Iran, which was using the profits to fund the Contra rebel guerilla army in Nicaragua. Richard Nixon who resigned as President of the US in 1974 in the face of an almost certain impeachment following the Watergate scandal was pardoned by Gerald Ford, who served as his Vice President and who also succeeded him as President after his resignation. Bill Clinton also came under fire for several of his pardons, including the pardon of tax evader Marc Rich.

There was also the case of Patty Hearst, the granddaughter of publishing magnate William Randolph Hearst. In 1974 Patty Hearst was kidnapped by the then-unknown radical group, the Symbionese Liberation Army (SLA). That same year she assisted the SLA in bank robberies and other crimes until the urban guerilla group's location was discovered by police. At her trial, Hearst claimed she participated in the criminal activities under psychological and physical duress but was sentenced to seven years in prison. She served two years of her sentence before it was commuted by President Jimmy Carter. Clinton pardoned her in 2001. Recently in South Korea, some pardons granted by the then outgoing President Lee Myung-bak in January 2013, generated national outrage because included in the list were the President's close friend Chun Shin-il and a close political ally, Choi See-joong, both of whom had been sentenced for bribery, as well as the former speaker of the national assembly Park Hee-tae and a former aide to Mr Lee, Kim Hyo-jae, who were both jailed over a vote-buying scandal.

Pardons are controversial partly because there is no scientific formula anywhere for selecting those to be pardoned. Presidents, being humans, often bring their own emotional and filial considerations in the exercise of this prerogative. This is why it is rather surprising that the American Embassy should openly condemn the pardoning of Alamieyeseigha – when the country routinely pardons drug barons, fraudsters and other criminals and the Embassy ought to be conversant with the controversies that often dog presidential pardons. This is more especially as they have a channel of privately making their feelings about the pardon known to the powers that be in Abuja.

The above is not necessarily an endorsement of the pardon of Alamieyeseigha but to put that exercise in its proper historical and global contexts. In our own type of society, where heroes and villains are defined by ethnic and religious boundaries, a hero in one enclave could be perceived as a villain in others. Alamieyeseigha may be seen as a villain by other Nigerians but may not necessarily be seen as such by his Ijaw brethren. And if he is seen as a hero in his region and President Jonathan is from that region, it is obvious the sort of pressure he will be under to grant him pardon. Being the President's benefactor will make that pressure even more overwhelming - unless we want to pretend that in this country our leaders are not influenced in their decisions by filial, ethnic and regional considerations. It is not the right thing to do but part of the diseases that constitute system dynamics in our country. Otherwise why will most Governors locate new Universities and industries in their villages? Why will political leaders play the ethnic and religious cards if not so that they will be in the good books of 'their people'? During the Second Republic top Igbo politicians were apparently under pressure to push for President Shagari to grant Ojukwu pardon. Not long ago, some top military leaders from the North converged and declared that Abacha was not corrupt – even though the rest of the country sees him as the poster-boy of corruption. It is therefore part of the character of the Nigerian State that since national political leaders often 'retire' to become regional and ethnic champions, their actions while in office are partly influenced by the way they want their 'people' to perceive them. In this sense, rather than blame Jonathan for pardoning Alamieyeseigha, we should blame it on the nature of the Nigerian State.

There is, in my opinion, at least one justifiable ground for pardoning Alamieyeseigha: while his corruption – alleged and confessed- in office is condemnable, the way he was removed from office smacked of impunity and vendetta – something that has often turned the fight against corruption in this country into a charade. You cannot rig the legal processes to achieve a desired outcome – even if you caught the thief with his fingers in the cookie jar. Gestapo methods were used to remove from office both Alamieyeseigha and the former Governor of Plateau State Joshua Dariye. The establishment of a rule of law must necessarily precede confidence-building in the justice system. I believe victims of such Kangaroo justice – whatever their crimes – deserve some form of reprieve, if not complete amnesty. And have we really forgotten the attempted abduction of Ngige in Anambra State? Why has nothing been done to fish out those behind such jungle justice as a way of sending clear message that impunity cannot be tolerated in a decent society?

The outcry over the pardon of Alamieyeseigha is good in so far as it shows that citizens are closely monitoring the actions of their leaders. But it also shows us to be a nation of hypocrites and people who like to play the Ostrich. Suddenly everyone is showing strong distaste for corruption. From a lecturer who demands 'sorting' to pass an undeserving student to the student leader who embezzles student union funds to the law enforcement officer who gladly looks the other way at a little inducement to the journalist who wants to be 'induced' before he can give a certain slant to his story to even the mechanic who will quickly exchange the new battery in your car for an old one, there is an outpouring of alarm and rage that a 'corrupt' man has secured a Presidential pardon. The outrage is in my opinion meaningful only if it offers us an opportunity for introspection: if I were in Jonathan's shoes, would I really have acted differently?

Daily Trust, March 21, 2013

CHAPTER 77

As Ali Mazrui joins 'Hereafter'

The word on the subject line of the email was simply 'Mazrui'. It was early Monday morning, 14 October 2014. The email came from Jakky Amadu, a former basketball player, who worked as a post-doctoral fellow under Professor Ali Mazrui between 2002 and 2005 at the Institute of Global Cultural Studies, Binghamton University, New York. Though I have never met Jakky, who is now an Associate Professor of Sociology at Seton Hall University, we have kept good contacts since 2005. When I opened the mail, the message in it was terse: "Mazrui has passed on."
I knew Mwalimu Ali Mazrui had been ill for quite some time but I did not suspect that the end was nigh for him.

As an undergraduate at the University of Nigeria Nsukka in the 1980s, I read Ali Mazrui and was impressed with his facility with the English language and the breadth of his knowledge of world history and politics. I had memorised several phrases from his books. Professor Okwudiba Nnoli, one of my lecturers at Nsukka, told us about an epic debate between Mazrui and the late Walter Rodney at the University of Dar Es Salaam, Tanzania, and how Rodney, a Marxist, intellectually battered the erudite Mazrui.

My path crossed Mazrui's in 2005. I had set up a publishing firm in London, Adonis & Abbey publishers (www.adonis-abbey.com), in 2003, and the following year had founded the journal *African Renaissance*. It was a period of intense Afro-pessimism. The journal not only got leading Africanists to discuss the African condition, but also to challenge theories and assertions which ruled out developmental and democratic possibilities for Africa. Even in the maiden edition in June 2004, we had great Africanists like Gamal Nkrumah (the late Kwame Nkrumah's son), Helmi Sharawy, Marcel Kitissou, Mammo Muchie, Bankie Forster Bankie and Kimani Nehusi as contributors. Professor Mammo Muchie, an Ethiopian scholar, who like me, was a regular contributor to the London-based *New African* magazine – gave me Professor Mazrui's number to call him and persuade him to become a contributor to the journal.

He was quite friendly when I called and I was pleasantly surprised that he was very generous with his time, given how big an intellectual he was and that I was just an unknown quantity who had started an innocuous book publishing company and a journal he had not even heard of. I reeled out his books that I had read and some of the quotable quotes I had memorized from them. Without knowing when I said it, I told him that of all his books I read the only one I did not like was *The Trial of Christopher Okigbo* (1971), in which, in a fictional 'Hereafter'; he had tried and found the late poet Christopher Okigbo guilty of abandoning his craft as a poet to fight for Biafra. I said something like: "Prof, how can you judge a poet in the hereafter and found him guilty for supposedly subordinating his art to the imperative of the survival of his community? Which one is precedent: art or community? Art outside a commitment to one's community is just art for art's sake. I just threw away the book after reading it. I was just disappointed."

As soon as I blurted out the statements over the telephone my heart started to pound: Was I saying these to the great Ali Mazrui? Had I abused his listening ears? Had I come across as rude? Had I abused the trust of the person who gave me his number? I quickly tried to do damage control by rephrasing what I just said in more polite ways. I believe Mwalimu Mazrui sensed my panic. He laughed and asked how old I was when I read the book and I told him I was about 18 years old. He asked if I thought I was old enough to understand the book and I replied that literature was actually my first love, that in fact I did postgraduate studies only because I was a failed novelist. I didn't need to tell him that as an undergraduate I had published my first novella with Fourth Dimension - before self-publishing became the vogue in Nigeria - but then went ahead to hold the record of the highest rejection slips from the defunct MacMillan's Pacesetter series and the Longmann's Drumbeat series – novels for young adults. As I mentioned the words "failed novelist", memories of how I visited several publishing houses to challenge them for their apparent love for rejecting my manuscripts flashed through my mind. From Pacesetters in Ibadan, Longman's Drumbeat in Lagos, Fagbamigbe and Ilesanmi in Akure, Tana Press and Delta Publications in Enugu, I visited them all. As an undergraduate I had read so many works on literary criticisms that felt I could hold my own on discussions of the literary merits of a work - even against the great Mazrui.

Mazrui challenged me to read the book again but I politely maintained that I found the idea that a writer's art should be superior to his commitment to his community difficult to accept. By the time the telephone conversation ended, Mazrui had given me his home telephone number and encouraged me to call whenever I felt like. From that telephone conversation, I came to confirm what I had read about him - he loved debates. I knew of his public spat and debates with other intellectual giants - Walter Rodney, Louis Gate jnr, Kwesi Prah, Abiola Irele, Biodun Jeyifo, Ochieng' Odhiambo Wole Soyinka and others. I did not know he would have the patience to debate an upstart like me. How wrong I was. Over the phone or emails, I felt the great Mazrui was surreptitiously encouraging me to debate him. Mazrui was an intellectual octopus and the intellectual slingshots I fired occasionally from a respectable distance was more like goading the master to open more his fountain of knowledge.

Mazui became an honorary adviser and regular contributor to *African Renaissance*. In 2006, my publishing firm published his very important work, *A Tale of two Africas: South Africa and Nigeria as Contrasting Visions*. Again in a book I edited in 2009 - *Who is an African?: Politics, Identity and the Making of the Africa-Nation* - Professor Mazrui not only graciously wrote the preface but also contributed two other chapters to the book. Ironically a number of Mazrui's critics – Wole Soyinka, Kwesi Prah and Ochieng' - had consistently questioned Mazrui's Africanity because part of his ancestry was Arab. In 2011 we also published *Public Intellectuals and the Politics of Global Africa: Essays in Honour of Ali A. Mazrui* which was edited by Seifudein Adem, Associate Director of Mazrui's Institute of Global Cultural Studies at Binghamton University. Professor

Mazrui was also to introduce me to his former student and scion, the eminent emeritus Professor of Political Science, Isawa J Elaigwu, arguably one of Nigeria's best in the field. Professor Elaigwu has remained "my oga at the top" since then.

The last time I met Mazrui was at the African Studies Association (ASA) Conference in Philadelphia, USA, in November 2012. Mazrui was a one- time President of ASA (USA Chapter) and regularly attends the Association's annual conferences. Though he was already wheel-chair bound by then, he was still intellectually alert, still ebullient, still looking to stir up a debate or dabble into controversy. Together with Seifudein Adem, we spent time chatting over lunch.

When I received invitation from his office to attend his 80th birthday celebration last year in New York, I sought to hide my worsening aversion for flying by joking that I would stay away from the celebration as protes that in the menu Mazrui asked his invitees to select from, did not include African cuisines – no egusi soup, no amala, no tuwo.

Ali Al'amin Mazrui was born in Mombasa, Kenya on 24 February 1933 and studied at schools in Mombasa before travelling to the UK where he obtained his B.A. (with Distinction) from Manchester University (1960). He later obtained an M.A. from Columbia University, New York (1961) and capped this with a doctorate (DPhil) from Oxford University (Nuffield College) in 1966. Until his transition, he was an Albert Schweitzer Professor in the Humanities and the Director of the Institute of Global Cultural Studies at Binghamton University in Binghamton, New York.

A teacher, orator, journalist, filmmaker, and public intellectual, Mazrui was arguably the most connected and best known African social scientist for over half a century. His research interests included African politics, international political culture, Political Islam and North-South relations.

In addition to the over 20 books he published, Mazrui was also the creator of the television series, *The Africans: A Triple Heritage*, (1986), which was jointly produced by the BBBC and the Public Broadcasting Service, WETA (Washington DC). A book by the same title was jointly published by BBC Publications and Little, Brown and Company. Mazrui was in 2005 voted Number 73 in a list of the Top 100 Global Thinkers compiled jointly by Prospect magazine (UK) and Foreign Policy magazine (US).

I was told that Mwalimu Mazrui, who in his last days was being fed intravenously, decided at a point that he no longer wanted to take food or drugs. He was ready to meet his Maker. He died on Sunday, 13 October and had left instructions that his remains should be buried at the family cemetery at Fort Jesus, Mombasa, the city of his birth. Adieu Mwalimu.

Daily Trust, October 16 2014

CHAPTER 78

Remembering Ali A Mazrui (1)

How do you go about immortalizing a man whose works already immortalized him while he was alive? That was precisely what Twaweza Communications of Kenya and Binghamton University of New York sought to do when they organized a symposium entitled 'Critical Perspectives on Culture and Globalization: The Intellectual Legacy of Ali A Mazrui.' The symposium, held in Nairobi, Kenya from July 14-17, attracted nearly 100 Africanists from all over the world. Those who honoured the invitation included Prof Horace Campbell, who gave the keynote address, Mahmood Mamdani, Kimani Njogu and Seifudein Adem (who were among the conveners of the symposium) Hamdy A. Hassan, Chris Wanjala, Peter Anyang' Nyong'o, Macharia Munene, Alamin Mazrui, Cassandra Veney, N'Dri Thérèse Assié-Lumumba, Timothy Shaw and Paul Zeleza, (the Vice Chancellor, United States International University, Nairobi). It was gratifying that among the invitees to the symposium were three Nigerians – eminent Nigerian political scientist J Isawa Elaigwu, who chaired a session and also gave the concluding remarks, Prof Adekeye Adebajo, who presented a paper on, 'Who Killed Pax Africana?' and my humble self who also presented a paper on, 'Who is an African? Reflections on Mazrui's notion of the African'

Mazrui had a rich academic life. With a Kenyan government scholarship, he studied at the University of Manchester, United Kingdom and graduated with Distinction in 1960. He subsequently obtained an MA in 1961 from Columbia University, and a doctorate (DPhil), from Oxford University in 1966. He began his academic life at the University of Makerere, Uganda, where he quickly rose to become a professor. He left Makerere after Idi Amin's military coup and was in 1974 hired as a professor of political science by the University of Michigan, USA. In 1989, he accepted the Albert Schweitzer professorship at the State University of New York, Binghamton where he became the founding director of the Institute for Global Cultural Studies. Mazrui has about 35 books and numerous academic articles to his name. He was also a renowned essayist and polemicist. Mazrui was equally famous for producing the TV documentary, *The Africans: A Triple Heritage*, which was later also published as a book. Mwalimu Mazrui transited to the Hereafter on October 12 1914.

Who is an African?

On face value the above will seem like a stupid question. Certainly all of us know who the African is, it would seem. However, the answer to this apparently stupid or elementary question becomes less obvious once other probing qualifiers are added to the question. How is the African identity constructed in the face of the mosaic of identities that people of African ancestry or people who live within the geographic space called Africa bear? How does African identity interface with other identities that people of African ancestry or those who live within the geographic space called Africa bear? For instance is Barack Obama, the 44th President of the United States, who had a Kenyan father but a white American mother, African? Is Jerry Rawlings, the former military ruler and former President of Ghana whose father was Scottish and his mother a Black Ghanaian, truly an African? Are people like Horace Campbell, Samir Amin, Walter Rodney, Mahmood Mamdani and even Ali Mazrui who have done perhaps more than most scholars in articulating African perspectives in global discourses, really African? Are all who proclaim themselves Africans accepted as such? And by the way who allots this 'Africanness' and why? The above are some of the questions one inevitably encounters when one tries to academically delineate who is an African and who is not. How did Mazrui try to grapple with these questions?

My Interest in Mazrui's notion of the African

As a young undergraduate at the University of Nigeria, Nsukka in the 1980s, we were exposed to the works of Ali Mazrui. One of our lecturers, Professor Okwudiba Nnoli, was a lecturer at the University of Dar es Salaam at the time Mazrui was teaching at Makerere. Professor Nnoli would tell us stories about the epic debate between Mazrui and the late Guyanese historian Walter Rodney and how Rodney thoroughly "messed Mazrui up". Rodney was the author of the famous book, *How Europe Underdeveloped Africa.*

As an undergraduate, we admired Professor Mazrui for his firm grasp of the English language and for the fact that it was impossible to read any of his works without coming out with several quotable quotes. One of my fond quotes from him in those days was his definition of an 'intellectual' as someone who was fascinated by abstract ideas and had acquired some capacity, through formal education, for handling such ideas. He also defined an 'ex intellectual' as an intellectual who has ceased to be fascinated by abstract ideas or has lost the capacity for handling such ideas. We would often label academics who went into government and began talking in sound bites like professional politicians as 'ex intellectuals'.

While we admired Mazrui, many of our lecturers were very critical of his works. They criticized his weaknesses in theory construction and his apparent inability to remain focused on a research theme to mature with the conversations in the field. Other critics accused him of being excessively defensive of the Arabs, including their role in the trans-Saharan slave trade. Several African academics questioned his Africanness. Mazrui had Arab ancestry.

I later found that while non-academics and non-political scientists were fascinated by Mazrui's works, several political scientists and Africanists were dismissive of him as at best an aloof polemicist with questionable commitment to Africa. Whatever the criticism, no one denied that Mazrui had a big voice in global affairs. You may disagree with him but it will be difficult to ignore him.

My interest in Mazrui's notion of the African

I had the first direct contact with Ali Mazrui in 2005. I had founded the publishing company Adonis & Abbey publishers (www.adonis-abbey.com) in London in 2003. The following year, I also founded the theme-based journal, *African Renaissance*. Our maiden edition was on 'Afro-Arab Relations: Co-operation or Conflict'. We had assembled an array of Africanists – Gamal Nkrumah (Nkrumah's son), Mammo Muchie, Helmi Sharawi, Kwesi Prah and others as contributors. The Ethiopian scholar Mammo Muchie gave me Professor Mazrui's number and suggested he might be interested in the sort of intellectual engagements we were pursuing.

Given his global stature, I wasn't exactly full of confidence that an obscure scholar like me who had set up a nondescript publishing company and an unknown journal would get much of his attention. Surprisingly when I called expecting that he would be so busy that he wouldn't give me more than a few seconds, he was quite generous with his time.

I told him of his books I had read and proudly recited some of the quotes I memorized from some of those books. However rather irreverently I told him that I didn't like his allegorical work – *The Trial of Christopher Okigbo* (1972). I told him that I threw it away in disgust after reading it. Mazrui was silent for a while and then asked me if I thought I was old enough to understand the message of the book since I said I read it as an undergraduate when I was still a teenager. I argued that it was wrong for Okigbo to be found guilty in the Hereafter apparently for subordinating his art as a poet to his community (Biafra). I argued that a writer's community preceded his art and that a writer who subordinates his art to his community is only celebrating art for art's sake.

There was a long silence through which my pounding heart told me I had blown the opportunity. When Mazrui finally spoke, it was to give me his home telephone number and ask me to call at my convenience. This was quintessential Mazrui – humble and tolerant of criticisms in a way his critics never were.

Mazrui later became the Editorial Adviser to *African Renaissance*. Our publishing company, Adonis & Abbey Publishers, also became one of his European publishers. Additionally Mazrui introduced me to his former student, eminent Nigerian political scientist J Isawa Elaigwu, who, when I finally relocated to Nigeria in 2011 found a University teaching job for me. In 2009, Professor Mazrui contributed three chapters to a book I edited entitled: *Who is an African? Identity, Citizenship and the Making of the Africa-Nation.*

Next week I will interrogate Mazrui's notion of the African based on those three contributions. I will also raise the question of whether Mazrui should really be called an African.

A Giant Tree Has Fallen: Tributes to Ali A Mazrui – a collection of the tributes paid to Mazrui globally from Presidents, Prime Ministers, public intellectuals and family members to academics and journalists – will be published by African Perspectives

Publishers (Johannesburg, SA) in September 2016. It is edited by Seifudein Adem, Jideofor Adibe, Abdul Karim Bangura and Abdul Samed Bemath

Daily Trust, July 21, 2016

CHAPTER 79

Remembering Ali Mazrui (II)

Obviously one cannot talk of the African without a prior conception of what Africa is all about. In the documentary, *Africa: A Triple Heritage*, written and narrated by Ali Mazrui in the early 1980s Mazrui argued that Africa (or Africa's identity as we know it) is formed by a triple heritage – "an indigenous heritage borne out of time and climate change"; the heritage of eurocentric capitalism forced on Africans by European colonialism and the spread of Islam by both jihad and evangelism.

In a paper 'Who are Africans?', which Mazrui published in a book I edited in 2009 entitled *Who is an African? Identity, Citizenship and the Making of the Africa-Nation*, Mazrui wrote:

> "If Africa invented man in places like the Olduvai Gorge and the Semitic invented God in Jerusalem, Mt. Sinai and Mecca, Europe invented the world at the Greenwich Meridian. It was the Europeans who named all the great continents of the world, all the great oceans, many of the great rivers and lakes and most of the countries."

He argued that Europe created the African or consciousness of being African through two inter-related processes – the triumph of European cartography and map making and through racism and the related imperialism and neo-imperialism.

Following from the above, Mazrui believed that what we call African identity is largely a fiction as it was merely a creation of European map makers, colonialism, racism and imperialism. The implication of this for Mazrui is that any attempt to define Africa and by extension delineate the African will inevitably bring one into the tension between Africa being an "accident of history" and "geographical facts".

While Mazrui might have been factually right about Africa being a fiction, his notion of Africa in this sense is static. One could argue that if Africa is a fiction, so also are several successful modern nations like Germany and France which at different points in their histories were made up of different peoples and principalities. We can therefore argue that Mazrui's notion of 'Africa' appears to have ossified history in time and space because several countries that are today successful nation-states today were once diverse, often warring nationalities and hence also fictions as nation-states.

Mazrui's Delineation of the African

From his theoretic notions of Africa and the African, Mazrui in an article on 'Comparative Africanity: Blood, Soil and Ancestry', (published in the same book I edited in 2009), sought to move into the more empiric exercise of how to delineate or identify the African. He identified the following types of Africans:

1. Africans of the blood who are defined in "racial and genealogical terms" and are identified with the Black race.
2. Africans of the soil who are defined in geographical terms and are "identified with the African continent in nationality and ancestral location."
3. Mazrui regarded White Africans such as F.W, de Klerk as "Africans of the soil by adoption". He said this also applied to East Africans of Indian or Pakistani ancestry.
4. Mazrui equally had another category of Africans: African-Americans and American- Africans. He argued that the 'American African', is "conscious of his indigenous Africanity, is aware of his immediate continental ancestry, is in contact with relatives in Africa, is bilingual (speaking at least one African language) and is at home with much aspects of indigenous African culture as cuisine" while the "African Americans are descendants of the Middle Passage, are not in contact with relatives in Africa, are not native speakers of the African language and are seldom socialized into African cuisines even when they are pan African."

Following from the above Mazrui argued that Barrack Obama, whose father was Kenya, has an intermediate identity between being an African American and American African.

Convergence

Mazrui talked about the remarkable history of convergence between the Arab people and the African people. He argued that there are today more than 100 million Arab Muslims in North Africa, which has created a new identity he called 'Afrabians'. He defined this group as "Africans of the soil in North Africa who are Arab without intermarriage with Africans of the blood." He had different types of Afrabians:

Geographical Afrabians – Africans of the soil in North Africa who are Arab without intermarriage with Africans of the blood (black Africans).

Genealogical Afrabians: who are products of intermarriage between Arabs and Black Africans such as the majority of Northern Sudanese, half of Mauritanians and "Swahilized dynastic Afrabian families like the Mazrui of Kenya."

Ideological Afrabians: Mazrui defined this category as Africans who refuse to recognize the Sahara as a divide and insist that all people indigenous to Africa (be they Arab or Black) are one people such as the late Kwame Nkrumah.

Cultural Afrabians – These are, according to Mazrui, usually Black Africans who have no Arab blood whatsoever but are highly Arabized culturally. He argued that many Sudanese – both Northern and Southern- are deeply Arabized in speech and values without being Arab genealogically.

Mazrui posed the question of where to locate the Hausa and Hausa-Fulani of Nigeria and answered it rhetorically: "Indeed, are not the majority of Islamized Africans of the blood (Black Muslims) automatically cultural Afrabians?"

Was Mazrui an African?

For some, the answer to this is obvious: Mazrui is generally regarded as a leading African intellectual. But there are several Africanist (such as our own Wole Soyinka and Chinweizu) who questioned Mazrui's Africanness and even his commitment to Africa. Among the reasons for this were Mazrui's Arab ancestry, his excuse (if not defence) of Arab slavery of Africans (Trans-Saharan slave trade), which he argued was for domestic purposes while condemning Trans-Atlantic slave trade (which he argued was for commercial purposes) and his strong condemnation of nationalism in Africa as a mask for dictatorship in the early years of his career. Many Africanists also did not forgive Mazrui for his critical article on Nkrumah shortly after he was overthrown as the President of Ghana. The article was entitled: 'Nkrumah: The Leninist Czar'. Mazrui was also said to have called for the recolonization of some African countries.

Does Mazrui see himself as an African on the same level of Africanity with say, my humble self? This brings us back to the question of whether identity should be a choice or an imposition – or both.

As we saw from the discussion in the preceding section, Mazrui identified his family and himself as part of "genealogical Afrabians" who are, according to him, bridge builders between Black Africans and Arab Africans. An interesting question is whether Mazrui's 'Afrabian' is a category in the hierarchy of Africanness, and if so, where he placed himself in relations to those he called Africans of the blood? Did Mazrui invent the Afrabian typology to show that as a bridge builder between African Arabs and 'Africans of the blood' he was morally superior to his critics, who continued to question to his death his Africanness or commitment to Africa?

Critique of Mazrui's Delineation of the Africans

While Mazrui's has successfully called attention to the inadequacies of each of the traditional taxonomies for defining or delineating the Africa – race, geography and consciousness of being an African – his own notion of an African is also fraught with major weaknesses. For instance the notion appears so universalist and elastic that virtually anyone one can fit into one category or the other (or can stretch the elastic to create a new category for himself or herself – after all Africa is the original home of man!).

In fact the elasticity of Mazrui's notion of the African reminds one of the 'cosmopolitans' whom Jean-Jacques Rousseau, the Francophone Genevan philosopher, accused of trying to "justify their love of their country by their love of the human race and make a boast of loving the entire world in order to enjoy the privilege of loving no one."

Related to the above is that Mazrui's creation of Afrabians as a new category of 'super Africans' or 'bridge builders' between 'Africans of the soil' and 'Africans of the blood' – could play into the hands of his critics who questioned his commitment to Africa. Given the occasional tension between Pan Africanism and Pan Arabism in Africa, where would Mazrui pitch his tent if such conflict exploded and Mazrui was asked to take a bold stand? Neutrality may be impossible because as they would say, behind every neutrality lies a hidden choice.

Daily Trust, July 28, 2016

CHAPTER 80

Are We Trying to Pull Down Barrack Obama?

Since Barrack Obama announced a visit to Africa, his relationship with Nigerian Internet bloggers seems to have soured. Initially, many Nigerians interpreted the choice of 'little' Ghana, over the 'oil-producing, giant of Africa' as Obama's subtle way of rebuking Nigeria's leadership for not getting its act together, and of rewarding Ghana for its assumed good governance and deepening democratic ethos.

Ghana has always had a sort of 'siblings rivalry' with Nigeria, from the time its national football side would routinely trounce the Nigerian Eagles. Despite the rivalry, Nigerians prefer to see Ghanaians as sort of younger siblings who nurse some ambitions of upstaging their older, stronger and richer brothers. It is possible that the new hostility towards Obama may be an unconscious frustration that the 44th American president appeared to have taken sides in the 'siblings rivalry' between Nigeria and Ghana. But the formal charge is that he 'talked down' to Africans, and tried to lecture them in that speech to the Ghanaian parliament on July 11, 2009. But did he actually do so? Apparently the offensive part of the transcribed version of the speech was:

> "In many places, the hope of my father's generation gave way to cynicism, even despair. Now, it's easy to point fingers and to pin the blame of these problems on others. Yes, a colonial map that made little sense helped to breed conflict. The West has often approached Africa as a patron or a source of resources rather than a partner. But the West is not responsible for the destruction of the Zimbabwean economy over the last decade, or wars in which children are enlisted as combatants. In my father's life, it was partly tribalism and patronage and nepotism in an independent Kenya that for a long stretch derailed his career, and we know that this kind of corruption is still a daily fact of life for far too many."

Critics of the speech however appear to have taken this passage out of context. In fact just after the above quoted passage, the next paragraph was:

> "Now, we know that's also not the whole story. Here in Ghana, you show us a face of Africa that is too often overlooked by a world that sees only tragedy or a need for charity. The people of Ghana have worked hard to put democracy on a firmer footing, with repeated peaceful transfers of power even in the wake of closely contested elections. (Applause.) And by the way, can I say that for that the minority deserves as much credit as the majority. (Applause.) And with improved governance and an emerging civil society, Ghana's economy has shown impressive rates of growth. (Applause.)"

Obama also narrated how his grandfather who was a cook for the British in colonial Kenya was called a "boy" for much of his life by his employers, even though he was a respected elder in his village. In the concluding part of the speech, Obama said mutual responsibility would be the basis of America's partnership with Africa.

For a black president, it takes remarkable courage to do what Obama has done so far. He has not tried to deny his identity – as many of our compatriots in top international positions abroad too often do. But he has at all times also been conscious of the fact that he was elected to be President of the United States, and by implication leader of the world, rather than to pander to his primordial identities. It is a tough balancing act that requires wisdom and courage. Read his speech to the National Association for the Advancement of Coloured Peoples (N.A.A.C.P) on July 17, 2009 and his reaction to the arrest and handcuffing of Professor Henry Louis Gates, the black director of Harvard's African-American research centre by the police from Cambridge, Massachusetts. Now compare this with a Nigerian female ambassador to Sweden who once told Nigerians in another Scandinavian country, before the leaders of that country, that Nigerians were thieves and should not be trusted. Her classical display of bleaching complex is often what we have come to expect of our leaders in privileged positions, especially when abroad.

In most of his speeches, Obama has shown he is nuanced as he tries to take on board most of the arguments in any given issue, conscious of the fact that the target of any speech goes beyond the immediate audience. In my book, he has displayed uncommon wisdom and level-headedness, and so far appear to have silenced critics who questioned whether a black guy could be trusted with such a highly complex office as the US presidency. Whatever is said against Obama's visit or speech, the fact remains that he visited sub-Saharan Africa within six months of his presidency. No other American President ever visited sub-Saharan Africa during his first term in office.

Obama has also been criticised for an interview he granted to CNN's "Anderson Cooper: 360" in July, shortly after the Ghana trip. Obama had compared the legacy of slavery to the Holocaust, saying both are horrible parts of history and that their lessons must never be forgotten.

It is thought the assertion displeased some Jews and Africans in equal measure. For some Jews, comparing the holocaust to slavery diminishes the centrality of 'holocaust' in the mainstream narrative of victimhood and evil. They suspect that Obama wanted to smuggle in the 'long forgotten slavery', which is hardly mainstream, to share the spotlight with the holocaust. For some Africans, the comparison is an 'insult', not only because of the differences in the duration of the two 'evils' but also because of the unique effects and after effects of slavery such as the inferiorisation, discrimination and racism against black people that it spurned. Can a former slave masters ever see his former slave as equals, some Africans ask?

While I am not against subjecting Obama's policies and speeches to critical scrutiny (we will actually be helping to strengthen his presidency by doing so), the way some bloggers are taking it these days appears to re-echo the familiar 'pull him down' mentality so common with our people. This begs the question of what we really expect from an Obama presidency, and what he can realistically offer us given that any

American president is often a captive of the system that throws him up? I believe Obama's greatest gift to black people would be to succeed as an American president for that would mean that yet another psychological barrier has been broken down for the entire race. Just as some people paved the way for blacks to be accepted in fields such as entertainment and sports, so will a successful Obama presidency perhaps also pave the way for future generation of blacks. Therefore, if we lead the battle cry to pull him down, or even lend hand in any effort that pulls him down, then of course the doubt in some quarters that a black person could operate successfully at such a level would be confirmed. And we would all be worse for it.

Daily Independent July 30, 2009

CHAPTER 81

The call for Asari-Dokubo to be arrested

The statement credited recently to Alhaji Mujahid Asari-Dokubo, leader of the Niger Delta People's Volunteer Force that there would be no peace in Nigeria if President Jonathan is not re-elected in 2015 has generated deserved condemnation from several quarters. The Niger State Governor, Babangida Aliyu, was quoted as calling for Asari Dokubo's arrest for treason while the House of Representatives reportedly called on the security agencies to investigate him. Asari-Dokubo responded by daring anyone to arrest him and boasted that such an arrest, if effected, could lead to the disintegration of Nigeria.

While Asari-Dokubo's purported statements are without doubt offensive, the truth is that across the fault lines, irredentists and merchants of parochialism abound, often competing on hate-speech, grandstanding and threats. Several of such characters from various enclaves have said far worse things and challenged authorities even more audaciously than Asari-Dokubo did – and nothing happened. The tragedy of our country is that we like to play ostrich – our enclave is the embodiment of virtues, which others are trying to undermine, while those who are not 'one of us' are merely animated by hatred or envy. The truth is that the foibles we find in others abound aplenty in us – just as no enclave has a monopoly of the virtues and strengths they like to appropriate.

Calling for Asari Dokubo to be arrested – as Governor Babangida Aliyu did, is in my own opinion not informed by wisdom. Similarly, I feel that it was an error of judgment for the House of Representatives to ask the security agencies to investigate him because the political message here is that both Governor Aliyu and the House of Representatives felt sufficiently threatened by Asari-Dokubo's threats to make their calls for him to be arrested or investigated. And it is precisely their 'unwise' interventions that helped to ensure that the matter remained on news headlines for days – boosting in the process, Asari Dokubo's political stock. If Asari-Dokubo had been ignored, or allowed to be dealt with his equivalents – which you find in every enclave - the issue would be taken for what it really was – a mere grandstanding.
Now by intervening as they did, both Governor Aliyu and the House of Representatives unwittingly energized the ethnic-watchers, who effortless began to reel out the list of people from other fault-lines who had made even more 'inciting' statements without anything happening to such people. So what would be Governor Aliyu and the HOR's responses to such long list of other offenders who went scot free? I believe such 'unwise' interventions by very top ranking politicians and political institutions end up widening the social distance among Nigerians by unwittingly fanning the embers of ethnic and regional discords.

Aside from what I believe is an inappropriate call for Asari-Dokubo to be arrested, dealing with offensive statements such as he made is often not a straight forward matter in free speech jurisprudence. An analogy could indeed be made between AsariDokubo's offensive statements and those made in the 1960s by a member of the Ku Klux Klan – one of the worst purveyors of racial hatred in the USA. In a landmark case, Brandenburg v. Ohio (1969), an Ohio Klansman named Clarence Brandenburg was arrested following a speech where he called for the overthrowing of the government. In a unanimous judgment which overturned his initial conviction, Justice William Brennan argued that: "the constitutional guarantees of free speech and free press do not permit a State to forbid or proscribe advocacy of the use of force or of law violation except where such advocacy is directed to inciting or producing imminent lawless action and is likely to incite or produce such action." In other words, unless the 'clear and imminent danger' test is passed, you simply cannot arrest or start investigating someone for uttering a threat, however offensive that threat may be. This is complicated by the fact that even what constitutes 'incitement' could be contentious. As argued in another landmark case in the USA (*Gitlow v New York* [1925]): "Every idea is an incitement.... The only difference between the expression of an opinion and an incitement in the narrower sense is the speaker's enthusiasm for the result". By this definition, even the opinions we express in articles and books could be construed as incitement.

I am not by any means condoning the type of offensive statements that were credited to Asari-Dokubo. My point is that such statements are usually inflamed by unwise interventions from higher-political ups which often end up reinforcing the suspicions and feelings of persecutions by members of the in-group. In societies where the basis of statehood is settled, there is often an in-built self-censorship, which would ensure that unacceptable statements such as those made recently by Asari-Dokubo would lead to his being shunned by his peers and mainstream political actors. However in a highly polarised country like ours, where the basis of statehood remains contested, his offensive statements will achieve the opposite effect: he will be lionized by members of his in-group for being bold and audacious and they will readily roll out the war drums in defence of a 'son of the soil'.

EFCC's jungle justice

I was filled with disgust after reading the report that the Economic and Financial Crimes Commission recently arraigned the Company Secretary of E-Barclays Micro Finance Bank Limited, Abuja, one Oby Onwukeme, before Justice Adeniyi Ademola Adetokunbo of the Federal High Court, Abuja on a one count charge of obstructing justice. According to the press release by Wilson Uwujaren, Acting Head, Media & Publicity at the financial crimes buster, MS Onwukeme allegedly declined to furnish the Commission with the account information of one of her customers, Chief Paulinus Enendu of Pamadas and Sons Limited who was being investigated for obtaining money under false pretences and issuance of dud cheque to the tune of N4.2 million. It was claimed that despite repeated appeals and citing of Section 38 (2) (a) of the EFCC Establishment Act which relates to the crime of obstruction, Ms

Onwukeme maintained that her client's lawyer wrote and informed her not to disclose the information to the Commission. When the charge was read to her, she pleaded not guilty and was reportedly granted bail on self-recognition.

There are several issues on this case: Did the EFCC realize that the relationship between a banker and his/her client is a confidential one? Did the EFCC try to obtain either the customer's (i.e Chief Paulinus Enendu's) written consent for such a disclosure to be made or a court order authorizing such a disclosure? Or did it just believe that simply because it is EFCC every other norm of business relationship should be turned on its head – even when Ms. Onwukeme maintained she was acting on legal advice? Why did the EFCC sue Ms Onwukeme instead of the E- Barclays Micro Finance Bank Limited, which she works for? With her photos splashed on such online media as Sahara Reporters, a casual reader could be tempted to conclude that Ms Onwukeme had been charged for corruption, not for insisting on doing her job as she saw fit. In this sense the mere publication of this charge and her photographs is capable of bringing her to public opprobrium and could, in the language of the law of defamation, lead to her being shunned by 'reasonable members of the society'.

Though contraptions like the EFCC and the associated media trial they often employ in their work do have a role in the whole fight against corruption, I have never been a fan of the Commission's method just as I have never believed it is making any dent on the endemic corruption in the society. For one, it has always been my opinion that the conflation of the fight against corruption with political vendetta, and the generalized belief that the Commission is a willing tool in the hands of power incumbents dents its work. Two, I also believe the Commission has an inappropriate or incomplete diagnosis of the cause of corruption, preferring to see it as a question of moral lapse on the part of those affected, rather than largely a systemic problem. This inappropriate diagnosis, in my opinion, means the Commission focuses on fighting essentially the symptoms of the problem. Three, contrary to the belief in some quarters I do not believe that the EFCC is succeeding. A key measure of its success, in my opinion, is not on how many arrests it makes or even the amount of money it has recovered but on whether its establishment has led to a decline in corruption in the country. If corruption is becoming more endemic and not less – as seems to be the case – despite the EFCC and similar other contraptions, it means in my opinion, that the EFCC has failed. I believe a sober impact assessment of our strategies for fighting corruption over the years is needed, because this will tell us whether we have been wasting valuable time and money in unnecessary showmanship.

Daily Trust, May 16, 2013

CHAPTER 82

Between Edwin Clark and Nigerian Governors

I have a lot of respect for senior citizens, especially those who have crossed the three score and ten mark and are still active. In most African cultures, there are certain benefits that come with advanced age: you can afford to be blunt, even have an acerbic tongue, because you are assumed to have passed the stage where your utterances are actuated by pecuniary or career considerations. For this, elders, especially 'Very Senior Elders' (VSEs), that is, those in their 80s and above, are often regarded as the conscience of their communities, with some licences such as to exaggerate or use insulting words without these being counted against them. A much younger man who embarks on essaying about a VSE therefore risks opening himself up to accusations of not showing proper respect to age in any portraiture that suggests a challenge to the Very Senior Elder's wisdom or speech form. At 85, Chief Edwin Clark is an elder in the VSE club. For his age, he is very sharp intellectually and physically.

Largely because he comments on many controversial political issues and is thought to be very close to President Goodluck Jonathan, Chief Clark's bluntness has been treated differently than it would have been if he were operating strictly in village and communal settings. He has been taken on headlong from several quarters and successfully labelled as the 'undisputed Ijaw leader' who is unabashed about his support for President Jonathan, his fellow Ijaw, and who essentially believes that the President is being undermined because he comes from the 'wrong' section of the country. His critics pigeonhole him as the Rottweiler against the President's enemies – real or imagined. The latest group to be taken on by VSE Chief Clark is the Nigerian Governors' Forum, NGF.

In an open letter to the NGF, Chief Clark was quoted as saying: "The Governors' Forum is now acting as an opposition party to the Federal Government. It deliberately breach (sic) with impunity the constitution of the Federal Republic of Nigeria and the constitution of the PDP, without any challenges. The Forum has now become a threat to the peace and stability of Nigeria. Most of the governors today, are more dictatorial than the then military governors" (National Mirror, January 25 2013, online). He also accused former President Olusegun Obasanjo of working in cahoots with the NGF to undermine President Jonathan.

Though Chief Clark's Open Letter to the NGF was infused with his characteristic bluntness and passion - with that licence to exaggerate, shock and awe often allowed to VSEs in village meetings - peel off these, and one will notice he has raised a few significant issues: No one doubts that Nigerian Governors are indeed too powerful. Virtually all the State Legislatures are mere rubber stamps of the State Governors. Several Governors have engineered the impeachment of their Deputies or Speaker of their State House of Assembly on a whim. In fact State Governors not only choose the principal officers of their State House of Assembly but also often engineer their removal at their convenience. It is also almost unheard for a State Government (read State Governor) to lose a case before its State High Court. While elections often hold on schedule since 1999 at the federal and gubernatorial levels superintended by the national electoral commission, INEC, at the State levels where the Governors determine when Local Government elections should be held, only a few Governors have been able to organise such elections. And even the very few that did, the state-appointed electoral commission usually ensures that the Party of the State Governor wins in virtually all the Local Governments, often without even a consolation prize to the opposition. In this sense, Chief Clark was right. At State levels, the Governors are Leviathans, meaning that liberal democracy, with all its imperfections as practised at the federal level, is yet to take off at the State levels.

Aside from the grains of truth in Chief Clark's position on NGF, several observations could be made about his position on the NGF:

One, is the inherent contradiction in calling for the proscription of NGF ostensibly because the Governors have become more dictatorial than military regimes and the forum is being used to oppose the President. The truth is that the words 'ban', 'proscription' and 'censorship' - which Chief Clark apparently endorsed in dealing with the Governors - smack of a certain nostalgia for the authoritarianism and dictatorship that were the hallmarks of military regimes. In other words Chief Clark was calling for the use of dictatorial methods to deal with the Governors allegedly because they have become dictatorial. This is a contradiction in terms.

Two, there is absolutely nothing wrong with State Governors forming a pressure group to promote and defend their common interests. If anything, the NGF, given the depth and politicisation of the fault lines in the country, could be said to be a force for unity and national reconciliation by showing, through their regular comingling, that despite the fault lines and regional differences they can sustain a forum to discuss common problems. The Governors have actually managed themselves and their differences under the NGF far better than politicians and all the political parties have done - despite such shortcomings as not developing a peer-review mechanism and not doing enough to stem the suspected looting of state treasuries by some of their colleagues. The Governors, despite their political, regional and political differences, once rallied together to successfully resist a suspected attempt by agents of the presidency to impose a chairman on the group.

Three, just as the powers of the Governors are enormous; those of the Nigerian President are simply imperial. The Nigerian President is in fact often said to be even more powerful than the President of USA - a situation that is aggravated by the federal government's control of oil revenues and the subsequent power of the purse that it gives to it. Largely because of this and the feeble character of Nigerian opposition groups, there is a need for a 'third force' powerful enough to serve as a restraint on the majestic powers of a Nigerian president. This is the role the NGF has been trying to play, though not always very successfully.

Four, pressure groups such as the NGF and civil society groups are normally ubiquitous in a democracy and are often used as barometers for measuring the strength of a country's democracy project. It is in fact remarkable that VSE Clark recently spearheaded the formation of one such pressure group, which he called the Southern Nigeria Peoples Assembly. It does not really matter the motive behind the formation of any pressure group provided that such a group goes about its business legitimately and peacefully. True, some pressure groups can aggravate the structures of conflict in our type of society. However banning such groups will often be counter-productive. Not only will such a ban amount to an invitation to dictatorship, they will easily drive such groups undergrounds, which will subsequently lead to the romanticization of the causes they espouse. The hope is that such groups could be countervailing - by balancing and cancelling one another or that they will come together under one umbrella organization that will formulate a code of conduct which will serve as a sort of self-censorship on the members.

Five, though Chief Clark pursues whatever cause he believes in with gusto and single-minded devotion, there is a feeling that the way he uncritically defends the Jonathan administration is counter- productive because the VSE's position is unwittingly defining the President as sectional when those who know him often swear by their mothers that he is no such person. There is also a feeling that regarding any criticism of the President Jonathan as an attempt to undermine his presidency is tantamount to using blackmail to muffle free speech and prevent the electorate from making the president to be on his toes. This apparent resort to blackmail can truly be alienating, especially to the undecided voters. Vigorous debates, including acerbic criticisms of elected officials, are the soul of politics in a democracy.

Six, politics is essentially a contest for power. It is in the nature of the game that the opposition will do everything legitimate to 'undermine' incumbents of power positions for this is the only way the electorate will reject such incumbents and vote them in as better alternatives. This happens in all democracies, including the mature ones. Those who often romanticize the way Americans close ranks after elections probably do not listen to opposition media houses such as Fox News or conservative radio host Rush *Limbaugh*. Limbaugh, whose show is broadcast in over 600 radio stations in the US, constantly lampoons President Barrack Obama and no one has called for his arrest or the banning of his talk show. Americans take pride in their free speech principle as guaranteed by the First Amendment to their constitution. And since we all like to point to the way Americans run their democracy as a model to be emulated, their respect and defence of free speech should be food for thought for those of us who are intolerant of dissents or criticisms

Daily Trust, January 31, 2013

CHAPTER 83

Deconstructing Babangida

I have never met Ibrahim Babangida, one- on-one. The closest I have been to a one-on-one meeting with him is the detailed attempt to deconstruct him and his eight year headship of the country by Dan Agbese, one of the four founders of the iconic Newswatch magazine. Entitled *Ibrahim Babangida: The Military, Politics and Power in Nigeria,* the 433-page volume was published by Adonis & Abbey Publishers (www.adonis-abbey.com) in 2012 but will only be made available to the reading public from 30 September this year.

In the interest of open disclosure, I should mention, that Adonis & Abbey Publishers, set up in the United Kingdom in 2003 to publish books and academic journals, is my firm. Several years ago, I was introduced to Dan Agbese by the eminent Nigerian professor of political science, Isawa J Elaigwu who was in turn introduced to me by Professor Ali Mazrui, who would definitely have been a strong candidate for a Nobel Prize had there been one in political science or political philosophy. I became Professor Mazrui's junior intellectual sparring partner after he published a very important comparative work with us in 2006 entitled *A Tale of two Africas: Nigeria and South Africa as Two Contrasting Visions.* Professor Elaigwu was to become my intellectual 'oga at the top'.

I took interest in Dan Agbese's manuscript, primarily due to the controversial subject matter but gave up on him because year after year he was still telling me that the manuscript was 'nearing completion'. When, sometime in 2011, he called to say he was ready to submit the manuscript, I did not take him serious. But when to my surprise I received the tome, I came to understand why it took him some twenty years to write it. It is, in my opinion, a bold and courageous attempt to deconstruct Babangida with a view to understanding some of the actions and inactions of his eight year rule.

One of Agbese's conclusions is that though Babangida generally means well and is enamoured by innovative ideas, he does not like to be predicted and may deliberately indulge in dance steps that contradict the big ideas he espouses just so that no one can predict him. This is probably what the Nigerian writer and academic Okey Ndibe had in mind when he nicknamed Babangida 'Maradona' - after the famous Argentinian football dribbler, Diego Maradona. The nickname stuck.

The book addresses another fundamental question: Does history have immutable laws such that it moves on its chosen trajectory irrespective of the will or actions of individuals or is it merely a record of the actions and inactions of individuals? Agbese seems to suggest a third way – that while the immutable laws of history influence the course a leader takes, a leader's personality can help shape the trajectory of such history. For instance Agbese noted that though the Babangida era formally began on August 27 1985 after the gap-toothed General overthrew the regime of Muhammadu Buhari, the forces that created that era were already in place even before Babangida was born. He also argued that throughout Babangida's tenure in office, those forces continued to cast a shadow on his era. As he noted on page 16 of the book:

"The Babangida era did not begin on August 27, 1985. The events that shaped it did not begin on that day either. Nor did they end on August 27, 1993 – the day he stepped aside from the presidency and became just another private Nigerian again.

"He was part of the story but it was not his story from the beginning. His decision to go into the army, for instance, may be seen as the beginning of his story. But it was not his decision. The decision was made for him and eight of his former classmates in the Provincial Secondary School, Bida, by the dynamics of the Nigerian political story."

Agbese further noted that we "are all subject to the fate decreed by the ubiquitous 'what if?' question. What if the northern establishment allowed the young Babangida to pursue his initial ambition of becoming a civil engineer? What if Nzeogwu and his fellow four majors had not dragged the army into our national politics on January 15, 1966?"

Agbese believes that Babangida is a complex character, "as complex and complicated as they come". To untangle this "complex character", he delved into his background, showing how some of the retired General's known traits such as his "genuine love for new thinking" and his aversion to being easily predicted were formed and how these traits in turn combined with the environmental variables of the Nigerian condition and the invisible hands of the forces that threw him up to define the choices he made as military president, including the decision to annul the June 1993 elections won by his friend, MKO Abiola. The annulment was to trigger a chain of events that culminated in the institution of Nigeria's Fourth Republic.

Agbese said he approached the research and writing of the book with the ingrained curiosity of a reporter but wanted it to be an intellectual rather than a reportorial inquiry. Perhaps because of this ambition, there are parallels in style between the book and Professor Isawa Elaigwu's highly regarded academic biography of General Yakubu Gowon, Nigeria's military Head of State between August 1 1966 and July 29 1975 - the foreign edition of which we also had the privilege of publishing.

I probably forgot Agbese's hypothesis that Babangida loathes to be predicted when I revealed in this column late last year what I picked up from the grapevine that the book was slated to be launched on 6 December 2012. I am not sure whether that revelation (or was it an attempt to predict him?) had anything to do with the retired General changing his mind about the launch date. None of the other dates supposedly slated for the launching or presentation of the book also came to fruition. When Agbese expressed frustration with this 'circular dance', I jokingly asked him if he was not contradicting himself by hypothesising that the man does not like to be predicted while at the same time hoping to predict him by holding him to his words.

Despite being a very bold work that tries to understand Babangida and how his personality and the forces that threw him up influenced the choices he made as military president, the book is not without fault. For instance some of the sources of the quotations in the book are not given and Agbese's discussion of the death, by parcel bomb, of Dele Giwa, one of the founders of Newswatch, does not provide any new insight on whether the Babangida regime was really culpable or not. Some Nigerians, led by the late Gani Fawehinmi, had blamed agents of the Babangida regime as being responsible for Dele Giwa's death. Agbese also does not account for the reasons why Babangida remains probably the most charismatic of all Nigerian leaders – despite the fact that he 'stepped aside' as military president more than 20 years ago.

Despite these lapses, I am very impressed by the objectivity and courage with which the book is written. It is neither an irreverent book that tries to pander to the constituency of Babangida bashers, nor is it by any stretch of the imagination a hagiography. It is rather a book that courageously searches for the truth as the author saw it, with respect rightly accorded to Babangida and the high office he occupied but without being intimidated by these. Credit must also be accorded to Babangida for endorsing the book despite its several digs and pot shots at him. I am convinced that Agbese's book will raise interesting new conversations about Babangida and his eight year rule (1985 to 1993).

Some quotes from the book:

> "Babangida used every opportunity to demonstrate his love for new thinking on the myriads of political, economic and social problems that hobbled the country since independence. He openly shopped for them. He encouraged dialogues between his administration and the people – as could be seen in the IMF and foreign policy debates...." (p.403)

> "Attempts have been made, and are still being made, to explain why [June 12] election was annulled. The easy pick in these attempts is that the military acted a northern script to prevent power shift to the south.... From what has been pieced together so far in researching for this book, the decision to annul the election was not 'collective', if by 'collective' Babangida meant that the members of the National Defence and Security Council were privy to it" (pp393-394).

> "In his eight years in power, Babangida, like the hurricane, tried to pull down every tree that stood in his path. He left almost nothing untouched.... Babangida attempted to do titanic things to create the Babangida Era that would be the veritable watershed in the history of Nigeria. It did not quite work out that way for him. He left office eight years later not in a blaze of glory but in circumstances that that put the Babangida mystique through the shredder." (p.405).

Ibrahim Babangida: The Military, Politics and Power in Nigeria is published by Adonis & Abbey Publishers (www.adonis-abbey.com). It is available in Europe, North America and Australia through Gardners, Ingram, Barnes & Noble, Bertrams, Amazon and other leading online retailers. In Nigeria, you can contact the company's Abuja office on 07066997765, 08050001501.

Daily Trust, September 26 2013

CHAPTER 84

'Fayemi effect' and Intellectuals in Politics

Dr Kayode Fayemi, the defeated governor of Ekiti State, is becoming a national icon by the way he has so far handled his defeat. He lost the governorship election in Ekiti but won a landslide victory in the hearts and minds of most Nigerians. In climes where dishonesty is banal, telling the truth is regarded as a revolutionary act. Dr Fayemi did the unthinkable: for an incumbent to concede an election to an opponent without whining that he has been rigged out, is a very un-Nigerian act. It is an act capable of revolutionizing our electoral politics. Many of the briefcase contestants in the election, who were in the race in the hope that they would be 'mobilized' (in Nigeria-speak) to play a role during the inevitable court processes, may not find Fayemi's action funny.

The larger victory of the Dr Fayemi in Ekiti, holds the promise of turning our politics away from its present character of zero-sum-game (winner takes all) to a relative gain situation (a win-win situation). The fear of vindictiveness by an opponent is one of the factors that animates 'sit-tightism' among African leaders. It also explains why many Nigerian governors and presidents want to impose on the electorate a candidate they hand-picked.

Though I do not personally know Dr Fayemi, watching him read his concession speech on TV, I felt tears swell in my eyes because he is one of the few Governors I really had very strong empathy for. The way he handled his defeat made him even a greater hero in my mind. Without any show of bitterness on his face, he declared that "election by its nature generates tension and hot exchange of words, but to me, once the whole exercise is over, all those involved should take such with calmness and stop all acrimony.

> "It is my belief that we must all start imbibing attitudes that will make us avoid activities that can threaten our peaceful co-existence. We must also avoid the bad loser syndrome. I believe we need to build this democracy to a mature end, rather than pull it down."

Dr Kayode has done his bit. He has extended a hand of fellowship to the winner, Ayo Fayose and has been rewarded by the public for doing so. For the Fayemi effect to take root will however now depend on whether Fayose will find the strength of character to resist the temptations of being triumphalist or vindictive – like virtually all the other Governors that succeeded in unseating incumbents (and even those handpicked by a former President and Governors to succeed them).

Fayose is most likely to come under pressure when he is sworn in as governor from his cronies, favour-seekers and the PDP to 'rubbish' Dr Fayemi in order to make himself look good (every governor creates the impression that before them there had been no governance in their states). Such provocations sometimes force people who have already accepted defeat to reverse themselves and challenge their defeat in courts as a way of fighting back. Fayemi must resist the temptation – despite any provocation.

It should be the duty of Nigerian media and Nigerians to take on both the sore loser and the triumphalist victor if we are serious about sanitizing our politics. Both the sore loser and the triumphant victor must be seen and treated as problems to the democratic processes in the country. We must begin to find answers to the question of why the phenomenon of the gallant loser has not become entrenched in our political culture despite the fact that Obasanjo became a global statesman by merely handing over power to a democratically elected government in 1979.

A very important issue raised by the Ekiti election is the role of intellectuals in politics. Many analysts believe that one of the reasons Fayose won was because he was a 'grassroots person', a man of the people, so-to-say, while Dr Fayemi, with his PhD and polished diction, was too much of an aloof intellectual. People who buy this thesis find support in the dictum by the former Speaker of the U.S. House Tip O'Neill that "all politics is local". The expression is often used to mean that a politician's success is directly tied to the person's ability to understand and influence the issues of their constituents. In other words, politicians must appeal to the simple, mundane and everyday concerns of those who elected them into office. In Ekiti, Fayose, who rode on 'okadas' was said to mingle with the people easily, attending to local burials, while Dr Fayemi, was aloof – as most intellectuals are wont to be.
I have problems with this type of analysis.

A starting point may be to pose the question of who is an intellectual. There is no consensus on the definition but I always find the definition by Professor Ali Mazrui, the Kenyan public intellectual, very illuminating.

According to Mazrui, an intellectual is someone who is fascinated by abstract ideas and has acquired some academic capacity for handling such ideas. Mazrui's definition means that one needs not be a Professor or PhD to be an intellectual. It also means that one can lose either his fascination with abstract ideas or his capacity for handling such ideas (such as through lack of refurbishments via readings and attending seminars and workshops). Mazrui called this category of intellectuals 'ex-intellectuals', suggesting that the possession of such honorifics as 'professor' or 'Dr' does not make anyone a perpetual intellectual. Quite a number of our intellectuals who dabble into politics quickly get engrossed with the politics of 'stomach infrastructure' and in the process either lose interest in abstract ideas or allow their capacity for handling such ideas to become obsolete (or both).

Following from the above, a Nigerian intellectual in politics is someone who, despite being involved in politics, retains his or her fascination with abstract ideas and also his or her capacity for handling such ideas. This often includes polished mannerisms and a belief that a vision of society he or she had before joining politics, is actually realizable. The intellectual in politics resists the system dynamics that try to turn him into a 'man of the people' – that is to say, a hypocrite that does things for expediency or simply to win elections. Unfortunately aloofness tends to be part of the definition of intellectuals (perhaps because they need their space to be themselves or to dwell on their abstract ideas). This is not the same as not caring about the needs of the people or being out of touch but a belief that leadership is not a popularity contest, that a leader should show the way, and that while the short term needs of the people are important, it is often the greater vision of the future that should be the driver of policies. In Nigeria, being 'a 'man of the people' (or 'grassroots' man) often means being a sort of Robin Hood who steals from the state and redistributes a tiny part of the proceeds to the people. I have no issue with people who are genuinely folksy. But to imply that going into politics means that everyone will have to acquire a 'man of the people' identity seems to me a fraud. I don't feel that I need to ride on okada to prove that I am not out of touch.

One of the lessons from Fayemi's loss therefore is for intellectuals planning to dabble into politics to start creating new narratives that will drive political discourses. Grassroots politicians in Nigerian parlance tend to be short-term oriented – they build new universities even when existing ones are not well equipped because it is what the people can relate with; they prioritize the building of roads over investing in qualitative education because the voters cannot immediately see the effect of the latter and the impact may not be felt before the next elections. Grassroots politicians may know how to win the votes with 'amala', 'tuwo' or 'garri' politics but it is not certain they know what it takes to build a society that will be competitive in the 21st century. Therefore the danger of glamourizing 'grassroots' politicians is not only the unacceptable subtext that we need to lose our individual identities in order to thrive in politics but even the more dangerous innuendo that the gratification of the immediate physical and sensory needs of the masses is the only way to be a good politician. What then happens to the age- old adage that leadership is not - and ought not be - a popularity contest? In a largely illiterate and poor society like ours, both the visionary leaders and the grassroots politicians have complementary roles to play: we need the 'grassroots politicians' to remind the visionary leader (intellectual) that in the long-run the people will be dead if their immediate needs are not gratified; we also need the visionary leader to remind the grassroots politicians that a society that is not driven by a big vision will forever remain ordinary.

Daily Trust, June 26 2014

CHAPTER 85

Governor Aliyu's Challenge

Politics is in the air and jostling for 2015 has simply begun in earnest. Anyone telling you otherwise is either living in another planet, trying to undercut the competition or simply being dishonest.

We saw another evidence of this when Governor Babangida Aliyu of Niger State, who is also the Chairman of the Northern Governors' Forum declared recently that President Goodluck Jonathan reached an agreement in 2011 with leaders of the Peoples Democratic Party (PDP) and Governors elected on the platform of the party to serve only a single term. He was quoted by several media houses as saying: "I recall that at that discussion, it was agreed that Jonathan would serve only one term of four years and we all signed the agreement. Even when Jonathan went to Kampala, in Uganda, he also said he was going to serve a single term." The key word here is 'signed'. Did President Jonathan actually 'sign' any pact with the leadership of the PDP and the Governors elected on the platform of the party? The Presidency, speaking through Alhaji Ahmed Gulak, Special Adviser to the President on Political Matters, denied the existence of any such pact and challenged anyone who thought otherwise to produce evidence.

I believe the 'salvo' from the Chief Servant of Niger State is merely adding a moral dimension to the numerous angles through which the key contending forces are fighting over 2015. There is already a legal challenge from sources suspected to be testing the waters on behalf of the presidency on Jonathan's eligibility to contest in 2015 just as the opposing sides have also sponsored contrary legal opinions on why he is legally barred from running. There is nothing really wrong in this because the contest for power is usually fought from various dimensions, including psychological mind games. But the categorical nature of Governor Aliyu's allegation put's the credibility of both the Niger State Governor and the President on the line. The onus of proof is however on Governor Aliyu to produce a signed pact between the Governors and PDP leadership and President Jonathan.

If it is proven that President Jonathan indeed 'signed' a pact to run for only one term and then is contemplating to jettison it, then the moral burden will be quite heavy. It will be one reneging of an agreement too many. It should be recalled that in 2011 President Jonathan chose to contest the presidency even though he was the 34th signatory to the expanded PDP caucus meeting in December 2002 which allegedly endorsed zoning and power rotation for the party. Proving the existence of another 'signed' deal that is about to be disrespected will be just too damaging - coming on top of whispers of ingratitude in the current face-off between Jonathan and Olusegun Obasanjo who literally made him Governor of Bayelsa State, Vice President and President of the country.

My personal opinion is that given the furore Jonathan's candidacy generated in the run-up to the 20011 elections, there must have been an 'agreement' of sorts between President Jonathan and the PDP leadership and Governors. In fact the Governors were at that time seen to be exceedingly powerful and were openly playing hide and seek with President Jonathan, who was then seen as weak and diffident. An apparently frustrated Jonathan was once quoted as telling the Governors and the leadership of his party: "Everything I have asked for, you have refused to give me. No President anywhere has been treated by his party the way you are treating me. I am the captain of this boat. I am not going down alone. I am going to sink this (political) boat and go down with all that are in it." (Weekly Trust, 19 December 2010). Again former President Obasanjo, who was a staunch supporter of Jonathan's candidacy in 2011 and who was then the Chairman of the Party's Board of Trustees alluded to the President's one-term decision at the PDP convention/presidential primary of January 15, 2011 at the Eagle Square, Abuja: "We are impressed with the report that Dr. Goodluck Ebele Jonathan has already taken a unique and unprecedented step of declaring that he would only want to be a one-term President. If so, whether he knows it or not, that is a sacrifice and it is statesmanly [sic]. Rather than vilify him and pull him down, we, as a party, should applaud and commend him and Nigerians should reward and venerate him" (ThisDay Live, 23 February 2013). In the same vein the Vanguard of 22 February 2013 reported that the PDP's NEC meeting which held on December 16, 2010 (allegedly after the Governors had tried to frustrate it) reached a number of agreements embodied in a communiqué which was read by Governor Ibrahim Shema of Katsina State. The paper quoted part of the communiqué as reading: "The Governors also recognize the Yar'Adua/Jonathan ticket and therefore hereby support President Goodluck Jonathan (GCFR) to contest the 2011 election as the PDP presidential candidate for a period of four years only."

Anecdotal evidence therefore suggests the existence of an 'agreement'. What is not clear is the nature of the agreement, what it was supposed to achieve and whether Jonathan signed or not. Nigerian politicians often say things they don't mean. Virtually all the major presidential candidates in 2011 – Buhari, Babangida and Atiku – promised to do only one term even though most people took such with a pinch of salt. Buhari, regarded by many as the most 'straight forward' politician in the country, even reversed himself on his public pledge not to seek the presidency again. Similarly Governor Peter Obi of Anambra State, who has a public persona of a 'saint' among some Nigerians, also promised to do one term in office but ended up going for a second term. Being double-faced is therefore in the gene of Nigerian politicians, not just in that of one politician.

Nigerian politicians simply cannot be trusted and the government cannot be trusted. The pervading distrust percolates into inter-ethnic and inter-religious relations. Did Nigerians not rally behind then Vice President Jonathan when a cabal tried to prevent him from becoming Acting President by lying about the true health conditions of Yaradua? And did the presidency under Jonathan not do exactly the same when Dame Patience Jonathan became ill and recently revealed she had nine surgeries?

From Taraba State to Enugu state, sick Governors lie on their conditions in order to cling onto power – the same thing we all found reprehensible about the cabal around the late Yaradua who held the nation hostage.

It is possible that the concession 'extracted' from President Jonathan to run for only one term in 2011 was part of political double-talk, only meant to pacify the public anger in some parts of the North. Despite the apparent street opposition to Jonathan's candidacy in the North, I believe that many of the Governors would still have been inclined to support him – purely from a perspective of self-preservation. At that time most of the Governors were to run for a second term and would not want an angry President who had threatened to do a Samson (pull down the structures so everyone goes down) setting the EFCC after them. There was also an apparent dread of a Buhari presidency that could amend the constitution to remove the Governors' immunity and herd as many of them as possible into long jail terms on corruption charges. Atiku, some Governors might have calculated, would have been too 'politically smart' for the sort of games they were playing with the then malleable Jonathan.

If I were Jonathan I would try not to run in 2015 – not just because of the general perception that he has underperformed - but even more importantly to make a bold statement about sacrifice and integrity and that there should be life after power. Handled properly such a bold step could help in healing a highly divided nation and rebuild trust. My fear however is that even if Jonathan does not want to run and assuming he has the will to resist pressures from those benefitting from his presidency, the politics of the opposition, with its embedded intimidation, can actually force him to run and 'let the heavens break loose'. There is also the often overlooked vendetta by power incumbents, especially against their predecessors in office. Just look at some of the States where the Governors lost in the last elections.

Nigerians rightly condemned Obasanjo for seeking tenure elongation. Given the nature of our politicians, I am not sure any future President of the country would not contrive ways to elongate his tenure. Obasanjo accepted defeat when his pet project of tenure elongation was defeated. We never really know how others will handle challenge to their attempts to elongate themselves in office.

Premium Times, March 1, 2013

CHAPTER 86

Ike Ibeabuchi: The Greatest who never was

He was billed to be one of the greatest heavy weight boxers of his generation. He said he took to boxing after watching journeyman James Douglas knock out the then invincible Mike Tyson in Tokyo in 1990. Before leaving Nigeria for the United States of America in 1993, he had in the amateur ranks twice defeated Duncan Dokiwari who would later win a bronze medal for Nigeria in the 1996 Olympics.

Ike Ibeabuchi, born September 21 1973, quickly took to boxing in the USA, where his mother, Patricia, had moved to in 1990, and was working as a registered nurse. He came under the tutelage and guidance of former world welterweight champion Curtis Cokes, who said of the young talent: "He was raw when he walked in my door, but each day you would have to teach him something new because he improved so fast. It was tough to keep up with him." In 1994, just one year after arriving in the US, Ike won the Texas State Golden Gloves. He turned professional the same year with a second round knock-out of one Ismael Garcia on October 13.

After winning 16 straight fights against carefully selected opponents, mostly club fighters and journeymen, Ike got an opportunity to prove himself in the big league when he was squared against the Samoan hit-man David Tua, for the WBC International Heavy weight title on June 7, 1997. At that time, Tua who had a record of 27-O, was considered the 'next big thing' in boxing and a massive favourite to win the fight. The fight was nothing short of spectacular, with both men throwing bombs at each other without either taking a backward step throughout the duration of the fight. They ended up setting a world record of the highest number of punches thrown in a heavyweight fight after exchanging a combined 1,730 punches through the 12-rounds that the fight lasted. Ike also set an individual record of the highest number of punches thrown by a heavyweight: he threw 975 punches throughout the fight, averaging over 81 punches per round, against the average of 50 punches per round for heavyweights. The 6ft 2inches strongly built, extremely quick and power-punching Ike Ibeabuchi was declared the winner of the fight by a unanimous decision of 117-111, 116-113 and 115-114. Boxing enthusiasts can watch the highlights of the fight on Youtube (visit www.youtube.com, and search for Ike Ibeabuchi v David Tua). It is a fight that needs to be watched to appreciate Ibeabuchi's potentials.

Ironically Ibeabuchi's troubles started or deepened after the David Tua fight. Though Ike complained of a terrible headache after the fight, several tests in the hospital, including an MRI scan, found nothing wrong with him. But from then it was alleged that he began nursing feelings of being plagued by demons and occasionally acting it out. For instance it was reported that a couple of months after the Tua fight, he became depressed over a perceived snub in the WBC rankings. He was alleged to have abducted the 15-year old son of his former girl friend and slammed his car into a concrete pillar on Interstate 35 north of Austin, Texas. According to the criminal complaint, the boy suffered "numerous injuries" from the accident "and will never walk normally again." Ike was charged with kidnapping and attempted murder, but the courts concluded he was perhaps trying to commit suicide and sentenced him to 120 days in jail after he had pleaded guilty to false imprisonment. He also paid $500,000 in civil settlement. Several other instances of bad behaviour were reported against him, reminding one of Tyson at the height of his fame.

Ibeabuchi returned to the ring after thirteen months of inactivity and of reportedly exhibiting other weird behaviours to score a first round knockout over journeyman Tim Ray in July 1998. Two months later, he stopped another journeyman Everton Davis in nine rounds. Ike's next fight would be against Chris Byrd in March 1999. Byrd, a highly elusive southpaw with an awkward style, won the silver medal in the 1992 Barcelona summer Olympics as a middleweight. At the time of the fight with Ike, Byrd, who would later become both the IBF and WBO champion, was undefeated in 26 fights and was touted as 'knock-out proof'. But with only 48 seconds left in the fifth round, a left-handed boo punch from Ike followed with a right hook sent Byrd to the canvas, face first. He was knocked down once more before the referee stopped the fight after being severely punished with power punches when he got trapped between the ropes. With the victory over Byrd, no one in the boxing world could afford to ignore Ike or doubt that he had truly become a top contender for the World heavyweight title. He turned down an offer of $700,000 to fight fringe contender Jeremy Williams and $1m for a showdown with the undefeated Michael Grant.

The fight with Chris Byrd however turned out to be Ike's last fight.

In July 1999, it was alleged that Ibeabuchi who was staying at The Mirage Hotel and Casino in Las Vegas had called a local escort service for a prostitute. The 21-year old woman claimed the deal was only for her to be there to strip for him and nothing more but that Ike wanted to get physical and attacked her in a walk-in closet after she demanded to be paid up-front. The Police was called in but Ike barricaded himself in the bathroom and the police had to discharge pepper spray under the door to coax his surrender. Following the incident, the police re-opened a similar sexual assault allegation from eight months earlier that took place next door to the Mirage hotel. Ike, who was alleged to exhibit symptoms of a bipolar disorder, was deemed incompetent to stand trial and was sent to a state facility for the mentally ill where a judge granted permission to force-medicate him. Eight months later and some two-and-half years after his arrest, he was ruled cogent enough to plea.

He entered an Alford plea (also known as Kennedy plea in the state of Virginia), where a defendant concedes that the prosecution had enough evidence to convict him while not admitting guilt. Had he gone to trial and been found guilty of rape, he could have received 10 years to life in prison, but instead he got two to 10 years for battery with intent to commit a crime and three to 20 years for attempted sexual assault, to be served concurrently.

Ibeabuchi was paroled on the first charge in 2001 and has been denied parole on the second charge four times. He was denied parole in August 2004, in August 2007, in February 2009 and on May 1, 2012. He is believed to have gone for another parole hearing in May 2013 but the details are not yet made public. At the end of his time in Jail, Ike who has obtained two college degrees while behind bars also faces a likely deportation to Nigeria.

No one can excuse the crimes Ike was accused of committing. But there are also issues of whether his punishment is proportionate to his alleged crimes. He has been behind bars for 14 years for 'attempted sexual assault' while Mike Tyson who was actually convicted of rape served only three and half years in jail.

Opinions also differ on whether he was really nuts or just had a hard time adjusting to life in the USA and to instant fame and wealth. For instance Chris Byrd, whom he knocked out in fifth round, believed he was nuts and his evidence was: "Before our fight he spent time just walking around the parking lot of the hotel. Sort of acting like he was in a military march. I thought it was some type of game then I realized, this guy is just nuts." Ike's former trainer Curtis Cokes however disagreed: "It wasn't that he was nuts, he just had a hard time adjusting to life in the US compared to Nigeria. Things he would do there were ok, and here they weren't. He just didn't get that."

I have a strong feeling that both Ike and his mother who resigned from her nursing job to work fulltime with his son, made mistakes in managing their instant fame and affluence, which probably got them on the wrong side of boxing politics. What is important here however is whether depriving Ike of his freedom and the opportunity to earn a living from his craft for over ten years is not enough punishment for his crime of 'attempted sexual assault' and other shortcomings?

Sadly missing in the Ike Ibeabuchi saga is the voice and legs of the Nigerian government. Despite his shortcomings, Ike fought as a Nigerian and brought glory to the country with his victories in the ring. But where is the Nigerian government in Ike's greatest hour of need? What would fire the Nigerian patriotism in him if he is eventually released?

In a country that truly value its citizens, the government would have been very actively involved in the diplomacy of ensuring that while Ike paid for his alleged crimes, it would be in such a manner that would correct rather than destroy and in such a way that his punishment would not be disproportionate to his alleged crimes.

Daily Trust, August 15 2013

CHAPTER 87

Jack Straw, Governor Amaechi and the Nigerian condition

Former British Foreign Secretary Jack Straw and former Prime Minister of Ireland, John Burton were among the high-profile speakers at a one-day international conference on democracy and good governance organised by the Rivers State Government at the Banquet Hall of Government House, Port Harcourt on March 11 2014.

Apart from the oddity of a state government appropriating a talk-shop of this nature from those best suited for such – relevant departments of our Universities, research institutes, NGOs and other think-tanks - my interest in the live-televised conference was aroused by the presence of John Whitaker "Jack" Straw, who has been a Member of the British House of Commons for Blackburns since 1979. Straw served in the British Cabinet from 1997 to 2010 under the governments of Tony Blair and Gordon Brown. During this period, he held two of Britain's traditional Great Offices of State' (juiciest political offices in Nigeria-speak) - as Home Secretary from 1997 to 2001 and Foreign Secretary from 2001 to 2006 under Tony Blair.

My strongest memory of him however was in late September 2004 when he was embroiled in a controversy that nearly cost him his ministerial position for 'shaking Mugabe's hand'. No, Mugabe's hand was not leprous. Mugabe was and remains a man British politicians love to hate.

The then Conservative spokesman Michael Ancram, called the handshake a "scandalous betrayal of the men and women of Zimbabwe who are suffering at the hands of Mugabe's blood-stained regime".

BBC Newsnight, which had been following Mr Straw around the United Nations, filmed the controversial handshake during a reception for the then South African president, Thabo Mbeki, at the UN building in New York. In his defence, Straw who had just started wearing contact lenses, said:

> "I hadn't expected to see President Mugabe there. Because it was quite dark in that corner ... I was being pushed towards shaking hands with somebody just as a matter of courtesy, and then it transpired it was President Mugabe. But the fact that there is a serious disagreement between Zimbabwe and the United Kingdom does not mean that you should then be discourteous or rude" (The Guardian [London], 28 September 2004).

Later Straw's aides, in what was meant to be damage control, claimed that the hall was dark (and Mugabe being dark too) did not help matters in Straw not knowing the hands he was shaking.

The UK government remains Mugabe's severest critic, a mode of criticism, which in my opinion, has made the man resolve to die as his country's President knowing that if he ever relinquishes power Britain and his international critics will ensure he ends up at the Hague as a guest of the International Criminal Court (ICC). Britain has for instance denounced all the elections in which Mugabe, 90, was returned to power and has sponsored various opposition groups and parties against him. Mugabe on his own regularly criticises the UK. In 2003, Mugabe withdrew Zimbabwe from the British Commonwealth. Members of his government, and senior members of Zanu PF, are in turn banned from entering the EU.

I was honestly pissed off by the furore caused by the Mugabe handshake. Here was a group of politicians who lauded Desmond Tutu and others for their Truth and Reconciliation Commission, which forgave White South Africans for the sins of apartheid and even criminalized the anti-apartheid struggle. I saw the whole handshake affair as British double standard. But this is only a digression.

My main concern with the live-televised one-day conference was what the whole conference was intended to achieve. Rivers State government organising what was essentially an academic conference - not even a policy-oriented workshop – to understand the relationship between democracy and good governance is akin to Anambra state or any of the States of the country not directly affected by what is happening in the North-eastern part of the country organizing expensive talk-shops to understand the challenges of terrorism in Nigeria.

Several questions agitated my mind after listening to the televised conference on TV: Why does the Rivers State government deem it necessary to organize an international 'academic' conference on 'democracy and good governance in Nigeria' rather than a policy-oriented roundtable or workshops on issues of local concerns? Knowing that former high profile politicians like Straw and Burton command extremely high speaking fees from mostly governments of 'Third World' countries, what was the cost of such talk-shop to the Rivers State government? If Rivers State government was genuinely interested in understanding the relationship between democracy and good governance, would it not have been more cost effective and better rewarding if it had commissioned consultants, a research institute or even a relevant department of any of our Universities to carry out a research on the topic? Did Jack Straw or John Burton bring any special perspective on the topic to warrant the astronomical fees they were most likely paid? Or are their invitations a hangover of the colonial mentality in which we needed colonial endorsements of the political options we embrace as a proof of our wisdom? Is the sharing of the same platform with them a proof of our putative global statesmanship? Simply put is Governor Amaechi losing it?

In his lecture titled: 'Democracy, Nationhood and Citizenship Rights, Freedom and Responsibilities in a Global Order,' Straw argued that a strong opposition party would boost Nigeria's democracy and welcomed the formation of the All Progressives Congress (APC). Understandably APC apparatchiks had gone to market with this, wrongly giving the impression that Straw endorsed APC as a party rather than what it represents as a strong opposition party.

But even this apparent 'obvious truth' by Straw that a strong opposition party boosts democracy is simplistic in fragile societies with deep fault lines as ours. In other words, while the mantra of strong opposition parties boosting democracy may be true in countries where the bases of nationhood are accepted by all the citizens, it is not the whole truth in multi-ethnic and multi-faith countries like ours where even the basis of statehood remains contested. The fear in democratizing fragile states is that democracy and strong parties (especially those that converge with the fault lines) will aggravate the structures of conflicts in such countries and widen the social distance among the citizens. In essence, if a strong opposition party complicates the nation-building process, it cannot *ab initio* be said to help in deepening democracy.

I am not in any way against the emergence of a strong opposition party. My position rather is that in our euphoria or desire to get rid of PDP or President Jonathan (or both) through a 'strong opposition party', we tend to gloss over what I believe should be a precedent question: how do we ensure that the sharp contestation of ideas in our democracy with a strong opposition party is not hijacked by a cabal or fissiparous forces to unravel the state if such forces do not get their way?

It is instructive that at the conference Governor Amaechi expressed disappointment that the people of the South-south had stopped their campaign for resource control, stating that the region might not have the opportunity to press for their rights again. His words: "In 2005/2006, the mantra was resource control. Where are we now? Are we controlling our resources, is oil in our hands? If tomorrow President Goodluck Jonathan leaves office, who will we say is controlling the resources? Why are we not talking now or is it because it is our turn to chop?" With the one-day jamboree in Port Harcourt funded by the Rivers state government, it is also important not just to talk about 'resource control' but judicious management of available resources.

Daily Trust, March 13, 2014

CHAPTER 88

Between President Jonathan and Governor Amaechi

First, it was a fight –to- finish between him and then Governor Silvia Timipre for the soul of Bayelsa State. A re-invented President Jonathan - not the one with the public persona of the guy-next-door but his resolute double - reportedly ignored all pleas for Governor Timipre's 'sins' to be forgiven from eminent Nigerians until he has fought and annihilated the former Governor of Bayelsa State Governor to surrender. Governor Timipre was not only denied nomination as the flag bearer of the PDP in Bayelsa State but was also handed over to the EFCC for prosecution for alleged corrupt practices while he was in office.

Now it is the turn of Governor Rotimi Amaechi to feel the punches of an apparently enraged but always calm Jonathan. The feud between the duo has been playing out on several fronts. On April 30 2013 for instance, the Vanguard reported that 27 lawmakers loyal to the Governor out of 32 in the Rivers' State House of Assembly were suspended by the new leadership of the Peoples Democratic Party, PPD in the state and their seats declared vacant. According to the new chairman of the PDP in the State, Felix Obuah, the suspension of the lawmakers followed an earlier ultimatum given to them to rescind the suspension they slammed on the elected Chairman, Vice Chairman and 17 councillors of the Obio Akpor Local Government Area of the State. While it is not clear whether a state legislature has the constitutional right to suspend the chairman of a local government, it is, in my opinion, an act of rascality and political illiteracy for the state chairman of a party to declare the seats of legislators vacant. Where does the Chairman of a party derive the constitutional power to act in such a reckless manner?

The presidency is also reportedly behind the formation of PDP Governors' Forum in an attempt not only to clip the wings of the governors but even more importantly to cut Governor Amaechi, who is also Chairman of the Nigerian Governors' Forum (NGF), to size. The Governor allegedly entertains an ambition of being a running mate to a Northern Presidential candidate. Recently, the Rivers' State-owned bombardier aircraft was temporarily blocked from taking off from Akure airport allegedly because the pilot failed to declare the flight manifest but more likely as part of the war of attrition between the two political leaders. The same plane was reportedly later banned from flying on Nigeria's airspace by the National Civil Aviation Authority, NCAA allegedly on grounds that the plane's clearance certificate has since expired.

Though it is easier to cast Governor Rotimi as a victim - given the unequal power relations between a Governor and a President - it is, in my opinion, necessary that any sympathy for Governor Amaechi should be qualified. If, as Jonathan's loyalists claimed, Governor Amaechi is preparing to run on a joint ticket with Governor Sule Lamido or any other Northern Governor, he should not expect the Jonathan camp to clap for him and sing his alleluia. True, any such ambition is legitimate, but a declaration of such intention whether verbally or by body language is putting the President on notice that his job is on the line. The contest for political power is rarely for the fickle-minded anywhere in the world, which is why Otto Von Bismarck, the conservative German statesman who dominated European affairs from the 1860s until his dismissal in 1890 by Emperor Wilhelm II, (the last German Emperor or *Kaiser* and King of Prussia) described politics as the "art of the possible". Simply put, if you cannot take the heat, do not bother to enter the kitchen. In the contest for power, each opponent fights ferociously using whatever resources it has at its disposal. In the duel between President Jonathan and Governor Amaechi, the state mobilizes the instruments of state power to intimidate while Governor Amaechi plays victim to garner public sympathy and paint his opponent as a political bull in a China shop. Governor Amaechi ought to realize that in his duel with the President even laws that are rarely applied to others will be applied to him if he infringes them and his immunity does not cover him from being sanctioned.

By the way I disagree with those who believe the quarrel between the President and the Governor is 'heating up the polity'. I think it is providing a needed excitement from a rather dull political environment and enriching our marketplace of political ideas at the same time. I don't think the contest between the two gladiators has degenerated to impunity – except the incident of a probably uninformed PDP chairman with an exaggerated sense of his self importance illegally declaring the seats of lawmakers vacant.

But let us for a moment assume that Rotimi Amaechi actually nurses the perfectly legitimate ambition of being a running mate to a Northern presidential candidate. If such an ambition is actualized, how is it likely to affect the outcome of the 2015 presidential election? Will it lead to the Northern minorities, the South-east and the South-south – which appear to be President Jonathan's current bastions of support - switching their support to Governor Amaechi?

In theory Amaechi's vice presidential candidacy will divide the 'Southern' vote, (assuming Jonathan is flying the PDP flag) with the populous and resource-endowed Rivers following him. Again in theory Amaechi will also defeat Jonathan in any contest for Igbo support because despite the 'Ebele Azikiwe' in President Jonathan's names, Rotimi Amaechi easily has more claims to Igboness than President Jonathan. My personal opinion however is that on the ground, things may not be as straightforward as it seems on paper. For one, the bottom part of a presidential ticket anywhere in the world rarely brings electoral votes – though it could hurt a ticket tremendously if it was not wisely chosen - as the choice of Sarah Palin did to the John McCain's ticket in 2008 and the choice of Philip Umeadi as Awolowo's running mate probably did to the UPN in 1979. Similarly though Amaechi has more claims to being Igbo, the Governors of the South-east often embrace the thesis of 'the goat following the man with the palm frond'. This essentially means a tendency to support the man in power at the centre – a reason, in my opinion, why they supported President Jonathan in the April 2011 election just as they supported Umaru Yaradua even at the time the cabal around the sick president held the country hostage. This means in essence that many of the South-east Governors, despite the perennial agitation for Igbo presidency, are likely to eventually queue behind President Jonathan. There will not be shortage of rationalizations on why they chose to do so.

Again with the re-invention of President Jonathan now transmuting into what one Daily Trust columnist called the 'Obasanjonization' of President Jonathan and its associated garrison command politics, it will not surprise anyone if some of the current fierce opponents of the President, when it matters most, begin to sing a different song as security reports of their misdeeds or contrived misdeeds are shown to them and the EFCC called upon to do its job, or as some are 'settled'.

The 'Obasanjonization of Jonathan however means that the President has lost his assumed innocence, which was part of his political capital before and during the April 2011 elections. This will make it much easier for his opponents to turn him into a hate or sneaky figure for counter mobilisation if he decides to contest in 2015. Prior to the April 2011 presidential election, Jonathan's public persona was that of a very humble and unassuming gentleman, who saw the office of president as a burden bestowed on him by destiny and which he was struggling with difficulty to carry, relying on his name of 'Goodluck' to help him carry it. I believe this persona of an uncomplicated guy- next- door who was in dire need of protection from the more sophisticated Goliaths in the political arena, was a key reason why many people during the PDP's presidential primaries and the April 2011 elections axiomatically declared him a good man, a sort of a biblical David chosen by God to take the country forward at this moment in our political history. It would also seem that for most of the Governors, GEJ's special appeal during this period was the same public image of a diffident and malleable man who could be easily swayed. That type of person, they must have reasoned, was someone they could do business with because they could always convince him with a 'superior argument' rather than Atiku, who could be too 'politically smart' to be swayed or Buhari who could remove the immunity clause in the constitution and herd as many of them as possible into jail for any infraction.

The above is by no means an indication that the President is assured of a re-election, especially given the general belief that he has performed below expectation. Also as the protest over the surprise increase in fuel price in January last year shows, Nigerians can temporarily close ranks to do what they perceive as the right thing.

Daily Trust, May 2, 2013

CHAPTER 89

When President Jonathan met ASUU Leaders

The report that President Jonathan met with leaders of ASUU on 5 November 2013 has raised new hopes that the four-month old strike would soon end, paving the way for lecturers to return to their classrooms. According to news reports, the 13-hour marathon meeting was attended by a high-powered delegation that on the government's side included the President Goodluck Jonathan, his Vice, Namadi Sambo; the Secretary to the Government of the Federation (SGF), Anyim Pius Anyim; Chief of Staff to the President, Chief Mike Oghiadhome, Minister of Finance, Ngozi Okonjo-Iweala and her counterpart in the Labour and Productivity Ministry, Chief Emeka Wogu. On the ASUU side were its President Dr Nasir Fage, Deputy President, Prof. Biodun Ogunyemi, three past presidents of the union - Professors Festus Iyayi, Dipo Fashina and Abdullahi Sule-Kano, among others.   Organized labour was represented by the Trade Union Congress (TUC) President, Bobbo Kaigama and other key officers from both the NLC and TUC.

Before the meeting President Jonathan was reported to have lightened the mood by telling the ASUU President: "My President, all the problems will be over today. Our children must go back to school." (The Sun, 6 November 2013). He also reportedly told the NLC President, Abdulwaheed Omar: "My President, with you here, we are covered. It is signed, sealed, and delivered" (Ibid). President Jonathan was said to have made a new offer to ASUU, which the negotiators said they would take back to their members.

Given the calibre of people that attended the meeting, and the President demonstrating (or appearing to demonstrate) the importance of ending the strike immediately by personally leading the negotiations, people will be surprised if the strike is not called off soon. The presidency will be counting on public opinion turning sharply against the striking lecturers, if after personal assurances from the highest political office holder in the land, the striking lecturers remain recalcitrant. Such a stubbornness, which we pray will not happen, might legitimate the wielding of a bigger stick against the striking lecturers most of whom have not been paid their salaries for months.

The flip side to this however is that if the lecturers choose to return to the classroom as many of us hope they will, then the integrity of the President as a person will be on the line. The government is notorious for not keeping agreements – not just to ASUU but to companies and the citizens. While promises made by others on behalf of the government could be reneged on account that the negotiators 'did not know their left from their right' (as Senate President David would put it – a position I disagree with), the one led directly by the President puts both the government and the President as a person on the spotlight. This could turn out to be a strong reason for the ASUU members to call off the strike – even if they did not believe that any promise made would be fulfilled to the letter. My feeling is that ASUU will not want to be seen as disrespecting the office of the President – just as they will be counting on the fact that the President is putting both the integrity of his administration and his on personal integrity on the line in whatever deal he offered them.

If and when the strike is called off, the academic calendar will be rushed – as usually happens in such a situation. For some courses the lecturers will just show up in class once or twice and the students will be told the areas to concentrate on while preparing for the examination. In such a situation, the quality of the education offered -already at its nadir - will take a further nosedive while the attractiveness of private universities where at least uninterrupted academic calendar could be assured, even if the quality of education there does not match the astronomical fees most of them charge. True ASUU has been at the vanguard of the fight against the deplorable state of our universities. However its method of going about this – almost exclusively through strikes- paradoxically exacerbates the crisis in university education. This should be at least one major reason why the body should now look for options with less unintended adverse side effects. It behoves on ASUU, which arguably is made up of the most educated segment of the population, to think out of the box on ways of maintaining its vanguard role in the fight for the improvement of the conditions of university education without being seen as a major part of the problem. Though the government often behaves like a deaf man with selective memory, it may be time to re-think the predictable strategy of strikes, which has since become a tool of blackmail used by both ASUU and the government to paint each other black.

The ASUU strike also brings to fore our fire-brigade approach to problem solving. Why will the government wait for the strike, which started since July 1, to go on for so long before showing a serious resolve to end it? The impression is unfortunately created that unless you use the leverage you have to the maximum in this country, no one will listen to your grievances, hence the wealthy bribe, organized labour go on prolonged strike, students riot, workers drag their feet and engage in moonlighting while terrorist and insurgency groups strive to normalize impunity. If there is any lesson from the current ASUU strike and the President's rather belated intervention, it is that the government unwittingly encourages disorder and impunity by ignoring grievances unless the affected group can demonstrate a certain capacity to hold everyone to ransom. This means in essence that the state treats groups that are law abiding or which believe in channelling grievances through appropriate formal channels with levity or as 'mugus'. Therefore if Nigeria today is one piece of chaos, in which life approximates the Hobbesian state of nature, it is only because the actions and inactions of the government encourage the citizens to be so. One may be tempted to ask: where is the country's Industrial Arbitration Panel? Where are the relevant committees of the National Assembly? I disagree with the Senate President that those who negotiated with ASUU in 2009 did 'not know their left from their right' because even if their recommendations were based on ignorance, the government that accepted such recommendations actually would be guilty of greater ignorance.

There are, in my opinion, other critical problems of university education that are not captured in ASUU's demands. Included in this is the length of time spent in pursuing an academic programme in the country which in some cases is nearly double the time spent to obtain such a programme in other countries? Why for instance will Nigerian undergraduates spend six years to read law, five years to read engineering and four years to read courses in the social sciences while their counterparts in say the UK will do a similar programme in three years? What is the sub-text here? That Nigerian students are not as intellectually endowed as their counterparts elsewhere? Agreed that the standard of education has fallen sharply, my personal opinion is that prolonging the time needed to obtain a degree for Nigerian students has nothing to do with addressing the problem of the falling standard of education. If anything, it compounds it as it embeds a self-fulfilling prophecy that subtly tells Nigerian undergraduates that they are slower learners and not as good as their counterparts in the UK and elsewhere.

As unfortunate as the ASUU strike has been, there are however certain unintended effects of the strike that hold good promise for the country. One of these is the inability of the government to break the strike by appealing to our traditional fault lines or by alleging that it was aimed at bringing down the administration of President Goodluck Jonathan. This will seem to suggest, in my opinion, that beyond the posturing and the shenanigans of the political elites, when the chips are down, the pockets will always trump geography and accidents of birth.

Daily Trust November, 7 2013

CHAPTER 90

Jonathan's reply to Obasanjo: Too Little, Too Late?

President Jonathan's reply to the letter written to him on December 2 2013 by Obasanjo was rather late in coming. Jonathan's letter, dated 20 December 2013 – some 18 days after Obasanjo wrote and leaked his to the press - raised punches but failed, in my opinion, to deliver devastating blows. Given the delay in replying, I had expected that Jonathan's reply would be loaded with finely decorated bombshells and polite but deadly uppercuts. I didn't get that. What I got was what rather appeared to be an apologetic piece - as if pleading with Obasanjo not to strike again. In a quick and terse reply, Obasanjo said he stood by his allegations and that he would not be offering any reply to Jonathan's letter.

While it is accepted that Jonathan should be presidential and restrained in his reply, I believe there is a difference between being apologetic and being humble or restrained. The former is actuated by fear, the latter by good manners. In my opinion, Jonathan's 'restrained' reply appeared to have been written by someone who wanted to avoid a dogfight at all cost. Also none of the counter allegations levelled against Obasanjo was new – just like there was nothing new in Obasanjo's allegations against him – except the issue of training snipers and having 1000 Nigerians on a political watchlist. I had expected new allegations that would have forced Obasanjo to go on the defensive.

Jonathan's reply however raises a very vital question: If a benefactor is magnanimous enough to buy a pair of shoes for someone but does not display the same magnanimity in allowing the benefactor the freedom to walk around in those shoes, how will the beneficiary defend his freedom without appearing to be ungrateful? Put differently, what should be the fine line between being captive to past benevolence and doing the needful to protect oneself from the unwholesome machinations of bad-wishers? Jonathan's reply must be analysed within the context of his efforts to navigate through this tough question.

Apart from the above, there are a number of other issues with Jonathan's reply. On a technical level for instance, I do not feel that it was necessary for the President to adduce as many as ten reasons on why he should reply Obasanjo's letter. For me, justifying the need to reply around those ten reasons made what should be a pungent preamble to be rather too lengthy and therefore a derogation from the main essence of the letter (akin to the subplot competing with the main storyline). These ten reasons would have been more pungent if they were collapsed into three reasons with additional two reasons on why the reply was late in coming.

I also find the format adopted in enumerating those ten reasons rather clumsy. For instance the President wrote that he felt obliged to reply Obasanjo for a number of reasons: "one, you formally requested for a reply and not sending you one will be interpreted as ignoring a former President". Now instead of counting, 'two', the next point was counted as, 'secondly'. After this there is a switch to the short adverb in the system of enumeration – "the third reason why", the "fourth reason for this reply", the "fifth reason is". After giving the fifth reason for replying, there was a switch back to the use of long adverbs - 'Sixthly you are very unique…". There is another reversion to the short adverb: "The seventh reason is.., 'the eighth reason is that…'" "the ninth reason…", the "tenth and final reason".

I also found his system of ordering his points of defence problematic. Given his public persona and perceptions of him as a humble and unassuming man, I feel he should have started with defending himself against the charge of training snipers and having 1000 Nigerians on a watch list. I think it was the most damaging of all the charges in Obasanjo's letter but also the one that will perhaps be most convincingly defended given Jonathan's public persona and the sharp contrast between absence of politically motivated assassinations under him and the impunity that took place under Obasanjo. Again instead of challenging Obasanjo to swear by the bible about his training snipers, (most of our leaders take oath of office holding the bible or Quran and violate the oath without anything happening), wouldn't it have been more effective to challenge Obasanjo to a television debate on the matter? Also for someone who felt unjustly accused, it will not be out of place to show restrained anger in the letter. I didn't' see such anger.

Again what was probably the most convincing defence in the letter –the statistical evidence showing that foreign direct investment inflow into the country in the three years that Jonathan led the country was nearly equal to what Obasanjo achieved in eight years - was tucked somewhere near the end of the lengthy letter. Though one could legitimately question whether the supposed improvement in FDI is due to the policies pursued by the Jonathan administration or because of a new wave of Afro-optimism, I feel the point should have been the second – after rebutting the charge of training snipers.

One of the most disappointing of the defences in Jonathan's reply was his argument that because of the demands of the high office of president, he "cannot possibly find the time to offer a line –by -line response to all the accusations and allegations made in your letter while dealing with other pressing demands of office and more urgent affairs of state". This defence creates the wrong impression that the President personally wrote the letter and by extension also writes his speeches. We know this is not the case. The truth is that people know that high political office holders need and use speech writers. There is no shame in that. There are also usually several research assistants employed by high political office holders. Therefore mentioning that he did not have the time to do a line-by-line rebuttal not only comes across as insincere but also reminds people of those points he failed to address in his reply.

In the same vein, the story that Jonathan has dragged Obasanjo to the Human Rights Commission and has called on the anti-corruption agencies – the EFCC and ICPC to investigate Obasanjo's allegations against him – will not be enough to convince the public of Jonathan's innocence. Does anyone really expect any of these agencies to find a sitting President culpable? After all, Obasanjo as President once asked the EFCC to probe allegations of corruption against him by Orji Kalu, who was then Governor of Abia state. As should be expected he was given clean bill of health. It would have therefore been more impactful if the President had announced the institution of actions for malicious libel against the retired general, especially over the charges about training snipers. At least by that Obasanjo would have been forced to reply, if not to his letter, then in court.

I think Jonathan challenging Obasanjo to name instances of his regime being soft on corruption removes the shine from some of his rebuttals. Everyone knows of people accused of corruption and committees set up by even the presidency to investigate those allegations without anything being heard about the recommendations of those committee – not to talk of implementing such recommendations.

While I believe it is right to make Obasanjo and others like him to realize that they do not own Nigeria, I also believe bringing the issue of his family life into it is in bad taste. The relevant assessment of Obasanjo should be as a political leader, not as a family man. Mandela and several iconic leaders are admired, not for their personal and family lives but for their political contributions. While I am not in a position to defend Obasanjo against some of the shameful allegations by his children – first Gbenga who claimed Obasanjo slept with his wife and then Iyabo- it may be tempting to pose the question of how many families are out there without at least one family 'shame'/'secret'? It is not abnormal for parents to fall out with their children. What I regard as shameful about the Iyabo letter is an educated woman apparently taking delight in the public humiliation of her own father. 'Honour your father and mother' is one of the Ten Commandments of God in Christian religion. And it is the only of the Ten Commandments that comes with a promise: "Honour your father and mother", says the Commandment, "that your days may be long". In this sense, Iyabo's letter tells me more about her and those trying to exploit it than it tells me of Obasanjo.

Daily Trust, December 26, 2013

CHAPTER 91

Will Jonathan Stepping Aside Solve Nigeria's Problems?

A report by Sahara Reporters on May 25 2015 entitled, 'A new government coming next year', quoted the President as saying that a "different government and leadership would be installed in Nigeria in 2015." The President was said to have made the statement on a "Democracy Day" church service held in Abuja. For effect it was also reported that before the president's speech, the head of Nigeria Pilgrims Commission, Reverend John Kennedy Opara, had told the gathering that this year's Democracy Day would be the last to be celebrated by President Jonathan.

If the above report was true, - it has not been denied to the best of my knowledge- it would be the clearest hint by the President that he may not contest next year's presidential election. If the story turns out to be true, it will be interesting to find out if the decision was forced on him or if it was his own.

For those who believe in prophecies by pastors, Malams and jujumen (I don't), there have not been shortage of prophecies on whether Jonathan will contest next year's elections, and whether he will win if he does. There have also not been shortages of threats by those who believe that Jonathan contesting or not contesting (or even contesting and losing) will lead to the disintegration of the country. Given the negative international media that the President received over his handling of the abduction of the Chibok girls, others have argued that the 'international community' is likely to prevail on the President not to contest in 2015 in order to prevent the country from falling over the precipice. Ranking US senator John McCain for instance derisively said there was no government in Nigeria in the heat of the furore over the kidnap of the Chibok girls. I declined to be part of a televised hearing by the Foreign Relations Committee of the US Senate on the Chibok Affair but it was clear from my telephone discussions with those who contacted me following a three part article on Brookings Institution's website on Boko Haram during the kidnap saga, that the government's handling (or lack of it) of the affair was a big issue for them.

The above raises a very fundamental question: If President Jonathan does not run in 2015, or is prevented from running, will that resolve the current crisis facing the country, especially the security challenge and the apparently heightened distrust among Nigerians?

There are a number of important observations in this regard:

One, while I believe that Jonathan could do better in several respects, especially mustering the political will to use the power he has decisively in the interest of the generality of Nigerians, it will be simplistic to equate him with the problems of the country. Boko Haram got radicalized in 2009 – before he became President, armed robbery and kidnapping also predated him. The country's fault lines especially that between the north and south, deepened markedly under Obasanjo's civilian presidency, especially during his ill-fated third term project. At a point Obasanjo was a figure many northerners loved to hate – though this seemed to have changed after his opportunistic open letter to the President. The current security challenges and crisis in our nation-building were therefore already evolving before President Jonathan stepped in as President. A valid criticism is that a leader with the right roadmap ought to have found ways to reverse some of the ugly trends rather than allowing them to grow worse under this watch.

Two, the focus on Jonathan to step aside misses the point that his candidacy has now grown larger than him – and this is irrespective of whether he is perceived as incompetent or not. In our peculiar form of identity politics and politics of 'our turn', some people privilege one of their own over someone from the out-group, even if the latter is far more competent than their own 'son'. Essentially, for many people from the South-south, the way Nigerians treat their son will determine whether the oil resources in their backyard will continue to be a common patrimony or not. This is another way of saying that Jonathan being forced to step aside might re-ignite militancy in the restive Niger Delta.

Three, if Jonathan is forced to step aside, or decides not to contest, it will throw up issues of two competing entitlements arising from the PDP's zoning and power rotation principles. Some people believe passionately that power should 'return to the north' as a condition for peace (I really do not like this phrase as it wrongly suggests that the north is power's natural habitat or that it is their entitlement), but the south south can also argue they have a right to complete Jonathan's second term in office and that if Jonathan is not willing to go for a second term, another person from the south- south should step in.

The danger in another person from the south south stepping in however is that there is no guarantee that such a candidate, at the end of that one term, will not demand for his constitutional right for a second term in office? Again if power 'returns to the north', how many years will the president of the northern extraction serve? Will that be the one year left in Yaradua's first term in office plus another one term of four years? Will such a candidate not be entitled to two terms in office? Will such a candidate demand to complete Yaradua's term before serving his own term in office?

Four, while I was among those who opposed president Jonathan's candidacy in 2011 on the grounds that he should respect an agreement he entered on his party's zoning and power rotation, I also believe that the way we handle him will in the final analysis determine the fate of the country. It will be a terrible mistake in my opinion to hound him out of office. Hounding him out of office will not only mobilize compassion for him and trigger fresh militancy in the restive Niger Delta; it will also encourage the militarization of other insurgency groups in the country. Essentially insurgency groups in different parts of the country may try to mimic Boko Haram in a bid to get political concessions for their parts of the country. My personal opinion is that getting Jonathan not to contest in 2015 will contribute in reducing tension in the land only if it is done as a political negotiation in which key stakeholders from the South-south and Christian constituencies are involved.

Five, I strongly feel that Jonathan may agree to step aside only if such a decision will enhance his political stature, not if he is hounded, or humiliated out of office. It is remarkable that in Nigeria, no Governor or President has ever declined a chance to run for a second term in office – all the Governors who claimed they would do only one term – from Fashola in Lagos to Peter Obi in Anambra state – ended up doing a second term. In fact Obasanjo became a global statesman simply because as a military Head of State, he handed power to civilians in 1979. Jonathan can attain such a global stature by being the first President in the country to give up his right to a second term in office and letting other politicians know that there could be life beyond power. For him to be able to set such precedence however requires a closer look at the politics of the opposition. I believe that in many parts of Africa, Nigeria inclusive, the cantankerous and vengeful nature of the politics of the opposition often make it difficult for power incumbents to give up power willingly. Opposition's grandstanding (the ruling parties are equally guilty but opposition parties tend to be guiltier of this) and threats often aggravate the structures of conflicts in our type of society and widen the social distance between Nigerians and the constituent parts of the country. Fears that without power leaders will be hounded are often at the heart of sit-tightism.

Six, Nigeria faces what the British novelist Frederick Forsythe would call the Devil's alternative. There will be no easy way out. Some believe that Nigeria has made hanging on the precipice its comfort zone and that at the end of the day 2015 will come and go and the country will remain on the same precipice. Others hang their hope on the fact that Nigeria is too big to fail and that the international community is unlikely to stand akimbo and wait for the worst to happen (the refugee problem alone from any unraveling of the country will destabilize the entire West African sub-region). Some are looking in the direction of the National Conference for some form of magic elixir that will save the country from the abyss. And yet many have adopted 'siddon look' or indulging in our favourite pastime – calling on God to intervene.

Daily Trust, May 29, 2014

CHAPTER 92

Between Keshi, NFF and Bleaching Complex

The no love-lost between Stephen Keshi, chief coach of the national team, the Super Eagles, and his employers, the Nigerian Football Federation, NFF, is playing out again. According to several media reports, the NFF wants an assistant technical coach to help pluck the technical lapses it claimed it identified in Keshi's teams. An official of NFF was quoted by the Vanguard of February 10 2014 as saying: "We want to do well in the World Cup and we strongly feel that he needs a technical assistant, it is about Nigeria and not individual aspirations.

"We want to break the African record of a quarterfinal berth in the World Cup and from all indications we know that Keshi needs a help. He will still lead the technical crew to Brazil and will remain the head coach. But we just want to attach somebody to him for the sake of improving Nigeria's lot in the World Cup."

Some of the alleged technical lapses identified by NFF include that though the Ghanaian team was reduced to ten men in the CHAN semi-final match, the Super Eagles could not find an answer to their power game and eventually lost to them. It was also alleged that during the CHAN match with Zimbabwe for the third place, the Super Eagles could again not find a way to convincingly overwhelm the team despite the fact that one of their players got a red card in the 17th minute of the game. NFF was apparently disappointed that the Super Eagles were able to score only three minutes to the full time. It was equally alleged that during the match with Mexico in Houston last year, Eagles failed to find a way to beat a ten-man team. It was further alleged that NFF's misgivings were not so much about the Super Eagles' inability to defeat their opponents but their inability to adapt to technical changes – as happened I their matches against Ghana and Zimbabwe during the CHAN tournament.

Apart from the above alleged technical lapses, there were also accusations, by innuendo, of bias in the selection of the team against Keshi. A source from NFF was quoted by the same Vanguard of February 10 2014 as saying that "a new hand could ask questions about certain things that may eventually help the team. Chigozia Agbim, for example, kept only two matches for his club throughout the season and has recently been dropped by his club, Enugu Rangers, who registered four goal keepers and found him not good enough to be among their keepers." The source continued: "That's the keeper Keshi used in the CHAN competition and he embarrassed the country. That cannot happen in football nations. We don't fold our arms while somebody leads us astray. If you closely watch our league you will find out that those who played CHAN in South Africa were not our best, some may not even make the second team of the bests in our league. We want to be sure that we make a true representation of the current best of Nigerian football in Brazil and a new hand may not give in to the kind of sentiments that we have noticed in the team now."

I am among those who kept wondering what Keshi saw in goalkeeper Chigozia Agbim who, by the way, looked more like a club bouncer than an athlete. I also believe it was right for NFF officials to ask questions, if, as Keshi's employers, they feel something is not just right. However given the long running battle between Keshi and NFF over who will call the shots in the selection of the team, I am inclined to believe the NFF is cleverly disguising its nostalgia for its traditional meddlesomeness in the job of a coach and Keshi's refusal to allow them to select his team for him. While NFF may have some points in some of its criticisms of some of the players featured in the CHAN game, one will also be bold to ask, "under whose watch has Nigeria made its best CHAN appearance so far"? - for a balanced perspective. The answer here is that so far Nigeria's best outing in CHAN has been under Keshi.

The no love -lost between Keshi and NFF apparently predated the nations Cup in South Africa last year where it was widely rumoured that the NFF had perfected plans to sack him after the tournament only for Keshi to shut them up by bringing home the Cup. Not long ago we also learnt that Keshi was owed several months' salary.

To be sure, Keshi's teams have not been without technical lapses – and no team is perfect. In boxing they say that styles make a fight. An invincible fighter will always have a journeyman whose awkward style gives him a bloody nose. Remember Mohammed Ali and Ken Norton? Remember Mike Tyson and James Buster Douglas? As it is in boxing so it is in football and other competitive sports. A team may appear invincible today only to be walloped mercilessly by a less fancied side. Your strengths and weaknesses as a side are often a function of the strengths and weaknesses of the team you are playing against.

Despite the drop in FIFA rankings, Eagles had never had it so good as it has under Keshi's guidance. Keshi has been one of the indigenous coaches who have been able to rein in the oversized egos of some of our big name professional players. Often forgotten when people discuss Keshi's achievements is the fact that he injected uncommon discipline to the team. He is not intimidated by the theatrics of the big name players, having been up there himself – in fact one of the pacesetters among Nigerian professional players. Unlike Samson Sia Sia, Keshi has the charisma and can be tough without appearing to be cantankerous.

It is obvious NFF would have preferred a foreign coach for the super Eagles – and let's be blunt about this, a White European coach.

I do not have anything against any ethnic or racial group in the world. If anything, my experiences in and outside the country convinces me of the universality of human beings, that you meet angels in all races and ethnicities just as every race or ethnic group also has its fair share of people who operate from the wrong side of the moral divide. However it seems to me a contradiction in terms that at a time the country is obsessed with launching its own version of industrial revolution and of protecting our infant industries, the NFF is obsessed with yanking open to foreigners - let's be blunt about it - to white Europeans, our putative infant coaching industry, of which Keshi has become the face of.

NFF's position is not just a continuation of its war without blood with Keshi but also a manifestation of the serious bleaching complex many of its top hierarchy suffer from. For these 'ogas at the top', they need the imprimatur of a White Coach to be assured they are preparing well for the World Cup in Brazil. NFF seriously needs to de-colonize its mind. Skin bleaching, fake 'accenting', and 'colonial mentality' are serious disorders, which are rooted in low self-esteem and manifest self-hate. The root of 'bleaching complex' is diffidence and self-doubt. And the remedy is a re-education to accept who you are, to de-colonize your mind and see reality from a balanced perspective.

NFF's position on foreign (read: White) coach reminds me of this saying attributed to an ethnic group in East Africa: 'Up above is God the omniscient, down below gathering strength from the dust, is the Blackman. Between the Black man and God is the Whiteman. The problem of the Blackman is to find a way to get past the Whiteman and talk directly to God.' NFF apparently still believes that a White European coach is needed to mediate between the Super Eagles and the god of soccer.

NFF says it wants to "break the African record of a quarterfinal berth in the World Cup". This sounds good. But how many of the foreign coaches African countries routinely engage in the run-up to World Cup every four years were able to deliver? Keshi qualified Togo for the World Cup for the first time. However the same 'bleaching complex' being currently manifested by NFF goaded Togo to jettison him in favour of a White coach. And how far did that get them? This is the 21st century. Nigeria has joined the league of vehicle manufacturers and is developing high ambitions in other fields. If the Eaglets could conquer the world with our local coaches, why not the Super Eagles?

If NFF has noticed some technical lapses in the Super Eagles, wouldn't it have been better to send Keshi to some refresher courses to bridge such skills gaps? I also believe the idea of an Assistant Coach makes sense but only if it is made in good faith and not as a guile to implement some hidden agenda. Even at that, Keshi should be allowed to select such an Assistant who will not only complement him but will also be able to work well with him as a team.

Daily Trust, February 13, 2014

CHAPTER 93

The Social Costs of Being Mandela

The recent transition of Madiba Nelson Mandela, 95, brings to sharp focus the whole idea that at one point or the other, we all have to face our mortality. Simply put, we will one day be called home by our maker - at a time and place we will neither have a pre-knowledge of nor be in a position to influence or control. There are individuals that people sometimes wish could be exempted from this inevitability. Mandela was one such person. However when he was hospitalized on June 8 2013 – his fourth in seven months - many people across the world gradually came to terms with his mortality. Given his age and how frail he had become, there was a general feeling that the end was nigh. Mandela was to defy all odds and live another six months before he was called home by his maker on Thursday, December 5. And when he was eventually called home – people were shocked, as if surprised that death did not show him any respect.

Mandela's memorial event on November 11 2013 - part of extended observances that will culminate in his burial on Sunday, November 15, 2015 in the rural village of Qunu where he spent his early childhood – brought together 91 serving Presidents, hundreds of former Presidents and A-list dignitaries across the world. The interesting thing is that sworn enemies found a common ground in Mandela. Raul Castro, President of Cuba and Obama, the US president even shook hands. It had been an article of faith that every President of USA inherited enmity with Cuba since Fidel Castro's revolution in that country in 1959.

In life, Mandela was celebrated and deeply revered as one of the greatest living moral voices. He was perhaps the only living soul that has a date set aside every year to celebrate him. July 18, Mandela's birthday, is globally celebrated as the Mandela Day. During last year's Mandela Day, the United Nations launched a campaign asking people to mark the day by devoting 67 minutes of their time to helping others - one minute for each year Mandela spent fighting for his cause. The Mandela Day is aimed at encouraging people to set aside some minutes to consciously do something that will help change the world or their environment for the better.

In death, Mandela was deified, with his position firmly assured in the pantheon of eminent human-deities the world has known of in the last 100 years and probably in the next 100 to come. If the voice of the people is indeed the voice of God, then given the global celebration of his life, Mandela is heading straight to heaven.

Mandela served 27 years in prison, many of those in the notorious Robben Island where he performed hard labour in a lime quarry. As a D-group prisoner (the lowest classification), he was allowed one visitor and one letter every six months. His letters were often delayed for long periods and made unreadable by the prison censors. Amid the hard labour Mandela was offered release several times on the condition that the ANC would renounce violence as an instrument of struggle. On each occasion he turned down the Greek gift. Following his eventual release from prison on 11 February 1990, Mandela led his party in the negotiations that led to the establishment of democracy in South Africa in1994, with himself as the first President.

Though *Madiba* was the President of South Africa from 1994 to 1999, his greatest legacy to the country is in creating a Rainbow nation and being a unifying symbol for the various cleavages in the deeply polarized country. I believe that another gift from Mandela is that his name has become a metaphor for knowing when and how to bow out gracefully when the ovation is loudest.

Mandela paid a heavy personal price for being Mandela. As he reportedly told a delegation that visited him in Johannesburg in 1994, his biggest regret was the way he found his family when he was released from prison in 1990. Before he became very famous, his first marriage - to Evelyn Ntoko Mase - unravelled in 1957 after 13 years largely because of the multiple strains of his constant absences, his devotion to revolutionary agitation against the apartheid policies in his country and because she was a Jehovah Witness - a religion that requires one to be politically neutral. Of the four children from that marriage – two boys and two girls – only one Dr Maki (born in 1953 and named after her older sister who died when she was only nine months) still survives. Mandela's first son - Madiba Thembekile (Thembi), who was born in 1946, was killed in a car crash in 1969 at the age of 23 while Mandela was in prison on Robben Island and he was not allowed to attend the funeral. His other son Makgatho died of AIDS in 2005, aged 54.

Mandela's second marriage – to Winnie Madikizela-Mandela - produced two daughters - Zenani (Zeni), born 4 February 1958, and Zindziswa (Zindzi) Mandela-Hlongwane, born 1960. Zindzi was only 18 months old when her father was sent to Robben Island. In 2010 Mandela's great granddaughter Zenani Mandela died in a car crash on her way home after attending the World Cup soccer tournament kick-off in Soweto. She was aged only 13. Recently Zenani's mother, Zoleka Mandela (33), Mandela's granddaughter, launched a book - *When Hope whispers* - about her battle with drugs, sex addiction and breast cancer. Zhindzi, Mandela 's 52 year old daughter and mother of four, in March this year, got married to Molapo Motlhajwa, 37.

In 1996, Mandela divorced Winnie after being separated since 1992. Winnie, alone for 27 years and often hounded into prisons and detentions by the apartheid regime, found solace in the arms of younger men and could not stop even after Mandela had been released. The open adultery and humiliation forced Mandela to divorce her in 1996.

Perhaps all these challenges in his private life were worth the gifts he bequeathed to the world. And I am not just talking about the gift of forgiveness – the ability or nobility of forgiving those who stole 27 years of his life. Many of us lesser mortals find it difficult to forgive minor slights until we have had a pay back time!

There are other less-sung gifts from Mandela: that the world has not passed you by if you have not 'made it' by the time you are 50. When Mandela was jailed in 1962, he was well in his forties – and he wasn't exactly a household name at that time. And when he became the President of South Africa in 1994, he was already 76. Your destiny can manifest anytime.

There is yet another lesson: When Mandela fell ill, he was treated in South African hospitals – even though the best hospitals in the world would have been happy to offer him free medical facility. Even if it could be argued that he did so because the Whites built world class hospitals in South Africa, he demonstrated the consciousness of embracing whatever his country could offer when he entrusted the task of chronicling his life's story to the South African producer of Indian descent, Anant Singh, said to be a personal friend of the late leader. There had been a stiff competition for a film on Mandela from Europe and US. Paradoxically Mandela's daughters Zindzi and Zenani learnt about the passing of their dad during the London premiere of the film - *Mandela: Long Walk to Freedom*. They excused themselves but asked that the film should go on – even though the producers had suggested that the film be stopped in honour of Mandela's transition.

Mandela did not become a globally adored figure by being a pleaser to all. He made tough choices and invariably disappointed many: the Black hardliners who longed for a payback time were disappointed in Mandela's reconciliatory posture; Mandela's former socialist colleagues were disappointed by his abandonment of the Socialist perspective, a number of the Western countries were disappointed that he refused to inherit their enemies such the Ghaddaffi and Fidel Castro who were treated as pariahs by Western countries. Even some church militants felt enraged by Mandela's pro-abortion stance. Yet even those who were disappointed in him appeared to intuitively appreciate why he had to disappoint them.

I have always maintained that the main trouble with Nigeria is the crisis in the country's nation-building, which conflates with the challenges of underdevelopment to create an existentialist crisis for several Nigerians. The latter in turn triggers a de-Nigerianization process as individuals and groups retreat from the Nigeria project into primordial identities where they seek meaning for their lives, often regarding the Nigerian state as an enemy of sorts. Following from this, my kind of President for the country is not necessarily one that is incorruptible or one with the best programme for economic development for the country but simply a leader, who like Mandela, is capable of unifying a fractious nation. I believe that it is only through this that the stalled nation-building process can be re-started.

Despite the challenges in his private life, Mandela, we were told by Graca Simbine Machel, whom he married on 18 July 1998 at the age of 80, was very much at peace with himself and the world at the twilight of his life. What else can a person ask for? Rest in Peace, Madiba.

Daily Trust, December 12, 2013

CHAPTER 94

Observations on Obama's Presidency and Re-Election

The 6 June 2012 presidential election in the US has just whizzed past. Barrack Obama has won re-election in what turned out to be the most expensive election in the US history. The tally in the number of Electoral College votes garnered by each candidate turned out not to be as close as the polls had suggested. And more importantly, the much feared 'Bradley effect' – the tendency for polls to be misleading when a Black candidate is running against a White candidate - failed to happen.

There are several observations on Obama's presidency and re-election.

One, it is to Obama's credit that he managed to avoid any major scandal during his first term in office, silencing those who feared that a Blackman in the White House would diminish the presidency with one scandal or the other. Many top Black American politicians and celebrities have not always been able to stand the test of public scrutiny that often comes with being in the public eyes. There is a long list of Africa-American politicians whose careers ended abruptly over scandals usually relating to sex, corruption or the use of illegal drugs. For instance, Herman Cain's strong bid to become the Republican Party's presidential nominee in the just concluded elections was torpedoed over scandals bothering on sexual harassment and infidelity. Similarly former New York Governor David Paterson became sucked into a scandal after he admitted shortly after taking office in 2008 that both he and his wife, Michelle, had engaged in extramarital affairs during a bumpy period in their marriage. Again former Detroit Mayor Kwame Kilpatrick's career unravelled in 2008 after he lied about having an affair with a city official named Christine Beatty. Some claim that African-American politicians and celebrities are more scrutinized than their counterparts from other racial categories. Obama deserves credit that he has so far carefully avoided matching on any banana peel.

Two, Obama won largely because the Republican Party was unable to successfully play the race card. Though the Tea Party – a largely White conservative movement which is anti-immigration and anti-compromise politics - tried to do so, Obama carefully avoided several baits such as when a particular radio talk show host called him and his family 'the trash in the White House'. Though some African-Americans felt that by not responding more forcefully to such insults he denied them the respect they felt they deserved by his being President, in retrospect, had Obama swallowed the bait, the issue of race would have become a prominent issue in the campaign which would have put Obama in an awkward disadvantage. Even when the right wing members of the Republican Party read race in the decision of the former Secretary of State Collin Powell to endorse Obama's re-election bid, Obama moved smartly to reject any endorsement based on skin colour. While rejecting race, he was however smart enough to recognize the changing demographics in the USA and the issues that would go down well with such key voting blocs as the Hispanics. This perhaps explains why on June 15, 2012 he granted deferred action - relief from deportation and the issuance of work permits to 1.4 million young undocumented immigrants. Immigration is a very sensitive issue among Latin Americans in the USA.

Three, the expectations in 2008 that the election of a Black man as President of the United States would lead to improvement in race relations in the USA and even globally appeared not to have happened. A recent poll by Rasmussen for instance found that only 36 per cent of voters believed that relations between Black and White people was getting better compared with 62 per cent a year ago and 55 per cent in April. I believe this trend is in line with what happens in Nigeria where the ethnic group that produces the President tends to court suspicion, if not hatred, instead of being better respected as they would hope. A possible explanation for this tendency is the interfacing of envy, jealousy, triumphalism with perceptions of bias by the President towards his ethnic group. Obama, it could be argued, demonstrated in actions and his rhetoric that he is the President for all Americans and that he was not just elected to pander to the special interests of his African-American constituency or the ancestral home of his Kenyan father.

Four, Obama's presidency appears to have triggered a me-tooist search for an 'European Obama'. In Britain for instance, Chuka Umunna, who like Obama is mixed race, is increasingly being touted as 'Britain's Obama', with some predicting that the 33-year old will be a future leader of the Labour party. A number of other European countries also appear to be 'searching' for their own 'Obama' – perhaps to show that their society has become post-racial. My issue with this however is that an impression seems to be given that there is a search for Obama's clone – someone who is male, mixed race, speaks well, is well- educated and good-looking - rather than Obama being used as a metaphor to show that one can overcome adversities that are tied to one's circumstances of birth to reach to the top of the society. This is where I think the 'me-tooist' search for Obama misses the point in some European countries. A crucial question now is how Obama's re-election victory will impact on the perceived hunt for a 'European Obama'.

Five, Obama's ascendancy appears to have led to a re-definition of colour and Blackness. Before he became taken seriously as a presidential candidate, the African-American community were concerned that he was not Black enough - his progenitors after all were not part of the civil rights struggles which meant very much to them. However once it became clear that he was going to be competitive in the primaries, the African-Americans embraced him. Under America's 'one drop rule', Obama is classified as Black. But in several countries such as the UK and South Africa, Obama would have been classified as 'mixed race'. It can be argued that with Obama the mixed race people in several countries are now being re-classified as 'Blacks' and they are not complaining.

Six, how would Obama's second term in office impact on Africa? There is a consensus that apart from being the first sitting American president to visit Africa during his first term in office, there has not really been any special benefit to Africa from having 'one of their own' there – apart from Obama's vacuous talks about promoting democracy and 'partnering' with the continent in its quest for economic development. I do not foresee any major change in Obama's policy towards Africa during his second term. Obviously there are expectation by some Africans that Obama will channel more development projects to the continent based on primordial sentiments - pretty much the way our politicians divert develop projects to their villages. Unfortunately or fortunately, America does not work that way because the institutions are strong and the system of checks and balances work well. It therefore behoves on Africa to articulate clearly areas it needs USA's assistance – or more appropriately partnership- and hope they will get more sympathetic ears from President Obama.

Seven, while our democracy is still evolving and America's has endured for over two centuries, it will still not be out of place to make a few comparisons: for instance it is instructive that Mitt Romney conceded quickly after it became clear he had lost. It is tempting to speculate on how this would have played out were it in Nigeria. Perhaps the newspapers would be screaming with such headlines as: "This is an open day robbery, which must be challenged – Romney". "Obama plans big party to celebrate victory". "Post election blues: violence breaks in xxx state, 15 feared dead".

HOR's Peoples' Public Sessions on the review of the 1999 Constitution

The recent announcement by the Lower House that it would organise a public session on the review of the 1999 constitution simultaneously in all the 360 Federal Constituencies in Nigeria on 10 November 2012 is a welcome development. It is in fact arguably the closest to the idea of a national conference being canvassed by some Nigerians to discuss some of the fundamental issues that have made the challenges of nation-building in the country intractable. The House plans to make the process as participatory as possible and is urging stakeholders to utilise the opportunity to present their ideas on how they want to see the polity restructured. While the thinking behind this is unassailable, there are a few concerns: is this just a subterfuge to douse the clamour from some quarters for a Sovereign National Conference? How will the House ensure that all the memoranda submitted to it – not just those that fit into its agenda – are collected and allowed to impact on any amendment of the Constitution? Since a Constitution review process involves also getting a nod of a majority of the State Houses of Assembly, what are the House's strategies for 'carrying along' the Governors who control the state legislatures?

Daily Trust November 8, 2012

CHAPTER 95

How Obasanjo Achieved his third term Ambition

Those who mock Obasanjo for failing in his bid to elongate his tenure as a civilian President may have been too hasty in their judgment or rather too naïve. From recent developments, Obasanjo is having the last laugh on them. His ambition for a third term has just been realized. Those who cannot see the genius – evil or angelic - in his political moves are perhaps too naïve or too partisan to deconstruct complex political plots.

Obasanjo was one of the gladiators intensely consulted by the disaffected members of the PDP, who formed the 'new PDP that eventually merged with APC to bolster the latter beyond the wildest imagination of its founding fathers. Obasanjo who offered to mediate between the disaffected PDP members and the then Tukur-led main PDP was accused by Chief Edwin Clarke and others of orchestrating or fuelling the crisis in PDP. Accusations and counter accusations are often the hallmarks of Nigerian politics. It is sometimes difficult to know when these accusations are wired just to force your opponents' hands or to put them on the defensive. What is not contestable is that Obasanjo was seen by most of the disaffected members of the PDP as their spiritual head. And when the 'New PDP' collapsed into APC and the latter's fortunes became bolstered, Obasanjo became more or less the spiritual guardian of a grateful APC. Obasanjo's angry letter to President Jonathan on December on December 3 2013 brought members of the APC closer to them in a classic case of the enemy of my enemy is my friend.

It could be argued that with the new found strength of the APC, and its overnight transmutation from a coalition of regional-based parties to a national party, Nigeria as a country has become factionalized between the segment of it controlled by PDP and its acolytes (APGA and Labour Party) and those controlled by APC. From what played out in Rivers State recently, APC-controlled States may have adopted Obasanjo as the *de facto* President of their faction of the country. APC apparatchiks may have found in him a match to President Jonathan in terms of media coverage, prestige (he was both military and civilian President) and knowledge of the country's political terrain and how to survive within it.

Like Jonathan who routinely goes to commission projects from loyal State Governors (hoping perhaps to also use such to showcase the achievements of the PDP), Obasanjo paid a two day 'official' (my word) visit to Port Harcourt between February 17 and 18. A press release from the Rivers State chapter of the All Progressives' Congress said Obasanjo was in the State to commission "16 world class projects". When was the last time we read of a big state project like that being commissioned by anyone else but an incumbent President?

Hailing Governor Amaechi for his administration's developmental strides, Obasanjo was quoted as saying: "I came to see developments and I have seen developments and I will confess developments! What I have seen is worth declaring! The area of Health, Education, Agriculture, Sports and Road Infrastructure is worth declaring. When I see development I earmark, eye mark and mouthmark." In Rivers State Obasanjo spoke, not as a former President, but as *de facto* President of the faction of the country controlled by APC. We are likely to see Obasanjo commission more projects in APC-controlled state. Despite his own limitations, he remains one of the few Nigerians who transcend the country's fault lines. APC needs to identify with them as a sign of how nationalistic the party has become. And Obasanjo needs the APC not just to re-invent himself as a statesman but also to fulfill his ambition of a third term, even if it is now only as a ceremonial President.

I have always been very fascinated by the Obasanjo character. As a younger man in the late 1980s, I had accompanied the political activist and publisher Chief Arthur Nwankwo to one of the nocturnal meetings at Obasanjo's Ota Farm. It was my first and only encounter with the Ota farmer. But I was very impressed. I recall he was wearing rather cheap trousers, his shirt was wrongly buttoned and he was walking around bare feet. His Raleigh (or so it seemed) bicycle leaned against the wall of the modest one storey building in the farm. I was just too full of admiration for a former Head of State that embodied such simplicity. Over the years I have been both his ardent critic and a passionate admirer of some of his attributes. True, when Obasanjo shaved off his trademark moustache and exchanged the simple shirts and trousers for which he was known for expensive agbadas, Rolex watches and designer glasses, something of the old Obasanjo seemed to have died in those transformations.

I concede that Obasanjo's critics are mostly right: Obasanjo is a hypocrite who is adept in seeing the speck in others' eyes but not the plank in his own; he could be vindictive and ruthless, he cannot be trusted to keep agreements or even be truthful about the existence of such agreements. I also concede that Obasanjo is almost always self-serving. But how come this Ota Farmer has been so successful in re-inventing himself and planting himself successfully at the frontal cusp of each turn in our history? How come the Tinubus, the self-appointed defenders of Northern interests and others who normally use the most demonic adjectives to describe Obasanjo glee in wild excitement whenever he pitches his tent with them? Tinubu, who had a long-running battle with him when he was governor of Lagos State led a delegation that included Buhari to Obasanjo and pleaded with him to be the navigator (read: spiritual head) of APC. By being the spiritual director of the APC, Obasanjo also by extension reconciles with his South-West home base, who often takes the charge in demonizing him. By taking a hard position that Jonathan should not contest in 2015 and implying that he supported him in 2015 only because he promised to serve one term, he probably also reconciles with a segment of the North that often sees him as betrayer. The crucial question now is whether the Lagos press which appears to have a bias for APC will now also temper its criticisms of the now beatified Obasanjo. In essence, the canonization of Obasanjo by APC could mean a pacification of those who are often most vocal in calling for the Ota Farmer's pound of flesh, ensuring that that the idea of his being a favourite character for demonization will be muted. For those who subscribe to the Machiavellian school of doing the needful to be in power or remain relevant, please let us give it to Obasanjo: he remains the master of the game. Combining his military courage with extreme cunning, Obasanjo knows how to place himself at the cusp of history. Some have called him opportunist but I think he has a good sense of timing. Whatever you may think of Obasanjo, you can ignore his deft political moves at your own peril.

There are several instances of Obasanjo positioning himself deftly to benefit from the turn of history or adding momentum to particular historical trajectory. For instance it was said that after his visit in hospital to the late Yaradua, his position that if Yaradua could not discharge the duties of his office effectively he was honour-bound to resign, added momentum to the forces that were clamouring for Jonathan to be made Acting President. And from there the rest is history and Obasanjo was on the winning side. It could also be argued that APC as we now know it benefited immensely from Obasanjo's angry letter to Jonathan which, by innuendo, painted Jonathan and the PDP as irredeemable.

Obasanjo will however always be an Obasanjo. He has declared that he remains a card carrying (not necessarily a loyal) PDP member. As the spiritual head of APC, he is the de facto President of APC- controlled states. However if the current excitement with the APC wanes and the momentum begins to shift back to PDP, trust Obasanjo to dig into his bag of tricks and find a magic wand that will make the PDP also eternally grateful to him for not being overrun by APC.

Daily Trust February 20, 2014

CHAPTER 96

Obasanjo's Agenda for 2015

It was first reported in August 2012. Three months later, the rumour (or is it speculation?) resurfaced again.

Several newspapers reported in August this year that Obasanjo had decided to back the Jigawa State Governor Sule Lamido as the PDP presidential candidate in the 2015 elections with Governor Rotimi Amaechi of Rivers State as his running mate. The *Leadership* newspaper of 20 August 2012 for instance quoted a source "close to Obasanjo" as confiding in the paper that the "former president is now drumming support for a power shift to the North on the grounds that the region deserves the development." Speaking through a media aide Garba Muhammad, Obasanjo had denied the story, saying he was too preoccupied with "more pressing national issues" to be bothered about 2015. Despite the denial, some believed there was no smoke without fire or that the Ota Farmer might even have planted the story in the media for other reasons.

Obasanjo, it should be recalled, was the mastermind of the late Umaru Yar' Adua/Goodluck Jonathan ticket in 2007 after his bid to elongate his tenure flopped.

On 29 October 2012, some three months after the story first broke out and was denied, the *Tribune* reported: "Few months after former president Chief Olusegun Obasanjo denied backing the speculated presidential ambition of Jigawa State governor, Alhaji Sule Lamido in 2015, the former leader appears to have unfolded his agenda ahead of the next general election". The paper further claimed that a source close to Obasanjo told it that the Ota Farmer's plans "include getting people to convince President Jonathan not to seek re-election and secondly, installing his favourite among the northern governors, Alhaji Sule Lamido of Jigawa, as president. He has been sending emissaries, some notable politicians, to the president; the idea is ostensibly to convince him (Jonathan) against seeking re-election in 2015."

Obasanjo is highly gifted – courageous, admirable guts, overflowing stamina, folksy wisdom, native intelligence and enduring capacity for working long hours. But he is also deeply flawed – extremely cunning, domineering, never forgetting or forgiving a slight and forever scheming to be at the centre of things. Given the critical roles he played in every turn of the nation's post independence life and the contradictions that define his person, stories that are linked to him are never taken at face value – and shouldn't. In this sense if there are reports that Obasanjo has said 'Good morning' to someone, it makes perfect sense to interrogate whether Obasanjo really said so, what that 'Good morning' meant for him, whether it was a decoy and whether the recipient of that 'Good morning' should be better advised to go underground or even on a temporary exile. There are rarely neutral views of Obasanjo: he is either a bugaboo or a genius.

Rewind to 3 April 2012 when Obasanjo resigned as BOT chairman of the PDP. The suspicion then was that Obasanjo jumped before he could be pushed or at least that it was an indication that his relationship with Goodluck Jonathan had begun going the way of most relationships between political godfathers and their political godsons: awry. Elsewhere I noted that Obasanjo has made a career of helping to pull down any regime he is not running or feels has slighted him. While it is difficult to know the truth or otherwise in the rumours of Obasanjo's estrangement from Jonathan, it is possible to count a number of instances in which the regime could be said to have slighted him. One such instance was when Presidential Assistant on Media Dr Okupe said Obasanjo was an 'ordinary citizen' after the Ota Farmer opposed plans by the CBN to introduce a N5,000 note.

It is within the context of Obasanjo's antecedents, persona and possible perceptions of slight by the presidency that we can interrogate the news of Obasanjo's reported agenda for 2015. There are several possibilities:

One, Obasanjo could have been planting the story as a bargaining chip in which he uses a subtle threat of embarking on his familiar job of helping to pull down regimes as a way of getting the President to make certain concessions to him. Obasanjo is conscious of the weight of his voice in the international arena and knows how to choose the most appropriate location and occasion to poke a regime for maximum effect. In this sense Obasanjo is an accomplished professional in the deployment of the echo of his powerful voice both as a testament of his courage and a tool of opportunism.

Two, it is possible that Obasanjo may be trying to curry favour with a wing of the Northern faction of the Nigerian elite who had helped to make him Head of State in 1976 and President in 1999 but who apparently feel betrayed by his civilian presidency. There is a feeling that Obasanjo is a character some people from the North love to hate and demonise. Therefore by championing a Northern presidency in 2015 Obasanjo could perhaps be hoping to launder his image in the region, especially given the position he took during the zoning controversy in the run-up to the April 2011 elections.

Three, it is equally possible that by leaking his supposed support for Lamido/Amaechi ticket, Obasanjo might be hoping to undermine Lamido's long-rumoured presidential ambition. The idea here may be that given the negativity that has continued to trail Obasanjo's foisting of a sick Yaradua on the nation and the various conspiracy theories about his motives for doing so, Obasanjo's declaration of support for Sule Lamido will be used to alienate many potential supporters for the Jigawa state governor, especially from the North. Obasanjo's supposed support for Lamido could also be calculated to ginger elements within the presidency into making moves that are designed to neutralise Lamido and Amaechi ahead of 2015.

Four, since nothing is impossible in politics, it cannot also altogether be ruled out that Obasanjo's supposed support for Lamido/Amaechi is the handiwork of the presidency. The idea here could be to create an illusion of a quarrel between Obasanjo and President Jonathan since Obasanjo's perceived closeness to Jonathan is thought to be viewed very dimly, if not with suspicion, by many elements from the North. In this way showing that Obasanjo and Jonathan have parted ways may be a deliberate calculation to bolster the standing of the President in the North.

Five, it is equally possible that Obasanjo's supposed support for Lamido could be the handiwork of people eager to cause or further the disaffection between the President and Obasanjo with the aim of opening up the political space ahead of 2015.

My position is that whatever may be the true reason for the resurfacing of this story about Obasanjo's support for a Lamido/Amechi ticket, the Ota Farmer should be encouraged to eschew any temptation to be strongly involved in the politics of 2015. He has done his bit, with successes and failures here and there. At his age, and given his experience, there is a higher calling, a vacancy if you must, which seems to be tailor-made for him. And that is to become a true statesman because one of the problems in the country today appears to be the lack of individuals with clout who enjoy sufficient legitimacy across the fault lines and who can be trusted to mediate impartially in the endemic intra elite, intergroup and inter-ethnic conflicts in the country. Obasanjo may currently not possess all the personal attributes for this job. But he can grow with the job.

Re: The Achebe book: a preface

Below are two of the several responses I received on the above, published in my column last week:

"Once again, you didn't disappoint your readers. Rather you have shocked those who were expecting you to jump into the vortex of the emotions that surround the reactions to Achebe's book. I hope the dispassionate manner you have approached the issue may help calm the overheated minds of those who are already at each other's throat over the book, majority of whom haven't even read the book. From Na' Allah Mohammed Zagga" (text message).

"Dear Mr Adibe, I think you wrote a very good piece on the Achebe book. I think you are one of the few unfortunate Nigerians who are so 'nationalised'. Trouble is, can you find a home here? As Apoi's reply you published would show, you have to be an 'Abujan', a Niger Deltan, an Igbo etc. which is why Achebe's book can only be viewed as a residual nostalgia or even downright advocacy for the 'Igbo cause'. Question is, isn't it? By the way I agree with Apoi's position. I think comparing Abuja to Olobiri is confusing logical justice. Do have a nice day, Chris Ojeikere,' (text message).

"Jide, I just finished reading 'The Achebe book....' Your great effort at dismantling rising xenophobic myopia even in the Nigerian intellectual realm is highly appreciated by me. Kudos and continue n'ejide ofo gi ofuma', Paddy Njoku, Asokoro" (text message).

Daily Trust, November 1, 2012

CHAPTER 97

Obasanjo v Jonathan: Cockcrow at Dawn

Obasanjo's 18-page letter to President Jonathan dated December 2 2013 has been causing expected ripple in the polity. What was the letter really designed to achieve? Is it achieving that? And how do we evaluate the responses of the presidency to the letter?

At this stage several tentative observations could be made:

One, the letter seems to be part of a carefully choreographed chain of events: first there was the walkout on the PDP Convention by some disaffected PDP members, which culminated in the formation of the New PDP (nPDP). Later five of the seven governors in the nPDP decamped to the APC. This was followed by allegations by Sanusi Lamido Sanusi, the Governor of the Central Bank that the NNPC failed to remit a whopping $49.8m to the Federation Account and that he wrote to the President about this and was ignored. Before the furore from this could die down came open criticism of the President by Speaker Aminu Tambuwal who alleged that the President's body language shows he condones corruption. Obasanjo's letter caps or adds to this apparently choreographed sequence of events. And the aim appears to be to create a narrative of an incompetent and corruption-condoning Jonathan which will either force him not to run in 2015 or make him unelectable if he chooses to run.

There is absolutely nothing wrong in opposition groups using apparently choreographed plots such as the above to weaken their opponents. On the contrary, it is the crux of politics and is what some people mean when they say that 'politics is a game'. Like in any game, there are a number of smaller moves (sub-plots) which when added together will create a storyline or reveal a player's game plan. Today (December 18, 2013), we read that 37 Members of the House of Representatives have decamped to APC and that former Vice President, Alh Atiku Abubakar might soon follow suit. If we connect the dots from the series of apparently small events mentioned above, a plot, which casts the PDP as a sinking ship is emerging. If PDP has a counter game plan, it has not worked so far and time may be running out. Obasanjo's letter, by its overdose of bile, and expected reactions from feature writers (both hired and otherwise), will diminish him without enhancing Jonathan.

Two, Obasanjo's claim that he wrote the letter in 'public interest' is suspect. Since Obasanjo's antecedents in taking on governments he is not running have been well documented since the publication of the letter, we need not waste time on it here. Suffice it to add that the impression that Obasanjo sought to create that he was forced to make his letter public because his efforts to offer wise counsels in private were repeatedly rebuffed, is unconvincing. For instance while Obasanjo claimed that "none of the four or more letters" he wrote over the past "past two years or so" elicited an acknowledgement nor (sic) any response", (p.1) on page 3 of the same letter, he created a contrary impression when he wrote: "Up till two months ago, Mr President, you told me that you have not told anybody that you would contest in 2015. I quickly pointed out to you that the signs and the measures on the ground do not tally with the statement". Again Obasanjo noted that at "the prompting of the governors from the two sides of the divide and an encouragement from the President", he spent two nights to intervene in the dispute of the PDP Governors and "I kept you [Jonathan] fully briefed at every stage" (p.6). These suggest that Obasanjo and the President have been working closely, if not in conspiracy. My suspicion is that the letter has several layers of motives- including a possible fight-back for perceived slights and a certain playing to the gallery perhaps in an attempt to return to the good book of some people in the North who felt he betrayed them. Only Jonathan and Obasanjo know for certain at what point 'water passed under the bridge' in their relationship. We do know however that Obasanjo once reportedly endorsed Sule Lamido for presidency (which was bound not to amuse Jonathan). We also know that the presidency has been taking measures to undermine Obasanjo, including in the South-western (which Obasanjo has not found funny).

Three, as should be expected, an euphoric APC, hoping to benefit from the anti-Jonathan plots, is calling for the resignation or impeachment of the President. This is what any opposition party in its position is expected to do – whether it really means it or believes it is feasible or not. The Presidency on its own is uncreatively raising the hammer of treasonable felony against those proposing such impeachment. Some elements are also proposing that the presidency move very strongly against Obasanjo.

My personal opinion is that the presidency and the PDP have responded very poorly to the political moves by its disaffected members. I had expected a much cleverer counter moves that will not only thwart further exodus from its ranks but also trigger a return of the 'prodigal sons' from APC (apart from taking concrete steps to address some of the issues raised in Obasanjo's letter). I find it baffling that more than two weeks after the Obasanjo letter was written, President Jonathan had not personally made a pointed and strong rebuttal of some of the allegations in the letter - and if need be, make his own counter allegations, at least to put his opponents on the defence and gain reprieve. I do not believe that it suffices to use aides to defend himself and his administration. I also find it puzzling that the regime was apparently unable to make any of the former leaders of the country such as Shagari and Gowon to come against Obasanjo's letter – at least the bile in it – to help defuse its impact. In the same vein some have wondered why the Presidency has been unable to exploit the known animosities between Obasanjo and both Babangida and Atiku Abubakar to do damage control. The impression is therefore unfortunately created that the presidency does not have any of the former Heads of State/President or their deputies on his side – at least on this issue. This impression unfortunately accentuates Obasanjo's charges. Presidential aides appear to rely on only two strategies – accusing those opposed to Jonathan of trying to undermine his presidency (as if that is not the day job of opposition political parties anywhere in the world) and threatening sanction against those who will move against the President (as if they forgot we are in a democracy which permits freedom of speech). With all due respect this cannot be called a counter game plan – which will necessarily be made up of little plans (sub plots) that will be linked up to create a counter game plan or storyline.

Four, despite the politics surrounding Obasanjo's letter (and 2015 is a big part of this), my personal opinion is that it will be a mistake for the opposition groups to believe they can intimidate Jonathan from contesting in 2015. In fact, rather than make him chicken out, intimidation and a cantankerous environment is likely to make him not only contest in 2015 but may make him dread a life without power – which is often at the root of the quest for life presidency in Africa. A president who feels that vengeance e is all that awaits him if he gives up power is more likely to 'do a Samson' – (i.e. pull down the structures so that everyone goes down with him or remain in power by whatever means as Mugabe does in Zimbabwe). For this, those opposed to Jonathan really have to take a second look at their politics if they truly want to stop him from contesting in 2015 or accept defeat if he runs and is defeated.

Similarly any attempt by the presidency to move too strongly and roughly against Obasanjo will boomerang. True, Obasano is not the darling of the Yorubas – just as Abiola was not. Yet any perceived ethnic slight if Obasanjo is hounded will not only boomerang across the country and beyond but will also bring back the triumphal memory of the fight by NADECO and Afenifere over June 12. Whether we like him or not, Obasanjo has loyalists across critical networks in and out of the country. He is a former President and Head of State, who deserves to be treated with respect – despite his shortcomings. It is part of statesmanship for any regime to know how to manage Obasanjo and the 'usual suspects' - the likes of Wole Soyinka, Balarabe Musa, Olisa Agbakoba, Femi Falana and others. These are individuals with strong anti-establishment credentials who thrive in picking fights with governments and are unafraid of the consequences of such fights. Like medical conditions such as High Blood Pressure or Diabetes, these individuals, if not properly managed, are capable of creating events that could be fatal for any regime.

Five, Obasanjo has made a career of positioning himself at the cusp of history, such that whenever he comes out very strongly against regimes like this, something untoward happens – from the time he was Minister of Works under Gowon and criticised the regime (and Gowon was overthrown shortly afterwards) to moving against Yaradua (leading to the doctrine of necessity that made Goodluck Jonathan Acting President). Following from this, my main concern with Obasanjo's letter is whether he knows something the rest of us don't know about?

Daily Trust December 19, 2013

CHAPTER 98

When Pastor Oritsejeafore acquired his own Jet

It is no longer rumour. Hard-talking Pastor Ayo Oritsejafor, President of Christian Association of Nigeria (CAN) and founder of Word of Life Bible Church, has joined the elite league of Nigerians who own private jets. According to reports, Oritsejafor's jet, marked N431CB, was delivered to him on 10 November 2012 at the celebration of his 40th year of being on the pulpit. The jet, estimated to cost some US $4.9m (or roughly N769, 300, 000 at the current official exchange rate), was manufactured in 1994 and previously belonged to two different owners in the US. Pastor Ayo Oritsejafor's anniversary, held at the Word of God Bible Church in Warri, Delta State, had eminent dignitaries in attendance, including President Goodluck Jonathan.

The rivalry among billionaire Pastors to own private jets appears to be the current wave of the competition among Pentecostal churches and their leaders who often proclaim themselves 'saved' and have no qualms unleashing themselves on us as the intermediaries between God and us sinful mortals. First there was competition on the size of churches, the number of people who attended them and the weekly returns from sundry offertories, tithes, collections and several donations and levies for 'doing God's work'. Then the competition pushed them into going 'world-wide' – in search of hard currency, prestige or 'winning souls for Christ'. Quite often they operate like franchises as they open offices across the world. As more money poured in, 'doing God's work' transmuted to owning schools and Universities, choice properties, farmlands and now aeroplanes. And as they compete on the material plane, competition to be seen as miracle workers, harbingers of prosperity and God's chosen intermediaries also intensified. If your church neither performs miracles nor brings prosperity, then you are on your own. 'Believers' want a happening place, not time wasters.

I am not trying to come between anyone and his or her belief or ridicule any one's faith. I know enough about faith to know it is a belief in things unseen – which means it has nothing to do with rationality or science. I am a firm believer in God, in the existence of an omnipotent and omniscience God who oversees the affairs of us little, sinful, mortals. However I believe that my relationship with God is a private matter, something between me and my Creator. Largely because of this, I have a morbid suspicion of people who flaunt their piety or who use what I will regard as subterfuges to prey on the gullibility and vulnerability of the underclass who often form the core of the followership of religious leaders. Pentecostal pastors are not the only culprits in this regard. Across the country and the religions, charlatans, rabble rousers and conmen and women also use religion and phony pious ambience to mask their lust for money and power. And this creates image problem for the few who are truly called to the spiritual vocation.

The excuse often used by our 'pastorprenuers' – (apologies to the writer Eddie Iroh) to justify their morbid craving for the epitome of the things of the world always reminds me of the book *Animal Farm* - an allegorical novella by George Orwell published in England on 17 August 1945. In that book, after the animals had succeeded in overthrowing their human oppressors, the leaders of the new regime, essentially the pigs, began to re-make the rules to enable them corner all the good things in the Animal Farm for their exclusive use. For instance they banned all the other animals from eating the apples on the Farm. And their justification? They never really liked apples but scientists had found they were good for brain work – which they alone did in Animal Farm!

Re-wind to the congregation of the Word of God Bible Church in Warri, Delta State on 10 November 2012. When it was announced that the church had acquired a 10-seater Bombadier/ Challenger 601 aircraft , the announcement was greeted with "loud ovation and applause" (Punch, 11 November 2012). The Vanguard of 11 November 2012 reported that the "jubilant congregation spent over 15 minutes congratulating one another even as the recipient did not make any comment on the jet said to have been purchased for him by the church". As far as the members (or most members) were concerned, it was not a piece of luxury for Pastor Oritsejafor. It was something to enable their Pastor maximize his time in 'doing God's work'.

Sometime in 2008, I found myself in a different area of London where I had to live briefly. One Sunday I was looking for a place to worship and by chance sauntered into a Pentecostal church – which had a Zambian as a Pastor. There were no more than 15 people in the congregation. The Pastor had apparently been having an issue with the landlord who wanted the church to vacate the place - a rather spacious lounge that could accommodate up to 200 people.

Just before the service ended, when people were giving testimonies of the good things the Lord had done for them during the week, the Pastor chose to be the last person to testify. "Many of you are aware of the issue the church has been having with our Landlord", he began in a low tone and then paused for effect. The congregation was wrapped in attention. The Pastor continued. He was, he said, led by the spirit a few days before to the landlord to talk about the church's tenancy. When he got to the landlord, he found him unusually friendly. He paused again amid shouts of "our Lord is good" and "Alleluiah". The Pastor claimed that as he discussed with the landlord he could see a halo over the landlord's head and knew immediately that the Lord was about to do a great thing that day. More shouts of 'Alleluiah' and the 'Lord is good all the time.'

Briefly, the landlord, who had all along insisted they should vacate the premise that day told the Pastor that he would not only allow them to continue with their tenancy but would also encourage the church to buy the place.

The small crowd was uncontrollable in its excitement and dabbled into several songs praising the Lord. From where I was, I began to wonder whether the landlord was not just being a smart business man rather than someone who had come under the influence of the spirit of God. It was the height of the collapse of the property market when many landlords were having a hell of time because securing mortgages had become almost impossible for most potential property buyers. Landlords were happy if they had tenants who paid their rents as and when due.

From my wonderland I heard the pastor lower his voice, almost to a whisper, and said: "Even though the price is £1.2m, I know our good Lord will do it for us". As be began a lengthy sermon of the benefits of the church having its own place where it can serve the Lord, I began to do a mental arithmetic of how this small congregation was ever going to raise the money to enable the pastor buy the building. Predictably, before the service ended, the Pastor said he would like to see all the men – about five or so were there - for a proper briefing on the plans about buying the building. I offered apologies that I had other engagements and left. I never went back. Admittedly not all 'men of God' are like the Zambian Pastor or Eddie Iroh's 'Pastoprenuers' but my suspicion of them is truly deep.

For Pastor Oritsejeafore's 40th anniversary on the pulpit I consider it an error of judgement that the announcement of the purchase had to be made in the presence of President Jonathan as it could wrongly suggest that the President supported the purchase or had a foreknowledge of it. Given President Jonathan's rather simple lifestyle and the level of poverty in the country, being associated with such ostentation could undermine his standing before many Nigerians.

I also consider it an error of judgement that the President had to attend the event at all. With all due respect, I find Pastor Oritsejeafore's hard line views on some political issues rather uncomfortable. By gracing the occasion, an impression could be created that the President supports those hard line views of the Pastor or that the Pastor was merely acting out the President's script.

For sure Pastor Oritsejeafore is not the only religious preacher who takes inappropriate hard line views on national issues. Several Islamic preachers are also guilty of the same offence. But such views should be sidelined, not mainstreamed by the President inadvertently legitimating their purveyors.

Daily Trust 22 November 2012

CHAPTER 99

The Resignation of Pope Benedict XVI

The entire world, especially Catholics, have been simultaneously shocked and dismayed by the recent announcement by Pope Benedict XVI that he would step down, effective from 28 February 2013. You need to go as far back as 1292 to find the time a pope willingly resigned from office. It is supposed to be a job or calling that you take on and know you will continue with it until death.

It is true that the last time a Pope 'resigned' was in 1415. But that was under a different circumstance. Pope Gregory XII, whose papacy lasted from 1406 to 1415, reigned during one of the most confusing times in Catholic Church history, known as Western Schism. At that time, while Gregory was the overwhelming preference of the cardinals in Rome, there was also a French pope, Benedict XIII, who also staked a claim to the papacy. In 1409, a church council decided that the best thing to do was to depose both Gregory XII and Benedict XIII, and elect a brand new one, Alexander V. Since the popes refused to step down and all had powerful protectors, the church now had three popes simultaneously in charge. Finally, in 1415, Gregory 'agreed' to resign and spent the rest of his life in obscurity.

Pope Celestine V's abdication in 1292 had a certain similar ring to it with Pope Benedict XVI's decision to resign. Born to a poor family, he worked his way up in the religious ranks despite his love of living as a hermit in caves for years at a time. It was from his cave that he learnt about the death of Pope Nicholas IV in April 1292 and promptly sent a letter to the College of Cardinals urging them to elect a new pope as soon as possible or God would be angry. Coincidentally the College of Cardinals decided to elect him the pope. But he did not want the job and was eventually convinced to give it a try. In his five months in office, he made only three decrees, the last of which made it okay for popes to abdicate, which he immediately did. Though several popes had previously resigned under pressure including Pontian (235) and Benedict IX (1045), Pope Celestine is generally regarded as the first pope to have resigned voluntarily. While Pope Celestine V did not feel he was suited for the papacy, Pope Benedict said his age would not allow him to give his best. In both resignations, there is a sense that they took the decision because they wanted to put the Church above self, and above the attractions of fame and media spotlight. This will certainly be a good lesson for our politicians who continue to hang on to their office even when they are terminally ill and know they cannot go on.

Born on April 16, 1927, in the predominantly Catholic southern German region of Bavaria, Joseph Ratzinger, who was the son of a policeman, gradually gravitated towards the priesthood, entering a seminary in 1939, the same year he was required to join the Hitler Youth Movement. He was ordained priest at the same time as his older brother Georg in 1951. After receiving his doctorate in theology from the University of Munich in 1953, *Fr. Joseph Ratzinger* became a professor of dogmatic theology at the

University of Bonn. The brilliant scholar, aged only 35, caught the eye of Cologne Archbishop Joseph Frings, a cardinal who brought him to Rome to work as an advisor to the Second Vatican Council (1962-1965), which addressed the relations between the Roman Catholic Church and the modern world. Pope Paul VI named Ratzinger archbishop of Munich in 1977 and made him a cardinal the same year. The four-year stint in Munich was Ratzinger's only real pastoral experience before he became pope.

For his 85 years of age and given his schedule, Pope Benedict XVI does not look especially frail. In fact the Rev. Federico Lombardi, head of the Vatican press office reportedly told reporters there was no specific health crisis or disease that forced the pope to take the decision to resign. So why throw in the towel when he is, by modern standards, not even particularly old, and still looking strong? The Pope's sudden resignation and break with a 600-year-old tradition has expectedly flung the door wide open to various forms of speculation and conspiracy theories: some have alluded to the weight of the controversies surrounding child abuse cases which darkened his reign and in which the Vatican was accused of not doing enough to bring the implicated priests to justice. Others say he is pained by allegations that he did not personally do enough in his earlier role as Prefect of the Congregation of the Doctrine of the Faith to prevent such abuses despite a general belief that he genuinely detested those crimes. Some have also alleged that Pope Benedict XVI's papacy is not the best managed and that information in the Vatican leaked freely under him. A case in point was Paolo Gabriele, who has been the Pope's trusted butler since 2006 and who was convicted for being one of the sources of 'Vatileaks' - leaked documents allegedly exposing corruption and power struggle in the Vatican. While all these may have played a role in the pope's decision to step down, I am more persuaded by the argument that as a close associate of the more charismatic Pope John Paul 11, he knew that the Catholic Church and its 1.2 billion flock – the largest organised religious body in the world – virtually grounded to a halt in the last five years of John Paul's pontificate because everyone was put on a death watch for the increasingly frail Pope. It was said that Pope Benedict XVI, a very humble intellectual, did not want to put the Catholic Church through such a course again.

There are also indications that Pope Benedict XVI had always planned on resigning at a point. At 78 when he became pope, he reportedly said that he anticipated his papacy would be short. Was he alluding to a possible resignation? It was also reported that before becoming pope, he had attempted several times as he approached the mid-seventies to retire but that Pope John Paul II would not accept his resignation. He was then serving his predecessor as the head of the Congregation of the Doctrine of Faith, the doctrinal watchdog for the church once called the Inquisition.

It is part of the ironies of life that Pope Benedict XVI, a traditionalist and staunch defender of Catholic orthodoxy, took the radical step of breaking a convention that has lasted for nearly 600 years. What this portends for the Catholic Church remains unclear. But the news of the resignation reminded me of the words in one of those 'Team Up with Balarabe Musa' posters I had in my room as an undergraduate in the early 1980s when the 'feudal'-minded members of the Kaduna State House of Assembly were trying to impeach the 'progressive' Governor: "We are living in times of great changes. The old order is crumbling fast. Our business is to seek to understand these changes and to utilize them for human progress – Balarabe Musa". My feeling is that the radical undertone of Pope Benedict's resignation may unwittingly embolden the liberal forces within the Catholic faith, which could lead to the Church grappling with a renewed challenge on how to remain faithful to its key dogmas without being seen as being too out- of- touch with reality.

Besides his academic articles and official Church documents, Pope Benedict XVI authored several books including the *Ratzinger Report* (1996), The *Spirit of the Liturgy* (2000) and God *and the World* (2002). He is the oldest cardinal to be named pope since Clement XII, who was also 78 when he became pope in 1730. He is the first German pope since Victor II (1055-1057). He will be remembered as a staunch defender of Roman Catholic orthodoxy, a diehard traditionalist and for the few gaffes he committed during his papacy.

As the media remains abuzz with speculations on the 'real' reasons for the Pope's resignation, commercially minded people and entities are moving in to profit from the situation. Bookmakers for instance are already offering odds on who will succeed the pope. The bookmaker Paddy Power has anointed Cardinal Marc Ouellet of Canada the favourite at 5/2, followed by Cardinal Francis Arinze of Nigeria at 3/1 and Cardinal Peter Turkson of Ghana at 4/1.

Daily Trust February 14, 2013

CHAPTER 100

Sanusi's 'democratic-conflict' Theory

On 15 January 2013 Mallam Sanusi Lamido Sanusi, the irrepressible and talkative Governor of the Central Bank once again chose to stir the hornet's nest by calling for the proscription of ethno-religious groups in the country. Speaking at an inter-faith dinner organized by the Northern Reawakening Forum (NRF) in Abuja, Mallam Sanusi was quoted by the Vanguard of 16 January 2013 as saying: "I almost didn't want to attend this occasion because I am opposed to regional, ethnic and religious groupings in this country. In fact, I would like the Christian Association of Nigeria (CAN), Jamatul Nasril Islam (JNI), Afenifere and all such other groups to be banned."

There are three fundamental issues here: the first is whether it should be seen as an act of courage or betrayal on the part of Mallam Sanusi to use a platform offered to him by NRF to tell them to their face that they they are part of the civil society nuisance groups in the country that ought not be allowed to exist. The second is whether as CBN Governor he should be called to order for his penchant for making political speeches. The third is the relevance of Sanusi's call for these groups to be banned, which is my only concern in this piece.

As should be expected, Sanusi has been taken on by various interests, including the associations he called to be banned. My personal opinion is that the attacks on Mallam Sanusi have been as simplistic as Sanusi's call for these groups to be banned. In fact on this issue, Mallam Sanusi seems to be nearer the truth than his traducers because his call mirrors current concerns among some theorists of democracy of the potential of groups such as those he mentioned to aggravate the structures of conflict in deeply divided multi-ethnic societies, especially those with fragile economies, where the nation building process has either remained in a state of flux or completely stalled. My friend, Kenneth Omeje, a professor of international relations at United States International University, Nairobi, Kenya has called this 'democratic-conflict' theory. This is the crux of the issue raised by Mallam Sanusi. Aside from the inherent contradiction in a very conservative banker being a radical system critic, I believe that Sanusi's position on this issue has been largely misunderstood. I shall return to this later.

There are three major criticisms of Sanusi's call: one is that the constitution of the country guarantees freedom of speech and association, the other is that the associations he called to be banned are 'countervailing', meaning they could actually be helping to stabilize the polity through a sort of balance of fear or balance of threats. This is another way of saying that these groups actually help to restrain one ethnic or religious group from attacking another or carrying out acts that will undermine others because of the fear of reprisals – not necessarily physically. The other criticism of Sanusi's call for the banning of ethno-religious groups is that these groups are part of the civil society and that their vibrancy is often a good indication of the strength of a nation's democracy.

In free speech jurisprudence, freedom of expression, (even as indulged by the ethno-religious groups Sanusi mentioned), usually enjoys a high level of protection in several advanced democracies. In the UK for instance, long before the European Convention on Human Rights and Fundamental Freedoms (ECHR) was incorporated into its laws by the Human Rights Act 1998, freedom of speech was regarded as such an important right that government had to produce strong evidence to justify restraints on its exercise. In the US, the First Amendment explicitly provides that "Congress shall make no law… abridging the freedom of speech or of the press."

There are four principal arguments for a free speech principle: its importance in discovering the truth, as an integral aspect of each person's right to self development and fulfillment, its importance in citizen participation in democracy and more importantly the deep suspicion of government. Aside from these, there are those who have drawn an organic and seemingly universal connection between neo-liberal democracy and sustainable peace. The argument here is that liberal democracy promotes an enduring peace based on accountable government and the tendency towards shared libertarian values both within and amongst states. The belief is that because democracy is based on popular vote, the rule of law and an accountable government, democracies are unlikely to go to war with each other because the government, mindful of the feeling of the electorate, is likely to have a vested interest in exploring non-violent options to resolve any dispute. Proponents of this view will always find rationalization for the 'unjust' wars waged by stronger states against the weaker ones.

But how do the various theories of democracy and their relationship to peace and nation-building play out in Africa, which since the late 1980s has witnessed various forms of democratic transitions? No one in his or her right mind will recommend a return to Africa's inglorious past with its authoritarian impulses. But has democracy really facilitated the nation-building process, which in my opinion, is the fundamental problem facing many countries in the continent? Or has it empowered groups such as those mentioned by Mallam Sanusi to aggravate the crisis in the nation-building process by politicising the we-they dichotomy? What is the nexus between a noble role for them such as in articulating and aggregating the interest of their members and their aggressive politicisation of their supposed marginalisation as a strategy for recruiting and retaining members?

In our type of societies, where there is a deep institutionalised memory of hurt and unfair treatment by virtually all the ethnic and religious groups, the type of groups that Mallam Sanusi mentioned often turn themselves into 'ethno/religious watchers' on who has got what from the state and who is being marginalized and by whom. Any comment made by one group triggers a reaction from others, often deepening the distrust among such groups. In this sense, these groups could be said to negate the goal of nation-building as they often engage in shouting matches with their counterparts from other parts of the country. And in these shouting matches, hate speeches and occasionally violence are readily deployed or caused to be deployed by the more fanatical members of the in-group. This is the danger posed by these groups in our country despite their potential for more constructive roles in deepening our democracy. It is in this sense that Mallam Sanusi's call for them to be banned must be located. I strongly share his views about the menace these groups could cause. His panacea of banning them, however, I will distance myself from.

Even in the more mature democracies, dealing with hate groups is often problematic. A good example here is the Ku Klux Klan – one of the worst purveyors of racial hatred in the USA. In a landmark case, Brandenburg v. Ohio (1969), the arrest of an Ohio Klansman named Clarence Brandenburg on criminal syndicalism charges based on a KKK speech that recommended overthrowing the government was overturned in a ruling that has protected rascals of all political persuasions ever since. In a unanimous judgment, Justice William Brennan argued that "the constitutional guarantees of free speech and free press do not permit a State to forbid or proscribe advocacy of the use of force or of law violation except where such advocacy is directed to inciting or producing imminent lawless action and is likely to incite or produce such action." Even what constitutes 'incitement' could be contentious. As argued in another landmark case in that country (*Gitlow v New York* [1925]): "Every idea is an incitement.... The only difference between the expression of an opinion and an incitement in the narrower sense is the speaker's enthusiasm for the result". In other words, if we ban ethno-religious groups, we are not only inviting dictatorship but a police state since any speech could always be construed as an incitement.

What is perhaps needed by the various ethno religious groups is a form of self censorship by an umbrella group created by these groups themselves.

Daily Trust January 24 2013

CHAPTER 101

Sanusi has raised a very Important Question but...

Whenever Lamido Sanusi Lamido says anything, be it an ordinary 'good morning', then it has to be like Sanusi Lamido Sanusi – dramatic, colourful, controversial and 'roforofo'. The most controversial Central Bank Governor in the country's history is very adept in raising very critical questions but not always successful in providing the right answers. And it is not because he is not brilliant. He is exceptionally one.

In late November 2012, at the Second Annual Capital Market Committee Retreat in Warri, Delta State, Sanusi lamented the high cost of servicing the nation's civil service and called on the Federal Government to fire at least 50 per cent of its entire workforce, arguing that it is unsustainable for the country to continue to spend some 70 per cent of its earnings on salaries and entitlements of civil servants. Understandably labour leaders and many others lampooned him, with some even calling for his sack. The Nigeria Labour Congress specifically said Sanusi must be sacked before he destroyed the Nigerian economy. I will return to this later.

Why has controversy dogged Mallam Sanusi ever since he became the CBN Governor? Does he court it? Or does it run after him?

Sanusi's 'problem' in my opinion stems from two sources: The first is that I feel he is a radical in a job that is decidedly conservative in nature. The second is his fascination with the English Language, which he writes with remarkable authority and even speaks better. On the positive side this could make one appear cleverer than one really is. On the flip side, too much 'grammar' (*turenci*) could lead to an undue love for the podium and limelight and a fascination with the echo and musicality of one's words - with the attendant risks of gaffes in moments of rhetorical flourishes. I do not for a moment believe the crap that Sanusi is driven by any hidden agenda. But this is a different thing altogether.

At an event in London in 2009 to talk about the reforms in the banking sector, I asked Sanusi, if professionally speaking, he saw a tension between where he found himself, and where in his heart he felt he ought to be. Sanusi denied being a radical but admitted that when he was in merchant banking, he did feel that tension. I have read a few of Sanusi's writings on Gamji.com and never ceased to admire his brilliance. I always felt his 'natural' calling would be as a radical academic – in the mould of the late Bala Usman or as the life Chairman of a brief case political party that will provide him a platform for slinging shots at the establishment – as the likes of Femi Falana and Balarabe Musa do.

Despite Sanusi's protestations, I am inclined to see him as a 'radical' or 'revolutionist' – in the sense of someone who favours extreme or fundamental changes in the way the society is organised. Remarkably, while I regard Sanusi as a radical in criticisms of the system, as a banker, I see him as a conservative, a traditional regulator who is excessively concerned with risk management at a time Nigerian banks seem to have become more competitive and entrepreneurial. There is therefore in my opinion a tension between Sanusi the banker and Sanusi the system critic.

As with most system critics or revolutionists, Sanusi's approaches to complex issues tend to be simplistic and as the contradictions in his chosen options become obvious, the proffered solutions tend to appear contradictory or hastily taken. A clear case in point was his recommendation that the bank executives he sacked for fiddling with depositors' money who were then standing trial at various courts in the country deserved to die by firing squad for eroding public confidence and raping the institutions that were entrusted to their care through reckless credit and loan administration processes. Sanusi was later to recant, perhaps after he realised the enormity of the statement, saying that Nigerian bankers are honest, hardworking professionals and not the crooks he had made them to appear.

There have been several of such apparently hastily thought-out recommendations from the Mallam Sanusi, including the recent issue of N5000 bill. The typical mind-frame of a revolutionist is: we reject the institutions that govern us, let's pull them down and erect brand new ones that will serve us better. This dictum is fine on a philosophical plane but creates enormous challenges at the level of implementation. This is another way of saying that it is OK for such recommendations to come from theorists and social critics but not from policy-makers. The problem on the ground is that if you pull down your house because you want to erect a brand new one that will be more befitting, you risk making yourself homeless while the new building is being put up   with the attendant dangers from the elements - unless you have made alternative arrangements. The less radically inclined will embark on an incremental renovation of the same house, moving their belongings from one part of the house to the other as the work progresses.

It is within the above premise that we should try to locate Sanusi's recent recommendation about sacking 50 per cent of the civil servants to save cost.

On face value, Sanusi is right because there is no doubt that the public service, in particular the civil service is bloated. Just visit any PHCN office and you will see several of their staff loitering outside their buildings like touts – largely because there seems not enough for them to do, which also explains why ten staff should visit one household to do 'metre reading'. But Sanusi was wrong that firing 50 percent of the civil servants will lead to cost saving. It will not. Rather it will actually increase the cost of governance. There are three options here: The first is t reduce the staff strength without trying to professionalize the service. Under this scenario, there will be an increase in red-tape and corruption within the service as the fewer staff will increase their asking price to move your file from table A to table B. Here the civil service will end up being even more inefficient than it is now, leading probably to an increased use of outside consultants to get things done. The second option is to completely professionalize the civil service. This will include re-organising the recruitment modes of staff such that the service can attract the best talents available. But this also means paying competitive salaries and other emoluments commensurate with what they would get in private international firms in the country. This scenario means that having a 50 percent reduction in the size of the civil service will not necessarily mean a reduction in its wage bill. The third option is to do nothing – which shouldn't really be an option at all.

The service Sanusi has done for the country by his recent call for the firing of 50 percent of civil servants is to indirectly draw attention to the need to reform our civil service while boldly re-igniting the debate about the huge cost of governance in the country.

Let me return to my earlier assertion that Sanusi is a radical system critic in a job that is decidedly for conservatives and pro-establishment people.

Central Bank Governors are thought to possess so much crucial information about their country's economy that investors and analysts closely monitor their utterances even after they have left office. For instance when Alan Greenspan, who retired as chairman of the US Federal Reserve on January 31, 2006, predicted on February 26, 2007 that the US would enter into recession before or in early 2008, the Dow Jones Industrial Average dropped by 416 points (or 3.3 percent of its value) the following day. At that time, it was the worst one-day loss since September 17, 2001, when it lost 684 points (7.1 percent) after reopening in the wake of the 9/11 terrorist attacks.

It is perhaps because of the 'oracular' nature of being the boss of a country's central bank that many expect them to be rather taciturn. Willem "Wim" Frederik Duisenberg, first president of the European Central Bank (1998-2003) was noted for his bluntness and apparent inability to keep his mouth shut. In a special report on February 8, 2002, captioned, "The Wrong Man for an Impossible Mission", the *Financial Times* (London) summed up the angst against the late Dutch economist and financier: "The biggest criticism of Mr Duisenberg is not over the substance of his decisions, but over his presentation. His willingness to talk off the cuff and his often vivid turn of phrase has frequently raised eyebrows among other policy-makers." No, the Financial Times did not have Lamido Sanusi in mind, who is eminently intellectually qualified to be the CBN Governor, when it wrote that piece. But one sometimes wonders if he deliberately courts controversy by his choice of words – as system critics are wont to do.

Daily Trust January 3, 2013

CHAPTER 102

Sanusi and the Perils of a Two-Party System

Long before the country became effectively a two-party dominant political system, and the APC, which brought this about acquired its current swagger, Sanusi Lamido Sanusi (SLS) had become as controversial as they come. But there was a material difference between the way the controversies he generated were perceived before the APC and the way they were perceived after the party's emergence as a credible threat to the PDP and Jonathan's barely hidden 2015 ambitions. My position is that without the APC turning the country into a two-party system, the Presidency would perhaps have endured SLS as a garrulous gadfly until his tenure was up.

Since his appointment as the Governor of Central Bank on 9 June 2009, most of Sanusi's public utterances had been dramatic, colourful, controversial and cantankerous. His actions and off-the cuff remarks and the reactions they generated made him the most controversial Central Bank Governor in the country's history. He became a darling of some for raising very critical questions just as he achieved notoriety with others for being careless with figures while some held him in contempt for being less successful in providing the right answers to the numerous controversial questions he raised.

Sanusi's 'problem' in my opinion stems from two sources: The first is that I feel he is a radical in a job that is decidedly meant for conservative and pro-establishment people. Radicals by definition relish controversy and a fight. It is their oxygen. When a radical is given a public responsibility there is always the risk that he will turn a rebel and embarrass his benefactors because radicals often find the narrow confines of the system in which they work asphyxiating.

Sanusi's other problem is his fascination with the English Language, which he writes with remarkable authority and even speaks better. On the positive side this could make one appear cleverer than one really is. On the flip side, too much 'grammar' could lead to an undue love for the podium and limelight and a fascination with the echo and musicality of one's words - with the attendant risks of gaffes in moments of rhetorical flourishes. As with most system critics or radicals, Sanusi's approaches to complex issues tend to be simplistic and as the contradictions in his chosen options become obvious, the proffered solutions tend to appear contradictory or hastily taken.

The above has been the case with LSL not just with the contentious amounts he claimed the NNPC failed to remit to the Federation Account (he recanted when he claimed over $49bn was missing before coming up with a fresh allegation of missing $20bn). A clear case in point was his recommendation that the bank executives he sacked for fiddling with depositors' money who were then standing trial at various courts in the country deserved to die by firing squad. Sanusi later recanted saying that Nigerian bankers were indeed honest, hardworking professionals and not the crooks he had made them to appear. Again in late November 2012, at the Second Annual Capital Market Committee Retreat in Warri, Delta State, Sanusi lamented the high cost of servicing the nation's civil service and called on the Federal Government to fire at least 50 per cent of its entire workforce, arguing that it is unsustainable for the country to continue to spend some 70 per cent of its earnings on salaries and entitlements of civil servants. Understandably labour leaders and many others lampooned him, with some even calling for his sack. He had earlier wrongly claimed that the country spent 25 per cent of its revenues on Members of the National Assembly. Again shortly after he was appointed the CBN Governor, SLS announced on October 2, 2009, the removal of Dr Mike Adenuga as a non-executive director of Equatorial Trust Bank. About a month later, he changed his mind and restored the business mogul to the board of the bank, claiming that the CBN had not established any criminal activity against him. Virtually every major move since Sanusi became the helmsman of the apex bank, including the publication of the list of bank debtors shortly after his appointment, have been dogged by self-inflicted controversy, with the SLS often admitting errors.

The point of the above instances is to show that SLS's allegations that over $49bn were not remitted by NNPC to the Federation Account, his recanting and then coming back with other allegations of missing $20bn, had been his pattern since his appointment as CBN Governor. This raises two crucial questions: Why was the gaffes by SLS tolerated all along? And why was he suddenly seen as constituting himself as an opposition to the government when he has literally remained himself?

What has changed, in my opinion, is that the country has metamorphosed from being a one-party dominant system to a two-party dominant system. This in itself created a simplistic binary of 'we' versus 'they' in which if you are not for the government, then you are against it and by extension for the opposition. In essence while before, Sanusi's activism was seen as the minor irritations of a gadfly, under the new political configuration, the same activism was perceived as doing the bidding of the other side. The natural tendency of the opposition to come to the side of the 'enemy of my enemy' naturally accentuates the suspicion that SLS was doing the bidding of the other side to forestall President Jonathan's yet to be declared re-election chances. Despite the government's claims, it remains an open secret that SLS was suspended for 'embarrassing the government'.

Generally, a two-party system is a dichotomous division of the political spectrum, with one Party usually leaning on the right and the other on the Left: the Nationalist Party vs. the Labour Party in Malta, Liberal vs. Labour in Australia, Republicans vs. Democrats in the United States and the Conservative Party vs. the Labour Party in the United Kingdom.

In Nigeria where the two dominant parties are on the same spot on the political spectrum, and where there is a convergence between the fault lines of region, religion and ethnic, our two-party system will likely turn the country into a theatre of war without blood, akin to what one witnessed during the Cold War. The tension generated by the suspension of SLS is a foretaste of things to come. This is because under a two- party system, there is a tendency for the society to be polarized into two halves on the active controversies of the day – without a moderating voice of a third party since the other parties are either too small to be heard or have become appendages of one of the two dominant parties. In this scenario objectivity takes flight and those who strive for the truth will be accused of sitting on the fence.

In the current bipolar system, there are two perspectives on the Sanusi saga: One, favourable to APC sympathizers is that Sanusi is a whistle blower or even a revolutionary who got suspended for his anti-corruption crusade. In the same vein supporters of SLS's suspension accuse him of constituting himself as an opposition to the government or of going on the offensive to curry public sympathy after being indicted by the Financial Reporting Council for corruption.

Like in the Cold War days, the truth in all these is buried somewhere. What is clear is that SLS, though a clever man, talks too much, often thinks on his feet and did not go about his job with the requisite wisdom. Even if the President does not have the powers to suspend him as some contend – a position I disagree with - wouldn't common sense have told SLS that it was inappropriate to be seen opposing a government that he was part of (without first resigning), especially on the eve of an election year and when a credible opposition party had emerged? And wouldn't the same common sense have counselled him that you cannot run an establishment as complex as the CBN without incurring one or two things that your enemies could rope around your neck if the shove comes to push? In my opinion there is a difference between recklessness and courage. In his latest round of activism that many people believe led to his suspension, SLS simply appeared to be courting martyrdom. But amid all these and like always, SLS managed to raise some important questions – on subsidies on kerosene against presidential directive and without appropriation by the National Assembly and on likely corruption in the NNPC. Beyond these, the rest of the brouhaha surrounding his suspension is mere politics.

It is instructive that SLS left office pretty much the same way as Willem "Wim" Frederik Duisenberg, first president of the European Central Bank (1998-2003), who like Sanusi was notorious for his bluntness and apparent inability to keep his mouth shut. In a special report on February 8, 2002, captioned, "The Wrong Man for an Impossible Mission", the *Financial Times* (London) summed up the angst against the late Dutch economist and financier: "The biggest criticism of Mr Duisenberg is not over the substance of his decisions, but over his presentation. His willingness to talk off the cuff and his often vivid turn of phrase has frequently raised eyebrows among other policy-makers." No, the Financial Times was talking about Willem "Wim" Frederik Duisenberg, not Sanusi Lamido Sanusi.

Daily Trust February 27, 2014

CHAPTER 103

Margaret Thatcher: We remember differently

The title of this piece is not original. It was borrowed from Nigeria's nightingale of literature, Ngozi Chimamanda Adichie, in her tribute to Chinua Achebe when the 'fallen iroko' turned 82 last year. It was also meant to be a commentary on the controversy that dogged the writer's last work: 'There was a Country: A Personal History of Biafra'. In that piece, which Ms Adichie titled, 'Achebe at 82: We Remember Differently,' she essentially argued that we are all bound to re-tell any piece of story differently, based on our idiosyncrasies and the binoculars through which we filter reality. In social sciences some call such 'constructivist and interpretive' thinking.

How do we assess the Iron Lady, who transited on 8 April 2013? As an African, will it be fair to assess her strictly on how her policies as British Prime Minister (1979-1990) impacted on the continent especially given that she was elected as Prime Minister of Britain, not that of Africa? Even in the United Kingdom, assessing her legacy is a complex proposition: Will she be assessed from the perspective of the short- to- medium term impacts of her policies on the working class or the extent to which she helped to revive the UK as a country in 'terminal decline' and widely derided as the 'sick man of Europe' before her ascension to power? My personal opinion is that even if we choose to wear any of the binoculars and remember to adjust them properly, not just wear them perpendicularly, her legacy will also not be all that too straight forward to deconstruct.

One Chris Kitchen, a Briton, was quoted as saying: "We've been waiting for a long time to hear the news of Baroness Thatcher's demise and I can't say I'm sorry. I've got no sympathy for Margaret Thatcher and I will not be shedding a tear for her. She's done untold damage to the mining community. I don't think Margaret Thatcher had any sympathy for the mining communities she decimated, the people she threw on the dole and the state she left the country in. I honestly can't think of anything good I can say about Margaret Thatcher."

To fully understand this commentator, whose feelings have apparently not been mollified by a tradition of mortuary respect and the fact that Thatcher had been out of power for over twenty years, we need to go back to the miners' strike in the UK – the biggest confrontation between the unions and the Thatcher government. Briefly, when in 1984 the National Coal Board (NCB) proposed to close 20 of the 174 state-owned mines and cut 20,000 jobs out of 187,000, two-thirds of the country's miners, led by the National Union of Mineworkers (NUM) downed tools in protest. The leader of NUM had refused to hold a ballot on the strike, having lost three previous national ballots on strikes (January 1982, October 1982, March 1983). For this, the Thatcher regime declared the strike illegal and bluntly refused to bargain with the workers. In March 1985, after being on strike for a year, the NUM leadership conceded without a deal. Despite opposition the government in the same 1985 closed 25 coal mines it said were 'unprofitable'. The trend of closing mines continued after Thatcher's tenure with the eventual closure of 150 coal mines, resulting in the loss of tens of thousands of jobs, which devastated entire communities. So unpopular were the initial impacts of her policies, which centered on de-regulation, privatization and curtailing of public spending that the media started canvassing for a policy U-turn after the 1981 riots over the harsh impacts of her policies. Thatcher however retorted to the media campaign: "Turn, if you want to. The Lady is not for turning".

Supporters of Thatcher say she is not given sufficient credit for her role in arresting the UK's hitherto terminal decline as a great power. They argue that the competitive nature of the UK economy today is in large part due to Thatcher's policies. In fact Thatcher's supporters would argue that despite the short term adverse impacts of her policy options, by 1982, the UK had begun to experience signs of economic recovery, with inflation down to 8.6 per cent from a high of 18 per cent. By 1983 overall economic growth was stronger and inflation and mortgage rates were at their lowest levels since 1970, although manufacturing output had dropped by 30 per cent since 1978 and unemployment remained high. By 1987 however, unemployment was falling, the economy was stable and strong, and inflation was low, prompting a reversal in public opinion of her (her job approval rating was only only 23 per cent by December 1980 - lower than recorded for any previous Prime Minister). This turn-around in public opinion prompted Thatcher to call for a general election for 11 June that year, despite the deadline for an election still being 12 months away. In that election, Thatcher re-elected for a third successive term.

From domestic policy to foreign policy, deconstructing the legacy of the Iron Lady remains a difficult task: In Africa for instance Thatcher is often remembered unkindly, especially by those involved in the frontal struggle against Apartheid for her declaration that the African National Congress is a "typical terrorist organisation... Anyone who thinks it is going to run the government in South Africa is living in cloud-cuckoo land." Former ANC cabinet minister Pallo Alto, on hearing about Thatcher's death, reportedly said: "I've just sent a letter of congratulations...I say good riddance." My personal opinion is that this too is a rather simplistic appraisal. After all, the same Iron Lady that made that infamous statement and was opposed to sanctions also granted asylum to many of the ANC activists, including former president Thabo Mbeki. It should be recalled that in the mid 1980s, when the South African government was implicated in a plot that blew up the ANC offices in London and attempted to kidnap its members including Thabo Mbeki and Oliver Tambo (remember Umaru Dikko?), Thatcher provided armed body guard for most of the ANC's senior officials in London at the taxpayers' expense. Some of Thatcher's supporters even claim that she was privately doing more to end apartheid than her official gestures suggested. For instance in a confidential letter to P.W. Bother in 1985, Thatcher was quoted as saying: "I continue to believe, as I have said to you before, that the release of Nelson Mandela would have more impact than almost any single action you could undertake."

Born Margaret Hilda Roberts in Grantham, Lincolnshire on 13 October 1925, her father Alfred Roberts owned two grocery shops and was active in local politics and in the Methodist church. The young Miss Roberts won a scholarship to Kesteven and Grantham Girls' School, where she was the Head Girl (Senior Prefect) in 1942-1943. She was admitted into Oxford University in 1943 for a degree in Chemistry. While there she became President of the Oxford University Conservative Association in 1946 after reportedly being influenced by Friedrich von Hayek's book, *The Road to Serfdom* (1944), which condemned economic intervention by government as a precursor to an authoritarian state.

The road to Thatcher's ascent to the top in British politics was not paved with gold. She paid her dues, losing local elections a consecutive number of times (1950, 1951 and 1955) before she was elected MP for Finchley in the 1959 elections. Even when she applied for a job after graduating in Chemistry from Oxford University in 1947 at the chemical company ICI, she was also rejected after the personnel department assessed her as being "headstrong, obstinate and dangerously self-opinionated." In 1975, Thatcher became the Leader of the Opposition and the first woman to lead a major political party in the United Kingdom. Between 1979 and 1990, she was Britain's Prime Minister and the longest-serving British Prime Minister of the 20th century. She is famously known as the Iron Lady – a nickname given to her by a Russian journalist to capture her uncompromising politics and leadership style.

Largely because of her cuts in higher education spending, Thatcher was the first Oxford-educated post-war Prime Minister not to be awarded an honorary doctorate by the University of Oxford after a 738 to 319 vote of the governing assembly and a student petition. She left office in 1990, following a leadership challenge by Michael Heseltine.

For many, the last memory of Thatcher in office was her feminization of power when she left Downing Street in tears, regarding her ouster from the leadership of the Conservative Party and consequently of the government as an act of betrayal. After retiring from the House of Commons in 1992, she was given a life peerage as Baroness Thatcher of Kesteven in the county of Lincolnshire, which entitled her to sit in the House of Lords. She died of a stroke in London, aged 87.

Daily Trust, April 18, 2013

CHAPTER 104

The Achebe book: A Preface

I have not read Chinua Achebe's latest book, *There Was a Country*. The furore and shouting matches generated by the book are still evolving. For these, I do not feel ready yet to write about it but I have found a title for a future opinion on the book: 'Achebe's book: Now that the dust has settled'.

However following the conversations and hot exchanges generated by the book, it is possible to make the following observations:

One, the conversations and hostile exchanges about the book are incapable of undermining the mythical statures of of Chief Awolowo among the Yorubas, Ojukwu among the Igbos and the general perception of Gowon as a good- natured gentleman or of Achebe as one of the greatest writers to come from Africa.

Two, I disagree with those who feel that Achebe's book came at a wrong time. The institutionalised memory of hurt and pain by virtually every group in this country is one reason why our nation-building project remains in crisis. It is therefore important for aggrieved groups to speak up of their perceived grievances, even if for their cathartic effects. This is especially so in the case of the Biafran war where propaganda on both sides, repeated too often, became seen by many people as gospel truths. The war, especially the issues of 'kwashiorkor' and 'genocide' are embedded in the psyche of most Igbos. Therefore Achebe's book, when the dust settles, can help us as a country to soberly interrogate that part of our history, know where mistakes were made and revisit some of what we thought we knew about the war but which in hindsight could be mere propaganda or the natural triumphalism of victors in any war.

Three, we all engage in what we call in constructivist and interpretive thinking. In other words, we all have binoculars through which we filter realities. Therefore people who fought on opposite sides of the war are unlikely to agree on several fronts – from the causes of the war to the way it was prosecuted. It will be left to analysts, who are sufficiently detached, to listen to the sort of conversations and shouting matches stirred by Achebe to be able to piece together what really happened, including atrocities committed, especially in a war in which the key actors were in their 20s and early 30s.

Four, the way a writer, especially a protest writer interprets reality is different from the way a politician, an academic or a banker does. Protest writers, in their 'artistic temperament' often see 'cultural sensitivity' or 'political correctness' as cowardly attempts to mask the truth and may therefore sometimes 'offend' in exercising their 'poetic licence'. To 'offend' in fact is sometimes part of a protest writer's oeuvre. It is probably because of this that the 1989 Spanish Nobel Laureate in Literature Camilo José Cela declared that a writer is necessarily a denunciation of the time in which the author lives. It is also probably because of this that Wole Soyinka quickly jumped to Achebe's defence.

Five, I feel that the policy of blocking relief materials to those on the other side of the war was an error of judgment, even if it was meant to prevent Biafran soldiers from being fed as some have argued (as this clearly violates the 1949 Geneva Convention on war and I am not aware of any modern warfare where that policy has been applied even though soldiers would always benefit from relief materials).

Six, I am conscious of the fact that every individual is a composite of several identities. An Igbo man who is angry that he lost his brother during the Civil War could today have raised his children in Lagos, have a Northerner as his benefactor, his fellow Igbo as a betrayer or cherish his membership of several societies in which one's ethnicity or religion is not a criterion for joining. Let me expatiate with a personal example:

I am an Igbo born in Oturkpo, Benue State. Some of my mentors are from the North. I got the confidence to relocate to Nigeria after 22 years of living in Europe and elsewhere largely because I was invited to be a Director in Atiku's Presidential Campaign (September 2010 to January 2011). Since Atiku's media war with Obasanjo (where I pitched my tenth with Atiku), I have been consistent in my belief that Atiku is the best prepared person to be President of this country (despite rumours of his corruption that stuck from that media warfare with Obasanjo). My belief in him is not just because I worked in his campaign but because I admire his guts, his ability to identify and hunt for talents and his love for excellence in the things he does - from his American University in Yola to his other businesses. Obviously this belief deepened after working in his campaign and seeing how mountains of memos sent daily to him by 4pm would all have been read and commented upon by 10 am the following day.

I deeply admire Gowon's humility and remain grateful that he agreed to write the foreword to a book I edited in 2009 entitled, 'Who is an African: Identity, Citizenship and the Making of the Africa-Nation'. I have never hidden my admiration for Obasanjo's guts and belief that he is the best president the country has ever had 'despite his lack of grace' and other shortcomings. (In guts, strategy, vision, ability to network across the fault lines and capacity for working long hours, I rate Atiku a close second to Obasanjo). I feel honoured that my publishing firm, Adonis & Abbey Publishers (www.adonis-abbey.com) was chosen to publish what is arguably the most authoritative work on Babangida and his years in office by Dan Agbese, one of the founders of the now rested Newswatch. The book, 'Ibrahim Babangida: The Military, Politics and Power' is expected to be formally launched on December 6 2012. And by the way, did I need to become a Northerner or a Muslim to be given a back page column in Daily Trust and be made a member of the paper's Editorial Board?

I grew up wanting to be like the late Gani Fawehinmi. As a teenager I memorised Wole Soyinka's prison notes, *The Mad Died,* and his poem 'Telephone Conversation' and still hold him in awe and deep reverence. Chinua Achebe is for me, the eagle on the tallest iroko tree. All these are elements of my identity, not just my Igboness or Christianity. A person who abstracts only one or two elements from the mosaic of his identities and uses such to define his person or remains fixated on a moment in his history is often said to be bigoted. In essence identities are cross-cutting because a hurt suffered yesterday by someone or group could have been mitigated in one way or the other by people linked to that perceived hurt. This, for me is the key lesson to be learnt from the Achebe book after the dust has settled, even if we object to some of the great writer's choice of words or generalisations.

Re: Abuja indigenes: the fire next time?

I got a torrent of text messages, emails and phone calls from my last week's column. Virtually all the messages were to praise my position, some, mostly Abuja indigenes, in very emotional terms. Below is one of the two or three responses that had a different take on the issue:

'I read your above titled article on your column of Thursday 18, 2012 edition of the Daily Trust and cannot agree with you more that the indigenous people of the FCT deserve a better treatment from the Authorities that took over their land resources. However your effort to weep up sentiments by advocating for a Permanent Commission to attend to their needs on the grounds that such exists in the Niger Delta is quite appalling because there is no basis for comparison between the plight of the FCT indigenous people and their Niger Delta counterparts. At least the government is resettling the FCT indigenes with money from the Niger Delta while nobody has ever mooted the idea of resettling the Niger Deltans from Olobiri and Tebitaba in Bayelsa to Ogoni in Rivers, Otu Jeremi in Delta where Shell has been flaring gas since early sixties and whose lands, environment, ecosystem are under the very devastating effects of aggressive oil exploration and exploitation by the Nigerian government and its multinational allies. The lands in the FCT would not have been worth than a few naira if not for cheap money from the Niger Delta with which the FG and FCDA are pushing their expansion projects. It might also interest you to know that the Commission you are agitating for if eventually established will be solely funded with oil money from the Niger Delta. ..Thank you for drawing the attention of the world to the plight of Abuja original owners.
Biagboron Apoi (email)'

Daily Trust October 25, 2012

CHAPTER 105

The Mandela Example

The recent hospitalization of *Madiba* Nelson Mandela, 94, brings to sharp focus the whole idea that at one point or the other, we all have to face our mortality. Put in very blunt terms, we all will die one day, from causes we may not be able to predict - despite the pretensions of imams, babalawos, pastors, fortune tellers and others who hawk their ability to see what the future holds in stock for us yet are paradoxically unable to use such crystal balls to commune and convince the Infinite to exempt them from the same fate.

Mandela was admitted in a Pretoria hospital (not UK, German or American hospital, mind you),early Saturday morning (June 8 2013) after suffering a recurrence of persistent lung ailment - a legacy of the tuberculosis he contracted during the 27 years he was imprisoned for opposing apartheid. His health has recently been frail, and his latest hospitalization was the fourth in seven months. South African government officials have, until recently, been quite down beat about Mandela's condition, which they described as "serious but stable". Given his age (he turns 95 next month), there are concerns across the world on whether the end is indeed nigh for the living saint.

There are individuals that people wish could be exempted from mortality. Mandela is one such person. Across the world he is deeply revered as one of the greatest living moral voices. In Africa, he is seen as a jewel of inestimable value, a gem from a continent that is often a synonym for all that is negative and backward.

In her Nobel Prize lecture in June 2012 – a lecture that was delayed for nearly two decades because of her incarceration in her country, Burma - Aung San Suu Kyi, the 1991 Nobel Peace Prize winner and Burmese opposition politician, talked about Buddhism's six great *dukhas* (sufferings). The last two of these sufferings according to her are "to be parted from those one loves (and) to be forced to live in propinquity with those one does not love." It can be argued that Nelson Rolihlahla Madiba Mandela, who will turn 95 on July 18 2013, meets these two conditions, which arguably positions one on the path of sainthood.

Mandela's global saintly status has however not exempted him from the cruel joke that life sometimes deals on people. Before he became very famous, his first marriage - to Evelyn Ntoko Mase - unravelled in 1957 after 13 years largely because of the multiple strains of his constant absences, his devotion to revolutionary agitation against the apartheid policies in his country and because she was a Jehovah Witness - a religion that requires one to be politically neutral. Of the four children from that marriage – two boys and two girls – only one Dr Maki (born in 1953 and named after her older sister who died when she was only nine months) still survives. Mandela's first son - Madiba Thembekile (Thembi), who was born in 1946, was killed in a car crash in 1969 at the age of 23 while Mandela was in prison on Robben Island and he was not allowed to attend the funeral. His other son Makgatho died of AIDS in 2005, aged 54.

Mandela's second marriage – to Winnie Madikizela-Mandela - produced two daughters - Zenani (Zeni), born 4 February 1958, and Zindziswa (Zindzi) Mandela-Hlongwane, born 1960. Zindzi was only 18 months old when her father was sent to Robben Island. In 2010 Mandela's great granddaughter Zenani Mandela died in a car crash on her way home after attending the World Cup soccer tournament kick-off in Soweto. She was aged only 13. In 1996, Mandela divorced Winnie after being separated since 1992. On July 18, 1998 Mandela married Graca Simbine Machel, who was previously married to Mozambique's former president, Samora Machel who died in a plane crash on October 19, 1986.

Born on July 18 1918 in Mvezo, a small village located in the district of Umtata, Mandela's father Gadla Henry Mphakanyiswa served as the chief of the town of Mvezo but lost his position after being alienated from the colonial authorities and had to relocate his family to Qunu, where Mandela currently lives. Gadla died of tuberculosis when Mandela was only nine years old. In Khosa, Mandela's name *Rolihlahla* literally means 'to pull a branch off a tree' or more colloquially, a 'troublemaker'.

After attending a Wesleyan mission school located next to the palace of the regent, Mandela began studying for a Bachelor of Arts degree at the Fort Hare University, where he met Oliver Tambo, who was to become his lifelong friend and colleague. At the end of his first year, Mandela became involved in a Students' Representative Council boycott against university policies and was rusticated. However while in prison he studied for a Bachelor of Laws degree from the University of London External Programme. He had, before his imprisonment, while working as an articled clerk at a Johannesburg law firm, Witkin, Sidelsky and Edelman completed a B.A. degree at the University of South Africa via correspondence. He had got the job at the law firm through his friend and mentor Walter Sisulu.

Mandela joined the African National Congress in 1942 and for 20 years was involved in a campaign of peaceful, non-violent defiance against the South African government and its racist policies. With the non-violent methods of the struggle proving largely ineffective, Mandela became increasingly radicalised and co-founded *Umkhonto we Sizwe*, the armed wing of the African National Congress (ANC) (which is translated as Spear *of the Nation*, but famously abbreviated as *MK)*. He was arrested in 1962 and convicted of sabotage and other charges.

Mandela served 27 years in prison, many of these in the notorious Robben Island where he performed hard labour in a lime quarry. As a D-group prisoner (the lowest classification), he was allowed one visitor and one letter every six months. His letters were often delayed for long periods and made unreadable by the prison censors. Amid the hard labour Mandela was offered release several times on the condition that the ANC would renounce violence as an instrument of struggle. On each occasion he turned down the Greek gift.

Following his eventual release from prison on 11 February 1990, Mandela led his party in the negotiations that led to the establishment of democracy in South Africa in1994, with himself as the first President. Though *Madiba* was the President of South Africa from 1994 to 1999, his greatest legacy to the country is in creating a Rainbow nation and being a unifying symbol for the various cleavages in the deeply polarized country. I believe that another gift from Mandela is that his name has become a metaphor for knowing when and how to bow out gracefully when the ovation is loudest. This is unfortunately a lesson that has continued to be lost on most African leaders. Had several African leaders taken a cue from Mandela and bowed out at the right time, they should have been joint partakers in the halo around Mandela and in the global adulation he enjoys. Mandela's life tells us that an enduring legacy is not necessarily determined by how long one stays in office but on the impact one makes.

Mandela is perhaps the only living soul that has a date set aside every year to celebrate him. July 18, Mandela's birthday, is globally celebrated as the Mandela Day. During last year's Mandela Day, the United Nations launched a campaign asking people to mark the day by devoting 67 minutes of their time to helping others - one minute for each year Mandela spent fighting for his cause. The Mandela Day is aimed at to encouraging people to set aside some minutes to consciously do something that will help change the world or their environment for the better.

Frail as he may be today, his place in the pantheon of immortals is definitely assured. But the sharp reminder of the Madiba's mortality following his latest hospitalization raises the question of how and when Nigeria should have its own Mandela.

I have always maintained that the main trouble with Nigeria is the crisis in the country's nation-building project, which conflates with the challenges of underdevelopment to create an existentialist crisis for several Nigerians. The latter in turn triggers a de-Nigerianization process as individuals and groups retreat from the Nigeria project into primordial identities where they seek meaning for their lives, often regarding the Nigerian state as an enemy of sorts. Following from this, my kind of President for the country is not necessarily one that is incorruptible or one with the best programme for economic development for the country but simply a leader capable of unifying a fractious nation. I believe that it is only through this that the stalled nation-building process can be re-started. I also believe that since government is a continuous process, once the nation-building process is put back on track, we can come to another era where we will need a leader with a different set of skills.

Daily Trust June 13 2013

CHAPTER 106

Manipulators of Public Perception: Between Olisa Metuh and Lai Mohammed

There are lots of similarities between Olisa Metuh and Alhaji Lai Mohammed. Besides being the Publicity Secretary of PDP and APC respectively, both are lawyers and have had a long standing relationship with their parties.

Metu who was called to the bar in 1988, contested and won election as an Ex-Officio member of the PDP's National Executive Committee (NEC) in 1999 during the party's first National Convention. Being one of the youngest officers to be elected into the party's highest ruling organ, he was subsequently made the first Youth Leader of the party for the Southeast zone. Since 1999, Metu has worked in different capacities in the party and was in 2008 elected as the National Vice Chairman of the Party for Southeast zone and later became PDP's Publicity Secretary.

Alhaji Lai Mohammed, a lawyer and co-founded the law firm, Edu & Mohammed, has been a Director of Afromedia PLC since May 2011. He is also a fellow of the Nigerian Institute of Public Relations (NIPR). He worked as a Public Relations Officer for almost 10 years with the Nigerian Airports Authority, now Federal Airport Authority of Nigeria (FAAN). Lai Mohamed, a writer in his own rights, was Chief of Staff to Bola Tinubu when he was Governor of Lagos State. He resigned to contest for the Governorship election in Kwara State but was unsuccessful. He later emerged as the Publicity Secretary of the defunct Action Congress of Nigeria – one of the parties that merged to form the APC. Lai Mohammed is currently the APC's Interim Publicity Secretary.

Both now and when he did the job for A.C.N, Lai Mohammed was seen as an enfant terrible, taking the fight all the time to the PDP while defending his party with a combination of logic, filibustering and slanted truths. For instance when about 185 people were killed in Baga, Bornu State, by terrorists suspected to be Boko Haram members in April 2013, Lai Mohammed said the killing could constitute crimes against humanity which deserved to attract the attention of the International Criminal Court (ICC) and that the federal government could be culpable for being unwilling or unable to prosecute those involved. To say that Lai Mohammed has been a thorn in the flesh of both PDP and the federal government is to be charitable with words.

Until he became his party's publicity secretary Metuh was not known in the journalistic or literary world. He came into his current job as PDP's Publicity Secretary with a particular predilection for bombastic rhetoric that was for the most part ineffective. His profile shot up recently when he dismissed the manifesto unveiled early this month by the All Progressives Congress (APC), as a product of 'Janjaweed ideology'. "When last year in its first official outing, the leaders of the APC said terrorism in Nigeria would disappear within 100days of APC leadership, Nigerians did ask if they knew the characters in crime and their sponsors, APC gave silence as an answer while Nigerians kept wondering.", Metu was quoted as saying. Though Janjaweed is used to refer to the militia groups that operate in Darfur, Western Sudan, and eastern Chad, it was obvious Metu wanted an- easy- to remember onomatopoeic word that could be used to tie APC to Boko Haram.

It should be borne in mind that propaganda - the deliberate spreading of information, ideas, or rumors in an effort to either help or harm a person, group, movement, institution, or nation – is the kernel of party politics and often the central job description of a party's Publicity Secretary. Propaganda is usually associated with lies or half-truths – though this is not always the case. In fact, some of the most successful propagandas are based on the truth, though that truth may be hidden behind the propagandist's particular slant or style of delivery.

If a propagandist is someone who makes a living attempting to persuade others to their cause, perspective or perceptions and refuses to consider contrary perspectives or viewpoints as valid or worthy of consideration, then both Metuh and Lai Mohamed qualify as propagandists.

With the race for 2015 already in full swing, we have to pay special attention to these two propagandists and their strategies: How have they sought to market their parties? How do they define their rivals? And what are their strategies for damage control?

Defining their Opponents: Campaigns usually try to aggressively negatively define their opponents through the use of simple words, phrases or imageries in a bid to put them on the defensive. For instance during the 2008 presidential campaigns in the USA, Obama constantly reminded voters that a vote for his then rival, John McCain, would be 'four more years' for the then hugely unpopular George W Bush. Again when Jonathan was seeking the PDP's presidential party nomination in 2010, his strategists tried to define his opponent Atiku Abubakar by almost always wrapping 'corruption' or 'desperate for power' in most messages they sent out about him, hoping that the labels would stick. Atiku strategists themselves sought to wrap their criticisms of Jonathan and his policies in such labels as 'incompetence' or 'not to be trusted.'

When therefore Metuh called APC's manifesto a product of Janjaweed ideology, he was trying to create a Soyinkarist imagery of a party which would conjure in people's imaginations the imageries of Boko Haram and the horrors of death the name evokes in popular imagination. Here Metu was borrowing from the politics of language where the creation of scaremongering imagery could be used to prevent people from identifying with a particular party or label. For instance to accuse a regime of possessing Weapons of Mass Destruction – as George W Bush accused the late Saddam Hussein – would conjure in people's imagination imageries of impending Armageddon.

But has Metuh's imagery gone too far? If Nigerians believe that the Janjaweed imagery was merely an association with insurgents, not Muslims, and if PDP could make the label stick, it could hurt the APC. However, if Muslims see the attempt to create an association between APC and Boko Haram as a slight on them by innuendo, it could alienate some Muslim supporters of the party. Metuh's labeling could therefore cut both ways.

How do the parties define themselves? Another area we should pay attention is how the parties define themselves. For instance from the time he formally declared his interest in the 2011 presidential race, the Goodluck Ebele Jonathan (GEJ) Campaign built the thrust of its political marketing on a 'moving train' narrative - basically that everyone was queuing up to join its bandwagon. It constantly rolled out a wave of endorsements, some apparently contrived, to support this story line. Jonathan was also marketed as being divinely ordained to rule - and therefore likely bring good luck to Nigerians, if elected.

Ahead of 2015, PDP has made feeble attempts to define itself as the only party that is truly national and does not rely on the charisma of one or two founders. It seems however to have abandoned this narrative since APC became a national party, and with that a new swagger.

When five disaffected PDP governors in the defunct New PDP decamped to the APC, there was a feeble attempt by Lai Mohamed and others in the party to create the 'moving train' narrative for APC – that is, that there was a stampede to join the party. That narrative however seems to have been abandoned since Bamangar Tukur stepped aside as the party's national chairman. PDP also tried to contrive defections from APC to the party to show that the APC's moving train was just driving on false wheels. In essence, it is still not clear what the two parties stand for or how they define themselves – apart from the desire to remain in power or unseat the other.

Exploiting gaffes: For instance the GEJ Campaign in 2011 in exploited a statement made by Atiku during a stakeholders' conference on December 15, 2010 where he quoted Frantz Fanon's warning that those who make peaceful change impossible make violent change inevitable. The Jonathan Campaign deliberately omitted the part of the speech where Atiku said that such a violent change was not what the country needed at that time, and instead twisted the message to imply that he was preaching violence.

We have seen both Metuh and Lai Mohamed twist and take statements out of context in attempt to put the other on the defensive and gain political mileage. Metu did this in trying to tie APC to Boko Haram. In turn a spokesman for Buhari reminded Metu that the former NSA, Late Gen Andrew Azazi, was unequivocal in his assertion that the power play in the PDP was a major reason for the Boko Haram insurgency. They also reminded him that a confessional statement to the SS by one of the PDP stalwarts that the contact with Boko Haram was with the imprimatur of the VP Namadi Sambo!

Damage Control: In campaigns, mistakes are inevitable just as embarrassing documents docking up are always a given. Most campaigns have damage control strategies for such eventualities. We have to closely watch APC damage control strategies for some of the crises and violence that have gripped the party in the South

447

West. We also have to closely monitor how Olisa Metuh controls the damage done by Sanusi's allegations of missing $20bn oil money and attempts to label the Jonathan administration as corruption-friendly.

Daily Trust, March 27, 2014

CHAPTER 107

The re-invention of Goodluck Jonathan

Something is happening imperceptibly to our President, Goodluck Ebele Jonathan (GEJ). Shortly after he assembled a new cabinet following the April 2011 general elections, it seems there has been a gradual but deliberate abandonment of the public persona which GEJ used to good effect when, as Vice President, a cabal within the presidency sought to prevent him from being sworn in as the Acting President. GEJ's pre-April 2011 persona was that of a gentle, if diffident man, who would readily give a sympathetic ear to any argument and does not mind changing his mind several times on the same issue. This persona ironically made him come across to many people as a very humble and unassuming gentleman, who saw the office of president as a burden bestowed on him by destiny, which he was struggling with difficulty to carry, and relying on his name of 'Goodluck' to help him carry it. I believe this persona of an uncomplicated guy- next- door who was in dire need of protection from the more sophisticated Goliaths in the political arena, was a key reason why many people during the PDP's presidential primaries and the April 2011 elections axiomatically declared him a good man, a sort of a biblical David chosen by God to take the country forward at this moment in our political history. It would also seem that for most of the Governors, GEJ's special appeal during this period was the same public persona of a diffident and malleable man who could be easily swayed. That type of person, they must have reasoned, was someone they could do business with because they could always convince him with a 'superior argument' rather than Atiku, who could be too 'politically smart' to be swayed or Buhari who could remove the immunity clause in the constitution and herd as many of them as possible into jail for any infraction.

GEJ's pre-April 2011 public persona was solidified with his rather touching story of how he grew up and went to school without shoes. That public persona resonated well with many ordinary Nigerians making it extremely difficult for the proponents of zoning to turn him into an odious figure. In fact, my belief is that were GEJ a little more self-assured or strongly opinioned on anything during the hotly contested PDP presidential primaries it would have been much easier to demonise him and the zoning argument would perhaps have achieved a different outcome.

I believe the abandonment of GEJ's pre-April 2011 public persona became pronounced during the Justice Salami-Justice Katsina Alu saga. It will be recalled that in August 2011 the Nigerian Judicial Council suspended Justice Ayo Salami from office with immediate effect following his alleged disregard of the Council's directive to tender apologies to the NJC and to the then Chief Justice of Nigeria (CJN), Justice Aloysius Katsina-Alu, with whom he had been involved in an altercation bordering on allegations of corruption and influencing election tribunal proceedings. The NJC had recommended the compulsory retirement of Justice Salami for misconduct. Despite the hoopla in the media against the NJC's decision, the 'normally' indecisive President acted decisively, quickly accepted the recommendation of the NJC and refused to bulge despite the media campaign.

There was equally the case of the President's proposal for a- single term tenure for the President and Governors. Just when everyone thought he had quietly allowed the idea to die a natural death in the face of an overwhelming popular opposition, the President later declared that the idea was still alive and that contrary to media reports that the single term tenure proposal was for six years, it was actually for seven! He has stuck to his gun on the issue, insisting that the opponents of the idea had misunderstood his intentions.

The government's proposal for the removal of subsidies on petroleum products has followed the same emerging trend. Rather than recoil from a fight as people feel the pre-April 2011 GEJ would do, he has stuck to his gun, feeding into the impression that he is now being re-invented as a man of conviction, who will hold onto his belief, no matter the level of opposition. The emerging new GEJ, who will quietly but firmly defy pressures, reached a crescendo during the just concluded PDP gubernatorial primaries in Bayelsa State, the President's home State.

Though the PDP has continued to deny it, the general belief is that GEJ is behind the decision to disqualify Sylva Timipre from contesting for the PDP gubernatorial primaries because of his alleged political sin of campaigning against his being made the Acting President when the late Yaradua had become very ill and a cabal within his government held the country hostage. The significant thing here however is not that the President was opposed to Timipre's candidacy but that he remained adamant in his opposition despite the reported interventions of the South South Governors, the Governors' Forum and other eminent Nigerians that reportedly included former President Shehu Shagari and former Head of State Yakubu Gowon. Also though there was a court order (or 'motion on notice', depending on which side you are in the confusion), the PDP went ahead to hold the nomination – despite popular anger that the party was flouting a court order. The new GEJ, as if to damn the pressures, quickly congratulated the party for doing a 'good job' of conducting the primaries.

The new GEJ also showed in the way Mrs Farida Waziri was sacked as the Chairman of the EFCC. The issue here is not just the sacking but the manner in which it was done decisively. He sacked her just before he left for France, ensuring that the news would still be 'hot' in the media by the time he would be meeting with his French hosts. The art of 'making a statement' by finding a major scapegoat in the anti-corruption war just before a foreign trip was perfected by the wily Obasanjo who would often use such to demonstrate to his foreign audience that his regime was serious in fighting corruption in the country.

I believe the putative re-invention of the President holds opportunities and threats both for the country and for President GEJ himself. On the positive side, the persona with which he won the PDP primaries and the subsequent general election can hardly be counted upon to take the necessary tough decisions that will transform this country. Leadership is rarely a popularity contest so a more decisive President, who is not afraid to give rewards or sanctions, is what the country needs. If the new decisive

GEJ is able to bring immediate improvement in the economic circumstances of ordinary Nigerians, the re-invention will be deemed successful. If however nothing changes on the economic front, the new decisiveness will be perceived as emerging traits of dictatorship. Again, there is a risk that in a bid to show that a new tough guy has emerged, the President may fail to realise when his decisions or policy options are truly contrary to popular will. And with so many of his current decisions such as the single term tenure proposal and plans to remove petroleum subsidies being unpopular (at least in the short term), there could be a legitimacy crisis, especially if the implementation of these policies do not lead to an immediate improvement in the material circumstances of ordinary Nigerians. There is a further risk that a re-invented GEJ, seeing that he is able to get away with one tough decision after another, may misread the situation and react in ways that may lead to reversals in our democratic gains. There is equally a possibility that if Sylva Timipre contests and wins the Governorship election in Bayelsa State under another party's banner, the 'fear' of being an 'ordinary' citizen when Timipre will still be Governor, could affect the reported decision of GEJ to leave office in 2015. The re-invented GEJ also means losing the innocence that was part of his political capital before and during the April 2011 elections, making it much easier to turn him into a hate figure for counter mobilisation if he decides to contest in 2015.

However this re-invention of GEJ turns out for the country, what is clear is that the President seems to have become more comfortable with the exalted office he occupies. And that too has both its merits and flipsides – for GEJ and for the country.

Daily Trust December 1, 2011

CHAPTER 108

The re-invention of Goodluck Jonathan (2)

When I published the 'Re-invention of Goodluck Jonathan' in this column on December 1 2011, I did not plan to write a sequel to it. Let me give a brief summary of this re-invention as captured in what is now the first instalment of this piece.

Shortly after President Goodluck Ebele Jonathan (GEJ) assembled a new cabinet following the April 2011 general elections, there appeared to be a gradual but deliberate abandonment of the public persona which had helped to galvanize public sympathy and support for him when a cabal in the late Yaradua presidency sought to prevent him from being sworn in as the Acting President following Yaradua's terminal illness. GEJ's pre-April 2011 persona was that of a gentle, if diffident man, who would readily give a sympathetic ear to any argument and does not mind changing his mind several times on the same issue. During the last presidential elections this persona made it very difficult for his opponents to demonize him or turn him into a hate figure. GEJ's rather touching story of how he grew up and went to school without shoes helped to solidify this persona in the popular imagination.

The efforts to re-invent GEJ as a man of conviction became very perceptible during the Justice Ayo Salami and Justice Katsina Alu saga following the suspension of the former by the Nigerian Judicial Council in August 2011. The NJC had recommended the compulsory retirement of Justice Salami for misconduct. Despite the hoopla in the media against the NJC's decision, the 'normally' indecisive GEJ acted decisively, quickly accepted the recommendation of the NJC and refused to bulge despite the media campaign.

The government's proposal for the removal of subsidies on petroleum products followed the same trend. Rather than recoil from a fight as people felt the pre-April 2011 GEJ would do, he stuck to his gun, and eventually ambushed Nigerians on January 1with the announcement that subsidies had been removed.

Perhaps the clearest indication that the presidency wanted to re-invent GEJ as a man of cool exterior but granite interior was in the disqualification of former Governor Sylva Timipre from contesting the last gubernatorial election in Bayelsa State. The President was suspected of having a hand in the disqualification. The significant thing here however is not that the President was opposed to Timipre's candidacy but that he remained adamant in his opposition despite the reported interventions of the South-south Governors, the Governors' Forum and other eminent Nigerians that reportedly included former President Shehu Shagari and former Head of State Yakubu Gowon.

In what is now the first instalment of this piece, I noted that the re-invention of GEJ could have both positive and negative sides. One of the negatives, I underlined, is the risk that "in a bid to show that a new tough guy has emerged, the President may fail to realise when his decisions or policy options are truly contrary to popular will."

Latest events may seem to suggest we may be getting close to this threshold. Let me explain:

It is true that leadership is not a popularity contest and that leaders necessarily have to make tough decisions. However the difference between a dictator and a visionary leader in a democracy is the manner in which they make such tough decisions and their timing. Many leaders that take tough decisions in a democracy often do so by trying to win the argument or at least bidding their time until opinions seem to be evenly divided on the issue. For the handlers of the President it would seem that they prefer to do very little at the argumentation stage only to strike after opinions seem to be coalescing towards a consensus against the presidential preference. It is immaterial whether this consensus is driven by rabble rousers or opponents of the President. The issue is that if you want to stop the rabble rousers, you meet them argument for argument and prevent them from mobilising popular opinion behind their own preference. If you lose it at this stage and then use presidential fiat to take a decision that will appear to be against the popular will you unwittingly enlarge the army of your critics. Instances of the presidency doing very little at to be competitive at the argumentation stage only to wield the presidential hammer are legion:

There was first the issue of removing subsidies on premium petroleum products. Though recent events would indicate the presidency was probably right in its decision to completely remove the subsidies (the fuel subsidy cabal seems to be far more powerful than ordinary Nigerians realized), the manner in which this was done left a sour taste in the mouth. The decision was taken when the anti-desubsidisation lobby was clearly winning the debate and the presidency had given an impression that it had not made up its mind on the issue and was still consulting. But just on the first day of the year, it struck like a viper.

There was also the manner in which Arunmah Oteh, the Director General of the Securities and Exchange who was suspended by the Board of the SEC was recalled by the Government even when the House of Representatives' ad hoc committee on the near collapse of the Capital Markets had concluded that she was not qualified to be appointed the DG of SEC. The Committee claimed that the Act setting up SEC states that the DG must have at least 15 years cognate experience in capital market operations and that Ms. Oteh did not meet this demand at the time she was appointed.

The way the regime quickly approved the proposal by the CBN to introduce a N5000 note when the opposition to the initiative was at its peak also seemed to be daring the public to do its worst. The issue is not whether the regime is right or wrong in its decision but that it could have done far more at the argumentation stage before weighing in on the side of the CBN. It could at least have set up a committee (its favourite pastime) to examine the proposal – to give the impression that it had broadened consultations before embracing its preferred course of action.

Having a Presidential Rottweiler is never a substitute to being competitive at the argumentation stage. In fact such an attack dog could complicate matters as Dr Doyin Okupe, the Senior Special Adviser to the President on Public Affairs appeared to have done recently, when, in response to Obasanjo's reported opposition to the proposed N5000 bill he was quoted as retorting that "Obasanjo is an ordinary citizen" and that his "views are not sacrosanct." While it is possible that Dr Okupe misspoke (after all English is not our mother tongue), the way his response came out seemed like an affront. And as everyone knows, Obasanjo neither overlooks a slight nor ducks a fight. For someone who has made a career of helping to pull down several governments, including the ones he helped to engineer by being their acerbic critic, wisdom would have cautioned that if you cannot have him as a friend of the regime at least try not to push him to the camp of the regime's opponents.

The emerging new political machismo in a re-invented GEJ could lead to other costly mistakes. One such may be the recent sacking of the Power Minister, Professor Barth Nnaji for alleged 'conflict of interest' – at a time many Nigerians are beginning to say there have been improvements in power supply in the country. I am not by this condoning 'conflict of interest' by public officials - though when stretched virtually all top political officials are guilty of the same charge because 'conflict of interest' also includes favouring one's community and cronies in the authoritative allocation of societal privileges. Is there really any top political office holder in this country who is not guilty of this?

I would have thought that for a man who seems to be succeeding where all his predecessors have failed, a public rebuke of any malfeasance would have been sufficient so that whatever achievement that is being recorded in this highly technical area is not frittered away. In football, some of the most talented players often have behaviour deficits which are often accommodated or managed because of their perceived critical role in their team's success.

In his novel *Things Fall Apart* (1958), Chinua Achebe told of the Okonkwo character, a man whose palm kernels were cracked by benevolent spirits but who, for fear of being thought weak, self-destructs through some reckless decisions. I really hope that the handlers of GEJ will avoid the 'Okonkwo complex'.

The new GEJ means that if the President wants to contest in 2015 – as his body language seems to suggest he will do - the persona of a gentle, unassuming and humble man which has been a tremendous asset in his political career will come under intense scrutiny and contestation.

Daily Trust, 13 September 2012

CHAPTER 109

The re-invention of Goodluck Jonathan (3)

The first instalment in these series was published on 1 December 2011 while the second instalment was on 13 September 2012. In these series, which will not run consecutively, I will try to monitor the putative re-inventions of Goodluck Ebele Jonathan (GEJ) and the consequent transformations in his style and public persona.

In the first instalment I noted the effort to re-invent him as a man who could take tough decisions and stick to his guns. This was against his pre-April 2011 public persona, which was of a gentle, if diffident guy, who gives sympathetic ears to all arguments and does not mind changing his mind several times on an issue. This persona of the guy next door has been a great asset in GEJ's meteoric political rise. I will call the effort to re-invent him as a man of conviction who can take tough decisions as the First Wave of his re-invention.

In the second instalment I observed that the re-invented GEJ seemed to be enjoying the new image of a 'tough guy' and with time appeared to revel in taking contrarian decisions when opinions seem to have coalesced in a different direction on a probable belief that such would enhance his new image. I will call this the Second Wave of his re-invention. The persona in this Second Wave inevitably attracted an army of critics forcing the President to hyperbolically declare himself as the most criticised President in the world. With the House of Representatives dangling the impeachment axe and the Senate indicating it might concur with the Lower Chamber, the President knew something must give in. These seem to have spurred the Third Wave of his re-invention. I will explain.

In the Third Wave we see GEJ soft-pedalling on some 'tough' decisions – in a manner reminiscent of GEJ before the First Wave of re-invention. First, his tough stance on the single term tenure proposal, which he insisted there was no going back on, was surreptitiously leaked as having been shelved. Then came the backing down on the proposed N5, 000 bill apparently without first informing its author Sanusi– after the Presidency had thrown its backing behind the proposal at the crest of popular opposition to it. Though I find most of the arguments against the N5000 bill unconvincing (I have never by the way been a supporter of Sanusi's methods), the timing of the presidency's support was symptomatic of GEJ's way of doing things in the Second Wave of his re-invention. In what can be regarded as a reinforcement of this putative Third Wave of re-invention, the ThisDay of 24 September 2012 reported that President GEJ may give in to pressure from the National Assembly for the sack of the Director General, Securities and Exchange Commission (SEC), Ms. Arunma Oteh, and the Chairman of the Pensions Task Team, Mr. Abdulrasheed Maina.

It will be recalled that the Presidency had recalled Arunmah Oteh as DG of SEC after being suspended by its Board and had even unethically allowed her to attend meetings of the Economic Management Team while in suspension. She was also recalled despite a resolution by the House of Representatives on 19 July 2012 requesting Jonathan to remove her from office. The point here is not whether the House was right in asking for her sack but the 'I don't give a damn' manner in which the presidency handled the issue, which was reminiscent of GEJ in the Second Wave of his re-invention.

Several observations could be made about the various efforts to re-invent GEJ:

One, GEJ's pre April 2011 persona of a humble, diffident and unassuming guy– which I suspect to be closer to the real GEJ – had been an asset in his political career only because he started with being the Deputy Governor of Bayelsa State and later Vice President of the country. It is the sort of a 'weak' persona politicians in frontline positions normally want as their deputies. However while such personas could be good in playing second fiddles, they cannot survive in political frontline positions where tough decisions necessarily have to be taken. In other words, a re-invention of GEJ was inevitable and would have been done anyway if he had stayed long enough as the Governor of Bayelsa State. My suspicion is that we will still see more efforts at re-inventing GEJ as he seeks to find a comfort zone between his pre-April 2011persona and the persona of a President who has to take tough decisions.

Two, when President GEJ declared that "I am not David…I am not a General.…I am not a lion…." my reading of that statement was that he was indicating a resolve to succeed despite his simplicity and unassuming persona. GEJ had also promised to be a 'breath of fresh air'. Essentially, my reading of a combination of both declarations was that like the musician Frank Sinatra, the President was declaring that he would do it his own way. However rather than being loyal to these declarations, the impression one gets is that he has been doing it the way of others or has not really found a political persona that he is truly comfortable with.

Take the proposal about the N5000 bill for example. The impression one gets is that President GEJ seems to have been carried away by the CBN Governor's undoubted facility with English language. In both the fuel subsidy issue and the Arunma Oteh saga, one suspects the 'stubborn' persona of Dr Ngozi Iweala, the Co-ordinating Minister of the Economy, as the invisible hand of Esau. A key challenge in the re-invention of GEJ therefore is how to 'own' certain tough decisions and 'domesticate' their marketing to fit into his own persona. 'Owning' policies means becoming truly convinced about such policies – and not to embrace them simply because they are propounded by Cabinet members who speak eloquent English language or have 'intimidating' résumés. Because some policies that flow from the presidency do not seem to be sufficiently owned by GEJ, they are often marketed using the personas of their authors rather than that of the President who should give political covers to his Ministers and aides. Consequently when such policies are pilloried, they become vulnerable to reversals because the President simply does not strongly and passionately believe in them. Under Obasanjo for instance, no one is in doubt who is in charge because the impression is that he 'owns' approved policies from his Ministers and aides and then uses his rambunctious persona to market them. Under GEJ, where a few in his Cabinet behave like philosopher kings, it is sometimes difficult to know who is in charge, making it difficult for GEJ to use his own persona to market his political options.

Three, it is possible for GEJ to put to good effect his declaration that "I am not David....I am not a general.....I am not a lion......I will defeat the Goliaths in our land" and succeed. He has already done so with INEC simply by being himself and by apparently not interfering. Much of the credit for the improvement in the conduct of our elections should actually go to GEJ because the body language of the President of the country will always determine how independent INEC or any other body in the country can be. Though GEJ is not sufficiently credited with the successes in this area, the fact is that the success came because he seems to believe in INEC's neutrality and therefore does not need to prove any toughness. You do not need to beat the drumbeat of toughness to be seen as tough. It is tough to see your party routed in an election and still congratulate the person who mauled the candidate you openly supported. This is the sort of toughness that the handlers of GEJ may want to reflect on rather than the toughness exhibited in some decisions in the Second wave of his re-invention. It is also the sort of toughness that may seem to be more in tune with the pre-April 2011 persona of GEJ.

Four, as GEJ continues to evolve politically as President, one obvious urgent area is patching his soured relationship with the National Assembly. Owing to tendencies in the Second Wave of his re-invention, the House of Representatives has threatened him with impeachment and it is ominous that in the Senate it was Senator Uche Chukwumerije, from Aba, who volunteered to lead the impeachment move in the Upper Chamber – if need be - against him. Apart from the South-south, the South-east was GEJ's strongest base of support in the last presidential elections.

Five, a key question is the motive in the putative Third Wave re-invention of GEJ: Is it because of fear of impeachment or because GEJ has become truly worried about the avalanche of criticisms that now trail his political options in the Second Wave of his re-invention? Could it be a desire to return to his pre-April 2011 persona, which had served him well in his political career - as 2015 approaches?

Daily Trust September 27, 2012

CHAPTER 110

Between Strongmen and Strong Institutions

"Across Africa, we've seen countless examples of people taking control of their destiny, and making change from the bottom up.... History is on the side of these brave Africans, not with those who use coups or change constitutions to stay in power. Africa doesn't need strongmen, it needs strong institutions." These were part of the remarks by Barrack Obama, President of the United States, on 11 July 2009 to the Ghanaian Parliament at the Accra International Conference Centre, Accra, Ghana. Some months earlier Obama had been elected the first 'Black' President of the United States of America in an epochal election that carried emotional resonance in many parts of the world, especially Africa. Since then the phrase 'Africa needs strong institutions, not strongmen' has become a sort of mantra among politicians and other commentators on public affairs. Obama was of course not the originator of the phrase. He merely popularized it among non-social scientists. But what do people really mean when they brandish this new mantra?

Like most concepts in the social sciences, there is no consensus on what 'institution' means. What is easily discernible when people brandish the new mantra is the tendency to equate 'institutions' with structures, organisations or public bodies such as the civil service, the police, the parliament and contraptions that fight corruption like the EFCC. This manner of understanding 'institutions' is at best only partially correct because institutions are also rules, conventions, ethos that have endured over time. Even individuals, to the extent that they purvey a certain brand, which is consistent over time, can also be called institutions. I think this is what the late KO Mbadiwe had in mind when he talked grandiloquently about 'men of timbre and calibre, caterpillar institution and juggernaut'.

Institutions are crucial in any system because they help to structure social interaction, allowing for predictability or stable expectations by imposing form and consistency on human activities. For instance an electoral law which fixes election into public offices every four years and which requires those defeated to bow out honourably means that such law, if it has been observed for a sufficiently long period of time, has become 'institutionalized'. This is another way of saying that the law has been so consistently observed that it has become rule through habituation.

It is important here to make a distinction between 'laws' and 'rules'. For laws to become rules, they have to become customary and habituated over a relatively long period of time. There are several laws in every country which are ignored, meaning that such laws have not acquired the status of rules or that they have not been consistently observed over a period of time for them to be regarded as customary. In other words such laws have not become 'institutionalized'.

Another important thing to mention here is that 'institutions' both constrain and enable behaviour. For instance traffic rules, where they are consistently observed over a long period of time could be regarded as being 'institutionalized'. Such rules could constrain behaviour because they will for instance prevent a driver from driving over a red light – even if the driver is running late for an appointment with the President. The same rule that constrains the behaviour of the driver however overall enables traffic to flow more easily.

Many people believe that our electoral system has improved under Attahiru Jega's INEC. Does it mean that the system of organizing fairly transparent election has become 'institutionalized'? The answer is 'no' because for now it is not clear whether the improvement in the conduct of elections (compared to what was obtainable under Maurice Iwu) was because of the integrity of Professor Jega or because the body language of President Jonathan does not so far suggest that he sees elections as a 'do or die' affair. For us to say that we now have an effective institution for conducting elections will mean that the observance of the electoral law has become so habituated that irrespective of who is the INEC chairman or the President of the country, the expectations and outcomes will remain pretty much the same. In this sense, even if you have someone of less than average intelligence as INEC chairman or a rambunctious President, it will not make much difference because the laws have become so institutionalized that they will be obeyed.

Since I have argued that institutions are not just mere structures or public agencies as they too often are misconceived to be, the next logical question is how do we create 'institutions – public bodies whose rules are observed as a matter of habit and not just because of the fear of sanction? It is obvious from the above discussions that building institutions is not just the work of the leadership or a 'strongman' but also of the willingness of the citizens to consistently obey the law or to habituate the observance of a particular set of rules.

Chinua Achebe in his slim booklet, *The Trouble With Nigeria*, believes that the trouble with Nigeria is 'squarely that of leadership'. For him if we get the right type of leadership, such a leader will be able to make the citizens form the habit of observing rules, laws and regulations. Others will argue that the problem with Nigeria is 'systemic' rather than leadership, meaning that they believe that there are dynamics in the larger Nigerian environment that pose obstacles to the observance of rules and which often swallow good men and women who try to change too quickly the way the system works. Some of those hurdles in the larger environment could be the manipulation of ethnicity, religion and other primordial identities by the elites.

So do Nigerians need 'strongmen' or strong institutions? Some definitions here will not be out of place. I believe that many of those who brandish the new mantra of 'Africa do not need strong men but strong institutions', will not like to be drawn into the conceptual issue of what they mean by 'strongmen'. But we cannot make much progress unless we know precisely what they mean. If by 'strongmen' they mean leaders, who are firm, just and act out of conviction, then it is obvious that Africa certainly needs such people just as it needs good citizens who privilege the nation over their other identities. 'Strongmen' can also be used to describe people in leadership positions who are narcissistic about the positions they occupy and like to throw their weight around or want everyone to fear them. Certainly Africa can do without such people as they try to habituate the process of rule observance or institution-building. My feeling is that most of the people who brandish the new mantra of mistake charismatic individuals or autocrats with 'strongmen'. While the autocrat thrives on cowing the citizens and wants to be feared, charismatic leaders draw people to themselves because of the personal magnetism they possess. One of the major pitfalls of charismatic leadership however is that it is inherently unstable because loyalty is given to a person and not to any known institution. Therefore while charismatic leadership could be useful in some circumstances, it often creates problems of routinization and institutionalization of behavior. In other words, we cannot rely on charismatic leaders to build effective institutions for us. So what is the way out?

My personal opinion is that building effective institutions in the country will be difficult under the current climate of crisis in the country's nation-building. I have always believed that the key problem of the country is not economic underdevelopment, but politics. Unless we can resolve the crisis in our nation-building so that people will start privileging their Nigerian identity over the mosaic of other identities that they bear, I don't think that there will be sustained observance of the laws governing public bodies because there is no strong, emotive attachment to such bodies in the first place. Rather because virtually everyone and every ethnic nationality has one grouse or the other against the Nigerian State and its organs, there is an institutionalized memory of hurt in which the Nigerian state is the enemy. Everyone attacks the state and its organs with whatever instrument he or she can muster: those entrusted to guard the country's common patrimony steal it blind; law enforcement officers look the other way at the offer of a little inducement, students riot and cheat in examinations, organized labour, including University lecturers go on prolonged strikes on a whim while government workers drag their feet and refuse to give their best. The sum total of all this is a massive de-Nigerianization process, as people retreat into their primordial identities. Nigeria is at the risk of being a country without Nigerians.

In my opinion, the first step to building effective institutions is to create true Nigerians. And you cannot create Nigerians without resolving the crisis in our nation-building process. The country needs a strong leader, a father figure in the mould of the late Nyerere of Tanzania or Mandela who can command legitimacy across the main fault lines to begin the process of rebuilding trust among the constituent parts of the country.

Daily Trust March 7, 2013

CHAPTER 111

Atiku: Beyond the Call for Restructuring Nigeria

The recent call by Alhaji Atiku Abubakar for Nigeria to be restructured seems to have struck a chord with many Nigerians. If anything the call by the former Vice President has re-ignited our ceaseless conversations on what some people often euphemistically call the 'National Question'. There are four possible reasons why Atiku's call is receiving very positive media review.

One, it is generally believed that the former Vice President does not talk glibly, and that most likely, he must have commissioned several experts to study the issue before taking a position on it. For many people therefore, Atiku's call merits revisiting the arguments on both sides of the divide, especially the arguments of the proponent of restructuring.

Two, as one of the most urbane and cosmopolitan Nigerians, Atiku's voice comes without the sort of suspected regional agenda usually associated with the opponents and proponents of the idea. While advocates of restructuring from the southern part of the country are often suspected of planning to use it to weaken the North or even dismember the country, the Northern oppositionists are often suspected of opposing restructuring because they want to protect their privileges under the current configuration.

Three, related to the above is that for a prominent Northern politician who is a member of the ruling APC government to advocate for restructuring at this time would suggest a putative shift in the position of the North on restructuring. As Atiku pointed out at the launching of Chido Onumah's book, *We are All Biafrans* where he made the call for restructuring: "Our current structure and the practices it has encouraged have been a major impediment to economic and political development of our country. In short it has not served Nigeria well, and at the risk of reproach, it has not served my part of the country, the North well".

Four, as the economy continues to tank, challenges to the state are expected to grow. And if the Nigerian state follows a classic pattern, the state is expected to become more repressive in response, narrowing the democratic space and paradoxically also widening both the scope of the forces challenging it and the aggression with which they do so. The pervasive sense of foreboding in the land appears to have ignited a fervent search for options to avoid such a doomsday scenario. There appears to be consensus that Nigeria under the current configuration is either not working at all or working very sub optimally.

While Atiku is right in calling for Nigeria to be restructured, I believe that before 'restructuring' becomes the new mantra, we should be mindful of the fact that the term is loaded and therefore needs to be unpacked or defined because different people have different things in mind when they talk of restructuring – as they do when they talk of 'Resource Control' or National Conference. Depending on the speaker, restructuring could mean anything from minor constitutional amendments to greater devolution of powers to states and local governments. It could also mean a reconstitution of the country such that the six geopolitical zones will replace the current state system. The ambiguity over what we precisely mean by 'restructuring' has been one of the reasons why the term excites some anxieties and concerns among those opposed to it – even though technically speaking restructuring has been taking place throughout our political history such as when we change the formula for revenue allocation among the three tiers of government. Some have sought to complicate the conceptual ambiguity over the word 'restructuring' by advocating for 'true federalism' – when in fact there is nothing like that concept. The truth is that every federation is unique.

Related to the ambiguity over the meaning of 'restructuring' is also the ambiguity over the meaning of 'Nigerian unity', which opponents of restructuring historically use as a weapon in their opposition of the term. Is Nigerian unity the same as stasis? Is it right to argue that anyone who complains against the current structure is against Nigerian unity?

I will align myself with Reuben Abati's choice of concepts in his article 'Atiku is right, Nigeria Needs to be restructured' published recently on several online platforms. Abati used concepts like 'reset', 'redesign' and 're-thinking' in his description of a version of what others would call 'restructuring'. And talking of old and new concepts, I will also align myself with Professors Okey Ibeanu and Mohammed Kuna in a forthcoming book they edited on Nigerian federalism where they expressed a preference for the term 'federative units' rather than 'federating units'. According to them, the term 'federating units' wrongly suggests that these units (states and local governments) joined in creating the Nigerian federation in the classical sense of the term while the adjective 'federative units' will correctly capture the fact that these are the current units of the federation but not the federating units. At this stage one may be tempted to ask, what is in a name? Why should we bother with all these conceptual issues? I believe there is something in a name. Using new concepts and categories will allow us to avoid the hang-ups, fixations and suspicions which the politicised old concepts aroused in us.

Aside from the need to clarify meanings of our words and perhaps embrace new concepts to show a new mindset, there are other issues that need proper interrogation as we warm up to embrace 'restructuring' and its new variants as the new elixir to our endemic political and economic problems.

It should be important to bear in mind that while any form of restructuring (whether using the six geopolitical zones as the federative units and the only units that will partake in sharing revenue from the federation or not), may assuage some grievances, it will inherently animate other grievances. Every policy initiative has unintended consequences that must be thought through before being embraced. For instance if we replace the 36 state system with the six geopolitical zones, it will necessarily bring to fore secondary contradictions within each zone which were submerged by the current structure of the country. Some of these secondary contradictions might be able to checkmate the forces of separatism within the new federative unit while others will aggravate such. How do we deal with such and other unintended consequences of any re-engineering? Another challenge is which body should lead the restructuring/re-design exercise? Obviously the current National Assembly, because it is a reflection of the current configuration of the country being inveighed against, will, ab initio be de-legitimated from leading it as the issue is beyond constitutional amendment. On the other hand if we use a National Conference as both Obasanjo and Jonathan did, there will be the issue of the constitutionality of such a body. Can the outcome of such a confab be implemented without the legislative approval of the National Assembly? And will the National Assembly not see the idea of a separate body to lead the restructuring and redesign of the country as usurping its function? Even restructuring, redesigning or re-engineering of any form without a requisite re-orientation of our own values will not work. Will any proposed new structure on its own be able to engender such change in our political attitude and culture?

I believe that before we begin warming up for another constitutional conference, the above are some of the hurdles we may need to scale first. I am fully in support of Atiku's call for restructuring and for me it includes a conversation on the necessary questions we must find answers to before embracing a version of restructuring. I also believe that if history is any guide, a combination of mounting political and economic challenges as well as powerful voices joining the clarion call for 'restructuring' will eventually force President Buhari to conduct his own National Conference – perhaps towards the end of his tenure as both Obasanjo and Jonathan did. I cannot see Buhari revisiting the recommendations of the 2014 national conference – however the pressure. If Buhari chooses to organise his own conference it will be left to be seen whether it will achieve anything tangible or will be another jamboree that will at best serve the purpose of providing a forum for Nigerians to ventilate their grievances.

Daily Trust, June 16, 2016

CHAPTER 112

Funny Quotes from Robert Mugabe

Why should I be concerned about funny quotes from Robert Mugabe, the 92-year old President of Zimbabwe, when there are more pressing issues to interrogate in our political space? Does this not tantamount to one running after rats and rodents when one's house is on fire?

I have my reasons:

One, is that I need a break from our politics. Writing about politics all the time, essentially about the ever widening gap between 'what is' and 'what ought to be' embeds a certain 'kill joy'. You get frustrated and even angry at things you have no power to change. And this was precisely why I resisted pressure to study medicine in my younger days. Knowing myself, I did not want the empathy about the suffering of my patients to deny me a 'normal existence'. Political discourses can inflict as much pain. An article like this is therefore escapist, enabling me to write while at the same time living out the late Bola Ige's 'siddon look' philosophy.

Two, Robert Mugabe became Prime Minister of Zimbabwe in 1980, precisely the year I both completed my secondary education and gained admission to read political science at the University of Nigeria, Nsukka. Mugabe was then regarded as the greatest African reconciler. He forgave those who jailed him for more than ten years in Rhodesia (now Zimbabwe) between 1964 and 1974. After his release from prison he escaped in 1975 to launch guerrilla warfare against the illegal White supremacists from a base in Mozambique during the Rhodesian Bush War. After the war in 1979, Mugabe, who was a Marxist, surprised his enemies by calling for reconciliation between the former belligerents, including White Zimbabweans, some of whom he appointed into his cabinet in April 1980 when he became Prime Minister. This bit of history is important in contextualizing the current image of Mugabe as a reverse racist and bugaboo in the Western imagination.

Three, Robert Mugabe is a clear epitome of how a certain form of politics could encourage the phenomenon of sit-tightism in Africa. Some fervently believe that without political power, Mugabe's enemies, especially the West, in collaboration with their local allies, will make sure he ends up at the International Criminal Court (ICC) to answer for the apparent insults he heaved on them during his reign. If this is so, will anyone blame the old man for thinking that it is better for him to die in office than to be treated as a criminal in ICC? And what lessons can we learn from Mugabe about creating enabling conditions for peaceful handover of power by incumbents?

Four, despite his famed penchant for 'dozing off' during public functions, I cannot help but marvel at how a 92-year old is able to appear so strong, jetting around the world and making public speeches. On January 30 2015, at the age of 91, Robert Mugabe was elected Chairperson of the African Union. He had earlier led the AU's precursor the Organisation of African Unity between 1997 and 1998.

Recently some news started circulating in the social media about Mugabe's supposed immortality. One of such was from a Zimbabwean publication called Zimbabwe Newsday, which on April 20 2016 had the following screaming headline: 'UK Scientists CONFIRM President Mugabe can't DIE! He was born to live FOREVER'. The publication quoted one Dr. Irvin Koch, the supposed lead scientist in the supposed research as saying: "We have never seen anything like this. At first we could not believe it, but after running a series of tests, we then realized that Mugabe is really immortal." It was also claimed that Mugabe never cuts or dyes his hair. Though the piece was meant to be a satire, it went viral, with different versions.

During Buhari's First Coming, when he promulgated Decree No 4, which made it an offence to publish anything that was capable of embarrassing public officials whether such was true or false, Nigerian journalists devised what they called 'journeying to Afghanistan'. It was a sort of escapism where they concentrated on reporting foreign news because of the fear of being caught by Decree 4. Today with virtually no cheering political or economic news out there for most Nigerians, I have chosen to journey to Zimbabwe in search of something to cheer us all up. And what can be better than compiling the funny quotes from Oga Mugabe?

Let me mention that most of the funny quotes attributed to Mugabe were never really uttered by him, and it is not certain why he was 'chosen' as the sage extra ordinary. Is it because he has seven University degrees, six of which he gained by correspondence while in prison? Or because of his age? I am not sure. I will divide the quotes into the controversial ones which he certainly made and the funny ones that were simply attributed to him:

Controversial Quotes from Mugabe

"The only White man you can trust is a dead White man."
"So, Blair keep your England, and let me keep my Zimbabwe."
"We don't mind having sanctions banning us from Europe. We are not Europeans."

"I've just concluded – since President Obama endorses the same-sex marriage, advocates homosexual people[sic], and enjoys an attractive countenance – thus if it becomes necessary, I shall travel to Washington, D.C., get down on my knee, and ask for his hand."

"[Nelson] Mandela has gone a bit too far in doing good to the non-black communities …That's being too saintly, too good, too much of a saint."

"Even Satan wasn't gay; he chose to approach unclad Eve instead of unclad Adam."

Funny Quotes Attributed to Mugabe

"The only warning the African takes seriously is low battery."

"Sometimes you look back at girls you spent money on rather than send it to your mum and you realize witchcraft is real"

"If you like school girls, buy a uniform for your wife to wear for you"

"Racism will never end as long as white cars are using black tyres; if people still use Black to symbolize bad luck and White for peace, if people still wear white clothes at weddings and black clothes at funerals; as long as those who don't pay their bills are blacklisted and not white-listed. But I don't care as long as I am using the white toilet paper to wipe my ass".

"It is hard to bewitch African girls these days. Each time you take a piece from her hair to the witch doctor, either a Brazilian innocent woman gets mad or a factory in China catches fire".

"South Africans will kick down a statue of a White man but won't even attempt to slap a live one. Yet they can stone to death a Black man simply because he is a foreigner".

"Some women's legs are like rumours, they keep on spreading".

"Some girls have never seen the doors of a gym but look physically fit because of running from one man to another".

"And to those of you who do not actually go to church but watch it on TV, you will not actually go to Heaven, but you will be allowed to watch it on TV!"

"You smoke weed and you take some coke. Few minutes after, you hear 'chooboi chooboi' in your head. It's a set up. The moment you answer, "Yei"!, you are mad."

"The only public place Ghanaian ladies can be romantic is around the ATM machine."

"If you are a lady and you don't respect men, you will end up serving jollof at your younger sister's wedding."

"Dear ladies, if your boyfriend did not wish you a happy Mother's day, stop breastfeeding him".

"Whenever things seem to start going well in your life, the Devil comes and gives you a girlfriend".

"I stopped trusting ladies when my class 3 girlfriend left me for another boy all because he bought a sharpener with a mirror".

"When one's goat gets missing, the aroma of a neighbour's soup gets suspicious."

"Treat every part of your towel nicely because the part that wipes your buttocks today may wipe your face tomorrow".

Daily Trust, June 23, 2016

CHAPTER 113

Chinakwe: When the Law became an ass

Joe Fortemose Chinakwe, a 30-year-old trader, has been making major headlines since his arrest in Ogun state for naming his dog, Buhari. The man, also known as Joachim Iroko, reportedly spent three days in police cell before he was released after the intervention of the Serkin Hausa and President-General of non-indigenes in the state. He was however re-arrested and charged to court, which granted him bail in the sum of N50, 000 with two sureties who must be regular payers of their taxes in the state, in the like sum. Mr Chinakwe was charged for conduct likely to cause breach of peace. The prosecutor Inspector Itaita Ebibomini said the accused committed the offence on Saturday August 13, 2016, at the Hausa section of Ketere Market in Sango-Ota, in the Ota Magisterial District. It is not clear at the time of this writing if Chinakwe had perfected his bail condition.

As should be expected in a case of this manner, opinions vary on whether the state acted properly in clamping the man into detention and subsequently charging him to court. Human rights activists, democracy vanguards, soldiers of our natural fault lines and government apologists are all still feeling animated over the case.

For me, the issue goes quite beyond the freedom to name your pet whatsoever you want to name it. It is not even whether the President of a country can be insulted – I believe such comes with the territory of being in the public eye. If you are allowed to enjoy the fame and adulation that come with being a public figure, you must also be prepared to put up with the occasional insults that come with it. Anyone who wants a rainbow must be prepared to put up with the rain.

The larger issue in the case however is the manner in which Chinakwe chose to exercise his right to name his pet whatever pleased him to name it. Most people who keep pets confine them to their houses, and if they choose to call their pets their saviour, it will be up to them for as long as they do not use such pets to constitute nuisance to others. What was therefore the point that Chinakwe wanted to make by allegedly painting the name 'Buhari' on both sides of the dog? To attract attention? Or to provoke, especially given that such took place in the Hausa section of the community? Did he bother to find out how his action would be interpreted by others, especially in our type of ethnically and emotionally charged environment? Honestly, I do not think that Chinakwe displayed the sort of sensitivity to the feelings of others which is essential for inter-ethnic/regional amity. And there is really no point treating him as a sort of hero for he really misbehaved.

Let me mention that context is also very important in the evaluation of the conduct of Chinakwe. For instance it would have been a different matter if he had painted 'Buhari' on either side of his dog during a campaign season or during a strike or demonstration in which people try to vent their anger against certain public officials. The conduct could also have been pardonable if he was a comedian and was acting on a stage (in which case he could claim artistic freedom). Honestly I think Fortemose Chinakwe showed poor judgment and insensitivity to the feelings of his neighbours. I do not believe it is helpful to obfuscate about that.

Having said this however, it is also germane to interrogate whether the police acted appropriately under the circumstance or whether their own conduct exacerbated the matter. There are a number of issues that beggar clarification:

One, Chinakwe claimed that he was incarcerated for three days and that some of the police officers were determined that he should be detained for as long as possible. I believe that under our extant laws, you cannot detain someone for more than 48 hours unless a competent court of law grants the police the right to extend that detention. Did the police meet this condition in that initial three-day detention?

Two, our police showed uncommon speed in the case which aroused suspicion in some quarters that they were perhaps acting on orders from above. The Vanguard of August 23, 2016 quoted the Police Public Relations Officer (PPRO) in Ogun State, ASP Abimbola Oyeyemi as saying: "He was arrested last Saturday and we are taking him to court later today (Tuesday) or tomorrow morning (today). You know an average Northerner will feel bad over such a thing. It can cause serious ethnic crisis or religious confrontation because when you are relegating such a name to a certain person, you are indirectly insulting him." The speed at which the man was charged to court was uncommon for the Nigerian police and raises questions of why they are not displaying similar efficiency in confronting cases of kidnapping, armed robberies and the rampaging herdsmen across the country. Also, it was remarkable that Chinakwe was released from his initial detention after the intervention of Serkin Hausa and President-General of non-indigenes in the state – the group that was supposedly to be hurt by Chinakwe's rather thoughtless conduct. Why was it then necessary for Chinakwe to be re-arrested since the Serkin's intervention implied that some informal moves must have been on to soothe aggrieved nerves?

Three, I agree with the police that Chinakwe's conduct was capable of breaching the peace in inter-ethnic relations. But given the media hoopla around the case – amplified in fact by the case being charged to court – one wonders if the police handling of the case did not end up achieving the opposite effect?

That the law is sometimes not the most sensible tool to use in the resolution of certain types of disputes could be gleaned from what happened in the Australian state of Victoria some years ago where a law banning incitement to religious hatred led to Christians and Muslims accusing each other of inciting hatred and bringing legal actions against each other which only served to further inflame community relations. Issues bordering on inter-ethnic and intercultural harmony are rarely best resolved by rigid application of the law. Quite often the unintended consequences of such rigid applications of the law compound the problem hence justifying the calling of such laws an ass, or plainly stupid. I believe for instance that since Chinakwe claimed that he did not name the dog Buhari to spite anyone, asking him to go with some elders from his own community to apologize to the aggrieved person or persons would have been far more effective. And had that alternative dispute resolution route been followed, not many people would have known that there was a dog named Buhari. Now the young man has been turned into a social media celebrity for conduct that should not be acceptable in a polarized and culturally plural society like ours.

Four, the Chinakwe case brings to the fore issues of ethnic, regional and religious profiling – and how some of us can really be insensitive to others' feelings – whether in the way we play our music or generally conduct ourselves. For instance not long ago former President Olusegun Obasanjo reportedly donated a chimpanzee named Patience to a zoo. It is possible the former President meant no harm, but with all due respect, I considered that conduct (from a man I respect in many ways) similarly insensitive and the setting of bad example to others since Patience is the name of former President Jonathan's wife. And we all know that former President Jonathan fell out with him. Could it be that Chinakwe merely tried to play copycat to what Obasanjo did?

Five, the Chinakwe incident calls for an urgent need to have reconciliation and arbitration groups in many multicultural communities in the country to resolve disputes of this nature. Although such alternative dispute resolution structures could be found in putative forms in many towns and cities, they need to be recognized and utilized more often by our law enforcement agencies.

CJ to wade into controversial court orders

Report that the Chief Judge of the Federal High Court, Justice Ibrahim Ndahi Auta, might take steps to correct inconsistencies in court pronouncements, especially over the leadership tussle in the People's Democratic Party (PDP), is most welcome. Justice Auta was said to have cut short his vacation overseas and returned to Abuja to have a closer look at the matter which has really undermined the integrity of the courts in the eyes of right thinking members of the society. Justice Auta has reportedly requested all the judges handling matters relating to the PDP case to adequately brief him. It is certainly not healthy for courts of coordinate jurisdictions to be dishing out conflicting judgments. Good move Sir.

Daily Trust, August 25, 2016

CHAPTER 114

A new broom at the NPA?

The English say that a new broom sweeps clean. Generally the expression is used when a new leader in an organisation embarks on sweeping or innovative changes. Barely four months after being appointed the Managing Director of the Nigerian Ports Authority (NPA), are some asking whether Hadiza Bala Usman is a new broom at the government agency regarded as one of the juiciest of the juicy agencies in the country. It is partly because of the perception of the NPA as a cash-cow that her appointment generated negative reviews and conspiracy theories among sections of the media.

Born in Zaria, Kaduna State on January 2 1976, Hadiza, whose father, the late Yusuf Bala Usman, a distinguished historian who helped to define Nigeria's historiography, neither had maritime-related academic qualifications nor relevant industry experience. She has a B.Sc. degree in Business Administration and also did postgraduate studies in Development Studies at the University of Leeds, UK. She had worked as Enterprise Officer at the Bureau of Public Enterprises (July 2000-August 2004); Special Assistant to the Minister of FCT on project implementation (October 2004 - January 2008) and Director of Strategy at the NGO, Good Governance Group (2011 -July 2015) from where she was appointed Chief of Staff to the Kaduna State Governor, El-Rufa'i. She held the position until her appointment as the MD of the NPA. Ms Hadiza was a co-founder of the Bring- Back- Our Girls - a campaign group founded to advocate the rescue of the missing Chibok girls who were abducted in April 2014.

While her critics questioned her qualifications for the plum job, her supporters claim that her experience in both the government and the civil society sector adequately prepares her for the office. It could be argued that in a world that is paradoxically getting more complex and simpler simultaneously, the notions of qualifications and experience are also being redefined. And that was perhaps what goaded the American politician Bruce Lowell Braley to declare that being "a farmer is a great qualification to have to serve in the United States Congress." Donald Trump was to exemplify this further when he won the recent presidential election in the US - arguably the most powerful position in the world - without ever holding a public office.

When Ms Hadiza formally assumed duties on July 18 2016, she declared she would have zero tolerance for corruption. She also promised to enshrine best practices and professionalism in the NPA, which is one of the country's major financial arteries. Barely four months after she assumed office, the Sahara Reporters of August 26 2016, reported that the management of the NPA under her had uncovered fraud totalling N11.23 billion at the agency. The revelation did not surprise many because the NPA has always been one of the government agencies suspected of being a cesspool of corruption. Of the said N11.23 billion, $24.1m was allegedly traced to Heritage bank;

some six million Euros were reportedly concealed at the First Bank of Nigeria and First City Monument while another $5.4m belonging to the agency was allegedly moved to a TSA account in the CBN that does not belong to the agency.

Recently the management of the NPA announced that it has signed a Memorandum of Understanding (MoU) with the not-for-profit IT firm, BudgIT Information Technology Network. Under the agreement, which the NPA says costs it nothing; BudgIT will develop an online portal for the Open Agencies Budget System with a "Follow the Money" approach, which will provide linkages with other civic tools, as identified by both partners. Under the MoU, relevant initiatives and channels will be identified by both partners to help engage policy-makers and private sector stakeholders as well as permit inputs from critical stakeholders.

According to Ms Usman, the benefits of the MoU include the development of an open budget system platform, implementation of a public data dissemination programme, blocking revenue leakages and enhancing transparency in the running of the agency. The MoU, she said, would promote effective and efficient management of NPA's terminals across the country as well as ensure that key research and industry policies and innovations are effectively communicated. It is also expected to help ensure that critical data are generated and made accessible to policy makers, private sector actors, stakeholders and the general public.

While the objectives of the MoU seem noble, Ms Usman needs not be reminded that several of the country's agencies do not lack good, innovative and even revolutionary ideas. As always the devil is in the details. How does the NPA ensure that there is sufficient buy-in by the stakeholders, including the staff of the agency, to ensure that the policies are not undermined at the level of implementation? What plans are in place for sustainability and follow-throughs?

While the steps taken so far by the new MD of the NPA are encouraging, it may be germane to observe that the problems at the agency go beyond promoting transparency and blocking leakages - as important as these are. The MD also needs to design strategies that will help in achieving faster clearance of cargoes, quicker turn-around time for ships calling at the country's ports, removal of unnecessary duplications in security clearance and enhancing overall trade facilitations.

There is also a need to find ways of reducing port service costs for users so as to make the country the hub for international freight and trade in West Africa. There is equally the need not to overlook the small things that matter such as regular update of the agency's website. For instance on the agency's website, the most recent statistics on cargo throughput, container traffic, number and gross registered tonnage (GRT) that entered all the Nigerian ports is 2014. I am not sure such is good enough and the new management needs to address such lapses.

Is Hadiza a new broom at NPA or are all these the usual effusions and 'gra-gra' of a new sheriff in town? I think we can paraphrase Hilary Clinton's position on Donald Trump's victory in the recent US presidential election: we owe her an open mind.

Exodus from ICC

The recent indication by Russia that it is formally withdrawing its signature from the founding statute of the International Criminal Court (ICC) is ominous. The indication came a day after the court published a report classifying the Russian annexation of Crimea as an occupation. Russia accused the tribunal of being "one-sided and inefficient". Though Russia signed the Rome statute in 2000 and has cooperated with the court, it had not ratified the treaty and thus remained outside the ICC's jurisdiction. This means that its indication to formally withdraw its signature from the statute is merely symbolic. But it adds to a sense of exodus within the intergovernmental tribunal.

Currently, only 124 countries are party to the Rome Statute and therefore members of the ICC. Notable countries that have not joined include the United States, China, Russia and India.

In recent months, three African countries, which were all full members of the ICC - South Africa, Burundi and The Gambia - have signalled their intention to pull out on accusations that ICC prosecutions focus excessively on Africa. Only Africans have been charged in the six ICC cases that are either on-going or about to begin.

Withdrawal from the ICC does not happen automatically when a country announces it. For the withdrawal to be effective, the country must officially notify the U.N. secretary-general of its intention to leave, and the pull-out becomes effective only one year after the receipt of that notice.

Daily Trust, November 17, 2016

CHAPTER 115

Tinubu and the 'rational calculus of war'

Several of the ideas that flow from On War, the unfinished masterpiece of the 19th century Prussian general, Carl von Clausewitz, remain relevant today and could be applied in the analysis of any return on investment model (ROI). One of these notions is the 'Rational Calculus of War' in which Clausewitz argued that there should be a correlation between the value a state attaches to its goals and the means it uses to achieve them. Clausewitz argued that since war is not a senseless passion but a rational activity driven by clear objectives, the value a state attaches to these objectives must determine the sacrifices to be made during the war. In essence, there comes a time when we must pause to do means-end (or return on investment) analysis and decide whether the cost of pursuing a particular objective is really worth it.

There is no doubt that Asiwaju Ahmed Bola Tinubu, the Jagaban, invested tremendous resources - materially re and otherwise- in helping not just for the actualization of the mega merger that resulted in the formation of the All Progressives Congress (APC) but also in the historic victory of Muhammadu Buhari in the March 2015 presidential election. It is however not a secret that Tinubu has not been happy with his party for a while. Matters came to a head in September 2016 when Tinubu openly called for the resignation of the national chairman of the APC, Chief John Odigie-Oyegun, whom he accused of manipulating the outcome of the party's gubernatorial primary in Ondo state in which Rotimi Akeredolu (SAN) who is now the Gorvenor-elect, defeated his favoured candidate, Olusegun Abraham. From all indications, the party's establishment and the presidency took sides with Oyegun. Tinubu felt thrown under the bus. The general feeling was that he would use the opportunity of the Ondo election to pull his weight and teach his traducers one or two lessons. For that reason, many saw the Ondo state Governorship election as a proxy contest between forces loyal to Tinubu and those loyal to the presidency and the APC. This perception was accentuated when Tinubu and his loyalists stayed away from a rally for Akeredolu attended by the president and some top members of the party. During that rally the president was quoted as expressing confidence in the processes that led to the emergence of Akeredolu as the party's flag bearer in the state.

Well, the election has come and gone. Akeredolu has been declared the winner of the election by INEC. Though I have never been a fan of Tinubu's brand of 'brazen god-fatherism', I feel that the outcome of the election in Ondo state, in which a candidate he was opposed to won, was actually good for him. I actually feel things would have been made tough for him, if a candidate he was thought to have supported carried the day against a candidate supported by the President.

Until the Ondo Governorship election, Tinubu or his loyalists may have unwittingly given the impression that he was competing for political space with the presidency. For instance some of these loyalists even demonstrated against his perceived marginalization by the party and the presidency - an ill-advised move. They easily point out that for someone who sacrificed as much as Tinubu did for the APC, it is an act of betrayal for the party (and perhaps the presidency) to collude and work against his preferred candidates for the leadership of the National Assembly and also against his candidates in Kogi and Ondo states respectively. The Tinubu loyalists were especially incensed that what happened in Ondo State meant that the forces against Tinubu were determined to humiliate him in his South-west home turf.

Though Tinubu's supporters call him 'master political strategist', I always feel that it was a bad political strategy on his part not to begin conceding political space immediately he failed in his ambition of being nominated as Buhari's running mate during the 2015 election. In fact by wanting to be seen as a kingmaker - not just in Yorubaland but also in the National Assembly and even in Kogi state - he made himself very vulnerable to being shot-down by counteracting forces. His brand of godfatherism led to a whole series of conspiracy theories about his motive: is he nursing presidential ambition in 2019? Is he being actuated by the love of lucre? What does he really want?

Tinubu may have meant well but by not conceding space or not trying to exercise influence discreetly using his proximity and access to constituted authorities made him extremely vulnerable. So while I am morally against the 'use and dump' tendencies of many politicians, sometimes those who are 'dumped' after making many sacrifices are also guilty of not reading situations correctly and not properly appreciating human psychology. I believe this is at the root of the endemic conflict and feelings of betrayal between political godfathers and political godsons in the country. A wise kingmaker, as soon as he puts the crown on another's head, must deliberately 'decrease' to allow the new king to 'increase'. In fact, in our type of society, it is foolhardy to compete for space with the President of the country. It is not that a President cannot be challenged. He can. But historically political actors who have done so successfully have avoided frontal confrontations but fight sideways or only when they are backed up by a formidable organisation. The only person I know who has successfully confronted regimes frontally and triumphed (except under Abacha) is former President Olusegun Obasanjo. And that is because Obasanjo is Obasanjo.

There are a number of opportunities for Tinubu and useful lessons from the outcome of the recent Ondo Governorship election:

One, I think it offers Tinubu a good opportunity to have a deserved long rest. Since the formation of the APC, especially since failing to become the running mate to Buhari, the impression is that he has been spending too much energy and resources trying to maintain his relevance. Forget that he is called 'Leader of the APC'. It is a mere honorific. Everyone knows that the President calls the shot - just as Governors do at the state level. If I were him, I would just disappear from the political scene for months to take deserved rest and re-charge.

Two, the outcome of the election offers him a good opportunity to change his brand of god-fatherism. Tinubu himself gave some indications that this may happen by quickly congratulating Akeredolu who was declared the winner by INEC. In congratulating Akeredolu, Tinubu was quoted as saying: "I appeal to all party members including those who have been disaffected from the primary until today to come together for the good of our party and its progressive ideals." If that was meant to be an extension of the olive branch to the forces he believed was fighting him, the presidency responded in kind. Speaking through his Senior Special Assistant on the media Garba Shehu, Buhari was reported as denying that there was ever a rift between the leadership of the APC, himself and Tinubu. In fact, Shehu Garba dismissed such insinuations as "unfounded and mischievous." He also reportedly said that President Buhari regarded Tinubu as a priceless political asset to the APC and whose "immeasurable contributions" to the development and progress of the party were known to all. Garba further claimed that the President was in constant touch with Tinubu. I believe that the conciliatory tone of Tinubu's congratulatory message to Rotimi Akeredolu and the President's 'soft landing' response, provide good grounds for the re-setting of the relationship between the two political gladiators.

Three, because in our type of society no political leader has universal legitimacy across the country's traditional fault lines, national political players tend to be legitimated only by the offices they occupy. Tinubu does not have such a legitimizing office in this dispensation, explaining why an array of forces seemed interested in cutting him to size - when he tried to frontally exercise influence beyond his South-west home turf. My fear is that having cut him to size by the outcome of the Ondo governorship election, the same forces may want to completely neutralize him politically - if he fails to properly understand the logic of power. This means that as the music has changed the Jagaban must also change his dance-step. He can use Clausewitz's 'Rational Calculus of war' thesis to do a means-ends analysis of his political forays. But an essential starting point must be for him to honestly answer a few questions: What does he really want from his political engagements? What is the worth of the goals he wants to achieve? And what costs of pursuing of pursuing those goals is he willing to bear?

Daily Trust, December 1, 2016

INTERNATIONAL AFFAIRS

CHAPTER 116

Africa: From Military Coups to Constitutional Coups

The outcome of Rwanda's constitutional referendum held on December 18 2015 was one of the boldest affirmations that Africa has become afflicted with a new virus - constitutional coup making. Official results of the referendum showed that 98 per cent of Rwandans 'wanted' a constitutional change to permit Paul Kagame, 58, to run for a third term of seven years at the end of his current tenure in 2017. The country's newly amended constitution which reduced a term from seven years to five years will come into effect when Kagame's third term tenure of seven years will come to an end, enabling him to run for another two terms of 5-years each under the amended constitution. Essentially the Rwandan strongman's constitutional coup makes it possible for him to rule until 2034 – or longer if he is able to engineer another constitutional coup after that.

Until the 'third wave' of democracy in Africa which started with the National Conference in Benin in 1990, the continent was a playground for autocratic life presidents and military adventurists who usurped power under the veneer of little messiahs. Whereas enlightened dictatorship arguably helped some countries such as Chile under Augusto Pinochet, South Korea under Park Chung-Hee and China under Deng Xiaoping to develop economically Africa's dictators succeeded only in further under-developing their countries both politically and economically.

Today most of the countries in the continent are in a democratizing mode. Military coups have become passé. Constitutional coups appear to be the new cool. Simply put, a constitutional coup is an attempt to review or amend the provisions of a national constitution by an incumbent leader with the ulterior motive of capitalizing on such amendments to achieve tenure elongation.

There are a number of observations:

One, across the continent liberal or Western democracy is being universalized, usually with term limits. However the continent's liberal democracy project faces resistance from two forces: adventurist soldiers who nurse a nostalgia for the period when the military was the shortest route to power in Africa and civilian beneficiaries of this 'third wave' of democracy who nurse a nostalgia for the period of one party dictatorships and life presidencies that prevailed in most parts of the continent from independence until the end of the Cold War.

Since the early 1990s, at least 24 presidents in sub-Saharan Africa initiated moves to stay in office beyond the constitutionally allowed two terms. For instance in 2001 president Lansana Conte of Guinea organized a referendum that scrapped term limits. Similarly, in 2005, President Idris Deby of Chad held a referendum to delete Article 61 (2) of his country's constitution which restricted presidents to two successive terms. Mamadou Tandja of Niger abolished term limits through a referendum even though Article 49 of the Nigerien constitution expressly forbade such a procedure. In Burkina

Faso, President Blaise Compaoré, who had already served two terms argued in 2005 that the term limit restriction in Article 37 of the country's constitution could not apply retroactively to him. He won tenure elongation for another two terms but was still not content. In 2014 he tried to abolish term limits altogether. The move led to riots and street upheavals which forced him out of office and into exile. Meanwhile some military adventurists led by Gen. Gilbert Diendere tried to cash in on the situation by toppling the country's interim government. The coup was fiercely resisted both by the local populace and the regional organisations - the ECOWAS and the African Union. In Senegal, Abdoulaye Wade in 2012 argued that the term limits in his country's constitution could not apply retroactively to his first term in office. He won the case in court and ran for a third term – but lost. Burundi's President Pierre Nkurunziza who violently resisted months of popular discontent eventually got his third term in office but at a bloody cost. In Nigeria Obasanjo was believed to have plotted for tenure elongation as his tenure was to expire in 2007. It failed. Similarly, one of Jonathan's first initiatives after winning the 2011 presidential election was to push the idea of a single six-year term. The move was abandoned after it was roundly condemned as an attempt at tenure elongation. In several of the countries that tried tenure elongation, especially where the ruling party is factionalized, attempts at tenure elongation often led to violence.

However while several incumbents plotted constitutional coups, in countries like Benin, Cape Verde, Ghana, Kenya, Mali, Mozambique, Sao Tome and Principe and Tanzania leaders respected themselves and the country's constitution and stepped down honourably after exhausting their two-term limits.

Two, the trend towards constitutional coups illustrates the tension between democratic consolidation and democratic reversal in the continent. For instance, when Compaoré sought to amend the constitution in a bid to elongate his tenure in Burkina Faso, it led to days' of mass street protests and popular uprisings which eventually forced him out of power. Similarly popular protests helped to foil the 2015 coup in that country. All these are indications of growth in democratic consciousness and preference for liberal democracy – as imperfect as it is in the continent – over life presidencies and military dictatorships. Also with the number of attempted military coups in the continent (about 26 in the last five years) and the number of attempted constitutional coups (about 24 since the 1990s), one could argue that the possibility of democratic reversal remains real in the continent even amid democratic consolidation.

Three, another inference from the trend towards constitutional coups is that authoritarian impulses remain very strong in the continent. This is often a key feature in newly democratizing countries and the manifestations of this include disobedience of court orders, manipulating court rulings, commoditizing justice and criticisms of democracy by government officials as an imported Western doctrine that has to 'be adapted to African culture and realities'. I recently had a discussion with a retired army officer on what Nigerians now call 'Dasukigate'. My position was that under the separation of power doctrine that undergirds democracy, only a competent court of law can pronounce any one guilty or not, and if a court decides that the accused should be granted bail, it must be honoured no matter the gravity of the allegation against the person. The officer was vehemently opposed to any form of bail for Dasuki, saying he was convinced that Dasuki would jump bail if it was granted to him. When I asked why any evidence that he would jump bail was not given to prosecuting attorney to help persuade the judge against granting him bail, he began a lengthy lecture on how corrupt our judiciary could be. When I asked why we should bother to send anyone to court if court orders could not be respected, he accused me of being "brainwashed" by the West. For him, "democracy must be adapted to our culture." He was not able to convince me on how such adaptation should be done in this circumstance except to insist that "we must be realistic". Essentially therefore our putative democracy sits uncomfortably with a certain nostalgia for our authoritarian past.

Four, constitutional coups is a continuation of the sit tight syndrome for which African leaders were infamous for. As our democracy matures, we must also begin to ask ourselves tough questions: Why do some leaders refuse to leave office at the expiration of their tenure? Why is the character of our politics anarchic? Why is there a pervasive fear that the ethnic/regional group that captures state power will use such power to privilege its in-group or disadvantage the others? Why is our politics a do-or-die affair? As we strive to earnestly answer some of these probing questions, we will quickly realize why African leaders who do what is taken for granted elsewhere such as accepting defeat in an election or handing over power at the expiration of their tenures are rightly seen as heroes.

Daily Trust, January 6, 2016

CHAPTER 117

Can Happiness Really be measured?

The inspiration for this reflection is the World Happiness Report 2016, released recently in Rome ahead of this year's UN World Happiness Day, which was celebrated on the 20th of March. The World Happiness Report surveys the state of global happiness and ranks countries by their happiness levels using such metrics as wealth, health, freedom to make life choices, having someone to count on in times of trouble, freedom from corruption and the generosity of fellow citizens

The background to the introduction of a World Happiness Report was that in July 2011 the UN General Assembly passed a resolution inviting member countries to measure the happiness of their people and to use such to guide their formulation of public policies. The World Happiness Report 2016, which is the fourth of such reports, is published by the United Nations Sustainable Development Solutions. The first Report was published in 2012, the second in 2013, and the third in 2015. Authors of the Report are usually drawn from experts from diverse disciplines - economics, psychology, survey analysis, national statistics, health, public policy and so on and so forth. The 2016 Report includes the ranking of 157 countries based on survey data from 2013 to 2015. Each country had an average sample size of 3,000 people who answered questions pertaining to six variables: gross domestic product (GDP) per capita, healthy life expectancy, social support, freedom, generosity and absence of corruption.

In the 2016 Report, Nigeria was ranked the 103rd happiest nation in the world, down from its 78th ranking in 2015. It also slipped from being the second happiest country in Africa in 2015 to being the sixth happiest in the continent. Globally Denmark emerged the world's happiest country in the world while Algeria, which was ranked 38th globally, maintains its position as the happiest country in Africa. African countries dominate the bottom of the table.

I have some issues with the World Happiness Report:

One, the greatest utility of the Report, in my opinion, is in calling attention to the fact that happiness – just like the notion of work-life balance - deserves a priority place in government policies and ought to be part of the primary indicators of the quality of human development in any country. In fact following the first UN High Level Meeting on 'Happiness and Well-Being' on April 2 2012, Bhutan became the first and only country so far to have replaced Gross Domestic Product (GDP) with Gross National Happiness (GNH) as its main development indicator.

Two, from all indications, the Report appears to be concerned with 'national happiness' or the 'happiness of nations' rather than the happiness of people who make up the nations. For this reason, the variables of interest - GDP, healthy life expectancy, social support, generosity and absence of corruption – measure a country's well-being and not strictly speaking 'happiness' - defined as mental or emotional state of well-being characterized by positive or pleasant emotions that could range from contentment to intense joy. For instance if the rate of suicide is used as a metric for measuring unhappiness, (the opposite of happiness), then quite some of the countries which are ranked among the top 20 happiest countries in the world will also feature among the top 20 with the highest suicide rates in the world. A crucial question therefore is whether a country's well-being is synonymous with the happiness of its citizens. People in some rural areas who are abjectly poor but have no idea of what it means not to be poor cannot be convinced that they are unhappy because the GDP of their countries have dropped or because some unseen government politicians looted their country's treasury.

An even more important question is whether happiness is dependent on societal structures and environmental variables (as suggested by the World Happiness Report) or is strictly an individual's choice that is independent of his or her social and material circumstances? The 14th Dalai Lama would say that happiness "is not something readymade. It comes from your own actions." Mahatma Gandhi, the preeminent leader of the Indian independence movement in British-ruled India defined happiness as "when what you think, what you say, and what you do are in harmony." For the Russian writer Leo Tolstoy: "If you want to be happy, be." In essence, for Dalai Lama, Ghandi, Tolstoy and several others, happiness is an individual choice that is independent of the society, its structures and enabling or disenabling conditions and not something to be measured using variables that can only capture a nation's well-being. This means therefore that one cannot really talk of a happy or unhappy nation, but of happy or unhappy individuals.

Three, the World Happiness Report may unwittingly be reinforcing an essentialist construction of Africa and the narratives and innuendos that go with it. Since its chosen variables can only measure well being, wealth and democracy (freedom), which are areas that actually define Africa's condition of underdevelopment, it becomes axiomatic that African countries will not do well in such rankings. But a fundamental reason why they underperform in such rankings is the condition of underdevelopment which has already been captured in the key index that defines developed and underdeveloped economies. Several of the symptoms of this fundamental problem of underdevelopment are curiously being captured in a pick-and- choose manner by several indices such as the United Nations Human Development Index, the Ease of Doing Business Index among countries, the Sustainable Governance Index etc. It is like using four different indices, each ranking people according to how healthy they look, their physical strength, how briskly they walk and how fast they can run. A man who is severely ill with malaria and has suffered loss of appetite as a result will be poorly captured by each of the four indices even though his only problem is that he is suffering from malaria. This is Africa's major problem with several of these indices. And it is both essentialist and reductionist.

Four, how will the Buhari regime interpret the World Happiness Report 2016? Are Nigerians becoming more 'wailing wailers' under him, as his critics will argue and as the Report suggests on face value? The answer to this can be both 'yes' and 'no'. Though the 2016 Report was based on survey data from 2013 to 2015, Buhari was inaugurated as President in May 2015, meaning that part of the period covered by the data used in the ranking came from the time of his presidency. However he cannot take all the blame because a disproportionate chunk of the data used in compiling the report also came from the time of the Jonathan presidency.

Promoting education and health: The Bauchi state example

I am quite impressed with Bauchi state government's 2016 revenue and expenditure estimates. Of its budget budget proposal of N47, 306,964,985, it allocated 52% to capital expenditure and 48 per cent to recurrent expenditure. More importantly, the state has one of the highest (if not the highest allocation) to the education sector in this country. It allocated the sum of N26, 736,579,182 (a whopping 20% of its total budget) to the education sector. According to the state government, the projects and programmes it intends to pursue to realize its goal of qualitative education include the purchase of furniture, supply of instructional materials, library books and equipment, construction of more public schools as well as rehabilitation of existing ones. Though the allocation to the education sector fell short of the 26 per cent recommended by UNESCO and the 30 per cent allocation canvassed by some Nigerian educationists, it is certainly one of the highest (if not the highest ever allocation) to education by any government in the country – federal or state. Remarkably there is no elephant project (such as establishing a state University) to gulp this relatively huge allocation, which is commendable.

Bauchi state's allocation to education compares favourably with El-Rufai's ambitious education programme in Kaduna state. Of Kaduna state's 2016 budget of N171.7bn, education received N27.5bn (about 16%). It should be recalled that in 2014 the federal government made a big bone of the fact that it increased the allocation to the education sector to 10.7 per cent, up from 8.7 per cent in 2013.

In addition to an impressive 20 per cent allocation to education, the Bauchi state government also gave the second highest allocation of N19,685,311,922 (15%) to the health sector. This is one of the few times in the history of this country that budgetary allocation to the health sector by any government in the country – state or federal – has met the 15 per cent recommended by both the World Bank and the World Health Organisation. Thumbs up to the Bauchi State government and its Governor Mohammed Abdullahi Abubakar for these bold steps. I pray the state does not derail at the level of implementation.

Daily Trust, March 24, 2016

CHAPTER 118

As Boutros Boutros-Ghali bows out

Boutros Boutros- Ghali, the sixth Secretary-General of the United Nations (January 1992 to December 1996) has died aged 93.

As an Egyptian, many Africans were elated when he became the first 'African' to head the United Nations. When he also became the first Secretary-General of the United Nations to be denied a second term in office, there was a feeling among many Africans and Arabs that the historical disrespect for 'Third World' leaders 'who were not afraid to speak truth to global power' was at play. Paradoxically when Kofi Annan, a Ghanaian, was elected to succeed him, a simple question of 'who is the first African Secretary General of the United Nations?' suddenly required convoluted answers or answers with several qualifiers.

At the heart of that question was the whole notion of Africanity. Was Bourtros Boutros Ghali, an Egyptian and Arab, African? Are Arabs living in Africa Africans? If yes, are they Africans on the same level of Africanity with say Ghanaians and Nigerians? Is Obama whose father is Kenyan African? Who decides who is an African and why?

Debate about African identity has raged among Africanists for years. Inspired by renewed conversations on the theme, in 2009, I edited a book entitled: *Who is an African? Identity, Citizenship and the Making of the Africa-Nation.* I got several of the leading Africanists who had taken strong positions on the issue to contribute. They included the late Ali Mazrui, whose own Africanity had been questioned by his critics such as Kwesi Prah, Wole Soyinka and Chinweizu. Mazrui, who had Arab ancestry, contributed three chapters to the book. Other contributors included Gamal Nkrumah (Kwame Nkrumah's son), Helmi Sharawy, Kwesi Prah, Steven Friedman, Mammo Muchie, Marcel Kitissou, Bankie Forster Bankie and Garba Diallo.

Mazrui sought to answer the question of whether Boutros Boutros-Ghali was an African on the same level of Africanity with say Kofi Annan by making a distinction between 'Africans of the blood and Africans of the soil'. For Mazrui, "Africans of the blood are defined in racial and genealogical terms. They are identified with the Black race. Africans of the soil on the other hand are defined in geographical terms. They are identified in nationality and ancestral location". In other words, for Mazrui, Boutros-Ghali was as much African as Kofi Annan, but just a different African. His position was similar to that of Steven Friedman, a White South African. For Friedman, a White or Arab African is just a "belonging of another type". He contends that the view that White South Africans, "because of their European roots, lack insight into African culture misses the point that the continent is not culturally homogenous – there is no single African culture. "One implication is that excluding Whites (or anyone else on the continent) from Africanness is likely to do little to enrich African identity".

For Kwesi Prah, in "many parts of Africa, people who do not regard themselves as Africans are regarded as such by Africans. Being African is virtually equated with citizenship. I think this is often deliberate and wicked".

As the editor of the volume, my conclusion, was that a "proper definition and delineation of the African will involve the development of a taxonomy of elements used in identifying the African – geography, race, consciousness, place of birth, culture, residence and citizenship.

"This will of course imply that there are categories of Africans and that yes indeed some are more African (the more of these attributes they posses) than others. This will also suggest that one's Africanness can expand (as when one engages in projects that help to uplift the continent) or contract (as when one relapses into Afro-pessimism".

The debate on who is an African remains ongoing. Boutros-Ghali's election as the Secretary General of the United Nations and his succession by Kofi Annan merely animated that debate.

Boutros Ghali appeared tailor-made for the UN job when he presented himself as a candidate for the job. As an Egyptian, he was African enough to win the enthusiastic support of Africa's UN members. As an Arab, the Arab world was comfortable with his candidacy – as were the Jews, given that his wife was Jewish. Boutros-Ghali's grandfather was Egypt's first Coptic Prime Minister and his own father was once Egypt's finance minister. He was regarded as a sophisticated intellectual who had studied International Law at the Sorbonne. France championed his candidacy because French was his preferred language and he was at home in the Francophone world. He was also seen as "one of us" in the Western because he was fluent in the English language and comfortable in Western mannerisms. The Russians and the Chinese equally supported his candidacy because they were confident he would be his own man and not a Western puppet.

Boutros-Ghali worked on a radical reform programme for the UN. He was encouraged by the first ever summit of the Security Council, which commissioned him to draw up a blueprint for the improvement of the "UN's capacity for preventive diplomacy, for peacemaking and peacekeeping". In June 1992, he came up with the ambitious Agenda for Peace – regarded by many as one of the best reform proposals yet put forward for the UN. He envisaged a revamped UN, which would have enough muscle to stifle conflict and promote peaceful settlement of disputes.

Boutros-Ghali was later to anger Washington by his opposition to NATO's bombing campaign in Bosnia in 1995. He was also considered too arrogant, too close to France and too preoccupied with the problems of the African continent. During the Rwandan genocide in 1994, he was also criticized for the UN's failure to prevent the massacre.

Boutros-Ghali was born on 14 November 1922 into a Coptic Christian family in Cairo. He graduated from Cairo University in 1946 and received a PhD in international law from the University of Paris. Between 1949 and 1979, he was variously Professor of International Law and International Relations at Cairo

University. In 1977 he became Egypt's foreign minister under president Anwar al-Sadat.

After leaving the UN, Mr Boutros-Ghali served from 1998 to 2002 as secretary general of La Francophonie - a grouping of French-speaking nations. . He died in a hospital in Cairo, Egypt, after being admitted for a broken pelvis, on 16 February 2016.

From the Unknown to the Unknown

And talking of death, our inevitable transition, at God's own appointed time, from the unknown to unknown, can be quite painful. This is especially so if such transitions come suddenly. Dr Chiku Malunga, a Malawian prolific author and capacity development consultant became my friend when he approached my publishing firm, Adonis & Abbey Publishers (www.adonis-abbey.com) in early 2008 for us to publish his book, *Making Strategic Plans Work: Insights from Indigenous African Wisdom*. The book was well received. I later met him in early 2011 when he visited Abuja and I had just relocated from the United Kingdom a month or two before. When I visited South Africa a few years ago, he asked his niece to take me around.

Last year we began discussions about his fourth book with us, which he told me would be his *magnum opus*. The new manuscript, which he titled *Organization Paremiology: A New Approach to Organizational Improvement*, is already with the proofreaders. On January 11 2016, we exchanged about five emails between us. He was going to Ghana and we agreed to work to bring out the title by the middle of March this year. On February 15 2016, I got an email from his close friend Emmanuel Chinunda, who is also one of our authors, informing me that Chiku Malunga had died on January 13 2016 and had already been buried. Chiku had taken ill while in Ghana and had died of kidney failure. I refused to believe the story and immediately called his numbers but they rang without anyone picking them up. I sent an email which is yet to be replied. It is just too painful. I had on 6 February just returned from burying a brother in law.

Late last year, Ibrahim Auduson, former Opinion Editor of the Daily Trust, also transited. I kept close contact with Auduson throughout the period he was ill. I called him sometime in November 2015 after he moved from an Abuja hospital to a clinic in Kaduna. He was in high spirits and told me that they had taken off his dialysis machine the past ten days and that he was doing exceedingly fine. For him, his recovery was a miracle. He said he planned to return to work by the end of November last year. In December I got a text message telling me Ibrahim Auduson had gone to meet his Maker. Adieu dear friends and comrades.

Each time someone we are close to dies, it not only reminds us of our own mortality, but also challenges us to question life itself.

Daily Trust, February 17 2016

CHAPTER 119

Who is an African?
Navigating through the minefields of African Identities (1)

Who is an African? At face value the answer seems obvious. Surely everyone knows who the African is, it would seem. But the answer becomes less obvious once other probing qualifiers are added to the question: How is the African identity constructed in the face of the mosaic of identities that people of African ancestry living within and beyond the continent bear? Do all categorised as Africans or as having an African pedigree perceive themselves as Africans? Are all who perceive themselves as Africans accepted as such? Are there levels of "African-ness", and are some more African than others? Who allots this African-ness, and why? How does African identity interface with other levels of identity and affiliations in Africa? How are identities stylized, negotiated and defended? Are Jamaican Rastafarians who have a high conscious of their Africanity really Africans? Is Barack Obama, whose father is Kenyan and mother a White American and who is currently the President of USA an African?

At the heart of the question of who is an African is the underlying issue of identity. But what is identity?

Amin Maalouf, the Lebanese-born French author tells us that identity is "one of those false friends" that could appear deceptively too easy to handle until one decides to take a go at defining them and they will bare their complexity. For this I will eschew any outright definition. Rather I will couch my discussion of the notion of identity on three broad propositions:

Proposition 1: Individuals are a mosaic of identities

One of the clearest indicators of a person's identity is his or her Identity Card or Curriculum Vitae, which is a whole array of details about the person designed to show the person's uniqueness and affiliations. A person's CV or ID card, depending on where the person lives, could contain such information about the person as his or her gender, ethnicity, race, residence, religion, foreign travels, work experience, hobbies, height, weight and academic qualifications. This set of information sets the person apart. But it also allows us to decipher who shares same affiliations with the person such as who went to the same schools with the person.

Identity is also partly the way others perceive the person – as a clever person, a charlatan or an honest person. In essence an individual is a mosaic of identities and some of these could be quite complex.

Proposition 2: Identities are cross-cutting

The identities we bear could be cross-cutting. For instance an African living in Europe may belong to a radical anti-racist organisation which complains constantly about White racism against Blacks. The same African may also be a member of a charity such as Red Cross where he has come to deeply respect the care and humanness of some White volunteers or workers in the organisation who sometimes endanger their lives while trying to deliver relief materials to some countries struck by natural disasters or wars, irrespective of whether the country in question is predominantly Black or White. In essence this African is a member of two organisations where he experiences two contradictory narratives of White people.

Let me illustrate further the cross-cutting nature of identities with the furore generated recently by Chinua Achebe's latest book: *There Was a Country: A personal History of Biafra*. In the book, the famous author claimed that during the Biafran Civil War Awolowo, a Yoruba, who was the Federal Minister of Finance and the second in Command on the federal side together with the then Head of State General Yakubu Gowon carried out a policy of starvation and consequently genocide against the Biafrans. Many Igbo commentators took sides with Achebe while the Yoruba and the North differed and lampooned the great author.

While I strongly believe that the policy of starvation used during that war was an error of judgment –because it is clearly against the 1949 Geneva Convention on war and there is no known modern warfare where the policy has been applied – if we bear in mind that Biafra is not the only identity those who fought on the other side of the war bear, it may help everyone to put things in perspective. For instance an Igbo man who is rightly angry that he lost his brothers to Kwashiorkor during the Civil War could today have raised his children in Lagos, have a Northerner as his benefactor, his fellow Igbo as a betrayer or cherish his membership of several societies in which one's ethnicity or religion is not a criterion for joining. This leads to a logical question: If identities are cross-cutting, under what circumstances do we choose which of our several identities we flaunt or defend and which we should use to define our being?

Proposition3: Identities that are under threat or very successful are often the ones most flaunted or defended

My basic argument here is that which of our several identities we flaunt or identify most with may depend on several factors. A person who feels that his colour is ridiculed or that he is discriminated against because of his race is likely to associate with fellow 'oppressed' who may design different symbols of asserting their humanity or resisting the 'oppression'. For instance Africans in the Diaspora who feel conscious of their Africanness on a belief that their African identity is responsible for the denial of certain opportunities to them in their host country may flaunt their African identity – sometimes as a defensive mechanism or to affirm their humanity. However the same 'proud Africans', once back in their home countries, may lose this consciousness because in the home environment that identity may lose its relevance. In fact, a returning African, who used his Africanness to define himself while abroad may come back home to see himself primarily as Wollof, Yoruba, Akan or Muslim. He may actually come back to be socialised into new identities which he may now regard as more important than all the other identities he bears. For instance the returning African, who is for example socialised into a belief that the North Senatorial District in his home State of Anambra has been monopolising all the resources meant for the entire State because the Governor is from that area, may now relegate his 'Igbo-ness, Nigerian-ness and African-ness to the background, and see himself primarily as someone from the South Senatorial zone of Anambra State. He may join advocacy groups aimed at bringing to light the various ways the South Senatorial Zone has been marginalised. For him, at that point in time, his affiliation to the South senatorial zone may trump all other affiliations. The former Diaspora African, who may have been active in Black-empowerment or anti-racism movements in his country of domicile suddenly stops seeing himself as an African or even a Muslim, Christian, Igbo, Hausa or Yoruba but a member of a particular affiliation from his ethnic and religious group. In essence, not only are identities that are perceived to be most under threat the ones most flaunted or defended, identities actually have time and space dimensions. A feminist in say Niger Republic who immigrated to the Scandinavia where women empowerment has got to the level where men may now be seen as the oppressed gender may discover that being a feminist in her new country is a different kettle of fish.

Identities that are very successful could also be among the most flaunted - in part because of the instinctive human tendency to identify with success. For instance, if a Nigerian football team does very well in a football tournament, say they win the gold medal in football (soccer) at the Olympics – as they did in the Atlanta Olympics in 1996 – Nigerians everywhere, including those who wanted nothing to do with the country or have been advocating for its dismemberment are likely to forget or at least overlook their differences and flaunt their Nigerian-ness – at least for a while. Similarly if someone from a particular ethnicity makes a remarkable achievement such as becoming the President of Nigeria, people sharing the same ethnicity are likely to flaunt their membership of that 'successful' ethnicity. In essence the issue of which of our identities we give primacy at any given time has both space and time dimensions and may not be as straight forward as it seems.

Abridged from a paper presented at the African Studies Association Conference, Philadelphia, USA, 1 December 2012.

Daily Trust, December 6, 2012

CHAPTER 120

The identity crisis: Who is an African? (II)

In the first of this three-part series, I explored the notion of identity based on three broad propositions - namely that an individual embodies a mosaic of identities, that identities are cross-cutting and that identities that are under threat or deemed very successful will be the ones most flaunted or defended. I also argued that identities have time and space dimensions and thus could be quite fluid.

In this instalment, I will explore the notion of who is an African. It is obvious from our propositions that the African embodies a mosaic of identities with several affiliations which are flaunted or defended depending on the circumstances. Yet, when the question of 'Who is an African?' is posed, there is often an instinctive feeling that the answer is obvious or ought to be obvious. But is it really? Let me briefly examine some of the most common systems of identifying the African:

Racial identification
A starting point here may be to imagine what a non-African, say a Caucasian Briton, means when he talks of an 'African'. If a Caucasian British police officer describes the scene of a crime thus: "At the scene of the crime were four Africans and four white boys", what kind of images come to our mind, to differentiate the four 'Africans' from the four White boys? Here it would seem that physical attributes, especially attributes believed to be specifically 'African' or 'Bantu' (generally used as a label for some 300-600 ethnic groups in Africa) would be the primary organising category. If the same police officer changes the description to: "There were four Blacks and Four white boys at the scene of the crime", what sort of imageries come to our mind? Or better put, what sort of imageries do we think he is trying to convey?

I will argue that the use of 'African' – from the perspective of a 'non-African'- is much narrower than the use of 'Black' because our hypothetical Caucasian police officer would most likely think of 'Africans' as being different from Black Caribbean, Guyanese, Mixed race people or African-Americans even though they are all generically called Blacks in many societies. It would therefore seem that when our hypothetical Caucasian police officer used the word 'Black', he was trying to convey a broader racial category, extending beyond pure Bantu and Black skin pigmentation to culture and even the accent with which the non-Caucasian spoke English. This would seem to imply that while race does matter as an organising category in identifying the African, it would be inadequate in properly delineating, in the Western imagination at least, who is an African from who is Black.

Another problem of using race to delineate the African is that it would wrongly make all Black people Africans. While most Blacks obviously share a common bond, including of course that of skin pigmentation and possibly racial discrimination, does that really make all Blacks Africans? Are Black Haitians Africans? Would all Black Jamaicans be happy to be called Africans? Would all Africans from the continent accept the Black Jamaicans or Haitians as Africans on the same level of Africanity as themselves?

Again if we use race alone in the delineation of the African, a legitimate question is raised about non-Black people with African citizenship, say, White South Africans, who never knew any other country but South Africa. Are they Africans? And what of the White person, who, despite having lived all his life in the continent and has African citizenship, does not want to be regarded as an African?

Territoriality

On the face of it, a very simple way of delineating an African will be to look at the map of the world and categorise all those who were born in the continent of Africa or who hold the citizenship of one of the countries that make up the continent, or has ancestry in the continent, as African.

This option too has a number of problems. For example, is having the citizenship of an African country sufficient to make one an African? If being born or being a citizen of a country in the geographical expression called Africa is the pre-requisite, what of the millions of illiterate people living in the continent's villages who have never even heard of the word 'African' or 'citizenship'? Again, what of the descendants of African migrants say second or more generation of parents who migrated from Africa to Europe, America and other non-African countries and who do not hold the citizenship of any African country but feel deeply African? If we choose to call all who have 'African' ancestry Africans, how far back in time should we go?

Another problem of using geography or territoriality as a basis for identifying the African is that it assumes that all who are citizens of the countries that make up the continent of Africa accept that they are 'Africans'. Even within the countries in sub-Saharan Africa, there is often no unanimity among the citizens that they are all Africans on the same level of Africanity. For example the late Somali ruler, Siad Barre, who ruled between 1969 and 1991, was known to have actively discouraged Somalis from seeing themselves as Africans. Rather he encouraged them to see themselves as Arabs. Somali scholar Mohamed Eno has also documented the existence of a form of Apartheid in Somalia against the Bantu Jareer Somalis who have more Bantu than Arab features.

It is also common to hear some Ethiopians and Black South Africans refer to citizens of other countries of sub-Saharan Africa as "Africans" and to themselves as just Ethiopians or South Africans. Travelling to or from the rest of the continent, it is common to hear some Black South Africans say they are going to or coming from "Africa". Therefore, territoriality cannot be an adequate variable for delineating who the African is.

Consciousness

There are those who believe that 'consciousness' of being an African, or commitment to the cause of Africa, should be the only or main criterion for delineating who the

African is. This form of classification is quite popular with the remnants of the African left and those eager to wear the toga of universalism and cosmopolitanism. Ethiopian scholar Professor Mammo Muchie has for instance argued that any construction of African identity must be built on a rejection of essentialism, arguing that there is no such thing as an essential African character that has been frozen from time immemorial. He contended that African identity must be expressed through the rejection of racism, ethnicity, parochialism, exclusivity and barbarism. For him, African identity "must posit an inclusive, non-essentialist and emancipatory goals."

One of the dangers of using consciousness or commitment to the cause of Africa to define an African is that it is so fluid that any one expressing any sort of interest in African affairs could, by this definition, legitimately claim to be an African. Besides, using consciousness, which is subjective anyway, to delineate the African, could end up de-Africanising a majority of the people who non-Africans are likely to identify on face value as Africans because the consciousness of being African, at least for the rural dwellers and the non-educated, is non-existent. Again, if having the right consciousness is enough to make one an African, can Tony Blair, who as Prime Minister of Britain, said that Africa was a scar on the consciousness of the world and felt moved enough to set up the Commission for Africa, be called an African?

Different Africanities

There are those who believe that just one affiliation will be inadequate to delineate an African. Leading African political scientist Professor Ali Mazrui for instance believes that three affiliations are necessary – blood, soil and ancestry. Based on this, he identified different types of Africans – 'Africans of the blood' who are defined in racial and genealogical terms; 'Africans of the soil' who are defined in geographical and genealogical terms, 'geographical Afrabians' who are Africans of the soil in North Africa but without intermarriage with Africans of the blood (Black Africans) and 'Genealogical Afrabians' who are products of intermarriages between Arabs and Black Africans.

A major problem with the use of a hybrid form of affiliation in delineating the African is that advocates of such a classificatory scheme are often unable to tell us which of the different identified affiliations should be prioritised in identifying the African under different circumstances. They are also often unable to tell us if there is a hierarchy in the different Africanities they identified and why.

Adapted from a paper entitled 'Who is an Africa?: Navigating through the minefields of African Identities' presented at the African Studies Association Conference, Philadelphia, USA, 1 December 2012.

Daily Trust, December 13, 2012

CHAPTER 121

The identity crisis: Who is an African? (III)

In part II of this series, I interrogated the various conventional methods commonly used in identifying the African – racial, territorial, consciousness and a hybrid form of identification involving more than one form of affiliation. I showed the inadequacies of each of these conventional methods of classification. And this brings us back to square one: How then do we identify the African?

In a contribution to a book I edited in 2009, [*Who is an African? Identity, Citizenship and the Making of the Africa-Nation*] I took the position that there is a hierarchy of Africans and that some are more African than others – depending on the number of relevant affiliations they possess such as being Black, being born in Africa, speaking African languages etc. My position on this has however evolved and I no longer believe this because I wrongly assumed that identity is frozen in time and space. I also wrongly believed that an African identity was a sort of a badge of honour to be doled out to those who met the conditions. The truth however is that identity is both an imposition and an expression. My earlier position is also inadequate in knowing the circumstance under which an African decides that one element of his identity – his religion, race or ethnicity - should be the defining characteristic of his person.

My current position is that the notion of 'African' as an ascription or imposition – the way others identify one - must be distinguished from the notion of an African as an expression – people consciously choosing who they are. As an ascription, I believe that those ascribing African-ness to others will have in their mind a hierarchy of Africans in which the more one has of the relevant attributes, the more African one is taken to be. As an expression however - people consciously choosing who they want to be - the element of identity that is perceived to be most under threat or most successful will always be the one most defended or flaunted. And this will have time and space dimensions and could be very dynamic. In essence, Nigerians of different religious and ethnic affiliations finding themselves in a foreign country can easily leave their politicised primordial differences behind and be united under their common African-ness or Nigerian-ness. This common identity may however dissolve when they return back to the country and are persuaded to be socialized into other forms of identities. Depending on where they live in the country, the identity they flaunt or defend most may vary. In essence, identities are not ossified. They are fluid, with time and space dimensions. If a collection of people of different racial identities living in a very racist locality in say USA were to be attacked by aliens from an outer space, there is a likelihood that all the people in that locality will sink their racial differences and will be united under their common human-ness to ward off the threat from the aliens from the outer space.

Back to the question of who is an African. In the global context and as an ascription I believe that race will continue to be a critical, even if an insufficient index used in the delineation of who the African is. This is largely because of the role of race in the slave trade, colonization, de-colonization, the current system of generating technological progress and in the distribution of the fruits of economics and technical progress. In other words, the notions of 'Black' and 'White' are both ideological and political, conjuring images of oppression, victimhood, success and excellence. Therefore following the proposition that identities that are under threat or very successful will always be the ones most flaunted or defended, using race to identify people in the global context, especially the notions of Black and White, are likely to be with us for some time to come.

Applying the argument

How can we apply the notions of identity developed here to Nigeria? Why do Nigerians very easily take refuge in their primordial identities? Let's take another issue from the recent controversy generated by Chinua Achebe's book: *There was a Country: A Personal History of Biafra*. Why did many Igbo, including those not even born during the war feel an instinctive need to support Achebe in accusing the late chief Awolowo and General Gowon of genocide during the war? Why did many people from the North and the South West, including those who virtually knew nothing about the war come out in vigorous defence of the two?

In politics, language is commonly used to frame political discourses. For instance a word like 'dictatorship' implies a regime that represses its people, making 'mass revolt' against such a regime heroic since it implies a moral fight to ward off evil. Given Americans' love of freedom, tagging any regime a 'dictatorship' automatically justifies any state action against that regime in the eyes of many Americans. Similarly accusing any regime of possessing 'weapons of mass destruction' frames the discourse of an impending Armageddon, which then justifies any action to prevent it.

In Nigeria, emotionally charged words like 'marginalization', 'genocide', 'civil war hero', push people 'forward to the past', making them active participants in a past in which the event occurred. And following our argument that identities that are under threat or deemed to be very successful will be the most flaunted or defended, they will stake strong positions on the issues based on the affiliation that is perceived to be under threat or successful. Because agenda-laden language is used to frame discourses in the marketplace of political ideas, any language used in such wise will generate counter responses. You cannot for instance expect Igbo people not to respond if there is a newspaper advertorial celebrating someone as a 'civil war hero' (for in that phrase inheres a subtle narrative of victory and defeat, reminding them about the civil war and all they believed they suffered). In the same vein some Igbos often come out smoking whenever the late Emeka Ojukwu is described as a 'rebel' leader because they see in the word a certain triumphalism and moral/political righteousness, which they believe do not capture the reasons they believe they attempted to secede. Similarly when the Igbos accuse others of 'genocide', there is inherent in that word a subtle accusation of 'wickedness, cruelty and murder against a largely defenceless people', which will naturally generate counter responses from those being accused.

Therefore precisely because we deliberately use language to frame political discourses to favour us, and given the crisis in the country's national-building, it becomes understandable why any attempt to rationally discuss any issue in the country almost always degenerates into ethnic or religious shouting matches and finger pointing.

My friend and former colleague Na'Allah Mohammed Zagga asked how we can use some of the propositions we developed in the first part of the series to explain the case of the late Libyan leader Colonel Muammar Gaddaff who once formally denounced his Arab identity and proclaimed himself an 'African'. The simple explanation is that identity, as we argued, is both an expression (a conscious choice) and an ascription. As an expression Gaddaffi was free to decide who he wanted to be – just as many of people go to foreign countries and decide to acquire their citizenships. It can for instance be argued that Barrack Obama consciously chose to be Black by marrying a 'proper' African American woman, attending a Black Pentecostal church with his wife and working as a community organizer in a predominantly Black area of Chicago. As an ascription however, we have no influence over the identity others will assign to us – as a Black man, honest man, a fraud etc. Therefore even though Gaddafi renounced his Arab identity, he was bound to be seen as an Arab by many people – whether he liked that or not.

Traitor

And how do we use our propositions to explain the notion of a 'traitor'? We argued that an individual is a mosaic of identities some of which could be cross-cutting. For instance an Ijaw may choose not to support the presidential candidacy of Goodluck Jonathan, his fellow Ijaw, because he prioritises his common membership of an influential club with another presidential candidate over ethnic solidarity. He can also estimate that he stands to gain better if the other candidate wins. This is another way of saying that he believes that his networks, (which are part of his identities), can guarantee him better access to the non-Ijaw candidate than if his fellow Ijaw were to win. Therefore when we call someone a 'traitor', we wrongly assume that the person has just one identity, which is frozen in time and space or that there is a universally shared notion of what is good and bad or even what is just

Adapted from a paper presented at the African Studies Association Conference, Philadelphia, USA, 1 December 2012.

Daily Trust January 2, 2013

CHAPTER 122

The Military's Misadventure in Burkina Faso

The September 17 2015 coup in Burkina Faso against the country's interim leadership contains important lessons in democratic consolidation in Africa. Under pressure from demonstrators, striking labour unions and the continental regional organizations - the African Union and ECOWAS - the coup leader, Gen. Gilbert Diendere was forced to 'step aside'. President Michel Kafando and Prime Minister *Yacouba* Isaac Zida were restored to power as transitional leaders of the country.

The trigger for the coup was dissatisfaction by members of the elite presidential guard (RSP), which was set up by Blaise Compaore after he overthrew Capt Sankara in a military coup in 1987. Sankara, regarded as Africa's 'Che Guevara' who had changed the name of the former French colony from Upper Volta to Burkina Faso ("land of honest men") - lost his life in the coup. In 2014 a failed attempt by Compaore, (who had transformed himself into a civilian President and had then ruled for a total of 27 years), to extend his tenure beyond the constitutionally allowed two terms led to uprisings that forced him into exile. A new transitional government in the country came up with a new electoral law banning candidates linked to the failed 2014 bid to elongate the tenure of Blaise Compaore - mostly members of the elite RSP and the former ruling party CDP - from contesting in the elections scheduled for October this year. One of those affected by the ban was General Diendere's wife.

There are a number of lessons to be learned from the short-lived coup:

One, though democratic consciousness is growing in the continent, the coup reveals that the continent does not lack adventurist soldiers who may want to exploit popular discontent to supplant legitimately constituted authority. There have been over 26 attempted military coups in the continent in the past five years alone. The failed coup attempt in Burkina Faso was the second military coup in the country in one year.

After decades of military rule, the rationalizations for the military's intervention in African politics no longer wash with people who are old enough to remember what life was really like under military rule. The good news however is that only very few military coups succeed these days. General Diendere who led the recent coup in Burkina Faso was later to confess that "this coup was the biggest mistake…. One should not have taken such action". Certainly the current international environment does not encourage military incursion in politics and both the African Union and regional organizations such as ECOWAS are increasingly taking very hard line approaches to coup makers. In Nigeria, most of the current structural problems facing the country were arguably created by the military.

Two, Africa seems to have moved from the era of military coups to constitutional coup attempts. As military dictatorships and one party rule became passé with the end of the Cold War, Africa entered the so-called 'third wave' of its experiment with liberal democracy. Across the continent liberal democracy was being universalized, usually with term limits. However the continent's liberal democracy project faces resistance from two forces: adventurist soldiers who nurse a nostalgia for the period when the military was the shortest route to power in Africa and civilian beneficiaries of this 'third wave' of democracy who nurse a nostalgia for the period of one party dictatorship that prevailed in most parts of the continent shortly after independence until the end of the Cold War. Nearly all the beneficiaries of the current 'wave' of democratization which began in Africa in the 1990s tried to elongate their tenures beyond the constitutionally allowed term limits. Even those once lionized by the West as representing a new crop of African leaders such as Olusegun Obasanjo of Nigeria, Abdoulaye Wade of Senegal and Paul Kagame of Rwanda all tried (or in the case of Kagame suspected of nursing the ambition) to elongate their tenures. While Obasanjo tried and failed in Nigeria, Wade succeeded in changing his country's constitution in Senegal to permit him to run for a third term but then lost the presidential election in 2012. Paul Kagame, of Rwanda, who was much beloved in the West had been Rwanda's Vice President and Minister of Defence from 1994 to 2000 when he became his country's substantive President.   He won an election in 2003, under a new Constitution adopted that year and was again elected to a second term of seven years in 2010. Though his term expires in 2017 and should not be constitutionally extended, his body language has clearly shown an inclination to tinker with the constitution to elongate his tenure.

Resistance to tenure elongation has been fierce in several countries. In Burkina Faso, the 2014 coup was caused by attempts by Compaore to extend his tenure.   In Niger, where four successful military coups have occurred since 1974, the February 2010 coup in that country which ousted President Mamadou Tandja followed the grumblings that attended his decision to amend the country's constitution to remain in power beyond the constitutionally allowed two-term limit. Burundi's President Pierre Nkurunziza who violently resisted months of popular discontent eventually got his third term in office but at a bloody cost. From Burundi to Benin, Rwanda and Congo Kinshasha to Uganda, Algeria, Angola, Chad, Djibouti and Cameroun, there are or have been attempts at tenure elongation – often leading to violent clashes on the streets or animating the hunger of some military adventurists for a piece of the action.

Three, the fight against terrorism in Africa embeds in it a potential threat to democracy. Counter terrorism measures have not only led to measures that curtail citizens' freedoms such as imposition of curfews and roadblocks, but also people trained in the new techniques for fighting terrorism could become security risks to the state. For instance the leader of the recent coup in Burkina Faso Lt General Diendere was the president of the country's Flintlock 2010 Committee, which is a major US-led military exercise designed to "enable African partners to combat violent extremist organizations" and provide "increased interoperability, counter-terrorism and combat skills training while creating a venue for regional engagement." Remarkably, Lieutenant Colonel Yacouba Isaac Zida who served as Burkina Faso's acting head of state in November 2014 after seizing power in the aftermath of the 2014 uprising that forced the abdication of Compaore, also previously received US military training. Again Capt. Amadou Haya Sanogo, who led a renegade military faction that overthrew the democratically elected government in Mali in 2012 equally received US military training. We may therefore have to keep an eye on soldiers receiving advanced military training to help combat the current terrorist challenges. In the 1960s and 1970s, the 'modernization thesis' – the idea that relative to the civilian political leadership, the military, by its training could be considered modern and therefore better equipped to run the affairs of the country than the civilians, was one of the excuses used to justify military coups in Africa. With new training in counter insurgency, the soldiers may also get into the temptation of feeling that by their new training they are better equipped to confront the current challenges of our time.

Five, the impasse in Burkina Faso following the short-lived coup was resolved, not through military means but through dialogue. There were fears that the country would descend into chaos or factional armed conflicts after the ECOWAS mediators initially failed to reverse the coup. Though Burkina Faso's Army chiefs sent regular troops to Ouagadougou they refrained from leading a direct offensive against the RSP but rather were persuading Diendere's men to return to their barracks. The ECOWAS mediating group also toned down its rhetoric. Dialogue prevailed throughout as even rival generals sought to find a peaceful solution to avoid further bloodshed. By embracing dialogue, Burkina Faso's Army chiefs gave Africa's armies an important lesson in showing restraint and trying to avoid confrontation at all costs.

The above lesson is also applicable to other African leaders confronting other challenges - whether we are talking about terrorist groups like Boko Haram or insurgency movements such as MASSOB and OPC or dealing with other 'de-Nigerianized' Nigerians. Dialogue is never a sign of weakness. Rather it remains the best tool for achieving reconciliation especially in deeply polarized societies.

Daily Trust September 17 2015

CHAPTER 123

Issues in Nigeria's Foreign Policy

In my column last week on corruption, I mentioned that I was a discussant on the foreign policy segment of the recent 2-day Policy Dialogue – 'Implementing Change – from Vision to Reality' organised by the Directorate of Policy, Research and Strategy of APC's Presidential Campaign Organisation. My interventions borrowed heavily from my published criticisms of aspects of Nigeria's foreign policy under the Jonathan administration, viz: 'NEC Was Wrong on New Foreign Policy Proposal' (published November 3, 2010) and 'How Not to Formulate Foreign Policy' (published on August 20, 2011). It equally borrowed from my article on 'Debating Diaspora Voting', (published 28 August 2014).

In late 2010 the National Executive Council (NEC) took a decision that Nigeria would no longer play 'big brother' to countries in trouble "without getting anything in return", and that going forward the nation's foreign interventions and assistance would be guided by the 'national interest'. Briefing journalists after the Council's meeting at Abuja, Babangida Aliyu, who was at that time the Governor of Niger State was quoted as saying: "…we are going to shed that belief that we are big brother where we go to help other people and we never get something in return…So, wherever we go or whoever we relate with, must be because it will help us develop, rather than, as we normally say, that we have gone to help these or that people without getting anything in return." At a seminar to 'review Nigeria's foreign policy' organised by the Presidential Advisory Council on International Relations (PAC-IR) in collaboration with the Ministry of Foreign Affairs at Abuja from August 1- 4 2011, this point was re-emphasised.

While it is true that 'national interest' is at the heart of foreign policy, (in fact the French word 'raison d'état' - meaning 'reason of the state' -vividly captures this), rarely is a country so rude as to stick it to the face of other international actors that its primary concern in its relations with them is the advancement of its 'national interest'. For instance though the colonisation of Africa was in the main undertaken because of the interest of the colonists to find raw materials, it was couched on the morally acceptable ideology of the 'need to civilise the natives'. In the same vein, former US President George W Bush justified the Iraq war on the moralistic need to find Saddam Hussein's Weapons of Mass Destruction. Even the Opium Wars (1839-1842, 1856-1860), one of the most mercantilist projections of 'national interest' in history was still given a morally acceptable justification. Though the wars were caused by the smuggling of opium by merchants from British India into China in defiance of Chinese prohibition laws, Britain's formal justification for the war was a need to stem China's balance of payment deficits. Those calling for a more explicit embedment of immediate economic gratification in our foreign policy are therefore not only throwing diplomatese to the winds but also advertising the country's weakness to the world. As Wole Soyinka would tell us, "a tiger does not need to proclaim its tigeritude."

I was also very uncomfortable with the idea of announcing to the whole world that Nigeria was reviewing its foreign policy. Not only did this re-echo policy reversals and instabilities for which we have become infamous, my personal opinion is that you don't really need to have a Presidential Committee on Review of Nigeria's Foreign Policy to do this. How many times have we read about the US, Britain or Germany announcing a panel to review its foreign policy? My personal opinion is that this is the day job of the Ministry of Foreign Affairs and think-tanks such as the Nigerian Institute of International Affairs and similar institutions. Given the dynamic nature of international relations, a country through its Ministry of Foreign affairs, independent think-tanks and consultants is constantly reviewing its relations with different countries and institutions depending on changes in power configurations that create new opportunities or threats. I have a feeling that people who grandstand about trade and economic-driven foreign policy or immediate financial gratification from any international engagement, are mixing up the role of the economic/trade missions found in the country's various embassies with foreign policy.

I also feel that there is a little confusion about the meaning of 'national interest' – the totality of a country's goals and ambitions whether economic, cultural, military or otherwise. Contrary to the impression that 'national interest' is projected only when financial gains are expressly and immediately extracted from an interaction with other state and non-state actors, sometimes states invest in enhancing its influence in a country or region because of the leverage such influence could give it in the future (such as being allowed to station a military base in the country/region in the future or to avoid the influx of refugees that could overwhelm its social services). This too is projecting 'national interest'. I believe that contrary to popular belief, we have actually benefitted from the countries we helped in the past – South Africa, Liberia, Sierra Leone etc. I believe that we derived the intangible benefit of our international prestige rising as we 'helped' them. If we were not able to leverage on such intangible assets, it was more because of the failure of leadership or poor economic circumstances at home, not foreign policy. Usually forgotten in the discussion of how 'ungrateful' countries we have helped in the past have become is that we often 'unleash' our human capital on them after 'helping' them. It certainly seems that the population of Nigerians in countries we 'helped' increased astronomically after our 'help'. It seems that the role of such Nigerians in the remittance economy is overlooked. It is therefore misleading to assume that playing 'big brother' to other African countries means that the country's 'national interest' is not being projected. This is the whole notion of 'soft power' - winning over the minds of the people in the countries we play 'big brother' to. Converting this soft power to economic benefits will depend on the character of the country's political leadership, the cohesiveness of its elite and the level of development of its productive forces.

Related to this is that a nation's respectability in international relations is not wholly contingent upon its past benevolence but often more on the current leverages it can bring to the table. Even in domestic politics, past benevolence seems to count for little as we have seen in the face-offs between political god-fathers and almost all the Governors that they installed in office. The bottom line therefore is that if Nigeria wants to command influence and respect, it must improve and sustain its ability to bring leverages to the table. This is obviously where the interplay between domestic politics and foreign policy comes into play. As the street urchins would say in Pidgin English, "I get am before no be property".

I was miffed at suggestions in 2010 that Africa would no longer be the centre-piece of our foreign policy. Part of my critique of that proposal was that Africa being the centre piece of our foreign policy does not mean that we would always take Afrocentric position on issues – but that we should strive to be a leader in the continent. It is not unusual for a country to once in a while have a more compelling national interest which would require taking positions that is contrary to the position of most of its immediate allies. For instance during the Thirty Years' War in Europe (1618-1648) – a largely religious conflict between Protestants and Catholics - France chose to intervene on the side of the Protestants despite its overwhelming Catholicism because the regime was apparently more interested at that time in blocking the growing power of the Holy Roman Emperor than in protecting its religious faith. Similarly though Europe could be called the centre-piece of British foreign policy, Britain sometimes disagrees with other European countries (such as during the Iraq War) but would often return to rebuild burnt bridges after such disagreements in other not to undermine its leadership role in the continent.

I am not suggesting that all is well with our foreign policies. But the problem, as I see it, is not in trying to find one sexy phrase to encapsulate our foreign policies – Africa as the centrepiece of our foreign policy, the notion of concentric circle, citizen diplomacy etc. The problems in our foreign policy are largely symptomatic of the crisis of underdevelopment weighing down the country and which in turn feeds on our stalled nation-building project.

A key solution is re-starting the stalled nation building process (given the interplay between domestic circumstances and the vibrancy of a country's foreign policy), pursuing policies of inclusion, (including voting rights for our Diaspora, that in 2013 alone, according to the World Bank, brought into the country a whopping $21bn through remittances) and continuing and improving upon those economic policies that led to the country being included in the Next 11 emergent economies in 2005 and in MINT countries (Mexico, India, Nigeria and Turkey) that were predicted to become break-out economies. The global interest in Nigeria in the last five years has been unprecedented, leading to a huge inflow of foreign direct investments. We must sustain and improve on policies that helped to power such optimisms in the country – before the collapse of oil prices. The bottom line here is that we must not, for political expediency, throw away the good in Goodluck Jonathan.

Daily Trust June 4 2015

CHAPTER 124

Nation-building: The Mandela and Nyerere Examples

In my column last week, I re-stated what I have always believed is the fundamental problem of the country – namely the crisis in our nation-building process. I believe that unless Nigerians feel there is 'an imagined community' that has their overarching loyalty, the current wave of de-Nigerianisation will continue unabated and solutions thrown at our problems will end up compounding those problems. A central manifestation of the crisis in Nigeria's nation-building project is that no individual or institution enjoys universal legitimacy across the fault lines.

A fundamental question is how this crisis will be resolved amid the numerous developmental challenges facing the country.

The key responsibility for driving a reconciliation process in any polarized and fractious society lies with the leadership of that country. Since the leader of such a fractious society necessarily belongs to one of the fault lines or contending blocs in such a society, he or she has to make an early choice whether to deliberately transcend the extant fault lines (at the risk of displeasing his or her 'own people' in the short term) or politicize those fault lines by cultivating some and alienating others in a bid to entrench himself or herself in power.

In this piece I will highlight the examples of Mandela and Nyerere in uniting post-apartheid South Africa and Tanzania respectively.

Mandela

Mandela's story has been told so often that it needs no repeating. He died on December 5 2013 as one of the greatest moral authorities in the world. He was one of the few souls that had a date set aside every year to celebrate him. July 18, Mandela's birthday, was globally celebrated as the Mandela Day by the United Nations. During such celebrations, people were asked to devote 67 minutes of their time - one minute for each year Mandela spent in prison –to help others or consciously do something that will help change the world or their environment for the better.

Jailed for 27 years for his opposition to apartheid, Nelson Rolihlahla *Mandela* came out of prison in 1990 expressing no bitterness towards those who deprived him of 27 years of his life. When he was sworn in as post-apartheid South Africa's first democratically elected President in 1994, many Black hard liners wanted justice for the sins of apartheid while many White people were apprehensive of their fate under Black majority rule. Mandela opted to champion reconciliation among the country's fractious population, espousing the principles of nation-building and co-operative governance.

It would take more than a generous human spirit for any man to truly forgive people who jailed him for 27 years. More than that, Mandela had to deal with the initial disappointment of many of his hard line Black supporters who felt that he was subordinating reconciliation to the quest for justice. It was a gamble: if he alienated his

Black supporters and the Whites ended up despising him, he would have lost out completely. But the gamble paid off: he was able to transcend the fault lines in the country and by so doing became a unifying symbol.

When he set up the Truth and Reconciliation Commission in 1995, the emphasis was on reconciliation in sharp contrast to the approach taken by the Nuremberg Trials and other de-Nazification measures.

Even before he became President in 1994, Mandela had chosen to be a reconciler. A clear demonstration of this was in 1993 when a White right winger murdered Chris Hani (at the time arguably the ANC's most popular leader after Mandela). Many Black South Africans simply wanted war. But Mandela thought otherwise. In one of his most impassioned speeches, Mandela declared:

> "Tonight I am reaching out to every single South African, black and white, from the very depths of my being. A white man, full of prejudice and hate, came to our country and committed a deed so foul that our whole nation now teeters on the brink of disaster....

> "A white woman, of Afrikaner origin, risked her life so that we may know, and bring to justice this assassin."

Mandela's greatest legacy was his uncanny ability to steer South Africa through the crisis of its rebirth. Though today South Africa still remains a divided country, it would certainly have been worse without Mandela.

Nyerere

Assessments of Julius Nyerere, Tanzania's first president (1962-1985) tend to focus on his quest for *ujamaa* - a just social order based on community solidarity. While supporters hail *ujamaa* as a "creative adjustment of socialist thought to local realities", critics contemptuously dismiss it as an attempt at redistributing poverty.

Often overlooked by his critics is that Nyerere's concern with social justice had to be understood within the context of his commitment to building a true Tanzanian nation. For instance in his farewell address to the Tanzanian Parliament on July 29 1985, Nyerere was quoted as saying:

> "The single most important task, which I set out in my inaugural address in December 1962, was that of building a united nation on the basis of human equality and dignity."

While Tanzania remains seriously poor on many economic and social indicators, few doubt that his nation-building project was a huge success. And this was not because his nation-building strategies were unique – they were not. True, he introduced Swahili as a national language – but so did Emperor Haile Selassie introduce Amharic as the national language in Ethiopia and Siad Barre standardize the Somali script in Somalia and make it the sole national language in Somalia. While the Swahili language helped to further Nyerere's nation-building in Tanzania; the same introduction of a national language in both Ethiopia and Somalia failed to prevent the fragmentation of both countries. The crucial difference between the nation-building efforts in Ethiopia and Somalia and the one in Tanzania was simply Nyerere's leadership.

In fact despite continuing challenges of underdevelopment, Tanzania has largely avoided the tumultuous ethnic politics of most African states. In fact the country's sense of national identity is legendary and something of a pride in Africa. For instance a 2011 Afrobarometer survey by the London School of Economics, in which some Africans were asked if they identified more with their national or ethnic identity, showed that 88 per cent of Tanzanian respondents said they prioritized their national identity over their ethnic identity. This contrasted with the continental average of 42 per cent who prioritised their national identity over their ethnic identity. The figure for Nigeria was a paltry 17 per cent.

Lessons

Nigerian leaders can learn a number of lessons in nation-building from the examples of Mandela and Nyerere:

One, a leader has to make a conscious decision, even before coming to power, on whether he or she wants to be appropriated by his ethnic/regional base or whether he or she wants to transcend all the fault lines. This is not always an easy choice in a very polarized society like ours, where concerted efforts will be made to indoctrinate the new leader into the culture of "it is our turn". In Nigeria, national leaders tend to prioritise how their ethnic/regional in-group will remember them when they are no longer in power over how the country or even the world at large will remember them.

Two, how can a leader who means well be accepted in a fractured and low trust environment like ours where every action of the leader will be interrogated using cultural and ethnic markers? Here the leader has to learn that his intentions count for little and that perception is everything. This means that the leader has to think through the perception effects of every policy option he or she wants to embrace. Quite often every policy option has the politics that goes with it and such politics has to be managed. A leader needs to be aware of the cost of managing such politics vis-à-vis the gains from such policy options. For instance, in the current 'war against corruption', what do we really gain, from the perspective of nation-building, by announcing that only Jonathan's regime will be 'probed'? Since historically the word 'probe' is always associated with vendetta in our country(making it easier for anyone found guilty in such a probe to cry persecution), would we have lost anything if the government had set up technical committees (which historically tend to be more acceptable) to look into a range of ministries, parastatals and agencies? The only thing we would have lost, in my opinion, is the current media drama and media trial that I honestly believe are distractions.

Three, nation-building is not incompatible with doing the right thing – whether we are talking about fighting economic crimes or any other malfeasance. It simply means being very sensitive to how our actions and inactions would be perceived across the fault lines and deliberately using state instruments to promote feelings of oneness.

Four, a leader can exploit simple symbolisms to further the cause of nation-building. For instance during the last presidential campaign, a big part of the hugely successful rebranding of Buhari was making him dress in the local attire of different ethnic groups he visited. His photograph, on several websites, in which he was dressed in a suit and bow-tie made him look like an adorable school principal or a disciplinarian father figure. One would like to see the president rediscover those symbolic gestures to help widen his appeal across the fault lines.

Daily Trust, August 6 2015

CHAPTER 125

Lessons from the Scottish Referendum

Scotland held a referendum on September 18 2014 to answer just one question: Should Scotland become an independent country? The voters decided by 55.3 per cent to 44.7 per cent that they would rather continue to be part of the United Kingdom. Heading to the referendum, the polls were too close to call, with some suggesting that the "No" campaigners might carry the day by a narrow margin. The outcome is a testament that the loudest advocates of a cause may actually not be reflecting the wishes of the people they claim to speak for.

A very interesting question is why the passion for independence remains strong in Scotland, despite having been part of the United Kingdom for over 300 years and producing a number of Prime Ministers for the union, including Tony Blair (1997-2007) and Gordon Brown (2007-2010). The kingdom of England and the kingdom of Scotland, which were previously separate states with separate legislatures but sharing the same monarch since 1603 were joined together into a single kingdom of Great Britain through Acts of Union passed in 1706 and 1707 respectively by the Parliaments of England and Scotland.

It is generally believed that the desire for Scottish independence is rooted in current political differences between the country and the rest of the United Kingdom. For instance Scotland is believed to be more liberal than the wealthier but relatively more conservative England. This belief has led some Scottish nationalists to agitate for full independence so they would have more room to push for even more liberal political and social agenda. In essence, the independence referendum was not really about Scotland being marginalized in the scheme of affairs in the United Kingdom but about political differences. National pride was also a factor because Scots have a long history of scepticism toward the union.

There are several reasons why the "No" campaigners carried the day. The three major UK parties – Labour, Conservatives and Liberal Democrats- had for instance promised more autonomy for Scotland if independence was rejected. It is possible that the so-called "devo-max" option helped to persuade some undecided voters in the run up to the referendum. Already Scottish Parliament has the right to set and administer Scottish policies in several areas of national life, including on healthcare and education. Under "devo-max" Scottish parliament would be given control over of the items that are currently reserved to the UK Parliament in Westminster. Will Nigeria be willing to consider such flexibility to some nationalities such as sharia to those who clamour for it? Canada has a similar flexibility in dealing with separatist agitations from Quebec.

The "Better Together" campaigners also used fear mongering as they harped on the risks of independence including that it could leave the country's economy small and weak. The financial markets appeared to buy into such sentiments because when polls showed that the pro-independence campaign was gaining ground, stocks in

Scottish companies fell heavily on the news - the Royal Bank of Scotland, Standard Life, and the SSE utility company each fell by more than 2 per cent while the Lloyds banking group fell by more than 3 per cent. This must have rattled the undecided voters.

Other "No" campaigners point out that the Union goes beyond economics to emotional issues of shared heritage, family ties and centuries of joint contributions to the building of the UK brand - in economics, politics, diplomacy, culture, scientific innovations and technological progress. As J.K. Rowling, the famous Scottish author of Harry Potter who donated £1 million to the 'Better Together' campaign emotionally put it: "If we leave, though, there will be no going back. This separation will not be quick and clean: it will take microsurgery to disentangle three centuries of close interdependence, after which we will have to deal with three bitter neighbours."

Several lessons could be drawn from the Scottish referendum and its outcome.

One, the desire for some nationalities that make up a country to be independent is natural, and trying to use blackmail to suppress such feelings can only drive their canvassers underground and glamourize the cause they espouse. Just as there are several agglomeration of previously different nationalities that became successful nations – China, France, Tanzania and United Kingdom – there are also several federations and countries that have imploded after years, decades or even centuries of being together. Examples here include Yugoslavia, Czechoslovakia, the Union of Soviet Socialist Republic and the Federation of Rhodesia and Nyasaland. Even in the United States there are still groups that hoist the confederate flag of independence. The bottom line is that we need to find more creative ways of dealing with separatist tendencies as our current blackmail strategy appears counter- productive.

Two, referendum may be one way of resolving the apparently intractable 'national question' in Nigeria. There may be a need for a constitution which allows for the conduct of referendum among nationalities that want to secede from the union say once every 30 years. I believe that the idea of declaring that discussion about the unity of Nigeria is a 'no go area' to successive constitutional or national conferences is counterproductive as it only helps to romanticise the hush-hush agitations for independence. In Scotland, when the separatist Scottish National Party lost the referendum, Alex Salmond, a long-time canvasser for independence, announced that he would stand down as Scotland's First Minister and leader of the SNP. The outcome of the referendum was in essence an indication that his views on Scottish independence were not representative of the views of the majority of Scots men and women. How do we know if those agitating for separation in our country are truly reflecting the wishes of the people they claim to represent or merely presenting their personal agendas as the views of the people? Another advantage of a generational referendum is that it will force the country to be fair to all its constituent parts, knowing that those that feel marginalized may opt for independence during a referendum. It is instructive that the issue of 'marginalization' was not one of the issues of the 'Yes' campaigners in Scotland.

Three, if the 'Yes' campaigners had won; it would still not mean an automatic independence for Scotland. There will still be protracted negotiation around a number of knotty issues such as how to share assets and liabilities, the fate of the British Royal Navy's Trident nuclear submarines which is currently based near Glasgow, whether there would be a closed or open border between England and Scotland and who would be eligible for Scottish or dual citizenship.

For Nigeria, any decision by any group to go its way will also involve very complex negotiations: How do we share our assets and liabilities? How do we define the boundaries of the new nations? How do we deal with the internal contradictions in the new country?

Four, the clamour for a sort of return to regionalism based on the six geopolitical zones could be in the short term an antidote to secessionist sentiments. But as the Scottish case has shown, it could also in the longer term sharpen the demand for separation. For instance Scotland has enjoyed considerable autonomy for over two decades as a way of assuaging the demands for separatism, including having its own parliament: Despite this (or partly because of it), there was the ascendancy of the Scottish National Party in 2011, which duly began demanding for referendum for full independence. The good lesson from them however is that both the "Yes" and "Nay" campaigners were allowed to trade their ideas openly and freely in the political marketplace. The victory of the 'Better Together' campaigners is likely to blunt the demand for Scottish independence for a long time to come. In fact, SNP leadership indicated in the run up to the referendum that it would abandon its push for independence if the referendum backed continued union with the UK, saying that the vote was a "once-in-a-generation opportunity." This should be a big lesson to Nigeria, especially those who feign anger at any suggestion that the country should be restructured to serve everyone better. The Scottish referendum and its outcome should be a good lesson to Nigeria on how to manage separatist agitations without bloodshed.

Daily Trust, September 25, 2014

CHAPTER 126

South Africa: Beyond Xenophobia and 'Market Dominant Minorities'

The wave of attacks against foreigners in South Africa, mostly migrants from other African countries, has attracted justified condemnation from around the world. Seven lives have been lost in the orgy of violence, with soldiers now (rather belatedly) deployed to some of the key flashpoints to help contain the mayhem. In 2008 a similar anti-foreigner violence left 62 people dead with over 100,000 displaced. The Economist of 25 April 2015 quotes one Jean Pierre Misago, a researcher at the African Centre for Migration and Society in Johannesburg as estimating that at least 350 foreigners have been killed in xenophobic violence in South Africa since 2008. But Mr Misago told The Economist he only heard of one conviction for murder.

Xenophobia or Afrophobia?

How can one characterize the episodic anti-foreigner violence in South Africa, which some call Xenophobia and others Afrophobia? A starting point is to understand that in South Africa, the term 'foreigner' has a pejorative meaning and usually refers to African and Asian nationals. Other foreigners, especially Whites from America and Europe are usually seen and treated as "tourists" or "expats".

Some have called the attacks 'Afrophobia' (hatred of Africans) because they target essentially enterprising African immigrants from Somalia, Nigeria, the Democratic Republic of Congo, Mozambique and Malawi who often own shops and other businesses in the country's informal economy. But this is not quite the full picture since nationals from Bangladesh and Pakistan are equally profiled and targeted. Certainly hatred of Africans is pervasive as are also hatred of Asians.

To call the violence 'xenophobia' in the sense in which the word is usually defined as "the unreasoned fear of that which is perceived to be foreign or strange", will also not be quite correct since White people from Europe and America are usually exempt from such attacks. Perhaps a more apt term will be 'Afro-Asiaphobia'.

'Market Dominant Minority'

In her very important first book, *World on Fire: How Exporting Free Market Democracy Breeds Ethnic Hatred and Global Instability* (2003), Amy Chua, Professor of Law at Yale Law School explores the ethnic conflict caused in many societies by disproportionate economic or political influence wielded by "market dominant minorities". She notes for instance that though the Chinese Filipino community is 1% of the population of the country, it controls 60 percent of the economy, with the result being envy and bitterness on the part of the majority against the minority. Again in Indonesia, while the Chinese Indonesian community makes up only 3% of the population, it controls 70 % of the economy.

Other examples of 'market-dominant minorities' given by Chua include overseas Chinese in Southeast Asia; whites in Latin America and South Africa; Israeli Jews in Israel and the Middle East; Croats in the former Yugoslavia; Yoruba, Igbos, Kikuyus, Tutsis, Indians and

Lebanese, among others, in Sub-Saharan Africa for Chua tension and conflicts are often inherent in the relationship between the 'the economic dominant minority' and the poor majority in the context of liberal democracy. For her, when "free market democracy is pursued in the presence of a market-dominant minority, the almost invariable result is backlash" because "overnight democracy will empower the poor, indigenous majority. What happens is that under those circumstances, democracy doesn't do what we expect it to do – that is, reinforce markets.

> "Instead,] democracy leads to the emergence of manipulative politicians and demagogues who find that the best way to get votes is by scapegoating the minorities." She further notes: "As markets enrich the market-dominant minority, democratization increases the political voice and power of the frustrated majority." (p 124).

In essence what we call xenophobia or Afrophobia in South Africa, as condemnable as it may be is actually part of the problems of globalizing the markets in an era in which liberal democracy has become triumphant. South may be different only for not having done enough, early enough, to prevent the deep-seated anti-foreigner sentiments from flaring into uncontrolled violence.

In South Africa, the latest violence flared up in the Durban area earlier this month after King Goodwill Zwelithini, the traditional leader of the Zulus, reportedly compared foreigners to lice and said that they should pack up and leave. And the environment for the majority poor is very fertile for such messages. According to The Economist of 25 April 2015, unemployment in South Africa runs at 24%, though the real figure could be much higher, with more than half of under-25-year-olds out of work. South Africa's last census, in 2011, found that 2.3 million foreign-born people were living in the country, with some estimating the figure to be as high as between 5 million and 6 million in a country which has a population of only 54 million people.

While we strongly condemn the anti-foreign violence in South Africa, we should also bear in mind that xenophobia exists in virtually all parts of the world in different degrees and that this has only been accentuated under the twin conditions of the globalization of markets and the triumphalism of liberal democracy.

In 1969 for instance Ghana's Aliens *Compliance Order*, led to hundreds and thousands of Nigerian immigrants being forced to leave the country. Nigeria 'retaliated' on a much bigger scale with the *Expulsion Order* of 1983 (reordered in 1985) which resulted in more than 700,000 Ghanaian immigrants being expelled from Nigeria in a very short space of time, with some of their businesses inhumanely confiscated.

We certainly live in a world of contradictions: while globalization is making the world a global village, countries are resisting the 'impurification' of their environments by foreigners and the fear and envy of the 'market dominant minorities'. While countries spend huge sums of money on globetrotting and PR to attract foreign direct investment, they end up resisting foreigners who jump to seize the economic opportunities in their countries.

In Nigeria the indigene-settler issue - not too different from the problem of xenophobia elsewhere - remains unsatisfactorily resolved, both for the 'host communities' and the 'immigrants', including the 'market dominant minorities' segment of it. Indigenes resent the foreigners not just because they could be 'market dominant minorities' but also because the 'immigrants' citizenship and residence rights confer on them almost equal rights as the host majorities. The fears of both the 'host communities' and the 'immigrants' should be acknowledged and properly addressed and not be masked by political correctness – as has been the practice.

What has been lacking in the debate on xenophobia – found in different degrees in all countries across the world – is a realistic strategy of how, in this era of globalization of markets and liberal democracy, we can come with strategies for both the 'dominant economic minorities' and the host communities to engage each other.

Nigerian Political scientists mull the future of their discipline

On April 23 2015, 44 political scientists from across the country and generations gathered at the National Defence College (NDC), Abuja, to discuss the future of their discipline. Among those who attended the stakeholders' meeting were Professors Bola Akinterinwa, Director General, Nigerian Institute of International Affairs (NIIA); Oshita Oshita, Director General , Institute for Peace and Conflict Resolution (IPCR); Tijani Bande, Director General, National Institute for Policy and Strategic Studies (NIPSS); Nuhu Yakubu, former Vice Chancellor, University of Abuja; Shuaib Ibrahim, former Dean of Social Sciences, Nasarawa State University, Keffi and Hassan Saliu of the University of Ilorin who convened the meeting.

Participants also reviewed the state of their umbrella association, the Nigerian Political Science Association and bemoaned the body's long period of inactivity. They pledged to re-activate and reinvigorate NPSA to enable it engage actively in critical issues of our time.

It should be borne in mind that the idea of disciplines doing soul-searching is not uncommon and certainly not peculiar to NPSA. For instance political scientists in the USA found themselves in a similar situation in October 2009 when Senator Tom Coburn, Republican of Oklahoma, proposed prohibiting the National Science Foundation from "wasting any federal research funding on political science projects". One of the projects financed by the National Science Foundation that Senator Coburn attacked was the American National Election Studies. Senator Coburn maintained that commentators on CNN, Fox News, MSNBC and other news media outlets "provide a myriad of viewpoints to answer the same questions." He argued that the $91.3 million that the foundation spent on social science projects over the last 10 years should have gone to biology, chemistry or pharmaceutical science.

Though political scientists rallied in opposition to the Coburn proposal, even some of the most vehement defenders of the discipline acknowledged that they themselves vigorously debated the field's direction, what sort of questions it should pursue and even how to increase the policy relevance of their research. In fact as a mark of the intense debate among American political scientists themselves on the direction of the discipline, a movement, known as the Perestroika Movement, had arisen in 2000 criticizing what it called the 'mathematicization' of the discipline in political science's first academic journal, the American Political Science Review.

Seen in the above light, the idea of political scientists questioning the future of their discipline should be welcome It is hoped, that in conjunction with the National Universities Commission they will constantly review the discipline's curriculum at the universities to ensure it remains relevant to the needs of the society and employers of labour. Above all, we look forward to the NPSA helping to shape political discourses – pretty much as the Nigerian Bar Association- does in matters of the law.

Daily Trust April 30, 2015

CHAPTER 127

US-Africa Summit: Another Gesture Politics?

From August 4 (Obama's birthday), through August 6, President Obama hosted the US-Africa summit, which was promoted as the largest event any U.S. President ever held with African heads of state and government. All African heads of state or government in good standing with the United States were invited. Prominent business people and the Chairperson of the African Union also received invitations. Leaders of five African countries - Central African Republic, Eritrea, Sudan and Zimbabwe were however not invited. The Presidents of Liberia and Sierra Leone excused themselves to deal with the outbreak of ebola virus epidemic in their countries.

The three-day Africa Summit was without doubt President Barack Obama's biggest initiatives for Africa even though the event was somewhat overshadowed by the Ebola epidemic in some West African countries and Boko Haram's terrorism in Nigeria. US Commerce Secretary Penny Pritzker promised that about $900m (£535m) in business deals would be sealed during the event.

The theme of the Summit - "Investing in the Next Generation" – was officially meant to strengthen ties between the United States and Africa – now touted as one of the world's most dynamic and fastest growing regions.

But beyond the rhetoric and the sanctimonious proclamations, what was the summit realistically designed to achieve? And what was it really capable of delivering? Opinions differ widely on this including on why Obama chose to host the summit in the first place.

For context, Obama's popularity rating is at an all-time low, with just 40% of Americans approving of his job performance according to the latest NBC/WSJ poll. For Obama's critics, the whole summit was just a move by Obama to divert attention from his struggles at home and abroad. For them, it was simply a jamboree that would not achieve anything, just another gesture politics that world leaders facing difficulties at home often embark upon either to launder their images or to divert attention away from their problems.

Coincidentally when Tony Blair, as the British Prime Minister, launched the Africa Commission in 2004, he faced similar charges of trying to use Africa to humanize his image. Before setting up the Africa Commission, Blair toured a few African countries and concluded that the poverty and hopelessness he saw in the continent made Africa a scar on the conscience of the whole world. His Africa Commission, he said, would help to change that. At that time his approval rating had crumbled to an all-time low. From the start of the War on Terror in 2001, he had strongly supported the foreign policy options of George W. Bush: he participated in the 2001 invasion of Afghanistan and 2003 invasion of Iraq. The invasion of Iraq was particularly controversial and was widely opposed in Britain, including by 139 of Blair's Labour MPs.

While Tony Blair's popularity rating in 2004 is similar to Obama's poor approval rating today, the global perception of Africa has since changed. While in 2004, Blair likened Africa to a scar on the conscience of the world, in 2014, Africa is regarded as one of the world's most dynamic regions, with six of the ten fastest growing economies in the world being in the continent. In fact the IMF projects an average growth rate of 5.4 per cent for the continent this year and 5.8 per cent next year – higher than the global average. This probably explains why the theme of Obama's Africa Summit is 'Investing in the Next Generation'. Obama probably needed the Americans to feel that such a Summit is good value for money and has nothing to do with his father being African.

There is a general feeling that there is more to the summit than the Obama administration was willing to admit. There are for instance suspicions that the Africa Summit might have been – at least in part inspired by 'China envy'. For instance China has emerged as Africa's biggest trading partner, with a trading volume worth $200bn compared to USA's $85bn according to United States Census Bureau figures. Despite being the world's largest economy, the US is still only Africa's third largest trade partner – behind the European Union. Some therefore believe that American government might have bought into the Africa summit idea as part of its containment of Chinese expansion in Africa. This was probably what Ben Rhodes, USA's deputy national security advisor had in mind when he reportedly told journalists last week "We chose to do this summit to send a very clear signal that we are elevating our engagement with Africa." A recent editorial in South Africa's Business Day newspaper also argued that "the US government was running the risk of missing the African bus". If this thinking is right, then the US-Africa Summit was merely playing a catch-up. Even the idea of Africa Summit was started by China in 2001 and Japan, India and Europe had had several Africa summits.

It is also possible that Obama hoped to use the summit to embellish his standing with Africans, aware that his presidency has not really benefitted the continent much. For instance aside from the 2013 tour, he made only two trips to sub-Saharan Africa during his presidency - one brief stopover in Ghana in July 2009, and a visit to South Africa for Nelson Mandela's funeral. There was also a general belief that during Obama's first Africa tour in Ghana he talked condescendingly to African leaders (or lectured them on democracy and good governance) – contrary to the conciliatory posture he adopted in his other tours at that time. Though some Africans excused that as an expression of 'tough love' - being partly African through his Kenyan father - others felt the slight deeply and began to feel alienated from his presidency. It is possible that by getting some 35 African Heads of State and governments to come Washington DC, with all the media hype and hoopla, Obama might be hoping to make up for all that, including to countries like Nigeria that felt disappointed that he did not visit them during his African tours.

Obama can in fact argue that he brought Africa to Washington DC to promote and market the continent as a good investment destination. In this sense, the Africa Summit is at least in part all about Obama and his legacy. His memoir is certain to talk glowingly about how the summit changed the perception of Africa among American investors. It is, he will argue, his payback for all the support and enthusiasm he got from Africa during his campaign for the presidency in 2008. He can also tout it as the dividend of his presidency to the continent Africa for being partly African. However whether the Africa Summit will do anything to revive his plummeting popularity in the US remains to be seen.

Whatever may be the motives behind the Africa Summit, there is no doubt that it is good for Africa. Coming at a time of unprecedented Afro-optimism, it will only strengthen the new perception of Africa as a good investment destination, though a stronger message in that direction would probably have been made if the Summit was held in Africa.

Whatever may be the real motives for the summit, it was probably an opportunity for the West to interrogate why China has made so many inroads into the continent at its expense. Part of the answer is that not only does China invest in infrastructures in the continent it is also believed to treat the countries it deals with in the continent with more respect than the West does.

The West may not have missed the bus to Africa but the global balance of economic power is increasingly moving away from it. For instance on July 15 2014, the BRICS countries (Brazil, Russia, India, China and South Africa) set up a New Development Bank, which would offer low-interest credit for developing countries to actually build necessary infrastructure. This will basically mean that the significance of the two Bretton Woods institutions - the IMF and the World Bank – long used by the West to control the developing countries will diminish.

For Africa, it is nice to be treated as beautiful bride - for once. But the continent needs not be carried away by the attention or the rhetoric. It needs to be smart and play its cards well. It needs to maximize available opportunities without sentiments or undue emotionalism.

Daily Trust, August 8, 2014

CHAPTER 128

Brexit, Bregret and Scaremongering

The victory of the Brexiters (those who wanted Britain to quit the European Union) over the Bremainers (those who wanted Britain to remain in the Union) momentarily threw the world into a panic mode. Just a day after the official figures showed that the Brexiters won by 51.89 per cent to 48.11 per cent, the British pound crashed in value to a level not seen in almost 30 years. The London Stock Exchange and bourses around the world were also not spared. In fact one would think that the victory of Brexit amounted to an impending Armageddon, not just for the United Kingdom but for the entire world. One commentator in fact wrote that the result of the referendum was guaranteed to turn Great Britain into Little Britain.

The run-up to the referendum was characterised by scaremongering by both sides. Sir John Major, the former Conservative Prime Minister for instance branded the Brexit camp "the grave-diggers of our prosperity" who would have to answer for their "lies". Brexiters in turn talked about a disappearing British identity as a result of changing demographics occasioned by immigration.

I believe that beyond the scaremongering by both sides, there are several important observations from the referendum:

One, the remorse and regret that followed the announcement of the outcome reminds one of the aphorism: "Beware of what you wish for because you may get it." We are told that shortly after the verdict Google search for the meaning of European Union in the UK peaked – meaning that people just voted in a classical demonstration of negation being a form of affirmation. A few days after the result was announced, there were anti-Brexit protests in London, which voted to remain in the EU, with some suggesting that London should simply secede from the UK. Those who signed the petition for a second referendum numbered over 4 million by June 29. The petition said: "We the undersigned call upon HM Government to implement a rule that if the Remain or Leave vote is less than 60% based on a turnout less than 75%, there should be another referendum."

Another sign of Bregret is that UK officials have not shown any inclination of invoking Article 50 of the Treaty of Lisbon (signed in 2007), which made provision for countries that want to leave the Union. Rather there has been increasing emphasis on the advisory nature of the referendum and that it would need to be ratified by Parliament before it could be effectuated.

The crisis of confidence triggered by Brexit had precedence in Denmark. This was when the Maastricht Treaty (also called Treaty on European Union) was signed in 1992. At that time various counties held referenda to ratify their countries' membership. In Denmark, in the first referendum held on June 2 1992 those who did not want Denmark to be part of the new ambitious political integration agenda of the European Economic Community (as it was then called) won by a slim margin of 50.7

per cent against 49.5 per cent. After that defeat scaremongering by government officials who had supported the Maastricht Treaty was let loose and a second referendum was held on May 18 1993. In the second referendum, 56.8 per cent voted in favour of the treaty with the four opt-outs that the government had negotiated as 'sweeteners' to the naysayers. This may be the most likely route for Brexit.

Two, an important lesson from the outcome of the referendum and the remorse that followed is that a referendum, just like any election for political office, is often not about taking the most rational decision, but knowing what is desired by the majority of people. Voters across the world are largely driven by emotions and sentiments, which is why democracy is often caricatured as 'mob rule'. While the main supporters of the Bremain were the so-called 'thinking classes' – academics and captains of industry – those who had their way were mostly those concerned about the dilution of British identity by immigration. We also see in both the Danish nay vote in 1992 and the Bregret that followed Brexit, a version of the 'iron law of oligarchy' – the tendency for the dominant elite in any society to have a way of imposing their views of society on others. The dominant elite lost in the referendum but they are most likely going to win what they canvassed for by other means.

Three, various analyses of how Brexit would affect Africa and Nigeria in particular verge on hysteria. Several commentators have for instance pointed out that the bilateral trade between Nigeria and the UK – currently worth USD8.3 billion and projected to reach USD25 billion by 2020 – would be negatively affected. They also argue that Brexit could trigger recession in the UK, which will negatively affect Africa and remittances from Africans in the UK. This is purely speculative. I support Britain being part of the European Union but I am uncomfortable with the rash of scaremongering that followed Brexit. For instance those who inveigh about its possible negative effects on Africa often forget that once out of the EU, Britain could in fact be forced by imperatives to forge closer ties with blocs like the Commonwealth, the African Union and ECOWAS. There is also a wrong assumption that without being in the European Union a major country in Europe would fare badly. This is not supported by available evidence. Norway and Switzerland could join the EU if they want to but they are not interested. Russia is not interested and may not be wanted. Similarly of the 28 members of the EU, only 19 use the euro and there is no evidence that those using the euro have fared better than others. Similarly it is wrong to assume that being outside the European Union Britain would be in a better position to control immigration. It will all depend on the type of arrangement it is able to reach with the EU – if it triggers Article 50. Britain is a mature democracy and an old industrial power. It has the capacity to manage whatever may be the consequences of not being in the EU.

Steve Barrow, head of G10 Research at Standard Advisory London has noted that any trade deals that African countries had with the UK were in effect trade deals with the EU, which has the sole jurisdiction over external trade for all its members. He suggested that if Britain exits the EU and really wanted to, it could simply turn all its

EU trade deals with the rest of the world into UK trade deals with them, with the stroke of a pen.

Four, though a referendum does not necessarily guarantee that the most rational decision would be taken, it does ensure greater citizen participation in the political process. To this end it helps not only to extend the democratic space but also to deepen democracy. It is a principle that has become a template in mature democracies for resolving thorny issues, including on separatist agitations. In a referendum, people are allowed to aggressively market their opinions in the marketplace of political ideas. It is instructive that the contentious issue during the referendum was what Britain stood to lose or gain by being in the EU contra what it stood to lose or gain by being out of it. When applied to separatist agitations in a country like ours, it ensures that ideas are not driven underground and romanticised and their purveyors turned into heroes and heroines. Precisely because a referendum on such issues will be based on what the federative units gain from being in the union against what they will lose by being out of it, a referendum could force the country to be fair to all the federative units. Will Brexit energize separatist agitations or will Bregret be a counterweight to such agitations? There is no straight forward answer to this. The important thing in my opinion is that the recent UK referendum and the Brexit and Bregret it brought in its wake provide opportunities for fruitful conversations about what we sometimes call the 'National Question'.

Five, David Cameron, who had campaigned for the UK to remain in the Union duly indicated that he would resign as British Prime Minister from October 2016. In the UK, his resignation was not treated as a big deal and did not add much to his political stature. If anything, his resignation if Brexit won was widely expected. Do we expect any Nigerian leader to resign for losing a simple referendum – when there are enough people and events to blame for such?

Daily Trust, June 30, 2016

CHAPTER 129

AU Passport: Road to United States of Africa?

One of the key highlights of the 27th Ordinary Session of the African Union Assembly of Heads of State and Government, which held in Kigali, Rwanda in July 2016, was the launch of the African Union passport. Remarkably Idris Deby, the Chairperson of the African Union and President of the Republic of Chad, and Paul Kagame, the President of Rwanda, received the first AU passports. Their AU passports were handed over to them by the Chairperson of the AU Commission Nkosazana Dlamini Zuma.

Though the two Presidents received their AU passports, the full roll-out of the passport for ordinary citizens is slated for the end of 2018. And that is after each state has passed the necessary legislation that would legalize the acceptance of such a passport in its territory. The AU is however pushing for citizens of its member states to have the possibility of travelling and staying visa- free in member states for up to 30 days before the formal rollout of the AU passports in 2018.

There are some pertinent questions. What precisely does the AU passport intend to achieve? Do Africans really need it at this point of internal tensions in several African countries? Is the idea of a common passport a pathway to the United States for Africa along the lines proposed by Kwame Nkrumah in the late 1960s and the late Muammar Ghaddafi?

This piece is a reflection on some of the questions and concerns surrounding the African Union passport and African integration. I note the following:

One, the idea behind a common passport is to make it possible for all African citizens to be able to travel throughout the continent without visas. In fact, a report by African Development Bank on visa openness found that only 13 out of 55 African countries allow all Africans to enter their countries either without a visa or to get visa on arrival. Ghana became one of the latest African countries to change its visa policy when in July 2016 it introduced a new visa-on-arrival policy for citizens of AU member states.

Two, proponents of a common African passport argue that it will foster regional integration in Africa. The argument is that free movement of people along the lines of what the European Union and the Economic Community of West African States (ECWOAS) have for their citizens will further boost the cause of unity in the continent. This is true, though it is equally true that having a common passport will be insufficient to address the problem. There is for instance the whole question of travel infrastructure in the continent; it is often easier to travel from one African country to Western countries than from one African country to another. Quite often you may have to fly to a third country for a connecting flight to the African country you are travelling to and even where there are direct flights among African countries, they are often very infrequent. Supporters of a common passport accept that a common AU passport will be insufficient to promote the cause of unity in the continent but contend that it will be a bold statement in that direction.

Three, questions have been asked on whether a common African passport will not create problems for the relatively wealthy countries, which may risk being swarmed with economic and illegal immigrants or even those who want to use some countries as transit routes to the more prosperous parts of the world. Again supporters of a common African passport accept that such are real possibilities as the experiences with countries like South Africa, (where there have been periodic eruptions of xenophobia and Afrophobia), show. They however counter that every policy has unintended consequences – just as every medication has a side effect – which has to be managed.

Four, questions have been asked of the relationship between the African passport and the quest for greater economic integration in the continent. My opinion is that many regional groupings that started a process of economic integration discovered sooner than later that political integration would be a necessary complement. This was the experience of the European Union and ECOWAS. You can also argue that those that started as political unions such as the Organisation of African Unity (the precursor to the African Union) also discovered that economic integration would be a necessary complement to a political union.

It is therefore not surprising that the African Union, which succeeded the OAU in 2002, has continued the push for greater economic integration of the continent. The African Union wants to achieve a single currency – possibly called Afro or Afriq – for the continent by 2028. Proponents of a single African currency argue that such would lower transaction costs in the continent, facilitate pan-African monetary decision-making and promote greater African unity.

The OAU's quest for economic integration was given an impetus by the Abuja Treaty of 1991, which proposed the creation of an African Economic Community in 2023 to be followed by the creation of an African Central Bank in 2028. It was proposed that an African Monetary Union should be created for member unions which would create a new unified currency, similar to the Euro. One common concern is whether this is not being too ambitious given the wide disparities in the economies of the member states and the unpalatable experiences of some of the richer members of the euro countries such as France and Germany. The other concern is how to integrate the economies of the member states.

Supporters do not deny that challenges of integration will be there but they argue that there will be criteria to be met by countries aspiring to become members of the single currency. Supporters also argue that the idea of a single currency has been practised with success in some parts of Africa. For instance in West Africa, there are two existing currency unions – the West African CFA franc (made up of eight countries) and the Central African CFA (made up of six countries. The two regional currency unions have been in operation since 1945 and despite challenges have survived to this day. In Southern Africa, there is the Common Monetary Area, which links South Africa, Namibia, Lesotho and Swaziland. Though these countries use their own local currencies, the South African Rand is a legal tender in the CMA. Proponents of a single currency for African countries believe that Africa can learn from the experiences of the European Union and also build on the successes of its existing regional currency unions.

Five, how will the current push for both political and economic integration in the continent interface with the sharp contradictions of ethnicity, regionalism and even 'clash of civilizations' among the member states? Supporters concede that it is true that in many parts of the continent the basis of nationhood remains contested and many groups are delinking from the formal state system into primordial identities often with the state as the enemy. They however argue that the nation-states will not disappear overnight just because of the quest for greater integration. They contend that many of the contradictions in each state system will continue in one form or the other depending on the balance of the contending forces. They also argue that even separatist forces are not likely to be against the economic and political integration of the continent as that will not harm their interest. Supporters equally believe that the world is changing so fast that no one will be sure whether these contradictions and 'clashes of civilization' will still remain as salient as they are today a few years from now.

Six, those of us very supportive of the integrative efforts of the AU are proud that the members were not deterred by the outcome of the Brexit referendum in the United Kingdom. In fact the AU's meeting in Kigali came roughly one month after Brexit. Many had thought that Brexit would damp the enthusiasm for greater integration in Africa. The idea for both the African Union passports and the quest for greater economic integration should therefore be seen as part of the determination by African countries to look inward for solutions to their development challenges. It is precisely for this reason that some of us are very excited about it – despite the real challenges that such integrative efforts are likely to encounter 'on the ground' (as Nigerian politicians would put it).

Daily Trust, September 29, 2016

CHAPTER 130

Lessons From the 2016 US Presidential Election

It certainly came as a surprise to many people. Though all national polls in the USA indicated that the race was tightening in the run-up to the elections, almost all indicated a Hilary Clinton win. With 279 Electoral College Votes to Hillary's 228, the world increasingly has to come to terms with a Donald Trump presidency. There are several lessons we can learn from the election:

One, Trump's victory could signal the ascendency and ultimate mainstreaming of right wing populism. This is a growing phenomenon in Western democracies, which is epitomized in backlashes against multiculturalism, growing anti immigration sentiments and fears about the changing demographics that come with it. In the UK, this rightwing populism was very eloquently expressed in the Brexit. In smaller countries like Denmark parties that articulate right wing populism have managed to be part of the ruling coalition government. In bigger countries like United Kingdom, France, Germany, the Netherlands, such parties influence the agenda of campaigns without being allowed to be part of the ruling government.

In the US, Donald Trump was not the first presidential candidate to premise his campaign on right-wing populism or stoking the fears of the White majority. In 1964, the Republican presidential candidate Barry Goldwater campaigned against civil rights. In 1968, ex-Democrat George Wallace, who ran as an independent, built his candidacy on a combination of promises to repeal the civil right laws and continue the segregation of Black and White people in public institutions. There was also Pat Buchanan – who tried to get on the Republican ticket a couple of times in the 1990s but ended up running for president for the Reform Party in 2000. Buchanan built his candidacy on attacks on government's immigration policy, transnational corporations and global competition as well as trade deals that benefited Mexican workers.

In 1992 Ross Perot made a very strong showing as an independent candidate. He also ran as presidential candidate of the Reform Party in 1996. On both occasions, he built his campaign on opposition to the government's immigration policy and what he saw as the outsourcing of American jobs. Again after Obama's election in 2008, a movement known as the Tea Party emerged based on a combination of several different resentments about bank bailouts, taxation, big government and a Black President in White House.

If Trump's victory is the first time rightwing populism will triumph in a major Western country, how will that translate in governance? Will the famed American institutions be able to restrain his excesses? Or would his campaign rhetoric just be smart strategies to play up the fears of the White majority in order to win the election? Only time will tell.

Two, another important lesson from the American election is that the democratic space can contract or expand irrespective of how old a democracy is. American democracy is over 200 years old. During the campaign, we saw the prevalence of features that are usually associated with 'new democracies' or 'democratizing societies' such as allegations of 'rigging', questionable intervention in the process by the FBI only 11 days to the election and voter intimidation or what we call thuggery here in Nigeria. This has raised the question of whether American democracy has suffered reversals, has run out of steam or is under serious threat from anti democratic forces. Trump was probably the first candidate in modern American political history to question the integrity of the country's democratic process. And a poll conducted by Rasmussen Report published on October 24 2016 showed that many Americans agreed with him.

Three, though Hilary Clinton did not win, that she worked very closely with President Obama, was an important lesson on strategic planning and alliance. It should be recalled that Obama and Hillary Clinton fought a very bitter campaign in 2008 during the Democratic Party's primary. Though Obama triumphed, he eschewed all temptations to 'neutralize' her and her family – as our politicians here would have certainly done. In exchange the Clintons campaigned for him and after he won the election, he appointed Hilary to the powerful position of Secretary of State. Mrs Clinton resigned after four years on the job to prepare for another shot at the presidency. Once she got the Democratic Party's nomination, Obama and his wife Michelle campaigned enthusiastically for her. Clinton in turn promised to preserve Obama's legacy. This is an important lesson on how to build alliances and coalitions – despite hurtful words that both candidates used on each other during their bitter primaries in 2008.

Four, the election tells us that there are group dynamics in politics everywhere in the world. While in Nigeria we talk of the fault lines of religion, ethnicity and regionalism, in racially mixed societies these dynamics will coincide with race. This means that groups – racial, ethnic, regional, social classes- are often conscious of how particular government policies impact on them and will react accordingly or bottle up resentment that could be expressed in other ways such as by being silent supporters of candidates like Trump. In essence, there is a need for those in power to take cognizance of ideas and grouses expressed by opposition and even insurgent groups – however offensive such ideas may be. The unexpected victory of Donald Trump tells us that such 'lunatic' ideas may be shared by more people than openly express them. When therefore people talk of 'issue-based campaigns', they wrongly give the impression that there is a clime where campaigns are run like academic seminars – in arcane language that is devoid of emotions. The truth is that campaigns play up on people's hopes and fears.

Five, it is remarkable that though all the candidates in the election are rather old, age never became an issue in the election. Donald Trump is 70; Hilary Clinton 69, Jill Stein, the presidential candidate of the Green Party is 66, while Gary Johnson, the presidential candidate of the Libertarian Party, is 63. When Hilary Clinton tripped during the presidential campaign, Donald Trump capitalized on it to ask whether she was strong and healthy enough to be president of the USA. That trip negatively affected her poll standing for a while before she recovered from it. This will suggest to us that the vitality of the candidates should matter more than their chronological ages. In Nigeria, there is this abiding myth that younger people will necessarily bring vitality and new thinking to governance.

Six, now that Trump has beaten all the odds to win, what should we expect of his presidency? It is often said that politicians campaign in poetry and govern in prose. He promised several things but never bothered to elaborate on how he will deliver on them. As President, he cannot escape the 'how' question. It is remarkable that he sounded very conciliatory in his first public speech after being declared the President elect. Will he be a President who will heal the wounds of a bitter and polarizing campaign and unify Americans as he promised to do? Or will he further polarize the country? Time will tell.

Oyegun, Oshiomhole and APC's lingering crisis

As the internal crisis in the ruling APC lingers, with Bola Tinubu openly calling for the resignation of its national chairman Chief John Odigie-Oyegun, one is not surprised that various interests are beginning to use surrogates to subtly promote some candidates as Oyegun's possible replacement. There is nothing wrong with this. Politicians are political investors.

When I read that the outgoing Edo State governor, Comrade Adams Oshiomhole, whose second-term as governor ends today (November 12, 2016) has been "pencilled down" to replace the embattled Oyegun as the party's national chairman, I smelled a rat. When I add to this what I read earlier that the leaders of the APC in the south-south geopolitical zone have passed a vote of confidence on Oyegun, I concluded that the campaign for Oyegun's post is now in full swing.

There is no doubt that both the ruling APC and the opposition PDP need to get their acts together for our democracy to thrive. In particular, more than one- and- half years after it became the ruling party, the APC is still behaving like an opposition party that is mired in confidence crisis after losing an election.

The APC needs as its chairman, a calm-headed person and a good listener who has sufficient emotional intelligence to work not just with the President but also with other political gladiators of different ambitions and temperaments. It is not going to be an easy assignment for anyone. But my gut instinct tells me that there is sometimes too much of the labour activist in Adams Oshiomhole – too much of the love of the political podium and too much political combativeness – that makes one doubt if he really has what it takes to be a unifier for a party like the APC.

Daily Trust, November 10, 2016

CHAPTER 131

Till debt do us apart

The recent request from President Buhari for legislative authorization for an external borrowing of almost $39bn is a sharp reminder that history truly moves in circles and that human memories are short. It should be recalled that Africa's debt overhang was partly blamed for why the1980s and the 1990s were regarded as lost decades for the continent. The argument was that due to Africa's high level of indebtedness resources that could have been used to develop the continent were being used to service debts. In fact by the 1990s, the word 'crisis' was being used to describe Africa's debt burden. At that time it was estimated that the continent's total external debt was $230bn - about 13 per cent of what the country now wants to borrow in one fell swoop.

There were several studies on how the continent's debt burden was impacting on ordinary people. Some of the very impactful of such studies included Susan George's A Fate Worse Than Debt (1988) and Katama G.C. Mkangi's The African Debt Crisis: A Radical Human Perspective (1993). These studies articulated very powerfully and emotionally the social costs of the debt crisis. Basically they argued that debt-induced economic austerity was destroying the lives of countless people in the so-called Third World countries, especially in Africa. They also showed that those bearing the brunt of the debt burden were people who did not benefit from the loans and that the continent was spending as much as four times on debt repayment as it did on say healthcare. It was argued that high level of debt servicing meant that repayments to Western creditors were prioritized over the lives of ordinary people. It was also argued that people's access to education and employment was restricted by a chunk of the national resources being diverted to servicing debts.

Based on studies and polemics like the above, scholars and activists began calling for debt relief, arguing that in the highly indebted poor countries (HIPCs), the scale of unmet social needs are simply too vast and the rate of progress on human development too slow that it should not leave anyone in doubt about the need for something to be done about the debt burden. The United Nations Children's Fund for instance estimated at that time that about 1000 people were dying daily in Africa because of the debt crisis.

The concern about Africa's debt burden moved quickly from being an academic concern to something that was to engage activists. Campaigns flourished globally, especially in the Western world - all challenging international creditors to cancel the debts of the world's poorest countries. One of the most impactful of these civil society groups was Jubilee 2000, which was set up in London in 1994 and which campaigned vociferously for international creditors to cancel the unpayable debts of the world's poorest countries by the end of the year 2000. The group mobilized international petitions in several languages asking creditors to cancel 'Third World's' debts under fair and transparent processes.

Owing to pressures from campaigners, the International Monetary Fund (IMF) and World Bank set up the $7-10bn Heavily Indebted Poor Country (HIPC) Initiative in 1996 in a bid to provide relief to some of the world's poorest countries experiencing difficulties in debt repayments. Meanwhile, Jubilee 2000 was becoming more influential, having won the support of churches and key NGOs. For instance at the G8 Summit in Birmingham, England, in 1998, the group mobilized over 70,000 supporters to form a human chain around the building where the annual G8 meeting was to be held. The same day it presented 1,500,000 signatures from over 50 countries to Clare Short, the UK's International Development Secretary at the time. Just a few hours later, the leaders of the G8 announced that it would cancel $50bn of the debts of the world's poorest countries.

The above is very important in understanding the context in which Obasanjo in 2005 negotiated for the cancellation of $18bn of the country's debt by agreeing to pay off, in instalments, $12bn for its $30bn loan to the Paris Club. It is also important in situating the current conversation on whether the National Assembly should approve the President's request for $30bn external loan or not. The conversation about the President's loan request cannot be very meaningful if it is divorced from the context of Africa's debt crisis of the 1980s and 1990s. I also feel it will be wrong to ossify this important conversation into a simplistic binary of those supporting or opposing President Buhari and his initiatives. In this unhelpful binary, those who oppose the loans are automatically opponents of the President and his agenda while those who support it are loyalists or supporters of the President.

There are several issues that demand clarification:

One, the immediate thing that comes to mind, giving the above context, is a legitimate concern on whether the country is deliberately putting its finger on a trigger called 'self-destruct'. What will the activists who campaigned for Africa's debt forgiveness and debt relief in the 1980s and 1990s be thinking of us if we go for this heavy loan? It should be recalled that one of the arguments of those who opposed debt relief to African countries in the 1980s and 1990s was that forgiving the debts would not guarantee that the affected countries would not accumulate fresh debts, which would necessitate another round of campaign for debt forgiveness.

By going for this loan - the total amount of our debt to the Paris Club which we exited in 2005 - are we not proving the Afro-pessimists right? It is especially saddening that this new round of debt accumulation is coming after a period of Afro-optimism in which seven out of the ten fastest growing economies in the world were in Africa. Nigeria itself was listed as one of the likely breakout economies in the world: in 2011, it was listed as a member of the Next Eleven (also known as the N-11). The N-11 are eleven countries - Bangladesh, Egypt, Indonesia, Iran, Mexico, Nigeria, Pakistan, Philippines, Turkey, South Korea, and Vietnam - identified by the British economist Jim O'Neill in a research paper on December 12 2005 as having a high potential of becoming, along with the BRICs, the world's largest economies in the 21st century.

It was also included in the MINT emerging economies in 2014. MINT is a neologism referring to the economies of Mexico, Indonesia, Nigeria and Turkey. The term was originally coined by the Boston-based asset management firm Fidelity and popularized by Jim O'Neil, a former Goldman Sachs analyst, who had in 2011, coined the acronym BRIC to refer to the economies of Brazil, Russia, India and China. BRIC was later turned to BRICS when South Africa was bracketed into the group. So with the desire to take such a huge loan, one would be tempted to ask: How are the mighty fallen?

Two, while I sympathize with the government's desire to spend its way out of recession, question should be posed about how this money should be repaid. For instance latest figures from the Bureau of Statistics showed that the country's Gross Domestic Product (GDP) shrunk by 2.24 per cent in the third quarter of 2016. It had shrunk by 0.36 per cent in the first quarter and by 2.06 in the second quarter - the country's worst economic outlook since 1991. Given this scenario, does the country really have the capacity to repay? Does it have a history of prudent management of resources? Does it have the capacity to utilize the resources effectively? Has it exhausted other sources of raising money to reflate the economy? The idea that the loan will be used to improve the country's infrastructures and that this in turn would spur industrial growth that will give us the ability to repay, is too theoretical.

Three, how can the government be asking for loans when some of the root causes of the current economic crisis have not been adequately addressed? By this I mean not just the resolution of the Niger Delta problem that has led to a drastic drop in oil production but also some policies that clearly hurt the economy such as the current mode of fighting corruption, which as well intentioned as it may be, actually has the unintended effect of discouraging investment.

Four, since the beginning of this recession, we have been regaled with promises that the country was about to turn the corner. Many of us wished so and would also want to talk up the economy, realising the role of sentiment plays in upturning a comatose economy. Unfortunately with a third consecutive quarter of negative GDP growth, I think we may be better off thinking out of the box. Loan money is cheap money. It is devil's excrement in the same manner as oil money is. It is very unlikely to be very judiciously used.

Daily Trust, November 24, 2016

Index

A

Abiola, MKO, 31, 47, 177, 210, 274, 345
Abubakar, Atiku, 144, 231, 263
Abuja,, 45, 63, 107, 113, 175, 307, 523, 540
Achebe, Chinua, 91, 508, 516
Action Congress of Nigeria, 282
Adamu, Adamu, 283
Adesina, Akinwumi, 245
Africa Growth Initiative, 21
African Union, 486, 496, 519, 520, 543, 549
Africanity, 345, 352, 354, 503, 507, 512, 513
Afro-pessimism, 343, 504
Afrophobia, 537, 538
Akande, Laolu, 225
Akinterinwa, Bola, 540
Akunyili, Dora, 85
Akwa Ibom, 92
Aliyu, Babangida, 23, 261, 523
All Progressives Congress, 269, 273, 293
Alliance for a Green Revolution in Africa, 246
Almajiris, 93
Al-Qaeda in the Islamic Maghreb, 22
Anderson, Benedict, 36
Ansaru, 21, 22, 26, 36, 39, 46, 176
Arendt, Hannah, 26, 45, 175, 204, 311
Armageddon, 119, 120, 517, 547
Awolowo, Obafemi, 91, 122, 210, 267, 275, 508, 516

B

Babangida, Ibrahim, 31, 47, 106, 133, 177, 215, 217,
    226, 251, 261, 273, 311, 312, 523
Baghdad, 41
Baraje, Abubakar, 261, 263, 281, 283
Basic Education Curriculum, 144
Better Together campaigners, 534, 536
Bicameral legislatures, 298
Bida, 370
Bill and Melinda Gates Foundation, 246
Boko Haram, 13, 14, 17, 18, 19, 20, 21, 22, 23, 24,
    25, 26, 29, 30, 31, 32, 33, 35, 36, 38, 41, 42, 43,
    45, 46, 47, 48, 49, 50, 52, 53, 54, 55, 56, 57, 59,
    60, 61, 63, 64, 65, 115, 125, 143, 175, 176, 177,
    178, 204, 210, 216, 310, 313, 320, 321, 522, 543
Borno State government, 13, 20
Brexiters, 547
Brown, Gordon, 346, 533
Buhari, Muhammadu, 41, 42, 44, 53, 54, 55, 57, 61,
    63, 66, 104, 105, 106, 120, 121, 122, 131, 134,
    143, 204, 206, 207, 209, 211, 213, 214, 215, 216,
    217, 225, 226, 227, 228, 229, 230, 231, 237, 251,
    255, 256, 257, 262, 263, 265, 267, 269, 271, 273,
    274, 275, 286, 287, 295,297, 307, 308, 309, 310,

311, 312, 313, 315, 316, 319, 320, 321, 324, 484,
486, 489, 490, 491, 501, 531

C

Cameron, David, 550
Cape Verde, 496
Capital Oil, 83
Centre for Democracy and Development, 319
Chibok girls, 13, 14, 17, 19, 20, 29, 30, 45, 49, 50,
    54, 64, 175
Chinese Yuan, 256
Christian Association of Nigeria, 59
Christian Religious Studies, 143
Clausewitz, Carl von, 295
Code of Conduct Tribunal, 143
Common Agriculture Policy, 245
Compaore, Blaise, 519, 520, 521
Cross-conditionalities, 226
Cultural Revolution in China, 293
Czechoslovakia, 534

D

Damaturu, 63
Danjuma, Theophilus, 55
Democratic Republic of Congo, 537
De-Nigerianization, 36, 125
Diendere, Gilbert, 496, 519, 520, 521, 522
Directorate of State Service, 267
Drucker, Peter, 229
Durkheim, Emile, 203

E

Ease of Doing Business Index, 501
Eastern Nigeria, i
Ekwulobia, 59, 60
Emefiele, Godwin, 275, 276
Enejere, Emeka, 314
Eze, Arthur, 84

F

Faleke, James, 107
Fayemi, Kayode, 66, 289, 290, 291
Fayose, Ayo, 289, 290, 291
Federal Character principles, 127
Friedman, George, 230, 503, 504

G

Ghali, Boutros Boutros-, 503
Giwa, Dele, 105, 274
Golden Eaglets, 241
Gurr, Ted, 24, 216

H

Hani, Chris, 528

I

Ibrahim, Shuaib, 540
Igbos, 61, 62, 91, 93, 94, 268, 517, 538
Ihejirika, Azubuike, 49, 50
Independent National Electoral Commission, 267, 307
Indigeneship rights, 100
Internal Displacement Monitoring Centre, 53

J

Jega, Attahiru, 83, 206
Jonathan, Goodluck, 13, 17, 22, 23, 26, 30, 31, 33, 35, 38, 43, 44, 47, 49, 54, 55, 57, 62, 63, 64, 91, 113, 114, 115, 116, 120, 121, 124, 177, 205, 206, 207, 209, 211, 239, 246, 266, 267, 268, 272, 273, 282, 283, 286, 287, 293, 296, 307, 308, 309, 313, 320, 321, 483, 484, 491, 496, 501, 518, 523, 526, 530

K

Kagame, Paul, 495, 520
Kanu, Nnamdi, 308, 309, 312, 313
Kick Against Indiscipline, 91
Kingibe, Babagana, 274
Kitissou, Marcel, 343, 503
Kogi State, 107

L

Labour Party, 83, 218
Lama, Dalai, 500
Leviathans, 95, 265

M

Maier,Karl, 121, 132
Malawi, 537
Malunga, Chiku, 505, 506
Mandela, Nelson, 62, 254, 307, 308, 321, 487, 527, 528, 530, 545
Mark, David, 267
Market Dominant Minorities, 537

Mazrui, Ali, 323, 343, 344, 345, 346, 347, 348, 349, 350, 351, 352, 353, 354, 503, 504, 514
MIKT, 133, 241
MINT, 37, 133, 203, 241, 242, 243, 244, 526
Moro, Abba, 35
Movement for Unity and Jihad in West Africa, 22, 46, 176
Mozambique, 485, 496, 537
Mugabe, Robert, 485, 486

N

NADECO, 31, 47, 177, 210, 282
Nagy, Imre, 293
Naija-optimism, 133, 242
National Assembly, 90, 99, 125, 230, 297, 299, 300, 315, 316, 317, 483
National Association of Nigerian Students, 84
Nazi Germany, 119, 293
New PDP, 261, 281, 283, 284
New York, 343, 345, 346, 347
Niger Delta Avengers, 204, 209, 309, 313, 325, 326
Niger Deltans, 89
Nigerian Educational Research and Development Council, 144
Nigerian Governors Forum, 96
Nigerian Labour Congress, 43
Nigerian Pyrate Confraternity, 51
Night of Long Knives, 293
Nnoli, Okwudiba, 343, 348
Northern Governors, 262, 264
Nwodo, Okwesili, 95
Nyako, Murtala, 23
Nyerere, Julius, 254, 321, 527, 529, 530
Nzeogwu, Chukwuma Kaduna, 370
Nzeribe, Arthur, 274

O

Obasanjo, Olusegun, 25, 49, 120, 121, 133, 134, 209, 217, 226, 227, 232, 239, 251, 252, 267, 268, 283, 290, 297, 320, 483, 484, 491, 496, 520
Obi, Peter, 83, 84, 85, 91, 93, 313
Odi, 227
Ogbulafor, Vincent, 296
Ohaneze, 59, 60
Okechukwu, Osita, 60
Okiro, Mike, 128
Oklahoma, 65, 540
Okonjo-Iweala, Ngozi, 227
Okoro, Anezi, 143
Onitsha, 65, 93
Onu, Ogbonna, 62
Osibanjo, Yemi, 208, 323, 324

P

PDP, 30, 31, 84, 95, 108, 109, 113, 114, 116, 119, 123, 129, 218, 229, 230, 237, 246, 261, 263, 264, 265, 266, 267, 268, 269, 270, 272, 281, 282, 283, 284, 285, 286, 290, 293, 295, 296, 492
Perestroika Movement, 541

R

Razon, Enrique, 133, 242
Romantics, 294
Rowling, J.K., 534

S

Sanusi, Sanusi Lamido, 25, 247, 248, 249, 256, 275, 276, 297
Scottish Referendum, 533
Second Lebanon War, 18
Shagari, Shehu, 133, 251, 266
Sheriff, Modu, 49, 50, 52, 285
Sokoto, 23, 144, 267, 271
Soludo, Chkwuma, 232, 276
Sovereign National Conference, 35, 96, 320
Soyinka, Wole, 225, 345

T

Tandja, Mamadou, 496, 521
Tinubu, Ahmed Bola, 61, 92, 262, 265, 267, 269, 273, 290, 295, 315
Traore, Karim, ii
Truth and Reconciliation Commission, 254, 528
Turkey, 37, 132, 203, 241, 242, 243, 526

U

Uba, Patrick Ifeanyi, 83, 86
Umar, Wasila, 14
Umeadi, Philip, 275
UN Declaration on the rights of indigenous peoples, 89
UN General Assembly, 499
United Nations, 46, 59, 60, 88, 176, 499, 501, 503, 504, 527
Universal Basic Education Commission, 315
University of Nigeria, Nsukka, 314, 348, 485
US-Africa summit, 543

W

Wade, Abdoulaye, 496, 520
Weapons of Mass Destruction, 524
World Cup, 241
World Happiness Report 2016, 499, 501

X

Xenophobia, 537

Y

Yaradua, Umaru, 25, 296
Yoruba, 25, 79, 80, 91, 94, 210, 212, 274, 275, 283, 286, 325, 508, 509, 538

Z

Zaki Ibiam, 227
Zambia, 230
Zik (Azikiwe, Nnamdi), 51, 52, 271
Zikist Movement, 51, 52
Zimbabwe, 255, 485, 486, 487, 543
Zoning and Power Rotation, 30, 98, 114, 129, 130, 282, 284, 285, 296